KEN SCHULTZ'S
Fishing Encyclopedia

Worldwide Angling Guide

VOLUME 7

KEN SCHULTZ'S

Fishing Encyclopedia

Worldwide Angling Guide

Ken Schultz

IDG Books Worldwide, Inc.
An International Data Group Company
Foster City, CA • Chicago, IL • Indianapolis, IN • New York, NY • Southlake, TX

IDG Books Worldwide, Inc.
An International Data Group Company
919 E. Hillsdale Boulevard
Suite 400
Foster City, CA 94404

Copyright © 2000 by Ken Schultz

All rights reserved. No part of this book shall be reproduced, stored in a retrieval system, or transmitted by any means, electronic, mechanical, photocopying, recording, or otherwise, without written permission from the publisher. No patent liability is assumed with respect to the use of the information contained herein. Although every precaution has been taken in the preparation of this book, the publisher and author assume no responsibility for errors or omissions. Neither is any liability assumed for damages resulting from the use of the information contained herein.

Webster's New World is a registered trademark of Macmillan General Reference USA, Inc., a wholly owned subsidiary of IDG Books Worldwide, Inc.

The IDG Books Worldwide logo is a registered trademark under exclusive license to IDG Books Worldwide, Inc., from International Data Group, Inc.

For general information on books from IDG Books Worldwide's in the U.S., please call our Consumer Customer Service department at 800-762-2974. For reseller information, including discounts and premium sales, please call our Reseller Customer Service department at 800-434-3422.

For information on a multimedia version of this book, available from Tricom Intrtactive, Inc., please go to this Web site: intellipedia.com

To contact the author, please visit: www.kenshultz.com

Library of Congress Cataloging-in-Publication Data

This edition of *Ken Schultz's Fishing Encyclopedia,* which is published in 7 volumes, contains the entire contents of the work as previously published in a single volume: *Ken Schultz's Fishing Encyclopedia,* ISBN 9780028620572

This is Volume 7 of 7

Schultz, Ken, 1950–
Ken Shultz's fishing encyclopedia: worldwide angling guide/ Ken Schultz. — 1st ed.
p. cm.
ISBN 0-02-862057-7
Volume 7: ISBN 9781684427758 (hardcover) | ISBN 9781684427765 (paperback)

1. Fishing—Encyclopedias. 2. Fishes—Encyclopedias. I. Title.
SH411.S38 2000
799.1'03—dc21   99-033719
CIP

Manufactured in the United States of America

First Edition

Trademarks

All terms mentioned in this book that are known to be trademarks or service marks have been appropriately capitalized. IDG Books cannot attest to the accuracy of this information. Use of a term in this book should not be regarded as affecting the validity of any trademark or service mark.

Table of Contents

Introduction
vii

Acknowledgments
ix

Photo Credits
xix

Fishing Encyclopedia Entries

T
1

U
161

V
175

WXYZ
191

Appendix: Conversion Charts for Weights and Measures
261

Introduction

*"Ah, the gallant fisher's life! It is the best of any;
'Tis full of pleasure, void of strife, And 'tis beloved by many."*
—IZAAK WALTON

"All men are equal before fish."
—HERBERT HOOVER

WHILE PRODUCING THIS FISHING ENCYCLOPEDIA I SPOKE TO MANY HUNDREDS OF informed anglers. Nearly all of them thought the compilation of all things piscatorial was too overwhelming to contemplate because the angling universe is so enormous and diverse.

Certainly a modern fishing encyclopedia—if it truly provides a full field of knowledge—runs counter to the short and specialized tenets of today's journalism. Yet it is precisely because there is so much to the sport of fishing, plus an increasing profusion of specialized equipment and confusing terminology, that it was necessary to bring order and perspective to all of this in one definitive book.

Ken Schultz's Fishing Encyclopedia & Worldwide Angling Guide has been a long time in the making. I started thinking about it in 1991. Since work began in earnest in 1995, the project became even more expansive than expected, and indeed there were times when it was nearly overwhelming. As a result, the book grew much bigger than originally planned, becoming 50 percent larger than any fishing encyclopedia that has heretofore been published.

As a result, however, this encyclopedia contains the equivalent of thirty standard-length books, meaning that there is ample space to devote to the species, equipment, techniques, locations, and ancillary matters that encompass the angling universe. Consider that nearly one-third of the encyclopedia is comprised of the most comprehensive information on worldwide angling opportunities ever assembled. There is absolutely no place to find these details together; indeed, some elements of the *Worldwide Angling Guide* cannot be found anywhere else at all.

Likewise, the coverage of angling methods and equipment has never been addressed more comprehensively between the covers of any other book. In fact, *Ken Schultz's Fishing Encyclopedia* contains the most modern, illuminating, and extensive dis-courses on the basic elements of fishing tackle—baitcasting, big-game, conventional, flycasting, spinning, and spincasting—ever found in one place. Each of these entries undoubtedly contain more than all but the most scrupulous person will want to know.

Great lengths were also taken, however, to make sure that the less obvious subjects in the angling universe were included and reviewed in comprehensive fashion. For example, nowhere else is there a more extensive review of the principles, methods, and pros and cons of catch-and-release—perhaps the most important angling conservation development of the twentieth century.

Topics like fisheries management, angling-related travel, choosing guides and charter boats, and the care and preparation of fish for consumption, which are among many unglamorous subjects taken for granted elsewhere, receive complete explanation and review here. Likewise the otherwise oft-ignored subjects of ethics and etiquette—increasingly important issues as human pressures increase—are included.

Although there's an enormous amount of information in this book, every topic was approached with the intent to take nothing for granted and to present information in straightforward language. Angling is not like nuclear physics, and if it was half as complicated as some people try to make it, no one would enjoy it or have success. The extensive insertion of cross references is thus intended to direct you through a continuing stream of appropriate topics, so you can take any subject as far as you want to go. Some cross references appear within entry text next to topics that are more thoroughly reviewed elsewhere; many cross references appear at the end of entry text, either to direct you to the appropriate subject entry or to note related topics.

We've tried to make things easy to find and to place subjects where you're most likely to look for them, even if you're unsure of the proper terms or spelling. As an example, you'll find rainbow trout under the "T" entries (trout, rainbow) rather than under the "R" entries. Also, at the back of the book is a weights and measures conversion chart; this will be convenient for many readers since there's a liberal mix of metric and U.S. customary weights and measures throughout this book, just as there is at boat docks, fish camps, and tackle shops throughout the world.

Because the text is encyclopedic in format, however, it does not provide a full sense of the joy or spirit of sportfishing—the pleasure that makes it "beloved by many," as Izaak Walton said. Perhaps the accompanying photos help convey this. Photos and line art, incidentally, were planned and selected to reflect the broad, eclectic places and situations that so many anglers experience, as well as to reflect the great diversity of its participants. Angling is a very democratic recreation; as the quotation from President Hoover implies, the fish don't care who hooks them.

It is a special delight to publish this encyclopedia at the close of the twentieth century—a period with the most phenomenal sportfishing growth in the history of mankind—and at the advent of a new millennium. Knowing that the decades ahead will require proper stewardship of aquatic resources—something that anglers in particular have always demonstrated personal and financial support for—this text has been written and edited with sensitivity to conservation issues while also being realistic about the role that humans play as the highest predators and the diverse motivations they bring to angling.

In a sense, the sport of fishing is like a book with as many footnotes as main text. It is full of variables, especially individual skills, weather issues, peculiarities among species, habitat differences, and so forth. You may notice that the words "usually" and "generally" occur often in portions of the text. This isn't meant to be vague; it's because there are often no hard-and-fast rules in catching fish, no matter what you may have heard to the contrary. There are norms, but straying from norms is common for one reason or another, as any angler who has been humbled at a "hot" site at the "best" time of the season can attest.

While there is a wealth of reliable information here, a caveat is in order with regard to the contents of the *Worldwide Angling Guide*. Many of the countries profiled have not in the past provided, or do not currently provide, or may not in the future provide stable travel environments, especially to tourists of certain nationalities. Jungle fishing opportunities are especially among those that may present danger. Angola, Colombia, and Zambia come immediately to mind in this regard. Civil unrest can likewise make travel in certain places dangerous; recent troubles in Kenya, Indonesia, Russia, Uganda, and the Balkans serve as examples. The adventurous angler needs to use good judgment.

Things change the environmental order and aquatic resources, too. Yugoslavia hadn't been wrecked by bombs when that entry was written; Nicaragua and Honduras were leveled by Hurricane Georges right after those entries were written. Environmental changes sometimes radically alter the presence or availability of certain gamefish species, and in the more remote pockets of the world only native people and intrepid explorers are likely to know it.

On a final note, it is tempting to say, as marketers and publicists are wont to do, that this book contains everything an angler will ever need to know about fish and fishing. But new developments in fishing tackle will surely come along, changes in some habitats or in fish populations will alter the techniques and equipment used, and certainly natural changes will take place in some of the world's best angling spots. However, a lot of the fundamentals—the underlying principles of fish behavior, the function of basic equipment, and angling methodology—will be constant, making most of the information in this book relevant to the discerning angler even in years to come.

I expect to add to this body of knowledge in time, so if you think there's something that should have been included, if you have knowledge about fishing in a country that wasn't covered, or if you can suggest an improvement to any aspect of this book, please visit my website—www.kenschultz.com— and post a message about it.

Now, turn to any page and become absorbed.
—Ken Schultz

"If I fished only to capture fish, my fishing trips would have ended long ago."

—ZANE GREY

Acknowledgments

Producing a book of this magnitude required the involvement of a tremendous number of people and a great array of talents. This encyclopedia would not have gone beyond a mere suggestion, however, had it not been for the endorsement and encouragement of Natalie Chapman, a former publisher at Macmillan General Reference, now IDG Books Consumer Reference, whose confidence and vision made this book possible, and who gave me free rein to produce it as necessary. I'm also indebted to publisher Marie Butler-Knight, who took this project over in mid-stream, marshaled all the resources, and fervently shepherded the book to completion. Sincere appreciation is also extended to Renee Wilmeth and Kristi Hart, who directed the publisher's nitty-gritty editorial and production work with outstanding dedication and professionalism, plus a reassuring enthusiasm; to Pamela Benner, who paid excellent attention to details in the copyediting process and made good suggestions; and to many other directly involved personnel, particularly Beth Jordan, Faunette Johnston, and Jeanine Bucek.

This book could also not have been completed without the special assistance of my wife, Sandy, and my daughters, Alyson, Megan, and Kristen. They each helped in a variety of ways, especially by being patient. Sandy's assistance with a host of matters was very beneficial, and Kristen was particularly vital, pitching in for a second time during a desperate period with important research and writing assistance.

In order to make this encyclopedia truly comprehensive and of worldwide significance it was imperative to involve a host of contributors with expertise in technical fisheries matters, regional angling opportunities, and specialized sportfishing topics. I'm grateful for their participation and excellent contributions, the bulk of which made up the *Worldwide Angling Guide*. In particular, appreciation is extended to the incomparable Ed Migdalski, who provided technical scientific fisheries advice and vetted all of the fish art.

I'm also indebted to the late, and incomparable in his own right, A. J. McClane. His fishing encyclopedia of 1965 and 1974, though now outdated, was not only a phenomenal reference work, but a monumental achievement in an era before personal computers, electronic mail, fax machines, scanners, laser printers, and the various modern technology that made putting this book together far easier than it was in his time. Unlike me, he was unable to write and edit on a laptop computer in cars, planes, airports, hotel rooms, and other places, or receive electronically transmitted text. More significantly, McClane set a very high bar for what a real fishing encyclopedia ought to be, and provided a template for such a book for the twenty-first century. Without his accomplishment, it would have been much more difficult to plan and publish this book. (Aside to historians: four contributors to this project—Ed Migdalski, George Reiger, Jack Samson, and Bill Scifres—were also contributors to McClane's encyclopedia.)

Just as McClane, the contributors to this book, and the people at IDG Books Worldwide are the best in their fields, so is *Field & Stream* the largest and best fishing and hunting magazine in the world, and I've been privileged to be part of this publication continuously since 1973. I appreciate the confidence and opportunities provided me over that time by its editors. Those opportunities laid the groundwork for this encyclopedia. I'm especially grateful to Editor Slaton White and Managing Editor Mike Toth for allowing me leeway over the last several years that I've been working on this project.

Information, suggestions, encouragement, technical advice, reference paraphernalia, reviews and critiques, and assorted material assistance were received from so many individuals and organizations that some will likely be overlooked in these acknowledgments, for which I apologize.

I'm very grateful to the following individuals:

Blaine Anderson
John Anthon
Dick Ballard
Ron Ballanti
LaVerne Barnes
Cameron Baty
Susan Baumgartner
Gene Bay
Dick Bengraff
Virginia Benoit
Walt Boname
Toby Bradshaw
Eric Burnley
Cyril Calendini
Bill Chapman, Jr.
Jim Chapralis
Larry Columbo
David Cosby
Gary Dollahon
Lou Duarte
Todd DuPuis
Jack Erskine
Mike Fine
Paul Fuller
Riccardo Galigani
Ken Gangler

Acknowledgments

Guy Geffroy
Lois Gerber
Alessandro Giangio
Barry Gibson
Gary Giudice
Fred Golofaro
Jerry Gomber
George Gowen
Garry Gurke
Judy Hammond
Bill Hilts, Jr.
Bruce Holt
Dr. James Imai
Jimmy Kano
Nick Karas
Glenda Kelley
Gary King
Jason Klein
Bob Lang
Steen Larsen
Mike Leech
Bill Liston
Chun Liu
George Loechl
Paulo Loes
Frank Longino
Jim Matthews
John Mazurkewicz
Tom Melton
Paul Merzig
Ed Mesunas
Bill Miller
Gail Morchower
András Nagy
Andy Newman
Stuart Newman
Donald J. Orth
Tom Pagliaroli
Sheldon Pasternack
Dennis Phillips
Stanko Popovic
Norville Prosser
Jim Reist
Al Ristori
Milt Rosko
Gail Ross
Sharon Rushton
Pat Salimeno
Marty Salovin
Glenn Sapir
Christine Moore Serrao
Vin Sparano
Ron Speed, Sr.
Roy Stiner
Mick Thill
Roger Tucker
Jerry Valentine
Mike Walker
Ben Wechsler
Mark Weintz
Fenner Weller
Jim White
Anthony M. Williams
Dick Wood
Peter Yaskowski

I'm also grateful to the following companies and organizations (and specific people where noted in parenthesis):

American Sportfishing Association (Mike Hayden)
American Wire (Michael Shields)
Arkie Lures
The Atlantic Salmon Federation
Bay de Noc Lure Co.
Bead Tackle (Peter Renkert)
Bear Advertising (Dick Bear, Mark Malkin)
Big Jon (Jerry Livingstone)
Bullet Weights (Douglas Crumrine)
Bushnell Sports Optics (Barbara Mellman)
Cabela's Inc. (Tony Dolle)
Classic Fishing Products (Mike Richards)
C-Map USA (Pam Oldham)
Computrol, Inc.
Cossack Bait Products (Garry Shaw)
Cuba Specialty Mfg. Co. (Craig Osterhus, Dana Pickup)
Daiwa Corp.
Earie Dearie Lure Co. (Helen Galbincea)
EZE Lap Diamond (Donna Long)
Fin-Nor (Niels Stenhoj)
Flambeau Products Corp. (Jason Sauey)
Florida Keys and Key West Visitors Bureau
Flow-Rite of Tennessee (Don Zielinski)
Furuno
Future Fisherman Foundation
Garmin International (Steve Featherstone)
G. Loomis (Gary Loomis, Steve Rajeff)
Gudebrod
International Game Fish Association (Jim Brown)
Hudson River Foundation
Interphase Technologies
K-C Tackle (Raymond Packer)
L. L. Bean (Mary Rose MacKinnon)
L&S Bait Co. (Eric Bachnik)
Lowrance Electronics (Darrell Lowrance, Steve Schneider)
Luhr Jensen & Sons (Phil Jensen, Barry Ternahan)
Magellan Systems Corp. (Don Meyer)
Mann's Bait Co.
Marado Inc.
Old Town Canoe (Jim Kaiser)
O. Mustad & Sons USA (John DeVries)
National Freshwater Fishing Hall of Fame
Nomadic Expeditions (Denise Gogarty)
Normark Corp. (Ron Weber, Craig Weber)
The Orvis Company
Outdoor Technologies
Owner America Corp. (Kat Shitanishi)
Penn Fishing Tackle
Pradco (Joe Hughes, Bruce Stanton)
Scientific Anglers
Shakespeare Fishing Tackle (Mark Davis)
Sheldon's Inc.
Shimano American Corp.
Si-Tex Marine Electronics
Storm Lures (Sharon Andrews, John Storm)
Sufix USA, Inc.
Techsonics Industries
Len Thompson Lures (Richard Pallister)
Top Brass Tackle (Eric Cosby)
Tru-Turn Hooks (Wes Campbell)
Wisconsin Pharmacal
H. D. Wood Advertising
Worden's Lures
The Worth Co.
Wright & McGill Co. (George Large)
Yakima Bait Co. (Rob Phillips)
Zebco Corp. (Jenni Foster)

Gratitude is also due the following government agencies and government-funded programs (and the people noted in parenthesis), which provided research and reference materials, and, in some cases, other forms of assistance:

Alabama Cooperative Extension Service (Richard Wallace)
Alabama Department of Conservation and Natural Resources (Stan Cook)
Alabama Sea Grant Extension Program
Alaska Department of Fish and Game (Jon Lyman)
Alaska Sea Grant College Program (Kurt Byers)
Alberta Department of Environmental Protection

Acknowledgments

Arizona Game and Fish Department
Arkansas Cooperative Extension Program, Univ. of Arkansas (Nathan Stone)
Arkansas Game and Fish Commission (Keith Sutton)
Auburn University Marine Extension (Richard Wallace, William Hosking, Stephen Szedlmayer)
Brazil Embratur
British Columbia Ministry of Environment, Fisheries Branch
California Department of Fish and Game (A. Petrovich)
Canada Department of Fisheries and Oceans
Canadian Consul General
Cayman Islands Department of Tourism
Colorado Department of Natural Resources
Connecticut Department of Environmental Protection
Delaware Division of Fish and Wildlife
Florida Department of Environmental Protection, Marine Research Institute and Division of Marine Resources (Jim Lewis)
Florida Game and Freshwater Fish Commission, Division of Fisheries (Henry Cabbage)
Georgia Department of Natural Resources (Chris Martin)
Great Lakes Fishery Commission
Guam Department of Agriculture (Gerry Davis)
Hawaii Department of Land and Natural Resources, Division of Aquatic Resources
Idaho Department of Fish and Game (Jack Trueblood)
Illinois Department of Natural Resources
Indiana Department of Natural Resources (Jon Marshall)
International Center for Living Aquatic Resources Management/Food and Agriculture Organization of the United Nations
Iowa Department of Natural Resources (Steve Suman)
Kansas Department of Wildlife and Parks (Mike Miller)
Kentucky Department of Fish and Wildlife Resources (J. Beth Garland)
Louisiana Department of Wildlife and Fisheries
Louisiana Sea Grant College Program
Maine Department of Inland Fisheries and Wildlife (V. Paul Reynolds)
Manitoba Department of Natural Resources, Fisheries Branch (Carl Wall)
Maryland Department of Natural Resources (Eugene Deems, Jr.)
Maryland Sea Grant College Program (Jack Greer)
Massachusetts Division of Fisheries and Wildlife
Michigan Department of Natural Resources, Fisheries Division
Michigan Sea Grant College Program (Martha Walter)
Minnesota Department of Natural Resources (Tom Dickson)
Mississippi Department of Wildlife, Fisheries and Parks (Jim Walker)
Missouri Department of Conservation (John McPherson)
Montana Division of Fish, Wildlife, and Parks
Nevada Department of Conservation and Natural Resources
New Brunswick Department of Economic Development and Tourism
New Brunswick Department of Natural Resources, Fish and Wildlife Branch (Peter Cronin)
Newfoundland Department of Natural Resources
New Hampshire Fish and Game Department (Patricia Fleurie)
New Jersey Division of Fish, Game and Wildlife (Dave Chanda)
New Mexico Department of Game and Fish (Ruth Anderson)
New York Department of Environmental Conservation (Robert Brandt)
New York Sea Grant Program (David MacNeill, Mark Malchoff)
NOAA/Gray's Reef National Marine Sanctuary (Beth Kostka)
NOAA/National Marine Fisheries Service
NOAA/National Weather Service
North Carolina Division of Boating and Inland Fisheries (Fred Harris)
North Carolina Sea Grant
North Dakota Game and Fish Department (Terry Steinwand)
Nova Scotia Department of Fisheries (Murray Hill)
Nova Scotia Department of Lands and Forests (Barry Sabean)
Ohio Department of Natural Resources
Ohio Sea Grant College Program
Oklahoma Department of Wildlife Conservation (Nels Rodefeld)
Ontario Ministry of Economic Development, Trade & Tourism (Tom Boyd)
Ontario Ministry of Natural Resources
Oregon Department of Fish and Wildlife (Randy Henry)
Oregon Sea Grant (Pat Kight)
Parátur, State of Pará, Brazil
Pennsylvania Fish and Boat Commission
Portuguese National Tourist Office (Maria Joáo Ramires)
Prince Edward Island Department of Environmental Resources
Quebec Department of Recreation, Fish and Game
Rhode Island Division of Fish and Game
Rhode Island Sea Grant
Saskatchewan Department of Environment, Fish and Wildlife (Bruce Howard)

South Carolina Department of Natural Resources (Greg Lucas)
South Carolina Sea Grant Consortium (John Tibbetts)
South Dakota Department of Game, Fish and Parks
Spain Ministry of Commerce and Tourism
Tennessee Wildlife Resources Agency (Dave Woodward)
Texas Parks and Wildlife (Steve Lightfoot)
Tourism British Columbia
Tourism New Brunswick
Tourism Newfoundland and Labrador
Tourism Nova Scotia (Randy Brooks)
Tourism Prince Edward Island (Carol Horne)
Tourism Quebec (Siegfried Gagnon)
Tourism Saskatchewan (Gerard Makuch, Nadine Howard)
Travel Alberta (Peter Gregus)
Travel Manitoba (Dennis Maksymetz, Colette Fontaine, Gord Richardson)
University of Connecticut Sea Grant Marine Advisory Program (Nancy Balcom)
University of Delaware Sea Grant College Program
University of Florida Cooperative Extension Service
University of New Hampshire and University of Maine Sea Grant College Program
U.S. Fish and Wildlife Service
Utah Department of Natural Resources (Gerry Schlappe)
Vermont Department of Fish and Wildlife (John Hall)
Virginia Department of Game and Inland Fisheries (Mitchell Norman)
Washington Department of Fish and Wildlife (Nina Carter, James Chandler)
Washington Sea Grant Program (Kris Freeman)
West Virginia Division of Natural Resources (Hoy Murphy)
Wisconsin Department of Natural Resources (David Kunelius)
Woods Hole Oceanographic Institute (Tracey Crago)
Wyoming Game and Fish Department
Yukon Territory Department of Renewable Resources (Susan Thompson)

Finally, I'm also grateful to four student interns, whose early work compiling and organizing research materials was of much help—Kristen Schultz of Oberlin College, Alyson Schultz of Boston University, Mathew Kane of Hamilton College, and John Kuhner of Princeton University—and to Megan Schultz of Ithaca College, for Web site development and advice.

—Ken Schultz

About the Author, Artists, and Contributors

PRINCIPAL AUTHOR AND EDITOR

Ken Schultz has been a staff fishing writer and editor for *Field & Stream* since 1973. His feature articles and columns for that publication appear monthly, and he contributes to the magazine's nationally syndicated weekly radio show and to its Web site. Schultz is a frequent author of the outdoors column of the *New York Times*, and he previously was a syndicated newspaper columnist for Gannett. He has authored a dozen books on sportfishing and angling travel topics, has been a featured guest on CNBC, ESPN, and The Nashville Network, and appears regularly in assorted fishing segments for the Outdoor Life Network. A widely traveled angler, Schultz is a former holder of seven line-class world records and was inducted into the Fishing Hall of Fame in 1998. He lives in Forestburgh, New York.

THE ARTISTS

Steve T. Goione is a rising star in the world of fishing and boating art, working in mixed mediums to present his lifelong passion for angling in a dynamic and realistic style. Although he drew the distinctive pen-and-ink illustrations for this book as well as the dust-jacket cover, Goione is primarily a creator of fine art. From his studio in Toms River, New Jersey, he produces commissioned fishing scenes for private collections and limited-edition prints, and he has created original artwork for Sea World in Florida. Goione has also made a mark among boat builders and owners for commissioned renderings of big-game sportfishing craft, and he recently created original artwork for the latest products of Hatteras Yachts. A frequent guest artist on the big-game fishing tournament circuit, Goione appears at exclusive contests each year from Nantucket to Venezuela, and his work is regularly featured at fund-raising events for prominent conservation organizations.

David Kiphuth, whose renderings of fish appear in this book, has had a varied career in the field of art, having been a professional illustrator since 1969. His work has included portraiture, architectural renderings, maps, and book illustration. Kiphuth has created archaeological and scientific book and exhibit renderings for the Yale Peabody Museum, the Yale Department of Anthropology, and Yale University Press. He formerly maintained a studio and gallery in Branford, Connecticut, where he created and sold wildlife and nature art and animal portraits. Since 1989, he has been the staff illustrator for the *Gazette Newspapers* in Schenectady, New York. He lives in Saratoga Springs, New York.

THE CONTRIBUTORS

Brett Albanese of Virginia is a Ph.D candidate at the Department of Fisheries and Wildlife Sciences at Virginia Polytechnic Institute; he formerly worked at the Mississippi Museum of Natural Sciences.

Ken Allen of Maine is Associate Editor of *Maine Sportsman* and a prolific writer, photographer, newspaper columnist, book author, and guide.

Michael Babcock of Montana is Outdoors Editor of the *Great Falls Tribune*.

Ken Bailey of Alberta is Manager of Field Operations in central Alberta for Ducks Unlimited Canada; he is a prolific writer and President of the Outdoor Writers Association of Canada.

Dick Ballard of Missouri is President of Dick Ballard's Fishing Adventures and a foremost authority on Amazonian angling; he's sent anglers fishing around the world for 18 years, and established the first travel service for Bass Pro Shops.

Scott Bannerot of Pennsylvania and Florida has a Ph.D. in fisheries science and has worked in marine biological research and consulting; he is a photojournalist and a charter boat captain.

John A. Barnes of Bermuda is the Director of Agriculture and Fisheries for Bermuda; he authors a weekly fishing column in the Bermuda *Mid Ocean News*, and is an IGFA representative.

Rob Barraclough of Indonesia and England works in the oil industry and is a charter boat captain and freelance writer.

Carlos M. Barrantes of Costa Rica established the first two sportfishing camps in Costa Rica; he is an IGFA representative and was the first President of the Costa Rican Fishing Federation.

Cody Beers of Wyoming works for the Wyoming Game and Fish Department as Associate Editor of *Wyoming Wildlife* magazine and Editor of *Wyoming Wildlife News and Wild Times*; he is also a freelance writer and photographer.

Bob Berry of California is one of the world's top fish carvers and sculptors, and swept all divisions of the 1986 world championship of fish carving; he is a foremost competition judge, a former professional taxidermist, and author of the book *Fish Carving*.

Mike Bleech of Pennsylvania is a writer and photographer whose work has appeared in most major U.S. fishing and hunting magazines.

Larry Blomquist of Louisiana is Publisher of *Breakthrough*, the world's largest taxidermy trade magazine, and one of the top competition judges in North America; he is a retired award-winning taxidermist, and former President of the National Taxidermists Association.

Fred Bonner of North Carolina is Editor of *Carolina Adventure* magazine; he is also a syndicated newspaper columnist, fisheries biologist, and an IGFA representative.

Judith Bowman of New York has been a foremost sporting books dealer for over twenty years; she produces two sporting book catalogs a year, with special emphasis on fishing.

John Brownlee of Florida is Senior Editor of *Salt Water Sportsman* and a former charter boat captain; he has served on the South Atlantic Fishery Management Council, is former Chairman of the Florida Conservation Association, and is an IGFA representative.

Eric B. Burnley of Virginia is the author of *Surf Fishing the Atlantic Coast* and a radio show host; he is a charter boat captain and Regional Editor of both *Salt Water Sportsman* and *The Fisherman* magazines.

Erwin Bursik of South Africa is Publisher of *Ski-Boat* and *Flyfishing* magazines of Durban, a member of the executive board of the South African Deep Sea Angling Association, and an IGFA representative.

Mac Campbell of Great Britain works for *Angling Plus*, a match fishing magazine, and has previously worked for *Sea Angler*, *Trout Fisherman*, and *Angling Times*.

Jim Casada of South Carolina is the author of many books, including *Modern Fly Fishing*; he is Senior Editor of *Sporting Classics* magazine, and outdoor columnist for the Rock Hill *Herald* and Greensboro *News and Record*.

Göran Cederberg of Sweden has been Editor of several international fact-packed large-format angling books, including *The Complete Book of Sportfishing*; he contributes regularly to north-European publications and has been chief editor of a Swedish sportfishing magazine.

Matthew D. Chan of Virginia is a Ph.D candidate at the Department of Fisheries and Wildlife Sciences at Virginia Polytechnic Institute; he formerly worked as a fisheries biologist for the U. S. Army Corps of Engineers.

Dawn Charging of North Dakota is Outdoors Director for the North Dakota State Tourism Department; she is also a writer and photographer whose family owns a successful fishing resort on Lake Sakakawea.

Homer Circle of Florida has been Angling Editor of *Sports Afield* magazine for 34 years; the dean of American outdoor writers, he is the recipient of numerous media and achievement awards, a former member of the Arkansas Game & Fish Commission, and a renowned television and video host.

Barry Ord Clarke of Norway is a professional photographer and writer and the author of several books on fly fishing and fly tying; he contributes regularly to most European fishing magazines, and is fishing consultant to Norway's largest private sporting estate.

Soc Clay of Kentucky is an accomplished and prolific fishing writer and photographer whose work has appeared in every major outdoor periodical in North America.

Angelo Cuanang of California is a Pacific Regional Editor for *Salt Water Sportsman* and a freelance writer and photographer.

Paula J. Del Giudice of Nevada is Outdoor Columnist for the *Las Vegas Sun*; a freelance writer, photographer, and book author; and former President of the Nevada Wildlife Federation.

Arthur De Mello of Uganda is a representative for the IGFA in Uganda.

Hansjörg Dietiker of Switzerland is Editor of the Swiss Anglers Magazine *Petri-Heil*, and an IGFA representative.

Philippe Dolivet of France is the Chief Editor of the French fly fishing magazine *Plaisirs de la Pêche* and a professional photographer; he is a fly fishing instructor and competitor, an ichthyologist, and an IGFA representative.

Gary Edwards of Wyoming is a longtime fishing guide and a television show host; he is the former Editor and Publisher of *Salmon Fever* magazine, and a former fly rod world record holder.

D'arcy Egan of Ohio has been a sportswriter for *The Cleveland Plain Dealer* for over 20 years; he authored the book, *Guide to Ohio Fishing*, and is host of the American Outdoorsman Radio Network.

Bill Ensor of New Brunswick works for the Fish & Wildlife Branch of the New Brunswick Department of Natural Resources; he was formerly marketing manager of fishing and hunting for the New Brunswick Department of Tourism, and is a longtime fishing guide.

Jack Erskine of Australia is a foremost big-game tackle designer and technical innovator who has helped design many of the modern rods, reels, and drag systems in use today.

Stan Fagerstrom of Oregon is one of the world's best known trick and accuracy casters, and has been featured at sport shows worldwide for half a century; he is also a book, magazine, and newspaper writer.

Jan Fogt of Florida is Editor of *The Bahamas Sportfishing Guide* and was the founding editor of

Bahamas Blue Water Magazine; she is a contributing editor for *Sport Fishing* and *Marlin* magazines, and is also a book author.

Frank Fry of the Yukon Territory has worked with the Yukon Territory's Department of Natural Resources on various fishing projects.

Mike Garzillo of New Hampshire has been a newspaper columnist for 24 years; he is a regular contributor to various publications and a former regional editor for *Outdoor Life*.

Alessandro Giangio of Italy writes for Italy's premier fishing magazine, *Pesca in Mare*, and has been published worldwide; he has authored five books, is owner and master instructor of the Fishbuster Trolling School and Sportfishing Travel, and has a charter boat in Huatulco, Mexico.

Jerry Gibbs of Vermont is Fishing Editor of *Outdoor Life*, where his career as a staff writer has spanned three decades and made him one of North America's most respected angling authors; he has written several books and has been inducted into the Fishing Hall of Fame.

Barry Gibson of Massachusetts is Editor of *Salt Water Sportsman* and a longtime Maine charter boat captain; he is a former member of the New England Fishery Management Council, and former advisor to the International Commission for the Conservation of Atlantic Tunas.

Jerry Gomber of New Jersey has over twenty-five years of experience in design, development, and marketing of fishing rods and reels; during that period he has been responsible for several successful product innovations.

George Gruenefeld of Quebec and Saskatchewan is Editor of *Canadian Outdoor Publications*; he has written for many magazines in Canada and the U.S., is a book author, and was formerly Outdoors Editor for the *Montreal Gazette*.

Chris Hanks of the Northwest Territories is an anthropologist, freelance writer, and author of the book *Fly Fishing in the Northwest Territories*.

Steve Harper of Kansas is the Outdoors Editor of the *Wichita Eagle* and author of the book *Kansas Day Trips*; in 1995 he was named Conservation Communicator of the Year by the Kansas Wildlife Federation.

Dan Heiner of Alaska is an advertising agency executive and former editor and writer for *Alaska Outdoors* magazine; he is the author of four books on Alaska fishing, including *Fly Fishing Alaska's Wild Rivers*.

Bob Hodge of Tennessee is the Outdoors Editor of the *Knoxville News-Sentinel*; he was named the state's Best Outdoor Writer for 1996-97 by the Tennessee Sportswriters Association.

Grant Hopkins of Ontario is the outdoor columnist for the *Ottawa Citizen*, a frequent contributor to *Ontario Out of Doors*, and retired from the Royal Canadian Air Force.

John Husar of Illinois is the longtime outdoors columnist and general sportswriter of the *Chicago Tribune* and co-host of a Chicago radio show; he has worked for newspapers in Kansas, Texas, and New Mexico, and has covered the last nine Olympics.

Jim Imai of California has a Ph.D in physics and is Professor of Physics at California State University, Dominguez Hills; he is a Consulting Physicist for the Daiwa Corporation, and a leading authority on the design and performance of fishing reels and rods.

James Kano of Ontario is the Marketing Director of Japan Communications in Toronto and Outdoor Coordinator for the Press and Tourism division of the Ontario government; his articles have appeared online and in newspapers, guide books, and magazines.

Nick Karas of New York is the retired outdoor columnist for (New York) *Newsday* and a charter boat captain and ichthyologist; he has written for many national magazines and authored a dozen books, including *The Striped Bass* and *Brook Trout*.

Lee Kernen of Wisconsin is the retired Director of Fisheries for the State of Wisconsin; he is also a writer, fishing guide, and fisheries consultant.

Ronnie Kovach of California is a radio and television show host, educator, magazine writer, guide, and author of five books, including *Bass Fishing in California*, *Trout Fishing in California*, and *Saltwater Fishing in California*.

Steen Larsen of Denmark is one of Europe's leading sportfishing writers and photographers; he is a book author and lecturer, and contributes widely to many European angling publications.

Dick Lewers of Australia is Technical Editor of *Encyclopaedia of Australian Fishing*, author of seven books on angling, a former IGFA representative, 35-year columnist for *Modern Fishing Magazine*, and past President of the Australian National Sportfishing Association.

Bill Loftus of Idaho is the Outdoors Editor of the *Lewiston Morning Tribune* and the author of two guidebooks to Idaho.

Maurice Loustau-LaLanne of Seychelles is the Principal Secretary in the Ministry of Tourism and Transport for the Seychelles, and an IGFA representative.

Carl. F. Luckey of Alabama is a writer specializing in antiques and collectibles; he has authored ten books, including his best-selling, 618-page work, *Old Fishing Lures and Tackle*.

Joe Macaluso of Louisiana is an award-winning outdoors sportswriter/editor for the *Baton Rouge Advocate*; his weekly fishing reports have appeared in Louisiana newspapers since 1976.

Rosanne Macfarlane of Prince Edward Island recently received her Masters degree in Biology at

Acadia University; she works for the Department of Fisheries and Environment.

Dennis Maksymetz of Manitoba is Manager of Tourism Marketing for the Industry, Trade and Tourism division of the Manitoba government.

Don Mann of Florida is a longtime contributor to *Florida Sportsman*, a record-holding big-game angler, and book author; his articles and photographs have appeared in many publications.

Al Marlowe of Colorado has written numerous articles for outdoor magazines; he authored a trail guide for the Flat Tops Wilderness area and a fly fishing guide for the Colorado River.

Peter B. Mathiesen of Missouri is Executive Editor and Producer of the *Field & Stream Radio Hour*; he is also a magazine writer, photographer, and video and television show producer.

John McCoy of West Virginia is Outdoors Editor for the *Charleston Daily Mail*, Regional Editor for *Field & Stream*, and a frequent contributor to regional and national magazines.

Tom Meade of Rhode Island writes about the outdoors for the *Providence Journal-Bulletin*; he is the author of *Essential Fly Fishing*, and writes for various magazines.

Ed Migdalski of Connecticut is the retired Director of Yale University's Outdoor Education and Club Sports Programs, retired Ichthyologist for the Yale Peabody Museum, and holder of the current world record for the largest strictly freshwater fish (pirarucu) ever caught on rod and reel.

Kent Mitchell of Georgia has covered outdoor sports for the *Atlanta Journal-Constitution* for three decades; he has received the Communicator of the Year Award from the Georgia Wildlife Federation, and has authored three books on martial arts.

Bill Monroe of Oregon has covered the outdoors for his state's largest daily newspaper, *The Oregonian*, for 18 years.

Gary W. Moore of Vermont is a freelance writer and photographer; he is former Commissioner of the Vermont Fish and Wildlife Department and former Chairman of the Vermont Water Resources Board.

Sam Mossman of New Zealand is Special Projects Editor for *New Zealand Fishing News* magazine; he is the author of three books and hundreds of magazine articles, and has held five world and numerous New Zealand fishing records.

Perry Munro of Nova Scotia is a writer and artist who contributes to *The Atlantic Salmon Journal* and various other magazines; he is also an outfitter, master guide, operator of Maple Mountain Lodge, and a Director of Trout Unlimited Canada.

Iain Nicolson of Angola is an IGFA representative and has a Ph.D. in molecular genetics; he and his family pioneered fishing for blue marlin in Angola and collectively established six world fishing records.

Chris Niskanen of Minnesota is the Outdoors Editor of the *St. Paul Pioneer Press*.

Donald J. Orth of Virginia is a Professor of Fisheries Science in the Department of Fisheries & Wildlife Sciences at Virginia Polytechnic Institute.

Tom Pagliaroli of New Jersey is an advertising agency executive, freelance writer, and photographer whose work has appeared in various regional and national publications.

Ali Pasiner of Turkey is an attorney, the author of two fishing books, and a consultant to the Turkish version of the *Encyclopaedia Britannica*; he is also a writer, editor, and representative of the IGFA.

C. Boyd Pfeiffer of Maryland is a longtime journalist and photographer, a regular columnist for many angling magazines, and the author of numerous books on fishing topics, the latest of which is *Fly Fishing Salt Water Basics*.

Larry Porter of Nebraska has been on the sports staff of the *Omaha World-Herald* for over three decades and their outdoors writer since 1990; he has been named Nebraska Sportswriter of the Year three times, and is a former professional tournament angler.

Steve Price of Texas is a longtime Senior Writer for *Bassmaster* magazine and contributor to a wide variety of national sporting magazines; he is an accomplished photographer and author of several books.

Gareth Purnell of England is Editor of Britain's leading angling magazine, *Improve Your Coarse Fishing*, and former News Editor of *Angling Times*; he has fished annually in the World Freshwater Angling Championships since 1993.

George Reiger of Virginia is Conservation Editor of *Field & Stream* and *Salt Water Sportsman* magazines and the most widely respected conservation writer in North America; he has been a staff writer for *Field & Stream* since 1972, is the author of seven books on angling and marine ecology, and the recipient of numerous honors and awards.

Tim Renken of Missouri has been the outdoors writer for the *St. Louis Post-Dispatch* since 1963; he previously worked for the Nebraska Game Commission.

Len Rich of Newfoundland is the author of two books and many outdoor magazine articles; he operates Awesome Lake Lodge in Labrador, is a former Hunting and Fishing Development Officer for Newfoundland and Labrador, and is a past representative of the Atlantic Salmon Federation.

Tom Richardson of Massachusetts is Managing Editor of *Salt Water Sportsman* magazine, as well as a freelance writer and photographer.

Al Ristori of New Jersey is Saltwater Fishing Editor of the *Newark Star-Ledger*, Regional Editor of *Salt Water Sportsman*, Conservation Editor of *The Fisherman* magazine, and the author of several books; he is also a charter boat captain and has served on the Mid-Atlantic Fishery Management Council.

Jim Rizzuto of Hawaii is Hawaii Editor for *Salt Water Sportsman* and *Western Outdoors*, a longtime columnist for *West Hawaii Today* and *Hawaii Fishing News*, and the author of the books *Modern Hawaiian Gamefishing* and *Fishing Hawaii Style*.

Nels Rodefeld of Oklahoma is an avid angler and hunter who frequently covers Oklahoma's hunting and fishing scene.

Milt Rosko of New Jersey is a writer for *Big Game Fishing Journal* and various other publications and a longtime authority on saltwater sportfishing; he is a photographer, book author, magazine feature writer, and lecturer.

Terry Rudnick of Washington has been writing articles on Northwest fishing subjects for more than 25 years; he is the author of the book *Washington Fishing, the Complete Guide*, and co-author of *How to Catch Trophy Halibut*.

Bob Sampson, Jr. of Connecticut is a writer, photographer, science teacher, and fisheries biologist; his work has appeared in numerous national and regional magazines.

Jack Samson of New Mexico is the retired Editor-in-Chief of *Field & Stream* and a former Associated Press columnist; he is Saltwater Editor of *Fly Rod & Reel* magazine, author of twenty books, and the first angler to catch both Atlantic and Pacific sailfish and all five species of marlin on a fly.

Ray Sasser of Texas is the Outdoor Editor of *The Dallas Morning News* and a freelance contributor to various magazines; he has been writing about outdoor sports for over 25 years.

Carl Werner Schmidt-Luchs of Germany is a contributor to *Blinker*, the largest angling magazine in Europe; he is a photographer, writer, and author of a dozen angling books.

Kristen Schultz of Massachusetts is a writer who recently graduated from Oberlin College; she works for an engineering consulting firm.

Bill Scifres of Indiana has been the Outdoor Editor of the *Indianapolis Star* since 1953; he is a book author, freelance writer, and photographer.

Eric Sharp of Michigan is Outdoor Editor of *The Detroit News*, and was formerly Outdoor Editor of *The Miami Herald*.

Luis Sier of Argentina is a newspaper columnist, a former magazine publisher, and an outfitter who operates several Argentinian fishing camps.

Jeff Simpson of South Dakota is an information officer for the State of South Dakota, a book author and freelance magazine writer, and former project developer for Cowles Creative Publishing.

DeWayne Smith of Arizona is an information officer for the Maricopa County Parks and Recreation Department; he covered the outdoors for over 30 years for *The Phoenix Gazette*.

Ryan Smith of Virginia is a research assistant with the Department of Fisheries and Wildlife Sciences at Virginia Polytechnic Institute.

Michael Snook of Saskatchewan is a freelance writer, conservationist, outdoor educator, and television producer.

Frank Sousa of Massachusetts is a writer for the *Springfield Sunday Republican* and the *Union News*, Editor/Publisher of *Northeast Woods and Waters*, and a freelance writer and photographer.

Vin T. Sparano of New Jersey is Senior Field Editor and retired Editor-in-Chief of *Outdoor Life*, for whom he worked for over three decades; he is a former syndicated columnist for *Gannett Newspapers*, and the author/editor of fourteen books, including *The Complete Outdoors Encyclopedia*.

Vladimir Stakic of Yugoslavia is Deputy Editor-in-Chief of the Yugoslavian angling magazines *Ribolovacka Revija* and *Ribolovacke Novine*, a freelance writer, and the author of three books of short stories.

Bob Stearns of Florida has been the staff boating/saltwater fishing writer of *Field & Stream* for 20 years and is the Electronics Editor of *Salt Water Sportsman*; the author of two books, he is a renowned fly fishing and light tackle expert, and has held two fly rod world records for sailfish.

Larry Stone of Iowa has been a writer and photographer for over three decades, and writes about the outdoors for the *Des Moines Register*.

Keith Sutton of Arkansas is Editor of *Arkansas Wildlife magazine*, a conservation publication of the Arkansas Game & Fish Commission, and a prolific freelance writer and photographer.

Ferenc Szalay of Hungary is Editor-in-Chief of *Magyar Horgász*, Hungary's premier fishing magazine; he is also President of the Hungarian National Committee for Match Fishing and Executive Board member of the Federation Internationale de la Pêche Sportive en Eau Douce.

Allan Tarvid of Texas is a contributing editor for *Sport Fishing* magazine and has authored hundreds of articles on electronics for sporting and commercial fishing and emergency service use; he has been a fishing guide and search and rescue diver.

Rikk Taylor of British Columbia is Editor and Publisher of *British Columbia Sport Fishing* magazine.

Mick Thill of Illinois and England is one of the world's top professional match fishing anglers and the first and only person to medal in the open water and ice fishing World Freshwater Fishing Championships; he is also a prominent float designer, and coach of the U. S. World Championship fishing teams.

Albert A. W. Threadingham of Fiji is an IGFA representative for the Fiji Islands and Governor of the Hawaiian International Billfish Association and the Pacific Ocean Research Foundation; he is a former world-record fish holder.

Raj Tilak of Maryland and India is co-author of the book *Game Fishes of India and Angling,* and author of more than 200 research publications; he is experienced in fisheries and wildlife management, with extensive knowledge of gamefishes and their ecology in India.

Anssi Uitti of Finland works for the Finnish outdoor magazine *Metsästys ja Kalastus*, and his articles have appeared in *Urheilukalastus* (Sportfishing) and *Perhokalastus* (Flyfishing) magazines.

Luis Umpierre of Puerto Rico is a physician, Editor of *Notipesca* (Fishing News), President of the Puerto Rico Sportfishing Association, and advisory member of the Caribbean Fishery Management Council.

Rudy Van Duijnhoven of Holland is a freelance photographer and author; his work appears monthly in *BEET-Sportvissers* magazine, and he is European Correspondent for Fly Fishing in *Salt Waters* magazine.

Carlo Vernocchi of Italy and Zanzibar introduced modern big-game fishing to the Zanzibar archipelago of Tanzania in 1992; he is an IGFA representative and charter boat captain.

Victor Villavicencio of Manila is a representative for the IGFA in the Philippines.

Tsutomu Wakabayashi of Japan is the General Manager of the Japan Game Fish Association; he has written for several Japanese fishing magazines, and is an IGFA representative.

Steve Waters of Florida is the outdoors writer for the *Fort Lauderdale Sun-Sentinel* and occasionally writes for national magazines; he was formerly a newspaper writer and video executive in New York.

Tom Wharton of Utah has been Outdoor Editor of the *Salt Lake Tribune* since 1976; he has co-authored five books, and is past President of the Outdoor Writers Association of America.

Jesse E. Williams of New Mexico is the retired Chief of Public Affairs for the New Mexico Department of Game and Fish, and a former Colorado wildlife manager and environmental education supervisor.

Juergen Willms of the Yukon Territory has worked with the Yukon Territory's Department of Natural Resources on various fishing projects.

Jorge Xifra of Paraguay operates El Pescador, a sportfishing outfitting service; he is a writer, television show host, IGFA representative, and holder of four world fishing records.

Photo Credits

All photographs by Ken Schultz except for the following:

Erwin Bursik 135, 140
Cabela's 297, 304
Daiwa 187, 189, 201
Fin-Nor 193

Bruce Holt 14, 243
Nick Karas 44
Steen Larsen 286
Marado 184, 190, 200

Al Ristori 76, 293
Shakespeare 161, 200
Zebco 155, 157, 158, 174, 191, 196

TACKLE

A generic term for the man-made equipment used almost exclusively for sportfishing; also commonly referred to as fishing tackle. In prevailing use, tackle fundamentally refers to rods, reels, lines, leaders, and assorted terminal gear. The term "tackle box" is derived from this, obviously because it refers to a compact portable means of storing the assorted small items that comprise terminal gear: hooks, weights, lures, connectors, and so forth. Natural bait is not considered tackle, hence the common term "bait and tackle" shop.

In an extended sense today, tackle also refers to accessory equipment used in sportfishing, such as a landing net, a bait container, or a downrigger. Clothing items are not considered tackle, although waders and wading footwear blur this distinction, as do such items as electric motors and sonar; these and other products are often included in the broad designation "tackle," although they may be used for other purposes besides fishing. As time advances, most gear that is used in sportfishing, whether exclusively or not, is considered an item of tackle, especially by manufacturers and merchants.

Although rods and reels are considered intrinsic to fishing tackle, they are not absolutely necessary to the act of fishing. The most basic fishing tackle consists of a line with a weight and a baited hook, which is cast and retrieved by hand. This is the basis of handline fishing. Handlines today are primarily used in underdeveloped regions, primarily with a baited hook and sometimes with a (baited or unbaited) jig or jigging spoon, and predominately as a means of procuring food rather than providing sport. This is how most people fished throughout history for subsistence purposes.

Another basic item of fishing tackle is a line connected to a reel-less pole *(see)*. That line may feature a baited hook or a lure, but it cannot be cast or retrieved as the line is fixed to the end of the pole. A line attached to a pole is usually no longer than the length of the pole and therefore a bait or lure can be placed up to twice the length of the pole away from the angler. Such a pole may be made of cane or synthetic material, and it may be of one length or telescopic, but there is no reel for the storage of line.

Other than these basic forms, fishing tackle for practical sportfishing purposes includes a rod, reel, line, and terminal tackle. These items are reviewed in detail as individual entries elsewhere in this book. (Some of those individual entries are listed at the end of this entry.)

The major components of fishing tackle—rods and reels—were once easily categorized as being freshwater tackle or saltwater tackle. But as the world of sportfishing changes, it has become less and less appropriate to make this type of designation. With the advancements made in materials and features, many products can be used in both freshwater and saltwater. Granted, an outfit that is classified as medium-heavy for freshwater (say for Great Lakes chinook salmon trolling) would probably be classified as light for saltwater (and used by the inshore casting/trolling/bottom fishing crowd), but it would definitely be appropriate. And a light spinning outfit suited with 6-pound line, which might be employed for some types of freshwater trout or bass fishing, could be very useful for casting small jigs to bonefish or redfish in saltwater.

Clearly some tackle, such as big-game tackle and certain types of conventional tackle, are used only in saltwater. Otherwise, it is not the type of tackle that dictates usage; that is dictated by two factors: individual models and their features, and/or the type of fishing being done and the size and behavior of the quarry. Because there are so many variables in fishing for all species, such as the places that anglers fish, the size and strength of the fish they catch, the techniques used, and the circumstances under which they are caught (depth, current, and so forth), it is difficult to categorize tackle as being just for freshwater, just for saltwater, just for trolling, or just for bottom fishing. At the extremes of the fishing tackle spectrum, this may be so, but the vast middle ground is more of a gray area.

What often happens with tackle is that the length and action of a rod is the major factor in determining the preferred or predominant use of that rod and an appropriately matched reel. In some cases, the strength of line, or line-test, further refines the use of a rod and reel. The size of a reel is usually a factor in line capacity and in the range of line strengths that are used.

This does not stop the manufacturers of fishing tackle from marketing products for specific uses, however. Just as there are a dozen kinds of fishing boats and a slew of lure types, so, too, are there reels and rods, especially the latter, marketed and promoted for specific (and in some cases niche) applications. To those unfamiliar with sportfishing, this is indeed a confusing potpourri. In an effort to make this less confusing, this book reviews the rod and reel components of fishing tackle in detail in the following categories, which readers are urged to reference.

See: Baitcasting Tackle; Big-Game Tackle; Conventional Tackle; Flycasting Tackle; Reel, Fishing; Rod, Fishing; Spincasting Tackle; Spinning Tackle; Tackle Care/Maintenance/Repair.

Because there are so many aspects to consider for the other elements of fishing tackle, these, too, have been treated in detail under their respective entries
See: Hook; Line; Lure; Terminal Tackle; Weighted Line; Wire Line.

TACKLE BOX
See: Lure Storage.

TACKLE CARE/MAINTENANCE/REPAIR

Contemporary fishing tackle is a high-tech wonder of engineering, manufacturing, and design. Rods and reels use materials that evolved from aerospace applications, and they benefit from refined and sophisticated manufacturing techniques. Whether simple or complex instruments, they have the ability to last for years with a reasonable amount of care and maintenance, and sometimes even repair or refurbishing.

Fishing tackle requires care during use and storage. Maintenance should be performed on a regular basis, and repairs should be made when something starts to go wrong or breaks. Proper care and maintenance often mitigate a need for repair. It's a smart move to look after your rods and reels so that they aren't mistreated and don't malfunction (and a malfunction will always occur when you need your equipment the most). Some tackle represents a significant economic investment, which is another reason to care and maintain equipment. It is pos-sible to send rods and reels to service centers for repair, but many repairs can be made easily and economically in your workshop or in the field.

Tools

Tools for maintenance and repair vary with the extent of service necessary. For basic maintenance, almost no tools are needed other than perhaps those supplied with a reel for the purpose of taking it apart to check on lubrication and excessive wear. For repair, you may need glues, small screwdrivers, wrenches, rod wrapping devices, finishing brushes, polishing rags, etc. Some possibilities and their uses with tackle include the following.

Manufacturer's reel tool. This small tool will vary with the manufacturer but typically comes with the reel. Usually made from flat plate steel, with one or more screwdriver ends and an expanded center with hex holes to act as wrenches, it is designed for simple take-down of a reel, often in the field, for basic repairs.

Small screwdrivers and screwdriver sets. Since reels possess bantam parts and screws, small sets of a half dozen or more screwdrivers are ideal. They are usually available in hobby shops or through tool mail-order outlets.

Small wrench sets. These consist of sets of standard wrenches, Allen wrenches, and Torx wrenches for various reel fasteners.

Oil and grease. Tubes of oil and grease are often supplied with reels; if they are not supplied, or are misplaced, they can be obtained from hardware, hobby, and automotive stores. You'll need a light oil (like a sewing machine oil) for most parts and a medium grease for gears and shafts. It's best if the tubes have small, tapered applicator tips for reaching the small spots and crevices found on most reels. Make sure that you have the right oil for the right application, however, as will be discussed later. Read the manual that comes with the reel for the manufacturer's recommendations.

Compartmented box. This can be nothing more than an egg carton or biscuit tin for separating reel parts. Place parts in order in the compartments as you remove them from the reel to make reassembly easier.

Old toothbrush. These are ideal for cleaning around the crevices of reels and removing grime during regular care and maintenance sessions. To avoid scratching the reel, use with liquid soap in a soapy water solution.

Heat source. This can be an alcohol lamp, cigarette lighter, or similar flame source. These devices are ideal for heating the ferrule cement or heat-set cement that is used to secure a tiptop onto a rod.

Razor blades. These are necessary for cutting thread, removing old and damaged rod wraps, and doing similar tasks when you are working on rods.

Emery board. Use an emery board to smooth rough spots on a rod and to remove old epoxy rod finish at the edges of a wrap after removing the old thread and before making the new wrap.

Rasps and files. These smoothing tools are a must for shaping and rounding cork grips when you must repair or replace rod handle grips.

Sandpaper. Sandpaper is necessary for final shaping of a cork rod grip. Use several grades, finishing with the finest grade available to smooth the grip surface.

Rod-wrapping jig. Rod-wrapping stands or jigs allow the fishing rod to be held horizontally while at the same time supporting the thread spool and creating tension on the thread for wrapping new guides on a repaired rod. However, for repairs you do not need a commercially made rod-wrapping jig. (They are nice, though, if you do a lot of repairs. A fishing club might consider buying one to loan to members.) A simple substitute is a large cardboard box, about 1 foot high, 1 foot deep, and 2 feet wide, with the top and front side removed. With the open front facing you, cut notches in the top of both sides. Cut out the bottom of the back panel to hold a book. In back of the book, place a cup to hold the thread, and then run the thread between two sheets of clean paper held in the pages of the book. Place the rod in the notches, the thread in the cup (which keeps it from rolling around), and adjust the thread through the book to control the tension on the thread as you rotate the rod and wrap on new guides. This is a simple, no-cost, disposable method for easy rod wrapping.

Burnisher. This is available from rod component supply catalogs, but an easy substitute is a round-shaft plastic pen or pencil. Use the pen or pencil to smooth and burnish thread wraps and to close up any slight gaps in the thread that would otherwise occur.

Rodcuring motor. A rodcuring motor is nothing more than a slow rpm motor capable of holding a rod by the butt cap and slowly rotating the rod while the epoxy finish is curing; the slow rotation prevents sags and runs. The middle of the rod has a simple support. Such devices are available commercially, but often substitutes can be made by using a slow rpm rotisserie motor from a barbecue grill and fitting it with a rod to which a butt cap can be taped in place.

Field kit. You can add some of the items already mentioned to a kit that travels with you or is kept in your boat. An assortment of tools and reel parts is mandatory; the latter should include the extra parts that come with some reels, especially screws, nuts, bail springs, and reel oil. Other items could include a razor blade, rod-wrapping thread, matches, rasp, quick-setting epoxy, candle wax, and wire for temporary guides.

Basic Tackle Care

Rods and reels are not unduly fragile, but they still should be used, handled, and stored with care.

Storing. The best ways to store rods are to stand them vertically in a rod rack, support them horizontally on shelving or with several cup-type hooks, or place them in bags and cases designed for storage. Some rods are supplied with protective storage cases, and rod storage racks and systems are available from tackle suppliers or through catalogs.

Do not store a rod by leaning it against the wall; this will cause a permanent set or bend in the rod blank that will damage the rod over time. Adding the weight of an attached reel makes the matter worse. Also, do not run the line through the guides and place a hook or snap in a butt guide in a way that makes the rod curve; in time, this can cause a permanent bend. It is equally bad to hang up a rod by the tiptop, since some tiptops are glued on with a heat-set cement and may be pulled off. This problem is exacerbated with heavy rods or rods with reels still attached.

While traveling, keep rods in their cases or otherwise protected from bending. If carrying several rods, bundle and tape them together for added strength and security. On boats, store rods flat or in horizontal or vertical rod racks. For detailed information on transporting and caring for tackle when traveling, *see: Travel*.

A drying motor board is used to create a glasslike finish on rods.

Never store a rod in a bag or closed case when it is wet from fishing. To do so can cause damage to the finish and possibly corrosion to metal parts, such as reel seats and guides.

Reels should be stored apart from rods, if only to protect from corrosion or electrolysis that can occur when dissimilar metals of the reel foot and the reel seat become wet while fishing. When reels are not in use, reduce the drag tension to a loose setting so that pressure on the soft drag washers is eliminated. Pressure over time can make an impression on the soft washers and cause sticking and erratic drags, which might later cost you a fish.

While you are fishing, protect reels on rods by covering them with a reel case. Many such cases for casting, spinning, and flycasting reels are made to fit onto a reel, even when it is mounted on a rod. If you don't have a case, use an old sock.

Washing. Rods and reels often require a little extra care after a fishing trip, particularly if they've been used in saltwater or in dirty, muddy, or algae-filled water where tackle is likely to pick up line-damaging grit and grime. Through repeated casting and retrieving, the grime builds up on guide rings, and over time it also damages reel parts and wire guides, such as snake guides on a fly rod.

Be especially concerned with salt because of the corrosive effect that it has on tackle. This is true even for reels with components that are meant to combat saltwater. Plastics and graphites are impervious to corrosion, but aluminum and stainless steel only resist corrosion; they are not impervious to it. And the biggest concern is the interior components, the inner workings of a reel that are not as accessible as the exterior for cleaning. Of equal concern is caring for reels that have been submerged in saltwater, especially the surf where there is a lot of sand in the mix, and reels that have been dropped in the dirt or sand. Simply rinsing reels that have been exposed to salt is not enough to remove the little crystals of salt. Many crystals will still remain after a freshwater rinse, so you need to use soap or detergent with warm water to help remove all of the crystals.

Ideally you should wash rods and reels after each trip of a day or longer if they have been used in any of the aforementioned circumstances. An easy way to do this is to first separate the rods and reels and then wash the rods in the shower. An ideal time to do this is when you are also taking a shower, since you can easily scrub and rinse each rod. Use a sudsy washcloth and scrub the entire rod. Run a corner of the washcloth through the guide rings and around the guide feet, or use an old toothbrush for extra cleaning. Use a toothbrush on the collet nuts and threads of the reel seat, and move the nuts so that you wash all parts of each reel seat.

Separate two-piece rods, but try to keep water from getting into either ferrule end. Most male ends have a plug, and most female ends are at the lower end of the tip section and thus not subject to water when the tiptop is pointed up. Once the rods are completely clean, rinse thoroughly and allow to air dry in the shower or out of the way in a corner. They can be stored after they are completely dry.

Reels should be similarly washed to remove any salt or grime. First, remove spools from those reels where this is easy: flycasting reels, spinning reels, and a few baitcasting reels. A few baitcasting reels have easy-access ports on the palming sideplate (opposite the handle) by which the spool can be removed. In addition, most have thumbscrews on the handle sideplate that are easily unscrewed without tools to remove the spool. Take care that small parts are not dislodged; if the reel has centrifugal cast control, make sure that you do not lose any brake blocks.

Place the spools in a warm sudsy bath to soak for a while. Do the same with reel bodies, soaking them in warm water to help soften any grime or salt. To remove the salt or grime (soaking won't accomplish this), use a soft scrub brush or old toothbrush for crevices and corners. After the spools and reels are washed completely, rinse thoroughly and place on an old towel to dry. Flycasting reels are easy to dry this way by placing them open and face down to drain off any water. Spinning and baitcasting reels are best dried by shaking out any water that might have entered the gear casing or sideplates and then air drying, turning occasionally to allow drying or draining of any water puddles on the interior or exterior.

If you have access to clean freshwater at the dock or launch site, you can use it to clean your tackle. But don't spray the reels with a sharp stream of water from a hose; you may actually drive salt into important areas. A fine spray is better, and using warm water with soap is best. Fill a bucket with warm soapy water; then use a brush or sponge to go over the reels.

This combination washes salt away, but on many reels there is still reason to be concerned about getting anything into the critical drag washers. Therefore, you can tighten down the drag tension, wash the reels with warm soapy water and a brush or sponge, rinse with a fine spray, wipe dry, and then loosen the drag tension.

If a reel has been completely submerged in saltwater or exposed to the sandy surf wash, you should take the reel apart to get to the inner mechanisms. How quickly you do this depends on when you will be fishing next. If you'll be fishing with that item for the next few days, then you can probably wait a few days before giving it a thorough cleaning and possibly a relubrication. But if you will not be using the reel for a while, then you should clean it thoroughly soon after. At the very least, give it the regular soap and water treatment at the end of each day.

Another step that you can take after washing and drying is to apply an anticorrosion product. There are a number of rust-inhibiting liquids available; some can be sprayed, but you need to be careful about getting the product on the fishing line, because it could impact the strength of the line or at least impregnate the line with scent. Using a cloth to wipe all the metal parts will alleviate any concerns.

Practicalities. The aforementioned care recommendations are the ideal, and they are the highest standards that can be followed. Within reason, some lesser attention to these details will likely not harm your equipment. Obviously, saltwater anglers need to rinse, if not wash, their rods and reels after every single outing; most freshwater anglers do not need to do this on a daily basis, although it is a good idea to rinse them with clean fresh water occasionally and to give them a more thorough soapy cleaning once in a while. Clearly, it is a burden to remove reels from rods after every outing, especially if you finish angling late one day and start early the next with the same tackle. Many people clean their reels without removing them from the rods; this is generally okay, but remember that the connection between reel foot and reel seat is an area that is likely to retain moisture and that is especially subject to corrosion.

Use common sense about this, remembering that even if you do not feel obliged to take the maximum cleaning measures each time, you should at least do so periodically, and more frequently when circumstances warrant.

Tackle Maintenance

All anglers should check their tackle periodically to avoid later repairs or to catch problems while they are small and more easily corrected. A careful visual inspection is ideal for this, and for reels should include trying and testing all functions to make sure that they work properly. For rods and reels, the best time to check them is after cleaning them, although a thorough inspection isn't necessary after each trip unless you think that you might have damaged the rod or reel while fishing or you suspect problems. Inspect your tackle on a regular basis, according to

Tackle Care/Maintenance/Repair

how often and how hard you fish. Do so at least once a year, preferably soon after ending the season so that you have plenty of time for repairs or adjustments.

Rods. Begin to visually inspect the rod by using a bright light. Check the entire blank, turning the rod as you examine it from tip to butt for possible dings or cracks. Often you can do little about severe problems, other than to be aware of them in case they cause later rod breakage—and carry a backup rod for the one that is susceptible to breakage. Evidence of possible damage to a rod blank would be areas where the finish is separated from the blank itself, where the finish or underlying rod blank has a bruised look, where there is a noticeable visual crack, or where you can feel something in the blank surface.

If you do find obvious damage, you may want to notify the manufacturer or check your rod warranty. Your rod may be under limited warranty, although the warranty may not cover the specific problem. A few rods, primarily expensive products (often fly rods), have unlimited warranties that cover almost anything that might happen.

Check the wraps on each guide, at the tiptop, at the ferrules, and immediately above the rod grip. The wraps at the tiptop and above the grip are decorative but still must be protected, and they are indicative of wrap condition in general. All the wraps should be protected by a rod finish, preferably epoxy. Wraps in good condition will show no signs of fraying, damage, bruising, or color fading. The protective finish should be intact, without blistering, peeling, or flaking. Assuming that you use and store your rod carefully, such wraps and finishes should last for many years without requiring refinishing or rewrapping. The topics of refinishing and rewrapping are both reviewed here later under "Repairing Rods."

Take the rod apart if not already disassembled, and check the condition of the ferrules. Make sure that the ferrule wraps are intact and in good condition, since they provide a protective hoop strength to the rod at this critical junction point. If the male ferrule is soiled, clean it with lighter fluid to remove any grime, dirt, or wax. Use a cotton-tipped applicator dipped in lighter fluid to clean the inside of the female ferrule. Candle wax is often used to help ferrules grip tightly and work smoothly, but it can also attract dirt. Once the ferrules are clean and dry, reapply candle wax to help the ferrules work smoothly.

Check each guide frame and ring. Guide frames that are bent can often be returned to original shape by using flat-nose pliers. Use care to avoid pulling them free from the thread wraps. Most guides today are made of some form of ceramic: aluminum oxide, Hardloy, silicone carbide, silicone nitride, etc. They are well protected in a wire frame with a plastic (nylon) shock ring, but the internal rings are very hard and can crack with a sharp blow. Check visually for cracks, or run a piece of old hosiery through each ring to check for damage. The hosiery will usually catch on any slight crack or damage.

Check the grip next. Grips are made of cork or synthetic foams, usually EVA or PVC types of cushiony foam. Often both types of grip become dirty with use, but they are easily cleaned with a scrub brush and suds. This often takes extra work and may not have been completely accomplished with the normal cleaning. Any dirt left after this second thorough cleaning is best removed using a very fine sandpaper on cork grips and a medium sandpaper on the foam grips. If cleaning this way, protect the blank and the reel seat with several layers of masking tape to prevent scratches.

Check the reel seat for damage or wear. Reel seats are made of chrome (plating over brass on saltwater trolling rods), aluminum (saltwater and freshwater rods of all types), and graphite (all types of rods and is really a graphite-filled plastic). Slide the hood, which holds one end of the reel foot, up and down the reel seat to make sure that it works smoothly. Check for hairline cracks in the corners of the hood, which is the most common place that they occur. Turn and move the collet nuts up and down the threaded portion to check for function and any wear or damage. With some spinning and casting rods, the foregrip is built on the forward collet nuts. In these cases, unthread the foregrip completely and slide it up the blank to examine the underlying threads. For saltwater tackle, check for corrosion on the reel, especially if the reel is always kept on the rod. Treat this area with corrosion-resistant liquid; applying a light coat of grease can help prevent corrosive buildup.

Some fly rod reel seats have wood inserts, or barrels, between the threaded portion holding the sliding hood and the fixed hood. Check these for cracks and splintering, and protect them by regularly polishing them with a wood furniture polish.

Some saltwater rod butt sections, mainly in big-game versions, separate from the rod blank (tip) at the upper part of the reel seat, using a separate locking, keyed collet nut system that holds the metal ferrule on the butt end of the rod into the upper end of the reel seat. Check these and wash carefully if this has not already been done.

Reels. Maintenance of all reels is simple and basically involves periodic checking, oiling, and greasing. Ideally, you've saved the manual that came with your reel; it will suggest how to take care of the reel and will explain which parts you should regularly oil and grease, as well as recommended time-tables for doing so. The latter is important, because overlubrication can be a problem, especially if it causes oil or grease to get onto parts that shouldn't have it. If you don't have the reel manual, you may be able to get another from the manufacturer, especially if it is a fairly recent model.

Usually you'll notice if something is amiss with a reel while you're using it. If the drag sticks, a

 When polyvinyl-chloride powder, liquid plasticizer, and heat stabilizer are mixed, melted, molded, and cooled, they become the most popular bass lure of all: the plastic worm.

moving part binds, or there is a grinding sound, you'll know. However, if a reel hasn't been used in a while, if someone else has been using it, or if some of the features haven't been used recently, you may not be aware of any difficulties. In such case, you should check the operation of the reel before using it. Since the drag is a critical element for landing strong fish, and an improperly functioning drag is a common problem, this feature should be carefully inspected on all types of reels.

Check drag operation by running line off the spool and through the rod guides; have someone stand a short distance away, wrap line around a gloved or towel-covered hand, and pull line from the reel while the rod is at a 45-degree angle. Repeat this a few times while you check and adjust the drag tension setting through its full range to make sure it's working properly. Pull the line rapidly and evenly. If constant, even pressure is applied to pull line from the reel, the rod tip should not jump or move much, indicating an even, smooth drag. If the drag is erratic, you may need to replace the tension washers. Some spinning reels have a standard front drag but also have a lighter secondary rear drag for fishing with bait. If so, test both drags through their full range, realizing that the secondary drag will not be as resistant to line pull as the primary drag.

When testing the spinning reel drag, make sure that the line roller on the bail assembly is turning at the same speed as the line going out. If it doesn't, it will wear the line in time. Turn the handle to regain line, and make sure that the line lies down properly on the spool. Don't turn against the reel drag, since this will cause line twist.

With a spinning reel, you should begin maintenance efforts by removing the reel spool. Check the rim of the spool for any nicks or roughness. If the rim is rough, you have no choice but to discard it and replace with another spool. (This would probably indicate that the reel hasn't been properly cared for, so you should determine why this has happened and avoid it for the future.) Some reels are supplied with a spare spool when new, and spare spools are also available from your tackle dealer. Check the frame to make sure that nothing is twisted, broken, chipped, or otherwise damaged in a way that affects performance. Turn the handle to make sure that the gears are smooth. Move the antireverse switch back and forth several times to make sure that it is working. If it has a bail trigger, see if this works smoothly and opens the bail easily and completely.

Oil the handle nut, handle shaft, handle knob, line roller, ends of the level bail arms or fittings, drag knob nut and spring, antireverse lever or switch, the arm joint for the bail trigger, and the main shaft (remove the spool for this). Periodically remove the sideplate, using the right type and size of screwdriver for the job. Check the gear box for wear and proper grease on the gears. If necessary, grease the main gears. To do this properly, don't smear a dollop of grease

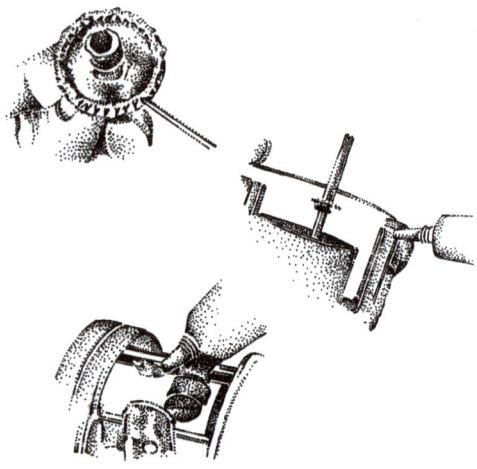

When lubricating a reel, apply a judicious amount of grease to the gears (top), oil to the bail of a spinning reel (middle), and oil to the levelwind pawl on a baitcasting reel (bottom).

into the gear box and close it up; use a toothpick to deposit a tiny dot of grease on each and every gear tooth, because this will distribute the grease better. Once greased properly, reassemble the reel and tighten all the screws. Gear systems and types will vary with the reel model and manufacturer, but this basic lubrication is easy to apply to every reel.

For spincasting reels, check the exterior for any damage, particularly the hood or nose cone for any cracks or dents that might interfere with line flow. Remove the nose cone, and push down on the line-release button (or trigger in some models), and make sure that the line becomes free (the pin drops on the rotor pickup) and that the spool or a bumper pushes forward to hold the line against the nose cone for casting. Check the antireverse switch if there is one, and make sure that the handle and gears turn smoothly.

Oil the rotary pin and spring (remove the cone or hood for this), the pushbutton line release, the handle knob and shaft, the knob or star drag adjustment mechanism, the antireverse switch or lever, and the main shaft (in back of or under the spool). Periodically remove the sideplate and check the gears, greasing the same as with spinning reels.

With a baitcasting reel, turn the handle to make sure that the levelwind runs smoothly back and forth on the worm gear and in the track. Make sure that the levelwind disengages when the reel is in freespool for casting. The same thing applies, and should be checked, with the drag engaged and line being pulled from the reel, as happens when a fish is taking line. Depress the freespool button or bar to place the reel in freespool; then turn the handle to make sure it pops out of freespool easily. Do this several times. Using a practice casting weight, make a few casts with the cast control at several different settings to check performance. If the reel has a flipping switch, make sure that this works properly.

Oil the handle fitting, shaft, and knob, the rack for the levelwind guide (not the worm gear or pawl), the shaft bearings on both sides of the reel (remove the sideplate and spool to do this), the drag controls, the flipping switch, and the antireverse switch if there is one. Grease the gears after removing the sideplate. Baitcasting reels typically have a small pinion gear and a larger main gear, so add small dots of grease to each gear tooth, as with spinning reels. Unscrew the cap to remove the pawl from the levelwind and check for wear, since this part wears most rapidly. Replacements should have been included with the reel, so replace with a new one if necessary. Grease the pawl housing and pawl at the same time, along with the worm gear in which the pawl rides.

The same things apply to conventional and big-game reels, which are larger and heavier. Putting a conventional reel into freespool means moving a lever rather than depressing a button, and most lack a levelwind feature. Big-game reels feature lever drag operation instead of star drag. Both types have a click alarm. Check this to make sure that it is fully on or fully off when switched back and forth; on older conventional reels, these often wear out. A few conventional reels have line counters, which are easily checked for accuracy by pulling measured amounts of line from the reel.

Oil the handle knob, handle shaft, star or lever drag, antireverse switch, and spool shafts (some reels have oiling ports for this and other parts). If greasing the main gears, use the reel manual for directions in disassembly, and use extreme care. Lever drag reels and many conventional reels are very complex internally, and they can be damaged by inappropriate care. Grease the gears as noted for other reels, one drop at a time on each tooth.

Flycasting reels are basically simple frames to hold a spool, the handle being mounted on the spool on direct drive reels. Antireverse reels (in which the handle will not turn when line goes out against the drag) have a separate plate or arm on which the handle is mounted. Multiplier reels are few, but they have additional gearing and a separate arm for the handle so that one turn of the handle makes more than one turn of the spool. Most flycasting reels have drags, but these can vary from a simple click, made by a pawl striking a gear tooth, to more-complex disk or caliper drag systems that are simple variations of car brakes. As with other reels, check the drag system through the range of settings. Note that fly line is thick and will be more erratic in coming off the spool, so that the drag will not initially appear to be as smooth as on other reels. To check for smoothness, pull out all the fly line and check the drag against the backing line, or pull off the front part of weight-forward lines to check the drag against the thinner section of the rear running line.

For direct drive, antireverse, and multiplier reels, remove the spool and arms and oil the moving parts such as click pawls, handle knobs, main shaft, drag adjustment controls, and spool locking catch. Use a very small amount of grease on each gear tooth of multipliers. For automatic flycasting reels, follow the reel manual for instructions, oiling the moving parts such as the spring control lever and spring ratchet. Because a spring is involved, follow the manufac-turer's instructions as to any further disassembly.

The following precautions apply to all reels. Avoid oiling or greasing them excessively, and do not lubricate drags or use demoisturizers. Avoid excessive grease or oil on the internal parts of anti-reverse mechanisms, flipping switches, click pawls, antireverse pawls, etc. Too much oil or grease on these mechanisms might slow their operating time or prevent them from working completely. Use light oil in all oiling procedures, and use it only very lightly and sparingly, especially in these areas.

Drag care and lubrication *must* be performed following the manufacturer's instructions. Some drag washer materials should not receive any lubrication, and if lubricated they will not perform properly. Some drags can be ruined by the application of greases or silicones to the drag plates and washers. Friction drag materials (usually as washers) used in reels today include cork, cork composite, graphite, graphite composite, Teflon, various other plastics, smooth metal washers (in disk drags), asbestos-like materials, carbon, etc. There is no general rule for all of them; some benefit from the use of pure neat's-foot oil (don't use a compound meant for waterproofing footwear on some cork drags), whereas others may need cleaning and light sanding only, silicone lubes, no oil at all, etc. Follow the manufacturer's instructions for each reel and drag system. The way to apply grease has been described, but it is also worth mentioning that you should not add more grease if enough already exists in a reel. If there is an insufficient amount of grease, then you can add more judiciously; it's better to clean off the old grease (it may have particles of grit in it that have gotten inside the reel) and reapply fresh grease.

De-moisturizers will help to repel moisture and "dry" reels after use and cleaning. Used selectively and with care, they can help keep reels in good shape. They should be applied to metal parts and are unnecessary on plastic, resin, or graphite. Be aware that de-moisturizers may damage the PVC coating on fly lines and may damage some of the plastics used in many reel parts today. They will not harm monofilament lines but may impart a scent to the line. However, some anglers have used these products as a fish attractant on lures, so such a scent may or may not be detrimental.

Repairing Rods

Rod repairs may involve only a few minutes to glue on a new tiptop or a full evening to replace all the guides. Many rod repairs are easy, even fun, to make, and don't require any special talents or tools. Some examples of easy repairs follow.

Replacing the tiptop. Tiptop repair on a rod

Trophy lake trout in the Far North are older than most anglers; 40 years old is common, and up to 62 has been recorded.

involves replacing the tiptop either because it is broken or worn, or because the blank has broken right at the end of the tiptop. In both cases, the repair is similar. If the tiptop is broken, the simple solution is to replace it with a new tiptop of the same style, finish, and tube size; you don't need to remove the wraps at all, since they are only decorative and don't cover the tiptop tube.

To replace the tiptop, cover the thread wraps with several layers of masking tape to provide insulation over the wraps. With the wraps protected, use heat on the tip-top tube and then remove it with pliers. Heat the tube only, using an alcohol lamp, cigarette lighter, or a hair dryer held close to the tube. In all cases, heat will break down the cement, including epoxy. Test frequently with pliers, since you don't want to overheat the area and possibly damage the blank. If the blank becomes damaged, then you'll have to cut back the blank at this point, remove the thread wraps, replace with a larger tube-size tiptop, and finally rewrap and refinish the thread wrap.

If the blank is not damaged after removing the tiptop, allow it to cool and then clean with an emery board or by scraping with a razor blade. Do *not* cut into the blank or reduce its diameter.

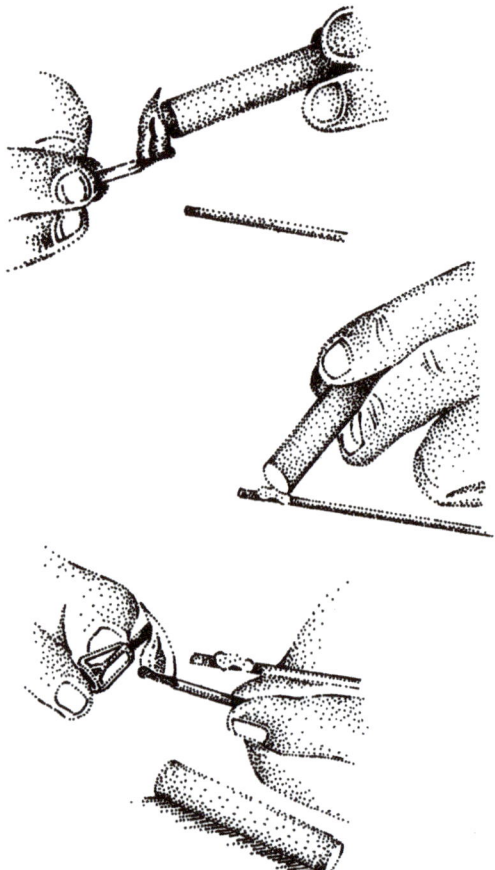

To put a new tip guide on a rod in the field, heat ferrule cement (top) and apply the cement to the rod shaft (middle); then heat the tip guide (bottom) and align it in position on the rod.

Use either heat-set cement (ferrule cement) or epoxy to glue the new tiptop in place. With heat-set cement, use a flame to heat it; smear it rapidly onto the blank, and just as rapidly slide the new tiptop in place. Immediately line up the tiptop with the guide rings. Do *not* try to remove any excess cement; you will be able to remove it easily after it sets and cools. Once the cement cools, peel off the excess with your thumbnail and then remove the protective masking tape.

An alternative method is to shave off splinters of the heat-set cement, place them in the tube of the tiptop, and heat the tube to melt the cement. Immediately slide the tiptop in place and line it up; remove the excess cement as described above. *Never* heat the blank when using heat-set cement.

If using epoxy glue, mix thoroughly; then use a toothpick to insert some glue into the tip-top tube. Smear more on the end of the blank, and slide the tiptop in place. Use a rag to remove any excess glue, line up the tiptop with the guides, and allow it to set. Keep the rod horizontal or at an angle while the glue cures, with the guides facing down to prevent gravity from moving the tiptop out of alignment. In both gluing methods, glue will sometimes ooze through a small opening in the end of the tube. Should this happen, remove it with a rag or toothpick.

If the blank is broken, remove the tiptop and then remove the thread wraps. An easy way to do this is to use a razor blade, scraping through the finish and wrap (using the razor like a carpenter's plane). After you've scraped away one side of the thread wrap, remove the wrap as if peeling the shell from a steamed shrimp. Lightly clean the area with an emery board. Measure for a new tiptop, and buy the right size. (Tip-top gauges are available from mail-order houses, and many tackle shops will have one to aid you in determining the right size of tube for your rod.) Then glue on as already described, using heat-set or epoxy glue. Finish with thread wraps and a protective finish as later described.

Replacing and rewrapping a guide. To remove a guide, use a razor blade to cut through the wrap along the foot; then pull the remaining thread to remove all of the guide wrap, or peel it off the blank. When the guide wrap is removed, use an emery board to sand down any excess finish at the ends of each wrap. Once the blank is clean, you're ready to rewrap. Make sure that you have guides of the same ring size and style as those being replaced, unless for some reason you wish to change them or upgrade them. Prepare each guide by filing the end of the guide foot for an easy, smooth transition of the thread from the blank and up onto the guide foot. Lightly file the underside of the feet to remove any metal spurs that could damage the rod blank.

Guides are best replaced in the same spot from which they were removed. If you're adjusting the position or number of guides on a rod, realize that, even when cleaned and refinished, the old wrap areas will likely be a different color (often lighter)

Tackle Care/Maintenance/Repair

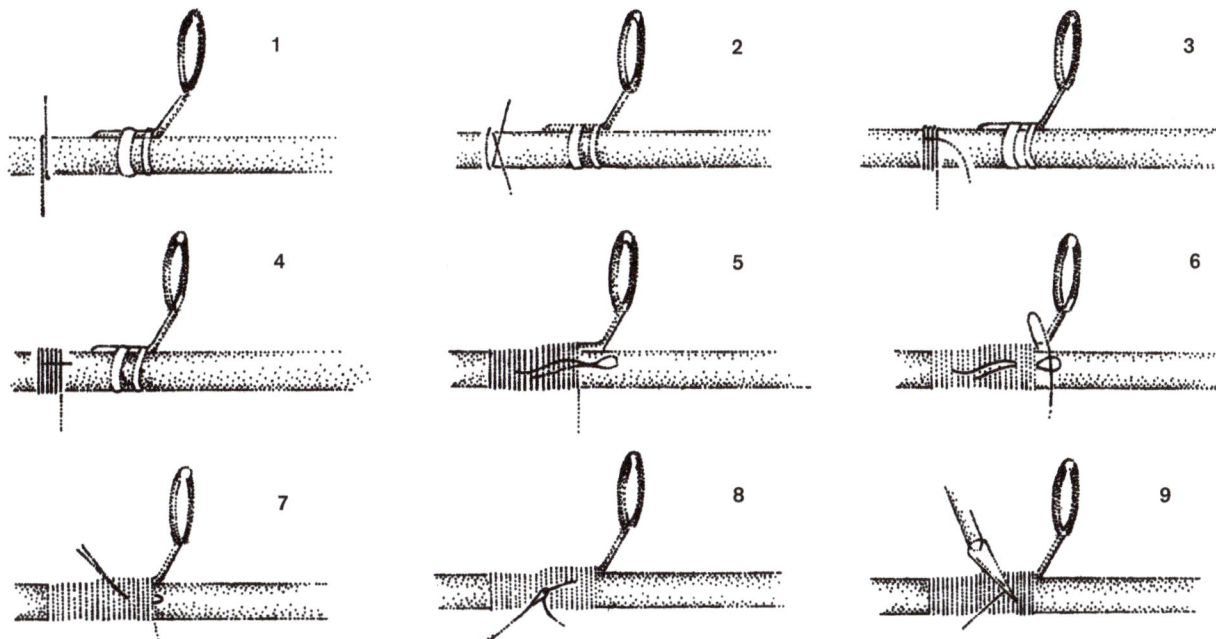

Depicted are the steps for wrapping a guide on a rod blank. In this case, a single-foot guide is shown. Note that in step 5 a loop of line is wrapped in, and in step 6 the tag end of the wrapping thread is run through the loop; this end is pulled through and then trimmed.

than the rest of the rod. This is due to the sun fading the blank and cannot be corrected.

Prepare the blank by taping the guide in place on the blank; make sure that it is lined up with the other guides, the tiptop, and the reel seat hoods. Use thin strips of masking tape, which can be cut from a standard-width spool or are available in narrow-width spools from arts and crafts stores; $1/4$-inch is best. Place tape in the middle of the foot, not the end; if you put it on the end, you won't be able to wrap the end with thread. Use masking tape also to mark the beginning of the rod wrap on the blank. (Note: all wraps begin on the blank and progress up onto the foot, ending at the frame.)

Thread for wrapping guides is available in different sizes (diameters). The 2/0 size is best for most fly rods. Size A is best for heavy fly rods and all freshwater spinning, spincasting, and baitcasting rods, and most light saltwater rods. Size D is best for heavy saltwater rods, and size E is used only on the heaviest saltwater trolling rods.

Use a rod-wrapping jig, or rig a modified cardboard box (described earlier in the tools section). Before starting, cut a 1-foot-long piece of wrapping thread, fold it over, and tie a knot to make a loop. This will be used to finish the wrap.

Most rod wrappers work from left to right, but either direction is all right provided that you wrap from the blank up onto the guide foot. Begin by bringing the thread over the rod blank and around it, wrapping over the thread by turning the rod while holding or pulling on the end of the thread. Make sure that the wraps are tight, and after a few turns clip any excess thread, since there will then be enough friction to hold the thread. Continue wrapping by turning the blank. Make sure that there are no gaps, and work slowly and carefully as the thread begins to cover the guide foot.

When you're about six to eight wraps from the end, lay down the previously prepared loop, with the loop toward the center of the guide. Continue wrapping over the loop until reaching the end of the foot (where the frame rises from the foot). At this point, hold the thread to prevent unraveling, clip the end, and tuck the end into the loop. Pull the loop tight, then under the wraps, which pulls the end of the thread with it and provides a neat, secure finish. With a razor blade, cut the excess flush with the wrap or open a gap and cut straight down to sever the excess thread. Reverse the rod on the wrapping jig, and make the other wrap on the other side of the guide (assuming it's a double-foot guide).

There are plenty of supplies for building and repairing rods, especially with regard to guides; shown here is a variety of wrapping threads.

This simple device is used for rod wrapping.

If you're redoing only one guide, try to match the thread color, although age and sun will make an exact match impossible. If rewrapping the entire rod or replacing all the guides, use whatever color you desire. Additional wraps are also necessary at the tiptop, at the junction of the blank with the rod grip, and at the ferrules. Those at the ferrules are necessary for hoop strength; those at the grip and tiptop are only decorative.

Emergency guide replacement. If you break a guide in the field, especially a tip-top guide, it could be a detriment to casting and to playing fish. You can make a temporary replacement guide out of stainless steel wire if you have some with you. Number 12 or 14 wire is good for this, and it can be rolled and formed into an appropriate ring shape with double feet. Take the straight piece of wire and wrap it twice over a round object of an appropriate size (about $1/4$-inch in diameter will do for tip-top guides). Bend the ends so that they are at right angles to the doubled wire and are parallel to each other; these will become the "feet" for securing the replacement guide to the rod. Align the replacement guide, and make several wraps over the feet with electrical tape (or better, use thread and epoxy if you happen to have them). Make a permanent replacement as soon as you can, since line will cut through the wire eventually.

Finishing or refinishing wraps. Once a wrap has been replaced on an existing guide or has been put on a new guide, the wrap should be protected with a sealer and finish. Most are epoxy finishes and very durable, clear, and flexible. If you choose, you can add color preserver, which will retain the existing spooled color of the thread. Without color preserver, dark thread colors will become darker, light thread colors will become lighter, and all will become somewhat translucent. If using color preserver, use the same brand as the rod finish; apply two coats, waiting 24 hours between each coat and before applying the rod finish. Add the color preserver with a disposable brush, liberally coating the wraps; after a few minutes blot any excess with a paper towel.

After applying the epoxy finish, the rod has to be slowly rotated for a few hours. You can rotate it yourself (maybe while watching a movie), or use a slow rpm motor made for the purpose and available commercially. You can also rig such a device using a slow rpm rotisserie motor from an electric grill.

Follow the rod finish manufacturer's directions, but a general procedure is to mix two equal parts of the two-part mix, stir thoroughly, then pour out on a flat surface; pouring on a flat surface helps dissipate bubbles and extends the working life of the mix. Any slight bubbles are easily dissipated by breathing on the mix. Using a small disposable brush, first wrap around the end of each wrap and then fill in the middle area. Use a bright overhead light to help detect missed spots or bubbles. Once all the wraps are coated with rod finish, rotate the rod to prevent the finish from dripping and sagging. Try to apply the finish in a clean environment so that dust, dirt, and pet hair don't soil the finish.

In some situations, the existing wraps on a rod are okay, but the original finish is starting to peel and flake. In this case, you can simply add an additional coating of protective finish. For best results, wrap the blank with masking tape at the end of each wrap that is to be refinished. Then lightly abrade with steel wool, and clean completely. Remove any loose or peeling finish. Remove the masking tape. Mix new rod finish and apply.

Regluing a reel seat. Rarely does the reel seat on a rod become loose, but when it does, repairing may be difficult. There are several possible solutions. If the reel seat is a skeletal type with the blank exposed in several areas, you can often wiggle the reel seat completely loose and then apply epoxy glue to the blank to reglue the reel seat in place. Tubular-type reel seats are more difficult to repair, since they are glued to a bushing or shim material, which in turn is glued to the blank. On a fly-rod reel seat, it is often possible to slide the reel seat completely off, clean the bushing and reel seat, and reglue.

Tubular reel seats on spinning and baitcasting rods can usually be repaired only by drilling holes through the reel seat (taking care to avoid hitting the blank), or you can drill holes at an angle from the rear or the fore grips. Then mix epoxy glue, and use a syringe to force glue through the holes to reglue the reel seat. This doesn't always work, but it's usually worth a try. The only other alternative with cork-grip rods is to cut off and remove the fore or rear cork grip, slide the reel seat up for cleaning and regluing onto the blank, and then rebuild the cork grip.

Replacing part of a cork grip. Badly damaged cork grips, and difficult reel seat repair problems, can be fixed by completely removing the old grip or a major part of it and replacing with a new grip, without removing the reel seat or guides. This method is appropriate when the damage to the grip is such that you could not effectively fill in a gouge with cork/glue filler. To make this major repair to the cork grips, you need a flexible waterproof cork glue (such as Ultra Flex, Pliobond, various cork glues, or others) and enough cork rings to fill in the gap you will create. Cork rings are usually $1/2$ inch thick and come in $1 1/8$-, $1 1/4$-, and $1 1/2$-inch diameters. Make sure that you pick rings larger in diameter than the grip, since some filing and sanding to shape will be necessary.

To make this repair, remove the old damaged cork by rasping down to the rod blank. Do not rasp or damage the rod blank. Remove all the cork in $1/2$-inch increments. Make sure that the resultant gap is squared off and even, so that the $1/2$-inch-thick cork rings will fit in precisely. If necessary, enlarge the hole in each ring to the diameter of the rod blank. Then cut each cork ring in half, numbering each half with the same number on the same side of the cork ring face so that the matching halves can be easily identified. Place the matching halves into the cut gap to check for fit.

Remove the halves; add glue to the rod blank, the facing cork halves, and the facing corks in the cut gap. Replace the cork halves into the gap on the rod blank, making sure that the halves match and face the right way. Fit them securely; then wrap with tape or cord to bind while curing. Once the cork is cured, remove the binding material; file, sand, and then polish with fine sandpaper to match the previous grip shape and diameter. Other than being a slightly lighter color than the handled portion of the grip, it will not be noticeable as a repair.

Repairing cork gouges. Small gouges and nicks in cork grips are easier to repair than large parts. The simple solution is to fill in these gouges with a glue/cork mix, overfill, and then sand after curing. To repair a gouge, first rasp and file some cork to make a cork dust. Cork rings are best to maintain quality, but bottle corks will also work. Then mix the dust into a thick paste with flexible, waterproof glue such as Pliobond or Elmer's Carpenter's Glue. Remove all loose cork from the gouged area, and coat with glue. Then fill with the cork/glue mix, overfill, and allow to cure overnight or longer until hard. (A prolonged curing time is often a must because of the high percentage of glue in the mix.) Then file and sand the excess, finally sanding with fine paper to polish the repair to a finish like that of the original.

Replacing a butt cap. Butt caps sometimes fall off or become damaged. If damaged, obtain a new one; reapply with a flexible glue such as Pliobond or Ultra Flex.

Repairing blanks. Cracked, broken, or damaged blanks are usually difficult to repair. One option for tip sections that are broken about an inch or two from the end is to clean the break and replace with a new tiptop (a larger tube size than the existing tiptop will be required). For this, follow the tip replacement, wrapping, and finishing instructions previously given.

Other breaks and damage are more difficult to repair. The only way to repair them is to smooth the cracks, breaks, and splintered edges as much as possible; insert an internal sleeve of blank under the broken area; and finally bind the outside of the rod with a long thread wrap. Unfortunately, the nature of the repair precludes repairs to the tip sections of all but the largest rods for three reasons: It's difficult to find thin scrap-blank sections that are strong enough and that will fit into the thin cores of tip sections; the repair makes the rod stiff in an area where you want it to be flexible; and the repair makes the tip feel heavy. This repair can be done, although it is chiefly recommended for the butt section of those rods for which flexibility and sensitivity are less important and additional weight is a secondary concern. Any repairs like this require access to the butt end of the rod, which requires removal of the butt cap. If the cap is rubber or plastic, often the best way is to cut it off and replace with a new cap. If it is metal, insulate the grip with several layers of masking tape and heat the butt cap to break the glue bond; then remove and replace it later.

It is important to be extremely careful when handling a broken rod, especially one with splintered ends. The sharp microfilament-like slivers, especially if they are graphite, can easily pierce your skin; so do not grab the broken area and be careful not to poke yourself with it.

To make this type of repair, you must find a scrap blank section in which the outside diameter matches the inside diameter of the broken area of the rod. To accomplish this, first clean and restore the broken splintered sections as much as possible; then insert the scrap blank section to check for proper length. Ideally, the insert blank should be 2 to 3 inches longer on each side of the broken area. Thus, if the break is sharp—almost like a transverse cut—the reinforcing insert might be no longer than 6 inches. If the break is splintered and about 6 inches long, then the total insert must be 10 to 12 inches long to overlap the end of the break.

Once the insert is sized and cut, roughen it with a light sanding, smear it with epoxy glue, and insert it into the rod. Since the glue will cause it to bind on the blank, use a thin dowel to push the insert into position. Use some glue in the splintered exterior area, and spiral wrap with cord to bind the glued areas together. Do not wrap too tightly, since the pressure can compress the rod and force the insert section out of position. When the glued area has cured for about 24 hours, remove the binding cord and use a file, followed by an emery board and then fine sandpaper, to smooth the repaired break area. Once smooth, add hoop strength with a thread wrap that completely covers and overlaps the ends of the break area. To blend the wrap with the blank, use a color closely matching the blank color and do not use color preserver before sealing with a protective finish.

Repairing Reels

Repairing a reel usually involves replacing one or more individual broken parts. If the necessary parts can be obtained, any angler can make the repairs; you simply need to follow instructions exactly, have a basic understanding of the mechanics of the reel, and use the schematic drawings provided with the reel. Some small tools, in addition to the one sometimes provided with the reel, are needed or useful for making certain repairs; these include needle-nose pliers, a small adjustable wrench or set of small wrenches, and a set of small Phillips and standard screwdrivers. It's a good idea to have oil and grease handy to lube the repaired reel.

A vital aspect of reel repair is using the manual or instruction sheet that comes with each reel when purchased new. These usually have schematic drawings to show how parts are assembled, a list of parts and ordering instructions, lubricating instructions, and suggestions for simple part replacements and adjustments. Some basic repairs to major reel categories follow. Keep in mind that most repairs are simply replacement of worn or broken parts and are not difficult to accomplish.

Also note that for anglers who put their reels to hard use in fighting strong fish, the friction drag washers on their reels need to be in top shape for maximum performance. These may need to be changed if the drag is not operating well. One of the major causes of poor drag performance is keeping tension on the drag washers for extended periods when the reel is not in use. Many drag-related problems could be avoided by getting into the habit of backing off the tension completely at the end of every fishing day so that there is no undue and prolonged tension on the drag washers; over time, the prolonged tension unnecessarily compresses the washers. If you don't back off the tension like this, you may need to service the drag washers more often than you otherwise should.

Spinning Tackle

Bail arm. Should the bail arm on a spinning reel become bent, it will need to be returned to its original shape; otherwise, you will not get the proper line pickup. Sometimes the repair can be done while the bail arm is still on the reel. If not, the bail arm has to be removed. In most cases, the line roller is part of the arm, so the bail arm is detached by removing screws from both ends of the bail assembly; it may also be detached by removing screws at the assembly point opposite the line roller and then removing the other end from the line roller. The latter method also facilitates checking the line roller and lubricating at the same time, and it lessens the chance of losing springs. Springs are used in one or both ends of the bail arm, so be careful that you don't dislodge or lose them. Once the arm is removed, bend the bail to reshape it to fit onto the reel; to avoid binding, make sure that the ends or end brackets are parallel to the body part on which they fit.

Line roller. The line roller is held in place on the side of the bail assembly by a bracket attached to the skirted spool or rotor. You can easily remove it with the appropriate tool. As you remove the line roller from the pin on which it turns, take care not to lose any washers, sleeves, or bearings that are part of this mechanism. Pay attention to any distinguishing marks that will indicate proper reassembly. Clean thoroughly, oil and replace, or replace with a new line roller if the original one is damaged.

Drag washers. Drag washers in spinning reels are located in the spool, in the rear part of the gear box (rear drag), or in the main part of the gear box (no-twist drag systems). Those in the gear box or under the sideplate are well protected and usually don't require replacement or care other than an annual check when the gears are greased, as previously outlined. Those in the spool are subject to more environmental damage through water and possible corrosion, and should be checked periodically. Most of these are multidisk drags and consist of metal washers alternately keyed to the spool or the rotor shaft, in between which are soft composition or cork washers. They are held in place by a spring that fits into the top of the drag stack. To check the drag washers, carefully remove the spring and then remove the washers, one at a time. Keep them in order so that you can replace them in the same order. Check for damage or wear on the washers. Sometimes the metal washers will become slightly rough or corroded. If necessary, polish the metal washers with steel wool, followed by abrasive cleanser; replace them if they cannot be restored to original smoothness. Grease or lube drag washers only if suggested by the manufacturer. Many are designed to run dry. If they are worn or are indented from compression, replace them.

Other repairs. Other repairs will be rare but could involve replacing gears or replacing the antireverse switch. Replacing gears can be time-consuming, since you will have to dismantle the reel almost completely to remove the main shaft (the reciprocating shaft that moves the spool in and out to put on line evenly). Usually, the drive gear is attached to the handle, and the main gear to the main shaft and rotor. Refer to the reel manual to remove the rotor, spool, and main shaft to replace the gears. To make reassembly easy, keep parts in order in a compartmented box.

The antireverse switch usually consists of a switch or lever that moves a pawl; the pawl catches a tooth to prevent the rotor from turning backward. These parts are easy to replace but are not always easily accessible on the sideplate or at the rear of the gear housing.

Bent or broken handles are easily replaced, since virtually all spinning reels have convertible left/right retrieve and, as a result, have easy attachment

Tackle Care/Maintenance/Repair

Proper storage of rods and reels, especially in boats where they can be accidentally damaged, helps prevent the need for repairs.

to the gear set. Most either are screwed into a shaft or have a hex or square shaft, which slips through a similar sleeve to be held in place by a machine screw on the opposite side of the reel.

Spincasting Tackle

Handle. Handles on spincasting reels also become broken, but they are generally screwed in place on the shaft, similarly to the attachment used with baitcasting reels. No tools are needed to replace a handle; unscrew the old handle and replace it with a new one.

Spools. Damaged spools are easily replaced by first removing the hood or nose cone (usually twisted off), then removing (unscrewing counterclockwise) the winding cup that holds the line pickup pin, and slipping off the old damaged spool. Replace with a new one, reversing the procedure to reassemble.

Pickup pin and snubber. The pickup pin and snubber are easy to check and replace when you are removing the spool. The pin operates on a cam or spring system on the winding cup. Metal and even ceramic pickup pins may become worn and should be checked periodically. The plastic or rubber line snubber on the forward inside of the hood can become worn or sometimes separated from the hood. If separated, it can usually be glued back into place by using epoxy or rubber cement. If worn, pry off and replace with a new one, also glued in place.

Washers and gears. The drag tension adjustment mechanism on most spincasting reels is located under the handle, in the same place as on baitcasting reels. To check or replace washers, remove the handle nut or screw, slip the handle off, unscrew the star drag wheel, and then remove the washers for examination or replacement. Follow the same instructions as those given for the washers on spinning reels.

Access to the gears on some spincasting reels is gained by removing the sideplate, the same as with spinning reels; on others, access is gained when the hood is removed. Replacing gears can be a little involved, as it is with spinning reels. Use the reel manual for guidance in removing the rotor, spool, and main shaft. To facilitate reassembly, keep parts in order in a compartmented box.

Baitcasting Tackle

Levelwind pawl. The levelwind pawl is the small-toothed pin that travels in the levelwind gear to spool the line evenly. To check or replace the pawl (spares are usually included in a small container of parts with each baitcasting reel), remove the small cap that holds the pawl in place and slide out the pawl. Check to see whether the pawl is worn or has become pinlike, in which case it needs to be replaced. Replace by sliding a new pawl into the housing; make sure that the tooth engages the worm gear, and replace the cap.

Levelwind worm gear. Levelwind worm gears seldom wear enough to require replacement; but if they do, they can be easily replaced by removing the handle sideplate, loosening and removing some retainer rings or screws and the levelwind pawl, and sliding out the worm gear. Replace and reassemble; then grease both the worm gear and the pawl housing.

Drag washers and gears. Drag washers and gears on baitcasting reels are both in the same location; the drag washer is usually mounted on the face of the main gear. To check or replace any of these parts, first remove the handle-side sideplate. Then remove the handle and unscrew the star drag wheel, following the manufacturer's instructions. Most require first unscrewing a small locking plate and then using a wrench to remove a handle nut, followed by spinning off the star drag wheel. With the handle removed, use a small screwdriver to remove the internal plate that holds the gears. This separates the external sideplate from the plate holding the gears and drag washers, and allows examination of the gears and drag washers. If the gear teeth have been stripped, then one or both gears in the set should be replaced.

Check for damage or wear on the washers. Sometimes the metal washers will become slightly rough or corroded. If necessary, polish the metal washers with steel wool, followed by abrasive cleanser; replace them if they cannot be restored to original smoothness. Lubricate drag washers only if suggested by the manufacturer. Many are designed to run dry. If they are worn or are indented from compression, replace them.

Handle. Sometimes the handle of a baitcasting reel becomes bent; more likely one of the knobs breaks. In both cases it's a good idea to replace the handle entirely. It is generally tightened in place on the shaft by a covering nut. The small tool supplied with the reel can be used to remove the nut. Make sure that you make the repair in a location where the nut can be recovered if you drop it. Some anglers have done this on a boat or dock and watched their retaining nut fall into the water, rendering the reel useless until a new nut is obtained.

Flycasting Tackle

Flycasting reels are simple and require little in repairs, provided that they are kept clean and maintained as previously outlined. In some cases, a reel foot or line guard, if these are separate from the reel frame, will become corroded or worn. For those that are separate from the frame, replacement is easy through the screws that hold these parts in place. Pawls that become worn as a click drag are easily replaced, often by just removing the spool and gently holding the spring apart to lift the pawl free and then replacing with a new one.

Drag components must be cared for on flycasting reels that feature disk or caliper drags; follow the manufacturer's instructions for care, cleaning, and any lubrication.

Conventional and Lever Drag Tackle

Making repairs to conventional reels and lever drag reels is something that must be done very carefully, since these products are put under tremendous strains and torque in some fishing situations. These products are meant for rugged use and are built accordingly, but you need to be careful when tinkering with them, especially if you take them apart and reassemble them. If you don't feel confident about doing this, have a repair shop or the manufacturer do the work.

Simple things like replacing handles or clickers or the levelwind pawl (in some models) are easy to do, and such repairs are accomplished as already noted for other products. Handles on conventional reels are held in place similarly to those on baitcasting reels, since they both have star drag operation. Thus, unscrew and remove the nut-locking plate, then use a wrench to loosen the nut and slip off the handle. Some conventional reels have multiple attachment for power or leverage advantages, so they may be frequently changed. Just be sure to use the right tool so that you don't strip the handle-fastening screw or nut.

It is unlikely that you will have to replace either the pinion or the main gear in these heavy-duty products, although such a repair can certainly be made if needed. These parts are typically located under the handle. To get to them, remove the handle and then spin off the star drag wheel. Remove the screws around the perimeter of the sideplate; for easy reassembly, remove them in order. After the sideplate has been removed, additional bracketing might have to be removed to expose the gearing. Once this is done, access to the gears and drag washers is similar to that of baitcasting reels, and they are relatively easily replaced.

The drag washers on conventional reels are critical to their performance, and all points that have previously been made about washers apply even more so to conventional reels. Lever drag reels are a distinctive product, operating differently, and they do not have a stack of washers. Nevertheless, the friction drag material that they use and the drag plate need to be inspected, and obviously replaced if they are worn. For some older reels, this material can be replaced with a better friction material supplied by the manufacturer.

See: Baitcasting Tackle; Big-Game Tackle; Conventional Tackle; Flycasting Tackle; Spincasting Tackle; Spinning Tackle.

TACKLE STORAGE
See: Lure Storage.

TAG
A mark on a fish made for identification purposes; also a physical device attached to a fish for this purpose.
See: Tagging.

TAG-AND-RELEASE
A term for placing a tag in fish that are captured by sportfishing and released unharmed.
See: Catch-and-Release; Tagging.

TAGGING
Tagging is a method of marking fish for identification purposes. In a very few cases, a visible tag is placed on a dead fish (such as Atlantic salmon in some Canadian provinces), much the same way that hunters place a tag on game animals or birds they have taken. Tagging is done when a limited number of fish are allowed to be harvested, and a tag (provided with fishing license) must legally be placed on harvested fish. Most of the time, however, visible tags are used to identify live fish that are returned to the water for the purpose of providing information about individual fish or particular species.

Tagging is commonly used by biologists for specific research and management purposes, and it has become an increasingly common voluntary practice by anglers, especially for pelagic and migratory species. Although tagging is generally viewed as the placement of visible objects on or in the bodies of fish, it is actually a method of marking, which also includes such practices as clipping the fins, coloring with long-lasting fluorescent pigment or short-term dye, tattooing, branding, and outfitting with electronic devices that transmit detectable signals. The most common item to anglers, however, is a visible exterior tag; anglers occasionally catch fish that possess such objects, and many actually place tags in fish that they release, especially saltwater anglers.

The Scientific Side
Biologists mark fish with visible exterior tags

Scientists say that most fish are color blind but can see color shadings, reflected light, shape, and movement.

and hidden body cavity tags, usually after weighing and measuring them. The tags usually contain an identification number and often a phone number or other information so that recaptured fish can be evaluated. Anglers are asked to return the tag to a sponsoring agency or organization and to provide information on when and where the fish was caught, as well as its measurements and weight upon capture. In some cases, there are rewards for returning the tag and/or providing necessary information.

Several things can be learned by biologists from a tagging program. The movement of a species, for example, is known if the release and recapture points are known. The rate of movement may be determined if the time between release and recapture is recorded.

Often the goal of a tagging program is estimating the size of a fish population, determining the rate at which fish are being caught, and verifying growth rates. A tagging program that records the size at the date of tagging and at the date of recapture provides an independent measure of the growth rate. When biologists tag a specific number of fish and later recapture a portion of them (through netting or other means), they can estimate the number of fish in that population. Likewise, when a biologist knows the number of tagged fish in a population, the death rate through angling can be determined when tags are returned for fish that have been kept.

Biologists conduct tagging activities for a wide range of fish in freshwater and saltwater; in North America, there is a distinct difference in the way programs are carried out within those environments, owing to the fact that many saltwater species cross state and even international boundaries.

In freshwater, the majority of tagging is done by technicians and biologists representing individual state fisheries agencies. Many tagged fish are ones raised in hatcheries and tagged prior to release in the wild, and others are fish that are caught in their natural environments, usually via netting and sometimes via electrofishing *(see)*. In a few cases, state agencies use angler volunteers to assist in getting wild-caught fish tagged more widely over a given time period, but these individuals are trained and provided with equipment. Most agency-related tagging efforts are locally targeted, geared to specific water bodies and certain species.

In saltwater, few states conduct tagging activities other than for inshore species and resident populations of fish, and then usually only for short periods and specific management purposes. However, private groups sponsor extensive tagging programs coordinated with federal agencies, especially the National Marine Fisheries Service *(see)*. Some mass tagging is done by federal fisheries managers in places where numbers of fish are available seasonally (such as anadromous species like shad in coastal rivers). However, limited resources and wide-ranging fish make it impractical for federal fisheries

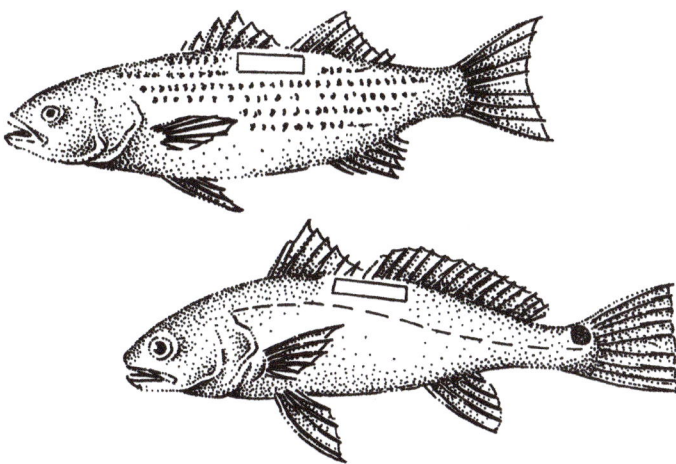

The bandagelike boxes on this striped bass (top) and red drum indicate optimal tag location.

managers to tag marine species in quantity over a reasonable period of time; therefore, they rely on angler volunteers to report taggings and recaptures to appropriate agencies.

Some of the more interesting and technologically advanced activities recently conducted by federal fisheries biologists are harness tags that send data to satellites, and in-body archival tags used with pelagic fish. The latter tags cost over a thousand dollars and are implanted by scientists in the body of a fish to record its swimming depth, water temperature, body temperature, and location by means of a sensor. A two-tone green alert tag, which is meant to bring attention to the presence of the archival tag, is also placed on the fish.

The National Marine Fisheries Service (NMFS) has placed these archival tags in a number of billfish, and in hundreds of Atlantic bluefin tuna. The tagging has particular value because it provides information about all the places that the fish visits between the point of tagging and recapture. Substantial rewards are offered for the return of an undamaged tag, and fish that are caught out of season or without the proper permit may be kept if they have such a tag. The most sophisticated and expensive of archival tags may be the pop-up variety, which are attached to the base of the fish's dorsal fin and detach after time, emerging on the surface and relaying data to a satellite.

Tagging by Anglers

As mentioned, the differences between tagging activities in freshwater and saltwater are extensive. Most freshwater fisheries managers discourage and do not favor tagging by the public because they feel that improper handling of fish and misguided tagging efforts are likely to be harmful to fish and because there is a chance (usually remote) that private tagging activities might interfere with agency efforts. Freshwater biologists note that tagging produces more stress on a fish than it would already receive through the process of hooking, landing, and handling for release, not to mention the possibility of in some way hurting the fish. Tagging

Tagging

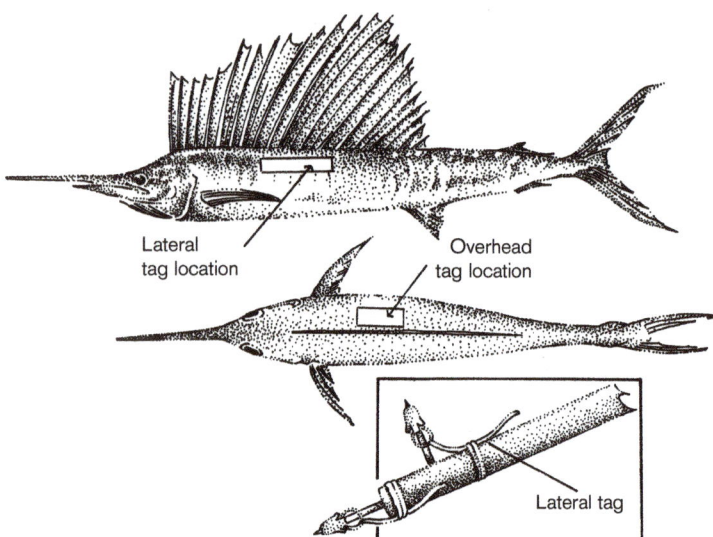

Patched areas show where a tag should be placed when a big fish, such as a sailfish, is approached from lateral and overhead vantages. A tagging stick (inset) rigged with two tags—one on the end for overhead tagging and the other on the side for lateral tagging—will permit tagging in either instance.

Tagging information. There are a number of different tag types, and suppliers provide information on the best method of tagging, angle of tag insertion, and placement location, depending on the tag type and target species. The Littoral Society, for example, which uses so-called spaghetti tags, recommends tag insertion behind the dorsal fin near the tail. Suppliers of barbed tags generally recommend placing it near the middle of the dorsal fin, well above the lateral line, with single-barbed tags at a 45-degree angle and double-barbed tags at a 90-degree angle. Some species have to be captured and handled for tagging; others (including billfish and large tuna) are tagged in the water with the use of tagging sticks (sticks to which tags are attached).

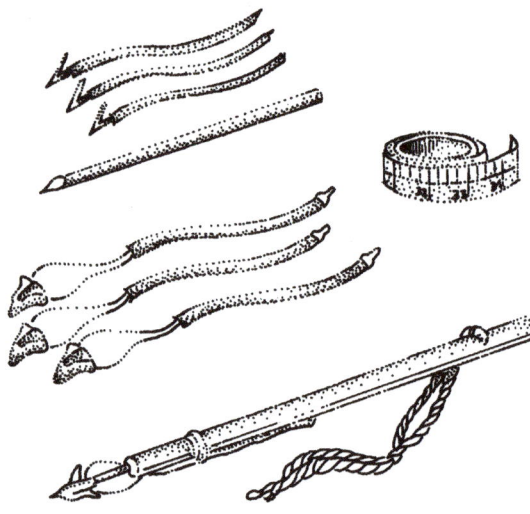

The tagging tools shown here, from top to bottom, include single-barb tags, hollow stainless steel small-tag applicator, double-barb tags, measuring tape, and solid stainless steel large-tag applicator.

T in public waters may be illegal in some places, and anglers should check on this.

In a practical sense, freshwater anglers have little reason to tag fish unless there is a coordinated research or management program associated with tagging, even though some companies have made fish tagging tools or kits available to the public. The end result of tagging should be to advance information that has scientific value, but without a program to use the information derived from tagging, there is little use for it other than curiosity. Even tagging anadromous fish is of little value without a program to utilize the information. However, tagging on private bodies of water (small lakes and ponds in particular) may have merit, even if just for personal reasons and curiosity, since these are closed environments.

In the marine environment, however, there is no private water, there are few public agencies that tag fish, and those that do are under severe budget constraints. Tagging and releasing fish has become increasingly popular here and is conducted under the auspices of a number of private organizations, which supply tags (for a fee) to the public or to members, as well as extensive tagging information. These organizations also report recaptures to participants, and they supply data to public agencies, such as NMFS or the Fish and Wildlife Service, for research and management efforts. The oldest such program was started in 1965 at Sandy Hook in Highlands, New Jersey, by the American Littoral Society, and tens of thousands of fish annually are entered into the database by volunteer taggers. Another organization, the Billfish Foundation of Miami, Florida, has reported over 40,000 billfish tagged since its program was initiated in 1990. The Cooperative Shark Tagging Program run by NMFS has over 6,000 participants and has been responsible for tagging over 125,000 sharks. And there are other programs as well.

Anglers who intend to tag fish need to keep the well-being of the fish foremost in mind. This means following all procedures for quickly playing and landing the fish *(see: landing fish; playing fish)*, as well as following the proper procedures for catch-and-release *(see)*. Fish that will be handled during tagging will benefit from having extra water poured over them and from having a wet towel placed over their heads while they are being held. With the proper tools already available, experienced taggers can accomplish the tagging very quickly and with no harm to the fish. The pertinent information should be supplied to the appropriate organization promptly. There is a lot of satisfaction in tagging and releasing a fish for science, and even more in recapturing one or in having one that you tagged be recaptured later at some distant place.

Proper tagging does reveal recaptures, although the overall percentage of recaptured fish is quite small. Some tagged fish have been recaptured many years after their initial tagging, and great distances from their original site. Some have been recaptured only minutes after first being tagged, some tagged fish are recaptured by their original captors, and some have been recaught numerous times.

If you catch a tagged fish. Although some tags are immediately obvious on fish, some are not. You should check both sides of a fish that you catch to see whether it has a tag, and check out any growths or trailing objects. A piece of "seaweed" could be the extension of an algae-covered tag.

If you're keeping the fish, then information can be obtained at your convenience. Otherwise, you'll have to act quickly. Copy down the serial number of the tag, and record the measurements of the fish, the location, and any other information, including the program to be contacted. If you keep the fish, clip and send the tag to the appropriate program.

TAGLINE

A heavy cord fixed either to an outrigger *(see)* or to a transom cleat and connected to a fishing line to provide hooksetting tension when a fish strikes. A tagline is used to help spread out offshore trolling lures *(see: trolling lures, saltwater)* behind the boat and adjust their angle of entry into the water for better running. It is used with lures and fishing methods that do not require a dropback for striking a fish when it attacks a fast-trolled lure.

The tagline consists of a short length of heavy, no-stretch line or cord (offshore trollers use 500-pound-test braided cord) connected to a cleat or clipped to the outrigger line. The business end sports a nonrelease clip or waxed line-tie. A rubber band (No. 64 is the preferred size for 50- to 130-pound-class line) is wrapped at least five times around the fishing line, then the two end loops of the rubber band are snapped into the clip, or secured to the waxed line-ties by a quick-release loop. When a fish strikes, the rubber band stretches considerably before breaking, providing some initial give, which helps in setting the hook.

Some offshore anglers attach the tagline to the fishing line via a slipknot in the rubber band, which is easily freed by yanking the cord when changing lures. Be careful that your knot doesn't bind onto the fishing line under tension; if it does, it will usually remain attached to the line even after breaking free of the tagline when a fish strikes. As the fish is subsequently fought to the boat, the rubber band, now knotted to the fishing line, will eventually arrive at the rod's tiptop, and unless the tip-top and lower guides are oversized, won't pass through them, which could prove to be an impediment to landing the fish. You can avoid this by wrapping the rubber band around the line at least five times, then securing the two free end loops of the rubber band to the tagline. This way, when the rubber band breaks, it flies off the line.

Incidentally, a similar system can be used for trolling spoons and plugs on flatlines, in both freshwater and saltwater, as a means of lowering

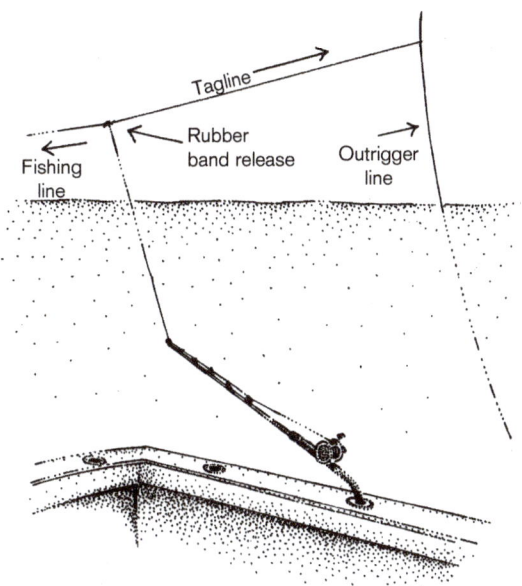

As shown, a tagline is a length of heavy cord or line between outrigger line and fishing line (or between boat and fishing line). A rubber band release, or spring tension release, is used to free the fishing line when a fish strikes the trolled lure or bait.

the angle of line entry into the water and also as a means of helping to set the hook. Some trout, salmon, and striped bass trollers attach a heavy (200-pound) 2- to 4-foot length of monofilament or microfilament line to a transom cleat and use a standard commercial release *(see)*, with tension tightened, to hold the fishing line. This is primarily used to hold a flatlined lure in a center position in the boat wake and keep it away from lures spread to the sides.

See: Big-Game Fishing.

TAHITI

See: French Polynesia.

TAILER

Also called a tail rope or loop, a tailer is a nooselike device that slips over the fish and cinches down on the caudal peduncle for landing. It is best for fish with a stiff rather than flexible caudal peduncle.

Hand tailers are used in freshwater, primarily for Atlantic salmon. Tail ropes and mechanical tailing loops are used in saltwater, primarily for large fish, especially sharks, that are hard to subdue, and they are sometimes used in conjunction with gaffing. A tail rope is usually slid down the fishing line and headfirst over the body of a fish, then drawn tight as it nears the caudal peduncle. The mechanical loop is attached to a long pole to reach out over the gunwale, and it is slipped onto the fish tailfirst.

See: Landing Fish.

TAILING

(1) A method of landing a fish by grabbing it around the caudal peduncle, either by hand or with a tailer.
See: Landing Fish.

(2) A term used to describe the observation of a fish's fins sticking above the surface of the water. It is sometimes used to refer to large fish in saltwater that are swimming along the surface, whose dorsal and tail fins are out of the water *(see: finning)*, but it is more commonly associated with shallow water feeding by fish, especially in saltwater. A bonefish, for example, when on a shallow tidal flat, may feed on the bottom at such an angle as to leave the upper tip of its tail fin exposed. Likewise, a redfish in shallow water may also expose its upper tail fin while feeding in the shallows.

TAILRACE

The disturbed and often turbulent section of river directly below a large dam, where water from the upstream impoundment is released. This term is often used interchangeably with tailwater *(see)*, which is actually the entire section of river below a dam whose flows are dependent upon dam releases. The tailrace is the section closest to the dam.

Tailraces often have varied fishing opportunities, even if one species usually dominates; catches may include a number of species. This section of water is often very good for fishing because of cooler and well-oxygenated water, an abundance of food, turbulent water conditions that are conducive to aggressive feeding, and the concentration of upstream-migrating fish, which can go no farther than the dam.

When the water is moving swiftly, which often depends on releases for power generation or flood control, fishing is likely to be prime. This is not unlike the movement of tides *(see)* in coastal rivers and their influence on fish activity.

In swift tailraces, much fishing is done from boats, since shore fishing limits effectiveness; and being situated on the bank has inherent danger when rising water levels are prevalent. Anglers in boats cast with lures or drift bait, both while anchored or while drifting. Fishing with live bait, especially shad that have been caught by dipping or using a cast net, is highly popular.

One of the often overlooked benefits of tailrace fishing is that the swift and well-oxygenated water here lends itself very well to releasing fish unharmed. This is especially true for striped bass, which are often difficult to revive and release in good condition, especially in summer months.

A drawback, however, is the extra safety precautions that must be taken in the turbulent below-dam environment. Rising water levels can sink improperly anchored boats, and extreme currents and roiling water can make boat operation very tricky.
See: Boat; Currents; Safety.

TAIL ROPE
See: Tailer.

TAILSPINNER

A small lead-bodied lure with a treble hook under its belly and a revolving spinner blade at its tail.

Tailspinners are used in freshwater fishing, primarily for largemouth bass and white bass in schooling situations, when the fish are near the surface and feeding frenziedly. These lures are aerodynamically shaped and can be cast a great distance, particularly with spinning gear and light to medium line. They're worked in a quick pump-and-go style, just under the surface in such a situation, always retrieving at a rate that keeps the blade turning.

Tailspinners can also be fished deep, in vertical jigging style, for suspended bass in deep water near some particular structure, or they can be hopped off the bottom in fishing submerged islands, rocky points, and such. Effective colors are white, silver, and gray.

TAILWATER

The entire section of river below a dam whose flows are dependent upon dam releases. A tailwater is sometimes also called a tailrace *(see)*, which is actually a component of the tailwater, being the often turbulent section of river directly below a large dam, where water spews from the upstream impoundment.

Tailwaters exist wherever rivers have been impounded, and they flow for varied distances. Some flow from one reservoir to another, which may be just a short distance or a dozen or more

Turbulent water in tailraces can attract large fish; this angler is fishing the Red River at Selkirk, Manitoba.

miles. Some flow to their merger with other rivers, which may or may not be tailwaters themselves.

In North America, tailwaters offer excellent fishing opportunities for a host of species, although most species that exist in these places aren't native. Many tailwaters exist, and have the environment that they do, because natural rivers and their habitats and native species were flooded by environmentally destructive dams. Those dams primarily support hydroelectric power generation, and downstream flows are dependent on water releases, which means that the species and fishing are likewise dependent on them. In some tailwaters, erratic release schedules, meager flows, and warm water from reservoir surface discharges adversely impact the fisheries, and there have been long ongoing struggles with water regulators to achieve sustained flows of proper temperature to benefit fish and other downstream aquatic life.

In the southern United States, the most prominent tailwater species is striped bass, but significant fisheries exist in many tailwaters for trout, catfish, walleye, smallmouth bass, and white bass. In western states, trout are the primary fish, and tailwaters there provide some of the best and most popular trout fishing that is known. Many of these species, particularly trout, feed well and grow to good, if not large, sizes but don't manage natural reproduction; their populations are supported through regular plantings in the river itself or in a downstream impoundment.

The type of fishery in tailraces is dependent on the temperature of the water that is released, especially during summer, and this is a function of the thermal stratification (see) characteristics of the reservoir and the location of the outlet in the dam. On many large dams, the outlet portals are located at or near the bottom of the dam, and this position ensures a constant flow of cold water. This water usually has good oxygen levels for most of the year, but may have poor oxygen during summer when the cold, deep waters of the reservoir become oxygen-deficient. However, in many tailraces, the discharge of great volumes of water creates enough turbulence to highly oxygenate the water in that area. In most tailwaters, discharge levels vary annually as well as seasonally; there may be shutdown periods, and water levels may be subject to extreme fluctuations. These conditions pose good fishing opportunities when current is strong but also present boating and wading dangers. However, a generally cool or cold water temperature year-round, often without much summer and winter fluctuation, makes them fishable all season and keeps fish active all year.

Boating and fishing in the actual tailrace section of a tailwater is a bit different than through the rest of the river because of its turbulence. Farther downriver, the tailwater becomes more like a normal river, except that water temperatures usually are constant, and there are often sudden increases in water level. In rivers that are waded, such increases

The long, shallow runs of the White River in Arkansas provide some of North America's best tailwater trout fishing.

can be especially dangerous; an unobservant angler may be quickly stranded on a rock with swift and rising cold water closing in.

The methods for fishing tailwaters vary with species and the rivers. In larger, heavier flows, a lot of fishing is done from boats, often power boats, some having jet drive (see) motors. Fishing is also is carried out by floating in inflatable rafts, canoes, jonboats, or drift boats (see). Wading is prominent also, especially by trout anglers, and occurs whenever and wherever shallow water and pools or runs can feasibly be approached by a wading angler—obviously in the smaller and shallow systems but also in the downstream reaches of larger tailwaters. Anglers who float down tailwaters often get out of their craft to fish some runs and pools.

For various species, a lot of fishing is done with bait. This includes live or cut shad or herring for stripers, assorted baits for catfish, minnows for walleye, and eggs and various processed baits for trout. Where stripers are found, live bait is best, but it usually has to be gathered, often by cast netting, and must be well cared for in proper wells. Jigs, assorted swimming plugs, jigging spoons, and bottom-bouncing bait rigs are among the mix as well.

Miles and miles of prime trout habitat exist in many tailwaters, and this opens up a range of fishing possibilities for primarily rainbow and brown trout. Bait is popular in many waters, but casting with spinners, small jigs, and small minnow plugs can be effective. Fly fishing is highly effective in many tailwater trout fisheries, and more common in western than southern rivers. The variety of food in downstream tailwaters—various types of baitfish, aquatic insects, terrestrial insects, aquatic worms, and crustaceans—means that a fly angler has a bulging vest in order to imitate everything that tailwater trout might feed upon.

For trout fishing, streamer flies are good when the water level is rising or falling, and baitfish may be a more prominent food item. The rising water will often bring fair numbers of terrestrial insects into the water, making it good for fishing with hoppers, beetles, crickets, and the like. Day in and day out fly fishing in tailwaters, however, sees the use of mayfly and caddisfly imitations, various nymphs, and a variety of flies that imitate scuds, worms, and the like.

See: Boat; Currents; Safety.

TAIMEN *Hucho hucho taimen.*

Other names—taimen salmon, Siberian taimen.

A member of the Salmonidae family, which includes salmon and trout, taimen are closely related to *Hucho hucho,* the huchen *(see),* and one of evidently four species in the same genus. These two fish cannot be separated by conventional scientific analyses but are distinguished by virtue of Asian versus European geographical location. Taimen have become a fish of greater interest to traveling anglers in recent years but are largely unknown to most and have been caught by relatively few Europeans and even fewer Westerners. They have white, sweet-tasting meat.

Identification. Taimen physically resemble northern pike or muskies. The body is round and elongated, and the head is flattened and has an enormous terminal mouth, which is equipped with small sharp teeth. Like huchen, taimen are specked with dark spots over the entire body, predominating on the upper portions, including the head and fins. The tail and anal fins are a crimson red. During the spawning period, most of the body becomes copper red.

Size/Age. Taimen evidently are capable of attaining the largest maximum size of any salmonid, as befits a fish of large rivers. An 1871 Russian report noted that taimen can reach 175 pounds in the Yenisei, Pyasina, and Khatanga Rivers in Siberia. A report exists of a 231-pound specimen taken in a commercial net in the Kotui River in 1943, but the largest authenticated record is a 123-pounder, which is slightly less than a commercially caught 126-pound chinook salmon, the largest of that salmonid species. The all-tackle world record is a $92^{1}/_{2}$-pounder. They are also evidently long-lived fish, as a 65-pounder was estimated at more than 50 years of age.

Distribution. The taimen is restricted to the Ural-Siberian-Amur drainages of Asia, most of which flow into the Arctic Ocean; it is reportedly found as far west as the Pechora River. This range is similar to that of another exotic salmonid, the lenok *(see).* The huchen, in contrast, is restricted to the Danube River drainage of Europe. The taimen and huchen ranges do not overlap and are separated by the eastern European flatland.

Habitat/Spawning behavior. The taimen inhabits large rivers with fast currents, especially the large lower reaches and often travels into their estuaries, although it is strictly a freshwater fish. It also occurs in lakes. In spring, it ascends rivers and enters shallow creeks, spawning in May in some Russian waters.

Food and feeding habits. As voracious feeders, taimen have a wide-ranging diet of other fish; smaller taimen, pike, salmon, and especially grayling are part of their diet. They are also reported to consume small mammals and birds. Lemmings are a staple during migratory periods, and this explains why they are attracted to mouselike offerings. They have been noted by observers to hunt in groups, and also to attract smaller fish into range through a tail-waving action that raises bottom sediment.

Angling. Taimen inhabit remote areas that have experienced little to no sportfishing until recently, and they are of no commercial fishing interest. Both factors contribute to a general paucity of information, especially scientific reports on life history.

Taimen fishing is accomplished with large streamer flies, surface and swimming plugs, spoons, and spinners. Live baits are used by native fishermen. These offerings run to large sizes and include fish and mammals (which may be attached to ropelike line and tied to a tree overnight). The voracious taimen reportedly will strike at anything resembling wounded prey, and in the remote Mongolian reaches of their range, they are pursued with huge natural baits, flies, and lures. "Huge" is not an exaggeration, as fly anglers have discovered that the biggest streamers primarily attracted only smaller fish.

TAKE
A strike by a fish.

TANK
A small pond, often called a stock tank, possibly used for watering farm animals.

TANZANIA
The land of Mount Kilimanjaro, Zanzibar, Ngorongoro Crater, and the Serengeti Plain, Tanzania is mostly associated with great wildlife viewing and stupendous natural beauty. Four times the size of Great Britain, its Selous Game Reserve is one of the last great wildernesses on earth, and its 938,000 square kilometers contains a significant part of the Great Rift Valley.

International visitors to Tanzania tend to focus on Africa's highest mountain and tremendous

Taimen

game, leaving sportfishing opportunities lightly explored. This is especially so in freshwater, even though Tanzania possesses several rivers and borders on Africa's three largest lakes. Tanzania shares Lake Victoria with Kenya *(see)* and Uganda *(see)*, Lake Tanganyika with the Democratic Republic of the Congo (formerly Zaire) and a small portion of Zambia *(see)*, and Lake Malaŵi (also known as Nyasa) with Malaŵi *(see)*. Its several large rivers flow eastward into the Indian Ocean, and its watershed feeds the great Nile, Zambezi, and Congo Rivers, all of which course through other countries.

In Tanzania, the focus is on saltwater angling along the country's 800 kilometers of coastline, which borders the Indian Ocean between Kenya to the north and Mozambique to the south. This coastline embraces the romantic islands of the Zanzibar archipelago, and the best sportfishing facilities are strategically situated in this region.

North of the capital city of Dar es Salaam, Zanzibar Island is separated from the mainland by a 40-kilometer-wide channel. Covering an area of more than 2,000 square kilometers, Zanzibar is a large coral island off the coast of Africa. Lying to its north and close to Kenya is 1,600-square-kilometer Pemba, and to the south of Dar es Salaam is Mafia. The banks to the east of Dar es Salaam and south of Zanzibar are known for excellent fishing. Still, many of the fishing opportu-nities in this area are hard to access and are lightly explored, but their potential is likely quite good. The most prevalent gamefish are marlin, sailfish, yellowfin tuna, shark, wahoo, dolphin, trevally, and rainbow runners.

Billfish are present year-round, but the two prime periods are during the Kusi and Kaskasi monsoon seasons. Kusi is the southeast monsoon, occurring from May through September. From August into September is the best period during Kusi for billfish, as blue marlin, black marlin, and sailfish are available in good numbers. Large schools of yellowfin tuna and wahoo dominate the action in October and November.

Kaskasi, the northeast monsoon, blows from November through March. This is the primary billfish season of the year. Striped marlin are present in vast numbers, black marlin move close to shore, and sailfish are most abundant. A grand slam of these species is a strong possibility during Kaskasi.

The billfish here have not been very large, but their plentiful numbers make the region a good light-tackle destination. Larger fish are in the area, but their precise locations have yet to be discovered.

Sportfishing in this region is primarily conducted out of two fishing lodges, one on Zanzibar Island and the other at Pangani Bay, about 200 miles north of the capital city. Both are located close to the most productive hotspots.

Situated high on a cliff overlooking Pangani Bay, Mashado Lodge has a stunning panorama across the sparkling blue waters of the Indian Ocean. Opened in 1996, and offering the comfort and feeling of an East African plantation home, Mashado provides boat access to the nearby Maziwi sandbank and reef, and to Pemba Channel and the northern reaches of Zanzibar Channel.

On the reef, anglers cast with spinning and fly tackle, surrounded by an exotic and private sand island. Big-game enthusiasts ply the channels for black marlin, blue marlin, striped marlin, swordfish, sailfish, sharks, wahoo, and yellowfin tuna, among other species. Anglers have access to modern equipment on large offshore charter boats, and inshore and river fishing are also offered.

Northwest of Pemba, Ras Kigomasha (Cape Kigomasha) and Pemba Channel are well-known gamefishing areas favored by Kenyan anglers since 1960. Most of Africa's billfish records are registered in this area, especially for striped marlin. Sailfish, giant trevally, wahoo, and yellowfin tuna are all excellent here. Pemba's best fishing is on its east and south, where swells and current action are prevalent. As one nears the reef, the bottom slopes quickly in deep water.

Zanzibar Island offers the only hotel accommodations on the archipelago; some of these are rated with four and five stars and provide other amenities and attractions. This island has good gamefishing opportunity, especially on the northeast at Leven Bank, Mnemba Atoll, and the south side of Pemba Channel. South of Zanzibar, at Ras (Cape) Makunduki and Kizimkazi, the fishing is also good. The Zanzibar Channel, which flows between the island and the mainland, is a known spot for sailfish, small tuna, and dorado—especially at Bumbwini, Bosa, and north of Tumbatu Island.

Zanzibar Fishing Club, situated on the island, can be reached from Dar es Salaam or Nairobi, Kenya, via a brief flight. The marine habitat around Zanzibar hosts many fascinating creatures, including the rare green turtle, and the offshore species caught here are the same as those previously mentioned. The club has one charter boat for fishing the nearly untouched waters of the Zanzibar Channel on the west and the dropoff shelf of the Indian Ocean on the east.

Anglers enjoy sensational gamefishing around submerged Latham Bank, which is 13 miles long and 6 miles wide. It is situated in the middle of the Indian Ocean, about 40 miles east of Dar es Salaam and 35 miles south of Zanzibar. The top of the bank rises out of the water only a few meters and drops off to 300 meters and more. All of the gamefish that populate the Indian Ocean are present here in big numbers and good sizes. In a good day of fishing many tuna are caught, and three to five marlin strikes are routine. Great white, mako, and hammerhead sharks are also present.

When lake sturgeon were abundant, their skin was sometimes tanned for leather, and their swim bladders were used as a component for pottery cement and waterproofing.

TAPER

The shape and diameter of a fly line, and a fishing rod blank, throughout its length.
See: Flycasting Tackle; Rod, Fishing.

TAPERED LEADER

The nylon monofilament line, tapering to a fine diameter and lighter strength, that connects fly line and artificial fly.
See: Flycasting Tackle; Leader.

TARPON *Megalops atlanticus.*

Other names—silver king, Atlantic tarpon, cuffum; French: *tarpon argenté;* Italian: *tarpone;* Portuguese: *camurupi, peixe-prata-do-atlântico, tarpao;* Spanish: *pez lagarto.*

The largest member of the small Elopidae family, the tarpon is one of the world's premier saltwater gamefish. A species of warm tropical waters, it would probably be recognized as the greatest gamefish in the world if it also occurred in temperate waters and was available to all anglers. It presents the foremost qualities that anglers seek in sportfish—it is very large, very strong, challenging to hook and land, often a target of sight fishing and casting in shallow water, and a spectacular leaper when hooked.

Also known as Atlantic tarpon, this species is sometimes scientifically identified as *Tarpon atlanticus;* it is a relative of ladyfish *(see)* and of a similar but much smaller species, the Indo-Pacific tarpon (*Megalops cyprinoides),* also known as oxeye tarpon or oxeye herring. In prehistoric times, there were many more species of tarpon; today, there are just these two.

A hardy giant that can survive in a variety of habitats and salinities, the tarpon can even gulp air for extended periods when not enough oxygen is present in the water to sustain it. Despite its popularity among anglers, many aspects of this extremely long-lived fish's life cycle and behavior remain a mystery. This especially includes its migratory habits.

Tarpon are edible but not rated high as table fare, although there is some commercial interest in them in parts of their range outside North America. In Florida, where tarpon sportfishing is a popular business, the sale of this species has been prohibited since it was declared a gamefish in 1953. There, a permit must be purchased to legally kill and keep a tarpon. Fewer than 100 tarpon a year meet this fate, and the fishery is almost entirely a catch-and-release endeavor.

Identification. The tarpon's body is compressed and covered with extremely large platelike scales and a deeply forked tail fin. Its back is greenish or bluish, varying in darkness from silvery to almost black. The sides and belly are brilliant silver. Underwater, they appear to shimmer like huge gray ghosts as they swim sedately by. This appearance, along with their impressive size, is likely responsible for their nickname, "silver king." Inland, brackish-water tarpon frequently have a golden or brownish color because of tannic acid.

The huge mouth of the tarpon has a projecting, upturned lower law that contains an elongated bony plate. A single, short dorsal fin originates just behind the origin of the pelvic fin and consists of 12 to 16 soft rays (no spines), the last of which is greatly elongated. The anal fin has 19 to 25 soft rays. The lateral line is straight, even along the anterior portion, with a scale count of 41 to 48.

Size/Age. Most angler-caught Atlantic tarpon are in the range of 40 to 50 pounds, but many from 60 to 100 pounds are encountered. Fish exceeding 150 pounds are rare in the western Atlantic, but western Africa, especially Sierra Leone and Gabon, have consistently produced heavyweights exceeding 200 pounds, including a reported 300-pounder that is believed to be the maximum size of the species, as is a length of 8 feet. The all-tackle world record is shared by two 283-pound fish, one caught in 1956 at Lake Maracaibo, Venezuela, and the

Tarpon

other in 1991 at Sherbro Island, Sierra Leone. The Florida record for tarpon caught with conventional tackle was a 243-pounder from Key West in 1975.

Some Atlantic tarpon live as long as 55 years. Most of the tarpon caught in the Florida fishery are 15 to 30 years old.

The Indo-Pacific tarpon is reported to attain a maximum length of 60 inches and a weight of between 32 and 40 pounds.

Distribution. Because tarpon are sensitive to cold water, their range is generally limited to temperate climates. Atlantic tarpon have been reported as far north as Nova Scotia and also off the coast of Ireland, although they prefer tropical and subtropical waters. In the eastern Atlantic, they are most common off western Africa, from Mauritania to Angola. In the western Atlantic, they are most common from Virginia to central Brazil and throughout the Caribbean Sea and Gulf of Mexico. Atlantic tarpon from the western Atlantic have also emigrated through the Panama Canal and become established in the eastern Pacific; large specimens have been caught along the western Panamanian coast and in the vicinity of some rivers.

Although scientists believe the western Atlantic stock is genetically uniform, they have observed regional differences in behavior and size. Tarpon in Costa Rica, for example, are generally smaller than Florida tarpon, and Costa Rica tarpon spawn throughout the year rather than seasonally as Florida tarpon do.

The Indo-Pacific tarpon occurs in the western Indian Ocean from the Red Sea to South Africa and eastward to the Society Islands, northward to southern Korea, and southward to the Arafura Sea and New South Wales. It is restricted to high islands in Micronesia, and reported as far inland as the lower Shire River in Malawi and the Save-Runde junction in Zimbabwe.

Habitat. Tarpon are most abundant in estuaries and coastal waters but also occur in freshwater lakes and rivers, offshore marine waters, and occasionally on coral reefs. Adults often patrol the coral reefs of the Florida Keys. In Costa Rica and Nicaragua, anglers frequently catch tarpon in freshwater lakes and rivers miles from the coast. Although tarpon do migrate, little is known about the frequency or extent of their travels. Tarpon captured in Florida have later been recaptured as far west as Louisiana and as far north as South Carolina.

Life history/Behavior. In May and June, Atlantic tarpon in the western Atlantic begin gathering together in staging areas near the coast in preparation for the journey to their offshore spawning grounds. Here, schools of tarpon may be observed swimming in a circular, rotating motion. This behavior, known as a "daisy chain," may be prenuptial activity that prepares the fish for spawning. The actual exodus to the offshore spawning areas is probably triggered by lunar phases and tides.

During each spawning season, each female produces from 4.5 to 20.7 million eggs. The heavier the fish, the more eggs she is likely to shed. Scientists have never observed tarpon spawning or collected their fertilized eggs. Although no one knows exactly where tarpon spawn, tarpon larvae only a few days old have been collected as far as 125 miles offshore in the Gulf of Mexico. Spawning in Florida occurs mainly in May, June, and July.

The eggs hatch into larvae called leptocephali. These bizarre-looking creatures have a transparent, ribbonlike body and slender, fanglike teeth. The leptocephali drift with the currents toward the shore, reaching estuarine areas within about 30 days. Storms may assist in pushing the larvae toward their inshore nurseries.

By the time the larvae reach these inshore areas, they are about an inch long. At this point, they begin an amazing transformation in which they lose their teeth and begin shrinking in length, winding up as miniature versions of the behemoths they will eventually become. Scientists don't know how long this metamorphosis takes. Tarpon, bonefish *(see)*, ladyfish, and eels *(see)* all undergo a similar leptocephalus stage, but the first three fish all have forked tails even at the larval state, whereas the eel does not.

Juvenile tarpon make their way into marshes and mangrove swamps, where they will spend the remainder of the first year of their life, often showing a preference for stagnant pools. They grow rapidly and are roughly a foot long within one to two years. Females usually grow more quickly and are larger than males, and both reach sexual maturity around age 10. The sex of a tarpon cannot reliably be determined until their second or third year and then only by an internal examination.

One particularly remarkable facet of tarpon physiology is the fish's ability to breathe both underwater and out of the water. When dissolved oxygen levels in the water are adequate, tarpon breathe like most fish, through their gills. When oxygen levels are depleted, however, they can also breathe by gulping air, which is then passed along to their highly specialized swim bladder. The swim bladder functions as an accessory lung and even resembles that organ, with its spongy, highly vascular tissue. The swim bladder can also be filled with air as needed to help the fish maintain its desired depth in the water. Scientists believe the tarpon's ability to breathe air is a nifty adaptation that allows it to survive in the stagnant, oxygen-poor pools and ditches it frequents.

Although tarpon can tolerate water of various salinities, they are vulnerable to cold snaps and become stressed when water temperatures fall below 55°F. Although adults can often seek refuge from the cold in deep holes and channels, young fish are less able to escape cold waters.

Food. Tarpon often travel in schools with other tarpon and are opportunistic eaters that feed on a variety of fish and crabs.

A tarpon clears the surface near Sugarloaf Key, Florida.

Angling. The tarpon's powerful leaps, sometimes up to 10 feet out of the water, and bone-jarring bursts of speed test the skill and fortitude of even the most experienced angler. The nature of their high and often frequent jumps is such that many anglers are happy simply to get a few jumps out of a tarpon before it shakes the hook.

The better fishing is in spring and fall, but they are caught in all months in some locales. Prominent fishing sites include rivers, bays, lagoons, shallow flats, passes between islands, mangrove-lined banks, and the like. Small, or "baby" tarpon, those up to 20 pounds or so, are usually located in estuaries and river mouths, even considerable distances up freshwater rivers and in sloughs and canals.

Fishing methods include drifting or stillfishing with live mullet, pinfish, crabs, shrimp, or other natural baits, or casting or trolling with spoons, plugs, or other artificial lures and flies. Trolling is generally the least-practiced method; casting is generally most favored, as it involves stalking, spotting, and skillful bait or lure presentations. It may not be appropriate, however, when the fish are deep or unaggressive. The best fishing can be at night when tarpon are feeding.

When casting, anglers usually sight-fish for tarpon, staking out a shallow-draft boat near a channel or hole or moving along shallow grassy flats, usually by poling. They wait for tarpon to come within casting range, or try to spot cruising fish and then move to intercept them. A variety of plugs are cast for tarpon, with shallow runners fished in a whip or jerky pull-pause retrieve being most effective. Surface plugs are also fished, and flycasters mainly employ large streamers. Lures and flies are cast just ahead of a passing fish. Often, casters get only one chance at a cruising fish or school, and poor placement of the offering can spook the fish. Sometimes tarpon strike readily, even turning and moving a short distance to take a lure or fly, although it is usually necessary to have the item right in front of the fish, in its path of travel. Tarpon seldom take a lure or bait with great authority, however. Sometimes they are quite finicky and ignore even a perfect presentation.

Live-bait fishing occurs with anglers drifting or anchored and stillfishing with a float. Such live baits as mullet, pinfish, crabs, and shrimp are used, usually in deep areas or in channels where the fish cruise through. Some anglers jig in deep-water holes and passes; others slow-troll along the edges of flats near deep water with big spoons, plugs, and feathers. Although tarpon appear to be sensitive to noise and boat traffic and may become skittish and reluctant to take baits when the waters are crowded with boaters, tarpon are unlike many other fish in that they are frequently found in highly urbanized areas with poor water quality.

Sharp hooks are an absolute necessity for tarpon fishing; these silvery fish have a tough, bony mouth that is hard to penetrate, and it is usually necessary to set the hook firmly several times in order to make a good connection. Even so, many tarpon are lost during one of their many jumps. They also have a tough gill plate that can cut the fishing line readily, so strong leaders are routinely used.

Standard tackle is a 7-foot baitcasting rod and reel filled with at least 200 yards of between 12- and 20-pound line. The heavier strengths are used most often, especially where landing large fish is a possibility. Flycasters use a 9- to 10-foot rod with plenty of backbone for 10- to 12-weight line, and a fly reel that has plenty of strong backing line.

Tarpon have to be thoroughly played out before being landed, although they revive well for release. Many are lip-gaffed for hook removal, a process that doesn't cause harm if done properly. Fish that are close to the boat and still green can be very dangerous, however. Some have leaped into a boat when the gaff was placed into the lower jaw; some have pulled the gaffer overboard; and some have jumped into the boat without being touched. A big, heavy fish with a wildly flapping body and tail, not to mention hooks and other paraphernalia lying about, can be enormously dangerous inside a boat, so it behooves anglers to be careful and observant at all times.

See: Flats Fishing.

TAUTOG *Tautoga onitis*.

Other names—blackfish, tog, Molly George, chub, oysterfish; French: *tautogue noir*.

Primarily known as blackfish, the tautog is a member of the Labridae family of wrasses *(see)*, which includes some 500 species in 57 known genera. It one of the largest families of fish. The tautog is not a fast or extremely active species, but it puts up a stubborn fight, and its flesh is edible and of good quality. These factors, plus year-round availability and good size, make it a popular inshore sportfish.

Identification. Blunt-nosed and thick-lipped, the tautog has a high forehead and a heavy body. It is brownish on the back and sides and lighter below, and it has blackish mottling over the entire body. Tautogs are darker over a dark bottom background and lighter over a light bottom background. The belly and chin are white or gray, and there may be spots on the chin. Females develop a white saddle down the middle of each side during spawning. The caudal fin is rounded on the corners and squared across the tip; the soft-rayed dorsal and anal fins are rounded.

The first dorsal fin has 16 to 17 spines of almost equal length. The short second dorsal fin consists of 10 somewhat longer soft rays. The anal fin has 3 spines and 7 to 8 soft rays. There is a detached area of small scales behind and beneath the eye, but none on the opercle. The lateral line is arched more or less following the contour of the back and has a scale count of 69 to 73. There are 9 gill rakers on the first branchial arch, 3 on the upper limb, and 6 on the lower limb. A number of small teeth are present along the sides of the jaws, and there are two to three large canine teeth in the tips.

Size. This fish averages 3 pounds or less in weight. Specimens weighing 6 to 10 pounds are caught with some regularity, however, and the all-tackle world record is a Virginia fish that was caught in 1988 and weighed 24 pounds.

Distribution. The tautog occurs in the western Atlantic from Nova Scotia to South Carolina, and the greatest abundance is between Cape Cod, Massachusetts, and Delaware Bay. It overlaps in range with the smaller and more northerly relative, the cunner *(see)*.

Tautog

Habitat. Tautog are known to move in and out of bays or inshore and offshore according to the water temperature, but they do not make extensive migrations up and down the coast. Preferred environs include shallow waters over rocky bottoms, shell beds, inshore wrecks, and the like, which it often inhabits year-round.

Food and feeding habits. The diet of tautog is mainly mollusks and crustaceans, with blue mussels being especially favored where abundant. It uses the flat, rounded, stout teeth located in the rear of its mouth to crush the shells of mollusks or crustaceans. The front teeth do the picking.

Angling. The place to look for tautog is around rocks. These fish are almost always found on a rocky bottom, and on or within a foot of it. Key areas include reefs, jetties, breakwaters, and boulders. The more extensive the area, the better. Shellfish beds are a popular locale, too. The edges of these structures are often the focal points, and early morning is a particularly good time of day to catch these fish.

Tautog don't school as such, but they will cluster in small areas. It's important to note the location of fish when they're caught, so you can place your baits back in the same spot. Being off a few feet may result in not catching anymore fish.

As with most bottom feeders, it is common to use baits with tautog. Crabs, mussels, and soft-shelled clams are mostly preferred, although worms are sometimes used. Tautog normally feed on hard-shelled food, and they have tough mouths for crushing it. Well-sharpened hooks are necessary as a result, and a quick, hard hooksetting action is also needed. A two-hook rig is commonly fished.

Tautog are stubborn battlers that often dive for rocks when they have been hooked. Although the average fish weighs only a few pounds, fairly stout boat rods are used to keep them from digging in behind a rock. That tackle is also employed because heavy weights are used to get and keep baits down near bottom, sometimes in heavy current. Tautog anglers lose a lot of terminal tackle, however, hanging it in the rocks, but that is to be expected.

These fish seldom exist in more than 60 feet of water, and they may remain much shallower and close to shore if the right bottom terrain is available. In shallow water, they are wary fish, and keeping the bait away from the boat, instead of directly below it, is a better presentation. They also do more nibbling than hard striking in shallow water, and you may have to give them a little time to move off with the bait before setting the hook. Sometimes, however, tautog move in with the incoming tide to feed on mussels that are normally above the low-tide level.

See: Inshore Fishing; Jetty Fishing.

TAXIDERMY

The field of taxidermy is probably one of the least understood aspects of outdoor recreation and one that is rarely discussed in popular periodicals, despite the fact that thousands of people every year hire the services of a professional taxidermist, and many people, especially youngsters, are taxidermy hobbyists. Fish taxidermy is more difficult than game and bird taxidermy, in part because it requires different methods, not to mention painting, and the field has greatly advanced in the past three decades because of new processes and changing public interests.

History

There is no clear record of when the practice of taxidermy began. The sixteenth century is the earliest period with records of animals preserved in a lifelike manner. Some writings on the history of taxidermy incorrectly associate the embalming of animals by ancient Egyptians as one of the earliest records of taxidermy. Embalming and taxidermy are two different techniques. Embalming refers to the preservation of skin and flesh with chemicals and/or herbs to protect it from decay. The Egyptians did this because of religious beliefs (they felt the soul would one day return to the body), not because of aesthetics and beauty. Embalming is not an appropriate method for longtime preservation of animals in a lifelike form.

Technically, taxidermy is the arrangement of a preserved or tanned skin over a sculpted form. The purpose of taxidermy is to reproduce the anatomy, attitude, and expressions of animals as they appear in life. However, there are many variations as to how taxidermy is performed, and this term, and the field, have become broader with time.

The first publication to offer information on fish taxidermy was a 1752 French manual by M. B. Stollas, *Instructions on the Manner of Preparing Objects of Natural History*. The main subject was birds, but it established the fact that fish taxidermy was being performed at that time.

The methods used to mount fish from the mid-1700s until 1900 were very inadequate. Most taxidermists employed a stuffing technique that made it difficult to portray anatomy correctly. It was during this early period of taxidermy when people began to refer to works of taxidermy as "stuffed" animals. In most cases, the term was appropriate a hundred years ago, but today it is very rare for a stuffing technique to be used. A more appropriate, modern term is "mounted," and modern works of taxidermy are referred to as mounts.

During those early days, it was not uncommon for natural oils to ooze from a mount because of improper degreasing. Fins were weak and fragile, shrinkage around the head and fin bases distorted the anatomy, and proper paints for restoring colors were lacking. Fish were much more difficult to work with than mammals and birds, so most people avoided them; thus, few advancements were made in fish taxidermy.

It was not until the early 1900s, with the increasing popularity of natural history museums, that fish taxidermy began to catch up with progress in mammal and bird taxidermy. It was museum curators, not commercial taxidermists, who found a better way than stuffing to prepare each animal in museum exhibits for longevity and a natural, lifelike appearance.

Several leading natural history museums had already begun reproducing reptiles for exhibits, using new, plasticlike or synthetic materials that were being developed, notably, celluloid acetate. The practice was soon applied to fish, and a new era for fish taxidermy began. The reproduction method is not true to the Greek derivations of the word "taxidermy," which comes from *taxi*, meaning movement, and *dermy*, meaning skin. There is no movement of the skin in the reproduction process. However, even though the skin is not removed and rearranged over a form or filled and reshaped, the reproduction process for fish is an accepted taxidermy procedure.

One of the early pioneers of reptile and fish reproductions was Leon L. Walters of the Field Museum of Natural History in Chicago, Illinois. In 1925, the Field Museum published Walters' manuscript, *New Uses of Celluloid and Similar Materials Used in Taxidermy.* This manuscript is considered by many to be one of the important turning points leading to the modern era of taxidermy.

An even earlier publication (1894), *Methods in the Art of Taxidermy,* by Oliver Davie, cited a brief mention of reproducing fish. It stated, "Stuffed fishes are not always a triumphant success. In many cases, it is better to cast them in plaster and paint them." This 360-page book was considered at that time to be the most complete book ever published on taxidermy. The method it promoted for mounting fish was the sawdust-fill method, which is still considered an adequate method for panfish such as bluegills and redear sunfish.

Museum taxidermists proved that reproduction processes were more permanent and exact processes for lifelike renderings of most saltwater fish and many freshwater species. Nonetheless, commercial taxidermists stayed with skin-mounting processes for virtually all fish. The main reason for this was that anglers wanted their real fish hanging on their walls, not copies of what resembled their prized trophies. Another reason was the extra time required to individually custom-cast and reproduce each fish. This lengthy process required a higher price, almost triple the cost of a skin mount. In museums, higher price was not a deterrent.

To avoid confusion, it must be noted that making reproductions is not the answer for all fish species, from a purely academic point of view. Many freshwater species of fish are very adaptable to skin mounting. Some of the popular fish acceptable for skin mounts are largemouth and smallmouth bass, walleye, crappie, and most members of the sunfish family. Trout and salmon are also skin-mount candidates, but in modern taxidermy a combination of skin and reproduction parts mounted on artificial bodies is the most popular method used for these species.

In the early 1900s, many improvements were still needed to produce skin mounts with a lifelike appearance and permanency. However, taxidermists continued to use skin-mounting methods in futile attempts at preserving fish trophies for their customers. After several decades of receiving and seeing aging, poor fish taxidermy, people began putting their prize catches in the frying pan more often than bringing them to taxidermists.

By the 1940s, the basic methods for skin mounting and reproducing fish had been further developed, but the refinements of these processes had a long way to go. This was especially true in smaller, commercial taxidermy shops. Taxidermy was a very secretive profession in the first half of the twentieth century. After museums completed their natural history exhibits, highly trained and knowledgeable museum taxidermists started their own studios or went to work for a few large, established taxidermy studios. Their wealth of new, proven techniques would rarely be shared with the smaller commercial shops, which were, for the most part, still using the techniques described by Davie in 1894.

It was not until the 1960s and early 1970s that advancements began to take place on an industry-wide basis. Taxidermy trade publications started, as did state and national associations, and this promoted sharing ideas and new developments. Taxidermy supply companies formed research departments and expanded their search for new products. Seminars and competitions offered incentives and stirred the imagination of gifted artists, who are today producing commercial fish taxidermy that equals or surpasses the best museum work of the previous 60 years. The process of taxidermy, which for many years was practiced more as a craft, now incorporates innovative compositions,

Creative displays are increasingly popular; this largemouth bass spawning scene by noted taxidermist Ron Kelly uses replicas.

design, accuracy, and permanency, and can truly be called an art. Today, fish taxidermy is alive and well, and people are having their trophies mounted and re-created in record numbers.

Skin Mounts vs. Cast Reproductions

Skin mounting is the most popular means of preserving fish. With modern taxidermy techniques, skin mounts of the highest quality can be produced from many fish. Some fish are poor candidates for skin mounts, however, because of their structure and chemical makeup. And others that would be good candidates for skin mounting legally cannot be kept or are voluntarily released. Additionally, in certain instances, transportation and/or storage may be a problem. In these cases, a skin mount is not an option, so a reproduction is done.

It is faster and easier for a taxidermist to complete a realistic skin mount than to make a reproduction. First of all, a taxidermist is working with a real skin. Even though this real skin will lose its colors as the skin dries, the natural markings of the fish will remain and can be used as patterns when painting the fish. The natural teeth, gills, and fins of a real fish add to the realism of a skin mount. The same holds true when the real scales are retained and the real inner mouth details remain as part of the mount. Because a skin mount takes less time and is easier to do than a reproduction, the cost will be less.

A reproduction is much like a blank canvas, with no patterns or natural markings to follow when painting. Without these natural markings to follow, it will take more time and skill for a taxidermist to realistically paint a fish. Some taxidermists can produce outstanding paint jobs on skin mounts, yet lack the artistic ability to realistically paint a blank fish reproduction. This is one reason some completed fish reproductions look fake. Most fish have variations of color tones and markings on each scale, and there are hundreds of scales on each fish. Painting techniques can reproduce this natural appearance, but many hours of practice and a thorough knowledge of paints and their properties are needed.

Many fish blanks available to taxidermists are molded in action positions, but with the gill covers closed. Since most fish in action have open gill covers with the gills exposed, even more work is required to achieve a realistic-looking reproduction.

Some fish species lend themselves to quality skin mounts more than others. Most warmwater fish such as bass, crappie, walleye, and many smaller panfish are ideal candidates for skin mounts. Coldwater species such as trout, whitefish, and charr, can also be successfully skin mounted but are more difficult and time-consuming to skin mount than the warmwater fish mentioned. Trout and charr are oily and have more delicate skins and fleshier heads, which have a high degree of shrinkage after drying. This shrinkage requires more work and time for a taxidermist to repair. Many taxidermists prefer to skin-mount the bodies of trout and charr and use reproduction heads in place of the real heads. In comparing the same size warmwater and coldwater fish, coldwater fish, on the average, will cost more to mount than warmwater fish.

Salmon and trout over 12 pounds are more difficult to mount and offer more problems when it comes to producing skin mounts that will hold up. The reason is the older (and bigger) these fish become, the higher the oil content of the skin. A skilled, professional taxidermist can produce a quality mount on these larger coldwater fish, but do not be surprised if a taxidermist recommends a reproduction.

Freshwater catfish are extremely poor candidates for skin mounting. A taxidermist who accepts one for a skin mount is asking for trouble. Reproductions are the only way to go for this family of fish.

The majority of saltwater fish are considered reproduction candidates. There are some exceptions, and there is one marine studio that still offers skin mounts on fish such as marlin and sailfish. This studio developed special methods many years ago when reproductions were a taboo subject with many commercial taxidermists. Even after fiberglass reproductions became the standard for most of the big coastal marine studios, this studio continued to be competitive and financially successful with its process.

The process was simple. Various sizes of hollow, molded paper forms (mannikins) were made for the many varieties of fish they accepted. As an example, a marlin form would have the body and head shape, but no tail, fins, or bill. The skin on each side of the real fish was removed separately from the fins, tail, and bill. The skin went through a secret degreasing and tanning formula and, when cured, was glued to the sides of the artificial mannikin. The bill, tail, and fins were degreased and reattached to the artificial form. Once the finishing work was completed, the fish was painted in the conventional manner.

Even though longevity has always been a problem with large marine species that are skin-mounted, this company has proven their process as one of the best. Nonetheless, specialists in saltwater marine taxidermy contend that fiberglass reproductions are the only viable means of properly displaying the beauty and action of big, blue-water gamefish.

Some saltwater fish that can be skin-mounted are the coastal species such as red drum, spotted seatrout, and sheepshead. For deep-water or bottom-dwelling fish like red snappers and groupers, reproductions are again the best alternatives.

Opinions differ on which fish are acceptable for skin mounts and which should be reproduced. If you select an established taxidermist with a reputation for quality work, it is best to go by his or her recommendation. The most important consideration should be the quality and realistic appearance of the finished work. After all, you have your trophies mounted, or in some cases reproduced, to admire and to beautify your home. How they were done is incidental if the results are beautiful.

Fish Reproductions and Replicas

In taxidermy, the terms "reproduction" and "replica" are both used when referring to any fish that are not skin mounts. Taxidermists also use the term "fish blanks." A fish reproduction is a cast copy of a real fish. A mold is made from a real fish. This mold is called the negative. From the negative, a positive is made by using any of a variety of plastic resin materials. The most common materials used for making reproductions are casting resins with fiberglass reinforcement. To have a reproduction made of an actual fish, the fish must be supplied in good condition to a taxidermist. Custom reproductions of an actual fish will be more expensive because of the molding process that must take place before the reproduction can be made.

The alternative is to request a reproduction positive of the same species that closely matches the size. These matching reproductions are made from molds already available to taxidermists; thus, they are less expensive than having a particular fish custom-reproduced. Using reproduction copies for many offshore saltwater species has been an option for years. Today this option is also becoming a popular practice for freshwater trophy fish. The catch-and-release practice established in many leading freshwater lakes has brought a new demand for freshwater fish reproductions. The big difference being noticed with freshwater reproductions is improved mold-making, giving even more realistic reproductions, and the capabilities of customizing the reproductions in more exact sizes. First of all, freshwater fish are much smaller specimens to work with than larger saltwater billfish. This smaller size has allowed taxidermists to use flexible mold-making materials and two-part epoxy resins that pick up exceptionally greater details than the traditional fiberglass and resins. These highly developed epoxies are also flexible and transparent, which, more than ever before, adds more realism and an appearance of fleshy depth to the painting.

Today, the term "replica" in taxidermy usually means a customized reproduction. Some taxidermists may describe an unaltered reproduction as a replica, but replica usually means an altered version of a reproduction to more closely match the particular measurements of a fish. A fish replica can also be a sculpted or carved likeness of a particular fish, which is not really the work of a taxidermist, although some excellent taxidermists have become outstanding fish carvers *(see: fish carving)*. Understandably, custom-made sculptures or carved wood replicas of a particular fish are extremely expensive. For this reason, it is more common and

Taxidermists compare a 20-pound peacock bass in the flesh and in unpainted fiberglass form.

less expensive to have a replica custom-made from reproductions of the species of fish you have caught.

Another means of re-creating a trophy fish is with a painting, and there are traditional canvas artists who do this. These paintings demand rather healthy prices, especially if a recognized artist is commissioned for the job. Original paintings that replicate the dimensions, colors of the fish, and story of the catch can range from $800 to $2,500. This would certainly be a collector's item, but it still gives only a two-dimensional effect as compared with a three-dimensional fish reproduction.

Artificial fish reproductions are here to stay; they've been increasing in popularity and will be playing a bigger role in fish taxidermy in the future. Catch-and-release *(see)* is the main reason for this increase. Voluntary release of fish, even trophy specimens, has become very popular and an accepted practice by many fishing clubs and individuals. In some places, certain fish cannot be kept no matter what size they are. Also, some people find it politically correct to have a reproduction or replica, especially if the original fish was released, instead of the skin-mounted original.

Other reasons may enter into the decision to choose a replica over a skin mount. The difficulty of properly transporting the fish when long distance travel is involved makes replicas a logical choice; this is especially true for anglers who travel to northernmost Canada and to South America, where a lot of travel time is involved, and transporting fish in a frozen state is difficult (and maybe impossible or illegal). The popularity of fishing for peacock bass in South America, for example, has made some excellent lines of peacock bass reproductions available to taxidermists.

For anglers who caught that special fish in their youth but could not afford to mount their trophies at the time, replicas become a nice way to commemorate youthful achievements. Also, old trophy mounts that were not up to par or have been damaged beyond repair are being replaced with realistic reproductions.

Skin Mounts

Skinning a fish for the purpose of mounting it is no easy task. Special care must be taken to prevent scale loss and to avoid cutting through the skin; there are no feathers or fur to cover mistakes. Each fin must be cut free from the body without tearing the skin, and the head must be detached with the gills in place and throat skin remaining. Once the body is removed, the tedious work remains of scraping flesh from the fragile skin, removing flesh and excess bone from the fin bases, and cleaning the cheeks and skull. All of these processes are vitally important in order to eliminate decay and shrinkage during the drying process.

Fish skins are not tanned like mammal skins. Some taxidermists will soak fish skins in a mild pickle (an acidic preserving solution) and degreaser. A full pickling and/or tanning process, like that used on mammal skins, will produce a very rubbery fish skin that cannot be mounted. Different fish will also require different treatments. This is especially true for skin-degreasing procedures. If this important process is not properly completed, a mounted fish can begin to leach grease from its skin anywhere from 1 to 10 years later, destroying the appearance of the mount.

The filler method and the artificial fish body method are two primary means of skin mounting fish, and there are many variations of both. The filler method is a holdover from the early days of taxidermy, and, until about 1980, it was very popular. It has declined in popularity with the emergence of accurate and fairly inexpensive artificial fish bodies made from polyurethane plastic. Today the filler method is used mainly for some smaller species of fish, such as bluegills, for which choices of artificial bodies are few. The filler material can be as simple as sawdust, or it can be a mixture of ground, low-density plastic foam mixed with a binder, such as plaster of Paris.

For best results with the filler method, a plaster cast must be made of the side of the fish that has been selected as the outer or "show" side. Once a mold is made, an incision is made on the other side in order to skin the fish. After the skin has been fleshed and prepared, the incision is partially sewn, leaving an opening large enough to insert filler material. The skin is laid in the half-mold, and the fish is filled with an appropriate amount of filler. As the fish is filled, it is gently pressed into the shape of the mold so that the skin regains the correct anatomical shape. A small piece of wood is sewn into the back of the fish for future attachment to an appropriate base. The fish is then removed from the mold and cleaned of any filler residue. The fins are positioned between cardboard or plastic splints to hold them open, and the fish is put aside to dry for a minimum of two weeks.

The more popular artificial body method utilizes artificial bodies that are sculpted to simulate the shape and musculature of the fish (minus the skin and head). Many taxidermy supply houses offer hundreds of sizes and poses for all species that are normally skin-mounted.

Before skinning a fish that is to be mounted over an artificial body, the taxidermist takes measurements of girth (circumference at the middle or largest area of the fish) and length (from the base of the tail to the "collar bone" behind the gill plate) so that the appropriate size body can be ordered. If the right size body has been selected, the skin of the fish should fit correctly around the artificial body and will meet on the back side.

Many steps in the mounting process must be followed to mount a fish accurately. Skin glues and a maché mixture that is the consistency of soft clay are used as a transition between the artificial body and the skin. Good live-fish references (photography and study casts) should be used to study the correct position for the head, how the mouth is opened, how the fins are flared, etc., all of which must be correctly done before the drying process begins. Drying can take from a few days to several weeks, depending on the size of the fish and the drying conditions.

Once a mounted fish is dry, glass eyes are properly positioned, fins are reinforced, and all other necessary finishing work is completed. The final step is painting the fish. Although all the mounting steps are important, it is the painting that will

It's getting hard to tell skin mounts from replicas.

make the biggest impact when a completed mount is viewed. If the fish isn't painted realistically, a customer will never be happy.

The entire process can take as long as six weeks from start to finish. The actual hours involved will vary, depending on the kind of fish and its size. For a 6-pound largemouth bass, for example, the actual work time for skinning, mounting, finishing, and painting for a professional taxidermist will be around 4 hours. In between are three to four weeks for drying. The steps for finishing and painting require another one to two weeks.

Selecting a Taxidermist

For years it has been debated whether taxidermy is an art or a craft. The answer is both, and much more. The processes and steps in performing taxidermy demand skilled craftsmanship. The composition and design of a mount involve art and creativity. A thorough working knowledge of paint types, their applications, and color blending is necessary. A taxidermist must be aware of chemical properties in order to tan and preserve skins properly, as well as know how to mix and use compounds to re-create and repair natural surface textures. A complete understanding of species anatomy, as well as species behavior and natural attitudes, is needed to re-create natural lifelike mounts. When artistic and mechanical talents have been combined and merged with a knowledge of nature and its properties, the foundation is there to be a competent taxidermist.

The old, musty unnatural-looking gameheads, discolored fish on boards, or distorted bird mounts that still exist in some older gas stations, bars, and clubhouses are things of the past. These old treasured antiques still have nostalgic value, but today you should expect much, much more. The taxidermy profession has made tremendous advances in education, professionalism, procedures, and products.

Selecting a top professional is crucial to getting a mount that will bring beauty to a home or office. Today there are hundreds of good taxidermists in every state, but, as in all professions, there are also those who lack ethics and a desire to produce quality work. Almost every community will have several taxidermists, and quite often there will be a wide range in the quality of work they offer. It is also very common to find taxidermists who excel in certain areas of taxidermy. Professional taxidermists often specialize in their favorite areas of taxidermy.

Choosing a taxidermist can be a perplexing task unless you know what to look for and what questions to ask. Two important qualities are honesty and competence. The best way to select someone is to check references and examine the person's work.

The first problem most people confront is time. Most trophy fish (and animals) will be taken unexpectedly, causing a person to make a rushed decision. It is therefore best to look for a taxidermist before you actually need one. Another way to eliminate a rushed judgment is to know how to handle and preserve a fish after catching it. This will be explained shortly.

A good way to start searching for a taxidermist is to ask friends, co-workers, and relatives if they've used a taxidermist recently and if they were satisfied with the service and quality of work. Sporting goods stores, bait shops, marinas, and professional fishing guides will often recommend taxidermists; however, you should not necessarily accept their opinions as fact. Sometimes friendships and/or personal feelings can cause misleading information about quality and service. Boat captains, guides, lodges, and sporting goods stores may also be on commission for referrals. Most established lodges in Canada, for example, work this way. That should not keep you from using a taxidermist they recommend, but it certainly can cause favoritism from the source.

Talking to personal contacts should produce several names to follow up on. If not, there is always the telephone book. In the United States, an effective way to get names of taxidermists is through a state taxidermist association. Call the state president or secretary and ask if a list of members in your area is available. You should be able to get the phone number for an association by contacting the National Taxidermists Association (NTA). The NTA has a national certification program that recognizes taxidermists who have proven their skills by winning taxidermy competitions. A list of taxidermists who have received certification in your state can be requested by contacting the NTA.

Instead of just dropping in on a taxidermist, call and arrange an appointment to view finished works. If the taxidermist has no work to view, you should wonder why. All busy, professional taxidermists have showrooms or at least displays. Usually you will see work on display that has been recently completed for customers. If a shop is empty, it could be a sign that business is bad or this taxidermist has little experience.

If you have never visited a taxidermy studio before, you are in for a real treat. First, you will be seeing the best trophies that have been taken by area hunters and anglers. Enjoy the display, but do not let yourself be overwhelmed by exceptionally large, trophy-class fish. You are there to check out the quality and service being offered. As an angler, your interest must be focused on the aquatic species on display. Here are some of the things you should look for and ask about:

Examine a mounted fish closely, looking at the base of the tail and along the edges of all fins for shrinkage. If these areas show evidence of shrinkage, it means meat or flesh was not properly cleaned from these areas, which will cause them to be distorted. The cheek area of the head and the throat below the gills should also be checked for shrinkage.

The body shape of the fish should have a smooth, clean flow and exhibit the proper contours and silhouette of the species. Check to see whether there are any lumps under the skin. All scales should be flat and not raised. If the gills are exposed, they should each be separated and symmetrically displayed. Check to see whether the dorsal fins are centered along the top of the body. The same should be noticed with the fins on the bottom of the fish. Are they located along the bottom center line? If they are off to one side, the skin is not properly aligned and the fish will have a distorted appearance. Compare all of these features to what you see when you catch a fresh fish. The best taxidermists will duplicate what is seen in nature. The prime objective is to complete a mount that mimics a live fish.

The paint job will be the most telling element of a taxidermist's ability. Even a fish that exhibits some of the above flaws will look outstanding with a quality paint job. Examine some of the mounted fish that you're familiar with. Do they have the natural colors and markings that you see in a freshly caught fish? The colors should have a blended, translucent appearance with proper shimmers and iridescence for that species of fish. Study the fish closely. A taxidermist should be able to answer any questions you may have about the fish.

It's also a good idea to ask how a fish is tagged so that you are assured of having your own fish returned. Most taxidermists will attach a tag to the back side of the gill cover, which will remain on the fish during the entire mounting process.

After you've visited several taxidermists, you'll see differences in the style and quality of their work. Like most artists, taxidermists tend to develop their own styles in mounting fish and will favor a certain color pattern for each species of fish. The more mounted fish you look at, the more you'll begin to see, and you'll likely become more conscious and aware of the anatomy and colors of the fish you catch. Anglers who begin a collection of trophy fish often develop a much deeper appreciation for the skill and artistic values needed to perform quality taxidermy.

Most of these evaluation tips can be used for inspecting both skin and reproduction fish taxidermy, but there are some additional elements that should be looked at when checking out reproduction taxidermy. If a taxidermist does not have any reproductions for you to see, ask if repros are finished with closed or open gills. Many freshwater replicas are available with transparent flexible fins that are difficult to tell from the real thing. Either look for or ask about this. Also look along the top and bottom lines of a reproduction to see if a seam is evident. A quality reproduction that has been properly finished should show no seams. Look inside the mouth to see if it exhibits detail. Detail in the mouth of a reproduction indicates quality workmanship.

Ask the taxidermist how long it will take to get your fish back. The average turnaround time for most shops will be three to six months, but some taxidermists require a year. The wait will be worth it for a taxidermist who produces top-quality work.

Last but not least is the question of cost. Ask what is included with the price, such as open gills/closed gills, panel, driftwood, or nameplate. You'll also want to know what sort of guarantee comes with the work. Good quality taxidermy will last a lifetime, and reputable taxidermists should stand behind their work. Do not let the price be the determining factor in whom you select, unless all things are equal. If you find a taxidermist whose work you like and you have confidence in his or her business practices, price should not be a deterrent. You usually get what you pay for. You will be admiring your trophy on a daily basis for many years, and it will be a symbol of good times and great memories. Cost should be secondary to selecting quality taxidermy.

According to a 1997 national survey of taxidermists in the United States, the majority of fish taxidermists charge by the inch. Taxidermists also have a minimum charge for fish skin mounts, which then averaged $100. Minimum charges for replicas were $150. The national average for skin mounts was $9.30 per inch, and for reproductions it was $13.65 per inch. Thus, for a 6-pound bass, which will have an average length of 22 inches, the average cost for skin mounting would be $205, and for a replica it would be $300.

Replicas averaged one-third more than skin mounts. The cost of fish replicas or reproductions can range from $12 to $20 per inch. The lower price range would be for stock reproductions with no alterations. The upper price range would be for custom replicas made to meet the exact dimensions of a fish with a lot of attention to realistic details, such as opening the gill covers and installing artificial gills. Prices will also vary in different regions of the United States. Taxidermists who have established national reputations for exceptional quality will get higher fees.

The survey revealed some extreme variations in pricing, due mainly to the types of fish most commonly mounted in various sections of the United States. In the South, bass, bream, and crappie are more commonly mounted, while in the North, trout, northern pike, walleye, and muskies are common. The southern fish mentioned are easier to mount because of a heavier skin texture. This is one of the reasons why southern prices per inch were a little less than the national average.

Anglers who have a trout mounted can expect to pay more than for bass of equal size. Since saltwater fish are more commonly completed as reproductions, they cost more.

Care in the Field

To get the best mount of a fish, you'll need to do some important things in the field. Proper care of a fish that will be skin-mounted should begin while you are still on or near the water. If you release the fish but desire a replica, you still need to do a few things before you return the fish to the water. With cellular phones being readily at hand, some anglers

It is estimated that 75 percent of the United States' population lives within 50 miles of a coastline.

are calling in their orders for replica fish within minutes of the catch!

Skin mounts. If you intend to have a trophy fish skin-mounted, it's best to keep it alive as long as possible. Care should be taken to prevent scale loss due to flopping in the boat or rough handling. If you have already selected a taxidermist, the fish should be delivered to the studio as soon as possible. If the fish cannot be taken to a taxidermist while it is still alive, immediately place the fish in an ice chest with plenty of ice. A fish begins decomposing as soon as it dies, so care for it in the same way you would if you were going to eat it *(see: fish preparation—care)*. Before you place the fish on ice, however, take good photographs of it in its natural colors; these will be useful to the taxidermist later.

Never eviscerate or scale a fish that you wish to have mounted! If you cannot take the fish to a taxidermist the day it is caught, it is best to freeze it. Prepare the fish for freezing by wrapping it in a damp terry cloth towel. Fold all fins close to the body before wrapping it. If an old bath towel isn't available, wrap the fish in good-quality white paper towels. After the fish is wrapped in at least three layers of paper towels, saturate the towels with water and place the wrapped fish into a plastic bag. The damp cloth or paper towels will form a layer of ice around the entire fish. This protects the fins, which become very susceptible to breakage once frozen. The layer of ice will also prevent freezer dehydration.

If you're away on a trip and freezing isn't an option, follow the same procedure of wrapping the fish, but place it on ice in an ice chest. Try not to let the fish float in ice water, which will bleach out and reduce the intensity of the fish's natural markings. These natural markings will aid a taxidermist in re-creating natural colors and details.

When placing a fish into a freezer, lay it on a flat surface and don't put anything on top of it until it is completely frozen. The fish will be fine in a freezer for several weeks, but it is always best to get it to a taxidermist as soon as possible.

In some situations, it is very difficult to save a trophy fish. If you are fortunate enough to have ice along or have some snow or ice packs in the area, you can follow the same procedures previously mentioned. If you'll be getting back to refrigeration within 24 hours and the air temperature is cool, you can possibly save a fish by packing it in powdered borax and wrapping it in damp towels. Place the fish in insulated storage to keep it cool. You'll have a fifty-fifty chance of getting it to a taxidermist in mounting condition. If you wish to give this a try, you'll have to bring along a box of borax. Chances are, however, that you will be better off just releasing the fish and having a replica made.

Replicas. If you catch a fish you want replicated, you need to be prepared to do one, and preferably all, of the following: Take measurements, weigh it, and photograph it. Of course, the greatest priority is minimizing the time a fish is kept out of the water so that you can release it unharmed; thus, you need to take these steps quickly and with proper care of the fish. Length and girth measurements are the most accurate means of ensuring a close replica to the body of the fish. The length should be taken from the tip of the tail to the tip of the lip, or jaw. Girth is determined by measuring around the largest circumference of the fish. If you don't have a measuring tape on the boat, monofilament line can be cut to record these measurements, then kept in your wallet for safekeeping. Weighing the fish is very helpful, since most reproduction bodies available to taxidermists from supply sources are listed according to the length, girth, and weight of the original fish from which the reproduction was cast, so the taxidermist who does your mount will try to obtain a reproduction body that matches, or very nearly matches, your fish. A good photograph not only will help a taxidermist select the closest replica available, but will be a color reference for your fish.

Care at Home

A professionally mounted fish will last a lifetime if it is properly cared for. The same precautions should be followed for protecting any medium of artwork. The elements of nature that promote aging are heat and cold, especially repeated extremes of each, plus humidity. Fortunately, in homes with central air and heat, these environmental conditions are controlled.

Rapid and frequent changes in temperature can eventually cause cracking in skin mounts. This occurrence is less likely in reproductions because the epoxy polymers used to make them are very durable. Even in homes with central air and heat, heat sources should be avoided. Hanging mounted fish over a fireplace has always been popular, but it is a bad location for all mounts if the fireplace is used during the winter. Avoid hanging a mounted fish in any heat source location, such as where air vents will blow directly on it. Another source of heat is direct sunlight. Sunlight can also cause bleaching after prolonged exposure.

Some other conditions can change the original beauty of a fish mount. Exposure to daily cigarette smoke, for example, will yellow a mount in only a few years. The same will happen if a mount is near a kitchen. Grease from frying or broiling meats is especially damaging. If a fish is displayed in a restaurant or tavern where these problems are apparent, it should be cleaned weekly with a soft cotton cloth dampened with a small amount of glass cleaner. The mild cleaning agents will clean the fish and should not harm the protective gloss surface. As a precaution, try the cleaning agent on the back of the fish first to make sure it will not mar the finish on the show side. Anytime a fish is being cleaned with a cloth towel, always wipe in the direction that the fins flow. The sharp points of the dorsal (top) fins can catch the towel and cause the fish to be pulled off a wall, or cause a portion of the fin to be bent or broken.

For normal cleaning, a feather duster works fine. A furniture oil cloth should not be used to wipe the surface of a fish mount. The oil tends to dull the gloss finish; this finish is very important because it enhances and amplifies the pigments and iridescent reflectors used to give a fish its lifelike colors.

If a fish mount is damaged through handling or shipping, it should be taken to a professional taxidermist for repairs. A damaged fish mount can be compared to a damaged car. After the repairs are made, a new or partial paint job will be needed to cover the repaired area.

After 10 or more years, the surface of a fish mount may dull. The gloss can be easily and inexpensively restored by a taxidermist, or you can take the fish to the taxidermist who mounted it, who will probably resurface it for nothing. Do not try this yourself because many different paints are used in painting and glossing a fish mount. Using a gloss that is not compatible with the original paints will cause big problems.

Taxidermy as a Hobby
If you're interested in taxidermy as a hobby or as a part-time or full-time profession, begin slowly to see if it is really something you want to pursue. There is no need to enroll in a school or spend hundreds of dollars on equipment, books, supplies, and video instructions before you're sure taxidermy is for you. You will soon find out that doing taxidermy may not be as simple as it appears, or as rewarding as you had hoped.

There are many inexpensive sources for information on taxidermy. Check with a local library for books or taxidermy trade journals. The classified section in the back of outdoor magazines will usually contain several vendors that offer catalogs with a wealth of information. Taxidermy trade magazines are probably the definitive source for general information. There you can find articles with step-by-step instructions, as well as information about association meetings, suppliers, schools, workshops, and additional resources covering every aspect of taxidermy.

If your interest is strictly fish, order a video on mounting and painting a largemouth or smallmouth bass. If you still feel like trying, save a bass from your next fishing trip and order the supplies as instructed in the video. A bass is a great fish to start with because it is easier to skin and mount than trout and many of the other gamefish that have more delicate skins. Mount the fish and set it up to dry. If you enjoyed the first part, then it is probably safe to invest in an airbrush, air compressor, and the paints you'll need to paint the fish. This is the area of fish taxidermy that is most costly, and there is no need to invest money in painting equipment if you did not enjoy skinning and mounting the fish.

If skinning and mounting a fish is not what you expected, but you're interested in painting, you have the option of finishing and painting replica fish. Some excellent videos on the market show these procedures. If you find an area of fish taxidermy that you would like to pursue, check out the many fine books, schools, and workshops that offer advanced training. One of the less expensive ways of learning more about fish taxidermy is to join a state taxidermy association and attend meetings and seminars. There you will also find many professional taxidermists who can offer advice on how you can learn more about this fascinating art.

For more information contact the following taxidermy trade magazines: *Breakthrough,* P.O. Box 2945, Hammond, LA 70404 (800-783-7266); *Taxidermy Today,* 119 Gadsden St., Chester, SC 29706 (803-377-7211); and *American Taxidermist,* P.O. Box 93476, Albuquerque, NM 87199 (505-771-1828). *Breakthrough* sponsors the World Taxidermy and Fish Carving Championships, held every other year in Springfield, Illinois. Over 1,000 taxidermists and carvers from around the world attend this prestigious event.

To get information about a state taxidermist association, contact the National Taxidermist Association, 108 Branch Drive, Slidell, Louisiana, 70461 (504-641-4NTA) for a list of affiliated state associations.

TAXONOMIST
A person involved in the science of classifying fish, animals, and other organisms according to resemblances and differences.

TEASER
A general term for several types of attractors used on the surface in offshore trolling. These include plastic teasers, trolling birds, and daisy chains.
See: Big-Game Fishing; Trolling Lures, Saltwater.

TEMPERATURE
Water temperature is an important element of all aquatic habitats and is relevant to the habits and habitat of baitfish and predators. A fish's body temperature approximates that of its surrounding medium, and its lateral line helps the fish to determine water temperature. Most species have preferred comfort zones as well as upper, lower, or upper and lower temperature thresholds. Spawning is related to water temperatures for many fish, and the hatching of eggs and the success of fry is dependent on suitable water temperatures for most species. In addition, feeding is related to temperature, especially for fish that live in a temperate zone, where seasons are well defined; these species eat more during warm months than during cold months, and their metabolism slows down greatly during winter.

Temperature is one of the many factors that anglers consider, consciously or unconsciously, when seeking gamefish in both freshwater and saltwater. In the extreme, some offshore big-game anglers rely on ocean surface temperature data provided by satellites to guide them to billfish and tuna hotspots. In the more commonplace, big-lake anglers in early spring use surface temperature gauges to find pockets of warm, nearshore water that are likely to hold trout.

Big-river anglers know that the upper region near the headwaters is colder and more conducive to trout, whereas the middle region is often more temperate and conducive to bass and walleye. Panfish that make nests in spring along the shores of lakes and ponds do so because the water temperature has reached a certain level and their eggs and milt are almost ready to be discharged.

The warming and cooling of water bodies, and especially the influence of tributaries in the spring (which bring warm water to cold lakes), are important factors in the presence of many fish species. Throughout the season, both surface and deep temperatures influence where to fish.

See: Anatomy; Finding Fish; Stratification; Thermal Bar.

TEMPERATURE GAUGE

For boaters. One of the most important aids for anglers who fish out of a boat is a temperature gauge. For many types of fishing, including shallow spring angling in freshwater, deep-water fishing, big-lake trolling for salmon and trout, and offshore fishing for pelagic saltwater species, the ability to find preferred temperature levels is a big help in catching fish. Some anglers believe in the importance of temperature so much that they seldom fish for any species without having some means of taking water temperature.

Fish are cold-blooded and their metabolism is keyed to the temperature of their environment. Knowing the temperature of the water can help you find fish and then determine how fast to move a lure to catch them. Ripping a lure through water cold enough to make a fish lethargic, for instance, isn't going to increase your fishing success.

Surface water temperature is a strong indication of where you might find certain fish and under what conditions the fish might become more active. In winter, surface temperature instruments can help find the warmest water available in hopes of locating the most active or most concentrated fish. In spring, these devices help identify the places where the water warms first. During the summer on freshwater lakes when the water can get too hot, temperature gauges can guide you to the coolest water available. Saltwater species often locate along temperature shears at the edges of ocean currents where warmer and colder water meet; these are often small variations and finding them is difficult without a temperature gauge.

You can use a stand-alone surface temperature gauge on a boat, with the sensor mounted on the transom, or you can use a handheld pool thermometer, or a combination temp/sonar or temp/speed electronic instrument. Many sonar devices have optional temperature and speed sensors, and the unit displays these measurements whenever the sonar is on. These devices read only surface temperature, but they are particularly valuable in the spring and fall when water temperature is changing on a daily basis. Some sonars have the sensing device built into their transducers, and some use optional, separate pickups that mount on the transom. Models have even been offered with the capability to display air, livewell, and water surface temperature readings.

To check temperature at greater depths, tie a pool thermometer to a snap, lower it to a specific depth on fishing line, leave it for a few minutes, then reel it up quickly. Or, tie it to a downrigger weight and lower it with the weight to a known depth, let it stay for a few minutes, then raise it quickly.

For some deep water trolling, it is helpful to constantly check deep water temperature. This has been done using probes attached to coaxial cable, but the coaxial cable has always broken down and generally not proven reliable for constant use. A better method of obtaining continuous deep-water temperature readings is to use a large, torpedo-like probe that attaches to the downrigger cable just above the weight. The unit has a 9-volt battery inside the probe, and sends temperature readings up to a meter without using the downrigger cable as a signal conduit. If it works right, it provides both temperature and speed data at the downrigger weight.

Temperature sensors on cables let anglers probe vertically for differences in water temperature. They can be used to confirm the depth of a thermocline (the boundary between the sun-warmed upper layer of water and the cooler layer below, where the water temperature changes the greatest number of degrees in the shortest span of depth) that is spotted on sonar, or to locate a thermocline if your sonar isn't capable of spotting one. If you believe that fish seek out their "ideal" temperature, you can find the depth at which that temperature occurs. If a thermocline was present yesterday in a freshwater lake, but no temperature stratification of any kind is apparent today, a lake turnover is indicated. When you find fish at a certain depth, a probe lets you check the temperature and record it. Over time, a pattern may emerge on a certain body of water that helps you locate fish on future trips.

For nonboaters. Small clip-on thermometers are available for anglers who wish to check the surface water temperature. Waders, tubers, shore anglers, and small-boat anglers use these, or a simple pool thermometer, especially in the spring and when looking for warm pockets of water. They can be tied to a weight or other device for checking subsurface temperatures, although it should be recognized that in flowing water, there is usually little variance in temperature from top to bottom.

See: Thermal Bar; Thermocline; Trolling.

In Minnesota, using leeches for walleye bait is a big business; one survey stated that more than $2 million was spent on these slippery critters, most of which are ribbon leeches.

TENCH *Tinca tinca.*
Other names—golden tench; French: *tanche;* German: *alia, schleie;* Italian and Portuguese: *tinca;* Spanish, *tenca.*

Tench are among the more popular coarse fish *(see)* of Europe, inhabiting many waters and providing a large measure of summer fishing interest. These members of the Cyprinidae family are relatives of carp *(see)* and are like these species in some ways. They are a popular food fish, widely sought for food and also raised commercially.

Identification. The back of the tench is dark green or olive, and the sides are greenish to coppery, often with an orange or yellow orange belly. Its color varies and may be darker in some locations. It has a thick caudal stem; a broad, rounded tail fin; and a rounded, erect dorsal fin. Small scales are set flat against its chunky body and are covered with a thick coat of mucus, making the fish appear scaleless. There is one barbel on each side of the mouth.

Size. Tench are common in the 1- to 4-pound class and are occasionally caught at 6 pounds; their reported maximum size is 18 pounds, although the all-tackle world record is a Swedish fish of 10 pounds, 3 ounces caught in 1985.

Distribution. With the exception of northern Scandinavia, the tench ranges throughout Europe, including the British Isles. It is also native in Asia in the Arctic Ocean drainage, the Ob and Yenisei basins, and rarely in Lake Baikal. It has been introduced into Australia and North America.

Habitat. Warm lakes and ponds with weeds and a muddy bottom are the primary environs of tench; they also inhabit sluggish rivers and occasionally hold in swifter flows, as well as over hard sand or gravel bottoms. They tolerate low oxygen levels, are known to bury into the mud, and are often found amid vegetation.

Life history/Behavior. These fish spawn in late spring and early summer, usually in weedy shallows, broadcasting numerous adhesive eggs rather than constructing a nest. The fry stay in schools and eventually gather in loose congregations. Adult tench form small groups rather than large close schools, but they are also sometimes encountered in an assembly of groups and caught in numbers in a given location.

Food and feeding habits. Tench are omnivorous and feed mostly, although not exclusively, on the bottom. When feeding on the bottom, tench assume a more angular, rather than horizontal, position, and their tail is pointed up as the mouth is positioned to pick food off the bottom. Their diet includes various invertebrates, snails, mussels, aquatic insect larvae, leeches, and bloodworms. They are renowned low-light feeders, and are especially pursued at daybreak by anglers, although evening, night, and overcast conditions are also favorable. They favor warm water and are more active when the water temperature exceeds 55°F; they are relatively inactive in cold water and hold fast to muddy bottoms in the winter.

Angling. Tench provide a dogged fight with persistent runs, although without aerial maneuvers, and are regarded very favorably by light-tackle anglers.

Feeding tench often send up a stream of small bubbles, which is the result of trapped gases escaping from soft bottom sediment as this fish roots while feeding. They may also roll at the surface, and both incidents are a sign of the fish's presence in a given location because tench do not stir up the water as carp do and are identified by means of disturbed water.

They tend to move shallower as light decreases, and deeper as it increases. In bright midday, they seek a cooler, deeper comfort zone, although there are occasional exceptions to this behavior.

Bottom fishing with assorted baits is almost exclusively the technique for tench fishing, and this usually involves prebaiting or chumming *(see)*, using groundbait *(see)*, and an assortment of prepared, processed, and natural baits. Maggots, corn, worms, cheese, bread, meat cubes, pastes, and other items are popular; anglers primarily bait hooks with those commodities that have been employed in prebaiting or chumming and which the fish have been conditioned to.

Hooked baits may be fished with a float or without one, but many tench anglers prefer a fixed bolt rig *(see)* and a bottom feeder (a device for precise-location chumming). Anglers use rods up to 12 feet in length, line from 6 to 10 pounds in strength, and No. 6 to 12 bait hooks.

TENNESSEE

Tennessee is best known for country music and the Smoky Mountains, but it also boasts superb freshwater opportunities—among the best in the United States. This is not a secret to resident and nearby anglers, and the news is beginning to spread far beyond the state's borders.

Home to more than 300 species of fish, Tennessee is among the most ichthyologically diverse of any state in the country. From the sandy-bottomed ponds and creeks of the coastal plains of western Tennessee, to the cold tumbling streams and large man-made reservoirs of the east, anglers have access to a multitude of environments that support gamefish. As a result of the fed-

Tench

eral government's attempts to control flooding and create inexpensive electricity, the Tennessee and Cumberland Rivers were converted into a series of lakes that step-stone from one end of the state to another. The 24 major reservoirs along these rivers attract the bulk of the angling interest in the state. In total, Tennessee has 29 large lakes that contain more than 500,000 surface acres of water; this is complemented by more than 2,000 miles of coldwater streams, 19,000 miles of warmwater streams, and more than a dozen family fishing lakes created by the Tennessee Wildlife Resources Agency (TWRA).

All of this water, matched with ample rainfall and a mild climate, makes Tennessee an angler's paradise. East Tennessee is home to some of the South's best trout fishing; here, stocked rainbows and browns offer a larger, more plentiful, and easier-to-find alternative to native brook trout. Since the 1960s, striped bass have been aggressively stocked statewide and are now the predominant fishery on some lakes. Largemouth bass thrive statewide in every significant reservoir and river, and they are usually the dominant species in thousands of farm ponds. In the clearer, cooler waters, largemouth are often joined by smallmouth and spotted bass. Smallmouths are also abundant in the many smaller rivers that have not been dammed or otherwise altered.

Reservoirs are the most popular angling destinations in the state, and some 440,000 individuals participate in these fisheries in any given year. Seventy-five percent of them pursue a particular species; largemouth bass are the most popular species by far and attract roughly half that number of anglers annually. In a recent Tennessee Valley Authority (TVA) rating of lakes according to angler success, fish quantity, and fish quality, Chickamauga in the eastern end of the state, Percy Priest in the middle, and Barkley in the west ranked as the best places to fish for Tennessee largemouths. Barkley, which gets surprisingly little fishing pressure, produced the most consistent angling across the state.

The TWRA manages a group of family fishing lakes in middle and west Tennessee, and another group is under construction. Some of these small lakes are operated by private concessionaires and offer everything from boats to baitfish; most require a daily angling permit.

Species Overview
Bass, crappie, and catfish. Quality largemouth bass fishing isn't limited to any one region of the state, and anglers can expect the same angling quality in the foothills of the Smoky Mountains as on the plains of the Mississippi River. Reelfoot Lake lies a stone's throw from the Mississippi, and, although it is best known for an outstanding crappie population, it also harbors fine largemouths. East Tennessee's Tellico and Douglas Lakes are gaining a reputation for springtime catches of largemouths weighing up to 12 pounds. Most of the largemouths taken from Tennessee reservoirs have a mean harvested size of about 15 inches. Although more Tennessee largemouths are caught in the spring than at any other time, bass are readily available year-round across the state.

The smallmouth bass is native to Tennessee but is not found in great numbers in the western third of the state. A fish of cool, clear waters, it has gained a reputation as a tough fighter, often pleasing the angler with its aerial displays. The best Tennessee lakes to fish for smallmouth bass are Watauga, Dale Hollow, Center Hill, Percy Priest, Boone, South Holston, and Norris. Dale Hollow is a designated trophy smallmouth lake and has special size regulations. The present world-record smallmouth bass—at 11 pounds, 15 ounces—came from Dale Hollow Lake in 1955. At one time smallmouths were more plentiful in Tennessee, but reservoir building by the TVA and the U.S. Army Corps of Engineers destroyed much of their prime habitat. In recent years, the fish has made a bit of a comeback and is again showing up in some of its old, but now impounded, haunts.

Black crappie and white crappie inhabit streams and reservoirs across Tennessee. Reelfoot Lake is by far the best crappie lake in the Volunteer State and even has a commercial fishery for panfish. Other good crappie lakes are Douglas, Percy Priest, Kentucky, Barkley, and Cherokee. Of the 22 catfish species found in Tennessee, the most popular are the blue, channel, and the flathead. In some locations—such as the tailwaters below hydroelectric dams and in the warm discharge canals of power plants—the majority of angling interest is often for catfish. Blues and flatheads are most often caught on live bait; the channels fall for a wider variety of natural bait—including nightcrawlers, chicken livers, and cut shad—as well as lures.

Stripers and walleye. Since the 1960s, striped bass have made a significant impact in Tennessee, but public opinion is still split over whether this is for the better. Norris and Melton Hill Lakes have produced freshwater world-record stripers, the latter having yielded two state-record specimens—one $60\frac{1}{2}$ pounds, the other $63\frac{3}{4}$ pounds. Each year both lakes produce several stripers weighing in excess of 50 pounds. Biologists in Tennessee developed many of the procedures currently used in many states for stocking striped bass. Although the fish is both popular and abundant in Tennessee, some anglers blame the striped bass for the decline of other species. Not only do the big fish compete for food with the likes of walleye, bass, and crappie, it is widely believed they often eat these gamefish. Studies are currently underway across the state to determine the impact stripers have on native species, although in the past there has been no scientific confirmation of stripers eating largemouth bass in any quantity. If new studies find that striped bass are detrimental to populations of native gamefish and panfish, however, it is possible that the stocking of striped bass will be halted.

Also not well known outside the state are Tennessee's healthy walleye and sauger fisheries. middle and east Tennessee are home to the South's best walleye and sauger fishing, and both species are actively managed by biologists. Old Hickory and Norris are probably the state's top walleye lakes; the former is home to the long-standing world-record catch, and Douglas Lake is tops for sauger. Kentucky and Pickwick Lakes also provide prime sauger fishing opportunities. The best time to fish for sauger and walleye is late winter and early spring, when the fish make spawning runs upriver.

Trout. Trout fishing is among the fastest-growing outdoor sports in Tennessee. Be it fishing for native brook trout in the mountains or for stocked rainbows and browns in the tailwaters of many dams in middle and east Tennessee, the state's trout fishing has never been better.

Tennessee's only native trout, the brookie, rarely reaches 12 inches in length, and even 6-inch specimens are hard to come by. Although their status seems to have stabilized, until recently brook trout were considered threatened by loss of habitat, acid rain, and competition from rainbow trout. Brookies are probably the most studied fish in Tennessee. Their populations are on the rise in some areas and declining in others.

Rainbow trout were introduced into Tennessee waters a century ago, and they have flourished in many streams where there is little fishing pressure, reproducing naturally in their adopted environments. Most of the rainbow trout caught in Tennessee waters, however, are stocked fish in put-and-take streams. The state-record rainbow trout is a $15^{1}/_{4}$-pound fish caught in 1994 at Boone Lake, and it was undoubtedly a stocked fish. The same goes for the record brown, a 28-pound, 12-ounce individual caught in the Norris tailwater in 1988. Although brown trout have not been stocked as extensively as rainbows, they, too, have been very successful. Probably the most difficult to catch of Tennessee's trout species, browns are found mostly in the tailwater fisheries.

In the east are roughly 250 miles of small headwater streams that are not stocked. Brook trout dominate nearly 95 miles of these streams, and rainbows dominate almost all the rest. Another 245 miles of small headwater streams flow through the Tennessee portion of the Great Smoky Mountains National Park, which is governed by a different set of regulations. These wild streams are preferred by growing legions of fly anglers, not only because these enthusiasts favor wild trout over stocked fish, but also because just getting to the fish often provides as big a challenge as catching them.

Another 1,000 miles of streams are managed by the TWRA and are stocked with adult fish on a regular basis. Of these waters, the Tellico River and Citico Creek in the Cherokee National Forest are among the South's most popular and intensively fished trout streams. Both waters receive weekly stockings of rainbows in the spring, summer, and fall.

Roughly 135 miles of water have been classified as tailwater trout fisheries, and these are also popular with anglers. Tailwaters receive regular stockings of adult fish, as well as thousands of fingerlings in the fall. With the cooperation of the Corps of Engineers and the TVA, minimum flow levels are now maintained below nine dams to help ensure the quality of trout fishing. Research in the 1980s showed the tailwater fisheries were often too warm or did not have enough oxygen to maintain viable year-round trout populations. The minimum flow agreements, along with many varied aeration projects, have helped make tailwater trout fishing the best it has been. The Clinch River below Norris Dam, and the Watauga River below Watauga Dam, are prime examples of tailwater trout fisheries that are thriving under intensive management. Watauga is best known for its rainbows, and the Clinch has produced many brown trout in excess of 12 pounds.

West Tennessee

Reelfoot Lake. By Tennessee standards, Reelfoot Lake is on the small side, but it is probably the best-known body of water in Tennessee. Unlike its dam-formed cousins, 12,000-acre Reelfoot is a natural lake that was created when an earthquake forced the Mississippi River to change its course. Crappie fishing in the saw grass and among the cypress trees is so good that the lake supports the United State's only commercial fishery for panfish, making these fish a popular menu item at local restaurants. And although Tennessee anglers often turn their noses up at bluegill fishing, at Reelfoot, the bluegills are almost as big a draw as the crappie. That leaves the state's most popular gamefish, largemouth bass, a distant third at Reelfoot, but that doesn't mean the fishery should be overlooked. Acre for acre, Reelfoot probably produces as many trophy largemouth bass as any lake in the state.

Kentucky Lake. At 158,000 acres, Kentucky Lake is the largest in the TVA chain and possibly the most productive. It has gained a national reputation for the quality of its crappie fishing and is also known as a top producer of largemouth bass. Although the best fishing for crappie and bass is in spring, the lake consistently produces both species year-round. Summertime night fishing on the lake is particularly popular. Kentucky Lake is also home to a superb sauger fishery, and the southern portion of the lake provides some of the state's best sauger, a fact overlooked by many anglers.

Barkley Lake. Running parallel to Kentucky Lake, Barkley has the same quality of fishing but receives hardly one-tenth the pressure. Considered Tennessee's "sleeper lake" by biologists, Barkley supports a better fishery than does Kentucky

Crustaceans, which are segmented hard-shelled invertebrates such as crayfish, shrimp, and crabs, are a major food source for fish; there are about 30,000 crustacean species, most of them marine.

Lake—according to data collected by the TWRA. Good for all species, Barkley offers crappie fishing that ranks with Douglas, which is widely considered the best of the man-made reservoirs. Although the lake is large at 57,920 acres (some of which is in Kentucky), 90 percent of the fishing occurs on only 10 percent of the water.

Pickwick Lake. With 43,100 acres to choose from, anglers on Pickwick usually head to the same place: the tailwaters. Tailwater fishing at Pickwick has always been popular, but it became more so when the TVA made several enhancements that provided more water, more oxygen, and cooler temperatures. Most of the state's species thrive in these tailwaters, but white bass, crappie, and sauger are probably the most popular. Although the sauger fishing is best in the late winter, crappie and white bass are caught year-round, and smallmouth bass fishing has been popular as well.

Family fishing lakes. Diverse opportunities exist at Browns Creek, Carroll, Glenn Springs, Herb Parsons, Humboldt, Graham, Maples Creek, Garrett, and Whitesville Lakes. These range in size from 87 to 500 acres, and most have good catfish and panfish populations. Browns Creek is noted for large bass as well.

Middle Tennessee

Center Hill. A top crappie lake from March through May, Center Hill receives much less pressure than some of its counterparts in the region, and it is the source of the state-record spotted bass, a 5-pound, 8-ounce specimen. The 23,060-acre lake also has excellent smallmouth fishing; March through May, and November through December, are the best months. Nighttime fishing for smallmouth is also exceptionally good in late May and June. Walleye fishing on the upper end of the lake is good from March through May. Fishing for paddlefish is popular from February through April.

Cheatham Lake. At 7,450 acres, Cheatham is small, but it produces decent seasonal fishing. Crappie are probably the lake's top draw in both spring and fall. Striper fishing in the tailwaters is popular from January through March. The lake suffers from fluctuating water levels, which impact angling results.

Cordell Hull. At full pool, Cordell Hull covers 11,960 acres and offers excellent year-round largemouth bass fishing. In August and September sauger are popular, making an annual run into the headwaters in late winter and early spring. Bream and catfish are favored targets as well.

Dale Hollow. At 30,990-acres, Dale Hollow is best known for its smallmouth fishing, which includes the recently disputed state- and world-record specimen caught in 1955. March through May provides the best smallmouth fishing, although nighttime fishing in June is also excellent. Good smallmouth fishing can be had during the winter months, but the action is considerably slower than in the spring. Largemouth bass and white bass are good in the spring, and crappie are also abundant in the lake. Muskie fishing provides an unusual December and January diversion for Tennesseans.

Lake Normandy. Lake Normandy is one of the state's better lakes for spotted bass, yet smallmouth bass and largemouth bass are also big draws. Crappie fishing at 3,160-acre Normandy is good in the spring, and walleye fishing is popular on the lake's upper end from February through April. Trout fishing in the tailwaters is good in spring but falls off in summer.

Old Hickory. Located just outside Nashville, 22,550-acre Old Hickory receives inordinate year-round fishing pressure, but it continues to produce good numbers of bass, crappie, stripers, and sauger. The lake is well known for its sauger and striper fishing from December through April, and each year the sauger run up the lake's headwaters, making for excellent early-spring fishing. Walleye are a top attraction at Old Hickory, too, although anglers cannot expect the likes of the state- and world-record specimen—a 25-pounder caught here in 1960.

Percy Priest. A Corps of Engineers impoundment on the Stones River, Percy Priest is a 14,200-acre lake that lies minutes east of Nashville. A deep, clear reservoir with an annual fluctuation of about 20 feet, it supports one of the better largemouth and smallmouth fisheries in the state, and a good crappie population. Smallmouths linger along the rocky outcroppings of the main channel and on clay and rock points lakewide, but the better fishing is closer to the dam. In late winter and early spring, the lower half of the lake has good crappie fishing.

Tims Ford. Probably best known for trout fishing in its tailwaters, Tims Ford is a 10,600-acre impoundment. It is also home to good bass, crappie, stripers, and walleye. Although striped bass stay deep in the summer and winter, during their run up the Elk River in early spring they are caught in the shallows. Walleye fishing in the Elk is also popular in the early spring.

Woods Reservoir. One of the states' smaller lakes, Wood Reservoir covers 3,910 acres. Its top attraction is smallmouth bass from March through May, and again in October and November. Among locals the lake is well known for its early-spring and late-fall crappie fishing. Despite its size, the lake does not receive inordinate fishing pressure.

Family fishing lakes. Diverse opportunities exist at Marrowbone, Laurel Hill, VFW, Williamsport, and Gaither/Bedford Lakes. These range up to 325 acres in size, and have bluegills, catfish, and bass.

East Tennessee

Chickamauga Lake. Chickamauga's bass fishing has become a lot more difficult since the TVA destroyed much of the aquatic vegetation. The lake

Though small compared to other Tennessee waters, Boone Lake has a notable striper fishery.

was once renowned for its bass fishing in stands of milfoil, spinyleaf naiad, and hydrilla, but today's anglers have been forced to change tactics. Those wanting to catch bass from this old 34,500-acre reservoir should target brushpiles placed by the TWRA or local anglers. Creek channels and old ditches hold bass in summer. Winter sauger are caught on small jigs and on minnows at the Watts Bar dam tailwaters on the upper end.

Cherokee Lake. Located amidst rolling farmland, 30,300-acre Cherokee Lake boasts good fishing for a variety of species. Striped bass abound near the dam in summer months. In fall and spring, stripers run upstream to the John Sevier steam plant discharge. Jigs and crankbaits take largemouth bass from rock outcroppings during the winter, when the water level drops as much as 28 feet. Crappie fishing is excellent in the large creek embayments; these fish strike small jigs or minnows on the flats in spring, and trolled grubs or jigs in deep creek channels in summer.

Douglas Lake. Nourished by three rivers, Douglas Lake is a 30,400-acre reservoir that has become the premier crappie lake in East Tennessee. It is considered second only to Reelfoot Lake. Despite an average 48-foot annual drawdown, fertile creek hollows and an ample supply of stump beds provide hot crappie fishing year-round. Successful anglers tight-line small minnows in the hollows during the spring spawn, and switch to deep trolling with small plugs, grubs, or small flies during the fall and winter. Bass fishing is best on the lake during the spring, but it is consistently good most of the time. Although anglers can catch a few bass here in the 8-pound range, the lake suffers from an overpopulation of largemouths, and most of the fish are small.

Nickajack Lake. At 10,900 acres and mostly river channel, Nickajack is a small lake with little seasonal fluctuation. During the summer months, spinnerbaits and buzzbaits take largemouth bass from stands of milfoil and around the many areas of shoreline riprap. Crappie concentrate near milfoil and woody structure, and the best crappie fishing is in the coves and around the islands on the lower end.

Watauga and South Holston. Although the total surface area of these two northeast Tennessee reservoirs is less than 13,000 acres, Watauga and South Holston nevertheless support a substantial two-story fishery. The most commonly caught species are smallmouth and largemouth bass, bluegills, walleye, and rainbow trout. The smallmouth fishery is one of the best in the state. The lower end of South Holston is better for smallmouth, and the upper end for largemouth. Watauga has an excellent walleye population.

Boone Lake. Tiny (4,300 acres) Boone Lake, near Johnson City and Kingsport, supports a tremendous variety of gamefish. Largemouth bass constitute the bulk of the annual catch, but smallmouths, striped bass, Cherokee bass (hybrid stripers), and panfish abound. In spring and early summer, largemouths stage at the mouths of the hollows and creeks, and on the dropoffs. The stump beds in Boone Creek and on the upper end of the lake are good locations for casting topwater plugs to largemouths. The best smallmouth fishing is on the South Fork of the Holston river arm of the lake, where 17-inch or better specimens are abundant. Try for stripers in the headwaters in the late fall and early spring. Drifting or slow trolling with live baits is favored, and there are some big individuals here. Boone produced the state-record hybrid—a 23-pounder—in 1994, and contains 40-pound pure-strain stripers.

Norris Lake. Norris is the oldest of the TVA reservoirs. An impoundment of the Powell and Clinch Rivers, it was completed in 1936, creating a lake of 34,200 acres. The annual fluctuation can exceed 45 feet, which doesn't allow shoreline vegetation to become established. In the winter, its clear, cool water provides excellent smallmouth fishing. Striped bass exceeding 50 pounds lurk here, making fall and spring runs far into the headwaters. The lower half of the lake is best for winter and summer striped bass fishing. Walleye are stocked annually and are caught by anglers trolling deep-running crankbaits. Bottom trolling with a spinner and worm combo is another favored technique.

Melton Hill Lake. Wedged between Knoxville and Oak Ridge, Melton Hill Lake gets surprisingly little fishing pressure, especially when you consider its propensity for producing record fish. The lake yielded a state-record 63-pound, 12-ounce striped bass in February 1998 and formerly held the world freshwater striper record. This big striper was caught from the warmwater discharge at Bull Run Steam Plant, which is probably the most intensely fished section of the lake for all species. The tailwaters below the dam are also productive and popular, but anglers would be remiss to fish just those two areas. Both largemouths and smallmouths are abundant throughout the lake. Spring and fall crappie fishing on Melton Hill is one of east Tennessee's better-kept fishing secrets.

Fort Loudon-Tellico. Located near Knoxville, Fort Loudon and Tellico are reservoirs joined by a canal near the dams. Tellico is a deeper, clearwater reservoir fed by mountain streams via the Tellico and Little Tennessee Rivers. The French, Broad, and Holston Rivers supply warmer, more turbid water to Fort Loudon. Every spring, several huge largemouths are caught on Tellico above the Highway 411 bridge, most falling to spinnerbaits or crankbaits. Bat, Clear, and Island Creeks provide excellent pre-spawn bass fishing. On Fort Loudon, white bass and crappie are caught in the springtime in Little Turkey, Sinking, and Ish Creeks, and near Louisville Point Park. Catfishing is excellent at Fort Loudon.

Watts Bar Lake. Probably the finest lake in east Tennessee, 38,000-acre Watts Bar has the best of just about everything. Largemouths and smallmouths are the big draws. April through June provide peak fishing for largemouths, and October through December offer the best fishing for smallmouths. Although the lake experiences the same summer doldrums as other Tennessee reservoirs, the nighttime bass fishing in July and August ranks with the best in the state. Crappie fishing in the spring is also exceptionally good on Watts Bar, as is the sauger fishing. October and November are the best times for striped bass, but big stripers are caught year-round. In August and September the lake's white bass fishing is second to none in the state.

TERMINAL RIG
An arrangement of terminal tackle items as a fishing unit; this usually involves some type of sinker, swivel, and hook or lure, plus a leader.

TERMINAL TACKLE
The individual and collective equipment used at the end of a fishing line.
See: Bait; Hook; Knots, Fishing; Leader; Lure; Natural Bait; Sinker; Snap; Split Ring; Swivel.

TERRESTRIAL INSECTS
Terrestrial insects spend all of their nymphal and adult stages on land. Like aquatic insects *(see)*, they are very diverse and abundant, especially in warm latitudes and during the summer in cold latitudes. Most occur near the banks of water-ways, except in periods of high wind. These insects accidentally fall into the water for various reasons and become prey for fish, especially trout in streams during the latter part of the summer; many terrestrial insects struggle noticeably when they land in the water. Thus, they are also the imitation object of many artificial flies.

Terrestrial insects most likely to be found in the water are ants, beetles, crickets, grasshoppers, leafhoppers (jassids), caterpillars, moths, and spiders. Generally the most important terrestrial insects to fish and to anglers are ants, grasshoppers, and leafhoppers. The life cycle of these insects is not a factor in imitation, although close resemblance of body forms is. Most float on the water, though some sink slowly. Artificial flies that imitate terrestrial insects are usually floaters and may float high or low depending on the type of insect and circumstances.

TEST LINE
See: Line.

TEXAS
For many Americans, Texas retains its old western movie image of a barren desert. In truth, Texas is a watery wonderland featuring 1.5 million acres of lakes; 80,000 miles of rivers, streams, and bayous; and 624 miles of beaches and shoreline on the Gulf of Mexico. From blue marlin in the offshore waters to bluegills in the Panhandle, Texas is an angler's dream.

Since the 1970s, a progressive fisheries division at Texas Parks and Wildlife Department (TPWD) has enhanced the natural bounty with cutting-edge limits and stocking programs. Texas was the first state to ban commercial fishing for saltwater spotted seatrout and red drum (redfish), a measure that has subsequently been adopted by other Gulf Coast states and has led to a resurgence of inshore fishing. Texas built the first saltwater fish hatchery and continues to stock millions of redfish and seatrout (known locally as speckled trout).

Texas likewise led the charge of progressive bag limits for largemouth bass and has a worldwide reputation for great bass fishing. In the 1970s, TPWD recognized the genetic superiority of Florida-strain largemouth bass and began stocking that subspecies in Texas waters. Florida bass genes plus restrictive limits pushed the envelope on what is considered a big bass in Texas. Where an 8-pounder was once considered huge, hundreds of lakes have produced bass bigger than 10 pounds, and 15- to 18-pounders have been caught.

The state agency also recognized the sporting potential of gamefish species that are not native to the Lone Star State. Stocking programs continue for striped bass, smallmouth bass, coppernose bluegills, walleye, and hybrid striped bass.

Freshwater
The opportunities for fishing in Texas vary widely, from huge lakes shared with neighboring states, to small lakes in or near municipalities, to many small and privately managed waters. Largemouth bass are the primary angling interest, but stripers have a strong following, as do catfish and panfish species.

The majority of opportunity exists in large lakes, which are profiled here.

East Texas. The climate and habitat of East Texas more closely resemble those of states in the southeastern United States. Thanks to the U.S. Army Corps of Engineers and other lake-building authorities, the region is dotted with more good lakes than can be mentioned in this space. Fishing in most of East Texas is acceptable if not downright good.

Lake Fork. A 27,000-acre impoundment, Lake Fork has redefined big-bass fishing in Texas. Fork dominates the state's big-bass records and attracts anglers from as far away as Japan. One economic study done in the early 1990s estimated the value of Lake Fork's sportfishing at $27.5 million per year.

A number of factors—some intentional, others accidental—make Fork so productive. Lake Fork was built by the Sabine River Authority, which left most of the lake's abundant timber in place. The lake filled in three stages. Each stage inundated many more acres of thick cover that was inaccessible to fishing boats, thereby protecting the fish.

When the lake opened to fishing in 1980, it did so under the state's first restrictive bag limit. The limit has since been fine-tuned to accommodate changes in the fishery. A catch-and-release following developed at Fork and has matured with the lake's big bass. Most fishing guides discourage their clients from killing big bass. Instead, they push replica mounts. One of North America's top replica taxidermists has a shop 10 miles from the lake and does a booming business.

An additional study indicated that Fork may well profit from the abundance of dairy farms around the lake. Cow manure that leeches into the water with rains may increase the lake's fertility. Finally, Fork has one of the most constant water levels among Texas lakes. This combination of factors is responsible for Fork's phenomenal bass fishery.

Late winter and early spring are the best times to catch a Lake Fork bass weighing 13 pounds or more, but the most consistent angling occurs during the hot summer months. Carolina-rigged plastic worms fished on submerged roadbeds, points, humps, ridges, and other structure may yield as many as 50 bass per day during the summer. Fish weighing 8 to 10 pounds are common at this time of year.

Sam Rayburn Reservoir. At 114,000 acres, Sam Rayburn is the largest lake totally within Texas boundaries. Rayburn and its nearby cousins, Toledo Bend Reservoir and Lake Livingston, put Texas on the national bass fishing map in the 1960s. Rayburn fell on hard times but has since enjoyed a renaissance of sorts, partly because of state stocking programs and restrictive bag limits, and partly because of fluctuating water levels.

Sam Rayburn has endured regular cycles of low and high water. When water levels drop 10 to 20 feet below normal, new vegetation grows along the exposed shorelines. When water levels rise, the new growth is inundated, creating a stimulant that is almost like a new lake effect.

Largemouth bass are the big draw at Rayburn, although the lake also produces excellent crappie and catfish action. An abundance of hydrilla is another factor that seems to have helped Rayburn's bass population. Hydrilla creates excellent bass cover that frustrates the efforts of most anglers. To tempt bass from the hydrilla, anglers will fish the edges of the plant beds with topwater plugs or buzzbaits. A heavy jig pitched into hydrilla will crash down through the growth and draw reaction strikes as it sinks. Jig fishing in hydrilla requires heavy tackle and a deft touch to determine strikes.

Although a popular lake among anglers, Rayburn's sheer size tends to disperse the crowds. Camping facilities and boat ramps are abundant at this Corps of Engineers lake, and an angler wishing to escape the crowds can usually find a secluded cove.

Toledo Bend Reservoir. Texas shares Toledo Bend with the neighboring state of Louisiana. Since it was impounded in 1967, T-Bend has sustained its reputation as a great all-around fishing lake. Toledo is great for largemouth bass, crappie, bluegills, and catfish, as well as for striped bass stocked by Louisiana.

At 185,000 acres, the lake is huge. It stretches 65 miles and includes 1,200 miles of shoreline. In fact, Toledo Bend is so big that it fishes more like three lakes than one.

Toledo Bend veterans enjoy a lengthy spawning season for largemouth bass by first concentrating on the upper reaches of the lake, which warm before the more southern waters. Spawning action begins as early as February in T-Bend's northern end and continues through April in waters near the dam. Big fish are possible in this period; a 14-pound lake-record largemouth was caught in March of 1998.

A little-known fishery occurs in the Sabine River below Toledo Bend Dam, where huge striped bass fatten on baitfish in the swift tailrace waters.

Sam Rayburn Reservoir is one of Texas's best largemouth bass fisheries.

Tailrace anglers who fish from the banks and use saltwater tackle regularly tie into stripers weighing 20 to 30 pounds. The best fishing in the tailrace waters generally occurs during cold winter months and continues through April.

The coldest winter months are also when crappie in huge numbers suspend over the Sabine River channel above the Pendleton Bridge at midlake. In January and February, the hotspot is obvious from the boats positioned over the fish. Most anglers use live minnows to tempt the succulent panfish, which will readily strike light jigs.

Caddo Lake. One of the most hauntingly beautiful lakes in Texas, Caddo is the Lone Star State's only large natural lake. It was apparently formed more than 200 years ago when a huge earthquake created a logjam that diverted water from the Red River into the Big Cypress Basin. A dam later increased the lake's size to 25,400 acres.

Caddo is a shallow, blackwater labyrinth of channels and bayous winding through huge cypress brakes. Newcomers should make certain they have a good map and pay attention to navigational markers in the channels. It's easy to get lost at Caddo.

The most unusual gamefish common to Caddo is the chain pickerel, a long, toothy fish that readily strikes bass lures. Pickerel seem especially fascinated by spinnerbaits. They're most readily caught during the coldest weather by anglers casting near weedbeds or lily pads. Unlike other fish, chain pickerel seem to favor a lure that's moving fast.

Caddo is a good lake for largemouth bass, but it's best known for panfish. Crappie, bluegills, and warmouth bass (locally called goggle-eye perch) are favorites. Panfishing is great in the spring, when locals often use cane poles or fly rods with earthworms or crickets for bait. With an electric motor or sculling paddle, they move from one cypress tree to the next, dunking the bait around the base of the tree until they locate a customer.

Lake Texoma. A sprawling 88,000-acre impoundment on the Texas-Oklahoma border, Lake Texoma is the most prolific inland fishery for striped bass in North America. Stripers were stocked in Texoma in 1965 and soon began to reproduce naturally. Texoma is fed by the Red and the Washita Rivers. The Red River, in particular, is high in dissolved salts and perfectly suited to spring spawning runs by Texoma stripers.

Although anglers remove thousands of striped bass from Texoma each year, the fish remain incredibly plentiful. Some of the most reliable fishing occurs during the summer months, when anglers using a vast array of tactics land stripers in most parts of the lake. Using live shad fished deep is a common method, as is flatline trolling with crankbaits and plugs in 10 to 30 feet of water. Others use downriggers for fish that suspend in deep water off points and creek channels.

Summer also offers some of the most exciting topwater action of the year. Stripers often break the surface of the water, particularly on calm days. Popping plugs are local favorites, but anything that splashes on the surface is apt to draw a bone-jarring strike. In fall and winter, the fish often school on the surface and will readily strike plugs or jigs. Fishing under flocks of circling sea gulls is a popular tactic for pursuing surfacing fish. The sharp-eyed birds can spot feeding fish from a long distance and dive to attack the hapless shad from above.

Probably because the fish are so numerous and the fishing pressure is so relentless, Texoma stripers tend to be small. A 10-pounder is a nice fish, and a 20-pounder is considered a trophy. Bigger stripers are frequently caught in the tailrace waters below Denison Dam, and the fishing is good for several miles downstream from the dam. Free-lining live bait is an effective tactic, but many large fish are caught on jigs and topwater plugs.

Texoma probably has more active fishing guides than any Texas lake. It's less crowded in the Red River below the dam, where a handful of guides use air boats to negotiate the fluctuating river levels.

Striped bass dominate the fishing at Texoma, but it's also a good lake for catfish, largemouth bass, crappie, and smallmouth bass; some smallmouths between 5 and 7 pounds have been caught here. February and March are best for big smallmouths; late spring through early summer is tops for overall action.

In winter, big blue catfish are often caught on natural baits fished on submerged river ledges. The blues average more than 20 pounds. Blue and channel catfish are numerous here, and many successful anglers drift with live or cut shad, concentrating on middepth flats, the shoreline, and deeper creek channels. Platter Flats, Willafa Wood, and Willow Springs are prime spots.

Richland Chambers Reservoir. At nearly 45,000 acres, this lake near Corsicana is one of the best all-around fishing lakes in Texas. Richland Chambers is excellent for largemouth bass, crappie, white bass, and catfish. When the lake was filling in 1987, anglers caught tremendous numbers of channel catfish by simply fishing with natural bait along inundated roadbeds. Richland Chambers remains a exceptionally productive catfish lake.

It's also an excellent lake for crappie, which spend most of their year suspended next to submerged trees on main lake points. For an angler unfamiliar with Richland Chambers, the best time to catch crappie is during the spring spawn, which generally peaks in April. During this period, you can find crappie around shallow spawning areas in virtually every part of the lake. Dabble for them with live minnows or jigs. Bona fide 2-pounders are common in this lake.

Also common are 2-pound white bass. From spring through fall, Richland Chambers is an excellent white bass lake. These fish hang out on mainlake structure most of the time and can usually be caught on jigging spoons or grubs bounced off the bottom. When white bass school on the surface, catching a mess of them is an absolute given.

The lake's Richland Creek arm contains an abundance of standing timber and is a favorite haunt for largemouth bass anglers. Richland Chambers has earned a deserved reputation for high-quality bass. The best action occurs during the spring spawn from March through April, and during the consistent dog days of summer.

Lake Ray Roberts. About an hour's drive north of Dallas, Ray Roberts, at 29,350 acres, is an excellent fishery for largemouth bass, white bass, and crappie. The best structure occurs in the lake's easternmost arm, which features numerous feeder creeks with abundant timber and brush. Emergent vegetation, including hydrilla, also provides good cover, particularly for bass.

A good bet for oversize bass at Lake Ray Roberts is to fish the shallow flats and coves in the backs of creeks when the early-spring water temperature creeps into the high 50s. That's when bigger bass stage near spawning areas and are often caught on big spinnerbaits, jigs, or soft-plastic lizards.

Crappie fishing is good most of the year around standing timber or submerged brushpiles in 15 to 30 feet of water. The lower end of the lake is mostly open water, but an abundance of humps and ridges hold concentrations of white bass. Whites often school on the surface during warm months.

Ray Roberts State Park is one of the most fully developed Texas state parks. It surrounds the lake in several different units, offering good camping facilities and lake access.

Cooper Lake. East of Dallas, Cooper Lake lies north of Sulphur Springs, about equidistant from that small town as Lake Fork is located south of Sulphur Springs. Cooper was supposed to become another Lake Fork, but this hasn't happened yet. Cooper is, however, a solid bass fishery in its own right.

Half of Cooper consists of flooded timber with occasional boat rows cut through the thickets. That's where most bass anglers concentrate their efforts, particularly during spring spawning season. The open-water portion of Cooper also contains interesting structure, however. Summer fishing is particularly good on humps and submerged pond dams in the main portion of the lake.

At 22,740 acres, Cooper is an excellent crappie lake and also very good for catfish. There's a particularly productive fishery for virtually all species in the Cooper Dam tailrace. Fishing for a variety of species, including catfish, crappie, and white bass, is best in late winter and early spring.

Cooper Lake has an excellent state park complex that provides good boat ramp access to all areas of the lake. The park also has excellent camping facilities and even has fully furnished cabins for rent.

Lake Livingston. One of the "Big Three" East Texas lakes that put Texas on the national fishing map decades ago, Livingston remains a good fishery. Livingston was originally known for largemouth bass but the emphasis has shifted to striped bass, white bass, crappie, and catfish.

Interestingly, top striper fishing occurs in the Trinity River tailrace below the lake, and superb white bass fishing happens during the spring spawning run in the Trinity River above Lake Livingston. Striper angling below the dam requires specialized equipment: rods capable of long casts, and reels that hold enough line to handle sustained, current-aided runs from a powerful fish. This tailrace fishery is likewise great for big catfish.

The white bass run above Livingston is historically one of the strongest spawning runs in the state. When water flows are good, the best spawning runs occur from late January through March. It's possible to catch hundreds of big whites (up to 3 pounds) per day. The best lures are light jigs with a spinner attached for added flash. The water usually ranges from murky to downright muddy. When water is muddy in the river proper, the fish move up various tributary creeks and often congregate in unbelievable numbers.

Fairfield Lake. Covering just 2,353 acres, this power plant cooling reservoir between Dallas and Houston is an unusual fishery. Fairfield is an excellent lake for largemouth bass, but it's also a literal hotspot for big red drum and hybrid stripers.

Like other power plant lakes, Fairfield uses its water to cool an electrical generating plant. The plant releases warm water into the lake. The outlet canal is a coldwater gathering place for an unlikely assortment of tackle-wrecking gamefish, the toughest being red drum.

These are the same redfish caught on the coast, but they seem particularly strong in the forage-rich waters of Fairfield and several other power plant lakes around Texas. The power plant reds also take on an incredible color, like the copper shine of a new penny. Reds take live bait, but they'll readily smash just about any swimming plug that resembles a baitfish.

Redfish gather in schools over humps and creek channels. For those unfamiliar with the lake, trolling is a good way to locate fish. Fairfield reds commonly weigh 10 to 15 pounds; you won't catch many on light tackle. The same techniques that yield redfish will also tempt the lake's abundant hybrid stripers.

Fairfield Lake is surrounded by an excellent state park with good camping facilities and hiking trails. The lake has become a hotspot for wintering bald eagles. They're visible from the hiking trails, but you'll get a better look from a boat or from the eagle tours run by park personnel.

Lake Tawakoni. A venerable 36,700-acre lake east of Dallas, Lake Tawakoni was impounded in 1960 and was originally known for largemouth bass. Tawakoni has developed into more of an open-water fishery, however. It may be the top white bass lake in the state.

 Collect Pond in lower New York City was once one-fourth of a mile long and contained a good population of brook trout; Federal Plaza now sits on the site of that pond, which was filled in by 1803.

When the whites, locally called sand bass or sandies, are feeding from spring through fall, you can catch them literally by the hundreds. Two basic fishing patterns yield huge catches. The fish often feed on the bottom, attacking shad as the hapless baitfish cross submerged humps or main-lake points. Use sonar to locate the structure and the fish. Sand bass often show up as giant schools on the sonar. At such times, any kind of small jigging spoon will catch them. A solid chunk of brightly painted lead called a slab spoon is most commonly used to jig the fish.

You may also see white bass schooling on the surface. When the fish are in a surface feeding frenzy, they'll strike just about anything that vaguely resembles a shad. Everything from slabs reeled like mad to keep them in the strike zone to buzzbaits and small topwaters will work. Fly anglers can catch these fish on nearly every cast by using a small white streamer.

Striped bass often mix in with the white bass and are caught with the same techniques. The best fishing for both white and striped bass usually occurs from the FM 35 bridge south to the dam.

Other notable East Texas lakes in this region include Cypress Springs, Conroe, Cedar Creek, Lewisville, Lake Ray Hubbard, Murvaul, Lake O' the Pines, Palestine, Monticello, and Nacogdoches.

Central Texas. The waters of Central Texas are not as large or well-known as those in East Texas, but they still draw many anglers. Some have excellent bass fishing, and the larger ones are briefly profiled here.

Guadalupe River. The scenic Guadalupe River below Canyon Dam is the state's only rainbow trout fishery where fish survive during the brutal summers. Water coming from the bottom of Canyon Lake maintains the same temperature, roughly 50°F, year-round. Thus, trout are present in the river for at least 10 miles below the dam. These are stocked trout, but a few fish do survive from year to year, so a fair number of 16- to 20-inch rainbows can be caught along with the typical hatchery 10-inchers.

The best fishing occurs during cold months, when hatchery trout are released on a regular basis. Guadalupe trout take a variety of dry and wet flies. Top dry-fly patterns include Adams on Nos. 14 to 22, Light Cahill No. 14, and Blue-Winged Olive in Nos. 18 to 20. Productive wet flies include San Juan Worm No. 8, Quill Gordon in Nos. 14 to 16, and Black Gnat in Nos. 12 to 14. Top streamers are a No. 6 Woolly Bugger in olive, black, or olive; a black Clouser Minnow No. 10; and an olive Clouser Crayfish.

Although the Guadalupe is best known for cold-weather rainbows, it is an excellent fly fishing stream for smallmouth bass and sunfish. Giant striped bass also prowl deep pools below the tailrace, fattening on trout. The big stripers aren't plentiful and are difficult to catch, but the river has yielded 50-pounders.

Lake Whitney. A scenic 23,000-acre impoundment on the Brazos and Nolan Rivers north of Waco, Whitney is arguably the best all-around fishing lake in Texas. It has excellent angling for striped bass, smallmouth bass, white bass, and largemouth bass, and is also a good catfish and crappie lake.

The lake's rocky substrata has made it the top smallmouth bass lake in Texas. Smallmouths aren't native to the state, but they've been stocked in several impoundments. Whitney dominates the state's smallmouth bass records. Five-pounders are caught here year-round.

The best time to catch a big smallmouth is in fall and winter. The fish readily strike crankbaits and spinnerbaits cast along rocky points and dropoffs in the lower end of the lake. Any submerged tree line will likely hold smallmouth as well as largemouth bass. For the best odds on a big smallmouth, try night fishing at Whitney for several nights before and after a full moon. That's when the biggest fish are historically caught.

Winter months also produce the best action at Whitney for big striped bass. Use sonar to locate schools of stripers, which like to feed on humps or points from midlake south. Live shad or large white jigs dropped into the feeding fish will draw strikes. Fifteen-pound stripers are common here, and 20-pounders are caught on a regular basis. There's also a scenic fishery for stripers, smallmouth bass, and largemouth bass in the Brazos River below the dam. The river is ideal for float fishing either with a canoe or an aluminum jonboat.

Fayette Power Project Lake. This is one of several very good power plant lakes scattered around Texas. Fayette Power Project (FPP) Lake's fame is based on surface schooling largemouth bass. This may be the best school bass lake in the nation and is certainly the best 2,400-acre school bass lake anywhere.

Surface activity is best from early summer through fall, with the peak occurring in September or October. During calm days this time of year, you may see 10 different schools of bass simultaneously murdering shad on the surface. Many of the schoolies weigh 3 to 5 pounds.

Because the water is clear and the fishing pressure is heavy, FPP schoolies are very sophisticated. It's best to experiment with different sizes and styles of topwater plugs, small crankbaits, or plastic grubs to find the most productive lure. Locate the right offering and you'll catch a bass on nearly every cast.

Other notable Central Texas lakes include Possum Kingdom, Buchanan, Belton, Brownwood, Aquilla, and Proctor.

West Texas. This region is characterized by arid country and fewer impoundments, but its major waters are very popular fisheries.

Lake Amistad. Situated in West Texas on the Texas-Mexico border near Del Rio, Amistad is known as "Big Friendly," but it could easily be called "Big Windy." When full, the lake covers

67,000 acres of open river canyons at the confluence of the Rio Grande, Pecos, and Devil's Rivers. The wind blows in this part of the world, and the water gets rough.

Amistad is an excellent lake for largemouth bass and a top Texas lake for channel catfish. Anglers using soured maize to bait catfish to their anchored boat will often catch a pile of channel cats. A good method for Amistad's bass is to fish Texas-rigged plastic worms along ledges on the river channels.

Other notable West Texas lakes include O. H. Ivie, O. C. Fisher, and E. V. Spence.

South Texas. *Falcon Lake.* Probably because of its location in South Texas and fluctuating water levels, Falcon Lake is one of the unsung fisheries in Texas. When full, Falcon covers nearly 80,000 acres. It's seldom full, but low water in these parts tends to congregate fish into a smaller space.

Falcon lies on the Rio Grande, 75 miles south of Laredo. It receives light fishing pressure for such a good lake. Five-bass catches totaling 30 pounds are common during the spawning season, which tends to peak in February because of Falcon's location. The weather is often pleasant early in the year when conditions are blustery elsewhere. Like many Texas lakes, Falcon is prime water for fishing spinnerbaits.

Choke Canyon Reservoir. An unstable lake level has caused problems for Choke Canyon, which appeared destined to be the Lake Fork of South Texas. Choke Canyon produced, and continues to produce, many bass weighing 10 pounds or more. The lake is cursed by a small watershed, however. Combined with an arid location 75 miles south of San Antonio, Choke Canyon has experienced a roller-coaster cycle of high and low water.

Fishing is dramatic during the spring, when spinnerbaits cast beside brushy or grassy cover are a good bet for big fish. Although bass fishing is the big draw at Choke Canyon, this is also an excellent year-round lake for crappie and catfish. An interesting sidelight is the abundance of wildlife viewing. The Calliham Unit of Choke Canyon State Park offers some of the best public-area wildlife viewing in the entire state.

An offbeat fishery at Choke Canyon revolves around alligator gar. The big, prehistoric-looking fish are incredibly plentiful. In summer, they surface to gulp air, and it's possible to sight cast to these rising fish, some of which top 100 pounds.

Other notable South Texas lakes include Texana and Corpus Christi.

Saltwater

Upper coast. From the Louisiana border to Matagorda, inshore waters of the upper coast consist of Sabine Lake, Trinity Bay, Galveston Bay, East Bay, West Bay, and East Matagorda Bay. Despite the proximity to Houston and the resulting fishing pressure, the upper coast is very productive for a wide variety of species.

Inflow from several large river systems keeps the water turbid and, during heavy rainfall periods, brackish. Eastern Texas receives more rainfall than the remainder of the state. This portion of the coast also features boggy bottoms and deeper water than most Texas bay systems.

Fishing is nonetheless good, and most of the pressure is directed toward trout and redfish. Both species are abundant year-round.

The upper coast is also good for flounder. Flounder in other Texas waters are seldom the target species for rod-and-reel anglers. Along the upper coast, particularly around Sabine Lake, anglers use live bait to tempt flatfish. The preferred baits are live gulf killifish, locally called marsh minnows or mud minnows. Marsh minnows are hooked through the lips on a light wire hook. The rigging includes a short leader about 6 inches long attached to the fishing line via a barrel swivel. A slip sinker just heavy enough to keep the bait on bottom is placed above the swivel. Fishing in this fashion for flounder is like fishing a plastic worm for bass. Flatfish often strike tentatively. Veteran anglers wait 5 to 10 seconds after the strike before setting the hook.

When water temperatures cool in the fall, flounder move out of the bays and head for the gulf. This creates a fall flounder run along jetties leading from the bays. Rollover Pass, a narrow cut that connects East Bay to the gulf on the Bolivar Peninsula, is a historic spot for fishing the fall flounder run.

Another major event that lures anglers to beachfront piers and the surf itself is the late summer run of bull reds. Big redfish spend their adult lives in deep waters of the gulf and move into the surf to spawn in August and September. Spawning runs are generally triggered by stormy weather. Redfish eggs must suspend in the turbulent water until they hatch. Bull reds are caught by anglers fishing cut mullet on the bottom. These fish typically weigh 20 to 40 pounds. Anglers can keep only one big redfish per year, but there's no limit on how many fish they can catch and release.

Middle coast. From Port O'Connor to Baffin Bay, Texas inshore waters take on a different personality. With more sand bottom and less fresh-water inflow, the middle coast features clear, shallow water. It also contains one of the least-crowded and little-known coastal fishing destinations: Port O'Connor. From Port O'Connor, anglers have access to hundreds of square miles of shallow, clear water, much of which is well suited to wade fishing.

Just offshore of Port O'Connor lies Matagorda Island State Park. The island is 38 miles long and virtually undeveloped. Access is by boat only. Primitive camping is permitted along 2 miles of beach and also in the bay-side dock area. No motorized vehicles are allowed on the island, but anglers who bring their own bicycles can have miles of pristine beachfront to themselves. Surf fishing is best during summer months, when schools of trout, redfish, ladyfish, and Spanish mackerel are common.

Just down the coast from Port O'Connor, Rockport is a more popular sportfishing destination. A booming guide business takes clients after trout and redfish. Fishing can be good during any month, but summer and fall yield the most dependable weather and the most consistent fishing. Trout fishing is best on live shrimp, generally fished 2 to 3 feet beneath a popping cork. The popping cork has a concave head and, when jerked through the water, makes a slurping sound that imitates feeding fish. Live croaker are a favorite bait for tempting oversize trout.

Corpus Christi is the biggest city on the middle coast, and it's the jumping off place for Padre Island, the longest barrier island in North America. Adventurous anglers with 4-wheel-drive vehicles can explore more than 40 miles down the beach through Padre Island National Seashore. When conditions are right, dozens of fish species cruise within casting range of shore. The best conditions occur in the summer and fall; action peaks around September, when a migration of offshore baitfish usually comes in proximity of the island and triggers a feeding frenzy that includes everything from tiger sharks to ladyfish.

The southernmost extremity of the middle coast is Baffin Bay, an isolated area known for big speckled trout. Two Texas trout records have come from Baffin Bay. Spring is the best time for a shot at a Baffin Bay trout weighing 10 pounds or more. Local pros cast shallow-diving jointed plugs and concentrate on ancient rock formations scattered around the shallow bay system. The rocks aren't rocks at all; these formations were excreted by marine worms and exist nowhere else in Texas.

Lower coast. Inland waters of the lower coast consist almost entirely of the Laguna Madre—the mother lagoon—which spreads over hundreds of square miles of clear, shallow water covering turtle grass and other vegetation from Baffin Bay to Boca Chica. The Laguna Madre incorporates among the best sight fishing for trout and redfish in the state. The habitat is more akin to the Florida Keys than the opposite end of Texas.

Although fly fishing is a favorite sport throughout the middle coast, the lower coast is perfectly suited to flycasting from the raised platform of a shallow-draft boat or by wading. Redfish are ideally suited to being stalked by anglers, especially flycasters. The copper-colored reds are easy to see in the clear, shallow water. Fish sometimes feed with their noses rooting on the bottom and their tails literally out of the water (tailing). Moreover, the fish are nearsighted and not particularly spooky. Fly fishing on the middle and lower coast is perfectly suited to floating fly lines. Best flies include shrimp and crab patterns, and small baitfish patterns in yellow and green.

Snook have made a comeback in the Lower Laguna Madre, an area that features subtropi-

Redfish, being held by the middle angler here, are a primary draw in the shallow waters of Aransas Bay near Rockport.

cal weather. Although snook are caught on the shallow flats, the deep waters of the Brownsville Ship Channel are more consistent for this species. During summer and fall, topwater lures fished along the edges of the ship channel draw enough strikes to make an interesting day.

Port Isabel is the best-known spot for catching Texas tarpon. Luckily, tarpon have also made a comeback in Texas and are more prevalent all along the coast.

Offshore. Texas offshore fishing is good from one end of the coast to the other. The best fishing generally begins in May, with the arrival of migrant species that spend the warm months in Texas waters. Fishing remains good through October.

Offshore fishing along the upper coast is good out of Sabine Pass, Galveston, and Freeport. Freshwater outflows, shallow inshore water, and general offshore currents combine for murky water conditions along this stretch. In May, you might not hit clear water until you're 40 miles offshore. By midsummer, the calm winds and favorable currents often push blue water very near the beaches.

Offshore favorites include king and Spanish mackerel, cobia (called ling here), dolphin (dorado), amberjack, red snapper, bluefish, and a variety of large and small sharks. Along the upper coast, angling concentrates around offshore oil rigs; these towering structures represent irresistible structure to migrant gamefish. The oil rigs are attractive to anglers because they are visible for miles across the open water and are thus easy to locate.

Anglers either troll around the rigs or tie up to the downcurrent side of the structure and put out lines baited with natural baits like sandtrout, cigar minnows, or menhaden. Good combination fishing is available by allowing unweighted or lightly weighted baits to drift downcurrent while you probe the bottom with jigs or heavily weighted squid or other baits. It's possible to catch an amazing assortment of fish using these techniques.

Veteran offshore anglers generally include light tackle in their arsenal. When the big fish are not cooperative, there are always spadefish, bluefish, and other small denizens that can be tempted to bite small lures.

During the shrimping season, working the shrimp fleet is another productive fishing style. Shrimp boats pull their nets all night, then anchor at daylight to cull the catch. The bycatch consists mostly of small fish that are shoveled into the water, creating a huge chum line that attracts predators. Kingfish, sharks, and other gamefish eat their fill and lounge in the shade of the anchored boat, where they can be tempted by lures or natural baits. Shrimp boat crews may be enticed to trade several pounds of fresh baitfish for beverages.

Although billfishing in Texas is a low-percentage sport, sailfish, white marlin, and blue marlin are caught on a regular basis, mostly from ports along the middle and lower coasts.

TEXAS RIG
See: Soft Worm.

THERMAL BAR
A sharp distinction between temperatures offshore, primarily a phenomenon of large lakes, including the Great Lakes of North America, that exists in mid- to late spring. A thermal bar is a mixing of water temperatures leading to the development of a thermocline *(see)*. A thermal bar may establish many miles offshore on huge lakes, starting at the edge of a mass of 39°F water.

Cooler offshore water on a distinct surface thermal break is a prime place to be looking for big-lake fish such as salmon and steelhead. Such an area is prime for trollers but may offer rare opportunities for casting to cruising steelhead or salmon.

A thermal bar does not form in some years and may last for only a few weeks at most when it does. The interface between differing temperatures may trap insects and small aquatic organisms, and provide feeding opportunities.
See: **Finding Fish; Temperature.**

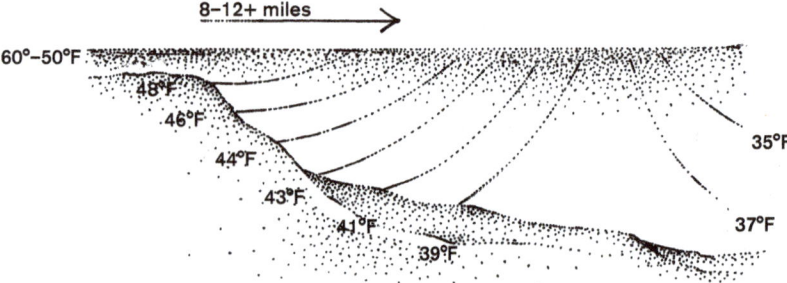

A thermal bar may form several miles offshore on huge lakes, starting at the edge of a mass of 39°F water. Fishing takes place on the edges where the temperature jumps several degrees, such as the area between 48° and 44°F illustrated here.

THERMAL STRATIFICATION
See: Stratification.

THERMOCLINE
The layer of water with rapid temperature change in a lake or pond that is stratified; the layer above is the epilimnion, and the layer below is the hypolimnion.
See: Stratification.

THERMOMETER
See: Temperature Gauge.

THREADFIN, KING *Polynemus sheridani*.
Other names—Threadfin salmon, Burnett salmon, king salmon, Sheridan's threadfin, gold threadfin.

The king threadfin, along with the four-fingered or blue threadfin (*Eleutheronema tetradactylum*; also called blue salmon, Cooktown salmon, Rockhampton salmon, giant threadfin, colonial salmon, blind tassel fish, and blunt-nosed salmon), make up a commercially viable fishery and are of considerable interest to recreational anglers in the northern half of Australia. Fast and sometimes spectacular fighters, they are also excellent table fish, preferred by many over barramundi, and their fillets have been substituted for barramundi by unscrupulous commercial fishermen, the difference being detectable only by scientific methods. Of the two species, the king threadfin is the more popular commercially, and in Australia is taken in gillnets used in the barramundi fishery. Anglers favor the king threadfin because of its larger size, although many anglers tend to ignore the distinction between the two species and characterize both as king threadfin or threadfin salmon.

Identification. Both species are similar in general appearance. The principal and definite identification characteristics, however, are the long filaments or rays located in the pectoral area, sometimes known as "fingers." There are five in the king threadfin and three or four in the blue threadfin. These are thought to be used for finding food and, possibly, for detecting obstructions invisible in the muddy water in which they are frequently found. Each has an adipose eyelid that is a thin membrane over the eye. Body coloring is bluish gray or bluish green above, shading to silver in the belly area. Yellowish pectoral fins and a deeply forked caudal fin are other features of both species. They lack real teeth.

Size. In northern Australian waters, king threadfin have been known to grow to at least 32 kilograms with a fork length of 140 centimeters, whereas the blue threadfin appears to maximize at a fork length of 82 centimeters and 18 kilograms. An Australian sportfishing record has been listed as 16.35 kilograms for the king threadfin, and 9.64 kilograms for the blue threadfin.

Distribution. King threadfin range over the top half of Australia from the Exmouth Gulf in Western Australia to the Mary River in southern Queensland.

Habitat. These fish are found in shallow and often muddy waters over sandbars and mud bottoms, although the blue threadfin is sometimes taken in clear, offshore waters and along ocean beaches. They mostly live in tidal streams, especially those places where feeder creeks enter the main stream and where runoff from mangrove areas brings food. They also favor tidal mud flats and feed on a rising tide there, and they are not averse to journeying far upstream into freshwater during the wet season.

Life history/Behavior. The king threadfin and the blue threadfin both appear to spawn during the summer months from October through March, and the most active month is December. The eggs are planktonic, and the nursery areas are known to be in shallow inshore waters of low salinity. The larval stage is not well documented, but it is known that specimens with a 3-centimeter fork length are present over tidal flats and in the lower estuaries from October through May. Fecundity is high; ripe blue threadfin contain more than 681,000 eggs. Like barramundi, mature threadfin exist as males for several years, then become females.

Food and feeding habits. Threadfin are carnivorous feeders that find the bulk of their food in surface waters. In some areas they hunt for crabs, prawns, and shellfish, but their main food consists of small fish such as herring, mullet, whiting, pilchards, garfish, small flathead, jewfish, squid, and octopus.

Angling. Whether specifically targeted, or fortuitously taken by the angler chasing barramundi, threadfin are highly respected for their fighting qualities. Fast moving, tackle testing, unforgiving, ornery, and as spectacular as any barramundi, they are a high priority among Australian anglers.

Because they are frequently found in turbid water, such areas are best fished using live or dead baits. Favorite items are crabs, live fish, pilchards, garfish, and whiting. The bait angler's tackle is generally a 2- to 3-meter rod, 10-kilogram line, and 4/0 to 6/0 hooks. Baits are fished near the bottom and under a float. Wire leaders may be necessary to avoid cutting on the threadfin's powerful jaws, and also because of the ever-present possibility of hooking a barramundi. Most fishing is from a boat due to the difficulties of shoreline access.

Lure fishing is increasingly seen as the most exciting threadfin fishing method. Both baitcasting and spinning outfits are used, similar to that for taking barramundi. Lures vary from diving minnow plugs to surface poppers. A common technique is to identify where the fish are feeding (surface activity can be frantic) and to cast a surface popper to the edges of the school of baitfish. Noisy swimming lures are worth trying, particularly where the water is clouded.

The best angling times are late afternoons on a rising tide, when threadfin move in over flats to feed. A falling tide can also be productive, especially in the vicinity of gutters that are draining water from mangrove areas and are carrying food.

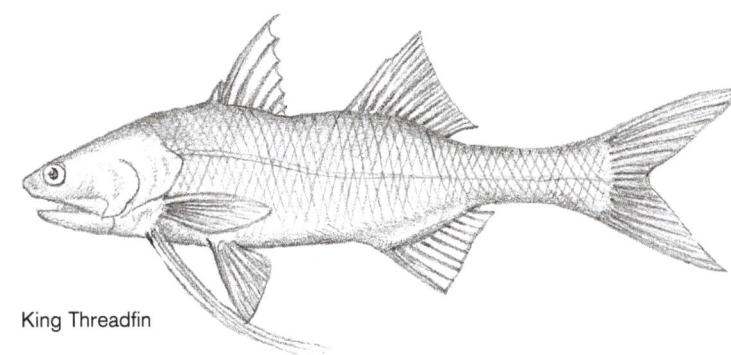

King Threadfin

THREADLINE
An uncommon term referring to light- or ultra-light-strength fishing line.
See: Line.

THREATENED SPECIES
In the United States, a species is classified as threatened if it is likely to become endangered within the foreseeable future throughout all or a significant portion of its range. Elsewhere, a species is classified as vulnerable rather than threatened, according to the International Union for the Conservation of Nature and Natural Resources (IUCN).
See: Endangered Species.

THUNDERSTORM
See: Safety; Weather.

TIDAL CURRENT
Horizontal movement of water in response to tide.
See: Tides.

TIDAL RIP
A spot where two or more currents collide or where a swift deep current confronts a shoal. Also known as a tide line, tide rip, rip tide, or rip, it is common in coastal waters in sounds, bays, estuaries, and inlets; the disturbed water that is generated here is often conducive to foraging for top predatory species, especially striped bass, bluefish, red drum, and snook as forage fish become trapped or disoriented in the strong flow. Some sportfish can be caught on or near the surface in a tidal rip, especially coho salmon, but most are caught by getting lures or bait close to the bottom. Drift fishing is popular, as is trolling.

Tidal rips result from the movement of currents rather than the movement of tides as the name suggests. Usually when two currents converge, one is stronger than the other, creating a seam or wall, often accompanied by debris at the surface, which is called a tide line and forms along the edge of the currents. Tidal rips are often visible from the surface, as currents push upward and disturb the surface, especially when the water is calm or nearly calm. Churned surface water is one indicator, as are surface debris and feeding birds. In rougher water a large tidal rip can be felt because boats require more power to maintain speed through the turbulent water, similar to running up a swift river. Disturbance through the entire water column also has a tendency to confuse sonar, which may not operate properly. Some tidal rips are smaller and less obvious, however. A small rip may be distinguished only by a short length of "nervous," rippled, or choppy water that fronts against calm or calmer water.

When tides are strong, as in spring tides, when a strong wind drives waves counter to the tidal rip, and when ocean swells are large, tidal rips can be dangerous, and boaters have to be careful and maintain constant control.

See: Currents; Tides.

TIDE LINE

The line of debris that often collects along the edge of a tidal rip.

See: Tidal Rip.

TIDES

A tide is the change in water level, at a given point on the earth, due to the revolution of the moon around the earth and to the rotation of the earth along its axis; these forces result in gravitational pull by the moon and the sun. This pull causes the water in the oceans to bulge on both sides of the earth, alternately raising and lowering the water level along coastlines, completing the cycle twice each day in most locales (some places experience one high and one low daily, and some have two of each that vary in range). Since the moon does not follow exactly the same path around the earth every day, tide frequency varies slightly. Usually, based on average time, the frequency between high tides is approximately 12 hours and 25 minutes, and each day the high tide will be approximately 50 minutes later than it was the day before; the same is true for low tides.

The lowest level of water is the low tidewater mark, also called the low water level; the highest level of water is the high tidewater mark, or high water level. The distance between these is the tidal range, or amplitude.

Because the tidal range depends on the basin containing the water and the contour of the coastline, tidal ranges vary widely around the world. Where the coastline provides open access to the sea or to larger bodies of water (such as rivers), the

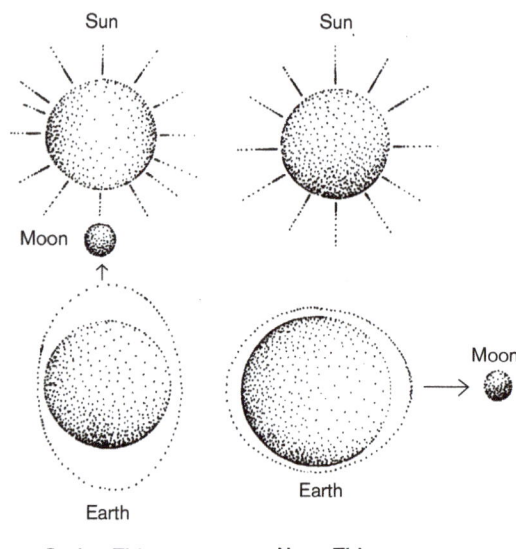

Spring Tide   **Neap Tide**

Spring tides occur when the sun and the moon lie in a direct line with the earth at full moon and new moon. Neap tides occur when the sun and the moon pull at right angles at first quarter and last quarter. Spring tides are more extreme than normal tides, being very high and very low, whereas neap tides are less extreme.

tidal range may be less than 1 foot. In the Gulf of Mexico along Texas, for example, the tidal range is 1 to 2 feet. Where an irregular coastline forms an inlet, the tidal range can be as much as 40 feet, as occurs in the Bay of Fundy in Nova Scotia.

When the sun and the moon lie in a direct line with the earth at full moon and new moon, their combined gravitational pull causes high tides to be very high and low tides to be very low. These are called spring tides. At first quarter and last quarter, when the sun and moon pull at right angles, tides are less extreme than usual. These are known as neap tides.

Since the moon rotates around the earth in an elliptical orbit, it is not always the same distance from the earth and it is not always directly over the same part of the earth's surface. The point of the orbit closest to earth is the perigee. The point of the orbit farthest from earth is the apogee. When the moon is in perigee, its gravitational pull affects the earth more and the tidal range is greater. When it is in apogee, the opposite is true.

Tides are predictable because the orbits of the earth and moon are predictable and the slope of the ocean basins is known. Tide charts or tables for specific areas are published for shipping purposes, and the tides for other nearby areas can be calculated by adding or subtracting correction factors. These tables provide daily high and low tide information, as well as the time at which the tide is going out or coming in. The incoming portion of a high tide is commonly known as a rising tide or a flood tide; the outgoing portion is known as the falling tide or ebb tide. The tide is said to be slack when tidal current velocity is near zero.

Tide levels or heights are measured in reference to a fixed point called "mean low tide," which is the average level of low tides in that location. If a tide height is listed as $2^1/_2$, for example, it will be $2^1/_2$ feet above mean low tide. These predictions are generally quite accurate, but they can be greater or less than predicted because of storms or strong wind.

Tides and fishing. In many aspects of sportfishing, there is a clear relevance between tidal activity and fish feeding activity. Tidal effects and tidal influences are visually most obvious in estuaries *(see)* and along the coastline by the shore and surf, rather than in the open ocean, except for tidal rips; they are especially obvious in rivers and marshes. In a salt marsh *(see)*, for example, with the incoming and high tide, large fish enter the marsh in search of small fish, crabs, or other food, and they depart when the tide gets to a certain ebb point. The incoming tide can present more food, and the outgoing tide can flush food out with it, making the activity of gamefish most likely at certain stages of the tide.

In this situation, and in most coastal fishing, anglers experience better angling at certain times of tidal movement. Many anglers find that the hour or so of flood tide before high slack, and the hour or so of ebb tide after it, tend to generate the most fish activity, with best results during the latter. This depends to some extent on species as well; fish that utilize cover, like largemouth bass in tidal portions of rivers, may be most receptive to angling at the opposite period; the last hour or two of the outgoing tide before low slack and the same period after it are good for bass action because the fish are more restricted in location. The high water period for this species scatters baitfish.

The change in tide movement, no matter whether it is changing to or from high or low tide, is generally a preferred time to fish; slack tides are often unproductive. Keep in mind what the current direction is and use it to proper advantage when presenting your lures, flies, or bait. Fish face into the current, which is moving in different directions when it is incoming or outgoing, so you need to present your offering so that it comes to the fish rather than from behind it.

See: Currents.

TIGERFISH

Tigerfish are members of the characin subfamily Alestiidae and endemic to Africa. A relative of African tetras of aquarium popularity, and of such South American predators as piranhas *(see)* and payara *(see)*, they are equipped with a massive and fearsome set of canine teeth and are one of the leading freshwater sportfish on the African continent. They are also valued as a food fish for native people, and are harvested commercially in some areas. Excessive fishing by commercial interests and, in some cases, poaching, have caused population declines in certain waters. Sportfishing for tigerfish has increased in popularity since the 1980s, and in some areas, especially Zimbabwe, catch-and-release has been widely adopted.

The most widespread and most frequently referenced species is the common tigerfish *(Hydrocynus vittatus)*. It is also known as *tiervis* in the Afrikaans language, *nsanga* in Zambia, and in other native languages as *ndweshi, maluvali, mcheni, muvanga, manga, shabani, simu-kuta, uthlangi, uluthlangi*.

The larger but less well-known species is the giant tigerfish *(Hydrocynus goliath)*. It is also known as goliath tigerfish.

Identification. Tigerfish have long conical teeth that overlap the outside of the jaws when the mouth is shut. They have an elongated compressed body with a raised dorsal fin, a deeply forked caudal fin, and an adipose fin. The body is silvery overall and dark on the back. The common tigerfish has a series of dashlike horizontal stripes that extend the lengthy of the body; actually, its heavy scales are blackened on the posterior, creating a continuous stripelike appearance from a distance. Its pelvic and pectoral fins, as well as the anterior part of the anal fin, are reddish orange; the caudal fin is also tinged with red or orange and fringed with black. Striping is absent on the giant tigerfish.

The common tigerfish has long gill rakers, which are approximately equal to the filaments, whereas the giant tigerfish has short gill rakers, which are less than one-third the length of the filaments.

A tigerfish from Lake Kariba, Zimbabwe.

Tigerfish

Tigerfish

Size. The common tigerfish can grow to 34 pounds; the Zimbabwean record is a Lake Kariba fish of 34 pounds, 4 ounces. The all-tackle world record is a 21-pound, 13-ounce fish from the Zambezi River in Zimbabwe. In most areas the normal catch is in the 1- to 4-pound range, although larger fish are common in some waters. The giant tigerfish is the largest characin, growing to more than 5 feet long and possibly weighing more than 100 pounds; the all-tackle world record is a 97-pounder caught in the Zaire River in Zaire in 1988.

Distribution. The common tigerfish occurs widely in rivers and lakes from West Africa to the Nile and southward to the Zaire, Zambezi, and Limpopo systems, as well as lowveld coastal systems to Pongola. It is present in Kenya's Lakes Victoria and Turkana, Malawi's Lake Nyasa and Shire River, Zimbabwe's Zambezi River and Lake Kariba, Uganda's Lake Victoria, Botswana's Okavanago Swamp, Mozambique's Zambezi and Shire Rivers, South Africa's Pongola Dam, Zambia's Lake Tanganyika and Zambezi River, Namibia's Caprivi Strip, and possibly in Angolan rivers, as well as other sites.

The giant tigerfish is more limited in range. It occurs in the Zaire River system, the Lualaba River, Lake Upemba, and Lake Tanganyika.

Habitat. Tigerfish occur in warm, well-oxygenated waters—mainly larger rivers and lakes. In rivers they are commonly found on the edges of fast-flowing water, and occupy channel edges and eddies. With the exception of large specimens, common tigerfish form roving schools of similar-size individuals.

Food and feeding habits. Tigerfish have terrific appetites and consume a wide range of fish in their respective habitats. Small bream are one of their favorite foods. They are capable of consuming fish that are up to 40 percent of their own body length. These are fit, strong, almost muscular fish, and they are quick to strike, which makes them especially interesting to anglers.

Obviously their formidable dentition allows them to be rapacious, but it also presents an unusual facet of their life history. Tigerfish naturally lose and regrow their teeth. New teeth are always present in the gum just below the functional teeth; these quickly rotate into position to replace the lost teeth. In 1972, biologists observed that dozens of teeth were discovered on the bottom of a tank that held eight large tigerfish, yet the captive fish had full dentition; it was assumed that the fish all shed their teeth and replaced them with new ones without anyone noticing. Anglers have (although rarely) caught toothless tigerfish, which is a stage of several days' duration. The temporary absence of teeth obviously does not hinder this fish's rapaciousness.

Angling. Although a vicious predator, the tigerfish does not attack humans as has been reported. It will strike readily at a variety of spoons, spinners, flies, and plugs, as well as live or cut baits, and it is caught by casting lures or flies, trolling, and drifting or stillfishing. The strike is strong and vicious and is followed by a series of spectacular leaps. The fish battles right up until boated. Many are lost because the line is cut, or because the teeth prevent the hook from imbedding. Tigerfish caught in fast water are even more tenacious than those in lakes, as they are more vigorous in fast water. The tendency of these fish to strike hard, leap when hooked, and fight aggressively, as well as to be caught by a variety of conventional angling methods, is what makes them such prized sportfish.

Medium-action rods of $6^{1}/_{2}$ to 7 feet are generally preferred, as is line of about 12-pound strength (although greater strength may be appropriate in heavily obstructed areas and where large individuals are possible). Terminal tackle should be protected by a wire leader to prevent the fish from severing the line with its sharp teeth.

Tigerfish schools vary in size from a pair of fish to 20 or more. In some waters, these schools become active, biting suddenly and for a period lasting up to 30 minutes. This activity ceases suddenly.

Many visiting anglers use small to medium spoons, spinners, and assorted swimming and diving plugs, as well as streamer flies. Local anglers in tigerfish waters are also fond of using live or dead baits.

A unique tigerfishing method, practiced on sections of some rivers, is fishing slightly downstream of a herd of wallowing hippos, where small bream are attracted by stirred-up detritus and can be easy pickings for tigerfish. Anglers need to stay a safe distance from the hippos, however.

See: Botswana; Zimbabwe.

TILAPIA

Tilapia are members of the Cichlidae family, which is well known to aquarium hobbyists and numbers approximately 1,300 species and 105 genera. Possibly 900 cichlid species occur in Africa, including the native tilapia, which number approximately 100 species in two genera. Tilapia are native to that continent and to the Middle East, and have been widely introduced around the world for food production.

It is believed that the fish that fed the biblical 5,000 was the tilapia. Even before that, some 4,000 years ago, the first identifiable fish ponds built by Egyptians contained tilapia (and Nile perch). Perhaps the most well-known member of this group, the Mozambique tilapia *(Oreochromis mossambicus)*, was transplanted to the Indonesian island of Java and eventually also became widely known as the Java tilapia; it has been widely cultivated in fish ponds.

Tilapia are generally small with a moderately deep and compressed body. They are characterized by the presence of a long dorsal fin, the anterior of which is spiny; a single nostril on each side of the snout; and an interrupted lateral line, which may be in either two or three parts. In North America, they may be confused with bluegills but can easily be distinguished from that species by the absence of a dark blue or black opercular flap.

Tilapia are common to the warm, weedy waters of sluggish streams, canals, irrigation ditches, ponds, and small lakes. Most tilapia are strictly freshwater fish, but some have adapted to brackish or saltwater environments, and some can tolerate environments with an extremely high temperature and very low oxygen. In freshwater, they are primarily algae and plant feeders. Many are mouthbrooders, although some build spawning nests, which they guard after the eggs hatch. Most are small, although some reportedly can grow as large as 20 pounds, and they are schooling species.

Despite their abundance, tilapia have little to no sportfishing value in some areas where they have been introduced, including North America, but some species are pursued by anglers in their native range, especially in southern Africa. As nonpredatory fish, they do not respond to most lures and casting presentations but are caught with coarse fishing methods.

Mozambique (Java) Tilapia

Tilapia have had mixed value in some areas where they have been introduced, crowding out some native species, stunting and breeding rapidly, and sometimes producing large crops of very small individuals, but also providing forage for larger predators, especially largemouth bass. They are important food fish that are harvested from cultured ponds and the wild for human consumption; tilapia are netted, for example, in Mexican lakes where they were introduced, and sold in U.S. markets.

TILEFISH

Tilefish are members of the Branchiostegidae and Malacanthidae families, which include roughly 50 species that are distributed worldwide. Most have little to no significance to anglers but are popular food fish, with firm white flesh, and are found in fish markets.

Most tilefish are less than 2 feet long and slender. The anal and dorsal fins are long and low; the pelvic fins are located far forward, directly under the pectorals. Some exist in temperate waters, but most are tropical.

A well-known species is the great northern tilefish *(Lopholatilus chamaeleonticeps)*, which inhabits the outer continental shelf from Nova Scotia to northern South America (including the eastern Gulf of Mexico, Venezuela, Guyana, and Suriname) and is relatively abundant from southern New England to the mid-Atlantic coast of the United States at depths of 44 to 240 fathoms. They are generally found in and around submarine canyons, where they occupy burrows in the sedimentary substrate and feed on crustaceans, shrimp, squid, and small fish.

This species is relatively slow growing and long lived, with a maximum age and length of 35 years and 43 inches in females, and 26 years and 44 inches in males. At lengths exceeding 27 inches, the predorsal adipose flap, characteristic of this species, is larger in males and can be used to distinguish the sexes. Tilefish of both sexes are mature at ages 5 to 7. The back and sides are bluish or greenish gray, sprinkled with yellow spots. The belly and cheeks are rose, grading into white at the midline.

Tilefish

Sand Tilefish

The dorsal fin is marked with yellow spots. The pectoral fins are dark and margined with black, as is the anal fin.

A mass die-off of this species occurred in 1882, after which it was rare for decades. A small recreational fishery for tilefish developed during the late 1960s in New York and New Jersey, but recent recreational catches have been virtually nonexistent; some are caught occasionally by deep-fishing party boat anglers. Commercial longlining efforts have resulted in overexploitation of this species in its northern range.

The sand tilefish *(Malacanthus plumieri)*, averaging 12 inches in length and occasionally reaching 24 inches, is a slim, almost eel-like fish found in reefs and sandy areas of warm Caribbean and Florida waters, rarely deeper than 50 feet. Like the tilefish, it has low, long dorsal and anal fins. The upper and lower lobes of the caudal fin are extended almost into filaments, and are more prominent than in the tilefish. The sand tilefish is light brown above and silvery below, marked with vertical bluish bars, the last of which forms a distinct blotch in front of the caudal fin.

A similar species to the sand tilefish is *M. hoedtii* of the western Pacific. Its tail, squared across the end, is white in the middle and has black upper and lower lobes. Another similar species, *M. latovittatus*, occurs in the Indo-Pacific region.

The ocean whitefish *(Caulolatilus princeps)*, found from British Columbia to Peru (including the Galápagos but rare north of California) is a relative found in eastern Pacific waters. It is known in Spanish as *blanquillo* and *peje blanco*. Reaching a length of about $3^{1}/_{2}$ feet, it provides some angling sport and is caught commercially and sold in markets. The ocean whitefish has a comparatively small mouth. The back and sides are usually brown, the belly light. The fins are yellowish, tinged or streaked with blue or green.

TIMBER

Flooded timber is a form of natural cover that exists in many impoundments and in the flooded backwater of river systems. It can be important in fishing for largemouth bass, striped bass, and crappie, and sometimes important for such different species as walleye and peacock bass. Fields of standing timber in relatively shallow water, or the remnant stumps that remain, are very obvious to anglers, but in many reservoirs timber is covered by water and not obvious to the eye. The latter occurs when the flooded land is left uncleared, so that live trees are flooded when the impoundment fills with water. They have a long life when submerged in the water, and though hazards to navigation, they can provide shelter and ambush feeding opportunities for some gamefish.

Fishing. Timber can be intimidating to anglers, especially those who haven't encountered it before. Many anglers take a pretty haphazard approach to timber, but not every tree is the same.

Where timber sticks out of the water, there can be visible clues to good places to fish. The most conspicuous is the leading edge of the timber, which many anglers treat like a shoreline, keeping their boat out from it and casting lures to the edge or just beyond the edge and by it. In young reservoirs, where fish may be highly mobile and schools of wandering fish are likely to swim along this edge in search of bait, particularly shad, it may be good to spend a lot of time in such places, using relatively noisy, vibrating lures and covering a lot of territory. This tactic is not as reliable in lakes where timber has stood for a long time and fish behavior is relatively stabilized, although it may be more likely at times for striped bass than for largemouth bass.

Almost as obvious, and for similar reasons, are timbered points. If a timbered point is being washed by wind, it could have a concentration of bait on it, so that would be a good spot to fish. Another prominent place in a stand of trees might be the edge of a clearing, which could be where an old pond existed. In many flooded timber environments, farmlands were inundated, and old ponds or lakes with fish were important to early angling.

Where largemouth bass are the quarry, you frequently need to get into the trees and maneuver around, fishing deliberately in those places that are just a little different. This might be as simple as finding leaning trees rather than perpendicular ones. Leaning trees offer more shade and are more

Fishing among treetops is common in some reservoirs and in the backwaters of large rivers; this scene is at El Salto Lake, Mexico.

conducive to hiding than straight ones. It might mean looking for the largest, widest trees, again for shade, but also because of the underwater protection they might afford. Large multi-limbed trees eventually lose their limbs, which usually fall around the base of the tree. If enough fall and get stuck on lower below-water limbs, they form a canopy, which is a great hiding place.

Watch for different species of trees, too. Pines among hardwood usually signal a change in bottom depth. Pines usually grow on higher ground, such as a ridge; in the water this would be like a hump, and that might be the best place to fish. Tight clumps of smaller trees can provide protection and may be the ticket as well. A clump of trees on the edge of a creek channel is a particularly good spot. Some channels through timber are fairly obvious and can visually be followed through the trees, but in some flooded timber it is easy to lose the channel visually, in part because trees have fallen or are leaning or have disintegrated at the water line. That is when sonar equipment becomes important.

A channel is one of the most important underwater terrain features to look for with sonar, with special emphasis on the outside bends, where it comes near a point or shore, and especially where two channels meet. A roadbed, a dropoff, and other features are worth looking for as well.

Sonar is absolutely invaluable for fishing completely submerged timber, where there are seldom visual clues to depth or tree conformations. In deep, submerged timber, fish are usually suspended, sometimes at the treetops and sometimes among the branches. To prevent fishing haphazardly, you have to know where you are and where your lure is. With a good sonar, some anglers are able to troll with downriggers over the tops of deep submerged timber to catch stripers.

You can vertically jig deep timber, too. The way to do this is to use a fairly heavy lead jig or preferably a jigging spoon. Spoons have treble hooks, whereas jigs have a single hook. Single hooks get hung up less so you might try replacing trebles with singles.

Spoons have an O-ring between the body and the hook, and this allows for a bit of swiveling, which facilitates de-snagging. In any event, lower the lure through the limbs, and retrieve by slowly jigging it; when it hits a limb, drop it down and then bring it back up over the limb. Keep jigging. As long as you haven't buried the hook, it will usually come free when the weight of the lure falls back on it. When it gets wedged in a crotch, however, you may not get it free.

This tactic is most effective when you use an electric motor for positioning (or are tied to a tree) and where there is no breeze. You have to be able to jig vertically, and when you move off the vertical line, you greatly increase the chance of hanging up the jig. Doing this jigging gently and using heavy line with a fairly stiff-tipped rod, you can have a

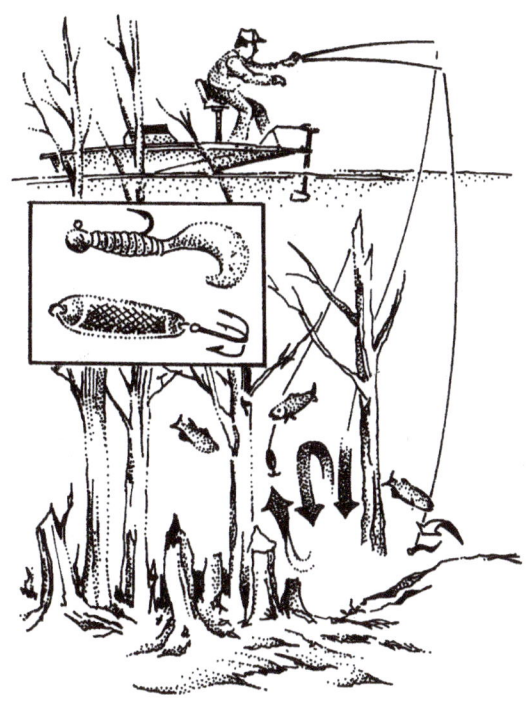

To fish deep in timber with minimal snagging, get directly over the tops of trees and fish vertically with jigs and jigging spoons (inset).

lot of excitement in the treetops with striped bass, hybrid stripers, or largemouths. Obviously, you need to be able to muscle a fish out of the branches and limbs very quickly.

Most of the angling done in trees is by casting, however, especially for largemouth bass and active schooling fish. Surface lures, when appropriate, are very productive. Because the water is usually stained or turbid in flooded timber, noise and action are important, so walking stick baits, poppers, and buzzbaits are good choices.

A rattling, vibrating crankbait is also a good lure choice, worked just below the surface. So is a spinnerbait. Floating-diving crankbaits have merit at times as well, although there is a knack to working these just right; don't set the hook when you tick a limb, and let the plug float up to get over obstructions.

For conventional casting as well as flipping, a plastic worm (use a pegged slip sinker) is a prime lure for largemouths in timber, as is a weedguard-protected jig with rubber tentacles and pork chunk. The latter is used for flipping in shallow to mid-depth water.

One thing about conventional casting in the trees is certain: you'll fine-tune your casting abilities. Spend enough time in the flooded timber and your accuracy will be sharp.

Be sure to follow some common-sense precautions while fishing in flooded trees. Watch where you put your hands, for example; ants, bees, snakes, tarantulas, and other creatures may be about. Tilt the outboard motor up when in use, and run only

at low-throttle speed. When standing in a boat, be aware of bumping into trees and be careful not to fall out.
See: Finding Fish.

TIN SQUID
An older style of metal spoonlike lure molded from block tin (and also called block tin squid), with a flat top and round or square keel, and used in saltwater fishing.
See: Spoon.

TIPPET
The terminal section of a fly fishing leader that is tied to the fly. Generally made of nylon monofilament like the leader, a tippet may be heavier and stiffer than the remainder of the leader, in which case it is called a shock tippet, or lighter and softer, which is necessary for most fly fishing presentations.

A tippet is a standard and especially important component of a tapered leader, which is used in most fly fishing. It may be the final link in a personally constructed knotted compound tapered leader, or a section that is added to a commercially manufactured knotless tapered leader. For most freshwater fishing, and especially when angling for trout, a tippet is the lightest and thinnest in diameter portion of a fly fishing leader, and thus the weakest link in the chain from fly line to fly, as well as the section most easily cut or broken. For most freshwater fly fishing, especially for trout and salmon, it is important to match the size of the tippet to the hook size of the fly.

The normal length is about 15 inches for most fishing, but may be several feet long, especially when a supple tippet is necessary to make a delicate presentation, to turn the entire leader and fly over properly, and to enhance the drag-free float of the fly. Less delicate and shorter tippets, however, are more useful where large flies (and poppers or bugs) are fished. A fly fishing tippet is frequently replaced as the length diminishes due to breakoffs and shortening from replacing and retying flies.

The strength of the tippet or tip section of a leader is characterized in a system that derived from European watchmakers hundreds of years ago and was used to draw silkworm gut for nineteenth-century leader construction. Thus, gradations are based on sizes that each vary by .001-inch starting at size 1/5, which is equivalent to a diameter of .021-inch, down to 10/5, which is .012-inch, and continuing from 0X, which is .011-inch, down to 7X, which is .004-inch. These categorizations identify the diameter, not the strength. Strength is somewhat related to diameter, but different products with different tensile strengths make for varying strengths in products of identical diameter *(see: line)*. Line spools and packaging, however, denote size, strength, and diameter. When in doubt, you can determine the classification in lighter tippet categories if you know the diameter; to do this, subtract the diameter from 11; for example, .004 subtracted from 11 is 4X, .011 subtracted from 11 is 0X, and .021 subtracted from 11 is (minus) 10, which translates into the 10/5 designation.

In some circumstances it is necessary to protect the end of the leader from being cut by the teeth, jaws, or gill covers of a fish. This is when a shock tippet, which is a short length of heavy monofilament or wire, is added to the end of the fly fishing leader. The breaking strength and diameter of the shock tippet exceed the breaking strength of the rest of the leader, sometimes by a great deal (often being from 30- to 100-pound strength). Shock tippets are generally no more than 12 inches long, especially to conform to world record specifications.

A tippet might also be identified as a class tippet. This is of primary concern to anglers trying to establish world records on flycasting tackle. According to International Game Fish Association *(see)* regulations, a class tippet must be made of nonmetallic material and either attached directly to the fly or to the shock tippet, and at least 15 inches long. The 15-inch shock tippet, whether part of a knotted tapered leader or the last 15 inches of a knotless tapered leader, must conform to exact breaking strength specifications (the "class"), and it is this portion that is tested and judged according to the tippet-strength categories of records that exist.
See: Leader; Line.

Shock tippets attached to tarpon flies are stretched on this board so that they're ready for instant, and natural-looking, use.

TIPPING

Placing live or dead natural bait on the hook of a lure, primarily a jig. In freshwater, a live minnow or a whole worm or piece of worm is often placed either on the bare hook of a jig or on a jig hook that is already adorned with a soft artificial bait. In saltwater, tipping is typically done with a strip of fish flesh, which may or may not be used in conjunction with a soft artificial bait.
See: Jig.

TIP-UP

A device for ice fishing with bait.
See: Ice Fishing.

TOMCOD, ATLANTIC *Microgadus tomcod.*
Other names—tomcod; French: *poulamon atlantique;* Spanish: *microgado.*

A member of the Gadidae family (codfish), the Atlantic tomcod is a small, hardy fish, resembling its relative the Atlantic cod *(see: cod, Atlantic).* Able to adapt to salinity changes and sudden cold spells, the tomcod can survive in both saltwater and freshwater. It is a delicious fish sometimes taken in large quantities by anglers and is caught commercially in small numbers due to its size.

Identification. Characteristic of the cod family, the Atlantic tomcod has three dorsal and two anal fins, which are rounded, as is the caudal fin. The body is heavy and has a large, subterminal mouth. Its eyes are small. The coloring is olive brown on the back, fading lighter below, and the sides are heavily blotched with black. The fins have wavy or mottled designs.

The Atlantic tomcod can be distinguished from the Atlantic cod by its long, tapering ventral fins and smaller body.

Size/Age. A generally small species that might be considered a saltwater panfish, the Atlantic tomcod averages 6 to 12 inches in length. It can weigh up to 1 pound.

Distribution. The Atlantic tomcod inhabits waters along the North American coast from Labrador and the Gulf of St. Lawrence south to Virginia. It is common locally north from Long Island.

Habitat. Primarily dwelling along the coast, the Atlantic tomcod is known to enter freshwater rivers during winter. It is also landlocked in some Canadian lakes. The tomcod lives close to the bottom and is usually found in depths of 2 to 3 fathoms.

Spawning behavior. The spawning season of Atlantic tomcod is from November through February. It spawns in brackish water or saltwater. The eggs sink to the bottom and attach to algae and rocks.

Food. The Atlantic tomcod uses its chin barbel and ventral fins to detect and inspect food. It

Atlantic Tomcod

consumes small shrimp, amphipods, worms, clams, squid, and small fish.

Angling. Tomcod are primarily taken on light line and while bottom fishing for other species, usually with small pieces of cut bait, shrimp, or worms.
See: Cod and Hake; Tomcod, Pacific.

TOMCOD, PACIFIC *Microgadus proximus.*
Other names—tomcod, piciata, California tomcod.

A member of the Gadidae family, the Pacific tomcod is a small fish with minor commercial importance due to its small average size. In central California, it is a popular recreational sportfish, usually taken incidentally by anglers pursuing larger-growing species. Its flesh is tasty, and it might be considered a saltwater panfish.

Identification. The body of the Pacific tomcod is elongated and slender. It has a small barbel on the chin. Characteristic of the cod family, the Pacific tomcod has three dorsal fins, two anal fins, a large head, and a large mouth with fine teeth. The body is covered with small, thin scales. Its coloring is olive green above and creamy white below, and the fins have dusky tips.

Three spineless dorsal fins and the small chin barbel separate the Pacific tomcod from any similar-appearing fish, except its cousin, the Pacific cod *(see: cod, Pacific).* The Pacific cod has a barbel as long as the diameter of the eye, whereas the Pacific tomcod has a barbel less than one half the diameter of the eye.

Size. The Pacific tomcod can reach up to 1 foot in length.

Distribution. It occurs from central California, at roughly Point Sal, to Unalaska Island, Alaska.

Habitat. Inhabiting depths from 60 to 720 feet, the Pacific tomcod prefers the shallower end of this range, and locations with a sandy bottom.

Food. The Pacific tomcod primarily consumes anchovies, shrimp, and worms.

Pacific Tomcod

Angling. Like Atlantic tomcod *(see: tomcod, Atlantic)*, these fish are primarily taken on light line and while bottom fishing for other species, usually with small pieces of cut bait, shrimp, or worms.
See: Cod and Hake.

TOMTATE *Haemulon aurolineatum*
Other names—tomtate grunt; Spanish: *ronco jeníguano*.

The tomtate is the widest-ranging member of the grunts, a small species and one that is fairly tolerant of colder water. It is not often caught by anglers, but it is important as a forage fish for larger species and may be used as bait.

Identification. Slim-bodied and silvery, the tomtate is silver white overall and has a yellow brown stripe along the length of its body, ending in a dark blotch on the caudal peduncle. The pelvic and anal fins are yellowish. The inside of the mouth is red. It has 13 dorsal spines and 14 to 15 dorsal rays, 9 anal rays, and 17 to 18 pectoral rays.

Age/Size. The maximum length is 10 inches but seldom exceeds 8 inches. Tomtate are reported to live up to nine years.

Distribution. The tomtate exists in the Western Atlantic from Massachusetts and Bermuda to Brazil, including the Caribbean and Gulf of Mexico.

Habitat. Tomtate prefer shallower water from nearshore to outer reef areas, and rocky and sandy bottoms. Schools are commonly seen congregated around piers or docks.

Behavior. Like other grunts, this species is a schooling fish often found in large groups around natural and artificial reefs. Fish are sexually mature at about $5^1/_2$ inches, and spawning takes place in the southeastern United States in spring.

Food and feeding habits. Tomtate are bottom feeders that forage on worms, snails, shrimp, crabs, and amphipods; they are in turn food for various snapper, grouper, and mackerel.

Angling. Tomtate may be cut on small pieces of cut baits.
See: Grunt.

Tomtate

TONGA
The only remaining Polynesian monarchy, the Kingdom of Tonga is located in the South Pacific Ocean about 650 kilometers southeast of Fiji. It has never been subject to a colonial power, which is unusual in this region, but it was visited by early European explorers. The famed "Mutiny on the Bounty" took place in Tongan waters.

Tonga is a chain of 170 islands, seamounts, and reefs that consists of three major groups: the Tongatapu Group, which is southerly and includes the capital and chief port of Nuku'alofa; the thinly populated Ha'apai Group to the north of Tongatapu; and the northernmost Vava'u Group. Roughly 40 islands are inhabited, and there is daily air service among the groups by the domestic carrier Royal Tongan Airlines.

The coral islands in the east are low, fertile, and more heavily populated than the more volcanic islands in the west, which include active volcanoes. The city of Nuku'alofa on the large island of Tongatapu is the site of Tonga's international airport, which is a three-hour flight northeast from New Zealand. Roughly 105,000 people live throughout Tonga; they are Polynesians who speak Tongan as a first language, but nearly all understand and speak English as a second language.

Most of the approximately 20,000 tourists who visit this island kingdom do so from June through October, when the weather is most settled and temperatures average an agreeable 20°C. December through April is the hottest period, averaging around 30°C. It is also the wettest period, although rainfall does not reach monsoon proportions, as it does at some island groups in the western Pacific. This is also the cyclone (hurricane) season. Consequently, tourist traffic is light at this time, and some facilities shut down for the off-season. Paradoxically, fishing can be excellent at this time, although few anglers are around to take advantage of it.

Domestic fishing pressure is light; this, coupled with a complex volcanic history that has produced a large number of reefs and offshore seamounts, produces the basis for an exciting sportfishery, the parameters of which are still being explored. Tonga is a popular destination for New Zealand anglers during their own winter off-season, and for some Australians and Americans. Sportfishing is administered by the Tongan International Game Fishing Association, which is affiliated with the Inter-national Game Fish Association (IGFA).

Sportfish taken in Tongan waters include blue marlin, sailfish, striped and black marlin, shortbill spearfish, mahimahi (dolphin), wahoo, dogtooth tuna, sharks, queenfish, yellowfin tuna, great barracuda, bluefin and giant trevally, shark mackerel, skipjack tuna, coral trout, red bass, bonefish, and a wide range of light-tackle and bottom fish.

Bonefish are present in lagoons from January through March, but this is the cyclone season, when tourist anglers are largely absent, so there is little angling effort for them. In addition, bonefish are not a popular eating species with village fishermen (they are known as "wire-fish" locally, for the large number of bones in their flesh) and are usually taken incidentally when netting for mullet. The extent of this fishery is consequently unknown.

Pacific sailfish in this region are present in moderate numbers but are of excellent quality. They average around 45 kilograms, and a 95.5-kilogram line-class world record was caught here in 1990.

Blue marlin make up roughly 70 percent of the marlin fishery, and striped and black marlin are also present. Several blues over 390 kilograms have been captured; the largest, a Tongan all-tackle record of 394 kilograms, was taken single-handed from a tiny 4.5-meter powerboat. A number of fish over 1,000 pounds have been hooked by anglers, but all have broken off. The average blue marlin captured weighs around 120 kilograms, but weights vary widely.

Another feature of Tongan fishing is the occasional appearance of schools of very large skipjack tuna, in the 13- to 15-kilogram range, which produced at least one (since defeated) IGFA line-class record.

Several fishing charters have recently been available out of Tongatapu, and include at least four modern, well-equipped boats in the 6- to 9-meter range. Most of these work out of the boat harbor on the Nuku'alofa waterfront, or from resorts on small islands a few miles offshore.

A number of seamounts, many reefs, and several fish aggregation devices (FADs) can be fished by the day from Tongatapu. Mahimahi are the most regular catch. Most of these fish weigh from 10 to 20 kilograms, and occasional catches reach 25 kilograms. Most Pacific sportfish are encountered in Tongatapu waters, however, including marlin, sailfish, tuna, and wahoo.

North of Tongatapu, the complex of atolls, reefs, shoals, and seamounts that constitutes the Ha'apai islands is an exciting proposition to explore. One charter operator works from the town of Lifuka, which is reached by air from Tongatapu. Another option is to access the area in a live-aboard charter boat from Vava'u. The fishery in these waters is very much a mixed bag, and all of the fish species previously mentioned are caught here.

North of the Ha'apai islands, the Vava'u group is a magnificent cluster of islands and has the second largest population after the capital of Tongatapu. This is a well-established fishing destination, and most Tongan big-game charter boats operate out of sheltered Neiafu Harbour; this recently included three modern game boats run by New Zealand skippers, and some smaller craft aimed at light-tackle fishing.

The picturesque Vava'u Group has produced exciting fishing action for visiting anglers, especially for billfish and mahimahi, and is the base for an annual international billfish tournament, normally held around September.

Commercial fishing pressure around Tonga is mostly from a small domestic fleet that targets red snapper using deep drop lines. As yet, there is no large-scale surface longlining or purse seining.

Blue-water trolling with lures and baits produces marlin, sailfish, mahimahi, wahoo, and tuna. Trolling the reef edges and passes with rigged baits or diving plugs can produce a wide range of predators, including wahoo, dogtooth tuna, jobfish, sailfish, and great barracuda. Downriggers are effective.

Offshore seamounts can rise steeply from over 1,000 meters deep to within 40 meters of the surface. These hold a variety of pelagic and reef predators. Baits, although effective, will often draw the attention of sharks over these structures. Dropping a large metal jig or heavy spoon to the bottom, then either jigging it up and down or retrieving it at high speed, is a good way to fish here. This technique can produce various species, but the powerful dogtooth tuna is a regular customer in lightly fished regions.

Casting surface lures, especially popping plugs, onto the reefs is an effective way to target giant and bluefin trevally, and is most productive in the northern island groups, especially in the hottest months, from December through April.

Light-tackle lure casting from the shore with small metal jigs, soft-plastic lures, and tiny bucktails also produces good sport with small trevally, longtoms (needlefish or houndfish), and various reef snapper and small grouper.

Most charter boats are equipped with good-quality modern trolling tackle, but anglers wishing to cast lures or flies or to use light tackle are advised to bring their own equipment. Tackle stores in Nuku'alofa and Neiafu have a limited selection of line, lures, and terminal tackle.

As in many parts of the Pacific, any fish caught on charters belong to the boat, although most captains are happy to release billfish at the angler's request. This should be discussed with the captain before fishing starts. Other species are usually kept for local consumption, and most skippers are happy when anglers take a share for their own table.

Visiting anglers should be aware that most Tongans are deeply religious and that fishing on Sundays is prohibited. Fishing is not considered a sport; it is work, intended to provide food. Other local customs to be aware of include dress standards. It is considered offensive and provocative for men to appear in public without a shirt. Traditionally, only warriors about to enter into battle go bare-chested. Likewise, women should not wear skimpy clothing or swimwear in public but may do so at the pool or beach.

TONKIN CANE
Raw bamboo cane used in bamboo fishing rod construction.
See: Bamboo Rod; Rod, Fishing.

TOPE
See: Shark.

TOPMINNOW
See: Killifish.

TOPWATER
A term for the surface of a water body, usually a pond or lake; for lures fished on the surface; and for surface fishing tactics (see: surface lure).

TOPWATER LURE
See: Surface Lure.

TORPEDO, ATLANTIC *Torpedo nobiliana.*
Other names—torpedo, electric ray, dark electric ray; French: *torpille noire;* Spanish: *tremolina negra.*

A member of the electric ray family, the Atlantic torpedo can generate a shock between 170 to 220 volts. The electricity-generating organs are located in the front half of the body, one on each side, making up about one-sixth of the fish's total weight. The Atlantic torpedo may use these to stun prey, to protect themselves from predators, and to identify or attract members of the opposite sex.

Identification. The Atlantic torpedo has a broad disk squared off in front and a short snout. It is uniformly dark olive to brown or black, occasionally with black blotches and small white spots, and whitish underneath. The Atlantic torpedo can be distinguished from its relatives by its large size.

Size. The average fish weighs roughly 30 pounds and has been known to reach 200 pounds in weight and 6 feet in length.

Distribution. Strictly an Atlantic Ocean species, it ranges from Nova Scotia and the Bay of Fundy to the Florida Keys and Cuba, but is absent from the Gulf of Mexico. In the eastern Atlantic, it ranges from Scotland to West Africa and the Azores.

Habitat. Atlantic torpedoes live on sandy or rubble bottoms, ranging from beaches to sounds, and appear to be more common in the cooler parts of their range. They are believed to be most common in waters 60 to 240 feet deep.

Life history. Reproduction takes place in deeper waters in warm areas, and the young are born alive.

Food. Atlantic torpedoes are sluggish bottom dwellers and feed on such fish as flounders and eels, although they are able to capture fast-swimming prey such as sharks and salmon.

Angling. There is little to no angling interest in Atlantic torpedoes.
See: Rays and Skates.

TOTAL ALLOWABLE CATCH
The annual recommended catch in saltwater for a species or species group set by a regional fisheries management council. This applies to both recreational anglers and commercial fishermen.
See: Fisheries Management; Fisheries Management Council.

TOTAL LENGTH
The length of a fish as measured from the tip of its snout to the tip of its tail.
See: Measuring Fish; Regulations.

TOTUAVA *Totoaba macdonaldi.*
See: Corvina.

TOURNAMENTS
See: Competitive Fishing.

TOWER
Originally called a "tuna tower," this is an elevated platform designed to give the captain a better view, enabling visibility at a much greater distance. Towers were developed for captains spotting bluefin tuna in the Bahamas, but have been adapted to most sportfishing boats and virtually all large offshore cruisers. Their purpose is not only to see farther on the horizon, but also to see down into the water. Seeing into the water is very helpful at times, such as when landing big fish, identifying fish

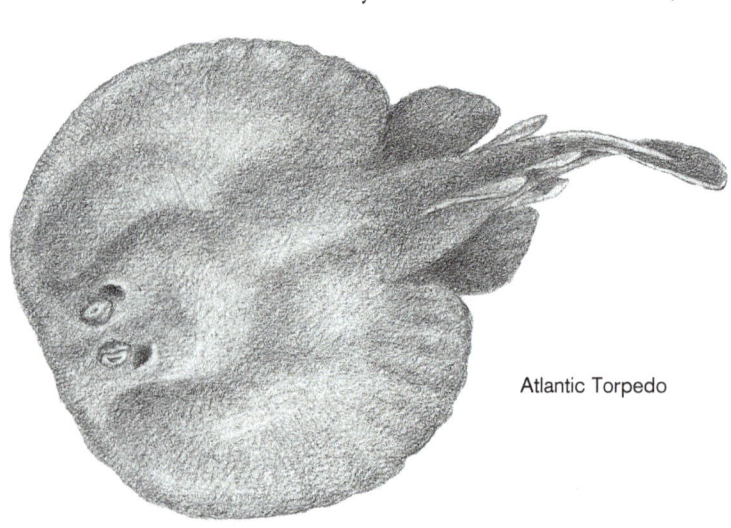
Atlantic Torpedo

that come into a chum slick, and spotting fish that casters can toss a lure or live bait to; in these circumstances, a guide or boat captain can direct the anglers or mates to action that cannot be as readily observed from deck level.

Towers these days come in many different shapes and sizes, but all accomplish basically the same thing: better visibility. They are made almost exclusively of aluminum to save weight, and can be rigged either with or without a remote helm station.

Though towers are primarily found on boats that are 25 feet or longer, mini-towers have been created for use on some smaller craft, including trailerable boats in the 18- to 25-foot range. Deck or console towers, mounted on the deck of center console boats so that anglers can walk around them easily, have become more popular in certain areas. Some, used on larger boats, have upper control stations while others are merely higher platforms without controls.

These small towers were created primarily for shallow fishing in calm inshore waters. Small towers improve visibility in small boats, just as poling platforms do, but they also come with some disadvantages, including safety concerns when used in rough water, and the possibility of altering performance, if added to an existing boat. On some boats, these small towers can, and must, be folded down for trailering.
See: Boat; Sportfishing Boat.

TRACE
A wire leader.
See: Leader.

TRACK PLOTTER
A display method used on electronic navigational equipment, particularly GPS, that presents a bird's-eye view of a boat and the surrounding area, and marks a trail to show the complete path that the moving boat has traveled. It is one of the most important features of GPS units and is used for practical fishing application as well as navigation.
See: GPS.

TRAHIRA *Hoplias malabaricus.*
Other names—guabine, haimara, tararura, tiger characin; Portuguese: *traíra, trairão;* Spanish: *guabina, tararira.*

An unknown number of trahiras are widely scattered throughout Central and South America; some reports mention 13, and most are undescribed. These are members of the Erythrinidae family of fish in the genus *Hoplias.* They are voracious, prehistoric-looking species that are unfamiliar to most anglers.

The trahira commonly caught by anglers in the backwaters of Amazon tributaries in Brazil is called

A large trahira, or *trairão*, from Brazil.

traíra (H. malabaricus) by Brazilians and references a fish weighing up to 3 kilograms; the *trairão (H. lacerdae)* is a larger, darker, but otherwise similar specimen.

Identification. Trahiras are cylindrical-bodied fish with a blunt head and a mouth full of canine teeth. They are partly air-breathing fish, and look somewhat like a bowfin *(see).* Most *traíra* and *trairão* are a mottled dark brown color. Their fins, with the exception of the dorsal fins, are rounded.

Size. *Traíra* are said to attain a maximum length of 60 centimeters and a weight of 3 kilograms; *trairão* reportedly grow to 1 meter and 20 kilograms.

Distribution. The range of *traíra* is from Costa Rica and Trinidad to Argentina and Ecuador, including the tributaries of the Amazon. Among anglers, they are most known in Brazil. This species was introduced into the United States in 1977 but was later eliminated.

Habitat. Trahiras inhabit rivers, streams, swamps, and lakes. They are encountered in backwaters, in slower sections of rivers, and around cover, especially fallen trees. They are usually found alone but sometimes travel in small groups.

Food. The specific diet of trahiras is unknown, although from their behavior toward lures and their dental structure, it is apparent that they feed voraciously on other fish. Their preference for lurking near cover-providing structure indicates that they are accomplished ambush feeders.

Angling. *Traíra* and *trairão* strike lures aggressively and provide a strong battle on appropriate tackle, although most specimens do not make long runs and seldom jump. They will make explosive strikes on various surface plugs, and also take shallow-running crankbaits; other lures, including large streamer flies, will likely be effective in the right circumstances. Wire leaders are useful, if not necessary, particularly if large fish are likely. Sturdy baitcasting tackle with 15- to 20-pound line is advisable.

Neither of these fish seems to stalk and follow a

lure from afar, but they strike at objects placed fairly close to their ambush spot. In slow-moving rivers, they are mostly found along the banks by fallen trees, logs, and similar cover, requiring pinpoint casting, often to tight spots. Sluggish near-shore backwaters are other locations favored by these fish, although they are usually taken by surprise rather than being deliberately targeted.

Trahiras require careful handling when landed. Their jaws are very powerful and sometimes have to be pried apart for hook removal. A lip-gripping tool, and possibly a jaw spreader, such as that used for pike, may be useful.

TRAILER, BOAT

Boat trailers run nearly as wide a gamut as do boats. Anglers are among the biggest consumers for boat trailers because they frequently fish in different waters and want the mobility, as well as the convenience of home storage, that is provided by keeping a fishing boat on a trailer. If you didn't keep a boat on a trailer, you would have to leave it permanently moored at a marina, incurring dockage, storage, and bottom-cleaning maintenance costs. The advantages of trailering come with a lot of considerations, however, from vehicular towing to insurance to proper support for the boat.

The vast majority of boats used for fishing can be towed, and a very high percentage are. It is generally accepted that boats in the 14- to 25-foot length are suitable for trailering. Boats under and over that length are sometimes trailered, and lightweight boats in the 14- to 16-foot range are even placed atop cars and trucks (by two or three sturdy anglers) with the right type of roof supports.

At the lower end of the spectrum, no matter what size the boat is, if you want to pre-rig it for convenience with various accessories, including motor(s), and you want to be able to put it in the water and quickly be on your way rather than assembling gear prior to fishing and then disassembling it later, you probably should consider putting it on a trailer rather than car topping. That is a matter of choice. Most fishing boats are too heavy for car topping and have to be towed if you are to fish in varied and distant places.

At the upper end of the spectrum, boats in excess of 25 feet are sometimes towed, but usually with custom-made trailers and special heavy-duty tow vehicles. Otherwise, it takes a professional transport service to "tow" the boat somewhere other than its home mooring. There can, in fact, be unanticipated problems with towing some boats in the 20- to 25-foot range if they are too wide for state and federal highway width requirements ($8\frac{1}{2}$ feet). Then, permits or special arrangements may be required.

The majority of fishing boat trailers fall in the middle ground, and most are acquired with a boat rather than separately, especially when a boat is purchased new. The packaging of boats, motors, equipment, and trailers today usually assures that a proper trailer is matched to the boat by the boat manufacturer and/or the dealer. But not always. Problems especially occur when people buy used boats and trailers, or replace the old trailer with a new or used trailer.

Some people who do a minimal amount of trailering, especially limited driving locally, opt for a cheaper and lighter-duty trailer, but this is pennywise and pound-foolish unless you will only use that trailer to take a boat to a marina in the spring and then haul it out before winter. Even then, you have to figure that the boat may get weighted with rainwater or snow, and could incur damage while sitting on the trailer if the hull is not evenly supported. Many anglers who skimp on a trailer eventually want to take their boat someplace they hadn't originally planned on, like a 500-mile trip on their vacation, or they miscalculate the effect that bad roads or even limited bumping and bouncing can have, or they don't take into account the times they decide to put a lot of gear into the boat to make space in their vehicle. So it is generally not a good idea to skimp.

Indeed, if you'll be putting a lot of miles on a trailer, and under all kinds of conditions in all types of places, then you may want to explore heavy-duty options or at least acquire the best you can for your budget.

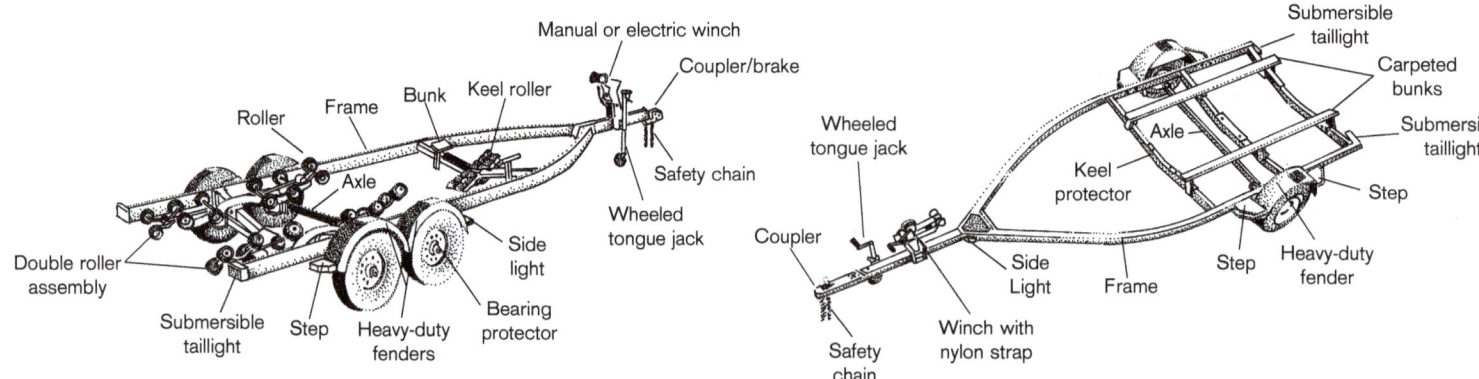

Selecting a Boat Trailer

The right boat trailer permits smoother towing, easier launching and loading, lower maintenance, and better appearance than the wrong trailer. It also makes for safer towing and optimum physical support for your boat. The best thing you can do when selecting a boat trailer is to get one that was made for your boat. Trailer manufacturers can figure out what trailer is best for your boat if they know the make, model, and year the boat was manufactured, or can determine it if they know the technical specifications (deadrise, transom width, and so on). The job of choosing a trailer is often made for you when purchasing a new boat as part of a preassembled package. However, you may want to opt for a different trailer, especially one size larger, as dealers will sometimes offer a trailer that is marginally appropriate in order to shave the package price. In the long run, that may not turn out to be a bargain.

There are many things to consider when selecting a trailer, but weight capacity and length are two of the most prominent. Boats are often toted with full gas tanks, assorted accessories, coolers full of beverages (or fish), and other gear that all adds up. It's a good rule of thumb, therefore, to consider a trailer that exceeds by 20 percent the gross weight of the boat and motor. You can do some simple arithmetic on this issue by looking at the manufacturer's weight of the unladen boat and the unladen motor, then add in the things that would normally be toted all the time, such as batteries, electric motor, miscellaneous electronics, storage boxes full of goodies, plus a full tank of gas (gas weighs roughly 6 pounds per gallon). This is what your rig might ordinarily weigh day in and day out. For extreme conditions, figure in other items. You need to have a trailer with the capacity to handle the extreme conditions.

Length is important both in regard to achieving desirable tongue weight (trailer weight as measured on the tongue) on your tow vehicle, and for getting the proper support for the boat, especially in the transom. A boat should fit on a trailer so that the transom is directly supported; the transom should not hang over the back of the trailer, which causes too much stress. However, if the bow is too far forward on a trailer, there will be excessive tongue weight, which is not good for the tow vehicle, and if it is not forward enough, there will be too little tongue weight, which can cause fishtailing (the swaying motion of a trailer behind a tow vehicle at highway speed). Most of the time you'll need a trailer that is a little longer than the boat. Although you need the right length of trailer, you may have some options in length (and width) between different models and different brands. This can be an important consideration for those who store their boats in home garages. Premeasure all your clearances to know what you'll need to fit a trailer and boat in your available space.

A trailer not only enables transportation, but it

Mobility is the prime asset of having a boat on a trailer.

takes the place of water as the means of support. Whereas a boat in water is supported equally, that is not the case on a trailer, so support for the boat is an important consideration, and it should conform to the contour of the hull. Carpeted bunks, padded bars, and rubber rollers are the primary hull supports on a trailer, and they have advantages and disadvantages. The size and type of the boat and how it will be launched and loaded have a large influence on desirable supports.

Rollers are used on trailers that tilt, as well as those that do not, but their primary purpose is to allow boats to ease into the water by gravity. They are good on steep boat ramps, places where you cannot back far into the water, and unimproved launch sites. Most trailers with rollers sit a little higher than trailers with bunks, so they can be better in off-road and unimproved locations. Rollers apply pressure to the hull of a boat, however, at specific places, which means that the pressure is not evenly distributed. The more rollers there are, the better this distribution is. If the rollers are designed to limit lateral movement, this is good, as they hold the boat in wind and current for easier loading. Some roller-support trailers also feature a self-centering keel cradle, which makes loading a boat under some conditions much easier than it would be otherwise.

Trailers with carpeted bunks distribute pressure more evenly. They provide more friction, so they can be harder to launch from the trailer by hand (pushing into the water) if it is necessary to do so (super shallow spots and places where the trailer cannot be backed far into the water). However, where launch sites are improved and with moderate inclines, a bunk trailer can be backed into the water until the boat floats off, and with the bunks partially submerged, the boat can be easily driven back on for loading. Many freshwater boat trailers, especially those for bass boats, have bunks; the boats are easily driven on and off the trailers, which also offer a low profile for easier towing.

Boat trailers are made of aluminum or either galvanized or ungalvanized carbon steel. Because most anglers have a tendency to put their trailers well into the water (although you should never submerge the hubs unless they have grease-fitted end caps and waterproof spindle seals), as well as travel over all types of trailer-wetting conditions, it is best to go with a material that resists corrosion. This is especially so if the trailer will be used in or around saltwater. The frame should be of welded construction, which is stronger than bolted construction and less likely to wear or rust.

When selecting a trailer, you also have to consider the size and quality of the tires. Small tires offer a low profile, but they turn faster than the larger tires on the tow vehicle, so they do not last as long and are best suited for light loads and short trips. Ideally, tires should be the same, or close to, the size of the tires on the tow vehicle. Some heavy-duty trailers have twin or triple axles and four or six tires, to distribute the load as well as to provide better tracking; these are harder to turn and tougher to maneuver in tight places. It's prudent to have a spare tire for your boat trailer, and to lock it to the frame. It's also good to have a fold-up jack for supporting the tongue when the trailer is off the hitch and also to help maneuver it around.

Brakes and Lights
Brake and lighting considerations are determined by vehicle laws. Lighter loads, usually those up to 3,000 pounds, can legally be handled by the brakes of most tow vehicles without additional help in many states, although you should drive with caution and realize that you don't have the stopping range and power with a trailer as you do without it. Laws aside, manufacturers recommend that you consider trailer brakes if the weight of the towing rig exceeds 40 percent of the gross vehicle weight of the tow vehicle. For heavy rigs, you may be required to have a trailer with hydraulic surge brakes, or you may opt for this even if it isn't required if you regularly tow in places where it is best to give the tow vehicle's brakes some help (steep terrain and wet roads are tough to brake on).

Trailers almost always come with sufficient lights, located on the frame, but anglers sometimes add lights onto trailer uprights. These should not replace frame lights. Remember to disconnect the trailer light wiring harness from the main vehicle before backing the trailer into the water. Lights are more likely to be inoperative on a boat trailer than any other element, so carry replacements. Putting some reflective tape on the back and side frame of the trailer could be helpful. Check for corrosion, bare wires, and cracked insulation, and put waterproof grease on plug and bulb contacts.

Wheel Bearings
One of the most likely problem areas for a boat trailer is the wheel bearings, which are subject to failure through overheating when a trailer is towed at high speeds and then taken to the water. If the wheels are submerged, there is a likelihood of water getting into the bearings and causing damage that will eventually lead to a breakdown, usually on the road and possibly at a high speed of travel, posing serious danger. Taking care of the bearings is essential for safety and for convenience.

Nowadays many boat trailers come with wheel end caps that have grease fittings (Buddy Bearings) to protect those bearings. If your trailer doesn't have them, they're easy and inexpensive to add. *Never* submerge a trailer that does not have this type fitting as well as waterproof spindle seals. These devices make it simple to pump a little grease into the bearings every two to three months, but don't pump too much, which could push the spindle seals out of place, allowing water and road dirt to get inside. Just add grease until the spring on the end cap barely begins to compress. Even if the hubs have grease fittings, the bearings should be removed, cleaned, and completely regreased every three years, more often if you submerge the wheels. Replace the spindle seals if they show signs of leakage.

Consider buying a complete hub with bearings already in place (and prepacked in grease), double-bagging it in big sealable bags, and always keeping it with you; if a bearing should fail while on the road, simply replace the complete hub with your spare. Have the old hub thoroughly cleaned and the bearings replaced at a service station to ensure there are no metal fragments left inside that could quickly destroy the new bearings, then keep it as a spare.

Winches and Tongue Weight
All trailers have a bow chock, which keeps the boat from moving farther forward. The location of this is relative to the position of the transom on the trailer and to the tongue weight. They also have a winch of some type. For smaller rigs, use a nylon-web strap instead of rope, and on larger boats, consider having a braided steel winch cable. The winch itself should not be high speed if you have a heavy load to pull up; some winches have dual speeds, using the lower gear for taking up slack and the higher one for the hard work. An electric winch is just about mandatory for the largest boats and for people who have physical impairments that make strenuous winching unacceptable.

The tongue weight should be between 6 and 10 percent of the gross weight of the objects in tow (boat, motor, trailer, etc.). You can determine tongue weight by placing the tongue on a bathroom scale covered by a piece of $2 \infty 4$. Move the winch stand and bow chock assembly forward or backward, and reposition the boat, until you achieve the right weight. Too much tongue weight will cause the rear wheels of the tow vehicle to drag and may make steering more difficult. Too little tongue weight means that there is too much weight on the rear of the trailer; this will cause the trailer to fishtail at high speeds and may reduce traction or even lift the rear wheels of the tow vehicle off the ground. So get it right before you ever start towing.

Towing and Security
When towing a trailer and boat, it takes longer to accelerate, pass other vehicles, slow down, and stop. Keep this in mind at all times, as you have to drive more cautiously than you do when not towing. Remember that the turning radius is greater for vehicles towing a trailer; you may have to give curbs, vehicles, barriers, and other items a much wider berth when cornering. At highway speeds, be careful not to make sudden movements, which may cause the trailer to fishtail; keep a steady hand and foot. The speed limit for vehicles with trailers may be different than for those without, and there may be restricted access on some highways, so be observant. Be aware that you will have to get into cash lanes at toll booths and pay a higher fee (usually per axle).

Take it very slow over bumpy roads and in places where the angle between trailer and vehicle is great; you can scrape the trailer frame, axle, jack, spare tire, or other parts in severe spots if you don't proceed slowly. And remember that no one should be towed in a boat, except at slow speed while launching or loading at an access site. If you are completely new to towing a trailer, you should take it first to an uncongested level area (like a mall parking lot in off hours) and practice backing up, turning, and parking. Some strategically placed cardboard boxes will help greatly as you practice.

With the proper tongue weight and proper tow vehicle, you should be able to tow a boat trailer safely. However, the weight of the boat and trailer determine what kind of vehicle you can tow with. You should check your owner's manual and speak to an auto dealer regarding towing specifics for your vehicle, but keep in mind that different circumstances create different needs. Towing in flat terrain is easier than towing in hill country. Launching at paved improved access sites is easier than at unimproved ones.

The majority of anglers who trailer boats use heavier-duty vehicles, including trucks, vans, and sport utilities, many equipped with four-wheel-drive, to handle the varied demands of towing. For serious towing and long distances, it is advisable to have a towing package installed by the manufacturer. Heavy-duty cooling for the engine and transmission, as well as heavy-duty brakes, turn signals, and shocks are among the necessities. While recommendations vary, it is generally wise to use Class II or III hitches for heavier loads. A load-bearing hitch attached to the frame, not the bumper, is best unless you will only be towing a light weight for short distances. Always use two safety chains to secure the trailer to the hitch of the tow vehicle so that it cannot run away from you if the coupler or stem of the ball breaks; cross the safety chains to keep the trailer following you. Put a lock onto the tongue hitch to ensure that it stays locked and does not pop free.

It is important to make sure that the tow ball (on the hitch) is the same size as the coupler, and that bolts with washers are tightly secured. Vibration during road travel may loosen them, so check them before you get on the road. The coupler should be completely over the ball and latched down firmly on it.

Lock the trailer when it is parked by itself or attached to your vehicle. There are various locking mechanisms for boat trailers. The best are those that immobilize the trailer and keep the wheel from turning. Others, which are padlocks or hitch coupler locks, can be cut with good bolt cutters or, in some cases, bypassed, and are lightweight short-term measures.

Make sure to properly tie the boat to the trailer before towing. Some boaters employ a single long nylon web strap that crosses the gunwales near the stern and attaches to the side frame of the trailer. Others prefer two separate straps that attach from port and starboard transom bolts to the trailer frame. Make sure that they are tight. Also use a safety chain from the winch stand to the bow eyebolt or a rope from the frame to the eyebolt. On bigger boats a turnbuckle may be necessary. The connection from winch to bolt should be firm as well.

When leaving the water to head home, drain all unnecessary water out of the boat. That includes the sump and unused wells. Water weighs 8 pounds per gallon, and if there is a lot of water in your boat, it can add significant weight to the towing package, perhaps producing a greater load than the trailer should handle, or perhaps changing the stress points on the trailer, particularly if the water shifts (as it might in the sump) with trailer movement. Besides lightening your load, this action will keep you from transferring any exotic or nuisance organisms from one place to another.

Maintenance
There is a small amount of maintenance required for trailer owners, especially those who launch in saltwater.

Washdown. There are two important reasons for cleaning your trailer down after every use just as you would clean your boat. The first reason is less obvious: to keep from bringing unwanted elements from one place to another. In fact, before leaving the launching site, make sure that there are no aquatic plants clinging to the trailer, and when at home, use hot water if possible to clean it. Taking steps to insure against the spread of exotic and/or undesirable plants and organisms is becoming more important than ever *(see: exotic species; zebra mussel)*.

Trailers that are exposed to saltwater are especially in need of cleaning for the sake of removing the salt and preventing corrosion. Salt is like an acid bath;

Published reports indicate that the industrial freezing of food was begun by Clarence Birdseye, prompted by a 1912 ice fishing expedition in –20°F weather in Labrador.

it can eventually eat away just about any metal. Even stainless steel will eventually develop small rust spots and pits if constantly exposed to it. It's also tough to wash off your boat and trailer unless you use soap. That's important because, unless all traces of salt are removed, it will constantly attract moisture and continue uninterrupted with its dirty work, even if you're far from the nearest ocean.

One way to wash the trailer is to stop by a coin-operated car wash and use the soapy water cycle followed by a rinse cycle. Another way is to buy a sprayer attachment for your garden hose and use that. Get one that can spray both soapy water and rinse water under very high pressure.

Lubricate and tighten. It's a good idea to periodically tighten all nuts and bolts and spot-coat them as well as other parts. If you even occasionally submerge your trailer in either fresh or saltwater, at least once a year remove all lug bolts or nuts, one at a time, and coat them with a thin layer of anti-seize grease. Otherwise, if you manage to go several years without a flat or other reason to change a tire, you might find it impossible to get that wheel off.

Also, check and oil every roller and replace those that are worn. A little oil on the roller spindles every few months will keep them turning easily and add years to their usable life. The time to do this is just before you put the boat back on the trailer.

Just like rollers, hull bunkers should be adjusted so that they support the boat evenly, thereby distributing the load over as much area as possible. Give these a quick visual check; look for supports that need attention, and rollers that might need to be replaced. Some trailers have carpeted bunkers. You can make the hull slide on them a lot easier by coating the carpet with silicone, which comes in pressurized spray cans.

Boat trailer springs should be kept out of water while launching if at all possible, especially around saltwater. In any case you can also protect them with a corrosion-resistant coating at the start of every season. One way is to apply a mix of 70 percent STP oil and 30 percent mineral oil (to enhance penetration within layers of the spring). A quicker way is to spray them with a heavy-duty corrosion protection, available at automotive supply stores. Spray this on nuts and bolts, too.

Inspect bearings. Check the bearings and replace corroding parts. Pump grease into the bearings periodically and repack them once in a while because water seepage and poor lubrication are the chief causes of bearing failure.

It's a good idea once a year to jack up each wheel, one at a time, and spin them by hand. Listen for grinding noises. Check for looseness (wobble), and tighten the spindle nut carefully if needed. You can do that by tightening as far as it will go without excess force, then backing it off just enough that the wheel spins freely. Visually inspect the spindle seal on the inside of the tire for grease leaks. If there is any leakage, replace the seal. If you have hubs with grease fittings on them, add a little more grease and then check to make sure you didn't overfill enough to force the spindle seals out of their seats. These steps take only a few minutes. If you find anything suspicious and you're not absolutely sure how to fix it, play it safe and let a pro do it.

If you have a dry, squeaky bearing while on the road miles from a service station, remove the cap that covers the bearings and squirt a generous amount of outboard motor lower unit oil into the bearing chamber. Replace the cap, and proceed slowly (45 mph or less) to the nearest service station where the proper grease can be added.

Tire check. Check the tires periodically. Improper inflation can cause steering trouble and tire failure. Under-inflation ruins most tires; it causes more flex in the sidewalls, allowing for a very high heat buildup, which leads the plies to delaminate and cause a blowout. Sometimes you can see a warning sign of this before it happens in the form of a large bubble in the side of the tire. But, if that bubble happens to form on the side of the tire where it isn't readily visible, you might not see it in time.

Check for proper inflation with a tire gauge when the tire is cool, before the start of a trip, and add the necessary air when you get to the nearest gas station. Make sure that the spare tire is properly inflated as well. Inspect tires periodically for uneven wear that could indicate a bent axle or balance problem. If you tow in the boondocks a lot, consider getting a 12-volt inflation kit or a tire repair kit.

Light check. Lights, of course, need to be checked for proper operation and appropriate steps taken to remedy problems for safety's sake and to avoid a traffic summons. Spray the connectors regularly with a moisture-displacing lubricant to ensure good contacts. The bulbs in the trailer lights themselves should be checked regularly to make sure that one of their filaments hasn't burned out. The housing for each light should be monitored to make sure it isn't collecting and trapping water. It's also a good idea to apply a light layer of grease to the base of each light bulb so there's no chance it can freeze in the socket because of rust.

See: Boat; Boat Launch; Launching.

TRAILER HOOK

An auxiliary hook attached to the main hook of a lure; this is primarily used with a spinnerbait *(see)*, but may be employed with other single-hook lures and with some bait rigs.

TRANSDUCER

The object that sends and receives sonar pulses.
See: Sonar.

The average discharge of an electric eel is more than 350 volts, but discharges as high as 650 volts have been measured.

TRANSOM

The furthest portion of the stern of a boat extending from port to starboard.

TRANSOM DOOR/GATE

A part of the transom on some sportfishing boats *(see)* that can be opened to facilitate bringing large fish into the cockpit. Very large fish (primarily billfish, sharks, and tunas), when kept, are difficult even for several people to bring into a boat due to the weight and length of the fish and the boat's freeboard. A latched gate that can be opened permits pulling and sliding a big fish into the boat instead of lifting it over the side.

TRAP

A device for capturing live fish or crustaceans for consumption or use as bait. Traps have been used for ages in procuring many animals from freshwater and saltwater, both for commercial and recreational purposes. The most popular trapping targets for anglers are minnows, crayfish, crabs, and eels. The use of traps for any of these or other purposes is subject to local regulations, so you should check on the legality of trap use before using any trap; placing a label on a trap, or otherwise identifying it, may be necessary, and there may be other regulations that pertain to their use.

Minnow/eel trap. When used properly a minnow trap is an easy and inexpensive way to catch fish for bait. The standard modern minnow trap is a wire mesh product that has been around for almost a century, and features two identical baskets of $1/4$-inch galvanized wire mesh that snap together at their large end and feature a cone-shaped opposite end with a 1-inch-diameter opening. In use the trap is baited with any number of items, but primarily with dry bread, crackers, dough balls, and meat. It is attached via cord or chain to some anchoring point, and positioned lengthwise in the water, and always with an opening facing upcurrent wherever there is a flow. In a good location, a minnow trap will produce results in a half hour or less. It can be left as long as overnight.

Some people like to paint a new minnow trap a dull color to make it less visible to detection (and pilferage or theft), and this is the only modification that might be considered. Such a trap can be converted into an eel trap by adding a separate cylindrical extension piece that connects to the two halves.

These traps can be placed near shore in a lake or stream if there is sufficient depth to cover the trap, and if it is a location likely to yield results, or it can be tossed up to 20 feet away via rope, provided that there is not too much current to sweep it sideways (the cone has to face into the current). Placing a trap by an undercut bank in a stream, near fallen trees and logs, and by other cover is usually best.

Crab trap. Although crabs may be caught

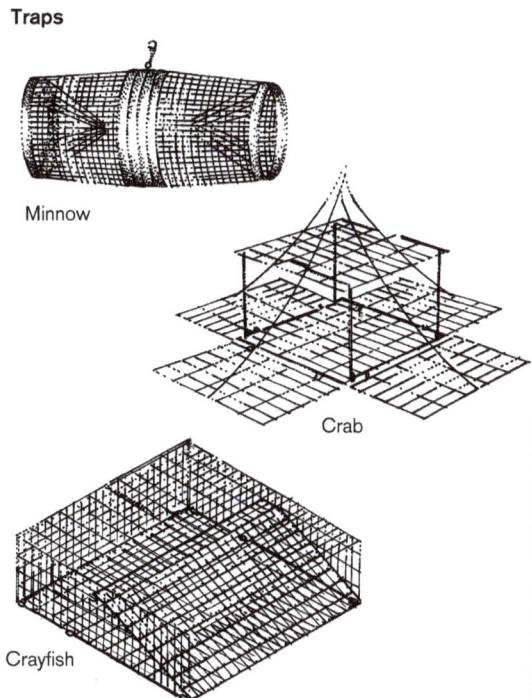

Traps: Minnow, Crab, Crayfish

on handlines or trotlines, they are able to escape those devices by letting go of them; traps have the advantage of not allowing a crab to escape, do not entangle crabs as nets do, and are more durable and longer lasting.

Crab traps are either of the box or pyramid variety. Both work the same way in that they have four folding sides that lie flat when lowered to the bottom of the water and close when the trap is raised to the surface via rope. Both are made of wire mesh; the box version has a fixed top and bottom whereas the triangular sides of the pyramid version preclude a top.

A crab trap should be baited with fish heads, pieces of eel, chicken necks or wings, or other meat that will not disintegrate too quickly. The bait is tied to the bottom of the trap, which has to be checked periodically. It is placed along a shoreline, fished underneath an anchored boat, and attached to a bridge or pier. When a trap is checked, it should be raised quickly to make sure that the crab is well enclosed. In time, an experienced user can lift the trap and feel by weight if it contains a crab, rather than pulling it completely to the surface.

Crayfish trap. A number of traps can be used to capture crayfish, and some people make their own. One commercial version is the same extended minnow trap that is used for catching eels. Another is a squared, galvanized wire model that lies flat on the bottom and has a rear section that opens to empty the trap; this type also keeps minnows.

A crayfish trap should be baited with fish heads, entrails, meat, or a can of cat food with holes punched in it. The trap is attached via cord or chain to some anchoring point when placed in the water. It may catch crayfish in a short time, but is best left overnight, especially since crayfish are most active after dark.

All of these traps should be rinsed with freshwater, especially if used in saltwater.

TRAVEL

Anglers have as big a yen to travel, probably more so, than other sports-minded people or hobbyists. The reasons are simple: to catch species not available where they live and to visit places where the angling is better, the fish larger or more plentiful, or the experience just different from what they're accustomed to. So they travel by auto, train, bus, horse, commercial airline, charter plane, floatplane, and even helicopter to reach near, far, or extremely remote destinations. Agents, outfitters, guides, captains, lodges, hotels, and many others cater to the traveling angler.

Fishing travel is big business. The livelihood of hundreds of thousands of people is all or partly dependent on fishing tourism. In some areas, small communities are completely dependent on visiting anglers for their survival. Some people have no other means of making the same amount of money in their community as they do from a sportfishing-related job; in one day, for example, a Mexican bass fishing guide earns what would take about a week and a half to earn in another job.

Fishing trips may be as mundane as toting a rod and tackle box during the family's car-camping vacation or as exotic as flying to an inaccessible spot for a rare and seldom encountered species. The more distant and involved, the more expensive the trips are, with far-flung international destinations costing thousands of dollars for a five- or seven-day excursion, plus airfare and incidental expenses. Spending five grand on a weeklong fishing adventure is not uncommon, and a few cost twice that amount. Getting to many places is not quite the ordeal that it used be; some prime fishing destinations that were once difficult to access can be reached in just a day of travel. Yet there are still places that take a lot of time, and possibly circuitous travel, to reach, depending upon where your journey starts from.

The following information pertains to fishing travel, especially that requiring air transportation and access to distant places. The needs for those who travel by auto or camper are more obvious and less involved than for those who trek to distant places on a tighter time schedule, although there is some overlap in considerations that need to be made. Since the issues of selecting a guide or a charter boat are detailed elsewhere *(see: guide boat)*, this information focuses on selecting destinations, trip planning, equipment considerations, and practical related aspects. There is also a special section devoted to major Canadian travel issues, since Canada is an enormously popular fishing travel destination in North America. Information about specific provinces and territories in Canada, and about issues for other countries, is contained in those entries.

Selecting

Every traveling angler is interested in having quality fishing and being in a quality facility. Quality is a nebulous thing and identified in different ways. The best fishing isn't all in the most remote or most costly places or, for that matter, accessed from the most deluxe facilities. Some remote Alaskan and Canadian salmon rivers, for example, are fished out of tent camp operations, with no running water and primitive showers, but they provide a great experience. Ditto for wilderness float fishing trips. Some terrific Amazonian fishing is accessed out of African Queen–style boats. Then, of course, there are places with five star lodges providing trained chefs, first-rate boats, and wonderful fishing. Great fishing spots and great facilities run the gamut.

One thing that has changed somewhat in recent years is that many top outfitters and lodge owners have upgraded facilities and put more emphasis on comfort. This is partly to attract the more pampered traveler, partly to attract corporate business, partly to keep up with competitors, and partly to be more amenable to women.

For a long time the traveling angler was almost exclusively male. Today that person is still most likely to be male, but in some camps the ratio of male to female in a given week might be 3:2 or 3:1; and many women accompany their spouse, boyfriend, or father, and they want better lodges and facilities. Fewer people are willing to put up with dubious sanitary conditions and "roughing it," even in many isolated and remote places. You pay for better facilities, of course, but you can find diverse creature comforts. The majority of angling destinations are not deluxe but are very good for all but the most fastidious person; they meet the major requirements of good (and ample) food, a comfortable bed, sanitary facilities, warm lodging, and the obvious fishing and boating necessities.

Some angling travel takes people far up jungle or rain forest rivers, such as this one in Brazil.

Naturally, your own requirements need to be focused a bit before you begin searching or selecting destinations, lodges, agents, outfitters, and the like. This is certainly the most obvious element of travel. The number of people in your group, the level of comfort you (and others) require, your willingness to share accommodations/boats/etc. if traveling solo (few people go solo, however), preferred methods of fishing, length of time and season you have available, budget, personal angling skills, personal fitness level, and personal expectations (how big a fish or how many?) are among the obvious issues that you have to confront before anything else begins. Be honest with yourself and your companions when it comes to what you can and cannot do. Your preferred method of fishing and personal abilities are probably foremost among these considerations.

Learning about locations, services, and sportfishing opportunities primarily comes from communicating directly with lodges and outfitters or their representatives, reading travel articles that appear in magazines and newspapers, and speaking to others who have been there. Having happy clients who provide repeat business is the most significant element in successful guiding businesses, lodges, outfitting operations, and travel agencies. Brochures, publicity, and appearances at shows have some value, and all have a part in the marketing of a site or service.

Shows. Sport shows include many exhibits by lodges and outfitters whose booths are generally staffed by owners and/or their families and employees. Speaking with these people is the best possible way to get direct answers to specific questions, as many as you care to ask. If you're seriously interested in visiting a particular place, a sport show is a prime opportunity to go beyond the obvious questions (When is the best time to visit? What lures should I bring?) to the most intricate matters (Are there reefs and shoals in the lake, how deep are they found, do you need sonar to locate them, and do they hold walleye throughout the summer?). Answers to such specifics will help an ardent angler make up his or her mind, as well as plan ahead.

Sometimes, booths are staffed by people who are filling in for the lodge owner and who cannot answer the most detailed angling questions; that doesn't mean the place is unsuitable, but you'll have to dig deeper for information. The person who digs deep and asks pointed questions is usually considered a more serious prospective client than someone who is collecting brochures and just kicking the tires, so the serious questioner usually gets detailed answers.

Many good operators do not have the time or interest to exhibit at shows. Shows are expensive and generally do not produce a lot of business for many lodges, particularly the pricier and more upscale ones. Shows have their pitfalls. Beware of people who use negative selling; be suspicious of those who criticize and downgrade their competi-

Many people get fishing destination information at sport shows.

tors. New lodges and new owners of existing businesses often exhibit at shows, and they may still be pulling their operation together. Shows are just a starting point, but if they provide an opportunity to interact personally with the owner or manager, then they can be very worthwhile.

Publicity. Articles in newspapers and magazines reflect the experiences of someone who has been there. They are relied upon for credibility by the average reader and, in general, are second in importance to repeat customers and word-of-mouth for helping to attract new clients. There are some pitfalls and problems associated with publicity but usually nothing that cannot be overcome by an astute angler/reader.

Seldom are articles published about places that you should not visit, nor are negative comments about places that are otherwise commendable. Sportswriters who review angling destinations nearly always focus on the positive. Keep in mind that they usually receive red carpet treatment, visit at optimum times, and may be hosted to some extent by the lodge; so it is easy to accentuate positives and bypass the less notable things. Some destination articles focus so much on the angling action, especially the number and size of fish caught, that you get little feel for other aspects. This is not always the case, although often some of the most important issues are addressed only in small print in sidebars.

Nevertheless, an article should help focus your interest and questions. Also, when photographs accompany an article, they can help establish the setting and the kind of place it is. Unfortunately, the photos are often too few or are of people holding fish, and little is seen of the other aspects of the lodge/locale/body of water.

One of the drawbacks of most articles is that they emphasize too much the exceptional catches and outstanding days, failing to note that every day was not fabulous and did not produce a monstrous fish, or that only one behemoth was caught all week even though 15 people were at the lodge, or that it took a particularly skillful angler to really do well.

The result can be that expectations are raised too high, and when people do not attain the same level of achievement as that described in the article, they feel that the author lied or that some special circumstances were at work. And they are disappointed when they do not experience what the author experienced. This is even more acute with television fishing shows; most people fail to realize that 23 minutes of constant video fishing action may have taken a week to actually experience and film (it may also take only half a day, but you can bet that the production value of such shows is very low). Seldom do all those TV lunkers fall cast after cast in real life, although it seems like they do on the screen. And the great shallow fishing or surface action depicted in a spring visit to a place shown on television will not necessarily be the experience from a fall or winter visit.

Many lodge owners say that television shows depicting far-off hotspots seldom bring clients to them, although they may be useful for helping to raise awareness. If the cameras do not spend all the time focused on the show host and his or her fish, this medium may provide a better visual feel for the camp facilities, the location, and the overall experience than an article with limited photographs. But if you haven't recorded the program, it's gone quickly from the screen. Many television fishing shows seem more inclined to depict a constant stream of fish catching rather than present a full view of the experience; granted the foremost purpose of fishing travel is fishing, but there are so many other issues influencing the selection of a place to visit, or a determination of what is a good place for you or what is not, that televised shows are of marginal value. Many issues are ones that you will want to learn about before placing a reservation, and they are discussed here.

It is important to realize that the skill level of many anglers and the skill level of the author of an encouraging article (or television show host) about a good fishing locale are often quite different. Some readers or viewers are better anglers than the author/host, and they may find even better fishing. That is not usually the case, but it happens. Many readers or viewers are much less proficient and may inadvertently be set up for disappointment. For example, just because an author caught a lot of bass at a great new lake by fishing heavy jigs in thick tree cover at 20 feet doesn't mean that you can do the same or that you will enjoy that.

By the same token, the fishing experiences of people at a camp at the same time are very different owing to their own skills (or lack thereof), so that while one person has a lot of success, another does not. Consider any article (or show), therefore, not as the last word but as something that motivates you to look further into the matter.

Finally, it is worth pointing out that savvy fishing travel marketers tend to get a lot of publicity, and the media tends to flock to the places that have good access, cheap access, a newly discovered fishery, and angling that provides good photo or video opportunities in a somewhat disproportionate manner. A review of fishing destination articles in major magazines, for example, will show far more attention to Costa Rican fishing or a hot new bass lake in Mexico, than to a lot of other equally deserving places. The Florida Keys, certainly one of the top angling destinations in the world, receives tarpon fishing publicity that is disproportionate to the number of people who can, or want to, fish for tarpon. Tarpon are more glamorous than walleye, to be sure, but the outdoor press and others who write about angling destinations often have a bias toward the more glamorous or renowned species, certain methods of fishing (have you noticed that most articles about bonefish emphasize fly fishing and almost never light-tackle spinning, which is just as much fun and equally demanding?), and some destinations.

This is not a recent phenomenon; it has been going on for over a century and is even more true where television shows are concerned; in this visual medium, producers and show hosts cater to activities that have more visible action and obvious drama. They would much rather show bass striking surface lures than being caught deep on jigs; if you can't see the strike or film the fish underwater, you wind up with more-than-the-usual amount of talking heads and after-the-hookset action. How many times do you see people on television trolling, unless it is for offshore saltwater species that will jump and look big in the camera?

As with anything else, you should approach all media attention with your eyes wide open and your brain thinking, and recognize that there are many excellent facilities and destinations that get very little, or no, popular press.

Literature. One of your first tasks is to look over the lodge's literature, usually a brochure, obtained from the lodge or its agent. This will range from a black-and-white photocopy to a glossy color folder. Be wary of the former and of literature that appears to have been hastily slapped together; that may reflect on the rest of the operation as well. Don't be too expectant based on the photos either. In the best brochures, the boats, rooms, facilities, and scenes usually look more impressive in photographs taken from the best possible angle, in the best possible light, with a telephoto or wide-angle lens, and under the best of circumstances, than they do in person. Of course, that is also true of most advertising photos, magazine pictures, and videos (some lodges now offer videos for prospective clients to review).

Most brochures depict large fish, especially camp record fish, but sometimes these are very old photos, of fish taken years ago. What have you done lately? is a good question to ask. Be wary of photos that show strings or piles of dead fish; lodges that appeal to meat hogs tend to emphasize that aspect more than others. The days of keeping limits has yielded to catch-and-release *(see)*, and the best camps advocate and practice catch-and-release. Many people are not pleased to be in a camp where the major interest of the staff and guests is in poundage and full coolers.

Look in the printed literature for a commitment to resource conservation and to the continuation of quality fishing. Far more lodges and outfitters are interested in advocating these issues today than in the past because the clientele has matured into one that recognizes the value of sportsmanship and conservation. A lodge whose policy allows keeping only one trophy fish of a particular species is one that is not attracting the meat hog element and is interested in having quality angling for the future. That means it plans to be around in the future rather than trying to make a quick buck now (if the fishing is lousy through overfishing, then the value of the business is hurt) and that it will be a place worth returning to. The merits of this have already been proven, especially in northern Canada, where most of the top lodges have had strict conservation policies that go way beyond the mandates of regulations established by fisheries agencies. The angling at these places continues to get better. But there are still operators—especially those whose facilities are accessible by driving—that emphasize limits and numbers and taking fish home.

Many lodge brochures give good details about accommodations, food, and services but are less specific about actual fishing information, which is described in general and glowing terms (perhaps because these places are leery of making promises that may not be fulfilled), although there are certainly exceptions. Ardent anglers usually want as many particulars as possible about the fishing (boats, angling styles, equipment needs, etc.). Some places provide detailed fishing information bulletins. This is very helpful and shows the commitment of the lodge to ensuring that clients experience good fishing.

The more traveling and fishing experiences that you have, the better you'll be able to satisfy yourself when selecting a fishing lodge. Astute lodge owners and their representatives make this chore a little easier by anticipating the kinds of things that you might want to know about (and anglers want to know different things than general tourists) and by providing you with those particulars to help make a decision.

A boat drifts the flats of the Florida Keys at sunset.

Speaking to others. Speaking to someone who has been to the lodge or waters in question is an excellent idea, and some places encourage this and will gladly supply a few references. If a lodge doesn't volunteer this, ask. Certainly a lodge is going to refer you only to someone who has had a positive experience, but in speaking to such a person, especially one who has recently visited that destination, you can learn some valuable things.

When you call someone to talk about their experience and recommendations, have a prepared list of specific questions in hand. Ask what they would do differently if they were to return (time of the season that they would go, gear they would bring, things they wouldn't do, etc.). Ask for a guide, cabin, or room recommendation, as well as a suggestion on specific places to fish (a certain pool, bay, flat, etc.). Be sure to talk about tackle requirements, especially productive types and colors of lures or flies. Find out if they paid for their trip, and make sure they aren't a relative of the owner or an old college roommate. Be sure to phone on your nickel, or if the person isn't home, leave a message to call you collect; don't expect someone who is doing you a favor to return your long distance call and help you at their expense. It is probably better to call someone than to write, but if you do write a letter, enclose a stamped self-addressed envelope to facilitate reply. Communication via e-mail may bring a quick response, but speaking one-on-one is still the best approach for getting detailed information as well as a sense of satisfaction that only the nuances of the spoken word can provide.

One of the best ways to find out about places that you might like to visit is by talking with other clients at a given camp or lodge when you are there. Many visitors to remote lodges and camps are experienced traveling anglers. For example, you might be visiting a bass lake in Mexico for the first time, but you find out that two of the people in camp have been to this place once before, to three other bass fishing lodges in Mexico, to two peacock bass fishing camps in Brazil, and to Alaska twice for salmon. Those people are likely to be excellent sources of information, and if they do not recommend a place, you can be sure they will say so.

Agents. Many people represent lodges, camps, and outfitters as agents. For some of these representatives, the world "agent" has a loose definition, although a small group of others offer all or most of the services that could be expected from a traditional travel agency, the difference being that these people specialize in outdoor (and maybe just fishing) travel. An agent who not only provides good information about prospective sites, but can also advise on scheduling and transportation issues and book air travel and lodging (if necessary) is very helpful. The cost of using an agent should be no more than if you dealt directly with the actual service provider; agents receive a commission from the service provider, so it does not cost extra to use an agent. And, you may get more and better information, especially if the agent has done a lot of the legwork. Some agents have newsletters that regular clients find very useful.

In fact, using an established full-service fishing travel agent has benefits that you cannot get elsewhere. The agent can often save you money on airline travel and can suggest or arrange the most advantageous travel routes. Although a regular travel counselor could do this, the regular travel counselor has not been to the off-the-beaten-path places that many anglers visit. More importantly, an established fishing travel agent who represents many clients is able to direct you to the place that is best for what you want. An agent usually is current on the places that he or she represents, so it is in the agent's best interests to look out for your interests so that you will be back for other trips.

If, for example, you ask an agent for a recommendation on where to go for the first-time experience of catching Arctic charr, the agent should be able to determine which site is best for you; he might suggest that instead of a location known for big charr, but tough fishing and less guarantee of success, you try another that has reliable action but nothing larger than mid-size char. Maybe after experiencing the thrill of catching small- to medium-size charr, you'll feel that you know that game better and next year will be ready for the big bruisers; the agent can work with you to accomplish this.

Furthermore, a fishing travel agent should know if a place that fits your interests is not suitable at the present time because of circumstances you would not be aware of (high or low water, unreliable transportation services, political or governmental concerns, etc.). The agent can steer you away from there until the situation improves. If something happens between the time that you booked a trip and your departure date, the agent can let you know and possibly change your reservation to another time. Would the lodge owner or outfitter call you if this was the case? Maybe, maybe not. Unfortunately, a lot wouldn't because they hope right up to the last minute that things will change, whereas a good agent will advise not taking the chance.

Usually agents have been to the places that they represent, or to most of them, and can give you a first-hand evaluation of a facility that interests you; or they can direct you to another place that is more within your means, interests, and abilities. The best agents try to visit every place that they represent to be sure that they are up to their own standards. This helps when they talk to a client who has specific interests and questions.

A final reason to use an established travel agent is that if the agent books a number of people to a given facility, the outfitter or camp manager will try to do his or her best for those clients and perhaps give them a little preferential treatment because the agent will not send people there if things go wrong. An agent who gets feedback from clients about the sites visited and the angling experiences is able to pass this information along to prospective clients, which provides a wider pool of information than what any individual could obtain on his or her own without a lot of time and effort.

Not all agents are equal, however, and not all provide a full range of services. Many so-called agents appear and disappear each year. Some are almost totally inexperienced at being an agent, even though they might be capable anglers. A few are totally inexperienced at fishing and thus are unable to evaluate a destination based upon what traveling anglers need or want. You are better off having a capable agent who is an adequate angler or has adequate knowledge of fishing than one who is a talented angler but has no skills at handling the varied tasks of being an agent.

An agent who has been in business for a while, probably five years or more, is likely to be reasonably good. An agent who has airline accreditation is probably financially responsible because the agent has to post bonds in order to work with the airlines, and this accreditation will be revoked if there are financial difficulties. Not all good agents have airline accreditation; some have an alliance with regular travel agencies to do their airline and hotel bookings. You could ask an agent for a bank reference and check it out if you are concerned; this is not a bad idea given the sums of money that can be involved, especially if you're taking family, business associates, or a group of friends on an excursion.

Bear in mind that many agents today are specialized. Some deal with fly anglers only, or fly fishing for trout only, or just largemouth bass and peacock bass adventures, or just remote Canadian and Alaskan operations, etc. It is getting harder to find a single agent who really can do it all, although the larger fishing travel agencies employ a number of people who collectively have diverse experience.

Liabilities. For the most part, dealings with well-established and reputable lodges, outfitters, agents, and the like go without incident. Everything doesn't always happen as planned, though, whether the mishap occurs through the actions of the operator or the people the operator has engaged, or the actions of a client or some other party. Planes have crashed, vehicles have been in accidents, boats have sunk, people have been thrown out of moving boats and injured, and so forth. Angling adventures are not without an element of risk. In a well-known incident in Costa Rica, a small boat capsized and the guide and at least one client were killed. Some people in Mexico have been robbed at gunpoint in their camp. A well-known South American outfitter was kidnapped. People at a Russian river salmon camp were simply thrown out. These are unusual and extreme cases, and not necessarily indicative of the ordinary perils of adventurous angling.

Disagreements or troubles with certain operators have prompted necessary lawsuits by clients; however, disgruntled clients have filed frivolous lawsuits as well. The byword in all of this is *caveat emptor*. Read the fine print in any literature, and be attentive to liability issues. Some agents and operators require that clients sign a total-liability release in order to be booked for a site. Some people balk at this, and you might want to have an attorney review any such release before you sign.

Keep in mind that there are many things that are not within the control of agents, lodge owners, or outfitters, no matter how reputable or attentive they are. Even though royal service is found at a select few deluxe lodges around the world, it is not possible in every phase of a fishing trip. If you aren't flexible, practical, and patient within reason, not to mention a little self-reliant, then exotic or distant international angling adventures are not for you.

Preplanning Issues

When selecting a lodge or service, you will be asking many questions of friends, lodge owners, references, and agents. Here are some thoughts on specific topics that will be a concern to many people and that may have some bearing on whether you visit a particular place or choose one site over another even though they access the same waters. Keep in mind that it is customary that all things except fishing tackle and personal incidentals are supplied at a site, especially when visiting a lodge or using an outfitter.

Distance to fishing grounds. Here is a subject many people don't think to inquire about. Great

Access to wild waters by floatplane is the dream of many an angler.

Bear and Great Slave Lakes in the Northwest Territories are excellent examples of this issue because they have good fishing, but much of it takes place considerable distances from the lodges. It is not uncommon to boat daily between one and two hours each way to get to the favored spots on these huge lakes. A lot of potential fishing time is spent riding. If you're assured of catching a big lake trout, you may find the long distances worthwhile; but since such assurances cannot realistically be made, long boat rides may be unappealing to you. These are extreme examples, but the issue of distance is pertinent to Caribbean saltwater or South American jungle fishing just as much as to big lakes in the far north. In a nutshell, the thing to determine is how long, on average, it takes to get from the lodge to the usual fishing sites.

A long boat ride may be worth taking once in a week, and then only if you pick the right day. When it's calm, this can be quite nice; but when the wind picks up and you have to venture out in rough open water for a great distance in a small boat with aluminum seats, little or no derriere padding, and no back support, it can be uncomfortable (and wet) for many, and intolerable for older anglers and those with back problems.

The distance issue is also relative to nonboat fishing and to getting to the boats. In some places, you may have to be almost a mountain goat to get from lodge to water, and bringing your gear back and forth each day is a real chore. In such cases, for older anglers, poorly conditioned anglers, and the clumsy, there is ample opportunity to twist an ankle while teetering from rock to rock. If you don't ask how far it is to the fishing or to the boats (especially important in periods of low water), you could be unpleasantly surprised.

Fitness and health concerns. It is a fact that many people visiting a fishing destination for the first time, especially if it is remote, have little or no idea what they are getting into from a physical standpoint. How rigorous will the activities be? If

Great moments to remember occur even when the big ones get away, as happened to these tarpon anglers in Costa Rica.

you're on an exploratory or pure adventure trip, you could spend many days bouncing in and out of boats, freighter canoes, and floatplanes, and walking through the bush. You might have to climb up and down banks to get to prime river pools, or you might have to negotiate a boulder-studded shoreline to get into casting position on a wild river, or help a guide pull a heavy boat from a cached shore spot. Climbing in and out of a floatplane is a chore for some people, especially when you're in a pair of chest waders. If you have a weak or bad back, consider bringing a brace along.

Such adventures have obvious fitness and medical implications and may be only for those who are up to the rigors. Some lodges and outfitters will properly detail the nature of things and forewarn clients. But this is not always true. When asked by a client, "Why didn't you tell me?" the response may be, "You didn't ask." So ask.

Guides. A guide can make or break a trip. Not all guides are good, not all guides have been guiding very long, and in some places anyone can hang out a "guide shingle." What makes a good guide? Ability to interact well with clients is foremost. That is closely followed by knowledge of the waters and fishing experience but also includes boat-handling ability and willingness to work to achieve success. A guide who takes you to one place and has no interest in going elsewhere, especially when the fishing slows, is a lazy guide.

The level of guide knowledge varies greatly, and expectations among clients vary greatly. Some people simply want a guide who will get them to and from the better fishing sites; some need expert tutelage in various aspects of angling or in presentation for the peculiarities of the situation. The range is as variable as the fish species and angling conditions.

Here is a general list of attributes of the absolute best guides: They carry themselves and behave as professionals; they will not violate game laws or allow clients to do so; they are courteous and helpful; they can communicate well; they can instruct a client on any element of the skills necessary for success at the particular type of fishing to be done; they have good equipment in good condition (important if you will be using the equipment supplied by a guide); they have safety equipment appropriate to the circumstances; they can provide accurate information about other elements of the experience (the place, the water, other species, etc.); they do not fish unless asked or invited to do so or unless they have to demonstrate something; and they have basic first aid and emergency skills. Very few guides have all of these, and many who don't are still very good guides. A great deal of variability exists here.

Likewise, the skills, personalities, and interests of the people who hire guides are varied. Some are unpleasant, unreasonable, overly expectant, and maybe not very capable anglers, and they may not treat a guide with courtesy or behave properly.

Every angler wants to get the lodge's top guide, which is impossible. It is reasonable to ask how many guides there are, how many years they have guided on the waters you will be fishing, if some specialize in certain areas (fly fishing, trolling, etc.), and other questions. You might ask if they are certified or receive any training. Some guides simply learn as they go, some are taught quite ably by camp managers, and some go through a formal training program.

Generally it is best to be with someone who has a few years of experience on that water, rather than with someone who is guiding for the first time as a summer job. Someone who is inexperienced on that water might be fine, however, if the person has had guiding experience elsewhere or if the lodge owner assures you that the person is a skillful angler. The concern here is not just being able to navigate properly in tricky places, but knowing where to fish when the obvious spots are not producing. If you especially want to learn about fishing techniques, ask if you can be placed with a good guide who is able and willing to communicate and show you how things are done.

If you are a well-traveled angler, and if you have experience in the kind of fishing that is done at a given site, then a guide need only be a boat driver. The guide should be able to navigate safely, get you back to camp at the end of the day from wherever you wind up, and be willing to position the boat however is necessary. You can pick the spots to fish and decide when and where to move and what to do from a technique standpoint.

For most people, a good guide is one who can suggest places, suggest or demonstrate technique, suggest lures or flies, and do the usual boat-handling and fish-unhooking activities. In Third World countries, in places where a foreign language is spoken, and in situations where the turnover of guides is high, such an individual is hard to come by, let alone a full squadron of them in a camp. You should give thought to what you need and what you expect out of a guide, and talk to the agent or lodge

manager about this. Fishing on your own without a guide may not be an option because of laws or liability concerns. The more angling travel experience you have, the more you understand guide concerns and can discuss these issues up front when selecting a destination. The entry for guides has more information about guides and being guided.
See: Guide.

Boats and motors. Although this maxim is not carved in stone, it is usually best to be in a place where the motors and perhaps the boats are replaced fairly often. In some places, the whole fleet of boats and motors is replaced annually, which impresses a lot of people. Most lodges replace their motors on a two-year cycle, sometimes a one-year. Motors are the lifeblood of many remote fishing experiences, and they have to work like a clock. In many places, they are put through their paces all season, being run a lot and also abused (striking rocks and such), so it is a good investment for a lodge to change them frequently. Few anglers think to ask about such matters, but it reflects well on the lodge when such matters receive attention.

Boats don't need replacing as frequently as motors, but it is not reassuring to arrive at a lodge where the boats are obviously old and battered. However, this is a variable issue; on the White River in Arkansas, for example, you will see a lot of older flat-bottomed boats in guide use, but these are specialized craft and well cared for, so a newer boat is not always a necessity. A good or new motor is more critical than a new boat.

Electric motors have become much more common, even in distant places, and especially where people fish for largemouth bass. Bass anglers are so accustomed to using electric motors (and sonar) for positioning and effective fishing that even camps in remote parts of Mexico and Brazil have electric-motor boats so that anglers can fish in their customary style. However, having an electric motor may not mean that the guide is skilled at using it for positioning. Not having an electric motor means that the guide has to pole *(see: pushpole)* or paddle to keep you in position. But poling is possible only in the shallows, and constant paddling just does not happen, and is ineffective in the wind.

If an electric motor is advantageous for the type of fishing being done (especially casting along shorelines and cover), then it should be on a guide boat. Make sure that you ask about this, and also inquire as to whether sufficient power is available to recharge electric motor batteries on a daily basis (this is hard to do in some remote places). Many Canadian lodges that offer pike fishing could benefit from having electric motors on the boats, but only a few enlightened lodges provide them; this is not quite as bad as it might seem, since the fishing is usually very good even without using an electric motor.

Safety equipment is a necessity, however, and life jackets are the foremost concern. It is dismaying to be out on a large lake in a 16-foot aluminum boat when the water is 40° and find no life jacket in the boat and perhaps not even a floating cushion. The orange kapok preserver that many lodges place in their boats is abhorred by most anglers, but it is better than a cushion—or nothing—when the chips are down. Almost no one wears life jackets, however, so when an accident happens, no one is prepared.

Lodges or outfitters should have Type III flotation vests *(see: personal flotation device)* in every boat if they want to be considered a top-quality operation. Ideally there is an assortment to choose from. Many of the life jackets provided in remote fishing camps are so small that a large, fully clothed person cannot get one on or cannot buckle it up.

Some anglers bring their own personal flotation device (PFD) to counter such issues. Compact inflatables now available make it easier to do this without taking up a lot of precious baggage space.

There is no harm in asking about the age of any lodge's boats and motors and about the availability of electric motors and life preservers. Your life could depend on the preserver, and possibly on the boat and motor.

Clothing and gear needs. Most lodges will advise clients what to bring; some provide more detailed and specific advice than others. It is more than a shame if you arrive at a choice fishing locale and are inconvenienced or severely hampered by not having things you need. This especially includes warm clothing; "warm" to a lifelong resident of Minnesota doesn't mean the same thing to a lifelong resident of Arizona. Foul weather gear is always important but often underappreciated by novice travelers, who don't know what good rain gear and truly nasty weather are. On the other hand, tropical climates demand clothing that is light and action friendly. Make sure you understand what is appropriate for the time of year that you'll be there. What is true for July may not be true for October.

Specific points about tackle needs (fly-rod length and fly-line size, for example, or baitcasting rod power) are useful. Experienced anglers can give themselves latitude, but the inexperienced need explicit instructions. A lodge that will provide you with such is one that is looking out for your best interests in all aspects of the experience. Invariably, a person who has not been to a specific place or has not obtained detailed advice from the lodge or from someone who has been there, will not have the full complement of tackle that may be needed. The more that you can narrow this down, and the more specific the information you receive, the better you can prepare and plan.

The best-time dilemma. The best times (or those perceived to be the best) are usually booked first by anglers-in-the-know, many of whom are repeat clients. How honestly a lodge owner or agent deals with this issue will tell you a lot about how he or she conducts business and whether you want to do business with that person.

Ideally, any time in a given season is a good time to visit, and in a few cases this may be true, but usually it is not unless there are overlapping seasons for three or four principal species. The best operators will tell you whether this is so, and they will squarely lay out your options and explain how things differ at nonprime times. They will also tell you that conditions may not be the same from year to year on given dates and that weather (cold, excessive rain, excessive heat, storms) and other forces beyond their control (such as drawing down a reservoir to repair a dam or prepare for anticipated heavy rains) can affect your success.

It is not uncommon to be at a fishing hotspot at what is ordinarily the "best" time, only to find the fishing uncharacteristically poor. Experienced anglers know this happens. But a lot of people who visit good fishing spots are not skillful or experienced anglers, and they do not understand this point. Many lodges do not warn people, perhaps because they fear losing a prospective customer, but it is better to be forewarned than to learn after the fact when disappointment and frustration have set in. Lodge owners and outfitters who are honest about varying conditions and can get this idea across to people, verbally or in their literature, deserve praise, and are likely to give you the straight scoop about all aspects of their operation.

What is "poor," of course, is also subjective. If you go to a Mexican bass reservoir that is renowned for plentiful shallow and surface action and find that, due to a cold front and/or dropping water, the fish are deep and being caught only on plastic worms or jigging spoons, you may consider your experience poor, even if you personally catch 20 fish a day. If you go fly fishing on tropical saltwater flats and find that, because of the conditions, regular success requires longer casts and more skillful presentations than you can make, you'll probably be disappointed. At times, the best fishing is experienced by only the most skillful anglers.

Occasionally the best spot in the world is a bust for everyone. Usually the reason is weather, especially cold fronts and high winds, but it could be drought, floods, or even commercial fishing. Anglers who have visited some prime salmon waters have been virtually shut out by commercial fishing activities. Sometimes these things are avoidable, but sometimes not. The troubles afflicting a remote region or fisheries are seldom newsworthy at home. However, thanks to satellites and world weather coverage through the media and the Internet, it is possible to get information about issues that might affect either your fishing or travel plans, even in remote places, so that at least you are forewarned and can plan or strategize accordingly.

Outposts. One of the options available at some lodges, primarily in northern Canada where outfitters are granted exclusive or near-exclusive rights to a certain territorial area, is staying at what are called outpost camps. The difference between outpost camps and established lodges is that the lodges supply almost everything, including guides. Not everyone wants or can afford this, however, so many places offer outpost camps; these can be as enjoyable as an established lodge, but they take an economical do-it-yourself approach.

Outfitters offer various kinds of outpost packages. The camp itself is usually a log or plywood cabin on a remote lake reached by floatplane. You bring your own sleeping bag and fishing equipment. Food supplies may be included, or you may bring your own. Boats, outboard motors, and gas are provided, and sometimes a guide or outpost camp manager/cook. Some outpost facilities are large enough to handle six to eight people, and they have a husband and wife team serving as camp managers and cooks, in charge of keeping things in order, providing firewood, and assisting guests with problems. In Canada, pike, walleye, and lake trout are the main species sought by outpost camp anglers. Some outpost sites provide opportunities to catch grayling.

If you're a reasonably able angler, if you don't need to be pampered, if you can unhook your own fish, if you want to *really* get away, and if you want to economize, then you should try the outpost experience. Envision a rustic cabin with bunks, a propane tank and cookstove, a wood-burning heat stove, an aluminum boat and working motor, a few housekeeping rules, and a lake or river with cooperative fish.

In most outpost waters, whether or not the fish are cooperative depends on your ability to find and catch them. There is pleasure in exploring wild and unfamiliar water, but the more you know about techniques and tackle for the species sought, as well as the places they're found, the better your angling experience will likely be. With few others to compete for the fish, however, it is possible to find good angling and a completely secluded wilderness fishing experience by going the outpost route.

A well-outfitted facility at Campbell River, British Columbia.

Other matters. Of course, you will have other concerns regarding the selection of a destination or service. Ask about extra costs (such as fly-out trips); travel routing (including overnight stays); special food concerns (almost every lodge that caters to Americans expects them to eat like Paul Bunyan, so quantity is seldom a problem; although when it is, it will override the good fishing for many people); language barriers, particularly with guides (a primary concern when English-language anglers fish in Spanish- and Portuguese-speaking countries); availability and cost (usually high) of tackle at the lodge; and so forth. If you have any special concerns or needs, be sure to bring them up. Many remote facilities are not conducive to people who are mobility impaired. However, there are exceptions to this. Some lodges exist in settings that permit easy access to boats from the camp, and they are able to accommodate people with special needs.

Few people think of everything to inquire about, and some of the final decision making rests on impressions and an intuitive "feel" for the people you are dealing with. You should go into the selection process with your eyes wide open and ask about anything. Naturally some things will escape you. You might not think to ask if a certain outpost camp has recently had bear problems, for example. And what about the wildlife? A place may have grizzly bears, crocodiles, lions, or snakes. Few people ever think about these matters.

Payments. Everyone understands the purpose of a deposit. Before making a deposit, however, find out the cancellation policy, the amount of time allowed for a refund, and whether deposits can be applied to a new date and a different booking. A cancellation fee may apply. Most cancellations made after a prescribed time period are subject to complete forfeiture. If you are a steady client with an agent or outfitter, you may be given some leeway.

Prepayment is usually required before the trip. This policy is no different from that of most general tourism operators and is meant to help ensure that you will be coming and to give the operator time to fill your slot if you must cancel. Many, though not all, lodges and outfitters will refund the cost of the trip minus deposit if you have to suddenly cancel and if you do so early enough. It is difficult, however, for many outfitters and lodge owners to fill a slot or two when there are last-minute cancellations. Find out beforehand what the cancellation policy is; if it is not clearly stated in the literature, get it in writing.

Most of the time a fishing trip to an international destination is priced to be all-inclusive beginning after your airport arrival. For example, if you're going to a northern Manitoba lodge, you are responsible for getting yourself to Winnipeg by a certain time; from there, the operator will take care of getting you to the camp, usually by charter plane. There are many exceptions and variations to this general rule, so you should have a clear idea of costs above and beyond the package price and of what services you are paying for.

You will probably be responsible for round-trip airfare from your home airport to that international airport. You may or may not be responsible for ground transportation to/from a charter plane, floatplane, hotel, etc. At the fishing site, all expenses, including food, lodging, boat, motor, guide, and gas, are usually included. In some cases, having a guide is optional, and an additional fee is required to reserve a guide in advance for select days or for the entire trip. Fly-outs are usually extra and optional, although some facilities include one or two days of fly-out fishing as part of the package. You pay for that at camp. Gratuities are usually extra, but a few outfitters include them. At some camps alcoholic beverages are extra, but increasingly these are simply included with the package.

At some camps you pay nothing extra except gratuities; others have lures and clothing and odds and ends to offer in camp, and you may have some incidentals to settle up at the end of the visit. For Americans, expenses are usually figured in U.S. currency.

Some operators make it easy for clients by including everything except gratuities in the prepaid package, which means that you don't need to carry a lot of cash. At certain sites, or at stopping points between an airport and the final fishing destination, there is more concern about cash and valuables than at others, so reducing exposure to theft or loss makes sense. Using traveler's checks (not for gratuities, however) further lightens concerns. In any event, be prepared with a good amount of money in ones, fives, and tens, for tipping porters, van or bus drivers, expediters, and the like.

Itinerary. In making plans for your transportation from home to your angling destination, you will need to pay special attention to the air travel arrangements, whether you make them or whether a fishing travel agent, outfitter, or general travel agent makes them. Missing a flight, or not allowing enough time for connections and delays, means extra expense, conceivably a ruined trip, and possibly arriving without your necessary clothes and/or fishing equipment.

Make sure that you have sufficient time between connections, particularly in case delays (due to weather or unforeseen circumstances) occur. Two hours connecting time between international flights (when making an international connection in Los Angeles or Miami, for example) is more than what the airlines require, but a good safety hedge. Remember that you will have to clear Customs upon return, so you may need more time, even though the minimum requirement is an hour and a half.

You should have a clear itinerary with dates, flight numbers, departure and arrival times, and the names and hopefully phone numbers of people or services that will provide ground transport or expediting when you arrive at a transfer point. It's a good idea to check on the flights and confirm your status and departure dates and times; occasionally departure times are changed. If your agent has not already gotten assigned seating, you can do this at that time if possible (there may not be assigned seating or you may have to wait until you arrive at the airport).

Many lodges use expediters who meet arriving flights and shuttle clients and their baggage to a hotel if an overnight stay is required, or to another terminal for a charter flight, or to the lodge itself. Make sure that you know who is doing this or where you need to go if you're responsible for getting yourself and baggage to a transfer point.

Packing and Preparing

The needs of traveling anglers are different from those of regular tourists. Seldom is tackle provided at fishing destinations, unless you'll be hiring a fully equipped sportfishing boat for big-game fishing, and even then experienced offshore anglers are likely to bring some of their own equipment. Most of the time, you have to arrive at a destination with the rods and reels that you expect to use, as well as the lures or flies and some ancillary equipment (scale, gripping tool, waders, etc.). For some places, and for extended stays, this amounts to a lot of gear; and it's hard to properly pack it all, plus appropriate clothes, and still be within weight limitations. This is especially true if your destination requires cold weather garb.

If you travel often for angling, it is helpful to prepare a standard list of things to consider bringing (some trips require things that others do not, so the list ensures that you review all possible choices). A comprehensive checklist is contained here, but a little commentary is required about certain items.

Lures/tackle. Ask well beforehand which lures work best at your destination, and purchase what you'll need before leaving home if possible. If you can't find what you need, some tackle shops cater to international angling travel, and they may have specialty items (especially offbeat lures) that your local shop doesn't carry. The agent or outfitter may be able to recommend these to you.

Your final destination may not have a supply of lures, or the camp may have a good but expensive selection. Don't count on the lodge or camp having what you'll need when you arrive (and there is always a run on hot lures/flies). It should be obvious that this also applies to rods and reels. Some people arrive at distant camps with rods and reels that are unsuitable for the angling conditions; some places have tackle that you can use, but most do not.

Trying to plan for all eventualities at a place you've never visited is difficult. Listen to the advice given by the outfitter, the agent, and people who have visited. The more specific they can be, the better. Once you've obtained the suggested equipment, you can consider bringing other items that have similar attributes or applications.

Whether you carry your lures/flies with you or pack them in checked baggage is up to you. A box or satchel full of hooks and metal sometimes requires close scrutiny by inspectors when it is carried onboard a plane; pack any knives in your checked luggage. Bringing these items as carry-ons could be useful if your luggage is lost or delayed. If you do carry them on, or if you check them as baggage, put duct tape around the latches and draws to prevent pilferage as well as to keep the contents secure in case the container breaks or inadvertently opens. Some boxes can also be locked.

There are all kinds of ways to handle the tackle storage issue. Some people use a bunch of individual plastic containers, stored in some type of bag; others use one multicompartmented flat-sided box that can also fit reels in it and some incidentals, plus a lot of lures. If you don't carry tackle onboard with you, it's best to put it in the same duffle that contains your clothing, and pack the clothing around the tackle for protection *(see: tackle storage)*.

Rod cases. Traveling with rods is a burden but a necessary evil, and there are two main issues to deal with: making sure that they arrive with you and making sure they are not damaged in transit.

The only way to be sure that your rods make it to your fishing spot with you is to personally carry them all the way. Occasionally you will see a traveler get onto a plane with one or two rods, without reels, banded together and carried in hand, to be stowed overhead. Airlines often do not allow this, and you cannot be sure that it will permitted. Furthermore, you don't want valuable unprotected rods exposed to overhead storage problems, like crushing and shifting. Even if you can get away with this for one flight, you have no guarantee that the rods will not get damaged when you have to stow them elsewhere, such as in a pickup truck, the back of a floatplane, or other place.

Rods should be placed in a protective case for all-around travel purposes. In theory, the best way to travel with fishing rods to distant places is to use breakdown rods that can be stored in a case and that are small enough to be hand-carried everywhere. The overhead storage compartments of some planes are so small that long tubes (3 or 4 feet might be a long tube) cannot fit in them. Airline personnel might require that these be checked as baggage, although you may be able to put a tube of such length under your seat. Three- and four-piece travel (or pack) rods break down into a smaller overall length that, inside a small-diameter tube, is small enough to be carried on any plane or even placed inside some duffel bags. Some companies make travel rods that are every bit the equal of two- or one-piece rods, but they are expensive, and they are limited to certain models.

Travel or two-piece rods that can be carried on planes are preferred by many fly anglers, particularly those who will mainly be fishing for one or two species that permit limited rod choices. A padded tube or carrying case for the rods is best; if not padded throughout, then it should be padded at least at the ends. The case should also be rigid enough to prevent bending and compressing and have a strap for easy handling. If you can carry one or more rods while traveling and pack your reels and essential tackle items in carry-on luggage, you will be ready to fish when you get to your destination, even if the rest of your luggage doesn't arrive with you.

This is the ideal way to travel with rods, but it is not possible, or practical, for the majority of traveling anglers. The limitation is that if the rod you bring (maybe two rods can be carried this way) breaks or is inadequate for the conditions, you're in trouble. Furthermore, not many high-quality travel rods are suitable for really demanding fishing, such as casting heavy lures, or for diverse use. For baitcasting and spinning tackle users, the choices are few (and the demand not that great); the choice is nonexistent for conventional and big-game fishing use. So, most people who travel and who are not fly fishing must bring longer rods, often one-piece, that must be stored as cargo for airline travel. This brings up a dimension of travel that is not encountered by many people other than golfers and skiers—checking oversize rod cases and tubes as luggage. (Incidentally, you might consider bringing a travel rod as a carry-on item strictly as a backup, and putting your other rods in a large case. This way, if the case gets lost, at least you have one rod that you can fish with at your destination.)

Thinking that you can bring just one or two fishing rods to a destination is optimistic but not realistic. A very short trip might permit this, but generally only the most seasoned travelers, repeat visitors to the same location, and veteran anglers who are very focused on one species or type of fishing, can do this.

Most traveling anglers realize that they have to be adaptable to the conditions that may exist (or change) at their destination, and the situation might require different methods of fishing that in turn require different tackle. Ditto for catching varied species of fish; at a northern Canada lake, for example, you might need one outfit for lake trout trolling, another for northern pike casting, and a third for light-tackle grayling fishing. Furthermore, extended trips and varied circumstances mandate that you have some type of backup, at least for the primary angling that you expect to do. Many rods have been broken on fishing trips, and since the main objective is catching fish, you don't want to be caught without your main equipment.

Carrying a selection of rods is accomplished by using some type of case *(see: rod storage)*. There are many commercial rod cases, and the majority of traveling anglers use a commercial case. A few are sturdy products that provide good protection under all but the most extreme circumstances; most com-

Rugged duffel bags and sturdy rod tubes are essential for traveling anglers; this is a scene at Scott Lake in northern Saskatchewan.

mercial cases, however, are suitable only for light applications and should be avoided.

Lockable flat-sided cases are available; these are similar to gun cases, with ample interior padding, and can be used for some rod storage but aren't long enough for one-piece rods. They are used mostly by people with multipiece rods, usually someone who is going both hunting and fishing at a destination (with fishing secondary) and needs maximum gun protection but cannot carry another case for rods.

Most commercial cases are tubular and adjustable. They are made out of fairly rigid material, but seldom out of a material rigid enough to withstand a heavy weight. You can test a rod case when empty by laying it on the ground and standing on it. If the sidewall flexes deeply, the product is inadequate. It should not flex at all, or just barely under heavy weight. Many commercial models have top and bottom sections that adjust for different rod lengths. At short lengths the cases seem very rigid; when extended to accommodate long rods, though, they are weak. Furthermore, the latch is likely to be a problem. Any case or tube that flexes is highly suspect, not only when weight is piled on it, but also when negotiating the corners and turns of a luggage conveyor belt.

Many people who use commercial cases do little to secure their rods; they simply lay the rods in the case and close it up. You can tell just by picking the case up and shaking it; you hear a bunch of rods rattling around. Do not pack rods this way. The rods should be wrapped, banded, or taped together; padding should be added to the top and bottom of the case so that the rods cannot move up and down; and the rods should be wrapped to prevent side-to-side movement inside the case. These measures should keep the rods (usually the tips and sometimes the guides) from being damaged.

Keep in mind that a rod case is likely to be subjected to all kinds of adventures depending on where you go and what you do. It might wind up being strapped to the struts of a floatplane or a helicopter; it might fall off the back of a truck and bounce down a hillside; it might get run over. When packing your rods in a case (tube), your mission is to make sure that the tube can survive the most severe punishment possible so that the contents are kept safe. Five premium rods in one case can be worth over $1,500. That is worth protecting, and since the airlines mainly treat rods as fragile merchandise not subject to damage claims, you had better protect them well. Imagine that a gorilla will be giving your rod tube the bash-and-thrash test.

The best solution for toting multiple one-piece rods is to protect them in a homemade PVC tube and to pack them with utmost care. You can construct such a tube yourself out of 4-inch (inside diameter) Schedule 40 PVC tubing. The overall length of the finished tube should be a few inches over 7 feet to accommodate one-piece 7-foot rods easily, or a few inches over $6^1/_2$ feet or 6 feet if that corresponds to the length of rod you use most often. You might make two, one shorter and one longer, for different needs. Shorter tubes travel easier and fit into more places (including vehicles). Do not go over 7 feet plus a few inches, or you will find situations where the tube doesn't fit.

You can use screw-on end caps if you like, but these tend to lengthen the tube and can be hard to get off if they crack or if the grooves fill with grit. Better to use flush end caps. You may only be able to find 4-inch diameter caps, which will not fit over the PVC pipe. The way to fix this is to apply heat to the end of the tube until the material is pliable; if you have a wood-burning stove, you can briefly rotate the end of the tube at the mouth of the stove. When the PVC becomes pliable, push the end cap over it fully; then let the tube cool to shape. You will now have a snug fit for the cap. Do this to both tube ends. Take one end cap and fill it with a foam pad that is several inches thick (you can cut the pad to shape from an old foam mattress); then epoxy the end cap permanently in place. You need a similar pad for the other end cap, but that cap will be secured to the tube with ample duct tape. To remove the rods at your destination, carefully unwrap the duct tape and save it for rewrapping the end cap on the return trip.

The case needs a handle, which is really the tricky part and should be done prior to putting the permanent end cap on. Without the end cap, you have more light to see by. A metal handle, like those used on storm doors, is cheap and adequate. Don't pick the largest handle, but something that your hand can grip with a glove on. The handle has to be secured with rounded Phillips-head screws that come from the inside out, so the nut is on the outside and only a small bit of rounded head is inside. This is tricky. One way to do it is to drill two facing holes on the opposite side of the tube that are large enough to accommodate a long-stemmed screwdriver; the screw can be gripped by the screwdriver and, working from underneath the tube to the top, you can then push the screw through the handle holes on the other side of the tube. Having two people makes this job easier.

Before the nut is tightened down, put epoxy on the screw stem; then tighten the nut fully and saw off the top of the screw stem. Do the same for the other screw, and fill the two screwdriver holes with silicone sealant, which should be trimmed flush when dry. Use a permanent marking pen to write your name and address on the tube.

Now you have a cheap, indestructible fishing rod tube that can hold 8 to 10 rods—more than enough for two people for even a two-week fishing trip. The absolute best way to pack the rods in it is as follows: Lay the rods alternately tip to butt (if you have six rods, for example, three should face in one direction and three in the other). Make sure that no rod tip extends beyond opposing rod handles and that the overall length is shorter than the rod tube; don't jam them in a tight fit. With the rods grouped and facing in opposite directions, bundle them close by wrapping in four or five places with masking tape or rubber bands. The rods should be firmly in place, not loose.

Take a bath-size towel and spread it out on the floor. Place one end of the bundled rods on the towel and near the end of the towel, but not extending beyond it. Roll the rods up in the towel and secure it with rubber bands. Take a second bath-size towel and do the same thing with the other end of the rod bundle. Make sure that both ends are covered with the wrapped towels. Now put the towel-protected rods inside the tube. Put the foam end protector into the tube; then put the end cap fully over the tube and wrap it securely with duct tape.

The contents should be very secure, with no forward, backward, or sideways movement inside. Packed like this, in such a container, the best rods in the world can endure the harshest treatment. Some anglers have not broken a rod through travel in over 20 years of using the same tube and the same packing method. A bonus: you have two towels to use at camp.

Duffels, not suitcases. Angling travel is much easier if you use duffel bags rather than hard- or soft-sided suitcases, because duffels can be stuffed almost anywhere. A large heavy-duty duffel without exterior or side compartments is best, and the better versions have rugged leather handles, twin zippers, and a full leather bottom that extends partway up the sides. The twin zippers can be fastened together with a small but reliable lock, although many people don't bother to lock them. Such a bag can store a lot of gear, handle plenty of weight, and be subjected to rough handling with relative impunity.

It's a good idea to treat the bag with a waterproofing agent, and especially to line the bottom

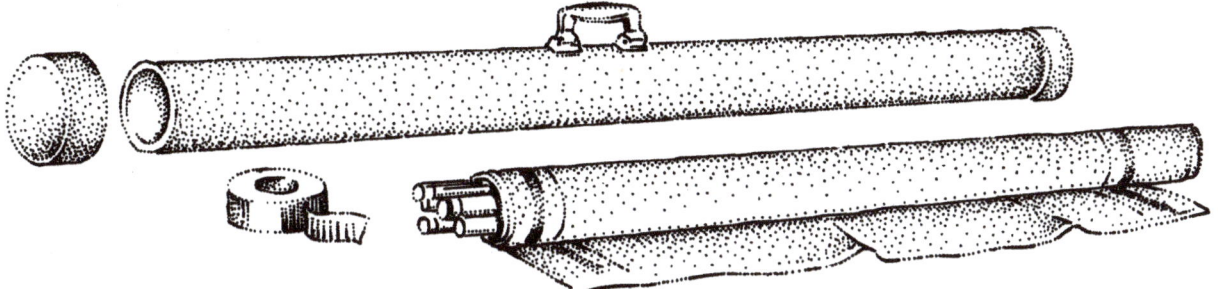

A cylindrical heavy-duty traveling case for rod protection can be made or purchased. It's essential to wrap fishing rods securely and fully before placing them inside the case. Towels make good wrapping material and should cover the entire rod bundle; in the illustration, one end of the rod bundle has been left uncovered to depict the rods, although in actuality one or more towels should cover the rods completely. The ends of the case should be padded.

and the top of the duffel with your rain gear (pants on bottom, jacket on top) for protection; a plastic garbage bag will also work and can be useful for other things during a trip. Outdoor travel often includes transport of gear in open trucks, wagons, boats, and the like, as well as temporary storage outside. A duffel may be exposed to the rain or sit on wet turf or airport pavement, and this protection could keep your clothes from arriving wet at camp.

Clothing. Clothing considerations are fairly obvious; expect to be cold whenever you head north, and pack for the worst-case scenario by including things you can layer up. You need to be flexible, but in a remote place you don't need a complete change of clothing for every day of the trip. Remember that you can always take clothes off if it's too hot, but you can't warm up with clothes that you don't have. Include a set of thermal underwear for north-country trips, even when you think it's silly; you'll be surprised how often this becomes practical. Several changes of socks and underwear are mandatory.

Consider carefully what you wear en route to your destination. It could be all that you have for a while if your bags are waylaid. Also, your baggage may not be accessible to you when you arrive at your final airport if it is being transferred to the camp. What if the weather is colder there than it was when you left home (which is almost always the case in northern Canada)? What if it's raining (maybe you should wear a waterproof jacket or windbreaker)? Could you go fishing for a day or two with what you're wearing if your luggage doesn't arrive with you?

Some lodges and camps are able to provide laundry service, which cuts down on your clothing needs. You should inquire about this beforehand. Many places do not offer laundry service; however, the creative traveler can bring some cold water detergent in a resealable plastic bag and hand-soak shirts and light pants in a tub or sink one evening, hanging them to dry in the sun or breeze the next day. You must be able to dry them in one day, however, for this method to be effective because if your other clothing gets wet, you might not have any dry clothes.

Some anglers who go to tropical climes wear short pants and short sleeve shirts only when in camp in the coolness of the evening, but not while out in the elements during the day. During the daytime they wear long pants and shirts to minimize sun exposure. Good-quality, supple, breathable clothing tailored for active people (casting all day and catching and releasing plenty of fish is active) is readily available today, so long pants and shirts need not be burdensome.

Footwear varies with the situation. Sneakers are useful almost anywhere, and sneakers or boat shoes with proper soles are best in many situations. In the north, you will need more rugged footwear, such as waterproof or water-resistant ankle-high boots with good-gripping soles. For warmth and all-around use, these are more practical than sneakers. To reduce baggage weight, you can wear the boots to and from the destination. For wet wading in warm locales, you can use old lightweight sneakers or wading booties that protect the ankle and help keep muck out of the shoe.

Waders and wading boots may be necessary at some locations and unnecessary at others. They certainly take up a lot of space in baggage, so you don't want to bring them if you don't have to. Hip boots are sometimes recommended, but you're better off with chest waders most of the time. Find out whether you need insulated or neoprene waders. Lightweight waders will not do in cold water and can lead to frostbite if you're exposed to the water for too long. Neoprene waders are great for cold water, but brutal if a lot of land walking is necessary. Ask whether felt-soled bottoms are adequate or whether you need grippers. Also, don't break in a new pair of waders on an adventure fishing trip; make sure that the waders fit comfortably and suit you before your trip. And bring some patching material with you just in case.

Necessities and desirables. Make absolutely certain that you have polarized sunglasses, a hat, and sunscreen with you. The benefits of these items have been discussed in detail elsewhere. Another must-have item in many places is insect repellent *(see: repellents)*. Keep insect repellent handy at all times, from the moment you deplane at a distant airport to the moment you leave for a scheduled flight back home. A small, full, screw-top lotion container that fits into a pants pocket will last you for a week. Use something that you know to be effective, not a product you're trying for the first time.

Other good items to tote include aspirin (or the equivalent), lip balm, bandages, and triple antibiotic ointment (for your wounded fingers after you catch and unhook a lot of fish). It's a good idea to have cortisone-type ointment for relieving itches from bites, needle-nosed pliers for unhooking fish, a pocket knife or multi-use tool), and possibly a small compass. Do not carry a pocket knife or fillet knife on your person or in your carry-on luggage if you're traveling by air through major airports; pack it into your checked luggage. A handheld GPS unit is a great addition to an exotic trip, provided you have room for it. It's best to carry this with you rather than check it with your luggage.

Keep in mind that if you're traveling with another person, you can probably pool your gear and bring less than if you both packed separately. You might be able to pack all your rods in one rod case, for example, thus freeing up another baggage allotment. Doubling up may allow you to tote something that might have otherwise been a burden, such as a portable sonar, an insulated float suit, a life preserver, or a camcorder (never check cameras as baggage).

Boat comfort. Travel by small boat for any distance on large waters can get very rough and can be hard on tackle as well as hard on your buttocks and back. Before you go, find out what kind of boats you'll be fishing out of and whether they have padded seats with back support (the best, but also the least common) or whether you will be sitting on the flat wooden or aluminum seats with no support (the worst and most common situation). If you have a bad back and will be traveling in unprotected waters that could get rough, you may want to think twice about your plans, or bring your own seat. Some anglers tote a stadium seat with them.

Ditto for life jackets. Every boat should be equipped with a Type III PFD for each occupant; nevertheless, you might find that there are no life preservers in your boat. Ask, and consider bringing your own. U.S. Coast Guard–approved Type III inflatables are compact and easy to tote if you have room in your luggage.

Some boats are liable to get wet or have puddles of water, so you should consider which footwear would be appropriate. In the north, where the water is cold, a leaky aluminum boat will puddle water on the bottom and you could wind up with wet, cold feet unless you have waterproof footwear. Remember that even a little puddle (like the kind that happens when everyone leans to one side looking at a fish) is enough to soak your feet.

Papers. For international travel, a passport and a visa may be necessary. American visitors to Canada technically do not need a passport, but it's a good idea to have it anyway. A passport is a must for visiting Mexico and for many other countries, some of which also require a visa. It takes time to acquire a visa, so plan accordingly. There are some services that can obtain a visa on short notice—they walk it through the embassy approval process—for a fee, and your agent or outfitter may be able to recommend them. This is necessary only when travel arrangements have been made on short notice. If you do not have a passport, or if it will be expiring within the next six months, allow plenty of time to get a new or renewed one before a trip; the process takes time when handled by mail. You might speed up this process by personally appearing at the nearest issuing office, but you can be sure that it will be an all-day sit-and-wait affair.

Make sure that you have your passport and visa handy at all times when traveling, and do not let them out of your sight. Do not tuck them in baggage that will be stowed away, since you will have to show them to Customs officials and airline agents, and possibly to others depending on where you travel; if they are stowed in a bag that is under a cart full of baggage, you'll delay everybody by having to dig them out, and if something happens to the bag, there go your important papers. If security is a concern when you are at your final destination, do not leave your passport in your room. Take it with you or store it in a secure place.

It may be necessary, or at least a good idea, to register items of value (cameras, personal computer, etc.) when headed to certain countries or when returning to the United States. This is to make sure that valuables that would be subject to taxes and import duties are not purchased elsewhere and brought back without payment, or sold while en route without payment of taxes. You might make up a list of these items, with date of purchase, cost or value, and serial numbers; the list can be kept with your passport and used to fill out any necessary declaration forms. The list might be notarized beforehand, or it might be stamped by a Customs official at a U.S. international airport. Check with the Customs offices of respective countries to see if this is necessary. If you have to fill out declaration forms or get a list stamped at an airport Customs office, recognize that this will add some time to your itinerary and plan accordingly. Customs officials usually don't check these items very closely, but if they do, and they have reason to be suspicious about valuable goods, you'll need some proof of prior ownership or proof that you had this merchandise with you when you departed on your trip. A copy of the purchase receipt would likely suffice as well as the registered list.

As for insurance, check to see what your personal insurance covers with regard to loss, theft, breakage, or damage of personal items when traveling abroad. There is no reason to bring valuable jewelry with you when traveling for fishing, so leave that items

---

Eighty-five percent of the salmon streams that existed in California in 1850 have been degraded to such an extent that they no longer provide spawning and rearing habitat for salmon.

at home. If you will be driving your own car in a foreign country, you may need a proof of insurance card or statement from your carrier or agent. There are special considerations for driving to Canada and Mexico, and you should check on these with regard to your own vehicle and to any boat and trailer that you might be towing. If you'll be renting a car in a foreign country, check with your carrier to see what provisions are made for this. It may differ depending on the country.

No matter what papers you have, you may get hassled in some places for no obvious reason. Mexico is notorious for unexplainable difficulties that are usually eased by greasing someone's palm. Having smaller bills on hand for this can smooth things along.

Last-minute check. The night before departing from home, make a quick check of your things to be sure that you have everything that you'll need, starting with necessary papers and then going through your entire checklist. Make sure that all baggage, including carry-ons and rod case, is tagged with personal identification. Some people like to use their business address instead of personal address on their luggage; others prefer just the opposite. It's a good idea to have identifi-cation both inside and outside the baggage. Some agents suggest including a copy of your itinerary, with destination phone numbers, in your luggage ID tags, so that your luggage can be forwarded if lost.

Consider marking the bags and tube with some common item (colorful tape, red cloth ribbon, decal, etc.) that makes your items stand out and easily identified. Make sure you include some reading material (a paperback book is good) with your carry-ons, since you will surely be waiting several times during the trip under ordinary circumstances, and even longer if there are transportation delays. Hurry up, then wait, is a common part of the itinerary when going or coming from many foreign destinations, especially in Central and South America.

The following is an all-purpose checklist that will cover just about all general travel as well as fishing travel (including auto travel) and that can be modified to suit your own needs. It's a good idea to print up two copies of your list on index cards; keep one at home and stick the other in your toiletries kit. By looking over the list before leaving home, and again before leaving the lodge or camp, you can be sure you haven't left anything behind.

Traveler's Checklist

- Underwear: pants, shirts, thermal
- Pants: work, dress, suit (and tie), sweat
- Shirts: long, short, tee
- Shoes: sneakers, dress, deck or boat, boots
- Socks: white, color, thermal
- Outer: sweatshirt, jacket, hat, rainsuit, snowsuit
- Bathing suit, gloves, goggles, belts, clock, pocket knife/tool, sunglasses, sunscreen, insect repellent
- House/car keys, watch, camera, batteries, film, cash, traveler's checks, personal checks, airline tickets, pad, pen, book
- Razor, soap, toothbrush, toothpaste, hairbrush, makeup, lip balm, deodorant, Q-tips, moleskin
- Lozenges, anti-diarrhea medicine, cold tablets, cortisone ointment, aspirin/ibuprofen
- Prescription medicine, anti-inflammatory drug, seasick tablets, Bacitracin, bandages
- Shampoo, towel, cloth, hand lotion, hair dryer, Walkman-type radio
- Rods, reels, line, lures, waders, wading shoes, sonar, compass, GPS, pliers and sheath
- Boat battery, battery charger, rod holder, downriggers and weights, fly tying gear
- Cooler, extension cord, thermos, large tools, weather radio, repair kit
- Rope, tie-downs, spotlight, tackle boxes, net, float tube, fins, scale, measuring tape
- Duct tape, electric tape, fillet knife, flashlight, lock and keys, fish-gripping tool
- Small duffel for boat, hook sharpener, binoculars, plastic bags

En route

Baggage considerations. Many frequent travelers prefer to use curbside check-in whenever possible, so they can avoid toting a lot of stuff any distance and shuffling a rod tube and luggage through waiting lines at the ticket counter. Technically there are weight limitations to all baggage; since porters seldom weigh baggage, it is to your advantage to use them when you have weight concerns. Be sure to tip the curbside porter and see that the routing tags are placed on your luggage. Unfortunately, for security reasons, international travelers cannot check luggage at the curb; it has to be personally checked in at the ticket counter. At U.S. airports, you are less likely to have your baggage weighed, and to be assessed if you are overweight. In a foreign airport, expect your luggage to be weighed at the ticket counter when you're returning home, and to be assessed if you are overweight.

Whenever an agent or porter checks your luggage, always be sure that the person has put the right flights and routing on the tags. Check your luggage receipt. It helps when heading home if you know the airport code for your home airport and can verify that.

For convenience, most travelers check their luggage all the way through to their final destination. However, if you have to board a connecting flight on a different carrier, you may have a problem if your luggage is lost, since the carriers always blame each other. Some people who have domestic travel connections to catch before they board their international flight (flying one airline to Miami, for example, then another from Miami to Manaus, Brazil) check their luggage from their starting point as far as the international departure point; then they claim their baggage and take it to the international carrier for check-in. This way they know where their luggage is and who lost it.

For international destinations, the ticket agent may ask to look in your bags; this should not be a problem, except for your rod cases with their carefully wrapped contents. Suggest that the rod case be run through the passenger carry-on X-ray machine and then hand-carried to the gate for baggage loading by the attendants. It will save having to unwrap and rewrap the case and contents in what is likely to be a cramped area in full view of the public, something that is not easily done with a 7-foot tube at a crowded, bustling ticket counter.

If you're worried about your baggage making a tight connection (and you know that if it doesn't, it will be hard to catch up with you at your remote destination), you can sometimes get peace of mind by watching the on-plane baggage-loading operations (either from the right side of the airplane or from the gate area) to see if your items come along. You might politely express your concern to the attendants and see if anything can be done to wait a moment longer or encourage that baggage transfer. Be pleasant about it.

Losing baggage containing fishing tackle and/or a rod case occasionally happens and is probably the number one worry of travelers. The more remote your final destination, the less likely it is that your bags will catch up to you if they don't arrive with you. It sometimes takes great luck, or exceptional effort on the part of the outfitter, to get delayed or waylaid baggage to you. If you're visiting a lot of places, or have several legs to your itinerary, the lost bags may reach you somewhere along the line. If other anglers are coming to the camp a day or two after you, it is possible that your items can tag along with them. But, in many cases, no one is coming to camp shortly after, and no flights are available to the area in question for several days. If you're headed to a destination that is serviced by a carrier with more than one flight per day, it's a good idea to book an earlier flight in case your baggage gets misplaced. It might come on the later flight, which you can wait for. However, if you're on the last flight to a destination, and your bags don't make it, then they will not be there until the following day at best, by which time you may well be in the hinterland.

You might consider purchasing optional trip insurance that covers lost baggage and/or trip cancellation or accidents.

When you and your bags have reached the final commercial airport before heading to the lodge or camp, continue to be vigilant about your luggage and carry-on bags. Watch your luggage at all times to make sure that it goes where you want it to.

When your luggage is unloaded at any destination, especially at far northern transfer points, check immediately to see that all of your pieces are there, and do your best to facilitate their arrival. Even if you're with a group and someone else is looking after the baggage transfers, keep an eye on your gear, not so much for pilferage, but to be sure that it gets from commercial airliner to transportation vehicle to floatplane to camp. Keep an eye on it whenever it is handled; you would hate to lose a bag that made it all the way to the hotel, only to have it placed off to the side during unloading of the vehicle, then be inadvertently overlooked, and subsequently found to have disappeared.

Customs. Most of the time you will have no problem when entering other countries and going through either foreign or U.S. Customs and immigration checkpoints. This is especially true for passengers on regularly scheduled airline flights; more attention may be paid to those arriving via private aircraft and small charter flights, particularly in Mexico. If you don't have the required papers, however, especially passport and visa, you could be denied entry, so be especially careful to bring, and not lose, these items. If you have a problem with a customs inspector, be courteous, patient, and co-operative. Try to avoid an argument or an unpleasant scene.

If you have to clear Customs before heading onto a connecting flight, you'll have to bring your bags through the inspection area and then take them to another dropoff point after clearing Customs so that they can be sent on. Time may be of the essence here, so don't delay, and be absolutely sure that the bags are left in the right place for continuing travel. Unfortunately, this is often where a duffel and rod tube part company. Tubes are oversized luggage, and in some places they will not be placed on a conveyor belt to the baggage holding site. They may get placed to the side to be hand-carried to that site, which might not happen expeditiously. Even if you have plenty of time between flights, a tube that gets placed off to the side can be overlooked for a long time, and you may find that when you arrive at your destination airport, your duffel is there but the tube isn't. Do what you can to see that it gets taken to the right place and is not neglected, even if that means waiting awhile to see it get picked up and carted off.

Reconfirmation. On international flights, it is a good idea (and may be required by the carrier) to reconfirm your return departure flights. You may have to reconfirm at least 72 hours in advance, which could be impossible for anglers headed to the boondocks. Reconfirming return flights might be possible when you arrive at a takeoff airport and have a little time to kill prior to moving on. A camp or lodge representative might be able to do this for you during your stay. If you reconfirm a flight on your own at an airport, go to the ticket counter and explain to the agent that you will be out of touch at a fishing camp for an extended period and ask the agent to immediately reconfirm your flight and place his or her initials on the ticket next to the outbound flight.

Exchanging money. Exchange some money at the first possible location (often the airport) to be sure that you have what you need. Local currency is especially useful if you will need to take a taxi somewhere. Some hotels will exchange money for you. In most countries, American paper money (no need for coins) is readily accepted; in a few, you need the local currency. American currency is more likely to be accepted at popular tourist stops than deep in the interior, and it doesn't hurt to have both your own currency and the local currency with you. Check with your agent or outfitter for suggestions. If you are paying a bill at the lodge or camp, make sure you know what currency is accepted. The pricing at many Canadian lodges is based on American currency. Know before you go.

At the Site

Guide matters. Most guides are excellent for navigating on local waters, and this is important because many remote locales are tricky. In some places, if you fish without a guide, and damage a motor or boat, you will likely be responsible for the damage.

When you use a guide, establish immediately what you want and how you care to fish, but accept the guide's suggestions and recommendations, especially at the beginning of the trip. If you are a knowledgeable and experienced angler, so much the better. Not all guides are professional anglers, and if you have enough experience, you can make a valuable contribution to the effort of finding and catching fish. Don't be afraid to experiment with lures and places to fish or to make suggestions to your guide regarding a place to fish and boat speed. The more that you and your guide communicate with each other, the better. Just do it without being obnoxious.

When there are language differences, communicating can be a struggle, and sometimes frustrating. Some agents and lodge owners have prepared a small translation list of useful terms in actual and phonetic pronunciation, so that clients can relay some basic fishing and personal interests to a guide in the guide's language. Knowing how to tell a guide to get closer to or farther from the bank, to put the boat in shallower or deeper water, to go to another place, etc., is very useful and will help both you and the guide (the guide always looks good when customers have had success).

It's a good idea to establish a rapport with your guide, especially those in Third World countries who speak a different language. Respect the guide's ways and culture, and give praise when it is due, especially when a big fish is caught. The large fish may be a moment of pride or even reward for the guide (some camps have big fish pools for the guides), and in any event let the guide know you are happy. If you remain positive and enthusiastic, even when the going is slow, the guide probably will, too. And if the guide is working hard, respect this; don't take advantage of the person, and don't expect the guide to paddle all day against the wind.

Treat your guide well, but don't spoil the person. If you take over the boat and run it, land the fish, unhook them, and leave the guide with nothing to do, the guide will be bored and probably lazy when you do want him or her to do something, not to mention that this treatment may be what the guide will expect of other clients. Guides should not fish unless they are asked or invited to, and you'll spoil a guide by having the guide do what you're there to do, not to mention adding additional pressure to the resource. You fish, your guide guides.

Talk to the head guide, camp manager, or owner, if you have a problem with a guide. They may be able to resolve it without problems or resentment on either side. Do not give a guide alcohol at any time, especially when running the boat, which could be dangerous if not illegal. Do not give a guide alcoholic beverages as a tip, and do not give the guide your alcoholic leftovers prior to your departure. This might send the guide on a bender that will cause problems for the next party in camp, or for the manager or owner.

Boating matters. You should check out your boat prior to departing the dock every day of a trip. Although it is the guide's business to see that everything needed is onboard, make it your business as well. This is especially true for the first day, when everyone in camp is eager to get headed to the fishing grounds. Take a moment to look over things and check that life preservers are available, that an adequate supply of beverages and ice is onboard (this is especially important in the tropics), that the boat has a net or gaff as necessary, that the seats are set up properly for you, that the lunch box is onboard, and so forth.

Before you start off, make sure that your gear is properly stowed and secured so that it doesn't get damaged while running across the water. An unexpected wave or boat wake, or some rough water, can smack a boat hard and send equipment flying. You don't want your rod left where something like an anchor might bounce onto it. Also, do whatever you can to keep your expensive graphite rods from being banged about on the seats, gunwale, or struts of an aluminum boat. Some guides have absolutely no concern for the value or condition of your fishing equipment, so it's your responsibility to keep it safe. Repeated banging will scrape the protective finish off rods and damage them, resulting in weak spots that may lead to breakage. Rod covers may help with this. Be especially careful when your rod tips extend overboard in brushy and weedy places; they could be snagged and pulled overboard or broken, or the hooks could get stuck in someone.

Stainless steel hooks will not corrode or break down in freshwater; they'll start to corrode after 7 to 10 days in saltwater and will take several months to break down.

Tipping. It is common to give the guide a tip for daily or weekly services and also to tip the camp or lodge staff. The dock manager and the transporter, as well as some others, might also be tipped, although a lesser amount. Check with the camp manager, who is seldom tipped, for customary policies. Many places ask you to tip the guides separately and to make a collective tip to the staff; the staff tip is pooled by all staff members, from the kitchen help to the workers around camp. In many distant places, a tip of $10 per angler per day to the guide is standard. A larger tip, however, is usually warranted, and a $25 daily tip is more likely in some places and situations. A similar amount is provided to the camp staff. An extra amount is warranted for exceptional performance and extra services, and a lesser amount is suitable for inferior service.

Keep in mind that the activities of a guide at one location may basically amount to being a boat driver, whereas at another place they may include being a full-fledged fishing advisor, shore lunch chef, the person who hauls the boat or motor around, and an indispensable factotum who assists with myriad chores. Even when both types of guides do their job well, the tip for the former should not equal the tip for the latter.

Many clients give guides a cash tip plus some equipment or give them some useful or valuable equipment in lieu of a tip. The equipment might be a rod, reel, some lures, or other merchandise. At many destinations, this is not a problem, but you may want to check with the manager about it. Some Mexican outfitters recommend not giving fishing tackle to guides because it may well be used by them or others for commercial fishing activities (legal or illegal) and contribute to depleting the resource. As mentioned before, do not give alcohol to a guide, as a tip or otherwise.

Incidentally, some camps will allow you to fish extra hours (in the evening perhaps for several hours) by private arrangement with the guide.

Food and water concerns. In some places you will have few if any concerns about the food, water, ice, or beverages; and the biggest problem is not stuffing yourself with all the breakfast, lunch, and dinner items that are made available. In tropical locations, where the heat can be intense, the quantity of food consumed may well be an issue. It is best to eat moderately and to drink a lot in such locations.

Where the quality of water is of concern, be careful about what you eat and about any contact that you might have with water. This could include the water that you use to brush your teeth, the ice cubes in your drink, and the salad that was washed in suspect water. Drink only pure bottled water, or bottled or canned soda or juice while you're out fishing, and recognize that the ice cubes that keep the beverages cold may come from suspect water, so you may want to clean the top of the beverage container before drinking from it. Some camps make ice cubes from pure water, so be sure to ask before using any ice cubes in your drink; likewise ask about any beverages (like lemonade or iced tea) that are mostly made from water. At the main camp, these matters should be less of a concern than while on the water, but find out about them when you first arrive in camp.

If you get diarrhea (Montezuma's revenge), the cause may be drinking the water, overeating fresh tropical fruit, or simply undergoing a change in diet. If the problem persists, you should take an anti-diarrhea medicine; Immodium works well for many travelers, and it's a good idea to carry a supply of this or something similar in your toiletry kit. You might want to put a few tablets in with your fishing tackle (you might do this for bandages and aspirin/ibuprofen, too). Don't wait too long to take remedial action, as you risk making the fishing uncomfortable as well as becoming dehydrated and invoking other medical concerns.

No garbage or fires. One of the things that makes remote fishing an enjoyable experience is the fact that relatively few others are able to do the same thing and visit the distant and (usually) pristine places that offer good fishing. Therefore, every effort should be made not to despoil these areas. There is no excuse for allowing garbage to fly out of the boat or for not properly disposing of refuse, including bottles, cans, old fishing line, etc. Pick up after yourself and encourage the guide to do likewise. Be attentive to fire concerns, especially in the wilderness; make sure that any fire is completely doused and that cigarettes and cigars are extinguished and then field-stripped. You don't want to be the cause of a forest fire. Finally, try to "tread lightly" in sensitive areas.

Be patient. Bring some patience and understanding with you. Be aware that no one can control the weather or unforeseen difficulties, such as a plane breaking down. In some far northern locales, floatplanes arrive or depart late because of a complicated chain of events; you may get fogged in at camp or at an airport, and you may have to stay somewhere for an extra day(s). Things don't always happen as planned, so leave time in your itinerary, be flexible, and maintain a good spirit. It will all work out eventually.

Canadian Issues

The stereotypical view of a Canadian wilderness fishing experience is more or less like this: postcard-quality scenery; dark, clean water; fragrant Jackie and birch; a rich and spongy undergrowth; deep-blue skies with marvelous cloud patterns; a star-studded night sky like what you'd see at a planetarium; possibly a view of the *aurora borealis;* maybe a loon, moose, or bald eagle sighting; maybe the discovery of old Indian camp ruins; fish that practically flop from the water into the frying pan; and fast angling action, big fish, not-too-sophisticated techniques.

There are 10 known living fossils in the world; 2 are fish: the Australian lungfish and the coelacanth, a deep dweller found off eastern Africa.

Of course, the fish are not everywhere in Canada. And they're not always easy. Some of Canada's good fishing waters actually have cottages on them. Some virgin-looking lakes have previously been netted. Even in remote Canada, the inhabitants have discovered propane stoves, fast food, and satellite television. When the fish do flop into the shore lunch frying pan, they land too often in a pound of artery-hardening lard. And it's a fact that beautiful secluded places can be hazardous or hostile when misfortune or bad weather occurs.

But if the fishing wasn't good for the most part, hundreds of thousands of anglers wouldn't be visiting the land of the maple leaf every year. The main focus of this attention throughout central Canada is northern pike, lake trout, and walleye. On the west coast, Pacific salmon and steelhead draw many people to British Columbia; back east, trout and Atlantic salmon hold sway. There is some fine but geographically limited fishing for bass and muskie, as well as grayling and charr, but it is fair to say that the greatest overall interest by far is for pike, walleye, lake trout, and Pacific salmon, so some specific information about planning to tackle these species will follow after these general observations.

Trophies versus action. Anglers want to visit a good lodge, fish in an attractive place, and have lots of action, but you can bet that they also want a chance to catch a trophy fish. Don't believe all the stories you hear about 20-pound Canadian fish. Who know what makes anglers stretch 15-pounders into 20-pounders, but it happens a lot in regard to Canada's plentiful pike and lake trout resources. Twenty is a magic number, and, to hear some returning anglers tell it, they caught that size pike or lake trout until their arms fell off.

While stupendous fishing does happen from time to time, be wary of so many grand claims. On the other hand, you could follow one pundit's whimsical assessment of this situation by deducting 25 percent from the size and number of the stated catch; hooking a lot of 15-pounders, by that standard, is still some mighty fine fishing. Indeed, simply having a lot of action is exciting.

Size notwithstanding, you simply cannot do as well in the states for northern pike or lake trout as in Canada. You cannot find consistently fast pike action in most of the United States, and trophy pike are increasingly rare. In the states, a 15-pound pike or lake trout is a darned good fish, but not one found regularly or with much certainty. Not so in these provinces.

Pike are as plentiful in Saskatchewan, Manitoba, and Ontario waters as bluegills are in American lakes. In many of the former, you can count on having lots of action, and in some of the more conservation-oriented waters you can catch and release your personal best. Any cast could do it. It is primarily this attraction, this abundance of riches, that brings anglers north.

The pursuit of trophy fish is an obsession for some anglers, but a steady dose of action is usually what turns on people the most. When you get into that kind of pike fishing, there are many thrills to enjoy: sudden strikes near the boat, fish that you see but that don't strike, fish that you can stalk, fish on odd lures, and opportunities to experiment with different tackle (the popularity of light spinning gear and fly tackle for pike has grown). If ever there was a cast-and-retrieve angler's fish, a pike is it.

The lake trout game is a bit different, however. Casting is a great deal of fun, but seldom the norm for these fish. You can cast for lakers with spoons, plugs, flies, and jigs early in the season, the time when lakers cruise shorelines and stack up below heavy-flowing tributaries to ambush suckers. You can cast around reefs at other times of the year, but seldom are the bigger fish caught this way. You can also jig for lakers through the year, but this doesn't seem to produce giants either. Trolling, therefore, makes up the majority of lake trout effort, whether fishing deep in midsummer, or shallow early and late in the season.

Whether you catch them by casting or trolling, Canadian lake trout are a different fish than their southern brethren. They have a fighting attitude. Southern lake trout are usually caught on heavy tackle at great depths; it's a tepid tussle. And in the Great Lakes, the fish are bleached-gray. To experience the other lake trout, you must go where there is perpetually cold water, brief summers, shallow angling, and old fish that are dark and richly vermiculated. No one experiencing the vigorous fight of a large Canadian laker, or the tenacious battling of smaller northern-water lake trout, would dispute their sportiness or the enjoyability of catching them. But you have to experience it to believe it.

Where walleye are concerned, be advised that plenty of this species is available to catch across the heartland, but trophy specimens are not as abundant as they are proportionately for pike or lake trout. If size is your standard for walleye, then you'd better not go too deep into the bush. Yes, a big (7 to 9 pound) walleye can be had occasionally in some remote waters, but think more in terms of near-border waters and the Great Lakes if you want giants. Smaller walleye, however, are abundant in many interior lakes.

Timing. Interest in fishing for the various species at prime time is always immense. Heavy outfitter bookings for the opening of the season confirm the most popular time. Many anglers want to be first, or among the first, to visit a lake each season. And some regulars book the same early week year after year. These anglers feel that the fish are shallow and most accessible then because the fish have had a long winter's respite from lures and boats and motors, they are more vulnerable to deception (although some anglers book the first week because the bugs are not yet bad). For anglers of moderate ability or skill, this may be true. And no doubt some fish, especially pike, are abundant in the shallows early in the season and you stand the best chance then for continuous action.

But first isn't always best. Sometimes, early-season anglers outfox themselves when a tenacious winter causes a lake to be mostly frozen when the camp opens. Then, everyone fishes in the same limited area, even on a huge lake. You could do that at home. And yet, a lot depends upon your skills no matter what time of the season you visit.

If you want fast lake trout action, for example, but are ill-equipped or inexperienced at fishing deep for them in the middle of the summer, then you probably shouldn't be there at that time. A good lodge owner/manager will be honest about season-long prospects. Nevertheless, it's a fact that some people will have terrific fishing on a mid-season week, while other people will have poor success at the same place at the same time. That is not necessarily attributable to luck, although it could be attributable to the guide, if one is used. The bottom line: Don't assume the fish will jump into your boat.

Weather. No matter where you go or what species you pursue, weather *(see: weather)* can be a factor, and there is nothing that you, a guide, or an outfitter can do about it. Virtually all the photos in advertisements, magazines, brochures, and tourism literature show moderately dressed anglers in idyllic lake settings on bluebird days. But it doesn't always happen like this, a fact that lodge owners, writers, and veteran travelers take for granted, but many other folks don't. You could be stuck in camp for a day or two in midsummer because of horrendous weather. And even when you can fish, it may not always be pleasant. Don't underestimate how cold it can be in mid-July when the clouds roll in, the wind blows, and the surface temperature on the lake you're fishing is much lower than you'd have back home. If you're not prepared, the fishing will have to be awfully good for you to forget your discomfort.

In the far north, weather can change quickly and frequently. Many days start with bluebird skies and budding warmth, and turn wet, windy, and miserable a few hours later. While fishing in locales far from camp, and where big expanses of open water are encountered, be attentive to increasing wind speed and changes in direction, so you can head back before conditions get unsafe. Your guide, if you have one, should be attuned to this, but may not be. You should assume this responsibility if the guide doesn't.

When you can see white on the tops of a few waves, you've already lingered too long in a small boat. Put rain gear and/or flotation equipment on before making a run across wind-whipped water. The person sitting on the windward side of the boat and those in the stern will get the wettest from spray. If you have inadequate rain gear, it is possible to get completely soaked and frozen on an otherwise clear sunny day while running across a wind-whipped coldwater lake.

Clothing, rain gear. Dress for cold weather, and use the layered approach. You can always take off clothes to get cooler. Bring thermal underwear as a precaution, plus two pairs of thermal socks (one in case the first gets wet). Bring waterproof pack boots (or wear them to your destination to save weight and space). You may need them for warmth, for hiking to hotspots, for getting out of the boat in shallow water when you can't step right onshore, for keeping your feet dry when it rains, and/or when there is water in the bottom of your boat, etc. A pair of shin-high rubber boots might do as well. Check with your outfitter, booking agent, or lodge operator to see if hip or chest waders will be helpful or necessary, and if the water will be cold enough to justify insulated rubber or neoprene waders.

Bring rain gear that will meet the toughest tests (most rainwear failures occur at the jacket collar and in the crotch or lower back) for water repellency, comfort while fishing, and wind protection (warmth). Bring a suit, preferably one with bib overalls, and make sure it will fit over all other clothes. Carry that rain gear whenever you go fishing or when you go somewhere for a day trip. Few lodges or camps supply rain gear; although on the British Columbia coast, most camps provide their guests with rain suits and rubber footwear.

Bugs. One positive side to cold weather and wind is that it keeps bugs at bay. Canada has black flies and mosquitoes like the ocean has salt. Fortunately, in Canada the wind is usually blowing, warm from the south and southwest till midsummer, and later cool from the northwest and north. As long as the wind is blowing and you're not in the lee, all will be well. It is back in camp, when someone has left the cabin door open for more than a nanosecond, that the invasion starts; when you get firmly tucked into bed or sleeping bag, visions of ferocious fish swirling in your mind, the critters divebomb your head. Be forewarned and prepared.

As a general rule, the fishing is best when the bugs bite the most. That may mean black flies in June in northern Manitoba or Saskatchewan, or mosquitoes in July in the Northwest Territories. Expect to have to deal with mosquitoes or flies, and be happy if they are not present or are less of a nuisance than you expected.

Keep insect repellent *(see: repellents)* handy at all times, from the moment you deplane at a distant airport to the moment you leave for a scheduled flight back home. If heavy concentrations of mosquitoes and/or black flies are a possibility, you might want to tote a headnet and bug jacket. Remember that some bugs will bite through a light shirt, so simply covering exposed flesh may not be enough. You can douse your clothes with repellent (although this could be harmful to the material), wear a treated bug jacket, or you can wear a light windbreaker that doubles as a rain jacket.

If you are allergic to bug bites, bring appropriate medication with you and advise your companions and outfitter.

Catch-and-release. Anglers with mostly meat on their minds have become increasingly less welcome in most of the Canadian provinces and territories. In the southern part of all of the provinces, drive-in access has resulted in extraordinary fishing pressure. The existence of more logging roads has meant access to places few could previously reach in the summer, and these sites have been hammered.

Overfishing is one of the reasons why travelers who can forgo the convenience of having their own boat will journey to fly-in locations, whether main lodge or outpost, to be assured of a Canadian experience that more closely resembles the stereotype. Such places have a growing emphasis on catch-and- release *(see)*, including trophy specimens (though small fish for your lunch can be kept); they also emphasize using barbless or de-barbed hooks, using single-hooked lures, and fishing without bait in order to minimize injuries to fish.

What is making this accepted policy are new owners, new customers, and a quality resource. Younger and progressive owners have stepped in at many lodges across Canada, especially in Manitoba, Saskatchewan, and Ontario. They have refurbished or newly built deluxe or near-deluxe accommodations and have made an enormous investment in the resource, most of which they have exclusive access to. Aside from offering a good service, they must sink or swim with that resource, which they, and most of their customers, recognize is finite. It used to be thought that the number and the size of fish that could be kept were unlimited, even in lightly angled wilderness waters, and that fishing pressure wasn't harmful. Now we know better.

Although resource-protection changes have met with resistance from a few anglers, these measures have been well received by most conservation-oriented visitors. Considering the cost of such trips, no amount of killing fish, trophies or otherwise, would be of comparable worth, so quality of experience becomes the real issue. The quality of experience is surely enhanced where there is enjoyable fishing opportunity.

Hot lure pattern. Certainly many different types of lures and color patterns catch Canadian fish. For pike and lake trout in far northern waters, however, you'd be remiss not to have a Five of Diamonds pattern spoon, which has been called the Lure of the North. It is arguably responsible for catching more modern-era Maple Leaf trout and pike than any other lure. So respected is it that you need but say the words and anyone who knows north country fishing is on your wavelength.

Although people speak about the Five of Diamonds as if it were a lure, it is really a pattern: five red diamond-shaped marks on a yellow background. In recent years, this pattern has become increasingly better known and more popular. In any article about fishing in the north, especially about lake trout, the Five of Diamonds is almost always the first lure mentioned. The effectiveness of this lure may be due to the fact that many far north waters are tannin-stained; this pattern shows up especially well in such water and in the depths of clearer water. The key to effectiveness could be the ratio of red to yellow on the lure, combined with a brass back; this pattern is not nearly as effective with a nickel back.

Guides and lodge managers can attest to the effectiveness of the Five of Diamonds, whether cast in its weedless mode for pike or trolled in dessert-plate-size versions for lake trout. It is heavily stocked and touted at camps and lodges, and many people say that if you had to bet the farm on one lure pattern to catch a fish, especially a lake trout, this is it. You can modify single-color lures and put the Five of Diamonds pattern on them with a waterproof marking pen. Keep in mind that using these colors or this pattern is in itself not a miracle solution. You still have to use a spoon with the right action, and you still have to troll or retrieve it in the proper manner.

Lake trout. Some anglers have no interest in going anywhere to fish for lake trout, even in the deep, remote, and fish-abundant waters of northern Canada. They don't like trolling; they don't want to endure long boat rides in small aluminum boats; and they have no appreciation for a fish that is known to be a deep-dweller and reputedly a sluggish fighter. But there are still plenty of anglers who prefer lake trout to Canada's other main attractions and who make a trip to one or more distant locales every year or two.

It is true that most Canadian lake trout fishing is trolling, but not all of it; many fish, including some over 30 pounds, can be caught by casting or jigging in the right circumstances. It is not true that these fish are sluggish. They can be sluggish if they are small and caught on heavy gear from deep water, but a lot of Canadian lake trout fishing is done in the upper 30 feet of water and these fish are scrappy. The smaller ones, which sometimes thrash and roll wildly near the boat, can be a spunky nuisance. And more than one angler, fishing in prime waters, has hooked and played a tenacious and drag-pulling laker for an hour or more, sometimes catching the monster, sometimes not.

In those far north places where the water stays cold all season, you can catch lake trout in the upper strata all year long. In places that warm up in the summer and where the surface water reaches the 60s, the trout will positively go deep. If you expect to fish shallow and use light tackle, and you arrive in the middle of the season, then you'll probably be disappointed.

The busiest time for most lake trout lodges is the first few weeks of the season. Camps are usually full. Most bookings are made 8 to 12 months in advance, prior to knowing what the winter will serve up. A severe winter and/or a long cold spring will delay ice out and possibly limit the places where you can fish if you're scheduled for a lodge on the first or second

Of the major oceans, the North Atlantic is the saltiest, averaging 37.8 parts per thousand of salinity; the Sargasso Sea is the saltiest part of that ocean.

Alberta's Bow River, one of North America's great rainbow trout waters, was stocked with these fish accidentally in 1905 because a fisheries wagon bound for Banff broke down.

week. But many anglers take that chance. Right after ice out, and for the first few weeks of the season while the thaw continues and lakes remain cold, is the best time for light-tackle fishing and shallow trolling. It's a good time for catching big trout, as well as many trout. It's also a good time for casting plugs, spoons, flies, and jigs around reefs, at tributaries (a big fish hotspot), and along shorelines. As the season progresses, casting becomes less practical in lakes, and trolling the norm. Don't overlook late in the season when some of the heaviest fish are caught. Not all lodges stay open late in August or into September, because of hostile weather and airplane delays, but those who do, cater to knowledgeable, hearty anglers searching for trophy fish.

The better lake trout angling is usually found in the upper half or upper third of the southern provinces, as well as throughout the Northwest Territories. Northern Manitoba and northern Saskatchewan provide some of the best opportunities for big fish, but the tundra waters of eastern and central Northwest Territories, as well as Victoria Island, are equally notable.

In the far north, rivers offer exciting lake trout fishing by casting but seldom are the fish big; however, larger fish will prowl the turbulent inlet. In lakes, trout are often structure oriented, and they migrate to reefs, shoals, and islands to feed. They also cruise the shorelines. In lakes that warm up and create a thermocline, lakers will go to cool water below the thermocline in large open-water bowls. This is where their primary food, ciscoes and other lake trout, is found.

Most veteran Canadian lake trout trollers use stout rods and 20-pound (minimum) line and large spoons (sometimes plugs). Big trout can be caught, however, on lighter tackle, including 12-pound line and conventional baitcasting tackle. In some places you can catch small trout on streamers, dry flies, and light spinning tackle with small spoons, spinners, and plugs.

The old standard technique in the far north is flatline trolling with a big spoon that gets down 20 to 25 feet when trolled behind about 120 feet of line. When fish are shallow or relatively near the surface, flatline trolling with various spoons and plugs is effective. When they're deep, you can use a diving in-line planer, weighted line, wire line, or a downrigger (a minority of lodges have these) to get down, primarily with spoons (big flutter spoons work well).

Wherever you're headed, find out what kinds of boats and equipment are available. Bring portable sonar if it isn't provided. Ask how long you'll spend, on average, to get to the prime laker grounds (on some big lakes you spend hours every day just traveling). Check on the camp's conservation policy. Many of the best lake trout lodges have strict catch-and-release/single-barbless-hooks-only provisions; they'll probably have good fishing for years to come.

Northern pike. Many people love to fish Canada for northern pike but wouldn't spend five minutes fishing for lake trout, and vice versa. For the most part, pike fishing is a different situation.

Pike fishing is almost always a casting fishery rather than a trolling one. You seldom fish in big open-water areas, although you may have to cross large expanses of lake (which can sometimes be rough) to go from place to place. Pike fishing often takes you to some of the northern lakes prettier locations: weedy back bays, meandering marshes, nooks and crannies that no self-respecting lake trout would ever visit.

This kind of fishing has a more visual element to it. You see a lot of pike, whether they're cruising the shallows or chasing a lure. And, because the fish are pretty voracious, you sometimes get to see a cavernous mouth open and inhale your lure. It's an active game.

As with lake trout, you can have some great action early in the season, especially for lots of fish. When northern lakes melt, the shallow bays and backwaters are the first to open and warm up, and pike get into these places big-time, sometimes resting in water barely deep enough to cover their backs. You can do a lot of sight casting then. Weeds are sparse at best, and the water is ultraclear. You can also catch large fish, but since pike spawn in late winter or early spring, the big pike now are not as hefty as they will be later, and the real monsters seem to be elusive.

Good pike lakes usually have no bad time. Later in the season, when the weeds are thick, most pike will be off the shoreline and in the weeds, and sight fishing opportunities are greatly reduced. Pike will have been feeding well and many will have better girth.

Except for the Maritime provinces and British Columbia, all of Canada has pike fishing to enjoy. The bigger fish seem to come from the remote northern lakes in the heartland provinces of Manitoba, Saskatchewan, Ontario, and, to a lesser degree, northern Quebec.

The pike action is good in some of the bigger rivers and lakes within big river systems, but the majority of the best fishing is in lakes, especially big lakes and places that aren't readily accessible from roads.

Pike are an ambush fish and in many ways are like largemouth bass in their habitat preferences. They aren't fond of current, but they'll hide in eddies and backwaters on rivers. They like wood and vegetative cover, especially if it's thick, and they can be caught in that cover and induced out of it to chase a lure.

Pike fishing tackle is very similar to bass fishing tackle. You can use baitcasting, spinning, or fly gear, and an assortment of lures. Line needn't be ultra-heavy, but you should use a short wire leader or heavy monofilament shock leader in case you hook a big fish that gets the lure inside of its mouth, or crosses the line on its sharp teeth. Experienced anglers can use an 8-pound outfit for spinning and 12-pound for baitcasting, although some use heavier-duty gear.

Some of the better pike lures are large and thus require at least a medium-action rod for casting. Line capacity on reels is seldom an issue. Drags should function well, but they come into play only for big fish or when using light tackle. Weedless spoons tipped with a plastic trailer, super-shallow-running plugs, and spinnerbaits with bright-colored blades are top lures but jigs, buzzbaits, bucktail spinners, and plastic worms are also effective.

Cruising and casting shallow backwaters in the early part of the season is the best bet. Shallow-running snagless lures are a hot item then, and so are many flashy plugs. As the season progresses, weed cover grows and lakes warm. Pike move into deeper cover, and lure selection changes to items with more vibration, more color, and more flash for active fish, and to jigs and plastic worms for inactive fish. Deeper running lures (heavy spinnerbaits, bucktail spinners, and diving plugs) may be necessary. Move away from shorelines unless they're steep and have ambush cover along them; cast around the mouths of bays, points, and where there is a tributary. Pike can move into deep water if there is ample food, but they are seldom deliberately sought in deep open areas.

Be extremely careful when using multihooked lures for pike. Try to avoid them if possible, not only for the sake of the person handling and unhooking fish, but also for the sake of the fish. Barbless hooks are the way to go; better yet, replace trebles with appropriate single hooks for lures that will still work well in this fashion.

Pike are mean and tough looking, but they aren't invincible and shouldn't be manhandled. Don't grab them by the eyes or the gills, and don't keep them out of the water for long. On many of the better pike waters, lodges practice catch-and-release; with the great replica taxidermy available today, anglers have no good reason to keep these fish. Some of the better lodges use a fish cradle to immobilize pike in the water for safe unhooking and release.

Walleye. From big fish to lots of action, Canada's got whatever suits your walleye interests, and the best part is that you don't necessarily have to go to remote waters to find it. Sure some distant spots have some fine walleye angling, but seldom are the biggest fish found in those places. A 6-pounder, which is a good-size walleye, is pretty rare in most northern waters. But get closer to the border, and include such havens for 8- to 10-pound walleye as Lake of the Woods, Rainy Lake, the Detroit River, Lake Erie, the St. Lawrence River, and the Bay of Quinte on northeastern Lake Ontario, and you can see that the biggest fish may be the closest ones.

Lots of people fish walleye in near and far Canadian waters, from Labrador to Saskatchewan, and much of it is fish-on-your-own angling, either piloting a boat by yourself at a resort or towing your own fish-catching machine to the designated site. The entire gamut of walleye tackle and techniques is employed, with fishing ranging from difficult to find in hard-fished waters to cast-after-cast easy in some remote fly-in lakes. The latter usually also offer good pike fishing, so there's combo angling available.

A big rush in Canada starts when the spring walleye season opens, a time that varies by province and by district within provinces. Walleye have usually spawned by the time that the opener occurs, but not necessarily. The people rush subsides after the walleye disperse and migrate to summer grounds and become temporarily harder to locate. Fishing early in the season can mean enduring some fickle weather and having plenty of company for the walleye's attention, especially in the more popular and heavy publicized places. It's not so frenetic yet very enjoyable in June, but when school is out and summer vacations have started, popular walleye waters see a lot of traffic.

Big and small lakes and big and small rivers, of which there are plenty in southern Canada, provide ample angling opportunity. Quebec, Ontario, Manitoba, and Saskatchewan lead the field, particularly the mid to southern regions of those provinces. Some of the finest small-walleye waters have been hit hard over the years by increasing accessibility; for bigger fish, the largest lake and river systems hold the most promise. But smaller waters have more charm and interest, and walleye eat well no matter where they come from.

For most of the season, from late spring through summer and into fall, walleye are located on rock reefs, sandbars, points, weed edges, and the like. In big lakes, some walleye suspend in open water where there are schools of baitfish.

Tackle for Canadian walleye fishing is no different than that elsewhere. Spinning rods with a medium action and sensitive tip for detecting jig strikes are common, usually with 8-pound line. Longer rods are necessary for trolling, where baitcasting gear is preferable. Jigs, bottom-walking rigs, in-line spinners, and assorted minnow-style plugs are the mainstays.

Bait is especially important in using bottom-walking rigs and for tipping jigs, but it is illegal to bring bait into Canada. You have to buy what you need there; plan ahead and make sure that what you want will be available where you're headed or en route there.

Drifting, stillfishing, jigging, slip-bobbering, and various forms of trolling are employed as conditions warrant. Casting with plugs or spinners is possible in some remote places where the fish are stacked up and not terribly sophisticated, but that isn't the norm.

Walleye are called pickerel in many parts of Canada and usually referenced that way in fishing regulations literature. But everyone knows what you're talking about when you say "walleye." People who keep walleye and return to the United States with them should check those regulations and be sure that their fish are readily identifiable as walleye to anyone who checks (that may mean leaving some skin on a fillet). Remember that in Canada you can fish only with one rod per angler, not two, no matter where or how you pursue walleye.

TRAVEL ROD

A multi-piece fishing rod whose sections are of small enough length to be packed inside a protective tube and easily transported for travel purposes, especially airline travel. Travel rods are usually three- or four-piece models whose individual sections are of equal length, and may be from 18 to 24 inches long; some models, especially pack rods meant for campers, may have more sections of shorter length, and others may be just two sections, which include a telescoping butt.

The purpose of a travel rod is to make the transportation of a rod for fishing practical in situations where longer rods can be problematic. They are especially designed for international travel via air. Longer rods, especially one-piece 6- and 7-footers, would have to be secured in a rigid and heavy tube of appropriate length, which provides ample protection but which becomes checked baggage and is subject to loss. When travel is to distant and obscure places, losing fishing rods can ruin a trip, so some anglers hand-carry one or more travel rods in a tube aboard an airplane, either as a backup in case their other rods are lost, or as the sole fishing implements.

Although some multi-piece travel rods are of mediocre fishability, high-end three- and four-piece travel products are eminently fishable. These can be found in 6- to 9-foot spinning, baitcasting, and flycasting versions, and are the equal of similar one- or two-piece rods in performance. The majority of these travel rods are fly models; spinning models are fairly common, but only a few baitcasting travel rods exist, in part because many baitcasters tend to use numerous rods while fishing.

Standard two-piece fly rods, which can be stowed into 44- to 50-inch tubes, are often carried onboard airplanes by traveling anglers, but these are not travel rods per se. They may be subject to luggage checking, but may also be permitted in the cabin; this may differ with airlines and also be dependent upon the storage capabilities of the specific plane.
See: Pack Rod; Rod, Fishing; Travel.

TREBLE HOOK

A hook with three points.
See: Hook.

TREVALLY

Trevally are members of the Carangidae family of jacks and are numerous in worldwide tropical, subtropical, and temperate oceans. Reportedly, more than 25 species of trevally inhabit Australian waters. Species of most importance to anglers include the giant trevally *(Caranx caranx ignobilis),* golden trevally *(Gnathanodon speciosus),* bigeye trevally *(Caranx caranx sexfasciatus),* silver trevally *(Pseudocaranx dentex),* and bluefin trevally *(Caranx caranx melampygus).* All are excellent sportfish whose strength, power, and stamina is esteemed, and their flesh is very good table fare.

Identification. All these trevally have moderately elongated and compressed bodies, deeply forked caudal fins, and pectoral fins that are long and sickle shaped (falcate). With the exception of the silver trevally, the soft dorsal and anal fins have a prominent anterior lobe. A row of scutes (varying from 25 to 38 in number) along the posterior section of the lateral line serves as a basis for identification. The anterior section of the lateral line has a pronounced upward curve. Of the aforementioned species, only the golden trevally has no teeth.

The silver trevally (also known as white trevally, silver bream, skippy, skipjack trevally, blurter, and ranger) has a black spot on the trailing margin of the operculum. Its body color shades from bluish green on the back to silvery yellow to silvery white on the belly.

Juvenile golden trevally are striped vertically (the first stripe is oblique and passes through the eye) and have a golden body coloring. As the fish matures, the stripes fade, and the gold changes to canary yellow, with a bluish tinge along the back. These colors also fade over time.

The giant trevally (also called turrum, ulua, and previously by the misnomer, lowly or lesser trevally) is identifiable by a small, oval patch of small scales within a larger scaleless area located on the breast immediately in front of the ventral fins. The breasts of other trevally are fully scaled. There is no opercular spot.

The bigeye trevally (also called turrum, ulua, and previously by the misnomer, giant or great trevally) has a body color that ranges from dusky above to silvery below, and eyes that are comparatively large. There is a black spot on the upper edge of the operculum. Its body is more elongated.

The back and flanks of the adult bluefin trevally (also called blue-spotted jack, starry jack, blue crevally, omilu, and bluefin kingfish) are a brilliant turquoise blue, silvery blue, or greenish blue, generously covered with small black or blue spots. The tail and other fins may be even more striking in color. The anal and dorsal fin lobes are often white tipped and the tail black edged.

Size. The silver trevally can grow to 15 kilograms, but specimens to 2 kilograms are the norm; the all-tackle world record is a 15.25-kilogram specimen caught in Japan in 1998. The golden

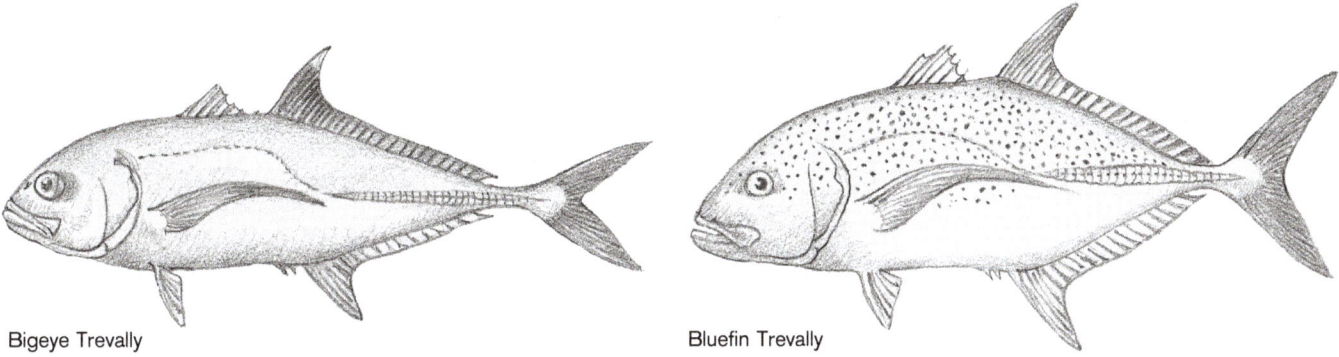

Bigeye Trevally

Bluefin Trevally

trevally can grow to a weight of 37 kilograms. The giant trevally is the largest of the species, growing to 65 kilograms. The bigeye trevally is generally smaller, with fish from 7 to 9 kilograms being large, although a record of more than 14 kilograms was established in the Seychelles. The bluefin trevally grows to at least 10 kilograms.

Distribution. Bigeye trevally range in the Indian and Pacific Oceans from east Africa to western America. Giant trevally are common in Hawaiian and Kenyan waters, and range from eastern Africa throughout the Philippines and to the Marquesas, as well as down to Australia and New Zealand. The bluefin trevally ranges from Japan and the Philippines south to Australia, west to eastern Africa, and east through Hawaii and to Baja, Mexico.

All of these species are encountered in Australia. There, silver trevally are found around the bottom half of Australia from Rockhampton in the east to the North West Cape in the west. The other species are mostly taken from subtropical to tropical waters from northern New South Wales in the east, across the top of Australia, to the central coast of Western Australia.

Habitat. Young silver trevally are found in estuaries, bays, and shallow offshore waters, whereas adults range from offshore waters around inshore reefs to the deep waters of the continental shelf. Giant, golden, and bigeye trevally are pursued near rocky headlands, in estuaries, around outer reefs and within tropical lagoons, and from ocean beaches; the bluefin is found in similar locations, in lagoons and outer reefs during the day, and in harbors, channels, and shallow reef areas in the evening.

Life history/Behavior. Little is known about the history or spawning behavior of the tropical species. Silver trevally spawn during the summer months, roughly from October through March, releasing their eggs in batches over a period of several weeks. Specimens in spawning condition have been found in both estuaries and offshore waters.

Food and feeding habits. All these trevally are carnivores. The golden trevally tends to prefer crabs and shellfish, whereas the bigeye, giant, and bluefin trevally prefer small fish but also eat crustaceans. The latter three species are often more active feeders at night. Silver trevally feed on crustaceans, small fish, worms, and mollusks at all times of the day or night.

Angling. Trevally are tough, powerful fish that fight tenaciously, characteristics that endear them to anglers. Baitfishing methods for the large tropical species depend on the use of live baits, or strip baits of mullet, garfish, pilchards, squid, and herring, and even prawns and worms (also fish liver if it can be kept on the hook). Hook sizes to 9/0 2X strong, and lines to 10 kilograms are in order, as are stout boat rods in the 6- to 10-kilogram class, and reels to match.

The smaller silver trevally feeds more on worms, prawns, and small shellfish but will not hesitate to take small fish baits. Hooks to 3/0 are usual, combined with lines to 7 kilograms on spinning or baitcasting gear.

Lures can be trolled along the edges of coral reefs or cast to surface-feeding fish. Feathered and plastic offshore trolling lures, metal spoons, plastic jigs, minnow-type plugs, and surface poppers will all interest the tropical trevally. Fly fishing, using up to 10-weight outfits, is popular for these species. Rock and surf anglers can choose between bait and lures.

The body shape of trevally gives them tremendous resistance in the water; this attribute, combined with powerful muscles, has an effect of sheer strength that can humble the most confident of anglers. Add to this their disconcerting habit of heading for the nearest reef in an effort to cut the line, and these characteristics quickly earn the respect of all trevally anglers. It's best not to exert too much pressure on a hooked fish; gentler tactics tend to contain the fish to the upper layers, where

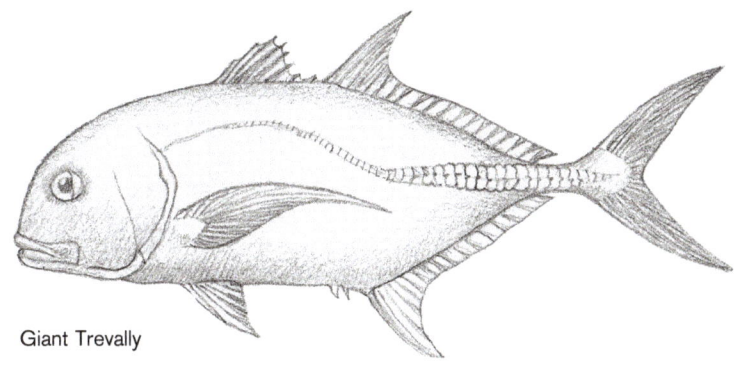

Giant Trevally

A giant trevally from the Arafura Sea near the Cobourg Peninsula, Australia.

it can be handled without the worry of underwater obstructions.

TRIGGER

A lever that permits one-handed disengagement of reel gears or opening of a spinning reel bail. On spincasting reels, a trigger performs the same function as a pushbutton, although it is used on a product that mounts underneath the rod instead of on top of it. On spinning reels, a trigger is an automatic bail opening mechanism. On baitcasting reels the finger grip located on the back of the handle is known as a "trigger grip."

See: Baitcasting Tackle; Spincasting Tackle; Spinning Tackle.

TRIGGERFISH

Triggerfish are members of the Balistidae family, which includes 40 species in 11 genera that inhabit coral reefs in the Atlantic, Indian, and Pacific Oceans. They are more common to divers than to anglers, although some are occasionally caught incidentally.

These fish have compressed bodies, and the stout first spine of the dorsal fin is locked into place when erect by the much shorter second dorsal spine, which slides forward. The long first spine can be lowered again only by sliding the second spine back. This can be done by depressing the third spine—the "trigger"—which is attached by a bony base to the second spine. By erecting the first spine and locking it in place, triggerfish can lodge themselves immovably in crevices.

The second dorsal and the anal fins are the same size and shape. Pelvic fins are lacking, and the belly has a sharp-edged outline, with its greatest depth just in front of the anal fin. Triggerfish are covered with an armor of bony plates. Their leathery skin lacks the slime or mucus usually found on fish, and they are capable of rotating each eyeball independently. They normally swim by undulating their second dorsal and anal fins but will use their tail for rapid bursts.

The queen triggerfish *(Balistes vetula)* occurs in warm western Atlantic waters northward to the Carolinas and also in the Caribbean, as well as in the western Atlantic from Ascension and Cape Verde Islands and the Azores south to Angola. It usually travels alone or in pairs but is occasionally seen in small groups. It has been caught to 12 pounds. Although its color varies considerably with its background, the queen triggerfish always has an iridescent bluish purple stripe circling the mouth and extending back on each side to beneath the pectoral fin. A second stripe crosses the snout and runs along the cheeks to the base of the pectoral fin. The base of the caudal fin is also bluish purple. The back is generally greenish, whereas the throat and belly are orange. The front of the dorsal fin and both lobes of the caudal fin are elongated.

The gray triggerfish *(B. capriscus)* is widely distributed in the warm Atlantic, Gulf of Mexico, and Mediterranean, ranging farther north than most triggerfish. It has been caught at more than 13 pounds. In the open water it is a dull gray color, but when swimming near seaweeds or over rocks it is usually mottled.

The ocean triggerfish *(Canthidermis sufflamen)* may also weigh more than 13 pounds and is found off the Florida coasts and in the Caribbean. It is dark brown to gray, with black spots at the base of the caudal fin. Like some other triggerfish, it emits noises, made either by grinding its pharyngeal teeth or by vibrating the muscles attached to the swim bladder.

Triggerfish can be eaten, but they have been associated with poisoning.

Queen Triggerfish

TRIM TABS

Small platelike devices on the port and starboard sides of the lower transom that adjust a boat's attitude when operated at planing speeds, producing a more stable and comfortable ride. Trim tabs, which operate like the wing flaps on an airplane, once were solely used for correcting hull performance deficiencies that caused porpoising, a rhythmic and uncomfortable rise and fall of the bow while underway at planing speed. The usual cause was too much fore-and-aft rocker in the bottom; trim tabs provided enough adjustable "hook" to correct or offset that.

Now they are commonly used on otherwise good-running boats for several reasons. Perhaps most importantly, they can control a boat's fore-and-aft, as well as side-to-side, attitude. This means lowering the bow in choppy seas to soften the ride and preventing the tendency to lean into the wind (lowering the upwind gunwale, which often makes for a miserably wet ride). The upwind gunwale can actually be raised higher than the opposite gunwale for a pleasantly dry ride. Trim tabs also allow a boat to stay on plane at much lower speeds, and they improve fuel economy throughout most of the planing speed range.

Using remote-adjusting trim tabs in conjunction with the engine's power trim also improves overall performance. For example, trimming the lower unit all the way forward and setting the tabs in the full down position allows most planing hulls to stay on plane comfortably in rough seas at speeds as low as 12 mph. By comparison, without tabs and with the lower unit all the way forward, minimum planing speed would typically be 16 to 18 mph, producing a much rougher ride. While the difference in miles per hour may not sound great, maintaining 12 mph in a subplaning attitude (if it could be done at all) requires a great deal more horsepower and burns 30 to 60 percent more fuel as compared to holding the same speed while on plane.

Even in a relatively small chop a light boat without trim tabs would require significant forward lower unit trim to ride comfortably. And as the lower unit is trimmed forward, the propeller shaft is no longer in its attitude of maximum efficiency, which is horizontal (parallel to the surface of the water). Part of the propeller's thrust is then wasted on pushing the bow down into the water. If the boat has tabs, the lower unit can be left with the prop shaft in its most efficient position, while the tabs do the work of keeping the bow lower. So although there is a slight amount of drag from the tabs, this is more than offset by greater propeller efficiency.

Trim tabs come in manual and electric versions. The least costly are the manually adjusted models, depending upon size and materials. Their disadvantage is that the boat has to be stopped while adjustments are made, and often tools are required to do this. Electric remote-controlled tabs allow precise adjustment while on the fly. They're operated from the dashboard by a lever or buttons. The tabs are moved up and down via an electric motor.
See: Boat.

TRINIDAD AND TOBAGO
See: Lesser Antilles.

TRIPLETAIL *Lobotes surinamensis.*
Other names—Atlantic tripletail, brown tripletail, dusky tripletail, sleepfish, buoy fish, buoy bass, chobie, triplefin, flasher; Afrikaans: *driestert;* Bengali: *samudra koi;* French: *croupia roche;* Japanese: *matsudai;* Malay/Indonesian: *ikan tidur, kakapbato, pelayak, sekusong;* Portuguese: *furriel, prejereba;* Spanish: *dormilona.*

The tripletail gets its name from its second dorsal and anal fins, which extend far back on the body so that the fish appears to have three tails. A member of the Lobotidae family, it is an excellent food fish with white, sweet, flaky meat. There is relatively little commercial fishing for this species.

Identification. The tripletail is characterized by its rounded dorsal and anal fins, which reach backward along the caudal peduncle, giving the fish the appearance of having a three-lobed, or triple, tail. It has a deep, compressed body that resembles the body shape of the freshwater crappie, and it has a concave profile. The eyes are far forward on the snout, and the edge of the preopercle is strongly serrated.

Compared with other saltwater fish, tripletail probably most resemble grouper but lack teeth on the roof of the mouth. The color is drab, various shades of yellow brown to dark brown, with obscure spots and mottling on the sides.

Size/Age. The tripletail may reach a length of $3^1/_2$ feet and weigh as much as 50 pounds, although $1^1/_2$- to $2^1/_2$-foot lengths and weights of less than 20 pounds are more common. The all-tackle world record is for a 42-pound, 5-ounce fish taken off South Africa in 1989. The tripletail may live as long as 7 to 10 years.

Distribution. Inhabiting tropical and subtropical waters of all oceans, tripletail are found in the

Tripletail

western Atlantic from Massachusetts and Bermuda to Argentina. In the eastern Atlantic, they are found from Madeira to the Gulf of Guinea, as well as along the southern coasts of Europe and in South African waters. In the eastern Pacific they occur from Costa Rica to Peru, in the western Pacific from Japan to Fiji and Tuvalu.

Habitat. Tripletail occur in coastal waters and enter muddy estuaries, commonly in depths of up to 20 feet. There is some suggestion of a northerly and inshore migration into warm waters in the spring and summer.

Life history/Behavior. Although little is known about their spawning behavior, tripletail are believed to be sexually mature by the end of their first year. Spawning occurs in the spring and summer, and although some fish may move inshore to spawn, young tripletails have been found in estuaries and in patches of offshore sargassum. Tripletail swim or float on their side in the company of floating objects.

Food and feeding habits. Tripletail feed almost exclusively on other fish, such as herring, menhaden, and anchovies, as well as on eels and benthic crustaceans like shrimp, crabs, and squid.

Angling. Anglers usually catch tripletail around wrecks, buoys, and offshore pilings and markers from May through October. They are generally ignored, however, either because they are viewed as an oddity, or because anglers don't notice them. Ironically, this species, which looks like it would fight like a bath towel, is a strong and determined battler, one that light-tackle anglers really enjoy catching, and also one that leaps. A 10- or 15-pound tripletail is a handful on a fly rod or spinning rod with 8- or 10-pound line.

Most tripletail are caught by sight fishing. Anglers observe surface-floating specimens, often near weeds, and pitch bait to them. Shrimp works especially well. Small jigs, tipped with baits or equipped with a soft grub body, and streamer flies, also catch these fish, as do small plugs on occasion. Lures and flies should be worked near the surface, usually with a pausing, twitching motion.

Anglers sight cast around floating debris in open and unobstructed water, typically for isolated cruising fish, and also near shore in shallow water, and sometimes on bottom near cover. In Mississippi and other Gulf States, some anglers place pine trees in the bottom to attract fish, somewhat like a brushpile *(see)* in freshwater, and cast a live shrimp or fish toward these trees.

Tripletail usually are best netted rather than gaffed, as they have tough scales. Anglers should use gloves when handling this species, as their gill covers can cause painful cuts.

TROLLING

Trolling is a commonly practiced method of fishing in both freshwater and saltwater for a wide range of species. In simplest terms, it is a method of presenting a lure or bait behind a power-driven boat. In a general sense, it is especially popular in wide-open waters, where it is used for fish that are deep and/or nomadic and where there are few underwater obstructions.

Despite the fact that it is a widely used technique, trolling is underappreciated both in popular angling literature and among anglers who primarily cast for presentation rather than use a boat. There is an image problem associated with an activity in which the angler doesn't cast and retrieve, and in which unseen fish are attracted to, and hooked by, lures pulled by a moving boat—television producers say that the action lacks drama. In many quarters, a myth has long been perpetuated that trolling is easy or too effective or less sporting than other techniques.

Trolling is an important means of searching conscientiously for fish that anglers rarely see until they are brought to the side of a boat. Trolling appeals to anglers who want to know more about the fish that live in wide open water and about the environment they inhabit. Modern trolling attracts those who want to master the challenge of catching fish—especially big fish—that are often far out of the reach of people using other methods. Trolling with proper tackle can be as sporting and enjoyable as fishing by any other method.

Many anglers troll for some or most of their fish. Trolling is *the* way to catch trout and salmon on lakes and reservoirs; it is *the* method on some muskie waters. It is a valued technique for walleye, an overlooked method for black bass, and an important means of catching striped bass. In saltwater, trolling is a critical method for catching many pelagic species, especially billfish, and important for pursuing many inshore species, including kingfish, bluefish, and various jacks. There is plenty of science and drama involved, whether the quarry is blue marlin, chinook salmon, walleye, or dolphin.

Knowledgeable anglers know that trolling does not entail dragging any old lure or bait an indeterminate distance behind a boat at an unknown depth, in an unplanned fashion. Successful trollers must know exactly where their lures are and how those lures are acting, and they must make a calculated, determined effort to entice a fish. That means being able to do many things well, including rigging lines, reading sonar, setting lures, judging when to change lures or locations, knowing the proper speed at which to fish, and understanding how to manipulate a boat to effect the kind of presentation that attracts fish.

General methods. Trolling can be broken down into the following basic methods:

1. Fishing an object on an unweighted monofilament, braided, or fly line.

    This method, known as flatlining *(see),* is popular for relatively shallow fishing in freshwater and saltwater because the depth achieved is entirely dependent on the weight or diving ability of the object being trolled. To know how deep you're fishing, you must know the depth that object will attain given boat speed, line size, current, trolling-line length, etc. To avoid haphazard effort and sporadic success, you must learn to evaluate the depth that the trolled lures or baits actually attain.

High-speed surface flatlining is also practiced in some situations, primarily in saltwater for billfish. Here, lures are trolled quickly on top of the water or through the surface foam.

2. Fishing an object on a weighted line.

Fishing an object on a weighted line involves using a weight *(see)*—drail, split shot, keel, bell, bead chain, or other type of sinker—to get a lure or bait deeper than it could be presented unaided. The problem of knowing the actual depth being fished is the same as with unweighted lines.

3. Fishing an object behind a lead core or wire line.

Here, the weight of the line causes the object being trolled to sink. The depth of the lure or bait depends on how much line is let out. This can be a more precise method of fishing than flatlining when it is important to achieve a specific depth. To gauge distance, lead core line *(see)* is marked by different colors at intervals, and wire line *(see)* is usually marked with tape by anglers. Although stronger than nylon or braided line, lead core line is bulkier, and it dampens the fight of a fish. Wire, which has to be used on stout tackle, is subject to kinking, crimping, and spooling difficulties; although it transmits the actions of the fish well to the angler, wire line and the corresponding tackle also blunt the fight.

4. Fishing an object behind a diving planer.

A diving planer *(see)* is a device used on a fishing line for the purpose of getting lures deep without weight or other attachments. Because it pulls so hard when trolled, a diving planer is fished off a very stout rod and is used with fairly heavy line. Diving planers run deep on a relatively short line; the length of line trolled determines how deep the planer will dive. A planer releases when a fish strikes, so you don't have to fight it along with the fish; nevertheless, the planer may impede the fight and activity of the fish, and its size or presence may deter some fish from striking. You have to set the lure no more than 5 feet behind the planer in order to land a fish.

5. Fishing an object behind a releasable cannonball sinker.

This is a deep-trolling system traditionally used for Pacific salmon fishing. A large, cannonball-shaped sinker *(see: weight)* gets the line down deep; the sinker is released and

Flatline trolling for muskellunge on the French River, Ontario.

drops to the bottom when a fish strikes. You lose a lot of lead weight in this system, and you need stout, heavy tackle. Also, you don't often know the depth at which you're fishing when you're off the bottom. Present and future restrictions on lead usage and disposal may preclude this approach.

6. Fishing an object behind a downrigger.

A downrigger *(see)* takes the burden of getting a line to a specific depth away from the fishing line. A lure attached to your fishing line is placed in the water and set at the desired distance to run behind your boat. The fishing line is placed in the release attached to the downrigger cable; the release frees the line when a fish strikes, and the angler plays the fish unencumbered. This affords the most controlled-depth presentation possible, plus the use of lighter and more sporting tackle. It has relegated wire and lead core line to near-antique status among regular and accomplished trollers, except in places where the lake or ocean floor is full of rocks and radical changes in depth. Downrigger trolling originated on the Great Lakes for trout and salmon fishing; it spread inland for muskies, stripers, and walleye, then to saltwater for inshore and offshore fishing.

Trolling speed. Most anglers are unaware of the vital role that speed plays in trolling, which perhaps explains why trolling is such a hit-and-miss proposition for so many. Routinely successful trollers have a special understanding of the behavior of the fish they seek; of the size, color, and style of lure that appeals to those fish under various conditions; and of boat maneuvering techniques for proper presentation. They also have a keen awareness of how speed relates to these other elements. The better guides and charter boat captains have a sixth sense about speed; they intuitively know if they are at the right speed, or they rely on

Deep trollers fish for salmon in the coastal waters of northern British Columbia near Dundas Island.

an instrument to gauge it. Many anglers, however, fail to recognize that boat and lure speed (there can be a difference) is an integral aspect of trolling and that they must be attentive to it. No matter what kind of fish you troll for, or what tackle and type of boat you use, you'll get more out of your lures by paying close attention to the speed at which they are working.

The key point about trolling speed is not speed for speed's sake: You don't necessarily go fast because your quarry is accustomed to out-hustling its prey, or slow because the target species won't run down an object moving quickly. The correct speed is the one that gets the right action out of your lures *and* is correct for the fish you seek.

The swimming action of a lure, perhaps more than shape or color, causes fish to strike. If it didn't, anglers might as well troll treble-hooked pencils. Action is the key. It is determined by lure design and the speed with which the lure is pulled. Complexity arises when you consider all the variables that affect trolling speed and lure action, including current, waves, wind velocity and direction, type and weight of boat, power of the engine, type of lure, and so forth.

One of the greatest mistakes made by trollers is to fish at the same boat speed when heading into the wind as when moving with the wind. On an otherwise still body of water, you will obviously go faster with the wind than against it, assuming you never reposition the throttle. The same is true of current. As an example, suppose you maintain a boat speed of 2 miles per hour (mph) downstream and then turn upstream at the same throttle setting; depending on the strength of the current, you may head upstream at only 1 mph, make no headway at all, or lose ground. Add varying wave heights, and think about the effect they would have. These factors affect the way your lure works and may explain why, on a particular day, you catch fish trolling in one direction but not in the other.

Boat speed, however, must be compatible with the lures fished. Trolling lures are designed to be fished within a certain range of speeds; there is a particular speed at which each lure exhibits its maximum action. Some lures work tolerably at slow or fast speeds, some can sustain action in a wide range of speeds, and others have a narrow range of workability.

Plugs that don't wobble, don't have a natural swimming action, or don't track true, or that run on their sides, roll, or skip out of the water, either need to be tuned to work properly or are being run too slow or too fast. Spoons that lie flat as they're trolled, have a lazy wobble, hang more vertically than horizontally, or spin furiously, aren't working right. You may find that a spoon will swim perfectly at a certain boat speed, whereas a plug will hardly wobble at the same speed. The two should not be fished together.

Most trollers have experienced occasions when one rod out of several consistently caught fish while the others had no action. Maybe the lure on that rod was at the magic depth or had the hot color, so you put other lures of that color out and/or more lures at the same depth. But the one rod still outproduced the others. Often the reason is that the lure on the productive rod was perfectly matched to the speed of the boat and exhibited the action the fish wanted or that it most accurately mimicked the movement of prey. The other lures may not have been swimming correctly because the boat was going too slow or too fast.

Trollers should check the swimming action of every lure before it is put into the water, even a lure that they have recently fished successfully. Put the lure in the water, point the rod tip at the water or lower it into the water with the lure several feet behind the tip, and watch the lure swim at the boat's current speed. You can alter boat speed to get the lure to run well, but this might adversely affect the action of other lures that you already have out.

Focus on the speeds that work well for the lures in your boat. If you do a lot of trolling, it is an excellent idea to make up a lure speed chart. Use a tachometer, an electronic speedometer, an incremental indicator, or whatever reference device you have. Spend the time to run all of your different lures in the water beside the boat to determine their ideal speed, and observe the range of speed they will tolerate. It may not be fun, but that information will be valuable, especially when you want to mix lures or change boat speed.

Knowing the range of speed your lures will tolerate is very helpful when you want to find out which lure speed is preferred by fish on a given day. It is no accident that many fish are caught when boaters speed up or slow down and when they make turns. On a turn, the lure on the outside of the turn speeds up and the lure on the inside slows down, unless the turn is very long and gradual. These changes in lure behavior often trigger strikes and may indicate that your speed was previously incorrect for the lure to be successful or that you needed a change in speed to trigger a strike from a curious fish. Making frequent alterations in speed, either by decreasing or advancing the throttle or by turning, is a valuable tactic—but you'll need to know whether your lures will work properly at the different speeds.

Even though you may achieve the proper speed and action for a particular lure, that speed may be inappropriate for the fish you seek. Thus, you have to experiment with different lures and different trolling speeds. Effective trolling speed varies according to species and season. Few anglers have the problem of not being able to troll fast enough (except rowers and electric-motor trollers headed into a wind), but some encounter situations when they cannot troll slowly enough. Some boats simply cannot troll slowly enough even at the lowest throttle setting, particularly if they're headed downwind. A light boat with a moderate-size engine will troll faster than many larger, heavier boats with powerful stern-drives or inboards. Some large outboard motors will not run below 600 rpm and, on a moderate-size craft, will push that vessel along at a speed greater than is practical. Consider using an auxiliary motor (9.9 or 15 horsepower) if you have a big boat, or use a trolling plate *(see)*, which baffles the prop thrust and stymies forward propulsion, or a sea anchor *(see)*, a bag that is dragged alongside or behind the boat, to slow it down.

Boat speed. To determine boat speed, you need some reference point. A tachometer shows engine revolutions per minute (rpm). Although rmp is not a perfect gauge of boat speed, lacking

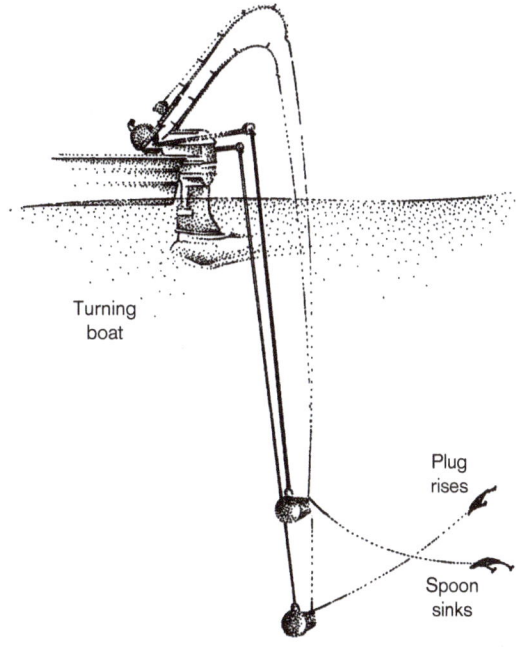

Turns are an important trolling maneuver because they change lure behavior and can trigger strikes. When a boat makes a sharp turn, a floating/diving plug rises momentarily in the water whereas a spoon sinks. Lures return to normal positions shortly afterward.

other references, you can use it to estimate speed when conditions are relatively calm. Stick with a certain setting if you're catching fish. You have to alter the rpm, however, when wind, waves, or current impedes your forward movement. If you're using a lure that has caught fish at a certain rpm setting, and if you encounter current or wind that is affecting your headway at that setting, run the lure alongside the boat and watch how it behaves. Increase the throttle until you get the lure to run perfectly; then note the new rpm and try to maintain it.

Small-boat trollers, including those with tiller steering, may not have a tachometer, so they have to guess at relative speeds or use some type of measuring device. Some boaters fashion a speed indicator by attaching one end of a 3-foot wire or heavy monofilament leader to a l-pound lead weight and the other end to an arrowlike indicator, which pivots along a plate that has incremental measuring units marked on it. The weight is dropped in the water, and the arrow points to a spot on the plate; the arrow's position changes as boat speed is altered. Commercially made speed indicators work similarly.

The units of measurement on these devices do not correlate to actual speed in miles per hour or knots, but simply to relative speed. When you put a lure in the water and get it to work properly, note the position of the arrow and run the boat at a speed that keeps it there.

Precise indications of knots or miles per hour are obtained by using relatively sophisticated, battery-operated electronic instruments. These sport paddlewheels are mounted on the transom; the paddle spins as the boat moves, relaying speed on a digital display. These units may read differently from each other, but they can be calibrated. Once you get accustomed to a particular unit, you'll learn to correlate what it reveals to fishing conditions. Another electronic device for calculating boat speed, and one with exceptional reliability and accuracy, is a GPS, which calculates distance moved over time and should be used in the fastest update mode.

The speed recorded on one boat may not be comparable with the speed recorded on another boat. You may be catching fish while motoring at 550 rpms, for example, yet friends in another boat are not catching anything despite the fact that their tachometer has the same reading. Or, you may be catching fish while traveling at 2.25 mph while someone else is catching fish at 2.50 mph using the same lures. Gauges do vary slightly, and boat speed is influenced by a host of factors, making exact speed comparisons between boats difficult.

How should you gauge speed if you don't have some type of indicating device? Become a rod-tip watcher when you flatline (this is a good flatline practice at all times because you can often tell whether your lure has picked up some debris that impedes its success). Listen carefully to the sound of your engine, and watch the action of your lures. Watch other anglers; come up alongside a boat that has recently caught a fish, duplicate the speed of the other boat, and then check your tachometer.

Lure speed. Most speedometers measure boat and lure speed at or near the surface. In many trolling situations, this speed will be the same, or nearly the same, as the speed of the lure at the level you are trolling. There are times, however, when surface speed has no relation to lure speed. If you have ever anchored your boat in a river and fished a lure on a fixed length of line behind the boat, you can readily appreciate this. This is how steelhead anglers work downriver with plugs; it is also how shad anglers use jigs or darts. The boat may be stationary, but the force of the current makes the lure swim. In effect, it's like trolling in place; the lure actually is going nowhere, but the speed of the current gives it action.

Imagine now that you are trolling upriver. The force of the current, in addition to the pressure of the forward movement of your boat, could be making your lure swim wildly instead of working naturally. How do you know? If the water is fairly shallow, you can watch your lure swim beside the boat and be fairly certain that it will swim the same when you drop it a little deeper. But in a deep river, or where there may be back currents or varying flow patterns, the lure may not swim at the same speed down deep as it does on the surface. What if you are trolling up a tidal river when the tide is coming in? Does that negate the force of the current, and if so, how does that affect your lure? If you are slow-trolling downriver when the tide is going out, it's conceivable that your lure might be hanging listlessly below your boat instead of swimming provocatively behind it.

These problems are not restricted to rivers and obvious current or tidal environments. There are currents in the ocean; there are also currents in open-water portions of the Great Lakes and in many large inland lakes. Few big-water anglers understand current's effect on lure presentation.

Current in lakes and reservoirs can be caused by tributaries entering the lake, by dam releases ("pulling water") or other outlets, and by wind and wave action. The presence of current may be obvious, but it is usually so subtle that a visual inspection of the surface and measurements of speed at that level give no indication of the presence of current. In some places, there is such a strong current at 50 feet or deeper that it is detectable by watching the action of downrigger weights and cables: With the boat at a slow speed heading into the current, the weights and cables sway back; going with the current, the weights and cables hang nearly vertically.

Below-surface or deep-water currents affect the speed and action of trolling lures. It is possible for a boat to be moving at 2 mph while the lure is acting as if it were running faster. You can troll all day, change colors over the entire spectral range, have no success whatsoever, and have no idea why. If you're flatlining under such circumstances, you may be able to detect the influence of current by watching your lines and rod tips, but most of the time this will not be an indicator. You can determine the presence of strong current by watching a downrigger, but even then you won't know how it is influencing your lures.

Electronic speed indicators can relay the speed of your lure or downrigger via sensors that attach to the downrigger cable above the weight and electrically transmit that speed to a readout. They also can indicate temperature at the depth of the sensor and at the water surface.

See: Backtrolling; Big-Game Fishing; Downrigger Fishing; Flatlining; Mooching.

TROLLING BOARD

A trolling board is a wooden or aluminum slat

that extends from gunwale to gunwale and either mounts onto a boat or, in smaller boats, slides under the rear handrails, and is used to hold various trolling accessories. Rod holders and mounting plates for downriggers are attached to the board so that down riggers can be readily detached from the board. On roomier boats, boards are easily acces-sible in the back, may also be fitted with sonar or speed indicators, and don't interfere with other types of fishing even when the board is permanently mounted. Most are homemade, although you can buy board installation systems.

On some small boats, the trolling board or downriggers might be mounted directly in front of the console. It's not bad for solo fishing, but the downrigger weights are close together due to the narrow beam of the boat, and this causes the fishing lines to be directly under the boat. When fishing near the surface, you may cut a line on the propeller if you turn too sharply.
See: Downrigger Fishing.

TROLLING JIG
See: Trolling Lures, Saltwater.

TROLLING LURES, SALTWATER
Most of the lures that are trolled in freshwater are also capable of being cast, and for this reason, there is no special category of freshwater trolling lures. Lures that can be trolled as well as cast, be that in freshwater or saltwater, are covered under their respective categories *(see: fly; jig; plug; spinner; spoon; trolling)*. The situation is different in salt-water, however, where there are many lures that are of use for trolling and which only have application for trolling. They are not designed to be cast, or jigged, or retrieved by some combination of rod movement and wrist action. They're too large, too hard-pulling, or too cumbersome for anything but trolling, and they often must be worked faster than would be prudent for any caster. The action they exhibit, the noise they produce, the water disturbance they make, and their passing resemblance to squid and flyingfish are important and intertwined elements— all of which are best accentuated when traveling at high rates of speed. Thus, special trolling lures have evolved for roaming the vast ocean expanses and, in some cases, for use with the heavier tackle that is often demanded for saltwater bruisers.

The category of saltwater trolling lures includes a number of distinctive items and some that are closely related or fished in conjunction with others. Teasers, for example, can be fished hookless as an attractor ahead of a hard-headed offshore lure or can be fished as lures when rigged with hooks. While teasers are primarily used as attention getting devices, similar to cowbells, flashers, and dodgers, which are all deep-trolling attractors *(see)* in freshwater, they are relatively

An offshore trolling lure is unhooked from a Pacific sailfish.

unique in fishing because they are only used in saltwater, only used on the surface, and only used for trolling.

Offshore lures, teasers, and feathers are essentially big-game products primarily targeted at pelagic species. Tubes, on the other hand, are an inshore trolling lure and about as unsophisticated as you can get.

Offshore Lures
Also called blue-water lures, big-game lures, and trolling lures, the category of saltwater trolling products known collectively as offshore lures are at the pinnacle of manufactured fish catchers and are specialized trolling items meant strictly for such dynamic offshore species as billfish, tuna, wahoo, and dolphin, usually at speeds that no other lure is capable of handling and under a wide range of sea conditions.

Offshore lures are fished either on the surface or under but fairly close to the surface, and though they look dazzling and sophisticated today, they evolved from fairly recent and humble origins. In part, their relatively recent evolvement is due to traditional and successful reliance on using live or dead natural baits for big-game species. Different types of dead bait have long been rigged for offshore trolling but these have always required brining, storing, freezing, thawing, and rigging, as well as repeated rerigging when the baits caught fish or were dragged to the point of no longer being serviceable. And, of course, if availability became a problem, or you used up your supply of bait while

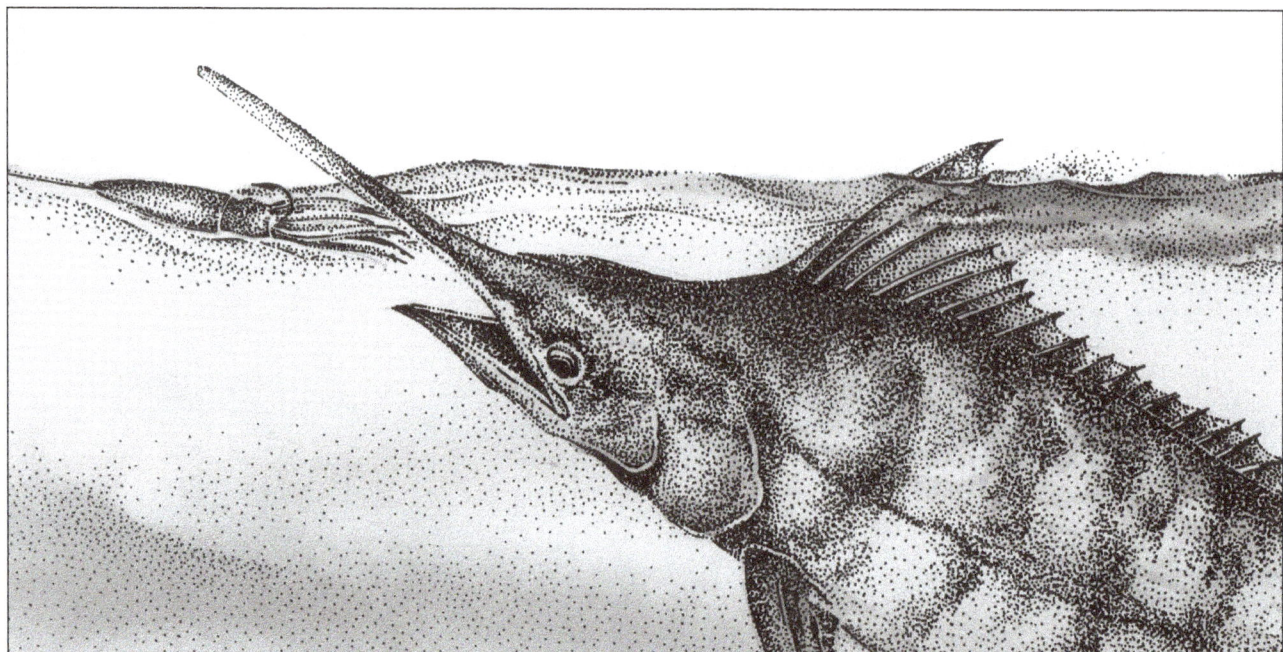

fishing offshore, then you had a dilemma. Artificials avoided these problems, required one-time rigging, and were always on call to catch fish; they offered a sensible substitute or option, and savvy anglers wisely broadened their outlook.

The earliest offshore lures were reportedly fashioned in the Pacific and their faces were either slanted or dished to provide maximum swimming action at the displacement speeds of the fishing boats of the time. The erratic pushing action of slant-faced lures and the darting actions of dish-faced lures swimming beneath the surface served to effectively attract attention at what were very slow trolling speeds by today's standards.

After World War II, when boat designs and more powerful marine engines allowed faster trolling speeds, lures were designed more to create commotion than to simulate swimming baitfish. "Smoking" bubble trails and occasional roostertails of water became the criteria for proper action, and trolling speeds increased to enhance the commotion of the lures. As sportfishing boats became faster and more sophisticated, anglers realized the value of covering as much blue water as possible during the fishing day, and modified their lures to work at faster speeds, resulting in flat-faced offshore versions. Broad, flat-faced lures that tracked straight at high speeds created impressive fish-attracting turbulence. Their intermittent but frequent trips to the surface to gulp air and create a solid bubble trail ("smoke"), along with an occasional roostertail, became favored actions for offshore trolling lures.

Then anglers started employing straight-running lures with concave faces (sometimes called chuggers), and slowed down a bit. The lure face here was not slanted, and the hole for the leader was still centered, but the scooped-out face provided bubble trails and roostertails over a wider range of speeds. The diameter of the concave head and the depth of the concavity determined the maximum speeds at which each lure performed best. Such lures that featured an up-front placement of the lead hook, combined with a short lure head, helped increase hookups and influenced future lure designs. Ever since, there has been a continuous refinement and hybridization of head styles, plus development of a potpourri of weights and a plethora of colors.

With increased use, anglers figured that if they could cover a great expanse of water at high trolling speeds, they might as well cover a still greater area by dragging lures while traveling to and from the fishing grounds. Doorknob-style lures (a patented shape with a narrowed neck, good high-speed tracking, and extreme turbulence) were designed to troll at the ultra-high cruising speeds of modern sportfishing boats, and anglers suddenly became aware of the incredible speeds at which blue marlin could spurt after a plastic meal. The weighted and aerodynamic offshore lures, when dragged far behind a speeding boat, resisted the tendency of more traditional shapes to "fly" and caught blue marlin at speeds from 10 to 20 knots.

A distinguishing characteristic of offshore lures is their ability and effectiveness—some would call it necessity—to be trolled at high speeds. High speeds in offshore fishing go way beyond the higher speeds that are used in most other forms of trolling, being on average in the 8 to 10 knots range, but on the low end starting at 5 knots and on the high end going into the upper teens (with some reports of offshore trolling lures catching fish up to 24 knots).

Despite the fact that offshore lures have proven effective for aggressive fish and in high-speed trolling, like any other lure, they are only effective when a combination of factors are at play; above all else, for a lure to be effective it has to "look right" in the water. The right look is a result of many variables, including the shape, weight, and color of the lure itself; the hull design and speed of the boat; the wake pattern of the boat; the position of the trolled lures behind the boat; and the sea conditions. Each can play a part in whether a marlin notices, and then strikes, a trolled plastic offering.

Types. Offshore lures consist for the most part of a weighted head and a synthetic tail or skirt. Most heads are made of durable hard plastic, and the skirts from soft plastic or vinyl. There are also soft-headed lures that are meant to feel more natural to a fish. There are a number of guidelines for choosing lures from among the plethora of head shapes and sizes available. Offshore lures can be divided into several categories, and each is designed to provide maximum visibility in a different manner and under different conditions.

In some cases, your choice depends on the habits of the species you're after. In the broadest sense, offshore lures either run on the surface or just beneath it. Surface runners create a silvery trail of bubbles (called "smoke") and produce a lot of surface commotion. They especially appeal to fish that strike from the side, like marlin. Underwater runners generally swim in a straight or near-straight manner, not far under the surface, and especially appeal to fish that strike from beneath, such as tuna or wahoo.

Some general rules of thumb can help reduce the amount of trial and error to achieve the right look. With surface lures, the desired effect is the densest possible stream of bubbles. The lure should make intermittent but frequent trips to the surface creating a solid bubble trail after each gulp of air, with an occasional roostertail of water pushed up by the lure on its forays to the surface. The lure should make a definite commotion.

Lures designed to stay continuously beneath the surface should swim fast enough to simulate a fast-swimming baitfish. Those with concave faces should be trolled fast enough to create a zigzagging, swimming action. It is their erratic, swimming action that is designed to attract attention, in addition to surface commotion and bubble trails.

At a given speed, most straight runners smoke more effectively when the angle between line and water is increased. Similarly, if they tend to fly at a given speed, or in rough seas, they are more likely to stay in the water if that angle is reduced. This can be accomplished by lowering the outrigger clip or outrigger tagline closer to water level, or in the case of flatlines, taglining them at the transom. This reduces the angle from that of simply trolling the line directly from the rod tip, and reduces the chafing of the line at the tiptop. When limited by a slow boat speed, action can be improved by bringing both flat and outrigger lures closer to the boat. This serves to increase the line-to-water angle and raise the head of the lure where it can gather more

Assorted offshore trolling lures.

air and produce more bubbling action. When seas are up, this effect can be reversed, and the lures kept from flying by letting them out farther from the boat. The reduced angle thus produced helps keep them in the water. Of course, in really rough seas, other options include switching to weighted lures, slowing the boat speed, and trolling the lures still farther back.

Although the different head faces of trolling lures get a lot of attention, this plus the length and weight contribute to performance. Some heads are short and some long, some are narrow and others wide. The face style is of special importance when the head is short; this contributes most to the action. When the head is long, the face style, plus the whole body design, contribute to the action. Weight may be added to any lures, and may be less necessary with heavier long-head lures.

Although they are described in various ways, there are basically four types of faces: cone, slanted, flat, and concave.

Cone-shaped faces are also called bullet faces and swimmers, and they have a narrow point to provide minimal water resistance. These run underwater and are usually weighted; they primarily run straight, but some versions swim from side to side. They are particularly effective when trolled short and flat, somewhat like teasers with hooks in them. They also serve well on boats that cannot get up to speeds normally considered minimal for artificial lure trolling. Swimmers tend to fly, however, and often become too active and erratic when trolled above 6 or 8 knots.

Slanted or angled faces provide a moderate amount of water resistance, less than flat models but more than cone-shaped faces. Although the angle of the slant can often vary widely from one brand to another, these lures track straight when trolled fast, and create quite a commotion in the water, moving up and down as well as diving. The roostertail raised by these lures is impressive, but you must be careful when setting out a full spread

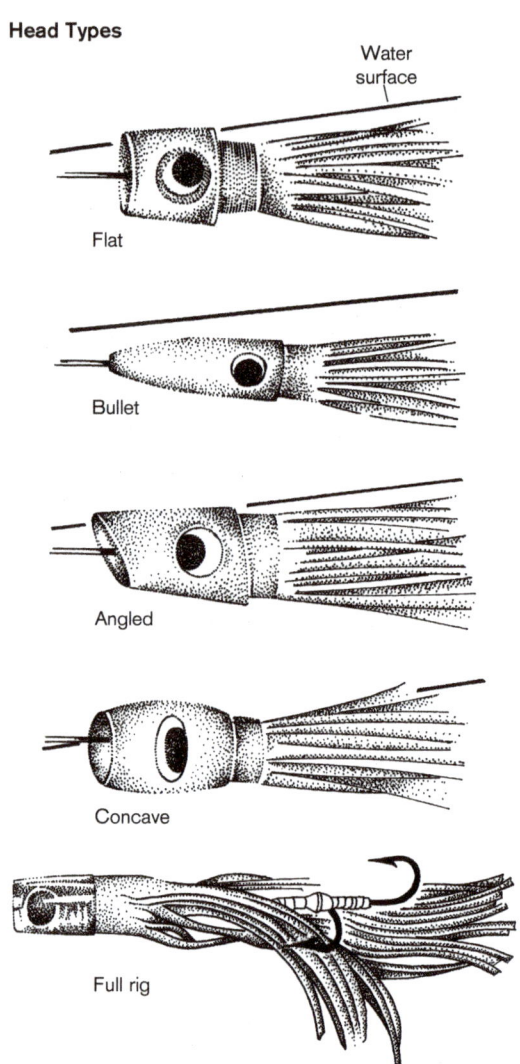

Head Types

of these. Slight differences in slant angle can result in markedly different actions from the lures in the spread. At a given trolling speed, the different lures in the spread may be tracking in dissimilar fashion, and when trolled too fast, slant-head lures tend to track erratically. This is sometimes rectified by arranging the two hooks 180 degrees from each other (rather than at the more traditional 90-degree-angle alignment), so that they act somewhat like a rudder or keel.

A flat-faced lure provides a lot of water resistance and a big bubble trail but without the motion of other lures. This style of surface lure handles a wide range of speeds, although it can fly out of the water in rough seas. Concave-faced lures, also called chuggers, track well and are designed for rough water; the cupped or dished face digs into the water so that it doesn't fly out. It pulls the water so well that it is also useful in calm or light sea conditions. Flat- and concave-faced straight runners bubble well at slower trolling speeds, and some models, which are hybrids with holes in the face and also called jets, are especially effective at both slow and fast speeds because their light weight, flat face, and holes serve to create long, sinewy smoke trails. Heavy lures with large-diameter concave faces troll best at slower speeds, while their flat-faced counterparts track well at considerably higher speeds. Concave-faced lures with small-diameter faces also track well at high speeds.

There are, of course, variations and hybrids of these that have created trolling lures that are hard to categorize. These include so-called jetheads and doorknobs, as well as shorter stubbier versions of conventional lures, and various designs with channels in them.

Size has become an aspect of change in modern trolling lures. Big lures in the 12-inch range used to be the norm, and they were fished off heavy tackle and from big boats, but the growth in small-boat offshore fishing and interest in lighter tackle has lead to many trolling lures that are suitable for use with 20- to 50-pound tackle, and which, perhaps most importantly, can be trolled more slowly. Smaller lures, including those from 6 to 9 inches in overall length, have been successful with various species, and have a greater tendency to be eaten rather than swatted.

Colors. The color scheme for offshore trolling lures varies widely and this is an area of much debate and little consensus among participants. Many offshore lure color preferences are regional, and sometimes based upon imprecise reasoning. When a particularly noteworthy blue marlin, for example, is caught on a particular color at a particular location, everyone in the area begins to troll the same lure and color thereafter. Because everyone is soon trolling the same color, it stands to reason that later catches are all made on that color lure. Soon, the word spreads that the particular color is the only one that produces in that area.

The compulsive use of green lures in the northeastern U.S., especially off New Jersey, is an excellent example of such a phenomenon, as perhaps may be the preference in Baja, Mexico, for green or orange and yellow. When the majority of anglers in an area predominantly troll one color, the majority of fish are caught on that color. Who's to say that another color combination might not produce just as well on any given day?

In Florida, the Bahamas, and much of the Caribbean, darker colors have been preferred in lure skirts. A majority of giant fish and tournament winners have been caught on combinations of black with (in approximate order of preference) purple, orange, dark blue, red, pink, and, especially in the northern Bahamas, green. All show a flash of light color beneath the predominant dark outside skirt, or consist of two dark shades. Some offbeat colors that have been favored by certain anglers include blue and white (or silver), pink and white, and blue over pink over yellow (which simulates dolphin).

Those few anglers who fish white marlin with lures instead of natural baits seem to prefer blue and white, as do the few Ecuadorian anglers who choose lures over giant ballyhoo for big black marlin.

This confusing potpourri does little to help the angler starting out. If you're on a limited budget, try a selection of darker colors, with a couple of light colors thrown in. You'll gather a personal list of preferred colors as soon as you catch some fish and get talking with other anglers.

Technique. The principal key to success with offshore lures is that they must "look right." They must create maximum visibility while still tracking straight and not flying, and to do this it may be necessary to make numerous adjustments when first setting them out. If you are new to the game, this requires some experimentation and experience to accomplish. There is a difference between looking good and looking perfect, and you really want them to be perfect. It's worth remembering that fish feed in certain ways and that their common foods behave in certain ways. Flyingfish, for example, exit the water sharply, and after gliding they dive back into the water and swim, but they don't skip. This is the action you want to imitate.

First, the boat speed must be adjusted to your choice of lures, or vice versa in the case of a boat with limited power, keeping in mind that you shouldn't mix lures that run best at different speeds. When the boat speed is limited by power or design or by sea conditions, the choice of lure design must be made accordingly. Flat- and slant-faced lures (with a shallow angle) have the widest range of application, while swimming lures are limited to slower trolling speeds. Concave straight runners work well over a broad range of boat speeds but tend to fly at the upper end or when seas are up. Weighted lures, pointy-headed styles, and doorknob styles can handle the highest speeds.

When seas are up, you must adjust, and your options include switching to weighted lures, slowing the boat speed and switching to lures that either swim erratically or create turbulence and smoke at slower speeds, or dropping the lures farther back behind the boat to keep them from flying.

In all cases, lures should ride the face of the wave for best action. Although there are many theories on placement, most pros prefer to set large lures out flat on the second to fourth wake wave behind the boat, and smaller lures on the fifth to seventh wave. Some put out a fifth line (called a "shotgun"), which is placed very short and center or very far back and center. Wherever you place them, make sure that they are getting the proper action. Many people new to this activity tend to troll at too slow a speed, and the lure action suffers. Remember that most offshore lures are designed to run best at 8 to 10 knots, and some even higher; 8 to 10 knots is generally considered an optimum range for marlin, tuna, and wahoo.

Because action, as well as a tendency to fly, increases when the angle of the line where it hits the water increases, many experts use a tagline on their flatlines. The angle of entry of the long lines can usually be lowered by running the outrigger tagline lower. Reducing this angle can also help prevent lures from flying out of the water in rough seas.

A tagline is nothing more than a heavy cord fixed either to the outrigger poles or to a cleat at the transom. Fixed, nonrelease clips or waxed line-ties are secured to the end of the cord. A rubber band (No. 64 is the preferred size) is wrapped at least five times around the fishing line, then the two end loops in the rubber band are snapped into the clip or secured to the waxed-line ties by a quick-release loop. When a fish strikes, the rubber band stretches considerably before breaking, providing some initial give, and helping to set the hook.

The size of the lure hook should be determined by the breaking strength of the line employed, and if possible, the distance between barb and shank should be greater than the diameter of the lure head. Remember that heavy, thick hooks require heavier strike drags and, hence, heavier line.

Most pros rig two hooks with artificial lures, connecting them with a variety of materials from heavy monofilament (usually snelled), to heavy wire or cable. Even the experts argue between using stiff rigs versus loose swinging "gaffer" rigs, but the beginner would do well to start with ready-made rigs. Many tackle shops sell pre-rigged lures, and that's a good way to start.

The second most important axiom for successful marlin fishing with artificial lures is paying close attention. When fishing offshore lures with tackle up to and including 50-pound-test class, the angler must set the hook and do so quickly. To accomplish this, he must be within a short step or

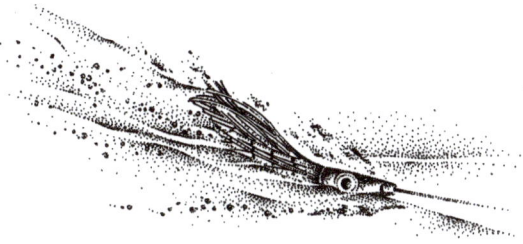

Offshore trolling lures are meant to create an attractive commotion on top of the water, as depicted here, just beneath the surface, or both, depending on design.

two of the rods and watching the lures at all times. Besides, it's more fun to see the fish approach and strike the lure. Although a good captain will hit the throttle the instant the rod bends and line begins to spill against the drag of the reel, the function of his action is simply to keep slack out of the line if the fish should charge toward the boat. With line of 50-pound test or less, this added momentum of the boat is not guaranteed to set the hooks for the inattentive angler. The angler must take the rod in hand and haul back hard and repeatedly to set the hook; failure to do so is the most frequent cause of "pulled hooks" and lost fish when using offshore lures, especially for big fish.

 Nile perch are the largest strictly freshwater gamefish; the best officially recorded on rod and reel was a 213-pounder, but this species reportedly is capable of attaining 500 pounds.

When fishing 80- to 130-pound-test tackle for marlin, the greater strike drag setting of the reel made possible by the heavier line does make it possible for the captain to set the hook by advancing the throttle. Although not foolproof, the inattentive heavy-tackle angler can count on a high degree of success as long as he has a capable and attentive helmsman.

Spread. There is a lot of discussion among big-game anglers about offshore trolling lure spreads. A commonly employed standard marlin spread is as follows: Two giant concave-face lures are fished flat and very close to the boat, within 30 to 40 feet behind the transom. These lines are rubber banded to taglines tied off at each corner of the transom. The outrigger-connected lines are either held directly by the outrigger clips, or taglined with rubber bands and trolled about 150 feet out, no farther from the boat than dead baits would be trolled. A fifth line is trolled either just behind the flat lines, dead center, or far away down the middle. The three farthest lures are either small teardrops or all-eyes with concave faces.

In all cases the lure distance from the boat is adjusted so that each lure rides on the face of one of the boat's wake waves. It's easy to tell when the placement is correct. The air gathering action is considerably greater when the placement is just right; you can see the difference as you let out or bring in the lure ever so slightly, seeking just the right spot on the wave. Here again, standard placement on this wave or that is nothing more than a guideline: flatlines on third and fourth, outrigger lures on fifth and sixth, and so on. What matters most is that the lures look right, that is, they are smoking maximally, tracking well, and not flying.

Once a spread is set and looks just right, it's best to resist the urge to keep changing things simply because no fish has risen immediately. Offshore trolling is a waiting game, and once you have confidence in the spread, stick with it. Troll up-sea, then down-sea, preferably with slight S-curve course variations. By not always trolling in dead-straight lines, you will alternately speed up and slow down the port and starboard lures. This slight alteration in lure speed is more natural than constant throttle changes, and often incites fish interest.

Soft Lures. It is reasonable to assume that a fish can distinguish between something the consistency of food it normally consumes and something that is the consistency of a chunk of granite, like the hard head of standard offshore trolling lures. Long ago, anglers made the reasonable assumption that if a billfish mouthed a soft lure once (like mouthing a natural bait), it might not be deterred from returning for a second try and chances for a hookup would increase, but that if the same fish mouthed a rock-hard acrylic lure, it was far less likely to try again. This assumption led to the creation of soft offshore lures, and their use has proven that many species, and especially billfish, do seem more inclined to try again when they hit and miss a soft lure.

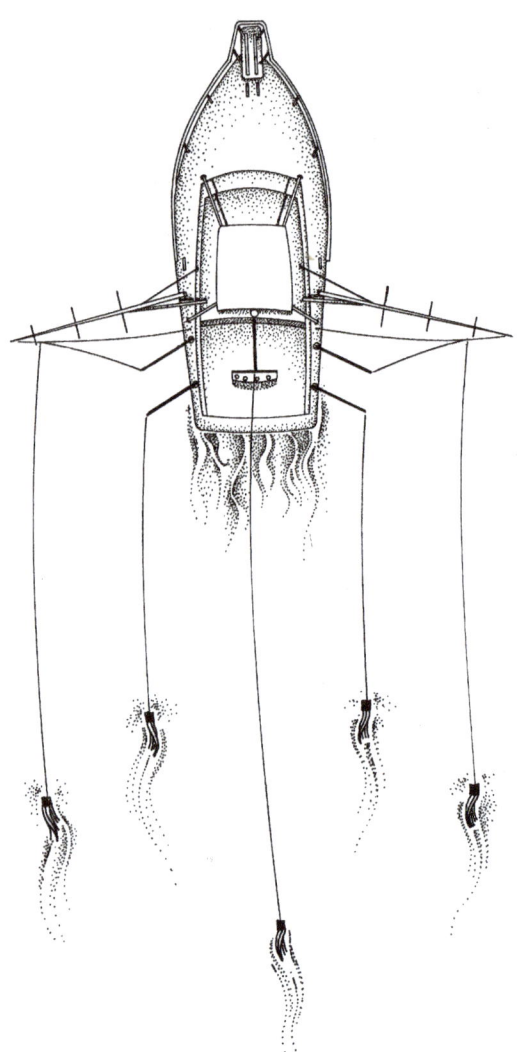

In a common spread for trolling offshore lures, the longest line is set down the middle off a rod placed in a holder on the flying bridge. The outrigger lines are about equal in length and deeper than the inside flatlines. The distance of lures relative to each other is proportionally greater than shown in this compressed depiction.

The use of soft trolling lures prompted anglers to use them in much the same way they fished rigged dead baits: freespooling the line the minute a fish strikes, then dropping the lure back as if it were a stunned baitfish before setting the hook. Now many anglers who use soft-headed offshore lures leave their rods in holders with the reels set at just enough drag to prevent line spilling from the pull of the lure being trolled through the water. Then, when a big fish strikes, it feels little or no tension on the "meal" it has just mouthed, and swims away with it. The angler has time to pull the rod from the holder and either adjust a stand-up harness or settle into a fighting chair before setting the hook. When the angler is ready, the drag lever is advanced to strike position, slack is quickly cranked back onto the reel, the rod tip is raised, and the hook is set hard. When done right, the technique delivers a high hookup percentage. There can be little doubt that this success is made possible in large measure by the more realistic feel of soft lures.

Because most soft lures are light in weight, they may tend to fly when trolled at high speeds or in particularly rough seas. The problem can usually be solved quite easily. When seas are up, simply reduce trolling speed until the lures track properly. This points out an important attribute of soft lures: They can be trolled a bit slower than hard, heavier lures and still create a splashing, bubbling commotion at the surface. Cup-faced (chugger-style) soft lures in particular smoke effectively at fuel efficient speeds as slow as 5 to 6 knots.

Feathers and trolling jigs. Known as trolling feathers, Japanese feathers, and feather jigs, the offshore lures commonly referred to as feathers are weighted trolling lures that can be fished hookless as single teasers or part of a daisy chain, or they can be run with hooks as a lure unto itself. The heads are either metal or plastic covering lead and the skirts are made of colorful feathers. Trolling feathers are perhaps the single most used type of offshore trolling lure, and are a key element in survival fishing packs. They are seldom used for really big gamefish, including billfish, because they don't travel right at the surface or make much of a surface commotion; rather, they are trolled for a variety of smaller species, such as dolphin, tunas, and wahoo, which often rise from the depths to feed just below the surface.

Feathers with a hook superficially resemble a jig, but they differ in that no hook is incorporated into the lure itself. They consist of a head, often weighted, in front of a binding over feathers as a skirt, all holed to allow the leader to pass through to rigged hooks, which nestle within the trailing end of the feathers. There are other lures that are similar to feathers, sporting soft plastic bodies and streamer-like skirts, and which are fished in a similar manner.

Feathers and similar lures differ in size and weight. They are trolled on or close to the surface, although the heavier versions run slightly deeper. Hookless heavy feathers are often fished in combination with a hooked natural bait, either a whole rigged bait or a strip. Those with heavily weighted heads are often slow-trolled deep or on wire line or downriggers for deep dwellers such as grouper.

Trolling jigs are lures with cone-, bullet-, or torpedo-head shapes, usually dressed with feather skirts or hooks, some of which have little or no practical value for vertical or deep jigging. They include cedar jigs and leadheads, and their single hook, which is part of the body or attached to it, may be adorned with a strip of pork rind or leathery fish flesh. A cedar jig is an old-time saltwater trolling lure made of rounded $3/4$-inch light or dark cedar about 4 to 5 inches long with a tapered lead head molded to it. A hole is drilled through the center of both and a leader is passed through the hole, then tied to a large hook, whose shank is drawn up into the hole. The lure may be fished in natural color or painted, and it is especially used for schools of small tuna, bonito, and albacore.

Both feathers and trolling jigs are smaller, on average, than other trolling lures, but move on and through the water easily and with an intrinsic action that appeals to some schooling species. They may also be effective at slower speeds when an angler works them occasionally with a quick, jerking rod action.

Teasers

Teasers are attractors designed to be trolled and create commotion in the water to attract gamefish to rigged baits or lures. Essentially, a teaser is a hookless lurelike device that is used ahead of a hooked lure or hooked baitfish, primarily while trolling. It's purpose is to draw the attention of fish by making a commotion in the water that imitates natural forage; it is followed by a lure or bait, rigged with one or more hooks, that may also look like the imitated forage (often a squid or flyingfish) or like a predator in pursuit. The following lure or bait is the item that is actually struck by the fish attracted to it and to the teaser, although there are times when the hookless teaser is struck first (which may or may not result in the fish striking a following hooked lure).

Teasers are essentially offshore fishing devices used (like offshore lures) for pelagic species, particularly billfish and, to a lesser extent, tuna. Tuna do not feed the same way as billfish, so they do not look at a teaser and than hang around to grab another lure. Similarly, dolphin and wahoo are species that use quickness and stealth to feed, so they are likely to attack a teaser but not likely to continue attacking the other lures in the trolled spread.

Remember that the ocean is vast and that it is usually necessary when roaming offshore waters to get your lures or baits noticed in order to be effective. No matter how big those lures or baits look to people, in the big water of the ocean, they are really small. The objective narrows to the task of making your offerings as visible as possible, especially from a distance. Visibility is the key to the trolling game, so the angler must do everything possible to draw attention to his small lures as they track across the boundless sea. That's what various types of teasers do.

It is well known that the vibrations produced by a boat in offshore waters—from the noise of the motor(s), the flash of the propeller(s), and the splashing sounds of the hull as it courses through the water—are considerable and attractive to fish. Likewise, the churning wake created by the boat's propellers attracts attention and raises saltwater gamefish. Whether or not fish confuse the frothy white water behind a boat at trolling speed for a school of baitfish is a debatable point. It seems clearer, however, that the more attention that is drawn to the area directly behind the moving boat, the more likely it will be that gamefish will find and strike the relatively small baits and lures that

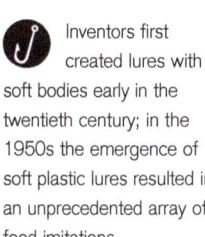

Inventors first created lures with soft bodies early in the twentieth century; in the 1950s the emergence of soft plastic lures resulted in an unprecedented array of food imitations.

are dragged there. Then, the action and appearance of the baits or lures can do their job of drawing a strike. So teasers are an important part of the attraction element of offshore fishing.

There are numerous kinds of commonly recognized teasers, made from assorted materials and in varied shapes; and although there are exceptions to all categorizations, in general such devices can be considered as one of several types: hard or soft conventional single teasers, trolling birds, and daisy chains. However, the entire category of lures known as teasers is rather broad and ill-defined. Some anglers refer to slender wooden popping plugs, for example, as teasers, and many items are used as a teaser when fished without a hook as well as a fish-catching lure when they have a hook. Conventional teasers are analogous to hard- and soft-headed offshore lures, which themselves can be used as teasers when run without a hook. Most devices that are used as both lures or teasers are best suited to heavier tackle because of the extreme tension they exert. The weight of water pressure on them as they swim or churn is considerable. When fishing light line, a teaser should be dragged separately, and strictly to draw attention to the other baits or lures behind your boat. And the lighter line can be directly attached to an appropriate size bait or lure. When fishing heavy tackle, a teaser can be employed with a lure or bait, or it can also be dragged separately.

Teasers can be employed at any time when trolling offshore. There's nothing to lose, and little doubt that anything you can add to your spread of hooked baits or lures that may attract gamefish is worth setting out. That teasers attract gamefish is born out by the fact that gamefish often attack the teaser first, proving that this device is what attracted their attention in the first place.

Single teasers. Fixed by heavy cord to a stern cleat, large single teasers crash and dive in the boat's wake directly behind the transom. There is little doubt that they effectively mimic a single large baitfish in apparent trouble.

These come in a wide array of sizes and shapes. The most common are simply large chunks of wood or plastic that dive and dart, occasionally rising to the surface to grab air and smoke a churning bubble trail in their wake. They may be nothing more than giant Kona head lures, or chuggers with broad faces, or they may be fancy affairs with air-grabbing holes drilled in their faces or flashing mirrors glued to their flanks.

Most single teasers were originally carved of wood and painted to resemble members of the tuna family. Now, molded bodies of plastic or hardened foam have replaced wood, but the effect is the same. The leading edges of these creations may be flat or scooped, holed or dished, depending on the amount of swimming or darting action desired. Those with dished faces can swing too widely if trolled at fast speeds, and may gather up the two flatlines trolled just behind them. Teasers with flat faces work well at higher speeds, while those with concave faces provide attractive turbulence even at slower trolling speeds. Both create sinewy bubble trails in addition to periodic roostertails when they rise to the surface.

You need only to inspect the teaser drawer of any busy sportfishing cruiser to find out if they work. Teasers that have been trolled for any length of time look like they've been through a threshing machine. Billfish leave broad scrapes from their filelike bills, while such toothy critters as wahoo or barracuda leave deep cuts and gashes from their attacks.

When such attacks occur, the trick is to move a hooked bait or lure into the vicinity of the teaser, while at the same time removing the hookless attractor from the spot. To facilitate this action, some people simply drag the teaser from a long heavy rod, rather than from a heavy cord fixed to a cleat. The fish's attention must be drawn away from the teaser and toward the bait with the hook in it. It's often not as difficult as it sounds. Indeed, the attacking or inspecting fish often will first strike the teaser, and then dart away and strike one of the other trolled offerings without any action on the part of the angler. The fish may simply be drawn within sight of the other baits or lures by the teaser itself, and, once in the spread, may decide to inspect each of them. To cover both situations, troll at least one flatlined lure or bait just behind the churning teaser.

If the fish doesn't attack the nearby lure, you can take matters into your own hands by reeling the hooked lure or bait to a position in front of the fish, diverting its attention. Then "feed" the fish the armed bait or lure, preferably with a rod-tip dropback when fishing lures. The rod-tip dropback is simply a maneuver in which the rod is held high above and behind the angler's head with a firm two-handed grip. When the fish grabs the bait or lure, the rod tip is instantly lowered to a position pointing at the fish, thus feeding the bait into his mouth. Then, the rod tip is immediately raised hard several times in a stabbing motion to set the hook. If the hook pulls free, the lure is rapidly reeled back to the surface and the procedure is repeated.

An alternative move, used more often with baits than with lures, is to raise the rod tip with the reel in freespool mode and the spool held firmly by the thumb. When the fish strikes, thumb tension is eased and the line is freespooled briefly to allow the fish to swallow the bait, taking care not to allow the spool to overrun and create a bird's nest. Then the reel is shifted back into gear, and when the line comes taut, the fish is struck by repeatedly and forcefully raising the rod tip.

Incidentally, bizarre makeshift teasers made from soda cans or plastic bottles have been improvised by clever anglers, and have done the job in emergency situations as effectively as expensive manufactured models. So it is not always neces-

---

Naturalist Louis Agassiz described and cataloged New Hampshire's silver trout in 1884; this fish was common in the early twentieth century but is thought to be extinct today.

sary to use manufactured and pre-rigged models, although they certainly look more dazzling than most improvisations.

It is also not always necessary to use artificials as single teasers. Using hookless natural baits as teasers, is nothing new. Single split-tail mullet and other baitfish, or strips cut from the shiny bellies of tuna or dolphin, have long been dragged in the wake of trollers. The manner of using them is usually to yank them away from an inspecting gamefish at the same instant that rigged baits, flies, or castable lures are presented. Attracted by the natural teaser and then subsequently angered by its sudden disappearance, the gamefish is more likely to cast caution to the wind and strike the new offering with reckless abandon. Such teasers are preferred to artificial ones in many parts of the world and are the teasers of choice for many fly anglers, although categorically speaking, they are not, in fact, lures.

For billfishing, a majority of today's experienced trollers favor soft teasers because the fish seem to hold onto them longer and are more likely to return to them because they feel like natural bait. While the objective is not to catch fish on these hookless teasers, the fact that they are soft is more likely to cause a fish that strikes one to return to take a hooked lure that is following in the spread. This is less of an issue with blue marlin, and more of one with white marlin and sailfish.

Teasers are usually attached to a flatline that is tied to the stern cleat; this is especially common on smaller boats. On larger boats, especially offshore charter boats, teasers are attached to lines that connect to reels mounted up on the bridge; this allows the captain to manipulate or retrieve them when necessary. Some of these are attached to electric reels or winches for fast retrieval; the line for these is run through glass eyes or locked-down release clips that are positioned low on the outriggers. Teasers can also be deployed via a rod and reel that is secured in a recessed gunwale or transom rod holder.

Large teasers are usually fixed close to the transom under the theory that they are easier to see in the frothy wake than smaller teasers, and that they are most likely to be the first thing that a billfish sees after it comes up to inspect a moving boat. This is especially so when trolling at fast speeds, such as 7 to 10 knots, for marlin. When fishing slower, smaller teasers can be fished close to the transom, and are more visible then because the area behind the boat is less disturbed.

Often billfish move away from the teaser and then inspect or strike one or more of the hooked lures that are pulled a few waves back. When they hit big teasers, the lures are pulled away from them by virtue of the motion of the boat or the action of the angler or mate, and this tends to make the fish mad and ready to pounce on the trailing lure.

Trolling birds. These are most commonly referred to simply as "birds," but they are in reality bird- or airplane-shaped trolling teasers. These

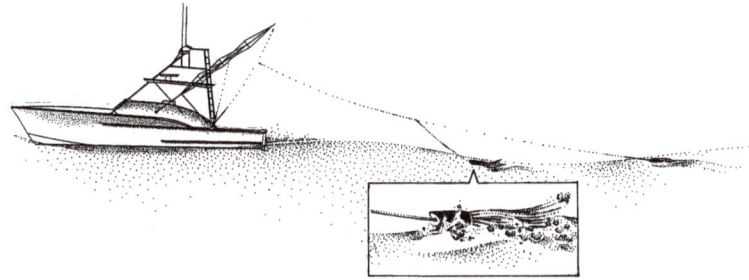

It's possible to run a commotion-making teaser ahead of a trolling lure as shown. The teaser (inset) is attached to a leader and snap, which in turn is connected to a snap swivel on the main line. The same connection is used for the trolling lure.

specialized teasers are designed to be used either in the conventional manner (dragged hookless behind the boat), or rigged in-line on the fishing line itself, and placed one leader length in front of the lure.

Developed originally by Japanese commercial tuna fishermen, and also called airplane teasers, birds gained rapid acceptance first among recreational tuna anglers and then among billfish anglers. Made of wood, hard plastic, or dense urethane foam, birds come in a variety of sizes for sportfishing, primarily from $4^1/_2$ to 13 inches long. They attract attention by creating a unique splashing action on the surface of the water with their fluttering and splashing "wings." In fact, birds produce more splashing, skittering, and spraying commotion than any other teaser.

Evidently, birds resemble baitfish (especially flyingfish) fleeing frantically from some predator. When rigged in-line, especially in front of a lure rather than a rigged bait, a bird unquestionably mimics a baitfish fleeing the smoking lure behind it, which itself might appear to be a small predator, like a bonito. Used singly or rigged as a group, birds add splashing flutter and very effectively draw attention to the spread of baits and lures. A chain of birds closely resembles showering ballyhoo or flyingfish, and fairly shouts to a gamefish to come and investigate. Some anglers, especially those in the Pacific, prefer to use them on calm days, but they can be used in rougher water.

Many people rig single bird teasers directly in line with leaders and artificial lures at the snap swivel, or, when trolling at slightly slower speeds, rigged on a separate trailer line attached to the swivel in front of the leader. The hooked bait or lure appears to be chasing the bird, or it may look like two fleeing baitfish. Both billfish and tuna react to bird teasers, whichever way they are rigged.

Several versions of birds are available, including some that are soft, and the design contributes to their action. Birds with more of a keel tend to track better, while others meander from side to side. Soft birds can also be rigged with hooks and fished as a lure, which may be advantageous if fish are striking the bird instead of the trailed offering. The size of the bird to use is generally dependent upon the tackle being fished: smaller birds for lighter tackle and bigger birds for heavier tackle. While small birds can also be fished on heavy tackle, large birds should not be fished on light tackle.

The number of birds and the pattern, or spread, will vary with sea conditions and fishing tactics. Yellowfin tuna anglers in Hawaii, who make tight turns when following schools of surface tuna, run just one bird on a long center line, to keep it from tangling with other lines. If you turn sharply and in any direction, you always have to be careful of crossing lines of dissimilar lengths or with differently behaving lures, so a single long-lined bird eliminates this problem.

Many anglers elsewhere, however, fish in wider turning or straight running patterns that allow them to fish from two to four or five birds, at staggered lengths and off outriggers as well as on flatlines. These are used ahead of the lures, with the main consideration being proper placement of the lures to get the best action out of them.

Some anglers prefer not to use birds when the water is really rough, while others merely lengthen their trolling line in rough water to get their lures to work most effectively. However, birds may flip in rough water. When birds attached to outriggers flip over, they cause a false strike by pulling out of the release, and may careen into other lines.

There has been concern in the past about the acceptability of birds for record-setting purposes due to a perceived problem with the drag created by a bird when a fish pulled it backward through the water and jumped with it in-line. The question was if this fit sporting definitions for record-setting purposes *(see: records)*. However, many anglers, as well as the record-tending International Game Fish Association *(see)*, determined that this is not so where standard sportfishing-size birds (as opposed to huge homemade versions) are concerned. The angler is virtually unaware of any added drag on his line as he fights a big fish that is also tethered to a bird. In the case of billfish, he is only reminded of the bird when a hooked specimen leaps clear of the water and the brightly colored bird can be seen flying behind the leaping fish, looking as if it's trying to catch up.

One word of caution needs to be sounded about using birds. When a large fish is brought to the boat and someone wires the fish (grabs the leader), an in-line bird can get in the way. This is generally no problem in the case of birds with wooden or plastic wings that have been sanded smooth at their edges. However, birds with sharp-edged aluminum wings have the potential to seriously cut the arms or hands in this situation and should be avoided.

Daisy chains and spreaders. A daisy chain is a combination of natural or artificial teasers rigged together in-line and trolled separately or on a fishing line. Born in the early days of giant tuna fishing off the Canadian Maritimes, daisy chains originally consisted of strings of dead herring dragged behind the boat while attached to the fishing line and meant to simulate a school of live fish. The last herring on the string hid a large tuna hook. Similarly, many Florida Keys skippers make natural bait daisy chains by stringing a succession of snap swivels on the line and then fastening ballyhoo to each snap through the lower jaw. The last ballyhoo is often rigged with a hook. This natural daisy chain works very effectively for everything from kingfish to sailfish, and often the angler is treated to the sight of gamefish violently eating their way down the string of baits before finally nailing the one with the hook in it.

Artificial daisy chains mainly consist of a string of lures, birds, or soft plastic baits (usually squid but sometimes other body types), and occasionally natural bait. Daisy chains made of artificials are primarily dragged hook-less behind the boat on a heavy cord exactly like a standard single teaser.

Although ready-made daisy chains are available, especially those made up of four or five plastic squid, many anglers simply string together a collection of old lures that have been irreparably damaged in the

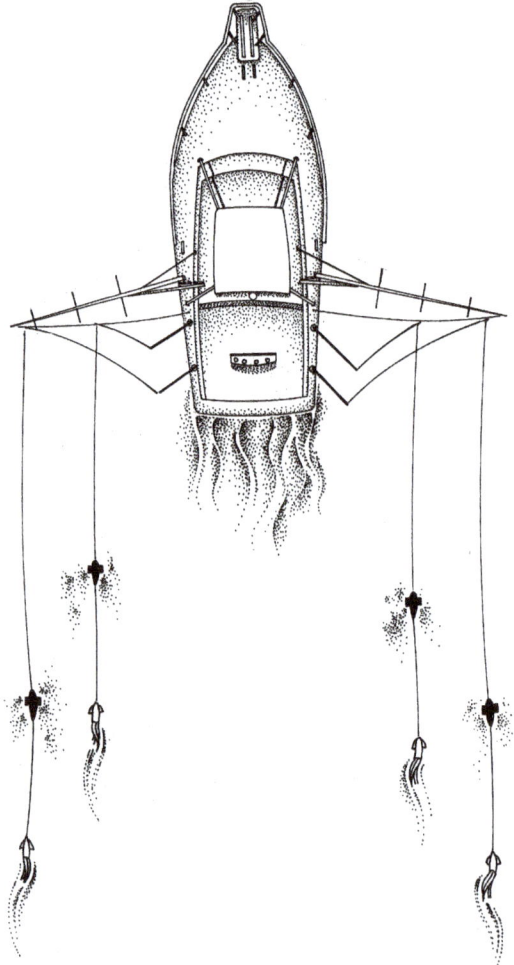

This is a typical setup for using four bird teasers (followed by plastic squid), all trolled off outriggers, with inside lines shorter than outside lines.

offshore trolling wars. The lures are held in place about 3 or 4 feet apart on heavy cord or monofilament by crimping small egg sinkers or sleeves onto the line. The daisy chain string of lures trails behind the boat on the second or third wake wave between the boat and the nearest lures and undoubtedly mimics a whole school of fleeing baitfish.

Although standard teasers and plastic squid are most commonly used on in-line daisy chains, trolling birds may also be rigged this way. Several birds (or small, plastic flyingfish) can be strung right on the leader in front of the lure to attract marlin. In the water they give the appearance of a small school of flyingfish being pursued by a larger predator, and marlin attack the lure perhaps as much out of a competitive urge as out of hunger.

Just as tuna anglers used to arm the tail-end bait of their daisy chain string of herring with a giant tuna hook, so, too, are modern anglers sometimes placing a stinger at the end of their daisy chain of artificial lures, rather than drag an unhooked daisy chain simply as an attractor. So the option exists to fish a daisy chain with a hook in it as well as strictly an attractor. By placing a hooked lure or bait behind, you can give the impression of perhaps a small school with the weakest member straggling behind, or of a small school being chased by something slightly larger.

The concept of daisy chains and imitating a group of baitfish may be expanded through the use of a spreader bar. Also known as a spreader rig, this is made up of a number of teasers mounted in a pattern behind a stainless steel bar, and instead of just imitating a straight-line formation, it broadens and increases it.

Egg-sinker stoppers or crimps squashed to the cord keep each component lure or plastic squid in place, and the rigs are dragged either alongside or directly in front of flatlined baits or lures. Some anglers, especially those after tuna, prefer to troll them farther back, in front of the trolled outrigger baits. Tuna anglers have been known to drag a large number of spreader rigs at the same time, presenting a pattern of teasers that resembles a large school of fleeing baitfish. The baits or lures with hooks in them probably resemble stragglers or larger predators that are chasing the pack.

In a pinch you can make your own daisy chain teasers by simply digging into your old tackle box and gathering a variety of offshore trolling lures, preferably about the same length. Old battered lures are fine. Then, all you need is a length of heavy monofilament leader and a bunch of small egg sinkers. By squashing the sinkers between the lures at intervals to keep them separated, and tying a large swivel at the end, you have made yourself a daisy chain. The fact that not one lure in the chain resembles another in either shape or color doesn't seem to affect their attracting ability.

Tubes

Tubes are long, slender, hollow trolling lures fashioned from rubber or plastic tubing. Most are made from pliable plastic and some from rubber; rubber versions were derived from surgical tubes and are also known as surgical tube lures. They feature a lead head, which may or may not have eyes, and two hooks that are attached to a wire leader that runs through the tubing; one hook is placed midway along the tube body and the other is at the tail. The tail is usually split or cut on an angle to taper to a point. The lure is fished with a ball bearing swivel and is trolled by itself on wire line or behind a downrigger weight, or with others on an umbrella rig *(see)*.

Trolling tube lures are available in sizes from 5 inches to 18 inches and in a variety of colors, with red and black being top preferences. Meant to imitate an eel or long sandworm, they are a top trolling lure for striped bass in saltwater, and also effective on bluefish and barracuda.

See: Offshore Fishing

TROLLING MOTOR

(1) A fuel-powered motor, usually of low horsepower, used for slow movement in trolling *(see)*. It is often an auxiliary means of propulsion, and is available as an emergency backup.

(2) Commonly used term for electric motor. In a strict sense, any motor can be used for the act of trolling. However, electric outboard motors are routinely referred to by many anglers and by the

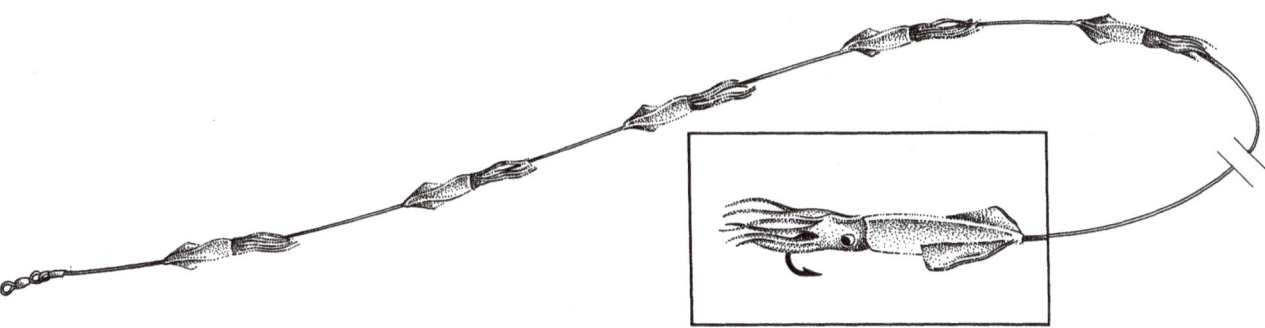

A daisy chain rig features a series of synthetic squid without hooks followed by one that is hooked.

This spreader bar is deploying soft teasers, the last of which is rigged with a hook.

general boating industry as "trolling motors," even though many people who own them never actually troll, but use them for positioning while casting or bottom fishing.
See: Motor, Electric.

TROLLING PLATE

A trolling plate is a boating accessory that baffles propeller thrust, and which is used by trollers who need to move slowly but whose big engines don't allow them to. With the plate up, the boat can be run at high speed without impairment; when down, the plate acts as a door behind the propeller and slows boat speed without sacrificing maneuverability.

Trolling plates are spring-loaded and flip down by pulling a cord. Some plates don't lock into position easily, so it may be necessary to put your engine in reverse momentarily to lock the plate down. Use super-heavy monofilament line or a length of low-stretch braided line to work the plate. A trolling plate is needed when headed downwind but not when headed upwind on very windy days. Be careful that you don't bang the plate on an underwater obstruction, and don't leave the plate down when you plane out, which can damage it.

TROLLING REEL/ROD

Anglers sometimes refer to a "trolling rod" or "trolling reel" when describing tackle used for that technique. No rods and reels are suitable for every type of trolling in freshwater or every type in saltwater, and some rods and many reels can be used for casting as well as for trolling. Whether a rod or reel is suitable for trolling depends to some extent on the type of trolling being done, the weight or pull of the objects being trolled, and the size of the fish to be encountered. Rods designed for downrigger fishing for trout and salmon, for example, are long and parabolic, and are not very useful in other fishing applications. Muskie trolling rods, by comparison, are shorter and stiffer than those used for downrigger trolling. Saltwater rods used for offshore big-game trolling tend to be of medium length and stout, while those for inshore fishing are longer and have more action, largely due to the type of lures and weights trolled.

Reel needs, too, vary widely, even among anglers trolling for the same type of fish. For instance, one could use a light-duty spinning reel that holds over 200 yards of 8-pound-test line for brown trout trolling, a narrow-spooled baitcasting reel (as employed when casting for bass) that holds 180 yards of 8-pound-test line, or a large capacity level-wind reel that holds over 300 yards of 14-pound-test line.

Line capacity and drag are the key factors to consider when selecting a reel to be used in trolling, matching them to the angler's abilities and the size of the quarry. Many reels used in trolling have a clicker to help alert anglers to a strike. In some freshwater trolling, reels with a line counter are preferred to regularly and reliably set lures at specific distances behind the boat.
See: Reel, Fishing; Rod, Fishing.

TROPHY FISH

A large specimen of gamefish, usually above an arbitrary size deemed notable by common consensus or one that exceeds the minimum requirements of an award or recognition program. Trophy fish are often candidates for replica or skin-mount taxidermy (see).

TROTLINE

A main line, usually of braided nylon, with drop lines to which hooks are attached and baited in order to catch fish. Trotlines are attached at one or both ends to a fixed object, often a stump or tree on the bank or shore at one end and a heavy weight or anchor at the other end; they are meant to catch nongamefish species and are especially used for catfish. They may be sunk to any depth, or they may be near the surface and have floats attached. Commercial trotlines are used by licensed commercial fishermen. So-called recreational trotlines are used by holders of a general fishing license who fish for personal consumption. Regulations govern the length of trotlines, the number of hooks, the spacing of hooks, and other issues. Trotlines are illegal in some places; where legal, they usually must be tagged or marked with the owner's identifying information.

Trotlines are not under the direct view and control of the person placing the line; however, they must be checked periodically, in some cases daily. Although using a trotline may be called fishing, and such usage may be covered under established regulations, a trotline is not a sportfishing instrument, and trotline fishing is not sportfishing.

TROUT

The word "trout" is used to describe various related members of the Salmonidae family, which also includes salmon, charr, whitefish, and grayling. As a group, these fish are endemic to freshwaters of the temperate and cool regions of the Northern Hemisphere but have been introduced widely outside their native range. Species that are commonly referred to as trout occur not only in the true trout genus *Salmo,* but also in the Pacific salmon genus *Oncorhynchus* and the charr genus *Salvelinus,* which complicates both a definition and an explanation of what a trout is.

Species

Among the most popular and widely known species of fish that are called trout are brook trout *(see: trout, brook),* brown trout *(see: trout, brown),* cutthroat trout *(see: trout, cutthroat),* rainbow trout *(see: trout, rainbow),* and lake trout *(see: trout, lake);* these have many strains, sea-run forms, and hybrid versions.

Some taxonomists would argue that the brown trout is the only true trout, as it was the first of its kind described by Linnaeus, the father of modern taxonomy, and that other fish species have been labeled as trout (especially in North America) largely because of their similar body form. This issue is best left to scientists, but from a technical standpoint it should be noted that such commonly known species as lake trout and brook trout are actually members of the charr group. So is the lesser-known bull trout *(see: trout, bull).* Likewise, the rainbow trout and its anadromous steelhead *(see)* variation, which was once placed in the trout genus, is now a member of the Pacific salmon group, as are the cutthroat trout, the lesser-known golden trout *(see: trout, golden),* and the Apache trout *(see: trout, Apache).*

Identification

In any event, true trout and would-be trout, as well as other members of the Salmonidae family, are primitive fish, with fossil remains dating to more than 100 million years ago. Evidence indicates that many of the more advanced or specialized families of modern-day bony fish have ancestral stocks closely resembling these primitive fish.

The most clearly evident primitive feature of the group is the lack of spines in the fins. Most of the soft rays in the fins are branched. The pelvic fins are situated far back on the body—in the "hip" region, where the legs of amphibians articulate with the body. This placement contrasts with the location of the pelvic fins in many other species, like largemouth bass, for example, whose pelvic fins are so far forward they are almost directly beneath the pectoral fins *(see: anatomy).* Other indications of their primitive nature are the possession of an adipose fin and a primitive air bladder.

Trout as a group are among the most distinguished-looking and prettiest freshwater fish. Some are especially colorful, particularly in spawning mode, and most have distinctive body markings, although there are great variations depending on the environment. Within each species there is considerable variation in color and markings from one river to another, as well as between river and lake populations. The brown trout found deep in a lake, for example, are more silvery and rather bland compared to brown trout caught in a rich limestone stream; so great is the difference that the casual observer would not assume that the two were the same species.

Habitat/Distribution

Like most members of the Salmonidae family, trout are in some way associated with cold, often rushing waters and high oxygen demands. Some—including the brown trout, cutthroat, and rainbow—have forms that are also tied to the sea and spend a portion of their lives there. The Pacific salmon, Atlantic salmon *(see: salmon, Atlantic),* and arctic charr *(see: charr, arctic)* are all examples of this. All trout spawn in freshwater and most require cold running water.

Some trout, especially the brown, have a lineage of historical, cultural, and angling significance, especially in Europe. All are good table fare and esteemed sportfish. They include species with limited range, especially various strains and isolated populations that are little known to most people, and species that have been distributed virtually around the world. Rainbow trout are likely the most widely spread gamefish worldwide, and have become important food fish through aquaculture production. As a group, trout are among the most widely cultivated fish, perhaps second only to carp *(see),* which are the mainstay of fish farming in China. Trout have been widely planted to supplement existing stocks, reintroduce species to waters where natural populations were extirpated, or introduce them to waters where they did not previously exist.

Like nearly all members of the Salmonidae family, trout have suffered from changes wrought by humans. These include overfishing, pollution, habitat alteration, factors that have caused a warming of waters, hatchery impacts, and competition from exotic species.

Gulf Coast marshes are home to mosquitoes termed Galinippers, so named by sailors who would see insect clouds so large that they were called "gallon-nippers"—a gallon of blood to the bite.

Some native populations of the various trout and their subspecies or strains have declined dramatically or have even been extirpated, although others have declined and recovered or expanded. Competition between species, especially between native and introduced trout, or trout and other introduced species, has often been a great problem. Unlike some other salmonids, trout (except steelhead and lake trout) are generally not a target of commercial fishing, or are a minor target, and recreational harvest regulations are well established.

Each of the major trout species is of great interest to anglers, although rainbow trout and brown trout have the greatest following because of their suitability to diverse habitats and wide international distribution. Trout are generally associated with rivers and stream fishing, especially wading and casting activities, although a great many anglers pursue these fish from various types of boats in large rivers and lakes, making it possible to fish for them in a multitude of ways. Because most trout are entirely freshwater in their existence, fishing methods are not centered exclusively around individuals that are preparing to spawn and undertaking migrations, as it true for sea-run salmon, and some species are available year-round.

Angling

Angling techniques for trout vary widely according to their environment; flowing water requires a different approach from that used in lakes, reservoirs, and ponds. The following information is a general overview and applies to the various trout except for lakers.

Rivers. To some anglers, the thought of fishing for river trout brings to mind a gentle flowage and small fish dimpling the surface during a profuse insect hatch, and using a light fly rod and fine-tippet leader to daintily drop a tiny imitation fly among the rising fish. To others it means tossing a flashy spinner in a roily cold flow and prospecting for an intermediate-size fish that will mistake the lure for a darting minnow. And to still others it means flipping a gob of fish eggs into a deep pool with a long rod and setting the hook into a 30-inch-long ball of silver fury that rockets out of the water and heads for the next area code.

Each of these is a classic view of river trout fishing, and this range of experiences highlights the extremes of this facet of angling. Fishing for trout in rivers—and, for simplicity, here "river" refers to all forms of flowing water—is a diverse activity, one that, in order to be consistently successful, requires proper presentation, a knowledge of the species' habits, and an ability to analyze the water and determine what places will likely hold fish.

Brook, brown, cutthroat, and rainbow trout, as well as steelhead, exist in a number of different-size flowages, and portions of these can be extremely fast or dramatically slow. Excellent trout-holding areas are available in nearly any flowage, however, and all of these fish are found in some of the same waters.

Brown trout tend to lie in slower and warmer waters than brookies and cutthroats, yet they will all inhabit pools and slicks in rapid-flowing waters. They primarily feed on various stages of aquatic insects but also on small minnows. Rainbows and steelhead tend to stay in deep main-flow water, and feed on aquatic insects as well as fish eggs and small fish. Yet all of these trout are often found in some similar locations, such as pockets behind rocks; fishing the so-called "pocket water" is a standard river fishing ploy, especially in low water and where smaller fish exist. Other such places include the slick water downstream from an eddy or pool; dark, swift water just above a falls or rapids drop; the sanctuary beneath a falls; and spring holes.

A great many river trout are caught by fly anglers, who typically use a light outfit (7- or 8-foot rod and 4- to 7-weight line) to fish small streams. They might use an outfit on the upper end of this range for larger or more open waters and/or places where big fish might linger.

Leader length should be about 7 feet long for small waters, slightly longer elsewhere (equal to the length of the rod is often a normal measurement), tapering to a 2X or 3X tippet. Flies must be selected according to the type of minnow or aquatic insect prevalent at the time. An enormous assortment of dry and wet flies, nymphs, and streamers are presented to these fish, depending on the circumstances.

Spring and summer insect hatches particularly attract river trout. In the spring these hatches may occur during the day, but later in the season they may be most evident around sundown and last long into the night. Trout, especially browns, will feed on meatier forage in the night as well. Small fish are often preyed upon in a long, shallow, gravel flat above a deep pool.

Fly fishing tactics vary, of course. Nymphs must be retrieved in short jerking movements, and at an angle downstream. Streamer flies, which primarily represent minnows, are retrieved at a steady pace across or upstream in rivers. Dry flies are cast upstream and float naturally downstream while the angler gathers line rapidly or mends line in order to get a natural, drag-free drift. To work a fly across stream or retrieve upstream causes your offering to drag or move in an unnatural fashion, and fish will seldom strike a fly presented this way. In a very slow pool or a midstream beaver pond, a dry fly should sit motionless and drift with a breeze if there is one. Give the dry fly enough slack by mending line so it drifts without line pull.

Spinning tackle users have a lot of success with river trout also, employing small spinners, small spoons, occasionally a light jig, and sometimes minnow-imitation plugs, as well as live worms and salmon eggs where baitfishing is legal, and large spoons and spinners in big, swift-flowing waters. Spinning equipment should be light or ultralight, with lines ranging from 4- to 8-pound test. In some smaller streams it's possible to use 2-pound line and a 5-foot ultralight rod. Line capacity and drag are seldom factors with reels used in spinning for trout. Where big steelhead are likely, line capacity and drag are more crucial.

Steelhead, rainbow, and brown trout are sometimes targets for big-river drifting, backtrolling, or back bouncing presentations, too, which are described elsewhere. Most of this is done with diving plugs or baits; winter-run steelhead, for example, are caught with pencil-lead-weighted spawn sacks or single-hook salmon eggs. Many different attractions, including plugs, spoons, spinners, flies, and bait, are used.

Lakes. Angling for trout in lakes—including in this term not only lakes but also reservoirs and ponds—is a completely different sport than angling for trout in flowages, not only because lakes usually harbor larger fish, but because such waters often provide suitable year-round water temperatures and have abundant forage fish opportunities, and their trout aren't readily accessible.

Trout in lakes move a lot and aren't always confined to readily identifiable terrain. Primarily they move in search of food, which is not made up principally of aquatic insects but such forage as alewives, smelt, cisco, chub, sculpin, assorted species of shiners and darters, and even yellow perch and crayfish. It is usually a certainty that the prominent forage species in any environment constitutes the major element in the trout's diet.

After ice out, or in late winter and early spring, trout lakes begin to warm on the surface. Trout are found at any level at this time, and are often within the upper strata (20 feet or less) of a lake or in shallow water close to shore. Thermal discharges, tributaries, rocky shorelines, and the like contribute to warmer water locales. In large lakes, a vertical surface distinction between water temperatures may exist until the weather warms. Known as a thermal bar, and found offshore in the spring, it is particularly attractive to steelhead.

As lakes get warmer, trout seek preferred temperature zones. Brown and rainbow trout prefer water in the upper 50s and low 60s, and once the water warms on the surface, they usually are found in waters of these temperatures, at whatever depth they may exist, provided that there is ample oxygen at that level. Often, their forage exists at or close to the same level. With brown and rainbow trout, the place where those temperatures meet with the bottom of the lake can be a productive locale for catching fish, especially if it is a prominent aspect of underwater terrain, such as a point or nearshore ledge.

An ideal situation in large lakes is to find a place where temperature, forage, and shore structure coincide. If you are looking for schools of baitfish, and monitoring preferred water temperature, try to find both of these where the thermocline intersects the bottom. This would be a prime place to begin looking for trout in the summer on large lakes. Trout may be more concentrated, incidentally, along a sharply sloped shoreline than a moderately sloped one.

Most anglers associate trout fishing with clear cold flows, such as the Blackwater River, British Columbia.

Trout orient to objects and edges. By identifying physical terrain, from depth contours to irregularities in the shore or bottom, you can discern which places attract baitfish as well as trout and pinpoint possible ways to fish them. A good locale is where baitfish get funneled, or where they might routinely pass by. The deep-water/shallow-water interface near islands can be equally productive. The edges of long underwater bars or shoals are places where baits migrate naturally, and logically present feeding opportunities for trout. In midsummer, deep trout may cruise over a large area, so in big lakes you may have a lot of scouring to do.

Fishing for trout in lakes is like blind prospecting. To have regular success means covering a lot of water. When trout are shallow and near the surface, trolling, casting from shore or from a float tube, or drifting with baits are all productive angling methods. Although casting is the most fun, trolling is often more popular because anglers can cover a large area in search of active, aggressive fish, particularly trout that perhaps have not been spooked or otherwise bothered by other anglers and boaters. Drift fishing with a boat usually is a live-bait proposition, but it is slow and, where motors are permitted on lakes, often less productive than lure trolling. If you cast from shore, you may simply be limited to one spot, such as a pier or breakwall, and must cast repeatedly in the hope of attracting a moving, incoming fish to strike your lure. This can pay off in tributary areas in spring when warm river water attracts a significant number of fish, or when fish are attracted here prior to upstream spawning migration. In most lakes, however, it is better to be mobile, concentrating shore casting efforts near prominent points, inlets, steep banks, rock- and boulder-studded shores, shorelines with sharp dropoffs to deep water, and warm bay and cove areas. Try casting spoons and plugs (crankbaits or sinking minnow-style lures) from shore.

Once the trout are deep, it becomes tough, if

not impossible, to catch them from shore, and here the boater with the ability to get lures down, to scout for fish with some type of sonar, and with the ability to ply a lot of water by trolling, has a distinct advantage.

In fishing for trout in lakes, once you have established roughly where and how deep to fish, the next consideration becomes what type of lure to fish, what color, and at what speed. Spoons, plugs, and spinners all catch trout, as do jigs at times. Many flatline trollers use fairly heavy spoons to get these offerings down to appropriate depths, but light spoons are preferred on downriggers. Fly fishing is predominantly done in small, shallow lakes and ponds, to rising fish with dry flies or to nearshore fish with streamers and wet flies and sinking lines.

There is seldom any reason to use extremely heavy tackle for trout in lakes, although large browns and steelhead can be powerful fish, and line capacity may be a factor. Spinning and baitcasting tackle is used for trolling, and spinning and fly equipment for casting. Rods are usually long, in the 7- to 9-foot range for all but brook trout and cutthroat fishing, and line strengths from 4- to 10-pound test are usually adequate, although big-water anglers who troll simultaneously for trout and chinook or coho salmon may use heavier line.

In many northern lakes, trout are a favorite target for ice fishing.

See: Charr; Salmon, Atlantic; Salmon, Pacific.

TROUT, APACHE *Oncorhynchus apache*.
Other names—Arizona trout.

The Apache trout is Arizona's state fish and was once so abundant that early pioneers caught and salted large numbers of them as a winter meat source. Since those times, a 95 percent reduction in range has resulted from hybridization with rainbow trout, brook trout, and other trout; in the early 1900s, nonnative trout species were stocked in the streams and lakes of Arizona's White Mountains to increase fishing opportunities, but they preyed upon Apache trout and out-competed them for limited food supplies. By the mid-1950s, pure Apache trout populations occurred primarily on the White Mountain Apache Reservation; in 1969, the Apache trout became one of the first species to be listed under the Endangered Species Conservation Act, and it was among the first fish species protected when the Endangered Species Act of 1973 was enacted.

This member of the Salmonidae family is currently listed as "threatened," or "likely to become endangered in the near future." The Apache Trout Recovery Team was eventually established with the goal of ensuring that healthy, self-sustaining populations of Apache trout exist in their White Mountain stream habitat. Currently, the Apache trout range is increasing due to joint conservation efforts by state and federal agencies and private organizations. These efforts have centered around reintroductions into streams where barriers have been constructed to prevent upstream immigration of nonnative trout species, and where "renovation" programs are in place to remove nonnative fish.

Identification. The Apache trout is a striking fish, with yellow to golden sides, an adipose fin, and a large dark spot behind the eye. The head, dorsum, sides, and fins have evenly spaced dark spots, and the dorsal, pelvic, and anal fins are white tipped. The underside of the head is orange to yellowish orange, with a complete lateral line of 112 to 124 scales.

Size. Adult fish usually range from 8 to 15 inches in length, although they can reach 18 inches. The all-tackle world record is a 5-pound, 3-ounce fish taken in Arizona in 1991.

Distribution. The Apache trout occurs in the upper Salt River and Little Colorado River systems (the Colorado River drainage) in Arizona. It exists in the West Fork of the Black River and a few small impoundments, such as Lee Valley Lake, and the largest population is on the Fort Apache Indian Reservation.

Habitat. Apache trout inhabit clear, cool mountain headwaters of streams and creeks above 7,500 feet and mountain lakes. They are dependent on pool development, shade-giving streamside vegetation, and undercut banks for cover, and are capable of tolerating a range of temperatures.

Life history/Behavior. Depending on the geographic elevation, spawning occurs between March and mid-June; the higher the elevation, the later spawning occurs, beginning when water temperatures reach 46°F. Females lay between 100 and 4,000 eggs in nests (called redds) at the downstream ends of pools; the lower egg counts occur in wild stream populations and the higher counts in hatcheries.

Food. As with other trout that live in flowing water, Apache trout eat both aquatic and terrestrial insects such as mayflies, caddisflies, and grasshoppers.

Angling. Fishing tactics are similar to those for other stream- and small lake-dwelling trout.
See: Trout.

Apache Trout

TROUT, AURORA
The aurora trout is a form of brook trout *(see: trout, brook)*, that has been considered extinct in its original form since 1971. The aurora trout was

native to several lakes in the Timiskaming region of northeastern Ontario, Canada. Desig-nated as *Salvelinus fontinalis timagamiensis* by some taxonomists, it was considered either a strain, color variation, or subspecies of brook trout by different scientists; it was distinguished by a lack of vermiculations or spots.

TROUT, BLUEBACK

This member of the charr *(see)* was once classified as a separate species with the scientific name *Salvelinus oquassa*. A landlocked, or nonanadromous, charr, it was reclassified as a subspecies of the arctic charr *(S. alpinus oquassa; see: charr, arctic)* along with its close relatives the Sunapee trout *(see: trout, Sunapee)* and the Quebec red trout *(see: trout, Quebec red)*. The blueback trout of Rangeley Lakes, Maine, were once extremely abundant but are now extinct; however, bluebacks are abundant in a few other waters of this state, and there is open-water fishing for them.

TROUT, BROOK *Salvelinus fontinalis.*

Other names—Eastern brook trout, speckled trout, native, spotted trout, speckled charr, brook charr, salter, coaster, squaretail, brookie, aurora trout, and mountain trout; French: *truite mouchetée*.

Brook trout are technically not true trout but are closely related to trout; they are charr and members of a family composed of lake trout, bull trout, bluebacked trout, Dolly Varden, and arctic charr. All of these species are members of an ancient order of fish that had their beginnings more than 100 million years ago in the Oligocene Epoch—a time period that is characterized by the development of higher forms of animals and today is represented by salmon, trout, charr, whitefish, and cisco.

As a native North American fish, and a sensitive one that has been displaced in some habitats as the result of fish stocking or water degradation, brook trout have long been a favorite of stream and pond anglers, especially in the northeastern region of North America. The transplanting and stocking of hatchery-reared brook trout, as well as brown trout, have been subjects of controversy both among anglers and members of the scientific community for more than a century.

Brook trout are, in general, more eager to come to the hook than brown trout, with whom they cross range and share some common waters. Today, large brook trout are fairly uncommon, except in some of the lake and river systems in Canada, particularly Quebec and Labrador, and in some locations where they have access to big-water forage, such as in certain Great Lakes tributaries. Native brook trout are virtually a delicacy, with bright orange flesh that is best sampled as soon as possible after a specimen has been taken. Commercially raised individuals are important to the restaurant trade.

Blueback Trout

Identification. Brook trout are among the prettiest fish in the world, both in color and body form. Their coloration and patterns are so unique that there is seldom any confusion with other fish, especially when one is looking at a native specimen (which will be richer and more brightly marked and colored than a hatchery specimen). Three external features allow immediate separation of brook trout from either brown or rainbow trout, or other charr. White pipings on the outer edges of all but the caudal (tail) fin identify it as a charr. On the interior of the white leading edges on the fins is a narrow black stripe. Body spots of true trout are on a light background but reversed in all charr. Trout have large scales easily seen by the eye, whereas charr have very small scales. The feature that is wholly unique to brook trout is the wormlike wavy lines, called vermiculations, on the back and head. These appear on the dorsal, adipose, and caudal fins like a series of tiger stripes.

Like all salmonids, brook trout sport a vestigial adipose fin on their back, located closer to the caudal than the dorsal fin. They also have paired pectoral and pelvic fins and a singular anal fin, just posterior of the vent. The body is generally fusiform (torpedo-like) in shape. It is slightly laterally compressed in young fish, but this becomes more noticeable in both sexes as fish age, especially older males.

Coloration can vary greatly depending on the environment; ranging from a light, metallic blue in fish that enter saltwater (which are called salters) or in fish that leave natal streams and spend part of the year in large, deep, clear lakes (which are called coasters), to dark brown and yellowish bodies in trout trapped behind beaver dams or in high mountain ponds whose streams drain leachates from surrounding conifer forest.

In general, its back coloration is olive drab or greenish brown, which fades down the sides into a light brown and somewhat yellowish color below the lateral line. On the abdomen, it merges into a pearly white that during spawning phases is replaced by roseate, then red and orange hues with a black swath along the very bottom. Upon this pallet, vermiculations are just a bit lighter green phasing into yellow; as these run down the sides, they break into pale yellow irregularly shaped dots and eventually become blotches. Over this collage are dispersed small, vermillion-colored dots surrounded by powder blue halos.

Body dots do not appear on the head or the gill covers, but green vermiculations from the back run

Brook Trout

forward onto the head and snout. Ventral (bottom) fins are red and almost transparent, whereas dorsal and caudal fins are dark and patterned. Both male and female brook trout undergo color changes as spawning approaches. In both sexes, all the colors intensify, but this is more pronounced in males. Young brook trout have 8 to 12 wide, vertical parr markings along the length of their body and usually a few red, yellow, and blue spots.

The head of a brook trout is large, encompassing nearly a quarter of its total length. The eyes are large and the snout is long compared to that of other charr (except lake trout) and true trout. In other charr, the maxillary jaw ends forward under the eye; in brook trout, it extends rearward for a longer distance and gives the appearance of a large mouth.

Size/Age. Brook trout are not a long-lived fish, generally surviving into their fourth or fifth year, although some fish have lived to at least 10 years of age. In most environs, the average brook trout caught is between 7 and 10 inches long and weighs considerably less than a pound. In many of their small-water natural habitats, the conditions do not exist to foster large sizes. A brook trout exceeding 12 inches in most Northeastern waters is a sizable fish, and one exceeding 2 pounds is uncommon. Nevertheless, brook trout are capable of reaching larger sizes; a 14-pound, 8-ounce brook trout caught in 1916 is the all-tackle world record for the species, and that individual measured 31 inches in length. It is the second-oldest all-tackle freshwater record chronicled, and in modern times, any brook trout exceeding 5 pounds is indeed a large fish. Few exceeding 7 pounds are caught in current times, and in those places where big brookies exist, the majority of anglers release them in any event.

Distribution. Brook trout populations still exist over much of the species' original distribution. Their range covers all of New York, New England, the Canadian Maritimes, Labrador, and Newfoundland. Brook trout exist in all the Quebec and Ontario rivers and streams that enter Hudson and James Bays. In Manitoba, brook trout are spread along all the streams that enter James and Hudson Bays. In all of Manitoba's east- and northeast-flowing rivers, brook trout do not appear, or are not significant, west of the 96° longitude. This longitudinal line, where it crosses into Minnesota, is also the natural western limit of brook trout in the United States, although they have been introduced elsewhere and as far west as California. In Minnesota, brook trout are found in the watershed that forms the beginning of the Mississippi River, but below its junction with the Minnesota River they appear only in the waters east of the Mississippi as far south as its junction with the Wisconsin River. They are spread throughout Wisconsin but not much farther south into Illinois. Brook trout are widely distributed on both Michigan peninsulas.

Brook trout range over all of Pennsylvania, but here their numbers are greatest on the eastern slopes of the Appalachians (Alleghenies), in the northeastern part of the state. Farther south, they spread into the eastern half of West Virginia and extreme western parts of Virginia, North and South Carolina, and the extreme northern part of Georgia. The most southerly brook trout distribution is the headwaters of the Chattahoochee River in Georgia. Brook trout also inhabit extreme eastern parts of Tennessee and Kentucky. Along the eastern slopes of the Alleghenies, they are native to Maryland north and west of the Chesapeake Bay. In New Jersey, the best brook trout fishing today is in the very northwest corner of the state.

Habitat. Compared to all other charr, as well as salmon and trout, brook trout are the least specialized in their habitat demands. This allows them to live in a great variety of environments with a wide range of tolerances. They inhabit small trickles, rivulets, creeks, and beaver ponds. They live in larger streams and any lake, from the Great Lakes to little lakes and ponds, to small rivers and big rivers with tumbling falls and rapids. Because of a unique organ (the glomerulus) in their kidney, they are anadromous and can move into riverine estuaries and are at home in brackish streams that feel the surge of tides, in a purely saline bay, or even the oceans themselves. They are, however, the classic example of a coldwater species, and thrive best in the northern half of the Northern Hemisphere.

The rate of water flow in a river or stream habitat is a factor in where brook trout are located. Slow, sluggish streams, or streams with plenty of backwater and pockets of little or no movement, are not brook trout waters. These fish are primarily "drift" feeders and prefer to lie in wait for food to come to them. But too fast a flow has a negative effect. In such a flow, fish must exert more energy to stay in place than can be replaced by the amount of food that moving water brings them. They cannot operate at a net loss for long, and seek out environments where the food en route is more than equal to the energy they burn to stay behind a boulder or even in midstream. In streams, brook trout are territorial and will defend their feeding station against other brook trout or fish. They give way only to larger brook trout or other, bigger fish.

Life history/Behavior. Brook trout spawn in late fall and early winter. The eggs grow throughout winter, remaining in the protection of the redd's gravel from 23 to as many as 80 days, depending on their latitude. They become free swimming at about $1^1/_2$ inches, and scales begin forming when they are 2 inches long. As they grow, they abandon the redd and work their way to the edges of the stream or, in a lake, into shallow water were aquatic vegetation provides protection from predators. Growth rates vary greatly over their range and depend on local conditions, that is food and competition with other larvae or fry, often of the same species. First-year growth depends on several factors, the most immediate of which is the length of the growing season. Other factors include water temperature, population density, and availability of food. Brook trout reach sexual maturity at ages 2 or 3.

Movements of brook trout in a stream are localized and especially likely during daytime hours, as indicated by their activity cycle. Biologists concluded that they are habitually inactive during the normal hours of darkness. During the day, they avoid being active during full-noon sunlight. Their activities are also controlled by the length of the day and even the time of day. Most food searches take place in early morning and again in late afternoon. When they aren't hunting, brook trout situate themselves out of main currents and find protected areas behind large rocks, under overhanging bushes and undercut banks. When rivers are up, the fish still maintain their general place in a stream. When temperatures rise or fall, they still like the place they chose.

Stocked brook trout undergo an immediate downstream movement when water temperatures are less than 50°F. When water temperatures are above 50°F at stocking, they show little or no movement. Limited movement by wild brook trout demonstrates the species' tendency toward a degree of territoriality. This is lacking in stocked fish because they are not born in the locale. Brook trout are a solitary fish, but, if alarmed or frightened, they will exhibit schooling tendencies.

Lake or pond habitat offers brook trout another set of living challenges. Immature and small, adult brook trout are likely to stay in a stream even when access to a lake or pond is nearby because stream habitats offer more protection from predators, especially larger brook trout. During summer months, larger brook trout typically inhabit the lake and move to rivers or streams only to spawn.

Big brook trout are also more likely to inhabit lakes and ponds in the summer because these environments usually produce more food, especially small fish upon which bigger trout prefer to feed as their size increases. In a lake, brook trout are more prone to inhabit the periphery, between 20 feet of depth and the shore, and in shoals in the lake where water depths are 30 feet or less. During summers with high temperatures, brook trout might be on the shoals that contain springs, where they can remain cool. During especially warm periods, they may be restricted from feeding in shoal waters until late in the night or early the next morning. In lake and pond habitats, brook trout cruise the lake, feeding individually or in loosely connected schools. Brook trout in a lake environment gather in more defined schools only when water temperatures are high and the fish find a source of cooler water on the bottom.

Some populations of brook trout migrate to sea for short periods. They move downstream and upstream in the spring or early summer and remain in estuaries and ocean areas where food is plentiful. After roughly two months, they return to freshwater. This migration may be in response to crowded conditions, low food supplies, or unfavorable temperatures in their home waters. Some overwinter in estuaries (in Nova Scotia, shore movements have been observed along the coast). Not all fish in a population migrate, nor do they necessarily do so every year. Sea-run brook trout live longer and grow larger than strictly freshwater brook trout.

Food and feeding habits. There isn't much living in the brook trout's world upon which this fish won't feed. They are predacious animals and need light to find their prey, and they feed as long as there is sufficient light. On evenings when there is sufficient moonlight, they feed into the night. There's a recognizable feeding pattern in both juveniles and adults. They feed best in early morning and late afternoon, when insect hatches are most likely to occur. They will be "off their feed," however, when water temperatures become too warm, such as during midday, especially in midsummer.

Brook trout are omnivorous, carnivorous, piscivorous, and even cannibalistic, and they occasionally feed on plants. Fry feed primarily on macroscopic crustaceans. At 1 to $1^1/_2$ inches, fry abandon crustaceans for insect larvae. They also begin taking their first terrestrial insects. At $1^1/_2$ to 4 inches, they shift to nymphs. Fish from 4 to 8 inches long feed mainly on aquatic and terrestrial insects. Between 8 and 12 inches, they begin feeding on small fish.

A brook trout from the English River, Labrador.

Large trout, particularly in northern waters during summer, are known to eat small mammals (mice, voles, shrews, and lemmings) that find their way into the water.

Angling. Brook trout readily take various lures, flies, and baits and generally provide a showy fight. The larger fish put up a particularly good fight. Their free-wheeling appetite and spunky disposition make them susceptible to a variety of tackle types and methods, although fly fishing and spinning are the primary means of catching these fish, essentially by casting, but also by trolling.

Unlike the rainbow trout, a brookie seldom jumps. This fish is a stubborn fighter, preferring to dig down and bore into the deeper, heavier water, employing a series of twisting, running rolls. It is during these heavy rolls that an angler with a limber, forgiving fly rod has an advantage over another angler with a shorter, stiffer rod. A fly rod, or a limber spinning rod, gives and provides leverage and constant pressure on a hooked trout.

Brookies are a terrific species for fly anglers, in part because of their nature but also because many of their habitats suit fly fishing's advantages, especially in rivers and streams. In those waters, brook trout hole up in some nearly impenetrable places, like an undercut bank, beneath a watery tree thicket, in a deep dark hole, and the like, where they wait for meals to come to them rather than chasing after the meal. When the waterway is narrow with overgrown banks, and the water is fairly shallow, a fly can be roll cast efficiently and quietly.

A 6-weight flycasting outfit will handle most brook trout that one can expect to catch in the United States on a small stream or river, as well as on a pond or lake. A $7^1/_2$- to $8^1/_2$-foot rod with a single-action reel, spare spool, and two 6-weight lines will do. You'll need a weight-forward floating line for use with dry flies, and either a sinking line, which is difficult to handle, or a floating line with only a sinking tip. The sinking tip is used to fish nymphs, wet flies, and streamers.

For those occasions when you might seek bigger fish, a heavier outfit is necessary, partly to play heftier fish, which are easier to land on a heavier rod, and partly to make longer casts and to deal with wind, but primarily to work lines deeper in heavier current, especially with all-sink lines. An 8-weight outfit will do the job. If most of your fishing is for small brook trout on small streams or with minimal room for backcasting, then you can try a lighter 4- or 5-weight outfit.

As with most aspects of fishing, the appropriate flies to use run a wide gamut. Time-proven flies that imitate natural forage and that are still effective include White Hackle or White Miller, March Brown, Pale Yellow Dun, Orange Dun, Royal Coachman, Hare's Ear Dun, Black Gnat, Red Ant, Stone Fly, Green and Gray Drakes, Black Palmer, Ginger Hackle, and Cinnamon Fly. More colorful and suggestive patterns include the No Name, Montreal, Silver Doctor, Grizzly King, Yellow Professor, Brown Hackle, Parmachene Belle, and Mickey Finn flies.

Fly fishing tactics vary, of course. Nymphs must be retrieved in short jerking movements at a steady pace across stream or upstream in rivers. Dry flies are cast upstream and float naturally downstream while the angler gathers line rapidly. To work a fly across stream or retrieve upstream causes it to drag or move in an unnatural fashion, and fish will seldom strike a fly presented this way. In a very slow pool or a midstream beaver pond, a dry fly should sit motionless and drift with a breeze, if there is one. Give the dry fly enough slack by mending line so it drifts without line pull. Pick an open area for your fly when a hatch is on.

One unusual aspect of note is the phenomenon of large flies for brook trout in northern waters, especially in Canada. Big deer-hair surface flies such as Bombers and assorted mouse imitations are effective for brook trout in places where rodents, lemmings in particular, occasionally are waterbound. These large offerings are dead-drifted on a slack line, skittered across the surface at a pace that will produce a slight wake, or floated in a drift-and-twitch manner. This produces fish of various sizes but can be especially productive for fish exceeding 3 pounds. The chase and capture of such offerings runs contrary to the usual stealth and ambush behavior of brookies, but large surface flies bring fish after them, and their take is usually explosive and exciting.

Spinners, spoons, and small plugs are the primary

nonfly hardware used by casters, and a variety of these are effective. Large lures, however, are seldom of great value in brook trout fishing, except where trophy fish and the aforementioned surface flies are concerned. Lure sizes are common in the $\frac{1}{4}$- to $\frac{1}{8}$-ounce range, seldom larger, and often smaller for low-water situations and shallow streams.

Lures and baits are fished across stream and downstream. It is almost always necessary to drift a lure or bait from above and let the current carry it, both to effect a natural look and also to induce the lures to swim, wobble, or waver as designed. Larger trout are likely to have a partial minnow diet and are susceptible to lures (including minnow-shaped plugs), although these usually have to be fished slowly and deep. Smaller trout are really more inclined toward flies and baits (worms in particular), with baits also fished slowly and close to the bottom. Because brook trout often lie in slack water and then dart out for a morsel as it goes by, be on the lookout for strikes during the drift rather than when the lure is swimming.

Spinning tackle users need different outfits for the entire brook trout fishing spectrum. The standard is an ultralight outfit, with a rod 4- to 6-feet long and a reel that handles 2- through 6-pound line and has an easy-starting drag that will cope with the fish's first lunge and remain uniform throughout the fight. An option is another spinning outfit that is a slightly larger version of the first: a rod between 7-and 8-feet long with a medium- to stiff-action tip and a proportionately larger reel equipped with a spare spool; this way the line size can be quickly changed if necessary. Terminal tackle, other than a bait hook, is small spoons and spinners, especially sizes 0 and 1, and small plugs. Weighting such lines with lead when using live baits (worms, minnows, grubs, grasshoppers, crickets, and the like) can be a problem if it is crimped so tightly that it reduces the line's strength.

Fishing for trophy brook trout, such as Canadian fish 5 pounds or heavier, may require a longer rod, especially for big, fast-flowing rivers. The rod should be between 8 and $9\frac{1}{2}$ feet long and have a long-handled grip. This heavier rod is not meant to overpower a trout; it simply leaves you prepared for an incidental catch of lake trout, or in some waters, northern pike or landlocked salmon. They live well in rivers and can grow to larger sizes, perhaps 20 pounds in the case of lakers and pike.

There are occasions, incidentally, both in ponds and small lakes, when trolling is the technique to employ, although trolling is not often associated with brook trout today, except on large bodies of water. However, washing a lure, fly, or bait behind a slowly rowed boat or paddled canoe is an old fishing technique. The most efficient method is to row or use an electric motor while trolling a large chub or minnow, although anglers intent on releasing fish should consider a small minnow plug or spoon, perhaps garnishing the spoon with a leech or worm. Trolling wet flies and streamers from a slowly paddled canoe is another possibility. Usually, a very slow troll is required, and it's important not to collect debris on the lure or line near the lure. In big bodies of water, deeper and more precise methods of trolling are sometimes employed.

See: Trout

TROUT, BROWN *Salmo trutta.*

Other names for brown trout (all forms): German brown, German trout, German brown trout, Loch Leven trout, European brown trout, English trout, von Behr trout, brownie, sea trout, lake trout, brook trout, river trout.

Other names for river and stream brown trout: Danish: *baekørred;* Finnish: *tammukka, purotaimen;* French: *truite commune;* German: *bachforelle;* Norwegian: *bekkaure;* Polish: *pstrag potokowy;* Russian: *forel strumkova;* Swedish: *bäcköring.*

Other names for brown trout in lakes: Danish: *søørred;* Finnish: *jarvitaimen;* French: *truite de lac;* German: *seeforelle;* Polish: *troc jeziorowa;* Russian: *forel ozernaya.*

Other names for sea trout, or sea-run brown trout: Danish: *havørred;* Dutch: *zeeforel;* French: *truite de mer;* Gaelic: *breac;* German: *meerforelle;* Italian: *salmo trota;* Norwegian: *aure orret;* Russian: *losos taimen;* Spanish: *trucha marina;* Swedish: *öring.*

One of the most adaptable members of the Salmonidae family, the brown trout was the first species of trout described by Linnaeus, the father of modern taxonomy, in his 1758 book *The System of Nature.* It was the foremost species of interest to Izaak Walton in *The Compleat Angler.* And it has been the darling of stream and river anglers over an expanding range for centuries.

The species called *Salmo trutta* (meaning respectively "salmon" and "trout") is the backbone of natural and hatchery-maintained trout fisheries on six continents, and is one of the world's premier sportfish, but it takes on many forms—river, lake, and sea-run—in many diverse environments, and is so varied in its appearance that it has been classified as scores of different species and subspecies over the years by scientists. This complexity has produced controversy, confusion, and many different scientific as well as common names. Some scientists have opined that there is one common ancestor for the various brown trout forms, and thus the brown trout of river or stream origin, the brown trout of lake origin, and the brown trout of sea-run disposition are specializations that have evolved. Throughout most of their range, brown trout are primarily thought of as residents of flowing water; therefore, those originating from lake environments—some capable of enormous sizes—are viewed as variations, whereas sea-run brown trout, which are anadromous and generically called sea trout (which differ from seatrout; *see*), are likewise a different form, also capable of growing very large, and obviously limited to coastal regions.

There are many populations (also referred to as strains or stocks) of brown trout that might well be individual races or subspecies; these are especially evident in the native European and Asian ranges of brown trout, although some have greatly diminished or disappeared for various human-induced reasons, including interbreeding with other races of brown trout. One of the more well-known strains is the *seeforelle*; this is a lake-dwelling brown trout indigenous to western Europe, which in the past has been scientifically designated as *S. trutta lacustris*. It has grown to huge sizes in its native waters and has been introduced to some waters in the United States.

The British were so enamored with brown trout that they introduced them widely. The Australian island of Tasmania, for example, received its first brown trout eggs in 1864. In North America, the brown trout is one of the few examples of an exotic species that was introduced with great success and general public approval, as it was not native to this continent until eggs from Germany arrived in February 1883, and fish were stocked that year in Michigan and New York. This was followed by eggs from Loch Leven, Scotland, introduced to Newfoundland in 1884 and then to the U.S. a year later; Canada received its first stocking of German brown trout in 1889. The brown trout eventually replaced native salmonids, however, like grayling, cutthroat trout, and brook trout, in some places, and would eventually become widespread. The North American brown trout came to represent what some scientists view as a mix of various different forms, resulting in a "melting pot" heredity, and a derivative form that was fashioned by its adaptation to a wholly new environment.

Although the brown trout is a true trout, its closest relative and a member of the same genus is the Atlantic salmon *(see: salmon, Atlantic)*. Like that anadromous species, regardless of its environment or geographical location, the brown trout is a challenge to anglers, a strong fighter occasionally prone to jumping when hooked, and a fish that can be caught using varied tackle and techniques.

The flesh of the brown trout is good, although not as esteemed as that of Atlantic salmon; native or sea-run specimens are gastronomically best. It is not sought commercially in most places, but it is intensively reared in public and private hatcheries to augment naturally spawning populations or to artificially sustain fisheries.

Identification. Brown trout get their common name from the typical olive green, brown, or golden brown hue of their body. The belly is white or yellowish, and dark spots, sometimes encircled by a pale halo, are plentiful on the back and sides. Spotting also can be found on the head and the fins along the back, and rusty red spots also occur on the sides. There is a small adipose fin, sometimes with a reddish hue, ahead of the tail. Sea-run brown trout have a more silvery coloration, and the spotting is less visible. Residents of large lake systems, especially the Great Lakes of North America, have a silvery coloration as well, dark spots without halos, and no colored spots.

Although the brown trout is a salmonid, it differs from Pacific salmon *(see: salmon, Pacific)* in having fewer than 13 rays in the anal fin. It differs from charr *(see)* in having larger scales and a pattern of dark spots on a light background (instead of light spots on a dark background). Stream-dwelling browns differ from stream-dwelling rainbow trout *(see: trout, rainbow)* in having red spots on the sides, larger spots on the head, fewer spots on the body, and few or no spots on the tail.

The brown trout is sometimes confused with the similar-looking Atlantic salmon; both have black spots on the back, upper sides, and gill cover, and sometimes have red spots. In freshwater, especially near spawning time, both species are bronze to dark brown in general coloration, with black and (usually) red spots on the body and head. In saltwater, both species tend to become silvery with fewer black spots and no red spots.

Although both brown trout and Atlantic salmon often occur in the same areas, they can usually be distinguished without laboratory analysis, although lake-dwelling specimens of both are much harder

Brown Trout

A distinctively marked brown trout from the Rangitaiki River, New Zealand.

to distinguish. In freshwater as a rule, brown trout are more heavily spotted than Atlantic salmon, and usually a good number of these spots are surrounded by lighter halos. The spots on the Atlantic salmon have no halos and usually some take the shape of Xs or Ys, which is not usually the case in the brown trout. The brown trout also has dark spots on the dorsal and adipose fins and vague or no spots on the tail, although nothing like the prominent radiating spots on the tail of the rainbow trout. The Atlantic salmon has no clear spots on any of these fins. Also, the brown trout's tail is squarish or very slightly concave or convex, whereas the Atlantic salmon's tail is slightly forked or indented.

In juveniles, the tail of the brown trout is slightly forked and the tail of the Atlantic salmon is deeply forked. Otherwise, these parr (young salmonids) look very much alike with small exceptions. A positive distinction between these two species, usually observed in the laboratory, is that the brown trout has well-developed vomerine teeth in a double zigzag row, whereas the Atlantic salmon has only a single row of poorly developed vomerine teeth.

Brown trout sometimes hybridize with brook trout *(see: trout, brook)* in the wild, and are also manipulated in hatcheries; the pairing of a brown trout female and brook trout male produces a deeply vermiculated fish called a tiger trout. Few of the eggs or hatchlings of this hybrid survive due to genetic differences between the two genera, and the offspring are unable to reproduce. The anadromous brown trout can also be successfully crossed with the Atlantic salmon to produce a fertile hybrid, sometimes called a "trousal."

Size/Age. Brown trout are capable of living up to 18 years, but most live no more than 12 years; sea trout can spend as long as 9 years in the sea. Technically, the brown trout is one of the larger salmonids, although growth and maximum size are especially relative to the particular environment. Most river and stream fish are only 9 to 14 inches long and weigh up to 4 or 5 pounds, rarely growing more than double that weight, although there are some notable exceptions. The White River in Arkansas has produced line-class world records exceeding 30 pounds, and the Little Red River, also in Arkansas, yielded the current all-tackle world record, a 40-pound, 4-ounce brown trout, in 1992.

Most large brown trout come from big lakes or from the sea-run form. Numerous brown trout exceeding 20 pounds have come from the Great

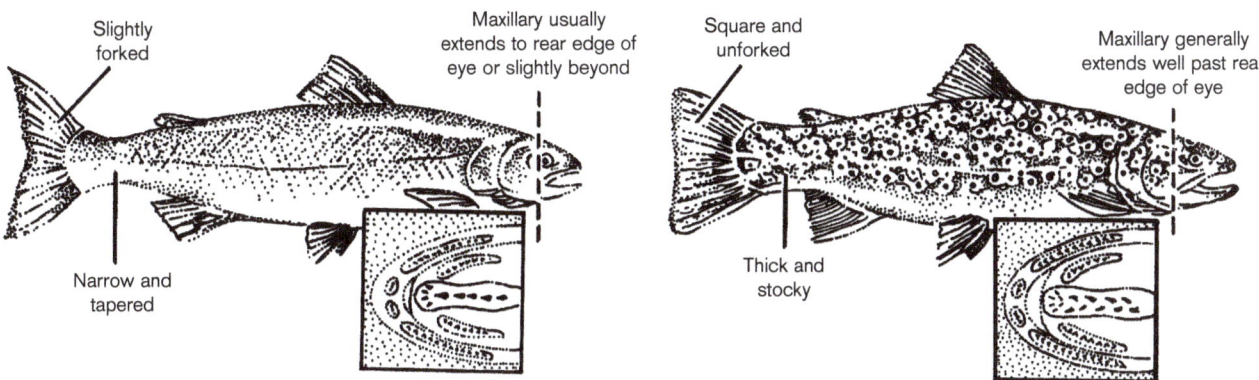

The most obvious differences between adult Atlantic salmon and brown trout are apparent in the head and tail areas. The vomerine teeth, which are inside the upper jaw, are depicted in the insets. On the salmon, these teeth are small and extremely sparse and appear in a straight row on the shaft; on the brown trout, they are well developed and form a zigzag on the shaft.

Lakes, including record-setting 34-pounders from Lakes Michigan and Ontario (respectively in 1984 and 1994), and a 37-pounder from Lake Strosjon in Sweden (in 1991). The large Alpine lakes of central Europe and the Caspian Sea drainage held fish exceeding 50 pounds in the past; Germany's Lake Wolfgang yielded a 68-pounder to a commercial handline fisherman in 1934, and a 60-pounder was caught in a net in an unidentified German lake in 1976. Sea-run browns, especially from the native range of the Caspian Sea, evidently grew even larger, and sea trout from Russia's Kura River have been reported to 72 pounds.

Distribution. The brown trout is native to Europe and parts of Asia, from Afghanistan and the Aral Sea across Europe to the British Isles and Iceland, and back across Scandinavia to Cape Kanin, Russia, on the Barents Sea. It is also native to the Atlas Mountains of North Africa. It has been introduced into all other suitable waters of the world, including Canada and the United States in North America, as well as South America, New Zealand, Australia, and other parts of the African continent.

It is now found in rivers and lakes in much of North America, with the exception of the most southerly American states, the most northerly Canadian regions, and Alaska. It is also found in some coastal rivers from Long Island, New York, to the Maritime Provinces and Quebec.

Habitat. Brown trout prefer cool, clear rivers and lakes with temperatures of 54° to 65°F. They can survive and thrive in 65° to 75°F conditions, which are warmer than most other trout can tolerate, but in streams they do best where the summer temperature is less than 68°F. In streams and rivers, they are wary and elusive fish that look for cover more than any other salmonid, hiding in undercut banks, in stream debris, surface turbulence, rocks, and deep pools. They also take shelter under overhanging vegetation.

Life history/Behavior. Brown trout spawn in the fall and early winter (October through February) in rivers or tributaries of lakes or large rivers. They return to the stream where they were born, choosing spawning sites that are spring-fed headwaters, the head of a riffle, or the tail of a pool. Selected sites have good water flows through the gravel bottom. The female uses her body to excavate a nest (redd) in the gravel. She and the male may spawn there several times. Females cover their eggs with gravel after spawning, and the adults return downstream. The eggs develop slowly over the winter, hatching in the spring. A good flow of clean, well-oxygenated water is necessary for successful egg development.

Brown trout fry are aggressive and establish territories soon after they emerge. They are found in quiet pools or shallow, slow-flowing waters where older trout are absent. They grow rapidly and can reach a size of $6^1/_2$ inches in their first year. Yearling brown trout move into cobble and riffle areas. Adults are found in still deeper waters and are most active at night. They mature in their third to fifth year and many become repeat spawners. Apart from moving upstream to spawn, adults tend to stay in the same place in a river with very little movement to other stream areas. They can be found at these stations day after day, even year after year. Others move to or from estuaries in the spring or fall.

In sea-run populations, brown trout spend two to three years in freshwater, then migrate downstream to spend one or two growing seasons in coastal waters near river mouths and estuaries, where they feed on small fish and crustaceans. Most return to their home streams to spawn, but some straying occurs. In lakes, brown trout seek out levels of preferred temperature, and are deep during summer months and shallower in spring and fall when the water is cooler. After ice out, they are in shallow and nearshore areas, often around warmer tributaries, but move deeper as the surface level warms.

Food. Brown trout are carnivores and consume aquatic and terrestrial insects, worms, crustaceans, mollusks, fish, salamanders, and even tadpoles or frogs. In small streams their diet may be largely insects; but in larger flows or where there is plenty of baitfish, it also includes assorted small fish. In large lakes, the primary diet is other fish, especially abundant pelagic schooling species, such as alewives; small fish are a primary food for sea trout.

Angling. Brown trout are a selective sportfish and challenging at times, no matter what environment they inhabit. Angling methods differ depending on whether the fish are found in rivers or lakes, and are similar to the methods used to pursue other trout species.

See: Trout.

A huge brown trout from Lake Ontario, New York.

TROUT, BULL *Salvelinus confluentus.*

A member of the charr group of the Salmonidae family, the bull trout is nearly identical to the Dolly

Varden, and these fish have many overlapping traits. It is therefore detailed under the entry for Dolly Varden *(see).*

TROUT, CUTTHROAT   *Oncorhynchus clarki.*

Other names—cut, native trout, coastal cutthroat, Clark's trout, red-throated trout, short-tailed trout, lake trout, sea trout, brook trout, native trout, Yellowstone cutthroat, Snake River cutthroat, Lahontan cutthroat, Rio Grande cutthroat, Colorado cutthroat, Utah cutthroat, Paiute cutthroat, harvest trout, blackspotted trout; French: *truite fardée.*

The term "cutthroat throat" and its scientific designation *O. clarki*—the species name in honor of Captain Clark of the Lewis and Clark expedition—is more like a name for a family tree than for a single species of fish. According to some scientific estimates, there are 14 subspecies, hybrids, and variations, forming what has been called an ichthyological jigsaw puzzle of fish that are endemic to western North America. All of these are members of the Salmonidae family of salmon, trout, whitefish, and grayling, and were reclassified from the trout genus *Salmo* to the Pacific salmon genus *Oncorhynchus.*

Of the 14 species, all but one inhabit only freshwater rivers, lakes, and streams; the exception is the coastal cutthroat trout *(O. clarki clarki),* which has both freshwater and anadromous forms; for unknown reasons, some fish migrate to sea, whereas others stay in freshwater. The coastal cutthroat is fairly well distributed and available to anglers, and is one of the more prominent cutthroat species, in addition to the West Slope (intermountain) cutthroat *(O. clarki lewisi),* the Yellowstone cutthroat *(O. clarki bouvieri),* and the Lahontan cutthroat *(O. clarki henshawi).* Others species include the Bonneville cutthroat, blackspotted cutthroat, greenback cutthroat, and Rio Grande cutthroat.

Cutthroats are popular with anglers and are generally not as selective as other trout species. They are not as acrobatic as rainbow trout *(see: trout, rainbow),* but they are strong fighters. Their flesh, which can range from white to red, has an excellent flavor. They hybridize freely in nature with rainbow trout (which are called a cutbows), golden trout, and other close relatives.

Perhaps as much or more than other trout species, all cutthroat species and populations are sensitive to overharvest, pollution, stream warming, and habitat alteration. Some strains have been greatly diminished and others extirpated.

Identification. This is a highly variable fish, in coloration and size. The characteristic that gives the inland cutthroat its name is the yellow, orange, or red streak or slash mark in the skin fold on each side under the lower jaw. The color of the body ranges from cadmium blue and silvery (sea-run) to olive green or yellowish green. There may be red on the sides of the head, front part of the body, and the belly. In some specimens there may be a narrow pink streak along the sides, but not as broad as in the rainbow trout *(see: trout, rainbow).* The body is covered with black spots, which extend onto the dorsal, adipose, and tail fins. Some are literally covered with spots, whereas in others the spots are sparse and larger, being more numerous on the posterior part of the body. On the tail, the spots radiate evenly outward, as they do in such species as the rainbow trout, golden trout *(see: trout, golden),* and Apache trout *(see: trout, Apache).* Although all these species are similar and closely related, only the cutthroat trout has hyoid teeth (teeth located on the back of the tongue). These may be difficult to see or are obsolete in some specimens. The tail of the cutthroat is slightly forked, and all the fins are soft rayed.

Coastal cutthroat coloration also varies with habitat and life history. Resident fish living in bog ponds are typically from 6 to 16 inches long; are golden yellow with dark spots on the body, dorsal, and caudal fin; and have a vivid red slash mark under the jaw. Free-swimming residents in large landlocked lakes can exceed 24 inches. They are uniformly silver with black spots and have rosy gill covers and a faint slash mark. Sea-run cutthroats are smaller, seldom more than 18 inches long. They are bluish silver with dark or olive backs and less conspicuous black spots; the characteristic slash is a faint yellow. Lack of a distinct slash mark in sea-run

A cutthroat trout from the Elk River, Colorado.

Trout, Cutthroat

Cutthroat Trout

and resident forms has led anglers to confuse the fish with rainbow trout, but a sure identification of the cutthroat is its hyoid teeth.

Size/Age. The largest form (or subspecies) of *O. clarki* was once the Lahontan cutthroat, which was native to the Lahontan drainage system of Nevada and California, including Lake Tahoe, Pyramid Lake, and the Truckee River. These specimens weighed roughly 20 pounds on average; a 41-pound Lahontan cutthroat caught in Pyramid Lake in 1925 is the all-tackle world record for cutthroats. In 1938, water was diverted from the Truckee River, and the Lahontan became extinct except for populations maintained by stocking, none of which attain the large sizes they once did. Yet a number of fish from there have become line-class world records in the 1980s and 1990s.

The smallest cutthroat occurs only in upper Silver King Creek, California, and does not exceed 12 inches. Coastal anadromous cutthroats have been recorded to 17 pounds but average under 5 pounds, whereas most inland specimens seldom exceed 5 pounds. Most cutthroats live 4 to 7 years, and they can have a maximum life span of at least 12 years.

Distribution. Cutthroat trout are the most widely distributed of all the western trout of North America, which is proven by the many names that refer to rivers, states, or drainages where unique forms occur. The coastal cutthroat trout normally does not exist more than 100 miles inland. They are known from the Eel River, California, north to Prince William Sound, Alaska. Inland non-anadromous forms occur from southern Alberta, Canada, to as far south as New Mexico, as far east as Colorado and most of Montana, and west as far as Alberta and eastern California. A small, disjunct population that may have been transplanted occurs in northern Baja California, Mexico. The species has been transplanted to other locations, including the east coast of Quebec, Canada, and Europe.

Habitat. Inland cutthroat and resident (non-anadromous) coastal cutthroat live in a wide variety of coldwater habitats, from small headwater tributaries, mountain streams, and bog ponds to large lakes and rivers. During their spawning migration, sea-run cutthroat are usually found in river or stream systems with accessible lakes; otherwise, they stay in saltwater near shore and their natal tributaries. In some watersheds, both anadromous and resident coastal cutthroats occur together.

Life history/Behavior. Cutthroat trout are late-winter or early-spring spawners, although sea-run fish typically ascend rivers from late summer through fall of the year prior to spawning. They spawn in small, isolated headwater streams; for anadromous coastal cutthroat, the selection of isolated spawning areas is thought to reduce interaction of young cutthroat with more aggressive juvenile steelhead and coho salmon. The female makes one or more nests; eggs hatch in six to seven weeks and, by the time they become parr, are difficult to distinguish from rainbow trout. Later, the young occupy beaver ponds, sloughs, or lakes. In lakes, smaller inland and nonanadromous coastal cutthroat trout hide among lily pads, sunken logs, or rubble from which they dart out and seize insects and small fish. Some fish abandon this "sit and wait" feeding strategy when they reach about 14 inches and become cruisers, pursuing and eating other fish. Cutthroat that adapt this feeding strategy can grow from 24 to 28 inches, weigh 8 pounds, and live to be more than 12 years old. These trophy-class cutthroat are always found in large landlocked lakes with populations of kokanee *(see)* salmon.

Sea-run juveniles can be displaced to downstream main-stem and estuarine areas where they reside for the summer, then migrate back upstream with the onset of winter floods. Sea-run cutthroat rear for three to four years in freshwater and migrate to sea in spring when they are about 8 inches long. Time at sea varies from a few days to more than 100 days before they return to their natal stream. During their migration, they follow the shoreline and do not cross open bodies of water, seldom venturing farther than 30 to 45 miles from their home stream. In the fall they return to their home stream, where they mature during the winter months. Homing is extremely precise; cutthroat can return to the same tributary stream from where they emerged and were reared. Fish mature at five to seven years. The rate of survival through the winter and return to saltwater is about

40 percent. About 60 percent of the migrants are sexually mature, a characteristic that tends to limit egg deposition and reproductive potential.

Food. Inland cutthroats mostly consume insects and small fish. Coastal cutthroats eat various small fish, shrimp, sandworms, and squid.

Angling. Angling techniques vary with the stream, river, pond, or lake environment, as also occurs with other species. These methods are similar to those used in fishing for other trout, and light tackle is generally appropriate for the smaller inland cutthroats. Cutthroats are aggressive fish, and a wide variety of flies, spoons, spinners, and other lures can be effective.

Sea-run coastal cutthroat can be taken in freshwater in the spring, or during the fall when they enter freshwater to overwinter. They are often caught by anglers fishing for steelhead *(see)*. They stay close to the bottom of deep pools or sloughs, and must be fished close to the bottom. During their migrations, they are caught in their home stream estuary or bays and salt chucks in the vicinity.

Because sea-run coastal cutthroat smolt are large, they are often confused with mature, catchable fish, and some runs have been depleted by overfishing the smolt run. Resident coastal cutthroats can be caught with spinners, spoons, flies, and baits fished deep in pools or along lake shorelines, especially where submerged debris is abundant. Dry or wet flies fished off inlet streams work well. A Muddler Minnow on a fast-sinking line fished along shores with submerged cover is often the best bet. Large trophy-class coastal cutthroat are best caught by trolling hardware or baits off steep shorelines of landlocked lakes.

See: Trout.

TROUT, GILA *Oncorhynchus gilae*.

Along with the Apache trout *(see: trout, Apache)*, the Gila is one of two native trout in Arizona, both severely threatened. Because of interbreeding with rainbow trout *(see: trout, rainbow)* and a similarity in appearance to cutthroat trout *(see: trout, cutthroat)*, it wasn't identified as a separate species until 1950.

A member of the Salmonidae family, the Gila trout is an olive yellow to brassy fish with small irregular black spots across its upper body, head, dorsal, and caudal fins. These markings protect the fish from predators. There is an indistinct rose stripe along the side, as well as a yellow "cutthroat" mark under the lower jaw and white or yellow tips on the dorsal, anal, and pelvic fins.

Growing to 18 inches, the Gila trout was originally found in tributaries of the Verde River in Arizona and still lives in small numbers in the headwaters of the Gila River in New Mexico. It prefers clear, cool mountain creeks above 2,000 meters in elevation and feeds on both aquatic and terrestrial invertebrates.

See: Trout.

Gila Trout

TROUT, GOLDEN *Oncorhynchus aguabonita*.
Other names—French: *truite dorée*.

California's state fish, the golden trout is classified as two recognizable subspecies, *O. aguabonita aguabonita* of California's South Fork of the Kern River and Golden Trout Creek, and *O. aguabonita gilberti* of the main Kern and Little Kern Rivers; an area of warm water where the South Fork joins the Kern apparently serves as a natural barrier separating the two subspecies. This attractive member of the Salmonidae family is highly desirable to anglers; its pinkish flesh is somewhat oily in comparison to that of other trout, but it is firm, finely textured, and delicious, especially when fresh or smoked. The meat does not keep for extended periods and should be cooked soon after capture or well iced and properly packed.

Identification. The golden trout is considered one of the most beautiful of freshwater gamefish because of its striking coloration and markings; it has a bright red to red orange belly and cheeks, with golden lower sides, a red orange lateral streak, and a deep olive green back. The sides have 10 parr marks centered on the lateral line, and the golden trout is the only salmonid in which these marks remain prominent throughout life. The tail is a brilliant golden yellow and is covered with large black spots that are also scattered across the back and upper sides as well as on the dorsal fins; the front part of the body may have spots above the lateral line on the back and top of the head, but not always. The lower fins are orange to red with no spots, and the dorsal, ventral, and anal fins often have white tips that are sometimes preceded by a broad black band. The golden trout loses its brilliant colors and becomes steely blue when at lower altitudes than its normal habitat. The lateral line has 175 to 210 scales, and there are 17 to 21 gill rakers and an adipose fin.

Size/Age. The golden trout grows slowly, usually weighing less than a pound, and is capable of reaching seven years of age. The all-tackle world record is an 11-pound Wyoming fish taken in 1948.

Distribution. In North America, golden trout occur in the upper Kern River basin in Tulare and Kern Counties in California, and has been introduced into Canada as well as the states of Washington, Idaho, and Wyoming, which have developed self-sustaining populations.

Golden Trout

Habitat. Golden trout inhabit clear, cool headwaters, creeks, and lakes at elevations above 6,890 feet.

Life history/Behavior. Spawning takes place when water temperatures reach about 50°F in early to midsummer. Stream dwellers spawn in their native streams or small tributaries, and lake dwellers spawn in inlets or outlets. Females dig several nests (redds), generally at the tail of a pool, depositing eggs in each and returning to their home pools or lakes afterward.

Many populations are believed to hybridize with cutthroat and rainbow trout, and apparently most trout in the Kern River basin are hybrids of recent origin. The only pure populations of golden trout are those limited to headwater areas.

Food and feeding habits. Golden trout feed primarily on small crustaceans and adult and immature insects, especially caddisflies and midges.

Angling. Fishing tactics are similar to those for other trout.

See: Trout.

TROUT, KAMLOOPS
See: Trout, Rainbow.

TROUT, LAKE *Salvelinus namaycush.*
Other names—laker, mackinaw, Great Lakes trout or charr, salmon trout, landlocked salmon, gray trout, great gray trout, mountain trout, tongue, togue, namaycush or masamaycush, siscowet, fat trout, paperbelly, bank trout, bumper, humper; Cree: *namekus, nemakos, nemeks;* French: *touladi;* Inuit: *iluuraq, isuuraq.*

The lake trout is one of the largest members of the Salmonidae family, which encompasses salmon, trout, charr, and whitefish. This fish is not actually a "trout" but a charr *(see),* and thus a close relative of the brook trout *(see: trout, brook)* and the Arctic charr *(see: charr, Arctic).* It probably should be known as "lake charr," but the whole name game is already confused, and, indeed, some scientists have placed it in a genus of its own *(Cristivomer).*

The lake trout was once associated with many variations, some of which have been termed subspecies or strains; some of these no longer exist, and others are deep dwellers that are not commonly known to anglers. The siscowet *(see)* or siscoet (which has been listed by some sources as *S. siscoet*) is one of these; a deep-dwelling (reportedly from 300 to 600 feet) fish of Lake Superior, it is known as the fat lake trout to commercial fishermen because of its extremely oily flesh.

Of all the charr, the lake trout is the least tolerant of saltwater and is the only freshwater fish ranging into the far north of Canada and Alaska that has apparently not crossed the Bering Strait. There are some northernmost stocks that evidently appear in brackish water, although the brackish water above the Arctic Circle is of low salinity.

Lakers are generally one of the least-accessible freshwater gamefish to most North Americans because of their preference for cold, dark, and mysterious nether depths, or because the greatest numbers exist in far-off or hard-to-access regions of northern Canada. Most of the fish that are geographically available to anglers are deep dwellers and are not regarded as exciting sportfish, at least not in comparison to salmon or stream trout species. This characterization is ill-deserved, however, and is partially a result of the heavy tackle many anglers traditionally use, the depths from which southerly lakers are often dredged, and the nature of the lakes in which they are found. There is a distinct difference between north-country lakers, which reside in waters that seldom warm up enough to establish a thermocline, and those that live in lakes where the upper strata become quite warm. Fish in the former are strong-pulling, head-shaking runners that give a fine account of themselves in all sizes, and are readily taken on all types of fishing tackle by versatile and accomplished anglers.

The flesh of lake trout varies from creamy white to deep orange and is excellent eating; the more colorful and flavorful fish come from the year-round cold waters of the far north. Historically, the lake has been eagerly sought by commercial fishermen, anglers, and subsistence fishermen. Some subsistence fishing still exists among northern native peoples. Commercial production via gill-netting occurs in winter and summer in northern Saskatchewan and the Northwest Territories. Lake trout flesh has a high fat content and is especially good when smoked. It is principally marketed fresh, or frozen as whole dressed fish and as fillets.

It is extremely vulnerable to pollution, however; this trait, combined with the introduction of the sea lamprey into the Great Lakes through the Welland Canal, had a devastating effect on natural populations. A campaign to control the sea lamprey and the level of pollution has helped restore the stocks in more recent years. Natural mortality is low in most lake trout populations; however, slow growth, alternate-year spawning, and older ages at maturity combine to make lake trout populations susceptible to overharvest by commercial and recreational fisheries. The number of large fish from the far north was severely hurt by overfishing from the 1950s through the early 1970s, and the lakers started to rebound only after conserva-

Lake Trout

tion measures were enacted. Most of the larger specimens in northern Canada are now fished with single, barbless hooks and are released alive.

Identification. Lake trout have the same moderately elongated shape as trout and salmon, as well as other charr, although they grow much larger than other charr. Extremely heavy specimens have a distended belly and a less elongated shape. Their tail is moderately forked (most people describe it as deeply forked, but in comparison to saltwater fish with truly deeply forked tails, this is incorrect, and certainly incorrect for large specimens), more so than other charr, their scales are minute, and they have several rows of strong teeth, which are weak, less numerous, or absent in other charr. Their head is generally large, although fast-growing stocked fish will have small heads in relation to body size, and there is an adipose fin.

Like other charr the lake trout has white leading edges on all its lower fins and light colored spots on a dark background, instead of the dark spots on a light background which is characteristic of salmon and trout. The body is typically grayish to brownish, with white or nearly white spots which extend onto the dorsal, adipose, and caudal fins. There are no red, black, or haloed spots of any kind.

Coloration is highly variable, depending as it does on seasons and specific populations, and is susceptible to much lighter and much darker variations from the norm. Lighter specimens are often the deep-dwelling fish of light-colored southerly lakes with alewife and smelt forage bases; darker specimens, including some with reddish and orange tones, come from less-fertile, tannin-colored shallow northern lakes. Males and females are similar, but males have a slightly longer, more pointed snout.

The lake trout has been crossed with the brook trout to produce a hybrid known as a splake *(see)*. The hybrid's tail is less deeply forked, and its body markings more closely resemble those of the brook trout.

Size/Age. The lake trout is evidently the second-largest of the salmonids (after chinook salmon), both in a historical and a modern sense (as more large lake trout than large Atlantic salmon exist today). Although the all-tackle world record for lake trout is a 66-pound, 8-ounce fish caught in 1991 at Great Bear Lake, Northwest Territories, larger fish have been caught in that lake since (including a 72-pounder in 1995) that have not met record-recognition standards. A 102-pound lake trout was netted in Lake Athabasca, Northwest Territories, in 1961, and was 50 inches long; according to legend, a 120-pounder was caught in 1818 in the Great Lakes, although this may not have validity.

In most of its range, a 20-pound lake trout is a very large specimen and is considered a trophy catch; fish from 30 to 45 pounds are caught every season in a few far-northern waters, most of them being released. The average angler catch in most places weighs 4 to 10 pounds.

Lake trout growth and age vary from place to place depending on diet, water temperature, altitude, and genetics. Lake trout in the cold, deep, infertile waters of the north are capable of long life spans. Some grow to 40 to 50 years of age and reportedly can live to age 62. In the more southerly portions of their range, however, they grow more quickly but do not live as long, and in most places they do not live longer than 20 years.

Distribution. The natural range of the lake trout is across the northern region of North America. It occurs from Quebec, the Maritime Provinces, and Labrador in the east, southerly through New York, and west across the north-central United States and all of Canada to British Columbia and Alaska in the west. It is widely distributed in the Nunavut, Yukon, and Northwest Territories, and in the northern sections of other Canadian provinces, including arctic islands. It has been introduced to northern deep lakes elsewhere in the U.S., as well as in Europe, New Zealand, and South America, and reintroduced to some parts of its native range, including the Great Lakes in North America.

Habitat. Overall, and especially in the southern portions of its range, or where introduced south of its native range, the lake trout is an

Teeth on Roof of Mouth

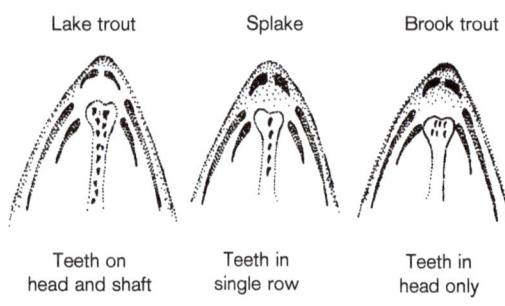

Lake trout — Teeth on head and shaft
Splake — Teeth in single row
Brook trout — Teeth in head only

inhabitant of cool waters of large, deep lakes. In far-northern regions it may occur in lakes that are generally shallow and that remain cold all season long, and it may occur in either the shallow or deep portions of lakes that have large expanses of deep water. It is also found in large deep rivers, or in the lower reaches of rivers, especially in the far north, although it may also move into the tributaries of large southerly lakes to forage. They rarely inhabit brackish water.

Life history/Behavior. Lake trout generally spend their entire lives in lakes, staying deep and often near the bottom at cool levels; in some places, including the Great Lakes, this level may exceed 100 feet. In far-northern waters, they may not be very deep even in midsummer, staying from 10 to 30 or 40 feet deep because of cool upper-level temperatures. They often orient to structure, cluster at tributaries, and wander in search of food; and although they are not school species like some of their forage, they are usually found in groups, often of like-size individuals.

Spawning takes place in late summer or early fall over clean, rocky lake bottoms. Rocky shoals or reefs, where they exist, are prominent spawning sites. Males reach the spawning sites several days before the females and use their snouts and fins to clean the substrate. Unlike other salmonids, lake trout do not make nests. Spawning usually takes place at night, with peak activity occurring after dusk. Females release from 400 to 1,200 eggs per pound of body weight, and the eggs hatch early in the following spring. In some populations, spawning occurs every year, whereas in others spawning may occur every other year or less frequently.

Food. As with other predacious fish, the diet of lake trout varies with the age and size of the fish, locality, and the food available. Food items commonly include zooplankton, insect larvae, small crustaceans, clams, snails, leeches, and various species of fish, including their own kind. Lake trout feed extensively on such other fish such as whitefish, grayling, sticklebacks, suckers, and sculpin in the far north, or cisco, smelt, and alewives elsewhere.

Angling. In spring, when lake waters are cold, trout are found near the surface and along the shoreline. As the season progresses, lakers go deeper; in waters where the surface temperatures warm considerably, they finally reside beneath the thermocline.

Some early coldwater lake trout fishing is done by casting from shore with spoons, spinners, plugs, and flies, especially along rocky shorelines and around tributaries. Most anglers then and throughout the season fish from a boat, occasionally by casting and jigging, but primarily by trolling. In the winter, ice anglers use jigs, live baits, and dead cut baits.

In most large waters, lakers are predominantly caught by anglers trolling slowly with flashy spoons and diving plugs. Jigging for lake trout is possible, as is casting with spoons, spinners, and flies in northerly locales.

In most places in the southern part of the lake trout's range, trolling for these fish is done at relatively deep levels, below the thermocline, and often near bottom and some form of hard structure (primarily shoals or reefs) from late spring through early fall, especially along dropoffs, around reefs and rocky structures, and along steep rock walls.

Not all trolling for lakers is done at decompression depths. Shallower rocky islands and reefs are prime foraging grounds for lake trout, which move into such spots to feed (even in the summer and even if the water temperature is higher than they generally prefer), then retreat to deep water. Also, early and late in the year are good times to find lake trout in the upper 20 feet of a lake or reservoir if the water temperature is favorable.

Lake trout are one of the most curious of freshwater fish, a fact that can make you more successful at catching them when you know how to appeal to this trait. Lakers may follow a lure a considerable distance, sometimes nudging the lure and sometimes staying just behind it for a long while, like a bird dog. When holding a rod, jerking or pumping the rod tip periodically, as well as dropping it back a few feet or speeding it up momentarily, are tactics that provoke these fish into striking. When rods are set in holders, changes in boat speed, turns, and manipulative boat operation momentarily affect the swimming pattern of a lure, and these are often factors that cause a lake trout to strike. It isn't the faster or slower speed of the lure that draws strikes so much as the change in behavior. Lakers basically like a slow presentation, quite slow, in fact, compared to salmon and other trout.

It is because of the laker's preference for slow-moving lures that the most successful lake trout tactic on the Great Lakes is to run a small plastic wobbling bait (called a Peanut by some) about 12 to 18 inches behind a dodger or cowbell attractor. Some spoons and small diving plugs are also worked in this fashion. In areas where there is a sandy bottom and when fish presumed to be lakers are spotted via sonar on the bottom in deep water (maybe 100 to 150 feet in summer), you can literally set your line by dropping the downrigger weight until it hits bottom, then raise it up a turn. The lead from weight to lure can be very short. Some bottom trollers like to use a banana-shaped downrigger weight for this, incidentally, dragging it right on the bottom.

Although trolling is the foremost method of lake trout fishing, jigging is also effective. Light jigs can provide exciting small lake trout action in north-country rivers, and for schools of small fish that prowl the shorelines of lakes in the evening. Large jigs are occasionally more effective than trolling spoons or plugs where lake trout are abundant. But it is best to limit jigging activities to known lake trout reefs, fishing for bottom-hugging trout that are spotted on sonar, or fishing where you've recently caught lakers. In north-country locales, it's worth jigging at river mouths, to the side of heavy current where a major tributary dumps into a large lake. You can also catch lake trout by casting and retrieving small spinners and spoons, streamer flies, and plugs, primarily in northern locales. In flies, try streamers when fishing in current and in the shallows, and possibly dry flies when small lakers are observed cruising shorelines for mosquitoes in the far north.

Tackle runs the gamut, from deep-trolling hardware to fly, spinning, and baitcasting equipment. Lakers give the best account of themselves on light line, which, because they inhabit open water, is feasible provided you don't need heavy weight to get down to the fish.

See: Charr.

A lake trout from Kaminuriak Lake, Nunavut Territory.

TROUT, QUEBEC RED

This member of the charr *(see)* was once classified as a separate species with the scientific name *Salvelinus marstoni*. A landlocked, or nonanadromous, charr, and also known as Marston's trout, it was reclassified as a subspecies of the arctic charr *(S. alpinus oquassa; see: charr, arctic)* along with its close relatives the blueback trout *(see: trout, blueback)* and Sunapee trout *(see: trout, Sunapee)*. The Quebec red trout exists as a remnant population in some waters of eastern Quebec.

TROUT, RAINBOW *Oncorhynchus mykiss.*
Other names—steelhead, rainbow, 'bow, redsides, Kamloops, redband trout, Eagle Lake trout, Kern River trout, Shasta trout, San Gorgonio trout, Nelson trout, Whitney trout, silver trout; Danish: *regnbueørred;* Finnish: *kirjolohi;* French: *truite-arc-en-ciel;* German: *regenbogenforelle;* Italian: *trota iridea;* Japanese: *nijimasu;* Russian: *forel raduzhnaya;* Spanish: *trucha arco iris;* Swedish: *regnbåge;* Turkish: *alabalık türü.*

The rainbow trout is one of the most widely distributed freshwater fish, and the one member of the Salmonidae family of salmon, trout, whitefish, and grayling that presently has global distribution. Endemic to western North America and now found on six continents, it was reclassified from the trout genus *Salmo* to the Pacific salmon genus *Oncorhynchus* (it was formerly identified as *Salmo gairdneri*), and occurs in both freshwater resident and anadromous, or sea-run, races. Seagoing rainbows, known as steelhead or steelhead trout, are briefly noted here but are reviewed in greater detail under a separate entry *(see: steelhead)*. One landlocked variety of rainbow trout from the interior of British Columbia is called the Kamloops trout, a genetically large strain called Gerrard trout exists in British Columbia's Kootenay Lake and its Lardeau River tributary, and there are many other variations (as well as hatchery created hybrids) of rainbows known.

One of the top freshwater sportfish, the rainbow is tolerant of moderate temperatures, which has allowed it to become available to many anglers around the world; this, plus its beautiful coloration and acrobatic tendencies when hooked, have helped make it a favorite in streams, rivers, and lakes.

The rainbow trout is one of the most heavily cultured species of freshwater fish, both for recreational use and for food production. Although natural populations of rainbows are not commercially fished, the species is pond-reared in North America, Europe, and Asia and sold as frozen whole fish. The flesh ranges from bright

Trout, Rainbow

Rainbow Trout

red in small lake and stream populations to pink or white in large lake and river populations in which the diet is largely piscivorous, and it has an excellent flavor. Commercial fishing for ocean steelhead, however, which have bright orange red flesh, is of significance, resulting in fresh and frozen market sale.

Identification. Rainbow trout possess the typical elongated and streamlined salmonid form, although body shape and coloration vary widely and reflect habitat, age, sex, and degree of maturity. The body shape may range from slender to thick. The back may shade from blue green to olive. There is a reddish pink band along each side about the midline that may range from faint to radiant. The lower sides are usually silver, fading to pure white beneath.

Small black spots are present over the back above the lateral line, as well as on the upper fins and tail. In some locations, the black spots of adults may extend well below the lateral line and even cover the entire lower side. The rainbow and its closest relatives in the Pacific salmon group (cutthroat, golden, Apache, and Gila trout) are known as the "blackspotted" trout because they are covered with numerous prominent black spots. These spots may cover the entire body or may be more abundant near the tail. The spots characteristically extend onto the dorsal fin, the adipose fin, and the tail. Those on the tail radiate outward in an even, orderly pattern. Spots may be present on any of the lower fins, and there are never any red spots such as occur on freshwater and spawning specimens of brown trout *(see: trout, brown)* and Atlantic salmon *(see: salmon, Atlantic)*. Rainbow trout are positively identified by the 8 to 12 rays in the anal fin, a mouth that does not extend past the back of the eye, and the lack of teeth at the base of the tongue.

The rainbow trout's coloration varies greatly with size, habitat, and spawning periods. Stream dwellers and spawners usually show the darkest and most vivid colors and markings. River or stream residents normally display the most intense pink stripe coloration and heaviest spotting, followed by rainbows from lake and lake-stream systems. By contrast, the steelhead is silvery and may not have a pink stripe along the middle of its sides.

The rainbow trout readily hybridizes with other "blackspotted" trout, especially with the cutthroat and golden trout, producing fertile offspring with all manner of confusing color combinations and intermediate characteristics. A short-lived but colorful (orange) hatchery-reared rainbow hybrid, crossed with a mutant albino form of golden trout, is called a Palomino trout, and has been widely stocked in Pennsylvania.

The absence of orange red slash marks on the underside of the jaw, and the lack of teeth near the base of the tongue, are good keys for distinguishing rainbows from inland or nonanadromous cutthroat trout *(see: trout, cutthroat)*.

Size/Age. In general, large rainbows are caught in large bodies of water and small ones in streams and ponds. Stream-caught fish commonly weigh a pound or so, whereas fish from larger rivers and lakes commonly weigh between 2 and 4 pounds. Rainbows that have migrated to a large inland lake (called steelhead), such as one of the Great Lakes, may attain double-digit weights, although most weigh 7 to 10 pounds, and sea-run fish likewise become heavyweights. The largest nonanadromous rainbow trout in North America presently come from Alaska and British Columbia waters. World records are kept for all varieties of rainbow trout as one species, meaning that the anadromous form dominates the record books. Rainbows from 20 pounds to more than 30 pounds have been caught, however, and Lake Pend Oreille in Idaho produced a 37-pounder in 1947. Rainbows can live for 11 years but typically have a 4- to 6-year life span.

Distribution. The rainbow trout is native to the West Coast of North America from southern Alaska to Durango, Mexico, and inland as far as central Alberta in Canada and Idaho and Nevada in the United States. It has been extensively introduced across the lower Canadian provinces, throughout the Great Lakes region and the northeastern U.S. to the Atlantic coast and south through the Appalachians to northern Georgia and Alabama, in the western U.S. easterly to western Texas, and sporadically in the central U.S. south of the Great Lakes. It has been transplanted to New Zealand, Australia, South America, Africa, Japan, southern Asia, Europe, and Hawaii. An Asian species known as the Kamchatka trout is believed to be a form of the rainbow trout. It is native to the Amur River in the eastern part of Russia as well as the Kamchatka Peninsula and the Commander Islands.

Habitat. Although rainbows do well in large lakes with cool, deep waters, they prefer moderately flowing streams with abundant cover and deep pools. In most streams they are found in stretches of swift-flowing water, at the edge of strong currents, and at the head of rapids or strong riffles. They prefer water temperatures of 55° to 64°F but can tolerate water to 70°F.

Life history/Behavior. Most varieties of rainbow trout spawn in the spring in small tributaries of rivers, or in inlets or outlets of lakes, but some strains spawn at other times. Rainbow trout usually return to the streams where they hatched.

During late winter or early spring, when water temperatures are on the rise, maturing adult rainbows usually seek out the shallow gravel riffles in their stream or a suitable clear-water stream that enters their lake. Spawning takes place from late winter or early spring through early summer, depending on the specific location and the severity of the winter. The female uses her tail to prepare a nest (redd) 4 to 12 inches deep and 10 to 15 inches in diameter. From 200 to 8,000 eggs are deposited in the redd, fertilized by a male, and covered with gravel.

Hatching normally occurs from a few weeks to as much as four months after spawning, depending on the water temperature. The tiny fry emerge from the gravel in a week or up to several weeks, again depending on the temperature. On emerging, the small trout assemble in groups and seek shelter along the stream margins or protected lakeshore, feeding on crustaceans, plant material, and aquatic insects and their larvae. Rainbow trout rear in similar habitat for the first two or three years then move into the larger water of lakes and streams and turn more to a diet of fish, salmon carcasses, eggs, and even small mammals.

Age of onset of sexual maturity varies markedly among individuals due primarily to such factors as population density, productivity of the aquatic environment, and genetic makeup. In the wild, male and female spawners as young as ages 3 and 5, respectively, have been found, but a majority of both sexes matures at ages 6 to 7. Spawning frequency ranges from annually to once every three years. Fish that live in large productive lakes generally grow largest and live longer than those of river, stream, or pond environs. In Alaska, rainbow trout that live in or migrate to large lakes with sockeye salmon runs generally grow faster and larger than fish that remain year-round in streams.

A close look at a rainbow trout from a Colorado pond.

Food. Rainbows feed on a variety of food, mainly insects, crustaceans, snails, leeches, and other fish if available. Some studies have shown that they feed less often on the surface than brown trout.

Angling. The beauty, strength, endurance, and spectacular leaps of the rainbow trout and all of its variations and strains have endeared it to anglers. It takes lures, flies, and baits well, leaps often, and fights hard no matter what its size, although larger individuals are especially exciting. In rivers that also contain salmon runs, rainbow fishing success is typically greatest in the spring and fall before and after the large salmon runs. Angling methods differ depending on whether the fish are found in rivers or lakes, and are similar to fishing for other trout species. Weighted spinners, wobbling spoons, streamer flies, Muddlers Minnows, and egg-imitation flies fished near the bottom are especially preferred in river and stream habitats.
See: Trout.

Sunapee Trout

TROUT, SUNAPEE
This member of the charr *(see)* was once classified as a separate species with the scientific name *Salvelinus aureolus*. A landlocked, or nonanadromous, charr, it was reclassified as a subspecies of the arctic charr *(S. alpinus oquassa;* see: charr, arctic*)* along with its close relatives the blueback

trout (see: trout, blueback) and Quebec red trout (see: trout, Quebec red). The common name is derived from a native population of Sunapee Lake in New Hampshire; Sunapee trout there hybridized with lake trout and are no longer believed to exist, and the species is not currently documented in that state. Sunapees do exist in Maine, where there is a remnant population in Flood's Pond, and reintroductions have been made into some other waters.

Trout-perch

Food and feeding habits. Trout-perch feed on aquatic insects and small crustaceans, and generally move from deeper water to shallower near-shore areas at night to feed.

Angling. These fish are an important food item for many larger predator fish, but not a source of angler attention. Trout-perch may be used as bait by some anglers, including those pursuing lake trout, although they are not a hardy species and do not keep well in bait buckets. In the northeastern U.S., people dipping for smelt sometimes capture trout-perch.

Tiger Trout

TROUT, TIGER
A hybrid trout resulting from crossing a female brown trout with a male brook trout.
See: Trout, Brown.

TROUT-PERCH *Percopsis omiscomaycus*.
Other names—troutperch, silver chub; French: *omisco*.

A member of the small Percopsidae family, the confusingly named trout-perch is neither a trout nor a perch, nor is it of angling significance, although it is an important forage species for predators.

Identification. The trout-perch derives its name from a superficial resemblance to trout by virtue of having an adipose fin, and to yellow perch or juvenile walleye by its body configuration. It has a fairly deep cylindrical body with a narrow caudal peduncle, large eyes, and a large unscaled head that is flattened on the underside. Its color is transparent yellow olive with silver flecks above, and rows of dusky spots appear along the back and sides. A related species, the sandroller *(P. transmontana)*, is smaller and slightly darker, with a more arched back.

Size. This species reaches a maximum length of 6 to 8 inches; 3 to 5 inches is common.

Distribution. The trout-perch ranges from Hudson Bay to the Yukon Territory and from the Potomac River west to Kansas. The sandroller is found in the Columbia River drainage.

Habitat. The trout-perch occurs in lakes, and in the backwaters and pool margins of midsize to large streams. It is primarily a deep-water resident.

Spawning behavior. This species spawns in late spring, usually on sand and gravel sections of tributaries and occasionally on lake sandbars. Most trout-perch die after spawning, although a few fish live to spawn twice.

T-TOP
Center console boats often have no overhead shading or storage feature; the first ones to do so had a console-shading option that was known as a Bimini top. Then someone invented the so-called T-Top. Shaped like the letter "T," T-Tops feature aluminum frames that mount either to the deck or to the console itself, and have an overhead top made of either soft (canvas or polyester material similar to boat covers) or hard (primarily fiberglass) material. The primary purpose of the top is to provide at least minimal protection from the sun and the rain.

T-Tops, especially the hard material models, have become much more functional, and designs exist that also provide a handy spot for mounting antennas, rod holders, spreader lights, and outriggers. Many of these items used to be mounted on the gunwales of a center console, compromising the T-Tops effectiveness as a fishing platform.

Some T-Tops can incorporate a lockable electronics box on the underside, which allows some or all electronics to be positioned away from the console. They can be fitted with weather enclosures, and some models allow vertical rod holding alongside the console.
See: Sportfishing Boat.

TUBE KNOT
A fishing knot for line-to-line connections.
See: Knots, Fishing.

TUBE LURE
(1) A hollow soft plastic body covering a jig.
See: Jig.

(2) A long, slender, hollow trolling lure fashioned from plastic or rubber tubing (once surgical tubing). See: Trolling Lures, Saltwater; Umbrella Rig.

TUBERCLE
A small hard knob on the skin that appears seasonally on some breeding male fish.

TUCUNARÉ
The Brazilian/Portuguese word for peacock bass (see: bass, peacock).

TULLIBEE
A name for cisco (see), perhaps derived from the Cree Indian language.

TUNA
Tuna are members of the Scombridae family, which includes mackerel (see) and numbers some 50 species in 15 genera. They are schooling fish found throughout the open waters of most of the world's temperate and tropical seas, and are among the most commercially important fish, as they are all good to eat.

Tuna are also great gamefish. Anglers consider them the most powerful gamefish of all, and the largest members of the bluefin tuna species are the strongest of all fish pursued with rod and reel. They are also among the fastest; schools of these swift swimmers may cruise at 30 miles per hour.

All tuna have an especially streamlined body shape, with a pointed head and a much-tapered tail. The large caudal fin is lunate (crescent shaped). The spiny and soft-rayed dorsal fins are separate, the soft-rayed dorsal matched in size and shape by the anal fin directly beneath it. Following each fin is a series of finlets, the number varying with the species. In all species, the scales are extremely small or lacking. Most tuna and mackerel are ocean blue or greenish on the back, grading into silvery on the sides and the belly, but some notable exceptions occur.

Whereas fish are generally cold-blooded, tuna expert and biologist Frank Carey of Woods Hole Oceanographic Institution in Massachusetts determined that tuna are able to maintain a body temperature up to 18°F above that of the surrounding water. Carey concluded that a rise in body temperature effectively triples the power and response of a muscle mass, and explains not only the ability of tuna to seemingly fight forever on light tackle but also their adaptability to both Gulf Stream waters off the Bahamas and frigid Nova Scotian waters.

The unique physiology of tuna is such that they must consume great amounts of food to maintain their constant-swimming lifestyle and fuel the rapid growth characteristic of the tuna. Thus, tuna are likely to be encountered where massive quantities of schooling baitfish are located and feeding can be accomplished with a minimum expenditure of energy. For instance, giant bluefin tuna tend to stay with schools of herring, mackerel, and squid during summer visits to cool northern areas, whereas school bluefins may hang around shoals of sand launce (sand eels), anchovies, and other smaller baitfish off the Mid-Atlantic States. Yet, these eating machines are often no pushovers, as they can also be surprisingly fussy about baits and very line shy.

Angling for tuna is fairly similar throughout most of their range, as they are seldom encountered anywhere but in open water. Trolling with rigged baits and lures, and fishing bait from a drifting or anchored boat, are the major angling methods. A minor amount of casting is done, usually when fish are attracted close to a boat via chumming.

Prominent Species
There are 13 species of tuna, 6 of which are intensively exploited by commercial interests. Most are considered overexploited, and some—especially both species of bluefin tuna—have declined dramatically. The bluefins are relatively slow to mature and are especially vulnerable to overfishing. Albacore and skipjack tuna are the species most frequently sold in cans in the United States; the yellowfin tuna fishery in the eastern Pacific is best known for causing the deaths of porpoises (a k a "dolphins"), which are encircled and then become trapped in the purse seining nets.

Most popular among anglers are members of the *Thunnus* genus, which includes the largest of the true tuna—the bluefin and southern bluefin, yellowfin, and bigeye—as well as the smaller albacore, longtail, and blackfin. The dogtooth tuna grows to about 300 pounds, but this relatively scarce Indo-Pacific species is actually part of the closely related bonito tribe and the only one with an air bladder.

Bluefin tuna. Perhaps more than any other species, bluefin tuna are categorized in terms of their size, but, unlike most other fish, there is a definite understanding of what these terms mean. The National Marine Fisheries Service (NMFS) has changed what used to be commonly accepted angler definitions of school (under 100 pounds), medium (100 to 400 pounds) and giant (400 pounds up) bluefins. The definitions they now use for management purposes are definitive. Small school bluefins are those under 27 inches curved fork length; these can never be retained. School bluefins are from 27 to 47 inches (about 14 to 66 pounds). Large schoolies range from 47 to 59 inches (66 to 135 pounds), and small mediums from 59 to 73 inches (135 to 235 pounds). All bluefin of these sizes in the U.S. are reserved for angling and cannot be sold. Large medium bluefins are from 73 to 81 inches (235 to 310 pounds), and giants are from 81 inches up. Large medium and giant bluefin can be sold.

Fishing for giant bluefins is fundamentally different from fishing for all other tuna in that the sheer size and power of the fish dictate the use of very heavy tackle. The International Game Fish Association (IGFA) limits sportfishing tackle to 130-pound line, and this was traditionally the standard for giant tuna sportfishing. Some anglers also used 80-pound tackle, but only those seeking records dropped to 50-pound, and they found it almost impossible to boat giants until the IGFA extended the allowable length of double line and leader.

Tackle got much heavier when Japanese fish buyers began paying big money for giants starting in the mid-1970s. Most giant tuna anglers from New Jersey through Maine now use lines even heavier than 130 pounds and "fight" their quarry out of pivoting rod holders by just cranking on the handle of a two-speed lever-drag 130-pound reel. Hardly any of the giants boated during the spring to fall northeastern U.S. season are caught in sporting fashion, as the objective is getting a valuable fish in quickly.

Sporting tackle still prevails during the winter fishery off Hatteras and Morehead City, North Carolina, and will as long as the NMFS continues to prohibit the sale of those fish, which are almost exclusively released. Most winter bluefins are also tagged and provide a wealth of information for scientists. Because those fish are encountered in relatively shallow waters, sometimes less than 90 feet, it's possible to not only fight them on standard 130-pound gear, but also for experienced anglers to release most in 5 to 15 minutes by using heavy drags.

Unlike most other members of the genus, bluefins are basically inshore fish that at times even enter the mouths of large bays, such as Rhode Island's Narragansett Bay. When much more abundant, giant tuna were even regularly caught in ocean fish traps along the northern New Jersey shore. Many popular fishing areas for bluefins, such as the Mud Hole in the New York/New Jersey Bight and Stellwagen Bight in Cape Cod Bay, are within 20 miles of shore. Boats out of North Lake in Prince Edward Island and in the Canso Causeway area of Nova Scotia can start trolling daisy chains of mackerel almost as soon as they leave their docks.

Bluefins are important to anglers along the U.S. Atlantic Coast from North Carolina to the Canadian Maritimes. Many spawning bluefins are encountered by longliners in the Gulf of Mexico during the winter, but few are caught by anglers in those waters. However, there is a traditional trolling fishery for giants off Bimini and Cat Cay in the Bahamas, as those giants head north in the spring. Bluefins also provide a major fishery in the Mediterranean Sea and in the Atlantic around Spain, although the formerly strong North Sea fisheries have long been depleted.

This fishery is managed by the International Commission for the Conservation of Atlantic Tunas (ICCAT), which has imposed severe restrictions on the depleted western Atlantic bluefin stocks but provides much more liberal regulations on the European and African fisheries, which harvest vast numbers of tiny bluefins as well as giants. Management has been based on a two-stock theory that assumes there is only occasional interchange across the ocean. Extensive tagging, however, now indicates there may be a much more regular interchange, which would dictate a change in regulations.

The same species occurs in the North Pacific Ocean, although it never seems to grow to much more than 500 pounds—as compared to a maximum of about 1,500 pounds in the Atlantic. Sportfishing for tuna started when Charles Holder subdued a 183-pound bluefin off Santa Catalina Island in Southern California in 1898, and the Tuna Club of Avalon record was pushed to 251½ pounds the next year despite the primitive tackle used during the infancy of big-game fishing. Commercial fishing pressure severely reduced that fishery within a few decades, and bluefins were eventually all but wiped out by purse seiners along the coasts of California and Mexico's Baja California, as the last significant sportfish-

A giant bluefin comes through the transom door off Provincetown, Cape Cod, Massachusetts.

ing catches of even small schoolies by the wide-ranging California sportfishing fleet were made in 1956. The decline of the San Pedro purse seining fleet, however, permitted a return of fair numbers of school bluefins in 1992, and they've built up since then, and ever-larger fish are now encountered.

School bluefins provided a consistent trolling fishery for slow private and charter boats along the mid-Atlantic coast from at least the 1920s, as they rarely had to run more than 20 miles offshore in order to fill their boxes. Large charter fleets developed in such ports as Beach Haven, New Jersey, and Freeport, New York, but most of those boats disappeared after tuna stocks were decimated by purse seining in the 1960s and 1970s, plus an extensive Japanese longlining effort on spawning giants in the Gulf of Mexico during a portion of the same period. Regulations adopted during the 1990s prohibit the sale of bluefins under 225 pounds and impose severe catch limitations on anglers but have failed to return that fishery to even a fraction of the early-1970s level, which was already only a shadow of what existed prior to the 1960s.

The southern bluefin is found worldwide from about 30° to 50° south latitude. It is distinguished from the bluefin only by a difference in the number of gill rakers and by being the only species of *Thunnus* in which the caudal keels are bright yellow. It is most commonly caught in Australia and New Zealand, and doesn't appear to achieve true "giant" sizes of 400 pounds or more.

Yellowfin tuna. Yellowfins are the most common warmwater tuna, and the most colorful. Indeed, many large yellowfins become particularly distinguished as they grow extremely long second dorsal and anal fins. These fish are often referred to as Allisons and were once thought to be a separate species. Although heavily pursued by purse seiners and longliners, yellowfins have managed to remain reasonably abundant in their ocean haunts. Although not strictly committed to the depths, yellowfins only occasionally wander relatively close to shore. One such exception occurred during the mid-1980s when vast quantities of sand launce (sand eels) lured yellowfins to banks and sloughs within 12 miles of northern New Jersey and Montauk, New York, for several summers. The only area along the U.S. Atlantic coast where they're regularly caught within 30 miles of shore is off the Outer Banks of North Carolina due to the proximity of the Gulf Stream.

A surface fish, yellowfins are a good target for trollers. Canyon anglers usually make their biggest catches by chunking for yellowfins at night and are often able to spot them racing through the slick to pick up chunks.

Most yellowfins are caught in sizes under 100 pounds, but they are common up to 200 pounds and can grow to 400 or more pounds. The largest yellowfins have been encountered by San Diego long-range party boats fishing in the Revillagigedo Islands off the coast of Baja California, Mexico. Specimens exceeding 200 pounds are common during many winter trips, and some in the 300- to 400-pound class are boated.

Bigeye tuna. Bigeyes are found in warm temperate waters of the Atlantic, Pacific, and Indian Oceans. Although the IGFA maintains separate records for the Atlantic and Pacific, the species is the same. They frequent the depths, particularly during the day, and, unlike other tuna, are rarely seen chasing baits at the surface.

Bigeyes are very strong fighters caught on baits primarily set at depths of 100 feet or more during the night and are irregularly caught by trolling, even at night around a full moon. They are just about as highly regarded as fresh fish by sophisticated Japanese food purveyors, as are medium and giant bluefins.

Anglers tend to troll for them with heavy tackle, such as 80-pound outfits, although most caught in mid-Atlantic canyons are only in the 100- to 250-pound class; any exceeding 300 pounds are exceptional. The maximum size of these fish in the Atlantic appears to be around 400 pounds. A Pacific fishery off Ecuador and Cabo Blanco, Peru, has produced bigeyes exceeding 400 pounds, although the once-large runs in that area have been depleted by commercial fishing.

Its large eyes, which probably facilitate feeding activities in low light deep below the surface, aren't sufficient to differentiate this species from yellowfins in smaller sizes, especially after the fish are dead. Sure identification involves the liver, as there are striations on the margin of the bigeye's liver, and the right and left lobes are about the same size. The yellowfin's liver is smooth, and its right lobe is longer than the middle or left.

Albacore. Albacore are the only white meat tuna and as such are highly valued by Americans as the finest canned tuna, but Japanese fish processors downgrade them for the same reason. Although much smaller than other members of their genus, these fish are good sport on lighter tackle. Often referred to as longfins, they are easily distinguished by pectoral fins that extend beyond the anal fin and by their somewhat slimmer form.

These oceanic wanderers are most important to anglers in the Pacific, and their summer appearances well off California lure thousands of anglers to the docks. Although Southern California is the focal point for that summer fishery, the migration takes them far north, and they are frequently found within range of boats from Northern California to Washington. El Niño years provide much warmer waters that bring albacore even closer, and can provide an unusual tropical fishery in British Columbia. Not only did that occur in 1997, but much larger than normal albacore were caught, and the 90-pound mark was finally broached off California when those fish should have been long gone, in January 1998. Anglers could thank El Niño for this.

Albacore are also important to canyon anglers in the western North Atlantic. Only a scattered few are normally caught from the more southerly canyons, but large schools tend to show during late summer into early fall from Hudson Canyon east. Anglers also enjoy good fishing for albacore across the Atlantic in the Azores, Canary Islands, and Madeira.

Longtail tuna. The longtail tuna is more elongated than the southern bluefin and much smaller, with a maximum size possibly around 80 pounds. It is an inshore species of the tropical and subtropical Pacific and the eastern Indian Ocean, and is caught in large schools off the western and northeastern coasts of Australia.

Blackfin tuna. The blackfin only runs up to about 50 pounds and is most common in the 10- to 30-pound range. It is Florida's primary tuna, and is most abundant from there south to Brazil and also in the Gulf of Mexico and Caribbean Sea. Blackfins are fine light-tackle fish, especially when chummed to the boat with live baits. Charter captains at Islamorada, Florida, specialize in that sport, cast netting hundreds of pilchards that are then distributed on The Hump (a mountain peak in the Gulf Stream) to attract blackfins, which can be hooked on the live baits or sometimes even by flycasters. Another popular but more complicated method involves rigging the wings of dead flyingfish to hold them straight out and then bouncing those baits in and out of the water from outriggers.

Little tunny. The genus *Euthynnus* includes three tuna species that tend to live closer to shore and are highly regarded as baitfish, although they are generally considered the least palatable of the tuna. The coarse red flesh of the Atlantic's little tunny results in its being looked down on, although it may well be one of the world's finest small gamefish. Indeed, they frequently fight so hard on light tackle that anglers find themselves boating dead or almost dead fish. Little tunny are almost never referred to by their correct name, instead being called false albacore in the northeastern U.S. and "bonito" (confusing them with Atlantic bonito) from Virginia south to the Gulf of Mexico. Identification is never a problem due to the several black spots always present under the pectoral fin.

Although they spread themselves out over the continental shelf, little tunny are most abundant within 30 miles of shore during a late-summer to early-fall run along the mid-Atlantic and southern New England coasts, when they average 5 to 15 pounds. Unlike the other tuna, the little tunny commonly chases baits into the surf and can be caught by surf casters retrieving small metal lures and jigs at high speed. Many are also caught by trollers seeking school tuna and in chum lines intended for bluefish. The same species is encountered south to Brazil and across the Atlantic to Europe and the Mediterranean and down to South Africa.

Black skipjack. The black skipjack is the eastern Pacific version of the little tunny. Primarily found from California to Peru, it is often conveniently available in large schools at black marlin hotspots such as Hannibal Bank and Piñas Reef in Panama, where ideal-size live baits in the 2- to 4-pound class will swim for hours when rigged Australian-style. The third very similar member of the genus is the kawakawa, which is primarily found in the western Pacific and Oceania. All three species would be considered large when weighing in the midteens, and they grow to a maximum of about 35 pounds in the case of the little tunny.

Skipjack tuna. The skipjack tuna (not to be confused with the black skipjack) is the lone member of the genus *Katsuwonus,* and has also suffered from name misidentification over the years with such misnomers as arctic bonito and oceanic bonito—even though it's a tuna, not a bonito. It is readily identified by the stripes along its belly, which are unique in the clan. This fine gamefish is widely distributed in temperate and tropical seas, and often travels in huge schools, making it a favorite of purse seiners, who capture it for cannery conversion into chunk light tuna. Despite that, many anglers turn their noses up at the softer skipjacks as being less desirable than most other tuna. Anglers catch skipjacks primarily while trolling. They are quite common from 5 to 15 pounds but may run as large as 50 pounds.

Sportfishing Techniques

Anglers pursue tuna by many means around the globe, but their basic physical characteristics largely determine the methodology. For instance, trolling occurs almost invariably at as high a speed as will work the lures or baits correctly. An exception involves the spreader bar rigs that have become popular for medium and giant bluefins in the northeast U.S. They're trolled somewhat slower than other tuna lures due to the action provided by multiple mackerel or artificial squid splashing on the surface. Live baits also can be trolled as slowly as necessary to keep them alive, and the same applies to live or dead baits fished from downriggers.

The vast majority of tuna trolling, however, involves rigged baits or lures being trolled at speeds of 6 to 8 knots or more. It's probably impossible to run away from a tuna that wants to eat at any speed at which that bait or lure can be kept in the water. High-speed trolling is particularly effective, as most species of tuna seem to be attracted by wakes and possibly engine noise. Some lures should always be placed in the whitewater very close to the boat and pinned down to stay there. Feathers and cedar jigs are ideal for that purpose. The wakes created by some boats seem to produce more tuna than others, and theories abound as to what the reason might be.

Trolling can be "blind" in areas where tuna should be present, or directed to surface schooling fish. Most of the yellowfin, bigeye, and albacore tuna trolled in U.S. East Coast canyons (100-fathom dropoffs at the edge of the continental shelf far offshore) are caught by blind trolling, especially where baits are marked and around temperature breaks. The arrival of a Gulf Stream eddy usually ensures a tuna bite.

In areas without such "structure," trollers often depend on sightings in order to focus their efforts. This is particularly the case with yellowfin tuna in the Pacific, as those fish associate with porpoises, a fact purse seiners learned long ago. Invariably, those feeding tuna are moving at a high rate of speed, and boaters may have a hard time keeping up with them.

Balao and large squid make good natural trolling baits. Straight-running high-speed offshore trolling lures work well for larger tuna; jethead versions are particularly favored for bigeyes. Lure sizes are scaled down for smaller specimens of large tuna as well as the smaller species, but even the largest tuna sometimes prefer short lures if they're feeding on similar-looking baits. Plugs that can be run at relatively high trolling speeds are also effective.

The lack of an air bladder is also a clue to hooking tuna on bait. Anyone who has watched tuna feeding alongside understands that no matter how much bait is provided, tuna always move through at a steady swimming pace. There is no such thing as a tuna "nibble." They either suck in or reject a bait as they swim through. Thus, it's possible to instantly hook a tuna by coming tight when it hits. Dropping back to those fish may result in deeper hooking, if that's the object, provided that the tuna doesn't spit the bait first if it feels something is wrong.

Chumming *(see)* is a popular method of attracting tuna in many areas. In some cases it's accomplished with ground-up fish that forms a slick. Tuna seem to be more attracted to meat than scent, however, so chunking with pieces of baitfish tends to be more effective. Chunking is the primary means of catching bluefins in the northeast U.S., from schoolies, which are sought primarily for sport and food in the Mid-Atlantic States, to giants, which are big business in New England for shipment at very high prices to Japan.

Chumming is also the basic method of yellowfin tuna fishing on Challenger and Argus Banks off Bermuda. Long-range party boat anglers from San Diego who used to fish yellowfins exclusively with live baits, found during the 1990s that chunking was sometimes more effective, particularly for the largest fish.

At first it would seem that tuna would be reluctant to eat dead baits in a chum line. But these fish have learned to adapt and frequently are found

Swirls and boils in the water off this boat's transom are made by frenzied school tuna ripping through bait and chum.

feeding on fish spilling out of trawler nets or being thrown overboard by commercial vessels as unmarketable. Bluefins are particularly noted for this tendency, and they rarely display any selectivity in eating everything provided free. It's only when a heavy hook and leader are attached to one of those baits that tuna become selective. Frequently they'll run through the chum line picking up every scrap of even old rotten fish while leaving the freshest item in the selection—the one with a hook in it that isn't drifting down at the correct rate.

The general rule in tuna chunking is to drop over just a few chunks and wait until the current carries them out of sight before repeating the procedure. Baited lines may be worked in the chum line by being dropped back with the chunks and fed out for a couple of hundred feet, after which it will be well below the chunks. Other lines are set at various depths with the aid of sinkers and held in place with floats. The depth selected may be based on recent experience, or by viewing marks on sonar. Many professionals use scanning sonar as well as conventional recorders in order to pinpoint tuna movements and bait placement. In earlier days, this was accomplished with a spool of 4-pound monofilament line tied to a bait and fed back into the slick where a tuna would surely grab it on such light line and give away its presence.

Anglers use a great variety of dead baits. Butterfish and menhaden are the most likely choices in the Mid-Atlantic, whereas New England anglers use mostly the herring and mackerel that attract giants to that area during the summer. These baits may be used whole or cut. When giant tuna are fussy, anglers often resort to a mousetrap rig in which a cable leader is bundled up on a short-shanked hook and secured with a rubber band or shrink tape before being sewn into the bait. The small teeth of tuna wear down leaders during the course of a long fight, but the cable eliminates that problem, and the mousetrap rig permits elimination of a heavy leader that could spook fish. Most tuna anglers are turning to fluorocarbon leaders in order to overcome the visibility factor with 300-pound mono leaders.

Any sort of small live bait found in the area is desirable. Mackerel, harbor pollock, silver hake (whiting), red hake (ling), menhaden (bunker), and bluefish are most commonly used in the northeastern U.S. Live baits are also used as chum in situations where large quantities can be obtained and kept. For instance, anglers fishing out of Southern California have long gone to sea with livewells full of anchovies to be tossed at schools of yellowfin tuna. Long-range party boats from San Diego also jig up quantities of mackerel and scad, which may be used in smaller quantities as chum in addition to live baits. Commercial fishermen at Madeira net mackerel at night and then chum with them during the day to raise bigeye tuna to their live mackerel offerings.

Relatively few tuna are caught on lures that are cast, but that method is very exciting and seems to be gaining popularity. Casting usually involves spotting surfacing schools of tuna and getting ahead of them to make a cast. Popping and swimming plugs that can be retrieved at a rapid pace are ideal for this method, which is becoming more common off Virginia and North Carolina. Watching a school of tuna attack a popper is among the greatest thrills in fishing. When tuna are feeding in chum lines, it's often possible to stir them up with a popping or darting plug, and that is frequently done with yellowfins in Bermuda.

Various types of jigs can also be worked effectively for tuna. Anglers in the northeastern U.S. catch many school and medium bluefins on diamond jigs. The usual method involves a fast retrieve, but the flutter of a falling diamond jig is often sufficient to attract tuna strikes when the lure is simply moved up and down in long sweeps at a level where the depth recorder indicates the fish are coming through.

Tackle for tuna fishing runs the gamut, from the heaviest gear to almost ultralight. Sportfishing for giant tuna almost invariably involves fighting them out of a fighting chair with 130-pound tackle, but a few have been caught when the angler was standing up—particularly during the winter fishery at Hatteras, where the abundance of tuna and relatively shallow water create a perfect opportunity for such an achievement.

Stand-up tackle *(see: stand-up fishing)* suitable to handle all but the largest of tuna was developed aboard San Diego long-range party boats, where anglers often fight yellowfins well over 200 pounds at anchor. The long, parabolic trolling rods that were once pressed into service for stand-up fishing worked against the angler, creating lots of back strain without putting enough pressure on the fish. Those Californians created short rods (5^1/$_2$ to 6 feet) with extended foregrips and tip action. This innovation brought the bend of the flexed rod almost back to the upper hand, putting leverage in the angler's favor. These rods, combined with dual-gear-ratio reels and rod belts and harnesses that are worn low and transfer pressure to the thighs, have made it possible for stand-up anglers to battle tuna to well over 300 pounds with fair success and a good chance of staying out of the hospital.

Trolling tackle for large tuna other than giants usually involves 50- and 80-pound outfits. That gear may be too heavy for the average catch, but most anglers want to be ready for the occasional large yellowfin or bigeye. In areas closer to shore, it's much sportier to troll with 20- and 30-pound outfits for smaller tuna such as school bluefins and yellowfins or blackfins, which may be mixed with such species as little tunny, skipjacks, bonito, dolphin, and king mackerel.

Light spinning and baitcasting tackle is perfect for chumming little tunny and skipjacks, and is still sufficient for handling most school tuna. Those fish are often leader shy, and it may be necessary to drop to 20-pound leaders to get strikes.

Tuna are difficult to catch on fly tackle due to their high-speed lifestyle. Even when it's possible to cast to moving tuna, it's hard to strip fast enough to interest them. The best bet for hooking up is in chum slicks, as the fish are then concentrated for each cast and they can occasionally be worked into such a competitive feeding frenzy with chunks that just about any fly flipped out to them will be inhaled immediately.

It is frequently necessary to run after large tuna to prevent reels from being stripped. Skippers fishing at anchor, particularly for giants, utilize an anchor ball that permits them to cast off their anchor within seconds in order to both follow the fish and avoid getting cut off or tangled in their own anchor line. Anglers who try to fight giants with their arms rarely last long. The technique from a chair uses the legs and lower back in a seat harness with a sliding motion across the chair to retrieve line.

The stand-up technique for large tuna works best with a short stroke, raising the rod only a few inches to gain line rather than lifting it overhead. The idea is to keep the tuna's head up and coming steadily, whereas the long stroke allows the tuna to get his head down no matter how fast the angler thinks he's reeling. Mastering the short-stroke technique can change excruciatingly long, painful battles with tuna into relatively short, pleasant ones.

Unless tuna are to be released, they are normally gaffed. As tuna don't jump or do anything unusual except continue to forge ahead when wired alongside, straight gaffs work well on them. Some anglers do prefer flying gaffs for large tuna, and most giant tuna pros now use cockpit harpoons (which aren't legal under IGFA standards) to ensure their capture.

Although the tuna remains a fish that is sought as much for its flesh as for sport, release fishing

---

One of the earliest laws regulating the taking of fish was the 1678 Virginia regulation that banned the attraction of fish with lights.

is increasing steadily in popularity even for this species. Tagging makes releasing fish even more worthwhile, and anglers are urged to participate in U.S. government programs that provide free tags. For Atlantic waters, contact Cooperative Tagging Center, NMFS/NOAA, Southeast Fisheries Center, 75 Virginia Beach Dr., Miami, FL 33149. For Pacific waters, contact Cooperative Marine Gamefish Tagging Program, NMFS/NOAA, Southwest Fisheries Center, P.O. Box 271, La Jolla, CA 92038.

Other Issues
Identifying tuna. There is often confusion about tuna species, especially those of small to intermediate size. Some external clues do exist that aid in making a quick identification, which may be necessary to enable the release of specific species and to comply with existing regulations. Most external clues involve fin length.

If the pectoral fin, when held flush to the side of the tuna's body, ends well before the origin of the second dorsal fin, the fish is probably a bluefin tuna. If the pectoral fin extends to or past the origin of the second dorsal fin, it is likely either a bigeye or yellowfin. A tuna with extremely long pectoral fins, extending beyond the origin of the anal fin, is most likely an albacore. A tuna exceeding 40 pounds with extremely long anal and second dorsal fins is most likely a yellowfin.

Other clues are useful only after the species has been landed and is dead. This includes counting the gill rakers on the first gill arch and observing the liver for its shape and presence of striations. Headed and gutted yellowfin tuna have a distinct, white, fleshy round node (like a fleshy cord) that runs along the top of the body cavity from front to rear. This is absent in bigeye and bluefin.

Headed and gutted bluefin tuna have a distinct pocket that can be felt by running a hand along the inside of the body cavity underneath the insertion of the pectoral fin. Yellowfin and bigeye tuna do not have this indentation in their body cavity.

Measurements. For some regions where tuna are found (especially the western Atlantic), total curved fork length is the sole criterion for determining the size class of whole (head on) tuna for regulatory purposes. Curved fork length means a measurement of the length of a tuna taken in a line tracing the contour of the body from the tip of the upper jaw to the fork of the tail, which abuts the upper side of the pectoral fin and the upper side of the caudal keel. When determining this length, the measuring tape must pass over (and touch) the pectoral fin and the caudal keel.

Atlantic tuna permits. Bluefin, bigeye, yellowfin, skipjack, albacore, and blackfin tuna, as well as bonito, are all regulated in U.S. waters of the western Atlantic. All owners/operators of commercial, charter, head boat, and recreational vessels harvesting regulated Atlantic tuna must obtain an Atlantic Tunas Permit issued by NMFS. These permits are issued in six categories, five of which are assigned as "commercial" permits: General, Charter/Head Boat, Harpoon Boat, Purse Seine, and Incidental Catch. The remaining permit category, Angling, is for recreational catches.

Only one category is assigned to a vessel. Atlantic tuna may be sold only by those permitted in commercial categories and may be sold only to permitted dealers. Atlantic tuna taken by persons aboard Angling category vessels may not be sold. Thus, charter boats may fish in a "recreational manner" for tuna, but they are classified as commercial vessels if it is their intent (which it is for many) to sell their catch. The propriety of doing this, of course, is questionable, especially when it is the angling community that clamors most for management of the fisheries and restrictions that would help rebuild stocks.

See: Albacore; Big-Game Fishing; Offshore Fishing; Skipjack, Black; Tuna, Bigeye; Tuna, Blackfin; Tuna, Bluefin; Tuna, Dogtooth; Tuna, Longtail; Tuna, Skipjack; Tuna, Southern Bluefin; Tuna, Yellowfin; Tunny, Little.

TUNA, BIGEYE *Thunnus obesus.*
Other names—bigeyed tuna, bigeye tunny; French: *patudo, thon obèse;* Hawaiian: *ahi;* Indo-nesian: *taguw, tongkol;* Italian: *tonno obeso;* Japanese: *mebachi, mebuto;* Portuguese: *albacora bandolim, atum patudo, patudo;* Spanish: *albacora, atún ojo grande, patudo.*

Like other tuna, the bigeye is a member of the Scombridae family and a strong-fighting species that is equally revered for sport as for its flesh. The meat of large bigeyes is as favored as that of medium and giant bluefin tuna.

Identification. A stocky body and large eyes characterize this species. Generally, there are no special markings on the body, but some specimens may have vertical rows of whitish spots on the venter. The first dorsal fin is deep yellow. The second dorsal fin and the anal fin are blackish brown or yellow and may be edged with black. The finlets are bright yellow with narrow black edges. The tail does not have a white trailing edge like that of the albacore.

The pectoral fins may reach to the second dorsal fin. The second dorsal and anal fins never reach back as far as those of large yellowfin tuna *(see: tuna, yellowfin).* It has a total of 23 to 31 gill rakers on the first arch. The margin of the liver is striated. The two dorsal fins are close-set, the first having 13 to 14 spines and the second 14 to 16 rays. The anal fin has 11 to 15 rays. On either side of the caudal peduncle is a strong lateral keel between two small keels that are located slightly farther back on the tail. The scales are small except on the anterior corselet. The vent is oval or teardrop shaped, not round as in the albacore.

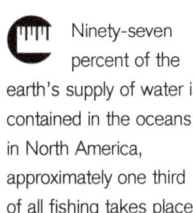
Ninety-seven percent of the earth's supply of water is contained in the oceans; in North America, approximately one third of all fishing takes place in saltwater.

Bigeye Tuna

At one time the bigeye was not recognized as a separate species but considered a variation of the yellowfin tuna. They are similar in many respects, but the bigeye's second dorsal and anal fins never grow as long as those of the yellowfin. In the bigeye tuna, the margin of the liver is striated and the right lobe is about the same size as the left lobe; in the yellowfin tuna, the liver is smooth and the right lobe is clearly longer than either the left or the middle lobe.

Size. Bigeyes are normally found from 16 to 67 inches in length but may attain 75 inches. They usually exceed 100 pounds in weight in U.S. waters. The all-tackle world record is a 435-pound fish caught off Peru in 1957. Although separate angling records are kept for bigeyes occurring in the Atlantic and Pacific, they are the same species.

Distribution/Habitat. Found in warm temperate waters of the Atlantic, Indian, and Pacific Oceans, this schooling, pelagic, seasonally migratory species is suspected of making rather extensive migrations. Schools of bigeye tuna generally run deep during the day, whereas schools of bluefin, yellowfin, and some other tuna are known to occasionally swim at the surface, especially in warm water.

Spawning behavior. Bigeye tuna reach sexual maturity at about 40 to 50 inches in length and spawn at least twice a year. This occurs throughout the year in tropical waters, peaking during summer months.

Food. The diet of bigeyes includes squid, crustaceans, mullet, sardines, small mackerel, and some deep-water species. They frequent the depths, particularly during the day, and, unlike other tuna, are rarely seen chasing baitfish at the surface.

Angling. Bigeyes are strong fighters and are caught on baits primarily set at depths of 100 feet or more during the night. Anglers irregularly catch them by trolling, even at night around a full moon. Fishing methods include trolling deep with squid, mullet, or other small baits, plus artificial lures, and live-bait fishing in deep water.

See: Big-Game Fishing; Offshore Fishing; Tuna.

TUNA, BLACKFIN *Thunnus atlanticus.*
Other names—Bermuda tuna, blackfinned albacore, deep-bodied tunny; French: *bonite, giromon, thon nuit;* Japanese: *mini maguro, monte maguro, taiseiyo maguro;* Spanish: *albacora, atún aleta negra.*

A member of the Scombridae family and one of the smaller tuna, the blackfin is primarily a sportfish with minor commercial interest. Found on or near the surface, it is readily caught on light tackle and is a strong fighter whose flesh is of good quality and flavor.

Identification. The pectoral fins of the blackfin tuna reach to somewhere between the twelfth dorsal spine and the origin of the second dorsal fin, but they never extend beyond the second dorsal fin as in the albacore *(see)*. There is a total of 19 to 25 (usually 21 to 23) gill rakers on the first arch (15 to 19 are on the lower limb), which is fewer than in any other species of *Thunnus*. The finlets are uniformly dark, without a touch of the bright lemon yellow usually present in those of other tuna, and they may have white edges. Light bars alternate with light spots on the lower flanks. The first dorsal fin is dusky; the second dorsal and anal fins are also dusky with a silvery luster. The back of the fish is bluish black, the sides are silvery gray, and the belly is milky white. A small swim bladder is present. The ventral surface of the liver is without striations, and the right lobe is longer than the left and center lobes.

Size. Blackfin tuna may attain a maximum length of 40 inches, although they are common at about 28 inches and weigh in the 10- to 30-pound

Blackfin Tuna

range. The all-tackle world record is a 45-pound, 8-ounce Florida fish.

Distribution/Habitat. Blackfin are a pelagic, schooling fish that occurs in the tropical and warm temperate waters of the western Atlantic from Brazil to Cape Cod, including the Caribbean and the Gulf of Mexico. They are most common from North Carolina south, and are Florida's most abundant tuna.

Spawning behavior. The blackfin's spawning grounds are believed to be well offshore. Off Florida, the spawning season extends from April through November with a peak in May; in the Gulf of Mexico, it lasts from June through September.

Food and feeding habits. The diet of blackfin tuna consists of small fish, squid, crustaceans, and plankton. Blackfin often feed near the surface, and they frequently form large mixed schools with skipjacks.

Angling. An excellent light-tackle species, the blackfin can be taken by trolling or casting small lures, flies, or natural baits, including ballyhoo, mullet, and other small fish, as well as strip baits, spoons, feathers, jigs, or plugs. They are also pursued by chumming or live-bait fishing from boats at the surface of deep waters 1 to 2 miles offshore. A popular method employed in the Florida Keys involves rigging the wings of dead flyingfish to hold them straight out and then bouncing those baits in and out of the water from outriggers.

See: Big-Game Fishing; Offshore Fishing; Tuna.

TUNA, BLUEFIN *Thunnus thynnus*.

Other names—Atlantic bluefin tuna, northern bluefin tuna, tunny fish, horse-mackerel; Arabic: *tunna;* Chinese: *cá chan, thu;* French: *thon rouge;* Italian: *tonno;* Japanese: *kuromaguro;* Norwegian: *sjorjf, thunfisk;* Portuguese: *atum, rabilha;* Spanish: *atún aleta azul, atun rojo;* Turkish: *orkinos.*

The bluefin tuna is the largest member of the Scombridae family and one of the largest true bony fish. A pelagic, schooling, highly migratory species, it has enormous commercial value, especially in large sizes. It is of great recreational interest, albeit only to the relative few who have the means and equipment to venture to appropriate offshore environs.

The red flesh of the bluefin has made the species coveted for food, especially in Japan, where giant specimens are sold at daily auction for prices far greater than those demanded for other species, especially late in the season when the meat contains the most fat. To date, the largest price paid for a single Atlantic bluefin was U.S. $90,000 at the Tokyo market, making this species the most economically valuable wild animal on the planet. Bluefin tuna are prepared for consumption in many ways but are most commonly associated with sushi and sashimi.

High demand for its dark red flesh has made the bluefin tuna the object of intense commercial and recreational fishing efforts and has resulted in a dwindling population of adult fish. This species, as well as its cousin the southern bluefin tuna *(see: tuna, southern bluefin),* is gravely overfished, and its numbers have declined dramatically in the western Atlantic, the eastern Atlantic, and the Pacific. According to some estimates, the population of the species in the western Atlantic has declined by roughly 87 percent since 1970. The southern bluefin tuna population may have declined by as much as 90 percent. Commercial fisheries continue to be active in the Bay of Biscay, off the Iberian Peninsula, in the Mediterranean, and off North America. Fisheries in the North Sea and off South America have collapsed.

Because both species are slow to mature, they are especially vulnerable to overexploitation. Although some catch quotas have been established, the con-

Bluefin Tuna

tinued landing of small bluefins as well as large ones (called giants) in some regions, the failure to restrict harvest in others, the ignorance of restrictions by commercial fishermen of some countries, the lack of punishment or enforcement, and the managerial treatment of bluefins on a separate two-stock basis instead of one interpolar migratory one are leading reasons for both species of bluefin tuna to be further troubled if not endangered. In 1996, scientists warned that existing worldwide catch quotas would have to be cut by 80 percent for populations to recover in 20 years, but they were raised instead.

Identification. The bluefin tuna has a fusiform body, compressed and stocky in front. It can be distinguished from almost all other tuna by its rather short pectoral fins, which extend only as far back as the eleventh or twelfth spine in the first dorsal fin. There are 12 to 14 spines in the first dorsal fin and 13 to 15 rays in the second. The anal fin has 11 to 15 rays. It has the highest gill raker count of any species of *Thunnus,* with 34 to 43 on the first arch. The ventral surface of the liver is striated, and the middle lobe is usually the largest.

The back and upper sides are dark blue to black with a gray or green iridescence. The lower sides are silvery, marked with gray spots and bands. The anal fin is dusky and has some yellow. The finlets are yellow and edged with black. The caudal keel is black at the adult stage but is semitransparent when immature.

Size/Age. Bluefin tuna can grow to more than 10 feet and are commonly found at lengths from 16 to 79 inches. Adults weigh from 300 to 1,500 pounds, although fish exceeding 1,000 pounds are rare. The all-tackle world record is a fish from Nova Scotia that weighed 1,496 pounds when caught in 1979. The species reportedly can live for 40 years.

Distribution/Habitat. Bluefin tuna occur in subtropical and temperate waters of the north Pacific Ocean, the North Atlantic Ocean, and in the Mediterranean and Black Seas. They are widely distributed throughout the Atlantic. Distribution in the western Atlantic occurs along Labrador and Newfoundland southward to Tobago, Trinidad, Venezuela, and the Brazilian coast; they are especially encountered by anglers off Nova Scotia and Prince Edward Island; Cape Cod; Montauk, New York; the canyons offshore of New York and New Jersey; the North Carolina region; and the Bahamas. Distribution in the eastern Atlantic extends as far north as Norway and Iceland, and as far south as northern West Africa. Atlantic bluefin tuna spawn in the Gulf of Mexico between April and June and in the Mediterranean Sea in June and July.

Life history/Behavior. Bluefin tuna are warm blooded and able to maintain their body temperatures up to 18°F above the surrounding water, which makes them superbly adapted to temperate and cold waters. They retain 98 percent of muscular heat, may have the highest metabolism of any known fish, and are among the fastest and most wide-ranging animals on earth. When hunted or hunting, they can accelerate to 35 miles per hour.

Bluefins are schooling fish and do congregate by size, although the largest schools are formed by

A small bluefin tuna from the offshore waters of Montauk, New York.

the smallest individuals, and the smallest schools are composed of the largest fish. They swim in a single file, side by side (soldier formation), or in an arc (hunter formation). Sometimes bluefins swim below a school of yellowfin tuna, relying on the skittish yellowfin to alert them of predators.

Extensive migrations appear to be tied to water temperature, spawning habits, and the seasonal movements of forage species. Specimens tagged in the Bahamas have been recaptured as far north as Newfoundland and Norway and as far south as Uruguay. In some cases, the recaptured fish had traveled 5,000 miles in 50 days. The giants of the species make the longest migrations.

During spawning, a giant female may shed 25 million or more eggs. Larvae have one chance in 40 million of reaching adulthood eight years later, but the survivors grow rapidly and may be 2-feet long and weigh 9 pounds by the end of their first year. By age 14 they may be more than 8-feet long and weigh 700 pounds.

Bluefins in the western Atlantic are sexually mature at approximately age 8 (80 inches curved fork length), and in the eastern Atlantic at about age 5 (60 inches).

Food. The diet of bluefin tuna consists of squid, eels, and crustaceans, as well as pelagic schooling fish such as mackerel, flyingfish, herring, whiting, and mullet.

Angling. Bluefins are not flashy fighters that jump out of the water like other highly prized species; however, they are tractor-pull strong and capable of great speeds. Fishing methods include stillfishing or trolling with live or dead baits such as mackerel, herring, mullet, or squid; and trolling with artificial lures, including spoons, plugs, or feathers.

See: Big-Game Fishing; Offshore Fishing; Tuna.

TUNA, DOGTOOTH *Gymnosarda unicolor.*
Other names—white tuna, scaleless tuna, lizard-mouth tuna, jackass, pegtooth tuna; Arabic: *moakaba, tomad;* French: *bonite à gros yeux, thon blanc;* Japanese: *isomaguro, tokakin;* Spanish: *casarte ojón;* various South Pacific Islands: *vau, atu, kidukidu, dadori.*

This generally lesser-known member of the Scombridae family has minor commercial value and is often an incidental catch for anglers. It is good table fare and has white flesh, which causes it to be named "white tuna" in some places.

Identification. The dogtooth tuna is noted for its lack of scales (except on the corselet and along either side of the lateral line) and for its large conical teeth—features that have earned it the names "scaleless tuna" and "dogtooth tuna" respectively, although it is actually a bonito. The first dorsal fin has 13 to 15 spines; the second is higher and has 12 to 14 rays followed by 6 to 7 dorsal finlets. The anal fin has 12 to 13 rays. There are 11 to 14 gill rakers on the first arch. The lateral line is prominent and wavy, ending in a keel on the caudal peduncle.

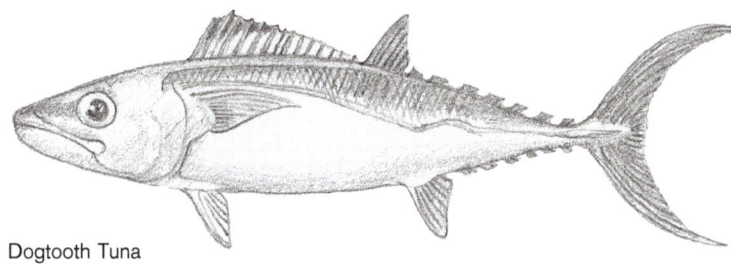

Dogtooth Tuna

The dogtooth is the only bonito that has a swim bladder and a large, single interpelvic process. It is similar to the Australian *Cybiosarda* in having two patches of teeth on the tongue. There are no dark stripes or spots on the body. The second dorsal and anal fins are tipped with white.

Size. The all-tackle world record is a fish that weighed 288 pounds, 12 ounces and was taken off Korea in 1982.

Distribution/Habitat. The dogtooth tuna inhabits tropical and subtropical areas of the Indian and western Pacific Oceans around coral reefs. It occurs from East Africa through the Red Sea to the Philippines and sporadically in southern Japanese waters, as well as around Australia, New Guinea, the Marshall Islands, the Society Islands, the Marquesas, Fiji, and other islands in the South Pacific. It is a pelagic and migratory species but is known to enter inshore waters during the warm season. It may be solitary or travel in small groups of six or less individuals.

Food. This species is usually found around coral reefs, channels, passes, or rocky areas, where it feeds extensively on reef fish. It also consumes mackerel, squid, and various pelagic schooling fish.

Angling. Like many of its relatives, the dogtooth makes a searing, long, fast run when first hooked, followed by a deep, circling, tough fight. It is usually taken incidentally by anglers deep trolling or fishing

A dogtooth tuna from Ujong Kulong, Indonesia.

deep with live or dead baits for other species in the vicinity of an offshore reef, although some are caught on rigs trolled on or near the surface. It has been known to take mackerel, mullet, squid, strip baits, spoons, plugs, feathers, and plastic lures.
See: Big-Game Fishing; Offshore Fishing; Tuna.

TUNA, LONGTAIL *Thunnus tonggol.*
Other names—northern bluefin tuna, oriental bonito; Arabic: *gebab, sahwa;* French: *thon mignon;* Indonesian: *aya, bakulan, kayu;* Italian: *tonno indiano;* Japanese: *koshinaga;* Spanish: *atún tongol.*

This member of the Scombridae family of tuna and mackerel occurs inshore in large schools. It is of some commercial importance, having good-quality pink flesh.

Identification. The longtail is more elongated and smaller than the southern bluefin tuna *(see: tuna, southern bluefin)*. Other traits that separate this species from the southern bluefin are colorless oval spots on the belly, the absence of a swim bladder, the lack of striations on the liver surface, and the lower gill raker count (20 to 23 mean total). The ventral surface from about the pectoral fin to the anal fin is covered with colorless elongated spots. The tips of the second dorsal and anal fins are yellow. The finlets are yellow and edged with gray.

Size. The longtail tuna has a maximum size of possibly 80 pounds and 53 inches. The all-tackle world record is an Australian specimen of 79 pounds, 2 ounces.

Distribution/Habitat. This species occurs in the tropical and subtropical central Pacific Ocean, and in the Indo-west Pacific region. Although largely coastal, it avoids low-salinity areas near the mouths of rivers. It is also seasonally migratory, occurring in large feeding schools off the western and northeastern coasts of Australia. Smaller schools occur off the coasts of India.

Food and feeding behavior. The diet of longtail tuna consists of a wide variety of crustaceans, squid, and fish, including hardyheads and garfish. Longtail tuna are often observed making dashing bursts through dense shoals of baitfish, showering spray as they do so.

Angling. Longtails are sometimes extremely aggressive and at other times frustratingly difficult to catch. Large schools are sometimes prevalent, and they may appear from nowhere to strike baits and lures. The fight is a tough one, both on the surface and deep down.

Anglers can work concentrations of fish by casting with lures or flies, and chumming helps brings boiling masses of fish to the surface. Trolling with live or dead baits and with lures over deep pockets and between coral reefs at high tide produces strikes. Live baits include small whiting, mullet, yellowtail, mackerel, crabs, and squid.
See: Big-Game Fishing; Offshore Fishing; Tuna.

TUNA, SKIPJACK *Katsuwonus pelamis.*
Other names—skipjack, ocean bonito, arctic bonito, striped tuna, watermelon tuna; French: *benite à ventre raye;* Hawaiian: *aku;* Italian: *tonnetto striato;* Japanese: *katsuo;* Portuguese: *gaiado, listão, listado;* Spanish: *bonito ártico, barrilete, listado.*

Although commonly called arctic bonito, the skipjack tuna is not a bonito and does not venture into arctic waters. This member of the Scombridae family of tuna and mackerel (which includes bonito) is an esteemed light-tackle species and has great commercial value. It is a mainstay of the California tuna fishery and is of tremendous importance in Japan, Hawaii, Cuba, and other areas. It is marketed canned, frozen, smoked, fresh, and dried/salted. In the United States, it is canned with yellowfin and bigeye tuna and sold as light meat or chunk light tuna.

Identification. The presence of stripes on the belly and the absence of markings on the back are sufficient to distinguish the skipjack tuna from all similar species. The lower flanks and belly are silvery and have four to six prominent, dark, longitudinal stripes running from just behind the corselet back toward the tail, ending when they come into contact with the lateral line. Although some other species do have stripes on the belly, they have markings on the back as well, and the latter remain the most prominent after death.

The top of the fish is a dark purplish blue, and the lower flanks and belly are silvery. The first dorsal fin has 14 to 16 spines, and the pectoral and ventral fins are short. The body is scaleless except on the corselet and along the lateral line. This fish has no swim bladder. On each side of the caudal peduncle is a strong lateral keel. There are roughly 30 to 40 small conical teeth in each jaw. The teeth are smaller and more numerous than those of bonito and are unlike the triangular, compressed teeth of mackerel. There are 53 to 63 gill rakers on the first arch, which is more than in any other species of tuna except the slender tuna *(Allothunnus).*

Size/Age. Skipjack tuna can attain a maximum of 40 to 45 inches in length but are commonly between 16 and 28 long and weigh from 5 to 15 pounds. The all-tackle world record is a 45-pound,

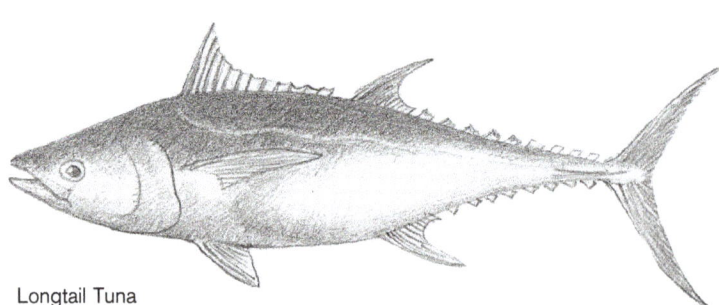

Longtail Tuna

Skipjack Tuna

4-ounce from Baja California, Mexico, but they are believed to grow larger. They may live for 12 years.

Distribution/Habitat. Skipjack tuna are cosmopolitan in tropical and subtropical seas, usually in deep coastal and oceanic waters. They are common throughout the tropical Atlantic south to Argentina, and may range as far north as Cape Cod, Massachusetts, in the summer months. A pelagic, migratory, deep-water species, it may form schools composed of 50,000 or more individuals, which makes it a prime target for commercial fishermen using purse seines.

Life history/Behavior. In the western Atlantic, skipjack tuna frequently school with blackfin tuna *(see: tuna, blackfin)*; in the Pacific and Indian Oceans they often school with yellowfin tuna *(see: tuna, yellowfin)*. Skipjack tuna reach sexual maturity at about 18 to 20 inches in length. Spawning occurs in spurts throughout the year in tropical waters, and from spring to early fall in subtropical waters, with the spawning season becoming shorter with increased distance from the equator.

Food and feeding habits. This is a gregarious fish and a fast swimmer. It feeds near the surface, and its diet consists of herring, squid, small mackerel and bonito, lanternfish, shrimp, and crustaceans.

Angling. The skipjack tuna is a fine gamefish caught by a variety of means. It will strike trolled strip baits, feathers, spoons, plugs, or small whole baits, and most are taken via trolling. Some anglers catch them by casting, jigging, or live-bait fishing offshore. Their soft meat causes them to be less favored by anglers than most other tuna.

See: Big-Game Fishing; Offshore Fishing; Tuna.

TUNA, SOUTHERN BLUEFIN
Thunnus maccoyi.
Other names—Japanese Central Pacific bluefin tuna, southern tunny, tunny; Japanese: *bachimaguro, indo (goshu) maguro, minami maguro.*

A member of the Scombridae family of tuna, the pelagic and seasonally migratory southern bluefin is an apparently smaller-growing cousin to the more widely dispersed Atlantic bluefin tuna *(see: tuna, bluefin)*. It is an important commercial species as well as a powerful, hard-fighting gamefish, but its population is estimated to be reduced to 90 percent of historic levels as a result of overfishing. Its red meat is excellent table fare; the raw flesh is prized for sashimi and draws a high price on the commercial market.

Identification. The southern bluefin tuna closely resembles the Atlantic bluefin and was once thought to be the same species. The primary difference is the number of gill rakers. The southern bluefin has a total of 31 to 40 on the first arch, whereas the Atlantic bluefin has a total of 34 to 43 gill rakers. Both have in common striations on the ventral surface of the liver, short pectoral fins that do not reach to the space between the first and second dorsal fins, and moderate second dorsal and anal fins that are never elongated like those of the yellowfin tuna *(see: tuna, yellowfin)*. The finlets are dusky yellow and edged with black. This is the only species of *Thunnus* in which the caudal keel is bright yellow, except in fish larger than 150 pounds, where the caudal keel tends to be darker.

Size/Age. The southern bluefin doesn't appear to achieve weights exceeding 400 pounds. The all-tackle world record is a 348-pound New Zealand specimen caught in 1981. It is believed to attain an age of at least 20 years.

Distribution/Habitat. A species of the southern oceans, the southern bluefin occurs worldwide from 30° to about 50° south latitude in oceanic to coastal waters. It is commonly found off the southern and eastern coasts of Australia and New Zealand.

Life history/Behavior. This species spawns in the eastern Indian Ocean, with one- and two-year-olds appearing off Western Australia in summer. Fish three and four years of age appear off Southern Australia in summer and New South Wales in winter. The migratory route from the Indian Ocean to the Pacific splits into two paths off southern Tasmania. Fish move either to northern New Zealand via South

Island or up the Australian coast. They travel in schools of similar-size fish and are relatively slow to mature. This occurs at roughly ages 8 to 9.

Food. The southern bluefin's diet consists of a variety of crustaceans, squid, and fish, including anchovies and pilchards.

Angling. The most popular method of catching this species is via trolling with assorted offshore lures. It can also be taken from boats or from the shore using live mackerel and little tuna for baits. It is rarely taken on dead baits, although very large specimens have been landed by this method. Hooked fish are prone to fast surface runs and deep sounding, like their bluefin relatives.

See: Big-Game Fishing; Offshore Fishing; Tuna.

TUNA TOWER

A term for elevated platforms on large sportfishing boats *(see)* designed to give the captain a better view, enabling visibility at a much greater distance. The name derives from the fact that they were developed in 1952 as lookout towers in the Bahamas for captains spotting bluefin tuna, but they have been adapted for wider use.

See: Tower.

TUNA, YELLOWFIN *Thunnus albacares.*

Other names—Allison tuna, albacore, autumn albacore, yellow-finned albacore; French: *albacore, thon à nageoires jaunes;* Hawaiian: *ahi, ahimalailena;* Italian: *albacore, tonno albacora;* Japanese: *kihada, kiwade, kiwada maguro;* Portuguese: *albacora, atum amarello;* Spanish: *atún de aleta amarilla, atún de Allison, rabil.*

Preferring warm waters, the yellowfin is the most tropical species of tuna in the Scombridae family. It is highly esteemed both as a sportfish and as table fare. Anglers throughout the world are familiar with the yellowfin, and they are heavily targeted commercially; hundreds of thousands of tons are taken worldwide annually by longliners and purse seiners. The meat of the yellowfin is light in color compared to that of most other tuna, with the exception of the albacore *(see)* and dogtooth tuna *(see: tuna, dogtooth)*, which have white meat.

Identification. This is probably the most colorful of all the tuna. The back is blue black, fading to silver on the lower flanks and belly. A golden yellow or iridescent blue stripe runs from the eye to the tail, although this is not always prominent. All the fins and finlets are golden yellow, although in some very large specimens the elongated dorsal and anal fins may be silver edged with yellow. The finlets have black edges. The belly frequently shows as many as 20 vertical rows of whitish spots. Many large yellowfins become particularly distinguished, as they grow very long second dorsal and anal fins.

Overall, the body shape is streamlined and more slender than that of bluefin or bigeye tuna. The eyes and head are comparatively small. Just as the albacore has characteristically overextended pectoral fins, the yellowfin has overextended second dorsal and anal fins that may reach more than halfway back to the tail base in some large specimens. In smaller specimens under about 60 pounds, and in some very large specimens as well, this may not be an accurate distinguishing factor, as the fins do not appear to be as long in all specimens. The pectoral fins in adults reach to the origin of the second dorsal fin but never beyond the second dorsal fin to the finlets, as in the albacore. The bigeye tuna *(see: tuna, bigeye)* and the blackfin tuna *(see: tuna, blackfin)* may have pectoral fins similar in length to those of the yellowfin. The yellowfin can be distinguished from the blackfin by the black margins on its finlets; blackfin tuna, like albacore, have white margins on the finlets. It can be distinguished from the bigeye tuna by the lack of striations on the ventral surface of the liver. The yellowfin tuna has a total of 25 to 35 gill rakers on the first arch, and it has an air bladder, as do all species of *Thunnus* except the longtail tuna *(see: tuna, longtail)*. There is no white, trailing margin on the tail.

Previously, large yellowfins with long second dorsal and anal fins were called Allison tuna or long-finned yellowfin tuna, and the smaller specimens were called short-finned yellowfin tuna in the mistaken belief that they were a separate species. It is now the general consensus that there is only one species of yellowfin tuna.

Size/Age. Yellowfins are commonly caught under 100 pounds in size but may grow to more than 400 pounds. Their maximum length is 75 inches, and the all-tackle world record is a 388-pound, 12-ounce Mexican fish.

Distribution/Habitat. This species occurs worldwide in deep, warm, temperate oceanic

A small yellowfin tuna caught off Virginia Beach, Virginia.

Yellowfin Tuna

waters. It is both pelagic and seasonally migratory but has been known to come fairly close to shore where there are warm currents. The largest yellowfins have been encountered by long-range party boats fishing in the Revillagigedo Islands off the coast of Baja California, Mexico. Specimens exceeding 200 pounds are common during many winter trips, and some in the 300-plus-pound class are boated.

Life history/Behavior. Yellowfins are fairly abundant in tropical waters. Young fish are known to form large schools near the surface. Adults inhabit fairly deep water but also live near the surface, and are caught close to the surface by anglers. They often mix with other species, especially skipjack and bigeye tuna. Yellowfin are sexually mature when they reach a length of approximately 40 inches, and spawn throughout the year in the core areas of their distribution, with peaks occurring in summer months.

Food. The diet depends largely on local abundance, and includes flyingfish, other small fish, squid, and crustaceans.

Angling. Yellowfins are a good target for trollers and also for bait anglers. Trolling with small fish, squid, strip baits, and artificial lures, as well as chumming and live-bait fishing are primary methods. Offshore anglers do especially well with this species by chumming with chunk baits at night.

See: Big-Game Fishing; Chumming; Chunking; Offshore Fishing; Tuna.

TUNING LURES

All lures must swim true to be effective. If they don't have the right action, they will probably not be as effective as they were designed to be—in fact, they may be totally ineffective. Plugs, for example, must run straight on the retrieve, not lay on their side or run off at an angle; spoons must have the right wobble and should not lay flat or skip.

Some anglers take already serviceable lures and make minor adjustments—such as bending the lip or changing the hooks—that make the lures work exceptionally well, and it can be worthwhile to tinker with some lures to see whether they can be improved through modification. Tuning, however, means more than modifying a lure that already works; it's making minor adjustments to lures that are not swimming properly. Lures don't always work just right, or as well as they could. Some that have been working properly may run awry after you catch fish on them, someone steps on them, or they get bashed against a hard object. Some lures work perfectly right out of the box, but others, especially diving plugs, do not. Moreover, you can buy a dozen identical lures and find that several need tuning to work right.

There are ways to tune lures to make them run true. Tuning is not difficult, but it does take a few minutes to accomplish, and it takes observation to know when to work on a lure to make it run better. Some plugs seem to need more frequent tuning than others, and some small lures need more frequent tuning than large ones. Others never get tuned exactly right. It is not uncommon to make many attempts to modify a new lure before you get it running to your satisfaction.

The majority of plugs have clear plastic bills of various lengths and shapes designed to make them dive. Into these bills are attached line-tie screws, and virtually all running problems involve the position of these little screws. When a plug runs awry, it is usually the fault of the line tie. The line-tie screw must be placed perpendicularly to the plane of the bill of the lure. Because this screw eye is partially positioned by hand at the manufacturing plant, human error can be introduced. If the screw is placed a fraction of an inch out of position, the lure will not run true.

Besides the line tie, other factors are at work as well. Plastic lures are molded in two halves that are joined and glued, and sometimes a change in the sealing of those halves, or some other aspect of mold design or construction, can affect a lure's performance. A few manufacturers tank-test each lure before they package it to ensure that it runs properly; however, most do not perform this labor-intensive activity.

A well-designed plug, with or without a lip, should have a good wiggling action. Some lures have a tight action, and some have more of a wide wobble. Whatever its action, a lure should come back in a straight line while swimming or diving. The body of a plug should swim on a vertical axis, like a real baitfish, not be canted off to either side; if it runs even a little bit off, it will have an unnatural action that will likely cost you fish. (This is not necessarily true for erratic-swimming and darting cut-plug lures that have no lip or bill. These lures appeal to fish, especially salmon, precisely because of their erratic movement.)

It is a good idea to check each plug before you fish it. Tie it on your line, drop a few feet of line from the tip of the rod to the lure, and then run the lure through the water next to your boat. If the lure does not run properly, adjust it immediately. If you can't tell by doing this, then cast the lure about 30 feet away, hold the rod tip out straight, and watch to see whether the lure runs off an imaginary straight line to either the right or the left

To adjust a plug, you need a pair of pliers to bend the line-tie screw. Watch the lure swim. If the lure runs off to the right, bend the line-tie screw to the left; and if the lure runs left, bend the screw right. Tweak the screw in small steps, bending it slightly and checking its action in the water to see the change. Keep adjusting and checking until the lure runs perfectly. (In serious cases, you may have to bend the line-tie screw far from its original position.) When bending the line-tie screw, be careful not to loosen it; the screw is epoxied in place, and loosening it may render the plug unusable. Sometimes you can take out the screw and reglue it, using clear, quick-setting epoxy. Also, make sure that you bend the eye, not twist it.

Before you tune a lure that seems to run awry, make sure you're not retrieving or trolling it too fast. All plugs have a top working speed beyond which they will not run properly. This speed is not the same for all lures. Some lures that run well at slower speeds will run awry at faster speeds, yet can be tuned to swim properly anyway.

Generally, most plugs will not run very well if a tight knot is tied directly to the screw eye. For this reason, it is best to use a split ring or rounded snap—not a snap swivel—for connection. Most plugs are supplied with split rings or snaps, and your knot should be tied to this. Snap swivels may alter the action of these plugs, making tuning difficult. A lure that is tuned to work without a snap swivel may have to be retuned to work with one. Moreover, a snap swivel poses a possible problem when you are fighting fish, and the fewer things that can go wrong the better. The only advantages to using a snap swivel are that it facilitates lure changing and prevents line twist, but diving plugs don't induce twist.

A new knot on a lure that was running fine may change the action because of the position of the knot. This is corrected by changing the position and alignment of the knot, or by retying the knot and snugging it tight. You may find that some plugs work best if you use a loop knot. With some deep-diving minnow plugs, tie a loop knot directly to the line-tie screw or the split ring.

Some of these comments about plugs and line ties apply to other lures. Spinners usually don't pose much of a problem except for the occasional bent shaft, which can be corrected easily if not too severe. Streamers need to swim upright, and usually you simply adjust the knot location on the eye of the fly to achieve this. Heavy spoons don't usually get bent out of shape, but wafer-thin spoons do, and this sometimes requires adroit remodeling. A few thin flutter spoons can be bent at the tip and base, to the left or right, to modify their action.

It pays to experiment with such tuning, if for no other reason than to compare actions. Remember

To tune a plug to run properly, bend the line-tie screw in the opposite direction from which the lure is running astray. Do this incrementally until the plug runs straight ahead with a good side-to-side wobble.

to watch for line twist with these lures; in the case of spoons or spinners, use a good-quality snap swivel to eliminate twist. In addition, be aware of the small things that might affect the way your lure swims. Sometimes plugs can be sensitive to the slightest adornment. If you pull a lure through weeds and get a tiny confetti trailer on your hooks or line tie, you'll feel the action of the lure change if you have the rod in your hand, or you may notice a change in the movement of your rod tip.

TUNNEL HULL

A term for a shallow-water style of boat hull with a raised center section that is flat and ductlike. This permits high-mounting of a transom engine to allow the boat to jump quickly on plane in bare inches of water.

See: Boat.

A little tunny from Montauk, New York.

TUNNY, LITTLE   *Euthynnus alletteratus.*

Other names—little tuna, Atlantic little tunny, false albacore, bonito; French: *thonine de l'Atlantique;* Italian: *tonnetto dell' Atlantico, tonnella sanguinaccio, alletterato;* Japanese: *yaito, suma-rui;* Portuguese: *merma;* Spanish: *bacoreta del Atlántico, merma, barrilete, carachana pintada.*

Although not part of the *Thunnus* genus like many tuna, the little tunny is a member of the same Scombridae family and one of the finest small gamefish available. Frequently misnamed as false albacore and bonito, this species fights so hard on light tackle that anglers are likely to boat dead or near-dead individuals. It has coarse red flesh, however, which does not endear it to many anglers as food, although it does attract some commercial interest.

Identification. The little tunny is most easily distinguished from similar species by its markings. It has a scattering of dark spots resembling fingerprints between the pectoral and ventral fins that are not present on any related Atlantic species. It also has wavy, "wormlike" markings on the back. These markings are above the lateral line within a well-marked border and never extend farther forward than about the middle of the first dorsal fin. The markings are the same as in the closely related kawakawa *(see)* but are unlike those of any other Atlantic species. The pectoral and ventral fins are short and broad, and the two dorsal fins are separated at the base by a small space. The body has no scales except on the corselet and along the lateral line, and there is no air bladder. Unlike its close Pacific relatives the kawakawa and black skipjack *(see: skipjack, black),* it has no teeth on the vomer.

The little tunny is often confused with the Atlantic bonito *(see: bonito, Atlantic),* the skipjack tuna *(see: tuna, skipjack),* and the frigate mackerel *(see: mackerel, frigate)* and bullet mackerel (genus *Auxis*). There are, however, differences among these species. The Atlantic bonito has a lower, sloping first dorsal fin. The frigate and bullet mackerel have the dorsal fins set apart. The skipjack tuna has broad, straight stripes on the belly and lacks markings on the back.

Size. Little tunny may attain a length of 40 inches but are most common to 25 inches. The all-tackle world record is an Algerian fish that weighed 35 pounds, 2 ounces.

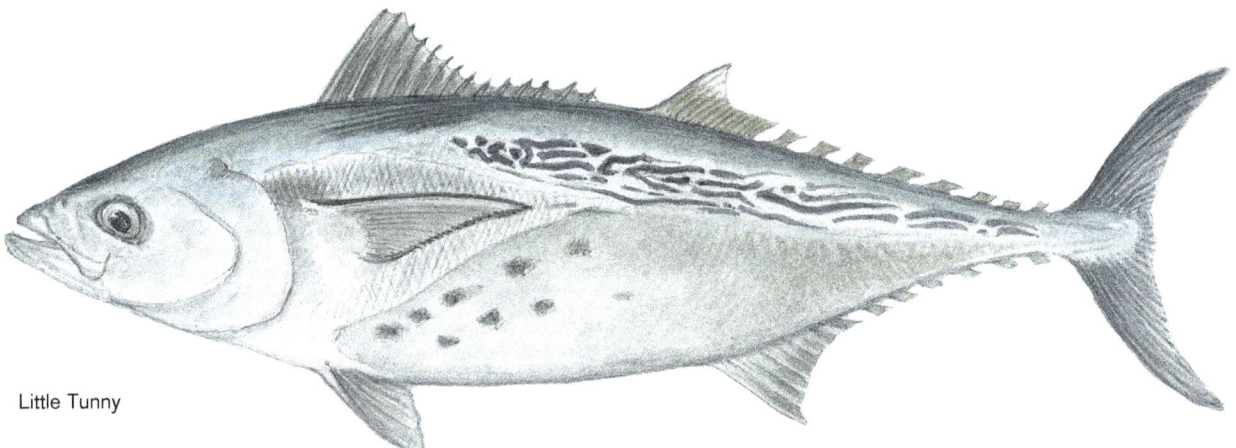

Little Tunny

Distribution/Habitat. This species occurs in tropical and warm temperate waters of the Atlantic Ocean; in the western Atlantic, it ranges from the New England states and Bermuda south to Brazil, and in the eastern Atlantic from Great Britain to South Africa, including the Mediterranean. It is not as migratory as other tuna species and is found regularly in inshore waters, as well as offshore, usually in large schools.

Spawning behavior. Little tunny reach sexual maturity at approximately 15 inches in length. Spawning occurs from about April through November in both the western and eastern Atlantic.

Food and feeding habits. Little tunny are common in inshore waters near the surface where they feed on squid, crustaceans, fish larvae, and large numbers of smaller pelagic fish, especially herring.

Angling. Flocks of diving seabirds often indicate the presence of a school of little tunny. Because this species feeds on small pelagic fish near the surface, any school feeding action tends to attract and excite birds looking for a meal. Fishing methods include trolling or casting from a boat and offering small whole baits, strip baits, or small spoons, plugs, jigs, and feathers.

These fish spread out over the continental shelf and are most abundant within 30 miles of shore during a late-summer to early-fall run along the Mid-Atlantic and southern New England coasts, when they average 5 to 15 pounds. Unlike the other tuna, the little tunny commonly chases baitfish into the surf and can be caught by surf casters retrieving small metal lures and jigs at high speed. Many are also caught by trollers seeking school tuna, and in chum lines intended for bluefish.

See: Big-Game Fishing; Offshore Fishing; Tuna.

TURBIDITY

The amount of suspended particles in the water column. Turbid water is clouded with sediment and in extreme cases may be muddy.

See: Water Clarity.

TURBOT *Scophthalmus maxima* (also *Psetta maxima*).

Other names—breet, britt, butt; Danish: *pighvarre;* Dutch: *tarbot;* Finnish: *piikkikampela;* French: *turbot;* Italian: *rombo chiodat;* Norwegian and Swedish: *piggvar;* Portuguese: *pregado;* Russian: *azovskii kalkan;* Spanish: *rodaballo.*

The turbot is a left-eyed member of the Scophthalmidae family of flatfish *(see)* that has long been commercially significant for European markets, and is mainly caught by commercial trawlers. Like other flatfish, it undergoes a unique maturation from egg to adult in which one eye migrates to the opposite side of the head.

Identification. The body of the turbot is

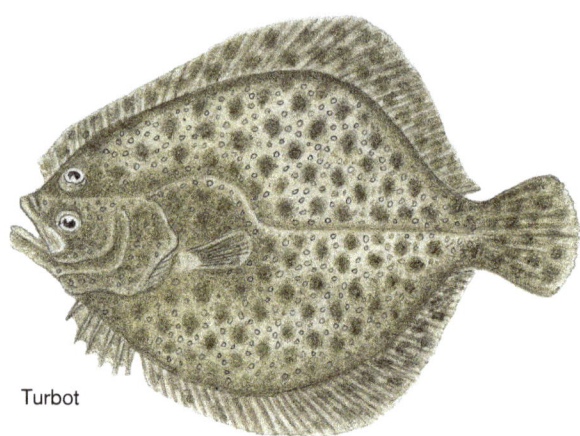
Turbot

diamond shaped. The eyed side is grayish brown with darker speckles and blotches, and the blind side is white. Although similar in appearance to the more oval brill *(see),* the turbot grows larger and lacks scales.

Size/Age. This species grows to 39 inches in length and is reported to reach a maximum weight of 55 pounds, but it commonly grows to 17 inches in length.

Distribution. The turbot occurs in the northeastern Atlantic throughout the Mediterranean Sea and along the European coast to the Arctic Circle; it is also found in most of the Baltic Sea.

Habitat. Turbot are located over sandy, rocky, and mixed bottoms in depths of up to 500 feet, but they normally range from the shore to a depth of 260 feet. They also commonly occur in brackish water.

Spawning behavior. Spawning occurs between April and August.

Food. The diet of turbot is mainly various fish and, to a lesser extent, larger crustaceans and bivalves.

Angling. Turbot are caught on standard, deep, bottom fishing methods, using heavy weights and natural baits, or heavy metal jigs.

See: Drift Fishing; Inshore Fishing.

TURKEY

Situated in southeastern Europe and southwestern Asia, the Republic of Turkey is seldom the focus of sportfishing interest by globe-trotting anglers. This is largely because its varied fisheries resources—found in mountain streams, rivers, freshwater lakes, and especially in four warm seas—are largely unknown outside its borders. It is also because Turkey has a scarcity of modern tackle, boats, and facilities for the visiting angler.

Situated centrally in the Northern Hemisphere, Turkey is both a Mediterranean and Middle Eastern country. Technically, 97 percent of its surface area of 814,578 square kilometers is situated in Asia and the remainder in Europe. Much of this generally east-west landmass is surrounded by warm salt-water: the Black Sea in the north, the

Marmara Sea in the northwest, the Aegean Sea in the west, and the Mediterranean Sea in the south. As a result, Turkey has 8,333 kilometers of coastline. Most of it is in the Anatolia region (between the Mediterranean and Black Seas) and includes 1,067 kilo-meters of island coastline.

Surface formations in Turkey show a wide variety due to high altitude. These include mountains in parallel ranges, a single or linear lineup of extinguished volcanoes, flat plateaus that are covered with lava or small rocks and that once belonged to ancient lakes, and plains with alluvial beds widening at river deltas.

Turkey is rich in rivers, and these flow to the Black, Mediterranean, Aegean, Marmara, and Caspian Seas, and to the Persian Gulf. Most contain rapids and are not suited to navigation, and some are important for hydroelectric and irrigation purposes. The amount of water flowing from the rivers, however, varies greatly during the year. In summer, nearly all the rivers are at their lowest, and some completely dry up. With the beginning of autumn rains and decreased evaporation, flows increase and continue during the winter, becoming highest during the spring.

In addition to its rivers, Turkey possesses more than 200 natural lakes. These cover nearly 9,000 square kilometers, although they are more abundant in some areas and nonexistent in others. In the Thrace (the small portion of Turkey in Europe) and Black Sea regions, for example, there are practically no lakes; the regions of Marmara, Central Anatolia, Eastern Anatolia, and especially the Mediterranean contain areas with an accumulation of lakes.

Turkey has three distinct climates. The climate of the Mediterranean region is dry and hot in summer, with mild rainy winters; this climate is also experienced in Western Anatolia and in the Aegean and Marmara regions. The Black Sea coast has a temperate climate, and it is rainy there throughout the year. The steppe, or plains, climate dominates Eastern and Central Anatolia; here the winter is cold with little rain, and the summer is dry.

Abundant water results in a rich overall harvest of fish for the people of Turkey, who number about 64 million. According to government statistics, the amount of combined saltwater and freshwater fish produced per person per year in the country is 11.4 kilograms. This includes mussels and shrimp, but of the saltwater finfish harvested commercially, the anchovy represents 55 percent of the catch, followed by horse mackerel (19 percent), chub mackerel (6 percent), and bonito (3 percent). The saltwater catch comes primarily from the Black Sea, which produces 87 percent of the harvest. Among freshwater fish, 46 percent of the commercial production is carp, followed by trout and chub.

Saltwater species caught by recreational anglers, which in Turkey includes the vast majority of people who use handlines and the lesser number who use rod and reel, are garrick, red mullet, sole, horse mackerel, Black Sea turbot, two-banded bream, comber, gray mullet, red gurnard, chub mackerel, European sea bass, bluefish, red bream, whiting, picarel, bluefin tuna, albacore, bonito, pilchards, mackerel, sturgeon, blue marlin, shad, lizardfish, moray eels, conger eels, sailfish, garfish (a type of needlefish), hake, Mediterranean ling, three-bearded rockling, John Dory, barracuda, stone bass (wreckfish), grouper, dentex, shortbill spearfish, gilt-head bream, bogue, salema, saddled bream, black bream, meagre, amberjack, pompano, dolphin (mahimahi), little tunny, frigate mackerel, swordfish, scorpionfish, brill, flounder, anglerfish, porbeagle sharks, hammerhead sharks, blue sharks, thresher sharks, spiny dogfish, smoothhound sharks, angel sharks, ray, and skate.

Freshwater species include river charr, lake trout, rainbow trout, brook trout, sea trout, perch, carp, roach, tench, chub, barbel, pike, eels, grayling, white bass, and wels catfish.

There are no fishing prohibitions for anglers in Turkey, a sportfishing license is not required anywhere, and there is no requirement to belong to a club or group in order to obtain permission to fish at particular sites. There are no overall limits and no size limits. Recreational anglers can use all kinds of natural baits and artificial lures, and they can fish at any time of the day or night.

In Turkey, a handline is generally used by resident anglers. The effectiveness of this method, as well as using rod and reel, varies according to the species, region, environment, type of boat, currents, and season. The type of natural and artificial baits used, and techniques employed, also varies according to region and environment; people who use flycasting tackle are extremely scarce.

In saltwater, such live baits as pilchards, garfish, scorpionfish, gray mullet, horse mackerel, chub mackerel, and small bream are commonly used. Other natural baits include crabs, squid, octopus, shrimp, mussels, clams, scallops, and pieces of fish. Artificial lures include spoons, plugs, and jigs. Fishing is primarily done from an anchored boat, by drifting in a boat, or by trolling.

The most productive fishing season in saltwater is from late summer until early winter, although this varies according to region. In summer, saltwater fish approach the shores; in winter, they retreat to open and deep waters.

The favored natural baits used in Turkish lakes and rivers are worms, frogs, rodents, certain flies, and insects. Some anglers use different shapes of spoons and plugs.

There are no specially designed open-sea fishing boats for hire in Turkey. At practically every saltwater fishing site, however, it is possible to fish with local fishermen and use their methods and tackle. For freshwater fishing, it is best to use a guide who knows the region being fished, although guides are not numerous.

Black Sea

The Black Sea is an inland body of saltwater bordered in the east by Russia and Georgia, in the north by Ukraine, in the west by Romania and Bulgaria, and in the south by Turkey. This huge sea covers 436,400 square kilometers, and its size impacts the nearby climate by making it milder; in winter it is noticeably milder along the Black Sea coast than inland.

With an average depth of 1,272 meters, the Black Sea is the deepest of the seas surrounding Turkey. Its deepest point, 2,234 meters, is north of the Turkish city of Sinop. There are shallow waters, less than 200 meters, in the northwestern region where the Danube enters, but apart from that area the entire coastline is very narrow, and the continental shelf drops off extremely sharply. The continental shelf between Giresun and the Strait of Istanbul (Bosphorus) widens somewhat following the Turkish coast toward the west, and is intersected by valleys of ancient rivers reaching a depth of 200 to 220 meters.

The Black Sea consists of two basins and has both surface and subsurface currents. The surface, or upper, current runs counterclockwise along the Anatolian coast toward the east, continuing along the northern and western shores eventually to the Strait of Istanbul. In general, the strength of this current diminishes the farther one gets from shore, but the coastal current is still felt 15 to 19 miles from shore. The complex current system in the southeastern region can be extremely strong, many times greater than the norm elsewhere. Along the coastal strip between the entrance to the strait and the Bay of Burgaz there are opposite currents.

In addition to this current flow, the Black Sea has low salinity, especially at the surface and near river deltas, and a rich upper water zone. The surface waters create a thin layer over the more salty and heavier water underneath. The differences in density created by the changes in salinity cause the surface and deep waters to remain in two separate, unmixed layers. This situation prevents oxygen from mixing into deep waters, so that no fish can thrive at the greater depths. Yet the area where these two layers meet, whether by virtue of temperature or salinity, provides an ideal living environment for many species of migratory fish. Thanks to the rivers that enter the Black Sea, which occurs primarily along the north shores, the upper layer of water is rich in oxygen, alimentary salts, and plankton, and this creates a productive environment for fish.

The surface waters of the Black Sea reach 20° to 26°C in the summer. The warmest waters are in the southeast and the coolest in the northwest. The difference in temperature is more evident in winter, when the temperature in the southeastern region is 13°C, and in the northwest it drops to 2°C.

Black Sea fish consist of permanent and migratory species. Permanent residents include horse mackerel, Black Sea bass, whiting, garfish, shad, silversides, anchovies, turbot, gray mullet, skate, spiny dogfish, and smoothhound. Perhaps most prized are sturgeon and herring; these anadromous fish are famous for their roe (caviar, in the case of sturgeon) but have decreased in abundance due to pollution.

Migratory fish that originate from the Mediterranean Sea include bonito, mackerel, bluefish, bluefin tuna, swordfish, sole, and red mullet. These species migrate in spring to the Black Sea to feed, and leave between the end of August and January. Their passage back to the Mediterranean is by way of the Strait of Istanbul into the Marmara Sea, then through the Dardanelles Strait into the Aegean Sea, and from there into the Mediterranean. Seventy-five percent of the fish fauna of the Black Sea originates from the Mediterranean. If the winter is mild, migrating fish stay longer in the Bosphorus area and in the Marmara Sea, and can be caught in large quantities.

Bluefin tuna and swordfish are among the premier fish that can be caught from a boat by drifting or trolling with live bait in the open waters of the Black Sea. They are caught respectively up to maximum weights of 360 kilograms and 110 kilograms; however, both have decreased in number due to extensive and uncontrolled fishing.

On the other hand, trolling with many feathered hooks for bonito is highly productive in August and September. Fishing for bluefish is done from a boat with handlines and live baits, or with spoons and jigs by trolling. August and September produce good-eating, fat bluefish. Bluefish are also taken from shore by anglers casting with lures.

Flatfish are found near sandy shores and can be caught on bottom bait rigs. The prime season for these fish is April and May. Fishing for mackerel is also done from boats by drifting and using handlines with many feathered hooks; the most productive fishing seasons for mackerel are August through November, and April through June. Sea bass are caught along the coasts with live baits or artificial lures in November, February, and May, where the rivers flow into the Black Sea.

As in every part of Turkey, local anglers plying the Black Sea fish primarily with handlines. In recent years, rods and reels have been used to fish from shore. Samsun, Ordu (Fatsa Bay and its coast), Giresun (around the small islands across the city), and Trabzon are all noted for their fishing. Visitors here are advised to fish with locals, and to realize that there are very few ports to take shelter in when sudden storms or strong winds break out. Winter is noted for being windy and rough.

A number of small lakes exist in the Turkish Black Sea region. Carp, whitefish, pike, and wels inhabit the lakes of Abant and Yedigöller (Seven Lakes area). Also, several species of trout exist in the Yesilirmak, Kizilirmak, and Sakarya Rivers and their branches. The Kizilirmak is 1,150 kilometers in length and is the longest river that flows entirely within Turkey, originating in the mountains east of Sivas.

Trout fishing occurs in every season in the high plateaus of the Black Sea region. In general, Turkish anglers fish for these species with rod and reel, using natural baits. It is advisable to hire a local guide for freshwater fishing.

Strait of Istanbul

The Strait of Istanbul, also known as the Bosphorus and sometimes called the Black Sea Strait, joins the Black and Marmara Seas. Along with the Dardanelles Strait, it separates Asia from Europe. The waters of the Bosphorus are rich in oxygen and provide a positive environment for sportfish, as well as tricky currents and challenging fishing.

This sharply bending strait is approximately 30 kilometers long. It is wide at the north and south entrances, and narrow in the middle. The widest point is 3.6 kilometers, and the narrowest 700 meters.

Two differing current systems provide an exchange of water between the Black and Marmara Seas, and these are related to differences in level and density. The less dense and less saline waters of the Black Sea, which is 25 centimeters higher than the Marmara Sea, flow from north to south on the upper level of the Bosphorus into the Marmara Sea. Underneath this, another current carries the more saline and more dense waters of the Marmara from south to north into the Black Sea. The boundary between the upper and lower currents in the southern Bosphorus is 20 meters deep, and in the north 40 meters deep.

The speed of the upper current increases in front of the capes and in areas where the strait narrows. Although its average speed is approximately 3.2 kilometers per hour, it reaches 5.2 kilometers per hour and may attain 9 to 10 kilometers per hour when aided by strong winds. The upper current also creates eddies in the small bays when it hits the capes.

The amount of water transferred into the Marmara Sea via the upper current is estimated to be double that of the water transferred into the Black Sea via the slower lower current. Sometimes important changes are observed in the currents. When strong and constant north winds blow, the speed of the upper current increases, and the waters of the Black Sea rise and overflow to fill in completely the strait channel, thus blocking the lower current. In contrast, when strong southwest winds blow constantly, the rising waters of the Marmara Sea enter the southern mouth of the strait and push harder against the upper current; as a result, the large water mass entering from the south joins with the lower current and fills in the strait channel, causing the upper current to flow from the south to the north.

A fishing scene from the Strait of Istanbul.

Fishing is very productive during the period when the speed of the upper current increases. From September through December, migratory fish move from the Black Sea to the Mediterranean, and, with the help of the fast current, large masses of fish enter the strait and provide good fishing. Fishing is poor when southwest winds create a stronger lower current, as the fish are more dispersed.

Depending on the species and their temperature preferences, migrating fish start leaving the Black Sea for the Marmara at the end of August, heading to the Aegean Sea and sometimes into the Mediterranean. This migration continues until the middle of January. In the spring, these species migrate from the Mediterranean, Aegean, and Marmara Seas beginning in April and continuing until early June, spending their summer in the Black Sea.

The direction of the winds and the currents plays an important role in the beginning of the migration. Bonito, bluefish, and bluefin tuna are the primary migratory gamefish. High numbers of bonito and bluefish begin to appear around the last week of August at the northern entrance of the Bosphorus and in the nearby waters. These species are present in the Bosphorus and in the Marmara Sea from the end of September until December. Bluefin tuna are in both areas in January and February.

Bonito can be fished from boats in the Bosphorus during the day with artificial lures and with multiple feathered hooks, and at night with pieces of bait. During the day, bluefish are caught from drifting boats with live bait, and with jigs and spoons. The favorite natural baits for these species are sliced or live horse mackerel, picarel, anchovies, and garfish.

Fishing for bluefish in the Bosphorus has an important place in Turkish sportfishing and is marked with traditional activities. These include the formation of special lures, as well as the preparation of tackle and attaching pressurized kerosene lamps on boats for night fishing. During the nineteenth century, master fishermen reportedly used to cast jigs out of pure silver. These were used only once, on the first day, to catch the first bluefish of the season.

When fishing at night for bluefish, the boat's motor is shut off and the anchor is not employed because the rope leaves a phosphorescent trail in the water. The boat is maneuvered with oars in the strong current, and the person doing the rowing also throws a handline and tries to hold it in a straight position.

Bluefish caught in September and October are juveniles, but larger fish appear in following months. Sometimes small coal grills are placed in the boats, and the fish caught are immediately cleaned and cooked.

The bluefish approach the shores following horse mackerel and are caught on rod and reel either with natural bait or lures. It is always useful to keep large amounts of live baitfish in the boat.

There are many villages on both shores of the Bosphorus, and it is possible to fish with local fishermen in a rented boat either during the day or at night. The best hours for fishing are generally from sunrise till 9 A.M., and from evening throughout the night.

Marmara Sea

The Marmara region covers just 8.5 percent of Turkey but includes the entire coast around the Marmara Sea, which joins the Black and Aegean Seas via straits in the northeast and southwest that are 290 kilometers apart. It also encompasses the city of Istanbul, and its 16 million inhabitants, and is the most populated region in the country.

Marmara is an inland sea completely contained within Turkey. The Bosphorus connects the Marmara to the Black Sea, and the Dardanelles Strait connects it to the Aegean Sea. It spans 76 kilometers at its widest point, and at its narrowest, 9 kilometers.

The European and Asian coasts of the Marmara Sea differ in shape. The Bays of Tekirdag and Silivri on the coasts of Thrace have suitable boat shelters. The major inlets on the Anatolian coast are Izmit, Gemlik, Erdek, and Bandirma Bays. The principal islands are the Marmara, Imrali, and Princess Islands.

The coasts and open seas of these islands are suitable for fishing. The continental shelf area is not particularly deep and takes up a wide portion of the Marmara Sea. All of the islands are located on this continental shelf. There are very deep places in the Marmara Sea, however, which is uncommon for small seas. One of the deepest spots is just south of Princess Island and reaches 1,238 meters. Another area over 1,000 meters deep is situated in the middle of the Marmara, and still farther west is a pit that reaches 1,112 meters. Large schools of fish typically gather around these regions, including bluefin tuna and bonito, which follow horse mackerel and anchovies.

The surface waters of the Marmara Sea are generally not very salty. The less saline surface layer ranges from the surface down to 15 to 20 meters. As depth increases, so does salinity. Mackerel and bonito prefer to live in more saline waters and can be found between 30 and 40 meters.

The Marmara's surface temperature reaches 24° to 26°C in summer and 7° to 9°C in winter. There is an upper (surface) current and an opposite lower current in the Marmara Sea, too. The surface current is caused by the difference in water level between the Black and Marmara Seas. The surface current leaves the Bosphorus and spreads out like a fan on the Marmara Sea, then accumulates in the west and, with increasing speed, enters the Dardanelles Strait.

The Marmara Sea, along with the Bosphorus and the Dardanelles Strait, is one of the most important waterways of the world and is subject to heavy traffic. Due to pollution created by large cities around the Marmara Sea, and excessive uncontrolled commercial fishing, aquatic life here has become much more scarce. There is still a local fish population, but pelagic species such as swordfish, mackerel, and bluefin tuna do not stay in the Marmara Sea, although these species do migrate through the Marmara from the Mediterranean and Aegean Seas.

Resident species include sea bass, red bream, dentex, comber, and striped bream. Fish like red mullet, sole, red gurnard, whiting, John Dory, flounder, ray, and skate prefer sandy bottoms. Migrating fish like horse mackerel, gray mullet, chub mackerel, bluefish, and bonito appear in April, May, October, and November.

Turkish anglers usually fish in the Marmara from a moving or anchored boat with a handline, primarily fishing at sunrise and sunset. The major baits used for bottom fishing are mussels, shrimp, crabs, and small live or sliced baitfish. Plugs and spoons are used to fish for dentex and sea bass.

In the deep waters around the Princess Islands, fishing occurs for mackerel and bonito from April through June, and October through December, with multiple feathered hooks and handlines. Live or cut bait are used for bluefish, and the most productive months for this species are October and November.

Even though they are near extinction in the Marmara Sea, bluefin tuna are still caught in December and January. Some specimens over 300 kilograms are taken on live bonito, bluefish, horse mackerel, and garfish. The prime area is off the Kumkapi and Princess Islands. It is possible to find 8- to 12-meter boats for rent from local fishermen, either from the islands or from Istanbul.

The Marmara region is rich in lakes and rivers. River charr, lake trout, brook trout, perch, carp, roach, tench, chub, pike, and wels are found in the Meriç River, which borders Turkey and Greece, and in Manyas, Ulubat, Iznik, Sapanca, and Terkos

---

Some of the earliest bamboo fly rods were round instead of polygonal; cork was not used as handgrip material until the 1890s.

Lakes. Anglers here favor rod and reel, and use live baitfish or artificial lures. Wels over 100 kilograms are caught in the Meriç River. The carp in Iznik Lake are very large and delicious. Pike over 4 kilograms can be caught on spoons in Terkos Lake, where it is possible to rent boats.

The Çanakkale Strait

The Çanakkale Strait joins the Marmara and Aegean Seas and is known in the west by the name Dardanelles, which is derived from the ancient city of Dardanos, 10 kilometers south of the city of Çanakkale. In the Ottoman era this was also known as the Mediterranean Strait.

Compared with the Bosphorus, this strait is straighter and longer at 94 kilometers, and its narrowest point is 1.2 kilometers wide. The Anatolian coastline is sharp, but there are many delta valleys where rivers enter. The current changes direction in the northern and central parts of the strait due to the narrowness of the coasts. The deepest spot is 109 meters, between Çanakkale and Kilitbahir, and the area experiences hot, dry summers and cold, windy winters.

As in the Bosphorus, there are two current systems—an upper surface current and a lower current. The waters of the Black Sea pass through the Marmara Sea and approach the Çanakkale Strait in a 25- to 30-meter-wide surface current. This current extends to depths of between 25 and 30 meters, where the more saline waters of the Aegean Sea (with a constant temperature of 14° to 16°C) flow toward the Marmara Sea. The upper and lower currents are rich in oxygen and organic matter. The nutrients found here, and the funneling of many fish species through this area on their migration routes, makes the Çanakkale Strait one of Turkey's most productive fishing sites.

Species that migrate through the strait include chub mackerel, horse mackerel, gray mullet, spiny dogfish, smoothhound, sea bass, bluefish, bluefin tuna, albacore, little tunny, bonito, and garfish. Resident species include garrick, red mullet, sole, comber, red gurnard, assorted sea bream, dentex, pilchards, picarel, moray eels, conger eels, John Dory, stone bass, grouper, solema, scorpionfish, and angel sharks.

Saroz Bay, reached by passing through the Gallipoli Peninsula from Koru Mountain in the northeast, hosts one of the richest fish areas in Turkey. In the center of this bay are Büyükada, Ortaada, and Kücükada Islands. Saroz is the spawning ground for many species of fish, and mackerel are seen in shoals here. Closer to the stony shores are sea bream. Sea bass and dentex are close to shore between the Büyük Kemikli and Kücük Kemikli Capes. Around the islands and in the depths are grouper. Moray eels lie in their holes, keeping a sharp watch for fish swimming too close. At nighttime, conger eels search for prey, and octopus watch from their holes, sometimes grabbing fishing lines.

Past Anafartalar is the island of Gökçeada, which is known for its fishing. The Mehmetçik headland has many garfish and produces garrick, which range up to 60 kilograms.

Southwest of this is the wreck of the battleship *Majestic* in Ertugrul Bay, and farther along is Morto Bay, whose western end marks the entrance to Çanakkale Strait. This area produces some 30 species of fish. Occasionally, a shoal of tuna weighing from 60 to 100 kilograms makes a foray into the bay. The waters that open onto the Aegean Sea at the end of Çanakkale Strait are very rich in variety of fish.

As the water warms during August, the fish approach the shore, and angling action increases. Bottom species are caught on mussels, shrimp, squid, pieces of octopus, and other items. Locals fishing for large species like garrick and dentex primarily use a handline. Live mackerel, scorpionfish, and garfish are the favored baits. Trolling is also popular. Plugs and spoons are sometimes used for dentex, which can weigh up to 12 kilograms. The garrick range between 35 and 60 kilograms.

The prime times for sea bass are November, February, and May. Fishing is done by drifting near the coast before sunrise, using shrimp or live small gray mullet. Anglers troll using small spoons to pursue sea bass, which sometimes reach 10 kilograms in November. When chasing smaller fish into the shallows, sea bass can be caught from shore on rod and reel, with spoons or plugs.

While it is possible to rent a boat from local fishermen for personal use, it is best to hire and fish with them in their boat.

Aegean Sea

The Aegean region, which encompasses 11 percent of Turkey, is in western Anatolia and abuts the Aegean Sea. The climate is usually hot, with dry summers and mild, rainy winters. The most populated area is around the large city of Izmir.

The Aegean Sea is situated between Turkey and Greece and is part of the Mediterranean, extending about 660 kilometers from north to south. It was once called the "Sea of Islands," due to the hundreds of islands here, most of which belong to Greece. Its coastline features many inlets, bays, straits, and peninsulas.

The temperature of the Aegean Sea is higher in the south than in the north, a difference that is most evident in winter. In most areas of the Aegean, the salinity of the surface waters is at conventional levels, although waters with higher salinity exist in the open areas of the west along the Anatolian shores. This is because the less saline surface current from the Black Sea, after passing through the Çanakkale Strait, moves close to the shores of Greece and spreads out, whereas the more saline waters of the Mediterranean pass close by these shores while moving toward that strait and then to the Marmara Sea.

The Turkish waters of the Aegean Sea, especially in the northern region, harbor red mullet, gray mullet, frigate mackerel, sea bass, dentex, red bream, grouper, gilt-head bream, little tunny, and stone bass, among others. Karaburun, Balçova, Çeşçme, and Ilica are the main fishing areas, and most fish are caught in waters within the continental shelf. Fishing in the southern Aegean Sea is poor.

It is possible to rent boats from local fishermen in fishing villages along the Turkish coast. Often these boats are 6 to 7 meters in length, with an inboard or outboard motor, and are not suitable for open-sea fishing. Turkish fishermen in this region strictly use handlines.

Mediterranean Sea

This region of southern Anatolia extends along the Mediterranean Sea and encompasses 14 percent of Turkey. It includes 1,542 kilometers of coastline. The most populated areas are around the cities of Adana and Antalya.

The coast of this region is less indented than that along the Aegean Sea and forms wide arcs that bear resemblance to the Black Sea coast. Summers are hot and dry, and the winters mild and rainy. Temperatures in the hottest month average 27° to 28°C along the coast, and 23° to 25°C inland. In summer, western and southern winds are dominant; in winter, the dominant wind is northern.

The Mediterranean Sea is a deep sea that extends from the western Atlantic Ocean to eastern Asia and separates the continents of Europe and Africa. It is joined in the northwest by the Çanakkale Strait to the Marmara Sea and thence to the Bosphorus and the Black Sea. Its deepest point, at 5,121 meters, is south of Greece in the Ion Basin.

In most places the Mediterranean coastline of Turkey is steep, with mountains rising immediately from the shore. These mountains create two big inlets in the bays of Antalya and Iskenderun.

In the eastern Mediterranean, a particular current moves along the Turkish coast from east to west. The origin of this current is the great southern current moving through the Aegean Sea along the western Anatolian coast toward Çanakkale Strait.

In winter, the temperature of the surface waters along the Turkish coast averages between 15° and 16°C, and in summer it averages 26°C in the western region and 28°C in the eastern region. Winter in the Mediterranean Sea is mild, rainy, and windy; in the summer it is hot, dry, and calm. Springtime is a rather changeable season, and autumn a short one.

Most fish species of the Mediterranean live in the upper layers and roam widely. These include bonito, mackerel, gray mullet, garrick, albacore, and dolphin. Some bottom-feeding species include plaice, sole, whiting, conger eels, stone bass, grouper, red gurnard, red mullet, comber, ray, and skate.

The major shark species that prowl deep waters are hammerhead, blue, thresher, and porbeagle sharks. These species follow shoals of bonito and albacore and enter shallow waters or sometimes follow the fish shoals up into the northern Aegean Sea. Sometimes they are caught in the nets of commercial fishermen, but they are not specifically pursued by anglers. No shark attacks on humans have been reported in Turkish waters.

A number of swordfish, blue marlin, sailfish, and spearfish are caught with longlines and nets by commercial fishermen in May, but there is little angling effort for these species. It is possible to rent boats from local fishermen in Antalya, and, using rod and reel and artificial lures or chub mackerel and garfish, to try for these species. Amberjack, garrick, pompano, and dolphin enter shallower waters in June and July and can be caught with live baits or spoons.

Turkey's largest freshwater lakes (some saline lakes have no sportfish) are in this region, and such locations as Beysçehir and Eğridir Lakes are important for freshwater fishing. Freshwater fish here include lake trout, perch, carp, roach, chub, barbel, pike, eels, and wels. Rods and reels are used with natural baits.

Central and Eastern Anatolia

Eastern Anatolia is a region with high mountains, crater lakes, and many rivers. Some of those lakes, however, including Turkey's largest—Lake Van—are saline. This highland region is the most rugged and mountainous area of Turkey, and includes Mount Ararat, which is cited in the Bible as the place where Noah's Ark came to rest. It is Turkey's highest peak at 5,137 meters (16,854 feet). Lake trout and rainbow trout are found in the eastern highlands. Trout up to 10 kilograms exist in the Ardahan area in northeastern Turkey, which is north of Ararat. This area is also the headwaters for the Tigris and Euphrates Rivers, which flow through Syria and Iraq to the Persian Gulf.

The lakes and rivers of central and eastern Anatolia also contain carp; these grow large, sometimes reaching 20 to 25 kilograms. Wels are also found here, and most anglers pursue them at dawn, dusk, and throughout the night, using frogs as bait. Pike, too, exist in the reservoirs of central and eastern Anatolia. They are fished with spoons and live baits.

TURKS AND CAICOS ISLANDS

The Turks and Caicos are a British dependency that are geologically part of the Bahamas, situated roughly 30 miles southeast of that island archipelago and 100 miles northwest of the Dominican Republic. There are two island groups here. The smaller Turks encompass six uninhabited cays, the inhabited islands of Grand Turk and Salt Cay, and numerous small rocky islands; the Caicos encompass numerous islets and six principal islands, which include Providenciales, and West,

---

Scientists calculate that there are about 23,000 different fish in the world; 40 percent inhabit freshwater and 60 percent inhabit saltwater.

North, Grand, East, and South Caicos, the largest of which is Grand Caicos.

With an awe-inspiring dropoff close to the reef edge, the Turks and Caicos offer excellent fishing for pelagic species, as well as lightly tapped reef fishing and hordes of small bonefish on flats. Miles of coral reefs make the islands a popular destination for divers. Established tourist facilities and resorts are available on the main islands, and airports exist on Providenciales, South Caicos, and Grand Turk.

Pelagic species are caught along the dropoff at the edges of these reefs, as well as farther offshore and at an impressive seamount that rises to 130 feet from the surface out of a depth of 7,000 feet. That great depth is part of the Turks Island Passage, and from Providenciales, which draws many big-game anglers and hosts a popular billfish tournament each summer, the deep-water fishing grounds are just a 15-minute run.

Blue marlin are the prime attraction here, and they are available year-round. The peak period is from June through August, when there's a good run of spawning fish and several blues a day can be raised. Most blue marlin are small, in the 100- to 200-pound range, and this provides good light-tackle fishing opportunities, including blues on a fly rod; indeed, the first blue marlin caught on a fly rod by a woman was taken here in 1994.

White marlin and sailfish are present from November through April. Wahoo are also available then but are especially abundant in November. Yellowfin and blackfin tuna are caught from December through June, and prime yellowfin action is in the spring.

Reef and flats fishing offer opportunities year-round. The reefs hold the typical array of snapper, grouper, jacks, and big barracuda. The flats reportedly have small tarpon, but they are mainly blessed with relatively unmolested schools of small bonefish. Large schools of 1- to 2-pound bones allow opportunities for catching good numbers in a given day.

The islands have an average annual temperature of 85°F, and the hottest months are September and October. Easterly trade winds help abate the heat, and the islands are subject to frequent hurricanes.

TURLE KNOT

A fishing knot for terminal connections, primarily used by fly anglers to tie a tippet to a fly.
See: Knots, Fishing.

TURNOVER

The complete mixing of all the water in a lake. Turnover occurs when a lake's temperature is essentially the same from the surface to the bottom, a process accomplished through water movement and wind. In deep lakes, this occurs twice a year, in the spring and fall, and is referred to as spring and fall turnover, respectively. In the spring, after turnover, the upper waters start to warm and eventually will stratify. In the fall, the upper waters cool and in some places will eventually freeze.
See: Stratification.

TWO-HANDED ROD

A loosely used term for any long-handled rod designed to be used with two hands when casting. These may be equipped with spinning, baitcasting, or conventional reels. A two-handed fly rod has a long butt section as well as long foregrip.
See: Casting; Flycasting Tackle.

TYEE

A chinook salmon *(see)* that is 35 pounds or larger. This Indian term, as well as the term "tyee salmon," is primarily used in British Columbia, but it may refer to large chinook, or king, salmon wherever they are found.

 Lake Chargogagog-manchogagogcharbunagungamog is said to be the longest place name in North America. Massachusetts anglers call it Webster Lake and know it for bass, pickerel, and yellow perch.

UGANDA

Sandwiched between the Democratic Republic of the Congo on the west and Kenya on the east, Uganda is a relatively small east-central African country with diverse topography and plenty of water. Elevated plains, low-lying swamps, broad forests, arid basins, and snow-capped mountain peaks all exist amidst Uganda's 93,104 square miles. The southern portion of the country, which borders on Lake Victoria, Tanzania, and Rwanda, is largely forested; the north is largely savanna. Although Uganda straddles the equator, its climate is relatively mild due to its generally high altitude.

Along its borders or contained within the interior are Lakes Albert, Edward, George, Kyoga, and a significant northern portion of the largest lake on the African continent, Lake Victoria, as well as the Nile River between Lakes Victoria and Kyoga, between Kyoga and Lake Albert, and below Albert to Sudan. The section of the Nile River below the dam at Lake Albert is referred to as the Albert Nile, and the section from Lake Albert to the Owen Falls Dam at Lake Victoria is referred to as the Victoria Nile.

As with other countries in the region, various game and coarse species exist in Uganda's waters, but tigerfish and Nile perch (locally called *emputa*) are the fish of most interest to anglers. Most of the waterways in Uganda have seen little or no sportfishing since the early 1970s, and the full extent of its angling opportunities for tigerfish and Nile perch in its rivers and lakes is generally unknown.

Nile perch originally inhabited rivers and lakes of the Rift Valley, mainly the Nile and its tributaries, Kenya's Lake Turkana, and Tanzania's Lake Tanganyika. They did not inhabit Lakes Kyoga and Victoria, or the waters above the renowned Murchison Falls (upstream a short distance from Lake Albert), which is also known as Kabalega Falls and resides within Uganda's 1,500-square-mile Murchison Falls National Park. Fossilized remains of both Nile perch and tigerfish were discovered in and around Lake Victoria, and were dated back to the great upheavals of the ice age, when the upper waters of the Nile had become shallow and deoxygenated.

In the 1950s, Major Bruce Kinloch, a keen and dedicated angler who was deputy head of the Uganda Game and Fisheries Department, undertook to revitalize Lake Victoria, which was then the least productive lake in Africa, and at that time contained no trace of predatory fish species. During that decade, Nile perch were introduced above Murchison Falls into the Victoria Nile and Lake Kyoga. In the 1960s, they were introduced into Lake Victoria above the Owen Falls Dam.

In 1967, anglers started landing large catches of Nile perch in Lake Kyoga, at Namasagali where the river enters the lake, and along the Victoria Nile upstream to the Owen Falls Dam. This included some specimens weighing up to 72 kilograms. Anglers from East Africa and Europe fished these waters—which are swifter upriver and broader and slower near Kyoga—mostly from the bank, and many stayed at Chobe Lodge (which was destroyed in 1979). This area has been seldom fished since Uganda gained independence from Britain in 1962, and hardly at all in the 1980s and 1990s.

Today Nile perch are well established throughout this system and in Lake Victoria. All 15 line-class, fly-rod, and all-tackle world records for the species have been caught in Lake Victoria—some in Tanzania, some in Kenya, and some in Uganda. The all-tackle record, and largest ever certified on rod and reel, was an 87-kilogram (191 1/2 pounds)

This large Nile perch was caught by trolling (note the heavy tackle) on Lake Victoria.

fish landed in 1991. An 84-kilogram fish caught in 1995 became a line-class record. Specimens of more than 150 kilograms reportedly have been landed with nets and longlines around Jinja; the largest specimen was a 160-kilogram fish taken from Lake Albert (still larger Nile perch have been reported in Egypt).

The phenomenal spread and growth of the Nile perch throughout Lake Victoria has occurred at the expense of indigenous species, and this has concerned ecologists. On balance, however, the outcome has been beneficial in terms of increased production of fish for the local market and export, and for anglers. More than 12 fish factories have mushroomed in each of the three East African nations, and exports of perch fillets earn valuable foreign exchange for them. Charter boat companies have recently been started, and this development is expected to attract anglers and tourists.

Although some huge Nile perch were landed in the lake in the early to mid-1990s, these days it takes a lot of luck to come by a big one. The fish factories do keep to the law and catch a certain size fish, but local fishermen break the law by fishing close to shore and catching small breeding fish. The water hyacinth has also spread rapidly in the late 1990s, and at times blankets Ugandan bays, making navigation and fishing difficult.

In Uganda, most access to Lake Victoria originates at Entebbe. Fishing is still productive around the Ssese Islands, but getting there can be difficult. A new boat service from Entebbe has improved transportation to the islands, however. The main fishing method there is trolling with plugs around rocky bays and inlets, where big fish lurk in pursuit of tilapia. Although tilapia are their main food source, Nile perch will also eat fellow perch and live bait. In the late 1990s, a small lodge opened on one of the Ssese islands.

Tanzanian authorities have banned commercial and local subsistence fishing around Rubondo Island, and this conservation effort has attracted many anglers from Africa and Europe, who are able to catch Nile perch there on large flies.

Little fishing has been done in the Victoria Nile in recent decades, although some anglers have made visits, no doubt seeking one of the larger Nile perch this area was known for decades ago (at least 10 fish between 54 and 72 kilograms were recorded between 1957 and 1966). An exploratory expedition below Murchison Falls in late 1997 revealed the presence of Nile perch in various sizes, including some monsters that were observed but not landed. The river perch are much more challenging to land than those in the lakes, as the swift currents and eddies, and the lack of accessibility by boats, mean that shore-based anglers struggle to handle behemoths that may take hundreds of yards of line from a reel on a downstream run. Heavy concentrations of water hyacinths increase the level of difficulty, making lures hard—if not impossible—to use in the areas that are accessible. Many anglers thus rely on live bait. Large catfish, incidentally, as well as tigerfish, exist in the turbulent river below these thundering falls.

ULTRALIGHT FISHING
See: Light-Tackle Fishing.

ULTRALIGHT TACKLE
See: Light-Tackle Fishing.

UMBRELLA RIG

A heavy wire multi-lure saltwater trolling rig used predominantly in the northeastern United States for striped bass and bluefish. The umbrella rig is one of the oddest and most effective saltwater trolling lures ever created. It started as the brainchild of a veteran Montauk, New York, skipper, who got the idea for trolling a school of lures while visiting his commercial fishing relatives in Nova Scotia and watching them troll with strips of beer cans rigged off a metal bar.

The original rigs were three-armed devices made with great difficulty by twisting three stands of relatively stiff No. 15 wire (a size used for sharks and giant tuna) with a trolling sinker at the head of the contraption. Attached to the arms were monofilament leaders, each with a plastic tube rigged with a bent hook, the same type of tube that had become popular as cod and pollock lures when rigged above a diamond jig. Small tubes without hooks were added in the middle of each arm to make the "school" look larger.

Others copied the concept with light single metal bars joined with a sinker in the middle, creating a four-armed trolling rig, which proved more effec-

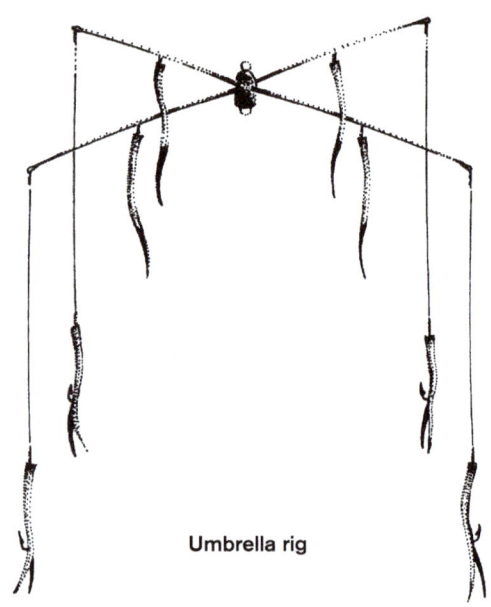

Umbrella rig

tive even if drag through the water increased. As use of the deadly setup spread, a variation was created in New Jersey called the gorilla rig, in which tubes were hung directly from the ends of multiple bars.

Umbrella rigs are primarily used with tubes and are most effective when schooling bait such as sand eels (sand launce) are present because the tubes closely resemble those slim fish. However, just about any lure that doesn't create excessive drag (such as small spoons or soft plastics) can be hung on umbrellas. In a standard setup, an umbrella rig has four teaser tubes, one each midway on the wire arm, and four hooked tubes, one each on a leader tied to the end of each arm. A larger lure, such as a longer unweighted tube or a plug, is often fished from the middle of these rigs on a long leader to create the impression of a predator chasing a school of baitfish.

There are variations, of course, and rigs of different size with different size lures. Fishing with these takes some practice. You can't just drop an umbrella rig in the water and keep trolling. You have to ease it over the side of the boat and make sure that the lures swim properly without tangling, then slowly drop it back while the boat is moving forward. Fish it uptide (moving against the tide) and be careful not to let it out so fast that it sinks to the bottom, where it will get snagged. Long lines are often employed with umbrella rigs, so sharp turns should be avoided.

Because of their size and the drag they exert, umbrella rigs are almost invariably trolled on wire line for striped bass and bluefish, although they also attract many other mid-Atlantic species such as bonito, weakfish, and even little tunny. They've never caught on in other areas, though such species as barracuda, king mackerel, and yellowtail snappers have fallen for them, even when trolled in shallow waters on monofilament line.
See: Trolling Lures, Saltwater.

UNDERHAND CAST
See: Casting.

UNDERWATER VIDEO
A system utilizing a video camera attached to a cable to view underwater activity. Underwater video systems (known as UVS) have become more prominent, particularly aboard charter boats used in clear-water environments, as a means of studying fish and lure activity.

UVS systems are primarily used in trolling applications. They consist of a low-light, wide-angle camera installed in a hermetically sealed waterproof hydrodynamic housing attached to a downrigger cable both inline and ahead of the downrigger weight. Some units feature coaxial-like cable, which provides a lot of water resistance; better ones have a thin-diameter stainless steel–jacketed cable, which offers less water resistance and acts as a conduit for the signal to a video monitor above on the boat.

Underwater video systems can be used in depths up to 200 feet, although this is dependent upon water clarity. Greater depths do not allow for much distance visibility, primarily allowing for seeing lures and fish that are within 6 to 8 feet of the camera. Watching fish come into the viewing area to inspect or take a lure provides interest to some anglers, and has entertainment value, which is why some charter boat captains are using them.

This is a fairly new phenomenon in sportfishing, and one primarily used for trout and salmon trolling, in part because of the clarity of the habitat of these fish and also because it is often feasible with these fish to run a lure a short distance behind the downrigger weight. However, there are other practical applications that do not have to be associated with trolling, although they do need relatively clear water. Ice fishing, for example, is a possible application (for those who have shanties and a source of power). Searching for weeds, surveying wrecks, monitoring lure and bait behavior, locating fish, viewing under objects and structures, and other actions are all possible. UVS systems can also be hooked up to a VCR for recording.

Although underwater video systems are unknown, expensive, and seemingly frivolous pieces of equipment to some people, they are likely to become more popular in the future.
See: Downrigger; Downrigger Fishing.

UNI KNOT
A versatile fishing knot that can be used for terminal and line-to-line connections.
See: Knots, Fishing.

UNITED STATES
Note: Specific fisheries and angling opportunities in the United States are detailed under individual state listings. This entry provides an overview of sportfishing in the U.S.

No matter how you measure it, as a country the United States has the greatest sportfishing in the world. Blessed with water throughout most of its landmass, and abutting two oceans with powerful currents, the U.S. has an incomparable variety of esteemed freshwater and saltwater gamefish, from trout to tuna, bass to bonefish, salmon to sailfish, bluegills to bluefish, and pike to permit.

America's abundant opportunities range from the pine-studded wilderness lakes of northern Minnesota to the mangrove-flooded backwaters of the Everglades, from fishing under the Golden Gate Bridge in San Francisco to alongside the Chesapeake Bay Bridge in Virginia, and from wading Rocky Mountain coldwater streams to using jonboats in Florida's reclaimed sea-level phosphate pits. These venues provide many great, almost-great, and

The 25-foot-long Alvin, a submersible belonging to the Woods Hole Oceanographic Institution, was once attacked at 1,700 feet by a swordfish, which left 2½ feet of bill in the vessel's seam.

The United States has an enormous amount of public fishing opportunity and access.

just-plain-good angling—from inlet to ocean, river to lake, highlands to lowlands, and region to region.

U.S. fisheries are, remarkably, publicly accessible with very few exceptions, although some excellent American waters—Alaska's in particular—are difficult, and relatively expensive, to reach because of their remoteness.

Abundant waters, diverse species, and easy access put sportfishing into the category of third most popular recreational activity in the U.S., surpassed only by the number of people who annually swim or ride a bicycle. A federal government survey in 1996 indicated that 35.6 million Americans over the age of 16 fished annually, and the value of their purchases relative to sportfishing—equipment, travel, jobs, wages, taxes, and the like—exceeded $108 billion. It is no accident that 75 percent of all people vacationing in the U.S. head for the water, and that two out of every five Americans on vacation will do some sportfishing.

A great deal of that angling is done from boats, perhaps more so in the U.S. than in any other country. It is estimated that more than 16 million recreational boats are in use by Americans, and more than 12 million of these are large enough to be powered and/or to require state registration. Many recreational boat owners trailer their boats, and many of these are anglers for whom being mobile and sampling different places are especially important.

Freshwater

In the U.S., anglers focus their effort predominantly on freshwater fishing, in part due to geography; most states are far from marine environments. In freshwater, bass—specifically largemouth and smallmouth varieties—are the most popular species.

The largemouth is a highly adaptable fish, one that is widely available in large and small bodies of water alike, including lakes, reservoirs, ponds, rivers, and streams, as well as in some low-saline tidewater environments. They are found in 49 of 50 states, the lone exception being Alaska. Texas, Florida, and California are especially noted for bass, in part because they have in the recent past produced, or currently produce, the larger specimens. Many states, however—especially in the central and eastern portions of the U.S.—have excellent largemouth bass populations and fish of good proportions.

Almost all sportfishing for bass is done by casting with lures, the vast majority of that from boats. The wide array of bass habitats and cover preferences, as well as the species' predatory ambush nature, lend themselves to virtually all types of lures and diverse presentations.

Smallmouth bass, which inhabit cooler and rockier environs than largemouths, are less widely distributed and on average smaller in size; they predominantly range from the southerly regions of Canada to the middle of the U.S. but are absent in warmer latitudes. A belt running from southwestern Ontario and Minnesota eastward to New Brunswick and Maine has long held the premier smallmouth fisheries, but some rivers and impoundments in the central U.S., including Tennessee and Alabama, are notable for big specimens.

A similar overall range exists for walleye, a species highly coveted for its flesh and one that attracts legions of anglers with the beginning of the open-water season each spring. Walleye have expanded westward to develop significant fisheries in some waters, however, including the mighty Columbia River in Washington State. In recent years, the emphasis in walleye fishing has shifted to the largest lakes and river systems. These tend to produce the bigger fish and abundant numbers of this species, which take advantage of prolific baitfish populations in large waters. Little directed casting is done for walleye; the main emphasis is on trolling, jigging, and presentation of natural bait.

Northern pike have a good following but are less widely available than the foregoing species, and muskellunge attract a small but ardent coterie of anglers who devote much effort to what are generally modest catch results. Other than Atlantic salmon, muskies are the least widely available established freshwater gamefish in the U.S., and they are considered difficult to catch with consistency. As with bass, the majority of muskies today are released. Muskies are most prominent in and around the states bordering the Great Lakes. They receive special attention in Minnesota and Wisconsin. Pike overlap muskies in many of the same waters and do not grow as large on average, but they are much more numerous and are susceptible to a variety of lures. Truly large pike are not common in the U.S., although the opposite is true in northern Canada.

It is the various species of panfish—crappie, bluegills, sunfish, perch, white bass, and the like—as well as assorted catfish and bullhead species, that collectively rank second to bass in total angling interest.

Panfish provide much satisfaction (as well as good eating) to many anglers but lack the glamour and publicity associated with other species. However, these fish are generally abundant and widely available, and they are accessible to people of all skill levels. Panfish anglers use spinning and spincasting tackle almost exclusively, and they place great emphasis on angling with small natural baits and jigs.

All of the species previously mentioned are largely self-sustaining in their respective environments, although some supplemental or introductory stocking by government agencies does occur.

Trout are widely available in the U.S., with a great deal of variety in both species and habitats. Brook trout, native to North America, are favored by many small-stream and high-pond aficionados, especially in the midwestern and northeastern regions, although they are rarely large specimens.

These fish are actually charr, and their family relatives—lake trout—do grow to large sizes, although they exclusively inhabit the cold waters of northern lakes, especially those that are large and deep. The object of many outings on the Great Lakes, lake trout are primarily caught by anglers trolling with medium- to medium-heavy tackle—shallow when the water is cold early in the season, then deep as it warms. Within the U.S., the Great Lakes offer the best opportunities for great numbers and large sizes of lake trout, although good fishing is available on smaller inland waters in a few states.

Rainbow and brown trout, which are more tolerant of warmer and less pristine waters than both brook and lake trout, are more widespread and thus a greater part of the American angler's catch. They are the primary river and stream trout species, although circumstances, sizes, and fishing methods vary widely. Small specimens, the product of regular stockings, inhabit waters where these fish cannot sustain themselves. The largest specimens, some over 20 pounds, exist in large lakes and rivers, and may also be the product of stocking.

Excellent fishing for rainbow trout and/or brown trout (and in some places cutthroat trout) exist in the highlands of various regions. This includes Northern California, the Rocky Mountain states, the Ozarks of Arkansas and Missouri, the Catskil and Adirondack Mountains of New York, and the southern Appalachian Mountains; but very good fishing also exists in Michigan, Pennsylvania, Washington, Idaho, Vermont, and elsewhere. Big rainbow (or steelhead) and brown trout also inhabit some waters scattered around the continent, most notably in the Great Lakes, where trolling in spring and summer, and bank or wade fishing in tributaries from fall through winter, are the favored methods. Some inhabit rivers in the Ozarks.

Salmon are intensely popular in the regions where they occur, but, as anadromous coldwater species, they are not available to the vast majority of Americans, who must devote substantial travel time and expense to access them. They are restricted geographically to naturally occurring Pacific stocks, and the greatest populations exist in Alaska. In New England, there is virtually no viable Atlantic salmon fishery, although fishable populations do exist in the Maritime Provinces of Canada.

With the exception of Pacific salmon (coho, chinook, sockeye, and chum salmon) in Alaska, native North American salmon have been under tremendous pressures due to environmental changes, especially damming of rivers and poor water quality, and to excessive commercial harvest in the oceans. Thriving fisheries for transplanted salmon in the Great Lakes, however, have provided exceptional angling in both lakes and major tributaries; this is sustained by extraordinary levels of stocking and is not subject to commercial fishing pressures.

Saltwater

Saltwater fishing in the U.S. varies considerably between the West and East Coasts, the Gulf of Mexico, and the Caribbean, where the Bahamas, although not technically part of the continental landmass, are a substantial light-tackle fishing destination for American anglers.

Along the East Coast, anadromous species such as shad and striped bass are popular attractions in large coastal rivers, and striped bass are among the most important coastal species from the Carolinas to Maine. Although striped bass were imperiled as recently as the mid-1980s due to commercial fishing and water pollution, stiff commercial controls and improved water quality have allowed their numbers to rebound dramatically. They have regained their place as the primary sportfish in the cooler middle and northern Atlantic waters, where they are caught on various tackle, with both bait and lures, and most fish are released due to regulations.

Stripers, incidentally, although naturally a saltwater species, have been widely transplanted into freshwater rivers and lakes, and huge landlocked populations of these fish occur in many impoundments throughout the middle and southern regions of the U.S.; few are naturally self-sustaining. In many locations, hybrid striped bass—the result of crossbreeding a pure-strain striped bass with a pure-strain white bass—are stocked by state fisheries managers and provide a fast-growing and aggressive sportfish that can be completely managed, as they are sterile.

Bluefish, weakfish, spotted seatrout, flounder, and assorted bottom fish are important species that thrive in the same inshore region as striped bass and, to some extent, drum; these are all suitable to presentations using lighter tackle. The upper East Coast offers offshore opportunities for big-game species, including marlin, tuna, dolphin, and sharks, although this is a more specialized and expensive endeavor involving heavier tackle. Blue marlin are caught off New York, New Jersey, and North Carolina, although not in great numbers, and white marlin are taken off Maryland. Bluefin tuna are sometimes caught in these regions, especially and most recently off North Carolina in the winter, but yellowfins are more likely targets.

Farther south, the emphasis is on a different mix of species, as the warmer climate leads to somewhat tropical conditions and the coastal sweep of the warm Gulf Stream current moves closer to the shoreline. This is why sailfish and dolphin are caught not far from the South Florida coast, as are king mackerel and other species. Some marlin and yellowfin tuna are likely catches, but these fish, and other pelagic species, are more prominent in the deep, blue water off various Bahamian islands.

Inshore, however, attention turns to drum (redfish), seatrout, snook, tarpon, and bonefish, as well as the occasional permit. Wading and casting for redfish and seatrout along the Gulf of Mexico is very popular, as are poling and stalking fish along shallow grassflats. Snook are probably the least abundant of these species and are mainly found in the brackish backwaters of the Sunshine State. Premier light-tackle fish, tarpon are extremely abundant, both on the flats and in passes and inlets, and are eagerly pursued and almost universally released after capture.

Bonefish are a glamour species, hotly pursued by anglers fishing from flats skiffs. In Florida waters, bonefish can run to large sizes but are solitary and skittish; in some parts of the Bahamas, they frequently travel in schools and tend to be less wary than they are elsewhere.

Coho and chinook salmon have long been the premier catches in the Pacific Northwest. These fisheries have been depressed in recent years, however, due to low populations. Their plight has drawn much attention in Northern California, Oregon, and Washington, although Alaska has good inland and coastal salmon fisheries as well as excellent angling for deep-dwelling halibut.

California is a hotbed for saltwater fishing, and its opportunities range from imported striped bass and shad fisheries in northerly coastal rivers, to offshore pelagic species, to the ever popular yellowtail and albacore, and a great diversity of surf and bottom-dwelling species. In Southern California, assorted rockfish, lingcod, and other species are always popular and available, whereas warm, bait-laden currents are necessary to produce good catches of bonito, barracuda, yellowtail, albacore, and tuna. Long-range fishing trips, some lasting up to several weeks, explore distant waters, especially off Mexico. Albacore and yellowfin tuna are the primary pursuits.

Possessing a considerably different topography than that of the East Coast, the West Coast does not offer the shallow flats found in the southeastern U.S. and thus has none of the East's inshore species; however, there is no lack of challenging opportunity for light-tackle enthusiasts.

It is easy to forget that Hawaii is part of the American fishing scene, too, because it is so distant from the mainland. Hawaii is in a league of its own for saltwater angling, however, and is certainly a hotspot in American saltwater fishing. The main emphasis is on pelagic species, especially yellowfin tuna and blue marlin.

General Information

Visitors to the U.S. will find no lack of guides, charter boats, and services catering to anglers, especially in the more well known and publicized areas. In freshwater, important lakes and rivers, and areas with abundant opportunities, have many guides, with and without boats. Charter boats are plentiful on the largest waters (restricted to four to six anglers with reservations only). Major coastal ports have fleets of party boats, capable of accommodating a large number of anglers for bottom fishing, and charter boats for inshore and offshore forays. Smaller guide boats—usually taking no more than three anglers and primarily used for near-shore, estuary, and flats fishing—are available as well and are especially numerous in southern regions. Lodges, camps, and other facilities dedicated to serving anglers are plentiful and are widely advertised in major outdoor publications. Outfitters exist who cater to canoe camping/fishing trips, houseboat vacations/fishing trips, horse or foot pack trips, and so forth.

If anything, the U.S. is so large and has such a plethora of angling opportunities that it can be a bit bewildering for the visitor from another country who aspires to do some fishing. Therefore, a prospective angler needs to focus either on the region that he or she is planning to visit (perhaps on vacation) and discovering both the opportunities available and the common means of angling, or on the species that he or she wishes to catch and then decide what place(s) to visit in order to catch either many of that species or large specimens (at some places it may be possible to do both).

Sportfishing in the U.S. is most popularly pursued from early spring through fall. Far fewer people fish during the cold weather months, although ice fishing is extremely popular in northerly regions, and the most southerly areas (especially Southern California, South Texas, and Florida) provide the most comfortable winter fishing due to a normally mild winter climate.

There are regulations that restrict sportfishing by season, usually to protect spawning fish or fragile populations; these are more prominent in fresh-water than in saltwater. During a limited time frame, the season will be "closed" for a particular species. This is especially prevalent for trout and salmon species; it also occurs for bass, walleye, pike, and muskies, especially in northern states.

For the most part, regulations regarding seasons, methods of fishing, catch limits, and licensing are determined by state governments. There is no national or federal sportfishing license in the U.S., although each of the 50 American states requires a license issued by its government to fish in freshwater. In some places, the same license also applies

---

It is said that in ancient China on moonlit nights, fishermen created an optical illusion with a white board sloping into calm water; this re-flected moonlight and induced fish to jump into the boat.

to saltwater fishing in the state's marine waters; in some places there is a separate license required for saltwater fishing; and in a few places there is no license requirement for saltwater fishing.

A fishing license issued by a state is valid only in waters within that state (although some states with shared water boundaries do cooperate), and in none is there a test or examination required to obtain a sportfishing license. Any person, whether resident or nonresident, can purchase a fishing license, although the nonresident fee is higher. Licenses can usually be purchased for varying time periods (a full year, a week, three days, and, in some cases, daily); they are most commonly acquired at stores selling fishing tackle but are also obtained at some government offices, marinas, lodges, and the like. Licenses are becoming increasingly available by telephone purchase with a credit card.

A license is valid for both public and private waters within a state. Most waters are publicly accessible, but a license does not grant permission to cross private property to reach or leave the water. Ingress and egress must be accomplished at places provided for such purposes. In privately owned waters—or in waters that are inaccessible because all the land around them is in private ownership—permission must be received to fish. There is no private licensing arrangement as exists in Europe, although an access fee may be charged by the owners of private land or waters who run a commercial business (such as a private marina or boat dock where people launch a boat, or a pay-to-fish facility).

There may be regulations pertaining to the manner of fishing; examples include a waterway where only barbless hooks are permitted, or where the use of live or dead baits is prohibited. These and other issues are addressed in a brochure or booklet provided with the purchase of a fishing license.

Although from afar it may seem that there is a complicated maze of regulations, species, waters, and opportunities associated with American sportfishing, a newcomer can obtain guidance at a local bait and tackle shop (which are sadly fewer in number these days), or from organized clubs, or while attending one of numerous regional outdoor shows that are held all around the country during winter months.

Although fishing in the U.S. is good to excellent by most standards, it is generally not as good as it was in the middle of the twentieth century, or even as recently as the 1970s. Pollution, habitat destruction and alteration, and commercial fishing are the biggest culprits. In saltwater, increasingly sophisticated and numerous commercial efforts have led to the overharvesting of many food fish as well as forage fish. This has directly or indirectly impacted gamefish species. The effects have been particularly evident with marlin, swordfish, tuna, salmon, cod, and haddock, but also with many other species, including redfish and striped bass. The latter two species rebounded after reaching near-catastrophic population lows and were subjected to long-term harvest moratoriums.

Recreational angling has played a role in diminished populations and/or fishing success, if not as a result of overharvesting, then as a result of intense pressure. This is especially so in freshwater, where water quality took a nose dive for decades before experiencing a reverse trend, years after passage of the federal Clean Water Act. Some fisheries are still recovering from excessive angling-related fish mortality in the 1950s and 1960s, when it was erroneously believed that angling effort could not wipe out or severely depress populations of fish in large bodies of water.

Fisheries management efforts have sometimes helped and sometimes hindered the situation. Attempts to propagate some species have resulted in successful stocking, transplanting, and fish restoration. Trout and salmon introduction into the Great Lakes is one of the greatest fisheries success stories of all time. Striped bass have been successfully introduced to freshwater, and management of bass has brought huge specimens of Florida strain largemouths to various states. The widespread introduction of carp, however, is recognized as a mistake, and these fish are greatly ignored or denigrated, although they are widespread and numerous and harmful to many environs.

Although many species of fish are retained by anglers for consumption (especially panfish, catfish, walleye, chinook and coho salmon, and stocked trout in freshwater; plus dolphin, yellowtail, bluefish, flounder, snapper, grouper, and other species in saltwater), the past 20 years have seen an evolution in attitudes toward preservation and a much greater inclination to voluntarily release fish. Catch-and-release fishing is not only common, it is accepted for some species in certain areas, no matter what the size.

This fact notwithstanding, fishing pressure is intense on many popular bodies of water, especially seasonally (for example, the opening of the season, in early spring, during the spawning run), and crowding is possible at the most popular waters. Much of this pressure is driven by media and marketing attention, which tends to be overly skewed toward a select few highly marketable species in both freshwater and saltwater. As a result, some species, some waters, and some seasons are neglected. Because of the many waters that exist in America, it is possible to find underutilized fisheries populations and locations that can be enjoyed in solitude.

A review of the species and opportunities in each of the states indicates that high-quality fishing can still be enjoyed; but sportfishing, and management of American fisheries resources, is still a relatively new phenomenon in the overall scheme of things, and thus a work-in-progress.

UNSNAGGING

Getting snagged—having your lure stuck on some object in, on, under, or near the water—is part of the fishing game. Many species of fish orient to bottom and to different types of structural cover, and, as the saying goes, if you aren't getting snagged occasionally, you're probably not angling where the fish are. Therefore, getting unsnagged is a practice you'll have to master unless you don't mind losing lures and breaking your line a lot.

An important point to realize about retrieving a snagged lure is that it doesn't pay to use brute strength and yank on a stuck lure unless you have very heavy line (and then you may straighten the hook) or you are stuck on something flimsy. You usually can't muscle that lure free. Moreover, in so doing you probably will sink the hook deeper into the snagged object; or you may break your line, meaning that you've probably lost the plug altogether, or you may free the bait but send it speeding perilously back to you.

Many lures will come free if you simply jiggle your rod a bit. Another tactic is to take line from the rod between the reel and first guide, pull back on the rod to get the line very taut, and then snap free the line in the other hand; this action may jolt the lure free, especially if it is a jig or single-hooked lure. This technique sometimes works when you are a distance away from an object that is fairly shallow and don't want to go into the shallow to retrieve it. It is especially worth trying on a snagged lure that is deeper than the length of your rod, in which case you position your boat directly over it.

Sometimes it pays to give the stuck lure slack line. A floating plug may float free, or another bait might fall back from the object it was hung on. In current, you can often free a lightly snagged lure by paying out 20 to 30 feet of line so that it drifts down current, and then retrieve the slack line slowly. The force of the downstream current provides a different angle of pull that frequently frees the lure.

Generally, you need to change the angle of pull to retrieve many snagged lures, which simply hang up by the lip or bill or head, usually by wedging into something. Changing position, whether that means walking down the bank or moving your boat so that you get a different angle of pull, usually does the job. In deeper water, position yourself 180 degrees from where you were when you got stuck and simply pull.

If your lure is stuck in water that is no deeper than the length of your rod, and will not come free by any other means, position your boat over the location, stick your rod tip into the water, reel up the slack line until the tip of the rod hits the lure, and then gently push or wiggle it free. You must be gentle when doing this so that you don't break the tip of the rod or jam the guide ring out of its retainer. Be especially careful when you're doing this around rocks. This technique is very effective when a lure is stuck on vegetation, dock pilings, or wood.

You might try using a long pole to poke a stuck lure free or to pull the lure free. Some of the pushpoles used in freshwater, which telescope to 12 feet, have a ring eye on one foot and a bent metal piece on the other. These are meant for reaching up to a stuck lure (tree limbs but no power lines, please) or for sliding down a fishing line to get to where a lure is snagged, and they are almost 100 percent effective for anything that can be reached within 10 to 15 feet.

For lures that are snagged deeper and can't be reached or snapped or jiggled free, you'll have to employ some type of retriever or knocker, which is a weight that slides down the fishing line and dislodges the stuck lure. This technique is most commonly used for plugs, which is why the knocker is often called a plug knocker, and also for jigging spoons. The knocker may be homemade or commercially manufactured. Sometimes an old sparkplug is used as a knocker by putting a split ring over the gap arm and pinching the arm to a closed position. The trouble with these free-falling devices is that they sometimes don't work, especially if a lure has been pulled hard into an object (a deep stump, for example); later, when the line gets broken, you lose both the lure and the knocker. Leaving large weights (often lead) and spark plugs on the bottom is really akin to littering, and not environmentally sensitive.

There are, however, string- or cord-fastened retrievers, which are meant either to dislodge the

Before applying direct, hard-pulling pressure in an attempt to free a snagged lure, first try taking the line ahead of the rod tip, bringing it taut (top), and then making a snap release (bottom).

snagged lure or to tangle around the hooks. When the lure is freed, you simply pull on the string to retrieve everything. These attach to the fishing line and slide down it also. They usually take some time to use, but if you have to retrieve a lure that is catching fish, or the last of its kind, or one that you paid premium dollars for, then it's probably worth the time. With either kind of device, you should position yourself over the top of it for best results.

When you can't get free by any of these means, then you have to try pulling up on the lure as a last resort. For last-chance unsnagging, try tightening the drag and pointing the rod directly at the lure while reeling up all slack and pulling back. When a lure is deep, because of the distance of water between you and the lure, you don't have to worry about it rocketing back at you if you are successful in freeing it. But beware of pulling on a lure that is stuck out of the water (on a dock or limb, for example) or close to the surface. Many people have been hit by multi-hooked lures, lead sinkers, and hard objects that suddenly pull free under great tension and fly back at them at the speed of light. It can be dangerous. Warn others in your boat to watch out before you pull on the lure if there is a chance of it coming back to the boat.

This direct pulling might break the line if it doesn't free the lure. If the line doesn't break, usually because it is very strong, then you should wrap the line over a short- or jacket-covered elbow and pull on it. Do not wrap the line around your hand, especially if the line is a slick, thin-diameter type, because it can slice right through the flesh.

After you've been stuck on an object, check the first few feet of line to make sure it isn't abraded. If it is, cut off the damaged section and tie a new knot.

UPSTREAM FISHING

Facing, casting, and fishing upstream in flowing water. This is the typical, and normally advantageous, presentation mode for fly anglers who wade and fish dry flies in rivers and streams, since the angler needs to face upstream and cast up, or up and across, and allow the fly to drift back to the angler. This means that the fly is likely to float most naturally with the current (there are exceptions), and the angler will be below and out of the sight of a fish that is ahead of the angler and facing the current.

A direct upstream presentation is suitable for an angler using spinning tackle when floating lures are fished, but generally not with any lure that sinks and requires retrieval and manipulation to give it life. Casting moderately up and across is better with lures, and requires retrieving, but casting down and across may be necessary.

See: Downstream Fishing.

UPWELLING

A rise in water from a lower level to a higher level, usually induced by current and wind. Upwelling is most prevalent in the ocean and may occur when current pushes water up and over a prominent seafloor structure. Upwelling may have sportfishing implications when it occurs over canyons, seamounts, humps, reefs, or other major irregularities. It can cause a temperature change and stir up water in the vicinity of these structures, and through effects on the food chain it can produce more forage and be attractive to predators.

U-TUBE

A term for a self-propelled float tube shaped like a U with one open end to improve entry and exit.
See: Float Tubes.

UTAH

About one in every four Utah residents goes fishing at least once a year. Big waters such as Lake Powell, Flaming Gorge, the Green River, and Strawberry Reservoir draw close to 200,000 people from outside the state annually.

There was a time in the not-so-distant past when most Utah residents considered trout the only fish worthy of pursuit. Most young Beehive State anglers grow up learning to fish by catching trout on a small High Uintas lake or a local pond.

These days, fish managers use an extensive hatchery system to raise hundreds of thousands of trout each year, which enables Utah's growing population to enjoy fishing. Because Utah is one of the driest states in the country, few waters exist in which enough sportfish can reproduce naturally to satisfy angling needs. Thus, most of the state's lakes, streams, and reservoirs are managed by planting either catchable-size or fingerling trout raised at hatcheries.

Although the emphasis remains on trout, a new generation of anglers fed by newcomers to the state has discovered the joys of warmwater fishing. The impoundment of huge Lake Powell in southeastern Utah in the middle 1960s created more interest. And, because warmwater species such as striped bass, largemouth bass, smallmouth bass, perch, crappie, and bluegills tend to be more self-sustaining, managers have diversified Utah fishing in recent years. Many "two-tiered" fisheries have been developed since 1980, catering to those who enjoy trout fishing and those who enjoy catching bass or other species.

The most difficult thing for a Utah angler is to find a stretch of blue-ribbon trout stream, a reflection of the emphasis on damming nearly every possible stream for culinary or irrigation purposes. But the tailwater fishery on the Green River below Flaming Gorge Dam is premier North American

 Small black spots on the outer skin of fish are parasites; they're harmless to humans, and the fish are safe to eat.

trout waters. And the close-to-the-Wasatch Front Provo River below Deer Creek Dam provides hundreds of hours of fly fishing pleasure for those seeking wild brown trout.

Northern Region

Bear Lake. Large, turquoise blue Bear Lake straddles the Utah-Idaho border. Although intensive management has improved the cutthroat trout fishery in recent years, Bear Lake is largely known for three unique species of fish believed to be remnants of ancient Lake Bonneville, a huge freshwater lake that once covered much of the Great Basin.

Although few anglers fish for Bear Lake or Bonneville whitefish, the Bonneville cisco is another story. These sardinelike 6-inch fish school by the thousands from mid- to late January each year during their spawning run. Anglers are allowed to use dipnets with long handles to scoop the minnowlike fish from the water. Dipnetting is best during the years when Bear Lake freezes over. A few anglers like to jig for the tiny fish. Although cisco can be eaten (they are best deep-fried whole), many Bear Lake anglers like to freeze them and use them later in the year as bait for the large lake and cutthroat trout that cruise these waters. Although cisco spawn throughout Bear Lake, the east shoreline tends to be most productive.

The Bear Lake cutthroat trout is a hard-fighting, voracious fish eater that the DWR is utilizing in many other reservoirs around Utah because it competes better than do rainbows with nongamefish such as chub. Managers have planted thousands of cutthroat in Bear Lake in recent years, greatly improving the fishing. Due to boating pressure in the summer, however, October through April is prime for angling. Trolling deep, jigging flashy spoons, and using cisco as bait are all common methods of catching trout, some of which weigh 5 or 6 pounds.

Willard Bay. A relatively shallow and somewhat barren reservoir, Willard Bay was created by diking a corner of the Great Salt Lake. Located just off Interstate 15 north of Ogden, Willard Bay had been known more as a close-to-home waterskiing area than as a fishery, but that image began to change in the late 1990s. Biologists have found several forage fish that could survive and serve as feed for the channel catfish, crappie, and walleye that traditionally inhabited the reservoir.

Biologists also introduced another popular gamefish, hybrid striped bass, known locally as wipers, to Willard Bay with good results. These hard fighters are popular with trollers.

Perhaps the best time to fish Willard Bay is in the spring during the walleye spawning run. Always a challenge to catch in Utah, walleye spawn along rocky shorelines, where anglers bounce jigs off the bottom for them. When the crappie cycle ends, Willard Bay is also popular with ice anglers. Because of its heavy boating activity, Willard Bay can be a difficult water to fish in the summer.

Pineview Reservoir. Located up Ogden Canyon, Pineview declined steadily as a trout fishery in the 1970s and 1980s as its waters warmed. But this is good news for panfish enthusiasts because Pineview might be northern Utah's most prolific producer of yellow perch, crappie, and bluegills.

Pineview is the place to take the kids to teach them to fish. On most days, the action is fast and furious. Just attach a piece of wax worm or nightcrawler to a small chartreuse-colored jig and cast along the shallow shorelines, or use a worm dangled below a float or bobber. Pineview also might be the best place in Utah for ice fishing, consistently yielding large numbers of panfish.

Because the panfish were stunting, biologists have added a new, interesting twist to Pineview fishing in recent years by planting limited numbers of fish-eating tiger muskies. The muskies have done their job, thinning the stunted populations of panfish. They also provide a thrilling trophy fish that is among the hardest fighting anywhere in the state. Young anglers targeting panfish are often surprised when a tiger muskie takes their bait and bolts off, stripping most of their light tackle with it.

Rockport Reservoir. Located between the tiny towns of Wanship and Peoa and near the thriving ski town of Park City, Rockport Reservoir is one of those frustrating waters that never managed to cut it as a rainbow trout fishery. But the addition of yellow perch and smallmouth bass actually seems to have helped trout fishing a bit. Trolling is best, although ice anglers enjoy sporadic success. Fishing with nightcrawlers near the rocky dam can be especially productive for yellow perch. Summer fishing is sometimes difficult due to heavy boat traffic.

East Canyon Reservoir. Located close to the town of Henefer, East Canyon Reservoir is among the nearest fishing and boating reservoirs to Salt Lake City. It is a put-and-take managed resource for catchable rainbows. Fishing is best when the ice leaves in late April, and bait angling is best near the dam. Trollers enjoying success lakewide. Late fall fishing can be fruitful as well. Heavy boating pressure in the summer can make trolling difficult, although many try.

Logan River. The Logan flows through Logan Canyon and is a good place to fly fish for wild cutthroat and brown trout. The fast-flowing upper stretches are particularly fertile. Three small impoundments grace the lower part of the canyon closer to the town of Logan, and these might be better suited to families using bait to land the rainbow trout planted there on a regular basis. But the edges of those impoundments can be good for fly anglers using No. 18 or 22 patterns and a light leader. This type of fishing, on the right day, can produce excellent results for enthusiasts of hard-fighting brown trout, which inhabit the upper edges of the impoundments or some of the deeper pools. The Logan is one of northern Utah's best river fisheries.

Blacksmith Fork River. Flowing through the Blacksmith Fork Canyon above the town of Hyrum, and located near the Hardware Ranch where the Division of Wildlife Resources (DWR) feeds hundreds of elk each winter, the Blacksmith Fork River is a classic wild brown trout fishery. Fly anglers look at its deep, green holes and know there has to be a lunker lurking down there somewhere. They often find one. This river receives less pressure than almost any other northern Utah river. Don't ignore the large schools of mountain whitefish, especially in the winter, when they are especially vulnerable to nymph anglers. In fact, fishing for these whitefish is a good way to introduce novice anglers to fly fishing.

Weber River. The Weber River is one of northern Utah's longest, flowing from the Uintas all the way through the urban environment of Ogden. A variety of trout coupled with many whitefish makes this a good, close-to-home river fishery, although much of the land along its banks is private. Anglers must know they are not trespassing, or have permission to fish the better stretches. The tailwater fisheries of both Echo and Rockport Reservoirs are open to the public and can generate good fishing. Angling for whitefish and trout near Morgan and the Devil's Slide area can also be worthwhile, especially in the winter months.

Ogden River. The Ogden River flows from Pineview Dam through Ogden all the way to the waterfowl management area at Ogden Bay. Biologists say it hosts a surprising number of trout throughout its length. In the 1990s, the advent of the Ogden River Parkway turned the Ogden River into Utah's best urban fishery. Try fishing with flies or spinners near Dinosaur Park at the mouth of the canyon, or well into town. Some trophy wild brown trout have been caught along this stretch. Avoid the river during the spring runoff, when the high water can be dangerous and difficult to fish.

Central Region

Strawberry Reservoir. Located on U.S. 40 east of Heber City, Strawberry Reservoir is certainly Utah's most fertile trout water and may rank with Yellowstone Lake as the West's greatest cutthroat fishery. This is a big reservoir, surrounded by marinas, boat ramps, and campgrounds, that yields prodigious numbers of 3- to 5-pound cutthroat or rainbow trout. Well over 1 million angler days are spent on this water, largely because it produces bigger trout faster than nearly any place in the world. From the time the ice leaves in mid-May until it returns in late November, fishing at Strawberry seldom slows. For the hardy few who can stand the cold and the deep, slushy snow, it even produces some good ice fishing.

Although shore fishing with bait can yield good numbers of trout after ice out and in the fall, especially near inlets, the best success at Strawberry comes to boaters. Trollers use weighted line and a variety of lures; most groups start with each angler trolling at a different depth with a different lure. Once the right depth, spot, and lure are found, fishing can be fast.

Strawberry also earns high marks from float-tube anglers who like to use dry flies in the early morning and late evening, or Woolly Buggers any time of the year. Where tributaries flow into the main reservoir are especially popular places with tubers.

Fisheries managers hope that one day Strawberry's many tributaries will be capable of naturally reproducing sufficient wild Bear Lake cutthroat trout and kokanee salmon that they will no longer have to plant fish. The tributaries are becoming more productive all the time, especially since the U.S. Forest Service bought the land around the lake and moved cattle out of much of the valley, improving the riparian areas. Sterile rainbow trout and thousands of Bear Lake cutts are planted each year to keep up with the high pressure Strawberry receives. But the reservoir is rich in insect life and seems capable of sustaining trout at an amazing rate. The size of the average fish is consistently bigger than in any water in Utah, and probably than any in the West.

Jordanelle Reservoir. One of the newest Central Utah Project reservoirs, Jordanelle opened with a flurry in the early 1990s. Fishing may have been too good and limits too liberal because trout angling quickly slowed after the first year, only to slowly build up again. Because of its proximity to Salt Lake City on U.S. 40 near the ski town of Park City and to some of Utah's best state park camping facilities, Jordanelle receives heavy boating and fishing pressure. Brown and rainbow trout fishing for bait anglers, trollers, and float tubers is best on the upper arm where the Provo River flows into the reservoir. Fishing can be quite good.

As of the late 1990s, the up-and-coming gamefish at Jordanelle has been smallmouth bass, which seem to be growing at a faster rate than was expected. Smallmouth anglers casting traditional bass lures along the rocky shoreline or the deep area near the dam can expect to enjoy good success, especially in the middle of the summer, when the trout fishing tails off.

Utah Lake. Many Utah anglers don't know that this shallow and muddy-colored reservoir, which has probably been hurt more than any single body of water by the industrialization of the Wasatch Front, was once a cutthroat fishery. But the warming, muddy water drove the trout away years ago, leaving a good place to catch channel catfish, walleye in the spring, an occasional black bass, and plenty of white bass.

Much of Utah Lake's fishing interest and pressure is centered around the walleye spawning run,

 The fat content of fish, 2.5 milligrams per 100 grams on average, is lower than that of beef, pork, or lamb.

which begins in mid- to late March. This brings dozens of lantern-carrying walleye anglers who bounce plugs and jigs off the bottom of the rocky shorelines at places such as Lincoln Beach, the Provo Boat Harbor, and the area just west of the Geneva steel plant. Some of the boat harbors are good places to fish through the ice for white bass in the winter. And stinkbait fishing for channel catfish and bullhead can be productive most of the year, especially near the structure found at the boat harbors around the lake, at Lincoln Beach, and near where tributaries flow into the Provo.

Northeastern Region
Flaming Gorge–Green River. It may be difficult to decide whether the 91-mile-long Flaming Gorge Reservoir, or the Green River below the Flaming Gorge Dam, ranks as Utah's most famous fishery. A case can be made for both of these waters inside the Flaming Gorge National Recreation Area.

The reservoir, which straddles the Utah-Wyoming border, became world famous in the late 1970s for producing lunker specimens of both lake trout and brown trout, which approached world-record status on occasion. Although the trophy brown trout fishery has all but died out, the big reservoir still produces 20-plus-pound lake trout on a surprisingly regular basis.

Of course, anglers must work to catch those trophies. Whereas lake trout are caught in the deeper areas of the reservoir year-round, the trophies are not plentiful and require hours and sometimes days of trolling or jigging before that one memorable fish is landed. But the big fish are there, and they certainly are a draw.

Other types of gamefish are easier to catch at Flaming Gorge Reservoir. Rainbow trout are stocked regularly and provide fair shore fishing and trolling, although trollers often have more success landing kokanee salmon. Shore anglers seeking rainbows do well fishing the lower part of the reservoir.

In spring and early summer, smallmouth bass are plentiful along the rocky shorelines, especially on the Utah side of the reservoir near Mustang Ridge and Antelope Flat. It's possible to catch smallmouths from shore as well; traditional bass plugs and small spinners provide some of the best fishing.

The Green River below Flaming Gorge Dam ranks among the West's top fly fishing rivers, drawing anglers from around the world. There may be more trout per mile in the stretch of river from the dam to Brown's Park than in almost any river in America. Wild brown trout and rainbows are the main species caught. Most are fat and healthy. More than one angler has been overcome by the river's beauty and clarity and decided to pass the time simply floating downriver, watching the 4- and 5-pound trout feed.

Dories operated by professional guides have become a popular way for first-time Green River anglers to learn the river. But several shops in nearby Dutch John rent rafts, and a 7-mile National Recreation Trail, which stretches from the dam down to the Little Hole take-out point, offers good access for wading anglers.

Scuds rank among the best patterns to use on the Green, although regular hatches send dry fly enthusiasts into ecstasy throughout the year. Good anglers can experience 100-fish days when they hit the river just right.

High Uintas. A 460,000-acre wilderness area with peaks exceeding heights of 12,000 feet, remote drainages, and gorgeous alpine scenery, the High Uintas region is the 17th largest wilderness in the U.S.

Although its season is short, usually from early July until late September, the area's 650 managed lakes and dozens of small streams consistently yield among Utah's best fishing for cutthroat, brook, and rainbow trout, as well as a few grayling. The DWR stocks many of the lakes from the air.

Wilderness anglers would do well to avoid more crowded drainages such as Henry's Fork, Naturalist Basin, and the Granddaddy Lakes and head into some of the less well-known drainages. The DWR publishes and sells a series of 12 inexpensive pamphlets called "The Lakes of the High Uintas," which indicate the species available in area lakes and streams and offer tips on avoiding crowds. Backpacking or horsepacking into the Uintas to fish for small, hungry trout is a delight.

Not everyone has to be a backpacker to enjoy the Uintas, however. This wilderness area is surrounded by lakes and rivers that can be reached by automobile. Although put-and-take rainbow trout are the focus, most of the waters are stocked two to three times a month, which keeps the fishing lively. The most popular campgrounds adjacent to alpine lakes are along Utah Highway 150—known locally as the Mirror Lake Highway—which connects Kamas, Utah, with Evanston, Wyoming. Don't ignore the Upper Provo River and Beaver Creek in that area as well.

Southern Region
Lake Powell. Although the Glen Canyon Dam is located in Arizona, most of 186-mile-long Lake Powell is in Utah. With 1,960 miles of shoreline cutting into twisting red-rock canyons, this designated National Recreation Area managed by the National Park Service has more nooks and crannies than a person could explore in several lifetimes.

This is good news for anglers in search of stripers, smallmouth and largemouth bass, crappie, walleye, catfish, and bluegills, which favor the shoreline. The frequent fluctuations of the huge lake actually improve the fishing by continually flooding new areas, giving fish fresh cover.

Stripers were planted as a trophy fish with the idea that they would not spawn. But the

Lake Powell draws bass anglers from throughout the West.

stripers fooled the biologists, creating a feast-and-famine fishery based on the number of forage fish available. As a result, biologists have lifted the limit on stripers and encourage anglers to bring home as many as they can keep. The stripers gather near the Glen Canyon Dam in the spring to spawn, and in the fall, when they "boil" on the surface during feeding frenzies, creating fast and fun angling.

Although largemouth bass were the primary gamefish in the early days of Lake Powell, the relatively recent addition of smallmouth to the mix has been successful. Other than the thousands of catfish, bluegills, or crappie that often cruise under the big houseboats found all over Lake Powell, smallmouths are the easiest of the gamefish to catch. This is especially true in the spring, when they head to their shallow spawning beds at the first hint of approaching hot weather.

Newcomers to Lake Powell can be intimidated by its sheer size. Don't be afraid to ask marina operators at Bullfrog, Hite, Wahweap, or Hall's Crossing for advice on what to use and where to fish. This is, after all, one of the world's largest man-made reservoirs.

Fish Lake. Located near Richfield in south-central Utah, pine-shrouded Fish Lake has lived up to its name for generations, developing a local lore built up around the occasional trophy lake trout pulled from its depths by trollers and jiggers. Although not as common as the lunkers at Flaming Gorge, 10-plus-pound lake trout succumb to several lucky anglers every year. A few old-timers still troll deep with steel line wrapped around paddles instead of using poles.

Anglers more interested in catching good numbers of trout usually head for the east shoreline of the lake, where rainbow trout are plentiful along the weedbeds. Some like to troll, some fish with bait, and a few even toss flies. Splake are also caught.

There has been a new wrinkle to Fish Lake angling in recent years in the form of plentiful yellow perch. Those who simply dangle a worm over the side of the bank in the upper part of this beautiful, natural lake surrounded by pleasant U.S. Forest Service campgrounds are usually rewarded by catching dozens of this species.

Ice fishing has also become popular in recent years, and at least one of the three lodges on the lake usually stays open, providing lodging and access in the winter months.

Scofield Reservoir/Electric Lake/Joe's Valley Reservoir. Located in southeastern Utah within an hour's drive of each other, Scofield, Electric, and Joe's Valley are the most popular trout fisheries in the Price area.

Scofield, which is surrounded by two state park camping and boat launching areas as well as some private land, is the most productive of the three, primarily offering large numbers of 10- to 16-inch rainbow trout to trollers, shore anglers using bait, and ice anglers in the winter. Although it can be plagued by invasions of Utah chub and is treated to remove these nongamefish every decade or so, Scofield ranks with Strawberry Reservoir in its ability to produce fast-growing fish quickly.

Electric Lake, with limited facilities and usually restrictive regulations, is primarily a cutthroat trout fishery. It supplies the cutthroat egg needs for many Utah hatcheries, so anglers should study regulations closely. Those seeking large cutthroats find success by casting flies or spinners from the shoreline or by trolling.

Joe's Valley can be spotty but does yield good splake and rainbow trout. Anglers should check out many of the smaller lakes and reservoirs on either side of the Wasatch Plateau that runs down the central part of the state. Some of these smaller waters produce good summer fishing, and the alpine scenery is spectacular.

Boulder Mountain. An alpine area full of small lakes known for their trophy-size brook trout, Boulder Mountain sits between Capitol Reef National Park and the Grand Staircase National Monument. This location attracted heavy pressure during the 1990s that has hurt the fishery, but numerous remote area lakes are still capable of providing good catches of trout in a scenic environment. Check with the U.S. Forest Service ranger station in the tiny town of Teasdale, or in Escalante, for maps and information.

Unlike the Uintas, Boulder Mountain is not a federally designated wilderness area, so some of the lakes can be reached by four-wheel-drive vehicles. Others require a short hike.

Southwestern reservoirs. Panguitch Lake, Otter Creek, and Minersville and Quail Creek Reservoirs rank as the top fishing waters in southwestern Utah. All are capable of growing fish fast, and—with the exception of Quail Creek, which has bass and trout—most feature nice-size rainbow trout.

Panguitch Lake has the most developed facilities. It is surrounded by private lodges offering boat rentals and places to spend the night. A couple of nice U.S. Forest Service campgrounds are on one end. Boat fishing is best for trout, usually between 10 and 16 inches.

Otter Creek typically yields the biggest trout. Although trolling is probably the preferred angling option, shore fishing can be good. There is a small lodge that rents boats, and a state park campground and boat launching facility. Infestations of Utah chub can slow fishing at times, but Otter Creek is a consistent trout producer most years.

Minersville is a state park that has been managed as a trophy trout fishery in recent years, largely due to problems with fish-eating birds and Utah chub. Because pressure is usually light, it's a great place for float tubers. Trout exceeding 20 inches in length are common. Expect to find restrictive limits.

Quail Creek is a few miles from the entrance to Zion National Park in the midst of southern Utah's red-rock country. It features open water year-round, and good trout fishing most of the year. Largemouth angling is excellent in the early spring.

VANUATU

Formerly the New Hebrides Islands, Vanuatu comprises a group of 82 coral and volcanic islands that runs roughly northwest-southeast over 1,300 kilometers of the Pacific Ocean. The group is roughly 1,000 kilometers west of Fiji.

Only 12 of the islands are of a significant size. Espiritu Santo (called Santo locally) and Malekula are the largest. The most developed is Efate, where the international airport and the capital city of Port Vila are located. Port Vila is one of the prettiest tropical towns on these Pacific islands. It is clean, with low crime rates, and has a wide range of shops and services.

Rainfall and temperatures increase to the north of the group. July through September are the wettest, and also the coolest, months. November through April is the cyclone (hurricane) season.

Vanuatu was jointly run by the French and British from 1906 until its independence in 1980. American influence was felt during World War II, and James Michener's book *Tales of the South Pacific* was set in these islands.

Outside influences are evident from Vanuatu's cosmopolitan atmosphere, one seldom encountered on other Pacific islands. For example, in Port Vila there are Chinese, French, Italian, Japanese, Mexican, Spanish, Thai, Indonesian, and Vietnamese restaurants, and others serve a variety of seafood dishes and European cuisine.

The local people are of Melanesian stock and are called "Ni-Vanuatu." They make up 90 percent of the population, which numbers roughly 200,000. The main languages are Bislama pidgin (which bridges the gulf formed by 105 indigenous languages), English, and French.

The main fishing base is Port Vila, where there's a wide range of quality accommodations and a handful of modern, quality charter boats equipped with good tackle. This includes two Australian-made 34-foot sportfishing boats and several smaller day boats. Many of these are based at the yacht club in downtown Port Vila.

Fishing can be excellent out of Port Vila. Besides fish attraction devices (FADs), the Erromango Seamounts are a hotspot, as is "marlin alley"—a stretch of water where the coastal shelf falls away into deep water; a parallel chain of seamounts exists out in the depths. During peak season, this area is hot! Regular pelagic captures are wahoo, yellowfin tuna, mahimahi (dolphin), Pacific sailfish, black marlin, and blue marlin.

Although yellowfin are available all year, the peak season runs from January through May. Fish average 40 to 60 kilograms, but 90-kilogram specimens are caught regularly. Mahimahi are best from June through October.

Peak marlin season runs from October through February, when there are good numbers of blue marlin about. There's also a run of striped marlin in October, as these fish head into the Coral Sea to spawn. Black marlin peak from January through May, but lesser numbers of blues and blacks are encountered throughout the year, along with sailfish.

Blue and black marlin in excess of 300 kilograms have been captured here on rod and reel, but the average is closer to 130 kilograms. Striped marlin are large and average around 100 kilograms. Skippers may release billfish on request, but this issue should be discussed before fishing starts. Custom dictates that the catch belongs to the boat, and most species are kept for sale on the domestic market. Lure trolling is favored for offshore fishing, as baits tend to produce sharks.

Big dogtooth tuna have been captured in this region, usually on the dropoffs around reefs and islands. These are taken on jigs, baits, and sometimes on trolled lures. Reef trolling with minnow-type diving lures and rigged baits, as well as casting surface lures and metal jigs, are ways to produce a mixed bag of tropical species that includes barracuda, rainbow runners, coral trout, red bass, and both bluefin and giant trevally.

Shore casting with lures can provide excellent fishing, although access is not open to all areas; visitors should check before starting to fish. Small lures and light tackle catch a wide range of reef fish, many of which have anglers running for fish identification books. Larger lures on more sturdy equipment will see hookups on larger reef predators such as coral trout, red bass, barracuda, and several species of trevally.

Anglers heading into the northern islands of Vanuatu will find frequent access by small aircraft. The most regular destinations are Espiritu Santo, Malekula, Tanna, and Pentecost.

Pentecost is known for its tower divers; at an annual festival, local men jump off high towers with vines attached to their ankles that stop their fall just above the ground—a primitive form of bungee jumping.

Varying levels of accommodation are available, including resorts on Espiritu Santo and Tanna.

Although fully equipped charter boats are not available, dive operators and local fishermen can often be persuaded to take adventurous anglers out on the water. Such boats are minimally outfitted for angling, and it's necessary to supply your own tackle.

North of Efate, malaria becomes a more common concern. Visitors should take antimalarial medication if venturing into this area.

V-BOTTOM

A term loosely used to describe a boat with a planing hull, and separated into modified-V or deep-V categories.
See: Boat.

VEER

To change direction or swerve; also, when the wind changes direction in a clockwise direction, it veers.

VEGETATION
See: Aquatic Plants.

VENEZUELA

It stands to reason that Venezuela is well endowed with fisheries resources. The country boasts more than 1,700 miles of coastline and in excess of 1,000 streams, and it possesses one of the greatest rivers in the world—not to mention the world's tallest waterfall (Angel Falls). With its huge peacock bass and payara far inland, tarpon on the coast, bonefish on island flats, and marlin in blue water, Venezuela is one of South America's most diversified, high-quality sportfishing destinations.

Freshwater

Six navigable rivers course through Venezuela, but the most significant one, the Orinoco, drains and influences nearly 80 percent of the country. One arm branches off into Brazil and heads to the Río Negro and eventually the Amazon River. The highland plains rivers, as well as the impoundments that have been formed on some of the major tributaries, provide excellent fishing for the likes of peacock bass, payara, piranha, and other highly prized warmwater species. The many rivers and fishing opportunities here are described in the Orinoco and Amazon watersheds review under Brazil *(see)*.

Saltwater
Inshore fishing. The Los Roques, Río Chico, and Río Aruca areas of Venezuela are relatively recent discoveries that rate highly for bonefish, tarpon, and snook, and provide good opportunities for light-tackle fishing.

Bonefish are plentiful and cruise the flats of some 20 islands that constitute Islas Los Roques ("Island of Rocks"), which lies almost 80 miles north of Caracas at approximately 12° latitude. To its north is the 2,000-fathom-deep water of the eastern Caribbean Sea; the next land to sight north of Los Roques is Puerto Rico, hundreds of miles distant.

Las Roques is one of Venezuela's national parks; further development is prohibited, and commercial fishing is tightly controlled. Out on the 30-mile-long Los Roques atoll are all manner of easily waded coral, sand, and grassflats. Tidal fluctuation is not great, so shallow water bonefishing is virtually always possible, and anglers encounter nearly every type of feeding situation.

Most bonefish here are caught on falling water, which is a bit unusual (rising water floods the flats and brings fish in to feed in most locations), and are found in classic tailing situations. Although singles and small fish are available, bonefish travel in large schools, sometimes numbering many hundred individuals and covering large expanses of the flats. The average bonefish here is small, in the 2- to 3-pound range, but 5- to 10-pounders exist.

The beautiful flats and reef edges provide opportunities for other quarries as well. Permit are scarce, but limited fishing for snook and small tarpon exists in lagoons and near mangroves in the summer. Of course, barracuda are often seen on the flats, and various snapper are taken as well. Few people bother with the reef edges, where action with a host of species is likely.

Although Los Roques is frequently windy, the area provides sufficient protected water to enable anglers to escape the brunt of the wind. With a water temperature that seldom varies from 80°F, the Los Roques flats are otherwise comfortable, with generally hard bottoms. Cold fronts and muddy water are not the problems here that they pose at other bonefishing sites.

Dirty water is another matter along the mainland coast, however, in the back bays, lagoons, and creeks that support hot fishing for snook and tarpon. A notable eastern site for this is in the Gulf of Paria, which is between Trinidad and the Venezuelan mainland, and several hours from Caracas. There, the Aruca River and assorted tributaries feed a brackish-water jungle-like estuary that hosts snook up to 20 pounds and tarpon up to 50 pounds. Anglers have reportedly seen larger tarpon here, but the average fish is in the 20-pound class. Snook are abundant in the mangrove- and deadfall-lined areas, and average several pounds.

The stained, milk chocolate water prevalent in these areas during the rainy season doesn't produce nearly as well as the darker, cleaner water, which one has to look for. The dry season, from November through April, produces cleaner water and good tarpon action. Schools of sardines are said to come into these waters beginning in September, followed by mullet in November, enhancing the tarpon prospects.

Light-tackle snook and tarpon fishing are equally productive in mangrove-lined Tacariqua Lagoon, a national park and wildlife refuge near Río Chico. Excellent small tarpon (up to 50 pounds) angling can be had here amidst small mangrove islands and in backwater bays and creeks.

The tarpon of Tacariqua are mostly under 15 pounds, and the snook average 2 to 4 pounds. Larger snook in the 6- to 8-pound class are caught as well, and some have been reported to 20 pounds. Casting tight to the edge of the mangroves is the norm in these dark, tannin-stained waters, with streamer flies and an assortment of surface and shallow-running plugs. Bigger fish are reported in the channels and in the open lagoon waters, however. As often happens in such places, early and late in the day are favored times for the bigger fish.

The absence of giant fish in these and other places may deter trophy seekers, but it's worth noting that Venezuela's Lake Maracaibo once produced a 283-pound tarpon. And the Boca Grande area of the Orinoco Delta, which is expansive by any measure, is mostly covered with mangrove swamps, but little has been reported about sportfishing there.

Offshore fishing. The North Equatorial Current sweeps westward from the northwest coast of Africa, coursing over 3,000 miles of the Atlantic and sweeping into the Caribbean Sea below Barbados and Grenada, striking the northern coast of Venezuela. There, just north of the coastal town of La Guaira, an eddy current works counter to the main flow. Added to this is the steady contribution of nutrients from the Orinoco River, one of South America's most prominent watersheds. Together, these natural circumstances create an environment that brings baitfish and large predators into the area and holds them there. The fish arrive in great quantities, quantities that at times produce fabulous action, especially for billfish, which are attracted by the abundance of baitfish along the dropoffs washed by the current. In the peak of their availability, these fish provide world-famous big-game fishing.

The tales of marlin and sailfish action off La Guaira Bank, although stupendous to anglers of today, are barely half what was experienced several decades ago, when the first anglers pioneered offshore fishing here. In intervening years, there was little exploration or exploitation of the area with sportfishing craft. It came as a surprise to many anglers when they ventured to La Guaira in the early to mid-1980s with better boats and equipment and raised 20 to 40 fish per day per boat.

Today the numbers aren't that high, but they are exceptionally good, and the variety is unmatched. Where captains in most other ports are glad to talk of hooking or catching a couple of sailfish and perhaps a single marlin in a day, success off Venezuela is measured in slightly better form.

There are many popular big-game fishing destinations that offer concentrations of particular species within a tight season, but few have excellent potential for catching a variety of billfish, and fewer still provide that potential at virtually any time of the year. The waters offshore of the north coast of Venezuela are perhaps unique in that they support year-round populations of a wide variety of pelagic fish, especially sailfish, blue marlin, white marlin, and swordfish. These species are augmented by wahoo, yellowfin tuna, and dolphin, which occur seasonally but are still found in varying numbers over much of the year.

Certainly there may be day-to-day and week-to-week variations in the numbers and cooperation of offshore species, but Venezuela's food-rich waters come close to predictability, and the notion of good or better seasons has less meaning when billfish are present in significant numbers year-round, and when a blue marlin, white marlin, or sailfish is a possible catch on any given day of the year. Indeed, a grand slam catch—a sailfish, a blue marlin, and a white marlin—is possible every day. Not many places can make such a claim.

The Venezuela recreational fishing fleet is headquartered in Caraballeda and generally fishes over La Guaira Bank or closer to shore off the power plant west of Maiquetia. Lines are usually in the water within 45 minutes after the boat leaves the inlet—sooner if you troll an artificial lure at high speed on the way out.

La Guaira Bank is a broad underwater plateau that rises to within about 350 feet of the surface a scant dozen miles from shore (a few miles farther out is a deeper bank, Playa Grande, but few boats venture there). The swift currents that sweep along the northern coastline of South America create tremendous upwellings around the banks, and the full range of the marine food chain is found in the area.

Squadrons of flyingfish, legions of bullet bonito, and clouds of seabirds overhead signal the richness of these waters. Southwest of the bank and slightly

Peacock bass anglers ply the flooded backwaters of Venezuela's Guri Lake.

inland, an occasional whale blows a plume of spray, and vast schools of leaping porpoises often stretch almost as far as the eye can see. In the spring, great schools of yellowfin tuna skirt the northernmost edges of the bank and beyond, under the traveling umbrella of screaming, feeding seabirds.

In spring and summer, pods of dorado feed over the bank. These schooling fish are not the ubiquitous "chicken" dolphin of Florida waters, but rather weigh between 20 and 50 pounds.

The constant trade winds and powerful currents responsible for the upwellings and concentrations of baitfish, however, also bring alpine seas. Although the bank can look like a millpond at times, it is more likely to have heavy swells rolling in from the east, accompanied by a sharp chop on top of the swells. This explains why most of the boats here measure 35 feet or more, and are of rough-water design. During the summer months, mornings may dawn clear and calm, but such blessings are rare and not dependable. October's popularity with anglers has nothing to do with calmer seas or greater comforts.

Seas notwithstanding, the abundance and variety of billfish is primarily what draws anglers from around the world. An ever-present possibility of trophy specimens makes every day on La Guaira still more exciting. Venezuela, in fact, has produced a number of blue marlin in the 850- to over 1,000-pound range in the last decade. Huge blues have come during such diverse months as April, July, September, and October.

The fall months have long been regarded as the premier billfish time here, especially September for sailfish and October and November for white marlin. In recent times, anglers have discovered that opportunities from February through June probably exceed those in the fall, if not for big fish then for quantity. And fishing during the summer can also be excellent. For swordfishing, the lighter summer breezes offer the most comfortable night angling; the winds and seas are far more likely to be calmer in June, July, and August than in the spring and fall. Three-hundred-fathom depths scant miles offshore provide good odds for swordfish success, even on a one-night trip. Conservation efforts make angling for swordfish generally less popular, however. A few charter boats still pursue swords here, but most leave the species alone.

In the past, white marlin fishing in the fall has been so productive that anglers often raised as many as 20 to 30 in a day. Although such banner days occur less frequently, undoubtedly because of commercial longline fishing pressures in the Caribbean, it is still common to raise a dozen whites in a day, and not only in the fall. If the number of whites raised is not as consistently high as it once was, it is still excellent when compared with any other locale.

As is true elsewhere, the presence and number of Venezuelan billfish are subject to various factors, not the least of which is excessive commercial fishing exploitation. Although many billfish off Venezuela are resident, others are migratory; some billfish from La Guaira Bank travel to and from the Cozumel/Cancún area of the Yucatán, and there is some white marlin movement between Venezuela and the mid-Atlantic coast in North America. What happens in one area or between areas can affect all of them. Local conservation efforts in U.S. waters, for example, afford protection to billfish populations only during that portion of their yearly wanderings when they fall within U.S. jurisdiction; elsewhere, they may be subject to less-restrictive commercial exploitation (something to keep in mind when you see billfish offered in a restaurant or fish market).

La Guaira Bank and surrounding waters also offer marvelous opportunities for other gamefish. Wahoo are frequent visitors and provide action for the angler willing to switch from monofilament to wire leaders. Although the wire may spook white marlin, it's a necessity for landing toothy wahoo. No such sacrifice needs to be made for dolphin or yellowfin tuna, and both are frequently caught here by anglers seeking billfish.

The dolphin (dorado), caught off Venezuela's verdant coast are larger on average than the schoolies familiar to most anglers. Schools of fish in which each specimen exceeds 20 pounds are common; 35- to 50-pound fish are taken with surprising regularity. Landed on the same rigged ballyhoo that produce sailfish and white marlin, giant bull dolphin provide an exciting diversion, even for the obsessive billfish addict.

Yellowfins are something else again, and for some anglers here, they may not be as welcome as wahoo or dorado due to their indefatigable nature. From 30 to 50 miles north of the coastal mountains, great clouds of screaming, diving seabirds commonly feed over schools of tuna. This is where commercial netters ply their trade. Tuna schools range far inshore to feed on swarms of baitfish, however, and billfish-seeking anglers are occasionally interrupted by crashing strikes, often in multiples, from feeding yellowfins. Averaging from 160 to 190 pounds, these tuna are often hooked on light lines intended for white marlin or sailfish, and anglers often are leashed to a seemingly inexhaustible monster by slim 20- or 30-pound-test line. One such angler, trolling close to shore on the way in from fishing on the bank one March day, latched onto a 245-pound yellowfin.

Not everyone fishes with conventional and big-game tackle here, of course. The bank attracts a growing number of anglers eager to tangle with billfish on fly tackle. Sailfish and white marlin are especially popular fly fishing targets, and some also pursue blue marlin. The smaller 100- to 200-pound fish that occur in incredible numbers over La Guaira Bank from April through June provide the most appropriate and realistic fly-tackle opportunities.

One of the joys of offshore fishing in Venezuela

Published in 1833, the Natural History of the Fishes of Massachusetts, Embracing a Practical Essay on Angling, by Jerome Smith, is believed to be the first American fishing book.

is its accessibility. Caracas is a 2½-hour flight from Miami, and a few anglers head there on Friday, fish for two days, and return on Monday morning. Although many of the available charter boats are booked months in advance, it's sometimes possible to slip in a brief, spur-of-the-moment trip.

As a bonus to the visiting angler, Venezuela adds aesthetic factors to the bare fishing statistics. These include shoreside comforts, delicious local delicacies, great shopping opportunities, and the awe-inspiring beauty of Venezuela's northern coastline, especially when viewed from offshore.

The offshore fleet originates at Caraballeda, a small town about a half-hour from the Caracas airport, which is actually in Maiquetia on the coast north of Caracas. Visiting anglers take a taxi from the airport to Caraballeda, a ride that leads through a succession of small towns nestled along a narrow strip of land beneath towering 7,500-foot-high mountains that separate the sea from the city of Caracas beyond. Visible from far offshore, these velvet-green peaks topped with whipped cream clouds serve as a constant reference point during the day's fishing, and as a magnificent backdrop for evening shoreside activities.

Most Venezuelan charter boats supply modern tackle from 20- through 80-pound class, but those who prefer to gamble with lighter lines are advised to bring their own tackle. Similarly, those who wish to do battle with stand-up gear would do well to bring their own fitted harnesses. Since many anglers seeking blue marlin prefer to troll artificial lures, they may wish to bring along a few proven favorites, although most boats carry a supply of rigged artificials. Everything else is supplied. The common fishing routine for charter boats is to start on or near La Guaira Bank, working the peak and the adjacent vicinity. If action slows, or for variety, the boats head southwest and inland.

VENTILATED-SPOOL REEL
A reel with perforations on the spool, also known as a perforated spool reel; this is an increasingly popular item in fly fishing for lightness and line drying; it has appeared recently on a few baitcasting reel spools, where it is mainly intended to reduce weight.
See: Baitcasting Tackle; Flycasting Tackle.

VENUE
A term predominantly used by British anglers to refer to a particular fishing site or location, be that a river, lake, reservoir, canal, etc. For example, an angler might say, "River fishing in the north has declined in recent years; previously the venues there produced excellent numbers of fish."

VERMICULATIONS
Short, wavy wormlike lines on the back and sides of some fish.

VERMONT
Vermont is a small state, but it offers greater variety in fish species and angling opportunity than much larger states. With 280 lakes and ponds that exceed 20 acres each, and 5,000 miles of fishable streams, good fishing locations are not lacking.

Among these possibilities is 110-mile-long Lake Champlain, one of the most formidable natural lakes in North America, and more than 200 miles of New England's most prominent river, the Connecticut. About half of Vermont's waters drain into Champlain, and about 40 percent drain into the Connecticut River, eventually reaching Long Island Sound.

The Green Mountain State's excellent offerings vary from big lakes and rivers to remote mountain trout streams and tiny beaver ponds. Almost every significant freshwater fish thrives in this state. Species of prominence in various waters include brook trout, brown trout, rainbow trout, lake trout, landlocked salmon, steelhead, largemouth bass, smallmouth bass, walleye, northern pike, pickerel, muskellunge, yellow perch, white perch, smelt, and several species of catfish.

Although Vermont is the only New England state that doesn't have a seacoast, it does offer anadromous fishing. The Connecticut River, which forms the state's eastern border, provides a good spring fishery for shad in its lower reaches. Time will tell if Atlantic salmon runs will be restored and with enough abundance to permit angling.

Access is rarely a problem in the state, as the Vermont Fish and Wildlife Department has been aggressive in purchasing land and building parking areas and boat ramps. Those who want to get away should look to the Northeast Kingdom or the Green Mountain National Forest. Lake Champlain in the west and the Connecticut River in the east offer great variety. In between is more good fishing than most people realize, and it all comes with beautiful scenery.

Lake Champlain
Lake Champlain is often referred to as the Sixth Great Lake and occupies much of Vermont's western boundary, or coast, as some call it. At 120 miles long, with 587 miles of shoreline and 435 square miles of surface, Lake Champlain is truly a great lake. Shared with New York and Quebec, its waters drain to the north through the Richelieu River into the St. Lawrence, and its fisheries are jointly managed.

Champlain's coldwater fishery consists primarily of lake trout, landlocked salmon, brown trout, and steelhead trout. The main warmwater species are large- and smallmouth bass, walleye, northern

pike, and pickerel. Yellow perch are the species taken in greatest numbers throughout the length and breadth of the lake, although white perch are also popular.

In addition to these prominent and sought-after species, however, there are channel catfish, crappie, bluegills, rock bass, brown bullhead, whitefish, and smelt in Champlain, as well as cisco, burbot, bowfin, carp, gar, suckers, eels, freshwater drum, and mooneye. If this potpourri isn't satisfactory, you can try for the occasional muskie that lurks near river mouths.

Lake sturgeon are also present, incidentally; this is one species that anglers should not be fishing for, although occasionally one is caught. The lake sturgeon grows to impressive lengths here, but it is an endangered species and protected by law. Release of accidental catch is mandatory.

Lake Champlain is divided into five sections for purposes of fishery management and assessment. From north to south the divisions are: Missisquoi Bay, Inland Sea, Mallets Bay, Broad Lake, and South Lake.

Missisquoi Bay is the northernmost part of the lake and extends into Canada. The Missisquoi River forms a delta that divides the bay, which is quite shallow and home to good populations of walleye, largemouth bass, northern pike, and perch. Along the delta is the Missisquoi National Wildlife Refuge.

The Inland Sea is the area from the causeway at Sandbar north, and is bounded on the west by the islands that form Grand Isle County. There are both deep water and shallow bays here, as well as a variety of guts around and between the many islands. The main species are landlocked salmon, northern pike, largemouth and smallmouth bass, walleye, and yellow perch.

Mallets Bay is south of Sandbar and north of the old railroad bed that connected Colchester Point and South Hero. Water depths exceed 100 feet in several places, yet there's a long, shallow flat along the causeway at Sandbar. Anglers do well here with largemouth and smallmouth bass, landlocked salmon, northern pike, walleye, and yellow perch.

The Broad Lake area is the biggest section and, at 12 miles, is the widest part of the lake. It is bounded on the south by the Champlain Bridge at Addison and on the north by the railroad bed, the Champlain Islands, and Quebec. Most of this section is deep and cold and naturally holds big lake trout and salmon, plus good populations of walleye, smallmouth bass, and smelt.

The South Lake sector extends from the Champlain Bridge to the Champlain Canal at Whitehall, New York. This section is shallow and apt to be turbid. Walleye, channel catfish, white perch, largemouth bass, sauger, and northern pike are the primary species.

Connecticut River

At 410 miles long, the Connecticut is New England's longest river, running the length of Vermont and forming its eastern border. From high in the New Hampshire mountains within sight of the Canadian border, the Connecticut flows south to Long Island Sound. Some 235 miles of its length abuts the Green Mountain State.

The big river offers excellent fishing and a greater variety of species than any other body of water in Vermont, with the possible exception of Lake Champlain. There is no better way to fish the river and enjoy its tranquillity and natural beauty than by floating it.

This great river was once an industrial and municipal sewer in Vermont but is now very clean and provides a variety of angling opportunities, from strictly trout waters in the north to the warmwater fishery in the south. Year after year the New Hampshire and Vermont annual records for several species of fish are taken from the Connecticut River.

The upper river holds brookies, browns, and rainbows. Much of the river between the upper and lower sections has a mix of species, including trout, largemouth and smallmouth bass, walleye, pickerel, northern pike, yellow perch, white perch, bluegills, hornpout, and the occasional tiger muskie.

The upper sections of the river from Beecher Falls to Guildhall are mostly easy to wade. From Guildhall south to Gilman there are plenty of trout, but smallmouth bass also thrive here.

Many anglers concentrate on a particular section of trout water in the upper river. From a point 250 feet below the Lyman Dam to a point 1,600 feet upstream of the Bloomfield/North Stratford Bridge, fishing is restricted to catch and release by flies or artificial lures with barbless hooks.

The Fifteen Mile Falls hydroelectric complex, which extends from Gilman to McIndoes, consists of three dams: Moore, Comerford, and McIndoes. The big reservoirs hold brook, brown, and rain-

Lake trout are a staple catch in Lake Champlain; note the lamprey attached to the flank of this trout.

bow trout, large- and smallmouth bass, and yellow perch. Many anglers consider Comerford one of the best smallmouth bass fisheries in the region. The tailraces of the three dams hold lunker brown and rainbow trout and can be productive year-round.

From McIndoes south to Wilder Dam, the fishery is mostly for warmwater species, but trout linger near the mouths of tributaries. This section of river holds both large- and smallmouth bass, pickerel, northern pike, walleye, and perch. Many anglers devote most of their time on this section to fishing for walleye. Also popular are perch, which are plentiful, or the monster pike that feed on them.

The lower river has anadromous fish, including American shad and Atlantic salmon. Shad arrive in late May and provide a particularly exciting and popular fishery below the dams at Bellows Falls and Vernon. These areas offer good walleye fishing, as do Sumner Falls and Wilder Dam farther upstream.

Those who fish the lower river for largemouth bass should concentrate on the many setbacks, such as those at Herricks Cove and at Retreat Meadows in Brattleboro. The mouths of the larger tributaries are good bets for both walleye and northern pike.

Northeast Kingdom

Rivers. The Northeast Kingdom consists of Essex, Orleans, and Caledonia Counties. A fabled region that offers excellent trout waters, it also provides as much seclusion as anyone could want. Much of the area is commercial forest owned by large forest-products companies. These large landowners have been exceptionally generous in keeping their lands open to the public free of charge.

The upper reaches of the Kingdom are referred to as the place "where the rivers flow north" because the Barton, Black, Clyde, Johns, and Coaticook Rivers do just that, as do their smaller tributaries, ultimately flowing into in the mighty St. Lawrence. The remainder of the Kingdom's rivers, however, empty into the Connecticut and drain south into Long Island Sound.

If there is one stream in Vermont as famous as the Battenkill, it is the Willoughby. This river, and its annual run of large rainbows, attracts shoulder-to-shoulder fishing in the spring. The Willoughby drains the picturesque glacial lake of the same name and empties into the Barton River in the village of Orleans. It also has a good population of brook trout. The main stem of the Barton between Orleans and Glover holds both rainbows and browns.

The Black River rises in the hill town of Albany and winds its way north to Lake Memphremagog. It is best known as a premier brown trout fishery but holds brookies and rainbows in many sections.

Nature took charge of the lower Clyde River in the mid-1990s, breaching a dam that had ended a once-heralded spring run of landlocked salmon. The Federal Regulatory Energy Commission ordered the permanent removal of the remaining dam, and the salmon have returned in increasing numbers, attracting anglers from afar.

Although less than 6 miles long, Johns River serves as an important spawning area for brown and rainbow trout from Lake Memphremagog. It starts and ends in Derby but swings into Canada for a short distance before emptying into the big lake.

The Nulhegan River and its tributaries drain one of Vermont's most remote and least-populated areas. Exploring the watershed is possible due to a network of private logging roads. Most of the watershed is populated with native brook trout, and the lower reaches of the main stem hold brown trout as well.

The Moose and Passumpsic Rivers and their tributaries drain southern Essex and northern Caledonia Counties. Both are good trout waters holding mostly brook trout in the upper sections and browns lower down. On the southern edge of the Kingdom, the Wells River is also a good trout stream, with browns in the lower reaches and brookies upstream.

Lakes and ponds. The Northeast Kingdom is dotted with clear, cold lakes and ponds holding trout and landlocked salmon. Anglers have so many options for trout and salmon that it is often difficult to choose a lake. Lake Willoughby in Westmore is the best known of these, and it produces the largest lake trout in the region. It is also one of the most picturesque lakes in the state. Lake Memphremagog is an international body of water that straddles the border at Newport. Until the water warms in early summer, the portion in Vermont provides good fishing for salmon, lake trout, browns, rainbows, and brookies. When the water temperature climbs, the trout tend to head across the border to deeper water. Another international lake is Wallace Pond in Canaan, which has rainbow, brown, and lake trout.

Great Averill and Little Averill Lakes are located in the border town of Averill and, along with good fishing, offer seclusion. Seymour Lake, and its neighbor Echo Lake, as well as Island Pond just down the road in the village of the same name, are all good bets for trout. On the east side of the Kingdom is Maidstone Lake, a beautiful trout water adjacent to Maidstone Lake State Park.

Shadow Lake in Glover, Crystal Lake in Barton, Caspian Lake in Greensboro, Harveys Lake in Barnet, and Joe's Pond in Danville are all easily accessed trout waters offering a variety of fishing opportunities.

Trout ponds are numerous, and two groups are especially worth noting. Newark, Bald Hill, Center, Long, and Jobs are located within minutes of each other in Westmore and Newark. To the south in Groton State Forest are Peacham, Martins, Osmore, Levi, Kettle, and Noyes.

Of special note is Noyes Pond in Groton, which is controlled by the Forests, Parks and Recreation

Department and restricted to fly fishing only. The pond covers only 39 acres, but the restrictive regulations imposed on it for years make the brook trout fishing very popular.

Exploring the remote Kingdom in search of trout ponds is best accomplished with a good topographic map. Many ponds, such as Lewis, South America, Notch, and West Mountain, lie far up paper-company roads that have no road signs and where visitors are guests who must give way to logging trucks.

Although best known for its trout and salmon, the Kingdom has some good bass fishing. Lake Memphremagog, the big lake that straddles the Vermont/Quebec border in Newport and Derby, has a sizable smallmouth bass population, as does Seymour Lake in Morgan. The Connecticut River in this region also offers both small- and largemouth bass fishing.

Northwestern Region

The Lamoille and Missisquoi Rivers are two good-size northwestern trout rivers that flow west into Lake Champlain, cutting deep valleys across the Green Mountains.

Approximately 85 miles long, the Lamoille holds browns, rainbows, and brookies in its various reaches. Perhaps the most productive section is between Morrisville and Wolcott, where trophy rainbows and browns await the dedicated angler.

The Missisquoi River winds back and forth across the border between Vermont and Quebec. Those who float it in canoes have to deal with Customs in both the U.S. and Canada. The availability of brook trout, rainbows, and browns varies according to the section of the river.

The northwestern region of the state isn't known for trout, but worthwhile trout waters do exist here. Good bets for brookies are Enosburg Reservoir in Berkshire, Kings Hill Pond in Bakersfield, and Adams Pond in Enosburg. At 2,920 feet in elevation, tiny Sterling Pond is Vermont's highest trout pond. A pleasant hike up the Long Trail from Route 108 leads to scenic book trout fishing.

A wide variety of warmwater fishing is available in Arrowhead Mountain Lake, Lake Carmi, Lake Iroquois, Shelburne Pond, and Green River Reservoir.

Central Region

Central Vermont extends from the Connecticut river on the east to Lake Champlain on the west. Consisting of lowlands on both sides and encompassing the backbone of the Green Mountains, this region includes high, fast-flowing mountain streams and meandering lowland rivers.

On the east there are three important rivers: the Waits, the Ompompanoosuc, and the White. Starting high in the mountains of Orange, Waits River flows eastward to empty into the Connecticut in Bradford. It is trout water all the way and holds brookies, browns, and rainbows. The Ompompanoosuc is best fished in its upper reaches, where water temperatures are more conducive to trout.

The White River and its many branches have a popular trout fishery. The river is very accessible and easily fished, and excellent trout populations draw anglers from afar. In the lower reaches, the trout share habitat with smallmouth bass, which are much sought after by local anglers.

The White also holds the hopes of those working to reestablish Atlantic salmon. The White River National Fish Hatchery was erected in Bethel to help meet the needs of the anadromous fish stocking program for the many tributaries of the Connecticut River. The goal here and throughout the Connecticut is to establish a self-sustaining Atlantic salmon fishery similar to what once spawned in the river before the first dam was built on it during the eighteenth century.

In central Vermont, the western trout flowages that empty into Lake Champlain consist of Poultney River, Otter Creek, and Winooski River.

The Winooski and its many tributaries offer excellent trout fishing throughout the central and western portion of this region. Brook, brown, and rainbow trout are found throughout the watershed, and the lower Winooski has an extremely popular steelhead fishery. Much of the Poultney River serves as the boundary between Vermont and New York. The Poultney is a good wild trout stream, offering angling for brookies and browns.

The Washington County towns of Calais and Woodbury have four rainbow trout waters in close proximity. Nelson Pond, Lake Greenwood, Mirror Lake, and Sabin Pond are all very accessible and have good fishing. Nelson Pond also has big lake trout.

To the west in Essex, Indian Brook Reservoir holds rainbows and browns, as does Waterbury Reservoir in Waterbury and Stowe. A short drive north of the state capitol in Montpelier is Wrightsville Reservoir, which boasts brown trout. To the south in Addison County, Lake Dunmore possesses lake trout, rainbows, and landlocked salmon, and there are rainbow and brown trout in Silver Lake nearby. Lake Fairlee in Thetford is well known for rainbow trout as well as for a winter smelt fishery.

Bass are not without some presence in this region. Buck Lake in Woodbury and Green River Reservoir in Hyde Park are notable sites, and the premier bass water is Lake Morey, located in the town of Fairlee on the east side of the state. Fairfield Pond in Fairfield, Arrowhead Mountain Lake in Georgia, Waterbury Reservoir in Waterbury, and Salisbury's Lake in Dunmore are prime bass waters.

Southern Region

The southern four counties of Windsor, Rutland, Windham, and Bennington are like those of the central region in that they encompass low-lying agricultural lands and high-mountain terrain along the north-south Green Mountain range.

Rising high in Sherburne, the Ottauquechee River meanders south and east to the Connecticut River and holds rainbow trout throughout its length, plus brookies in some areas. The river runs through Quechee Gorge, a picturesque natural attraction that holds large brown trout. Most of the smaller tributaries possess brook trout.

As one moves south, the next major trout streams are the Black, Williams, Saxtons, and West Rivers. Trout fishing in the West River consists mainly of brookies and browns. The section of this stream below Ball Mountain Dam is a whitewater course used for Olympic trials.

The Deerfield River flows south from its start on Stratton Mountain through a high basin between ridges of the Green Mountains until it enters Massachusetts. The upper reaches are scenic and remote, and hold brown trout and brookies.

The region's southwestern trout rivers drain into the Hudson, and the three most important are the Hoosic, Battenkill, and Mettawee.

The Battenkill is easily Vermont's best-known and most-fished trout stream. Its brook and brown trout are very wary and challenge the best anglers. Manchester, through which the Battenkill flows, is home to the world-renowned fishing gear supplier Orvis and the American Museum of Fly Fishing. Anglers flock to both just as they do to the river itself.

The waters of the Mettawee flow northwest from Dorset to the New York line in Wells, and are conducive to an especially good natural trout fishery.

Lake Bomoseen in Castleton is the largest body of water entirely in Vermont, and one of its best southern bass waters. It also has brook and brown trout. A bit farther south in Poultney and Wells is Lake St. Catherine, which is known for brown trout, lake trout, and a good warmwater fishery. Also in Castleton is Glen Lake, a favorite rainbow trout spot for local anglers.

The mountain towns of Chittenden, Mendon, and Sherburne are home to several good brook trout ponds. These include Lefferts, North, South, Colton, and Kent Ponds. Chittenden Reservoir also has brookies, as well as rainbows, browns, and salmon.

Vermont's scenic Route 100 runs the length of the state along the Green Mountains; a series of trout waters abut the highway between Ludlow and Plymouth. They include Woodward Reservoir, Amherst Lake, and Echo Lake. In the southwestern corner of the state, Lake Paran and Lake Shaftsbury, both in the town of Shaftsbury, offer rainbow trout.

High up along Route 9 are Searsburg and Harriman Reservoirs, which are part of the Deerfield River hydro system. Searsburg is known for its brook trout fishery, and the much bigger Harriman holds brook, brown, and rainbow trout, plus perch, pickerel, and smallmouth bass. Somerset Reservoir, which is a few miles up a road that follows the Deerfield River, is a remote lake that offers secluded brook trout angling.

The big Green Mountain National Forest has many trout ponds, most of which require a hike to get to. Bourn, Branch, and Beebe Ponds in Sunderland, and nearby Stratton Pond in Stratton, are among the notable sites here, and all possess brook trout.

VERTICAL JIGGING
See: Jigging.

VEST, FISHING

A compartmented sleeveless garment for storing terminal fishing tackle, including flies and lures, plus other accessories. Designed primarily for stowing readily accessible tackle while wading, and mostly used by stream and river fly anglers, a fishing vest is equally useful for anglers who hike a fair distance into fishing waters, for those who are mobile when fishing from shore, and for those who use spinning and baitcasting tackle.

Fishing vests are characterized by numerous pockets, which anglers, being tackle junkies, commonly fill to overflowing. Many also attach various tools to the exterior, so that they appear to be walking tackle shops. Vests for some anglers are so pregnant with supplies that a lot of weight is carried for long periods on the shoulders and back, which may be uncomfortable, and may even interfere with ordinary angling activities. Veteran anglers have learned to pare their streamside tackle down and carry in their vest what is most useful for the task at hand on a given day. This has also given rise to alternative carrying systems, some of which appeal to the go-light angler who does not need a great deal of equipment.

Vest features. Although there are vests with many pockets that may be fine for general outdoor or photographic use, fishing vests have a very specific design that is tailored to angling needs, and the various features are intended to accommodate specific types of equipment and have assorted angler-friendly virtues.

Fishing vests are categorized as standard or short length, the former extending to the waist and the latter to the chest. A chest-high vest, commonly called a shorty, is intended to permit wading in deep water with chest-high waders *(see)* without dunking the vest and its contents, which can happen anyway if you fall.

Among the most important items to stow in a vest are small boxes with flies or lures, and better vests have many deep-bellowed pockets to specifically accommodate these. Some are sized to accommodate the larger boxes that are used for streamer flies or lures, while others, both on the exterior and interior of the vest, accommodate other styles. Many of the pockets or compartments are suited to holding such objects as a penlight, stream thermometer, hook sharpener, sunglasses, sunscreen,

The ridges and spaces on some types of fish scales can be counted like the rings on a tree to determine a fish's age, and can be read to provide other information, such as the times it has spawned.

fly floatant, leader-dispensing spools, and so forth. Back pockets accommodate a light rain jacket and possibly a camera or extra reel or reel spool, and interior pockets are intended for keys, wallet, map, and the like.

Better vests are now made of quick-drying rip-stop nylon, have stretchable mesh shoulder construction to help spread the weight load, sport a comfortable rib-net collar, and have noncorroding zippers. A good feature on some is exterior loops, D-rings, or tubes for retractable tool holders, and Velcro loops for temporary rod holding.

While you can really stuff a vest, most of the contents go unused from day to day. This behooves you to cut out some of the items previously mentioned for comfort and practicality. Whether you really need a net, a compass, first aid items, a scale, a host of tools instead of one multi-purpose tool, six or more boxes of flies or lures instead of two or three, and food and water, among many other possible items, is up to you, your back, and the distance you'll be from the car, where you can stow everything that really doesn't have to be toted in the vest. However, you will definitely want to have a place to store insect repellent (it should not contact other items, which it can harm), fly line dressing, a split shot container or lead wrap, and a small knife.

Incidentally, some short-length wading-style rain jackets are designed for holding tackle boxes and a few accessories, and some personal flotation vests do likewise. Neither is as comfortable or functional as a fishing vest, however.

Alternatives. Other means of carrying gear for wading and mobile anglers include a wide array of rigid chest boxes, soft chest packs, and soft fanny packs. Non of these store the full range of items that a vest can, but they do offer short-trip, grab-and-go options, plus lightweight freedom, and may be very useful if you put the right things inside.

Rigid metal or plastic chest boxes have trays for fly storage, which is good for organization, and some offer quick-change options to suit the day's needs. Some also have a light, magnifier, tippet dispenser, and other elements. The box, which has shoulder and chest straps and is worn conveniently in front of the angler, is readily accessible, but its rigidity can be a disadvantage for travel, making it susceptible to breakage.

Soft chest packs are also convenient to use and available in a wide range of styles, from simple one-pocket items more like a small pouch to multi-compartmented products that are a step short of being a mini-vest. Many of these feature mesh or see-through material so you can view a pocket's contents without opening it. Soft fanny packs, too, range from single-pocket models to versions that can hold a few small fly boxes and several accessories.

See: Tackle Storage.

Fish names are not always what they seem. For instance, the dogfish is actually a shark, the buffalo is actually a sucker, and the sea robin is actually a sculpin.

VHF RADIO
Acronym for Very High Frequency radio.
See: Communications.

VIDEO SOUNDER
A type of sonar using a cathode-ray tube.
See: Sonar.

VIRGIN ISLANDS
The Virgin Islands lie east of Puerto Rico between the Atlantic Ocean and the Caribbean Sea. Forming part of the Lesser Antilles chain in the West Indies, the British Virgins consist of 36 small islands, the largest being Tortola and Virgin Gorda; and the U.S. Virgins consist of the three small islands of St. Croix, St. Thomas, and St. John, as well as 50 islets. The U.S. Virgins are the easternmost portion of that country. Tourism is important to all of the Virgin Islands but especially to the U.S. islands. St. Thomas lays claim to being one of the world's foremost blue marlin fishing centers.

For some big-game anglers, if you say "St. Thomas, blue marlin, North Drop, summer, and full moon" all in the same breath, you've hit the proverbial nail on the head. Look no farther. It's not quite that simple, actually, but for many marlin buffs, St. Thomas is a great place to hook up with a marlin. It is probably the premier location for this species in the western Atlantic.

The record books back this up. St. Thomas has produced more than its share of officially recorded sport-caught 1,000-pound Atlantic blue marlin (four) than any other location, certainly in the western Atlantic. Numerous line-class (and at least one fly-rod) world records for Atlantic blue marlin have been established in St. Thomas as well. And for many years it owned the one that all big-game anglers set their sights on, the former all-tackle and 130-pound line-class world-record catch of 1,282 pounds, which was established in August of 1977 and stood for 15 years.

Records aside, the hallowed billfish grounds are relatively near St. Thomas (and the other islands) and are uniquely situated to provide excellent opportunities and plenty of action. Relatively inexperienced anglers on a boat that sees (or raises) from one to three marlin in a day think that's pretty good. Regulars here call it slow.

On a good day, during the best of times, an angler will see six to eight fish raised, and two or three hooked. This kind of action doesn't happen just anywhere, and it has attracted sophisticated anglers and top boats from around the world, particularly in August for major tournaments, but throughout the summer as well.

The main reason for this highly productive fishery is St. Thomas's location in the Caribbean and the effects of currents and winds on the local environs. The deepest water in the Atlantic Ocean

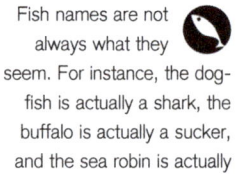

is directly offshore from the Virgin Islands, in the Puerto Rican Trench. Its depths plunge more than 6 miles. But within 10 to 12 miles of the Virgin Islands, the ocean floor slopes up to a bank that ranges from 140 fathoms up to 40 fathoms.

This is the site of the North Drop, and this is also where an upwelling of current and a prodigious amount of baitfish occur, due in part to the prevailing easterly trade winds. Bonito, tuna, and various predators routinely feed here. The marlin are primarily caught in an area that extends for nearly 10 miles and is about 2 miles wide, although anglers work the entire dropoff, from in front of St. Thomas to the island of Anegada. The so-called Corner, a section where the dropoff doglegs easterly, also causes marlin to congregate in the area.

The North Drop is between 10 and 12 miles from St. Thomas. In the peak of the season (July, August, and September, especially around the full moon) many boats descend on the dropoff. Deep water and dropoffs exist off each of the major islands, including off St. Croix in the Caribbean.

Anglers encounter white marlin and sailfish in area waters, although not as regularly as blue marlin. Other typical Caribbean offshore creatures also in the catch include wahoo (St. Thomas holds one long-standing line-class world record for this species), dolphin, yellowfin tuna, blackfin tuna, and various sharks. Lang Bank, east of St. Croix, is a place frequented for dolphin, king mackerel, and wahoo.

Although blue marlin are caught year-round, the prime time, as previously noted, is from July through September for the big fish. White marlin are most abundant in spring. Dolphin and king mackerel are best in spring, tuna in fall and winter, and wahoo through the winter.

Sharks sometimes pose a problem because of their relative abundance, and they have attacked many hooked marlin. Such an occurrence disqualifies a fish from record consideration and is especially hard to avoid when light tackle is employed. With the number of marlin to be raised out here, light-tackle fishing has grown in popularity, so sharks are a concern. Most of the marlin are released, and if they are too weak when freed, they can be vulnerable.

Some inshore fishing also takes place in and around the various Virgin Islands, especially around the reefs and on the flats. King mackerel, barra-cuda, and various jacks, snapper, and grouper are among the reef catch. These fish provide excitement for those not interested in the muscle fishing of offshore waters.

Tarpon prowl these islands, too, mostly off the northern shore of St. Thomas and along St. Croix, but also in the British Virgins. St. Croix provides bonefishing, incidentally, on flats along the southern shore, but the rest of the U.S. islands, with their steeper terrain, do not possess the flats and typical habitat that harbor this species. The British island of Anegada, however, is low lying, and it possesses shallows that have in the past been abundant with this species.

Permit are plentiful around these islands, especially St. Croix, and they are a lightly pursued fishery. Fifteen- to 30-pound fish are caught here by relatively few anglers, as the interest lies predominantly with offshore locations. Some visitors, however, have reported sighting high numbers of permit in a day, some actually in schools, on flats that surround St. Croix. The more reliable permit fishing is reportedly on the island's southern coral flats; the permit come into these areas from deeper water to feed, and winter is the prime season.

Subject to easterly winds, the Virgin Islands are also subject to rough water at times, especially in winter, although the prime billfishing period of midsummer is usually fairly calm. Late summer can bring hurricanes; St. Croix was nearly destroyed by Hurricane Hugo in September 1989. Well-equipped and experienced charter boats are available, especially in St. Thomas, and facilities are plentiful. The Virgin Islands draw many visitors for reef diving, and the local waters are rated among the best in the world for this activity. A favored spot is Buck Island Reef National Monument at St. Croix.

VIRGINIA

Not too many states can say that they offer anglers the opportunity to catch native brook trout from small mountain streams and also giant blue marlin from the vast waters of the Atlantic Ocean's Gulf Stream. The Commonwealth of Virginia can boast this and much more because in between these extremes are ponds, reservoirs, streams, rivers, and the Chesapeake Bay, all with varied species and multiple angling possibilities.

This may be a surprise to those unfamiliar with the Old Dominion state, but it shouldn't be when you consider that Virginia has 2,800 miles of trout streams, 112 miles of coastline, more than 1,500 square miles of the Chesapeake Bay, several major rivers, and loads of ponds, lakes, and small to medium reservoirs.

For freshwater devotees, some of Virginia's lakes and reservoirs offer first-class angling for various species, especially largemouth bass and striped bass, and the rivers and streams have terrific opportunities for trout and smallmouths. For saltwater enthusiasts, Virginia could be as good as it gets, with striped bass, bluefish, speckled trout, and drum heading a long list of highly desirable species that are often found in good abundance.

Freshwater

Virginia's varied topography ranges from the coastal plain to the Piedmont Plateau to the Blue Ridge, and the result is a plethora of creeks, rivers, ponds, lakes, and reservoirs. Largemouth bass, smallmouth bass, various panfish, and catfish anchor the warm-

water scene, with some opportunity for striped bass, muskies, and walleye as well. Brook, rainbow, and brown trout are staples in many locations, and having the brook trout as a state fish is perhaps indicative of how Virginians view their freshwater fisheries, particularly when there are 2,200 miles of wild trout streams in the state.

Notable small waters. One of the more noteworthy trout fisheries in Virginia is Whitetop Laurel Creek in the Mount Rogers National Recreational Area. Located near the appropriately named town of Troutville, this beautiful stream is filled with native rainbows and browns. The water cascades over huge boulders, forming deep pools where rainbows grow to 14 inches and a few brown trout reach trophy size. The trout here have seen every fly tied by anglers, however, so a delicate presentation is required. Dry flies will work during a hatch, and nymphs are the most consistent producers.

An old railroad bed follows Whitetop Laurel Creek, providing access to the water. The streambed is covered with loose and slippery rocks, making for some treacherous footing; felt-soled shoes or waders and a walking staff should be used here to prevent a nasty spill.

Those looking for slightly less challenge in their trout fishing but not wanting to give up beautiful scenery can drive a few miles north and west to the Clinch Mountain Fee Fishing Area. Roughly 7 miles from Saltville, this area is controlled by the Virginia Department of Natural Resources, which provides campsites and a small convenience store on the property.

At Clinch Mountain, Big Tumbling Creek and Laurel Bed Lake hold good numbers of rainbow trout. Fish are stocked in the creek every day during the season, providing good, and consistent, opportunities for success. Two launch sites on the lake can be used for small, shallow-draft boats. The lake covers 300 acres, and its usually smooth, quiet surface stands in sharp contrast to the roaring waters of Big Tumbling Creek. It takes the abilities of a mountain goat to reach the deep pools below the falls and rapids, but the fishing is worth the effort. The lower part of the creek near the checking station is easier to access and holds an equal number of trout.

Not far away, bass anglers find good smallmouth action along the North Fork of the Holston River in Saltville. At one time, this river was a mess, but efforts to remove the pollution have brought improvements, and fishing here is very good. Smallmouths are caught from shore, from a small boat, or by wading. Plugs and plastic grubs that imitate small minnows or crayfish work best.

Hungry Mother State Park near Marion is close to Mt. Rogers and Clinch Mountain, and contains a small lake with walleye, largemouth bass, bluegills, crappie, and muskellunge. The park has campgrounds and various facilities, and the lake has a small-boat launch site and a fishing pier.

Another site noted for diverse species is Lake Moomaw in the George Washington National Forest. Formed in 1981 with the completion of the Gathright Dam on the Jackson River, this 2,530-acre reservoir lies between Bath and Allegheny Counties near Hot Springs and Covington. Boats can be launched at Bolar Flat and at Fortney Branch.

Smallmouth bass have thrived in the lower part of this lake and in the headwaters; 3- to 4-pounders are common. Largemouths average 13 to 15 inches, and a few 3- to 5-pounders are taken each year. Local fishing clubs and the Department of Game and Inland Fisheries have improved fish habitat to benefit the crappie population, which is considered one of the best in the state. Crappie in the 1- to 1$\frac{1}{2}$-pound range are taken here in the spring.

Trout fishing at lake Moomaw is good for rainbows and browns. Anglers do not need a state trout stamp or a national forest stamp to possess trout from this lake. Shad are the primary forage species here and are fished live for bass and trout; crankbaits that imitate shad are cast or trolled.

Although small at just 118 acres, Skidmore Reservoir, which provides water for the city of Harrisonburg, has great fishing for trout and bass. West of Harrisonburg, the lake is clear and deep, offering excellent habitat for brook trout, some of which grow to 3 pounds. Brown and tiger trout have been stocked in Skidmore, and these fish grow to 4 pounds or more. Warmwater species in the lake include largemouth bass, crappie, and sunfish, but most are small. Access is via a primitive boat ramp and adjoining parking lot off the forest road. The shoreline is open to fishing on the west side and the upper end of the lake.

James and Rappahannock Rivers. Two bodies of water that flow through a good part of Virginia are the James and the Rappahannock Rivers. The upper parts of both rivers contain good numbers of smallmouth bass and can be fished from shore, by boat, or by wading. These are peaceful and pretty fisheries as the rivers flow through farmland and the foothills of the Appalachian Mountains.

Below the cities of Fredericksburg on the Rappahannock and Richmond on the James, the fishing takes a decided turn. The rivers here are swift and deep and provide excellent habitat for big blue and channel catfish. Channel cats over 20 pounds and blues approaching 50 pounds are taken out of both rivers each year. This is not a fancy fishery with lots of special tackle and equipment; most practitioners here use a stout rod with 20- to 30-pound line, and fish a big hunk of shad, herring, or eel in a deep hole or eddy.

Numerous access points and launch ramps are located along the banks of both rivers. Some of the best catfish action is in or close to Richmond and Fredericksburg.

Big waters. Virginia is home to big-water fishing on several lakes that have received national attention for their resources.

An ancient Chinese and Japanese method of catching fish is using tethered cormorants; this is still practiced today, and some birds are also used to catch turtles.

The biggest of these is Buggs Island Lake, which is also known as Kerr Reservoir. It covers 48,900 acres in Mecklenburg County and is the largest body of freshwater in Virginia. In addition to having an excellent largemouth bass population, the lake holds good numbers of big crappie, white perch, and striped bass.

Bass fishing is especially good in the spring, when the lake rises to its highest level, flooding trees and underbrush along the shoreline. Soft worms and lizards, and pork rind–decorated jigs, tossed to the base of this vegetation usually produce excellent results. Big crappie are caught here in the spring, when they school over submerged structure. A small jig tipped with a minnow is the favored offering.

Stripers spawn naturally in Buggs Island Lake, and the state stocks them to keep the population level in years of poor reproduction. Striper fishing has become more popular as the size and number of these fish increase. Live shad or crankbaits that imitate them are the most common offerings.

Lake Gaston is a 20,300-acre reservoir located in Brunswick County just below Buggs Island Lake. Largemouth bass draw most anglers here, but trophy striped bass have been vying for attention. Walleye are available in Lake Gaston, as are good-size black crappie and white crappie. The usual assortment of warmwater panfish, including sunfish, perch, and catfish, show up in the creel.

Access to both Lake Gaston and Buggs Island Lake is easy and convenient. Numerous boat ramps are available at both, and the nearby area offers every service necessary. Both lakes cross the Virginia–North Carolina border, and a license for either state will be honored throughout the waterway, although regulations may differ.

Smith Mountain Lake in Bedford County is the top place in the state to fish for big inland striped bass. A state freshwater record—45 pounds, 10 ounces—was established at this 20,600-acre reservoir in 1995, and stripers exceeding 30 pounds are caught each year. Stocking of 300,000 fingerling stripers every year helps to maintain a stable population. Live shad make the best bait, but various fishing methods are applicable.

The variety of species available at Smith Mountain Lake is excellent. Largemouth bass and muskies also get a lot of attention, and big flathead catfish, crappie, white bass, smallmouth bass, and walleye are caught regularly.

Largemouth bass are a good bet at Smith Mountain in cover and around boat docks. Pitching a jig-and-pork combo is particularly effective on largemouths. Spinnerbaits, plastic worms, and crankbaits all take their share of fish. Muskies are stocked each year, and most are caught incidentally by anglers pursuing bass and stripers. With fish to 20 pounds available, especially in the Roanoke River arm, a more directed fishery is developing. Flathead catfish have been strong in the Blackwater arm in recent years, and crappie fishing has been best in the upper ends, where there is structure. Smith Mountain has plenty of access, as well as many nearby facilities.

Lake Anna is the smallest of the big reservoirs at 9,600 acres, but it manages to flow over into three counties: Spotsylvania, Louisa, and Orange. It contains largemouth bass, walleye, striped bass, perch, pickerel, sunfish, crappie, and catfish. Numerous private marinas line the lake, and there's a public boat ramp near the Spotsylvania–Orange County line.

This lake supplies water to a nuclear power plant, and the warmwater discharge can create good wintertime fishing. Dike No. 3 is a good spot when the water temperature on the main lake drops. The warm discharge water attracts striped bass, walleye, and catfish; live shad, jigs, or chunks of cut baits are preferred choices for catching them.

Suffolk chain. A number of small water supply lakes are found in Suffolk, and, although their size may be dwarfed by the bigger reservoirs, the quality of the fishing stands up to any comparison.

Known as the Suffolk chain of lakes, they supply drinking water to the communities of Norfolk, Portsmouth, and Suffolk. These cities take every precaution to keep the lakes clean, including preventing the cutting of timber that surrounds each body of water. The result is excellent fishing in a beautiful setting.

Western Branch Reservoir, at 1,597 acres, is the largest of the seven lakes in the chain. The others range in size from 777-acre Lake Prince to 197-acre Speight's Run. Each lake has its own personality, but all hold a variety of angling opportunities. Bass, stripers, perch, pickerel, and catfish are taken in numbers each year; but redear sunfish, known locally as shellcrackers, draw the most attention. More citation-size shellcrackers are caught here than anywhere else in Virginia, and a few anglers are lucky enough to catch more than a dozen exceeding the 1-pound minimum weight. Special permits are required to launch a private boat, but rental boats and electric motors are available at a reasonable rate.

Saltwater

Virginia has one of the longest tidal coastlines of any state due to the many creeks and rivers that flow into the Chesapeake Bay, plus the barrier islands that line its Atlantic Ocean front. In all, this amounts to some 3,315 miles of tidal shoreline. All of this means good access to what many people consider the finest saltwater fishing available.

Chesapeake Bay and vicinity. The boats running out of Smith Point at the mouth of the Potomac River spend most of their time chumming for blues, striped bass, and weakfish. Trolling with spoons, bucktails, and tubes is common for the same species in the spring and fall. Bottom fishing produces spot and croaker along with flounder and weakfish; squid and peeler crabs are the most popular baits.

Trolling and chumming are practiced over the Middle Grounds to the north in Maryland waters, and over the Cabbage Patch and the wrecks southeast of Smith Point Light. Bottom fishing occurs closer to shore as well as along the shoals, wrecks, and channel edges.

A small charter fleet runs out of the Little Wicomico River, and there is a launch ramp at Kanyan. Several marinas in the area can service larger boats, and campgrounds are available on the south side of the river.

Anglers running out of the Great Wicomico River will chum and troll the same general area as those working out of Smith Point. They may fish a bit farther south around the Tangier Lumps or the Davidson Wreck, and travel north to Maryland only when all else fails.

A fair number of charter boats operate out of Reedville. They specialize in chumming or trolling for blues, stripers, and gray trout (weakfish). Bottom fishing for flounder, spot, croaker, and weakfish is the primary summertime activity.

Boat launch ramps are found at Glebe Point, Shell Landing, and Crane's Creek Landing. Fishing is possible from the shore in these locations, but parking is limited. Several marinas in the area can accommodate larger boats.

The coastline from the Great Wicomico to the Rappahannock River is populated by small creeks, bays, and marshland, giving the angler several choices of species and techniques. Speckled trout inhabit the shallow waters of the creeks, whereas bluefish and weakfish stage along the creek mouths and in the bays. Flounder, croaker, spot, and weakfish hold in the deeper water where the creeks and bays meet the Chesapeake.

Deltaville on the Rappahannock River is a center for recreational anglers fishing the river and the nearby waters of the Chesapeake Bay. A charter fleet runs out of here, and there are boat ramps at Kruses Wharf and Upper Mill Creek Landing.

Trolling for blues and stripers is the top activity in the spring and fall. Trollers here pull bucktail jigs, spoons, tubes, and plugs over shallow areas around Windmill Point Light, as well as in the deeper waters of the Cut Channel. The Cut Channel produced a state record 61-pound, 12-ounce striper in 1996; this early December fish was caught by trolling a spoon. When fishing solely for stripers, trollers continue up the river to the White Stone Bridge.

Bottom fishing takes over in the summer, when flounder, weakfish, spot, and croaker are the most popular species. These are caught throughout the river and over shoals, channel edges, and rocks in the bay. The Cell on the Eastern Shore side of the bay is a hotspot for big flounder, croaker, stripers, and spadefish. A relic of World War II, the degaussing cell was used to demagnetize ships and was blown up when the war was over. The remains litter the ocean bottom, attracting all types of marine life.

One of the better known speckled trout hotspots is just south of Gwynn Island at the Hole in the Wall. This narrow outlet to the bay is surrounded by sandbars and marsh—perfect speckled trout habitat. Small, shallow-draft boats are required to access this area, where small jigs and plugs take the majority of fish.

Hallieford Public landing on Gwynn Island provides access to the Hole in the Wall as well as the Piankatank River. Anglers take speckled trout from the river, along with weakfish, croaker, spot, and small blues.

Mobjack Bay and the rivers that feeds it are rich in fishing opportunities. Speckled trout attract most of the attention in the spring and fall. Croaker, spot, weakfish, small blues, and flounder take center stage in the summer. Specks are usually taken near the shore over grassbeds. Peeler crabs are the top baitfish in the spring, and live pinfish are a good bet in the fall. Plugs and jigs are effective throughout the year.

Warehouse Landing near Gloucester has a boat ramp and fishing pier with limited parking. One of the better speckled trout areas is at Ware Point, just a short run down the Ware River from the ramp.

The York River from West Point to the Chesapeake Bay offers various fishing opportunities for croaker, spot, striped bass, flounder, and bluefish. The shoreline along the Colonial Parkway from Yorktown to Williamsburg slopes gradually to the river, forming a large flat that is especially

Striped bass are a staple in Chesapeake Bay; this one was caught near the Bay Bridge Tunnel.

popular with light-tackle and fly anglers. Many people wade while casting small jigs, plugs, or flies. Others fish from small flats-style boats. Their efforts are rewarded with speckled trout, weakfish, striped bass, flounder, and bluefish. A boat ramp at Gloucester Point is the closest access. A fishing pier is located in the same area and is very popular with croaker and spot fanciers.

The Poquoson River also holds good fishing opportunities for spot, croaker, small blues, striped bass, and weakfish. Boat ramps are available on Back Creek and the Tide Mill Landing in York.

Bluefish Rock just outside the mouth of the Back River draws legions of cobia anglers each summer. They anchor up and chum with ground menhaden while soaking chunks of menhaden on the bottom. This area sees lots of trolling for striped bass and bluefish in the spring and fall. Drifting cut bait, squid, and shrimp produces spot, croaker, and flounder during the summer. Wallace's Marina and the nearby boat ramp are the center of fishing activity in this region; they are located at the end of Dandy Point Road in Hampton.

Hampton Roads is the junction of the James and Elizabeth Rivers before they fan out into the Chesapeake Bay. The entire area is heavily developed, but fishing is very good. The charter and head boats sailing from here seek spot, croaker, and weakfish from the Hampton Bar out to Thimble Shoal. In the fall, charter boats find striped bass in the same area.

The urban fishing available from shore, bridges, piers, and old boat docks can be good even if not aesthetically pleasing. Spot and croaker provide most of the activity, but stripers are taken in the spring and fall.

Little Creek and Lynnhaven Inlets are found between Hampton Roads and Cape Henry. Several marinas and boat ramps inside these inlets support a large fleet of private boats. Depending on the size of the boat and the preference of the owner, anglers can fish anywhere from inside the inlets out to the canyons.

A great deal of fishing activity in the lower bay is centered around the three bridge tunnels. The Monitor Merrimack, Hampton Roads, and the Chesapeake Bay Bridge Tunnel each act as artificial reefs and attract and hold a wide variety of fish species.

The Chesapeake Bay Bridge Tunnel is the longest of these spans, running 17 miles across the mouth of the bay, and it holds the greatest number of fish. Each year striped bass, bluefish, cobia, gray trout, speckled trout, croaker, spot, tautog, and flounder are taken along with such locally exotic species as jack crevalle, houndfish, spadefish, and mackerel. This is a true cornucopia.

Fishing piers are scattered from Hampton to Virginia Beach, and they produce good fishing from spring through fall. Small species like spot and croaker are the basis of pier fishing, but each year cobia, mackerel, bluefish, weakfish, and striped bass are caught from the piers. Grandview and Buckroe Piers are in Hampton, Harrison's Pier is in Norfolk, and Lynnhaven and Sea Gull Piers are in Virginia Beach. The Sea Gull Pier is located on the first island of the Chesapeake Bay Bridge Tunnel.

Small boat anglers and those who fish from shore will find good action inside Lynnhaven Inlet. The base of the Lessner Bridge over the inlet is a good bet for flounder, speckled trout, and striped bass. The sheltered waters inside the inlet hold the same species plus croaker and spot. Launch ramps at Bubba's Marina on the east side of the bridge and at First Landing State Park at the end of 65th Street in Virginia Beach provide access.

Rudee Inlet in Virginia Beach is the only direct outlet to the ocean between Cape Henry and Oregon Inlet. A large offshore charter fleet heads out to the Norfolk Canyon or the Cigar in pursuit of marlin, tuna, dolphin, and wahoo. Blue marlin are sometimes caught, but whites are the mainstays; white marlin action can be hot in some years. Inshore fishing is good for bluefish, mackerel, and striped bass.

The head boat fleet out of here and out of Lynnhaven Inlet fish for sea bass and tautog over inshore wrecks and reefs, as well as spot, croaker, and weakfish around the mouth of the Chesapeake Bay.

The two fishing piers in Virginia Beach are at 14th Street and in Sandbridge, and they attract spot, croaker, flounder, bluefish, striped bass, and mackerel. Surf casters along the beach can expect the same mixed bag. A boat ramp on Owl's Creek adjacent to the Virginia Marine Science Museum off of General Booth Boulevard provides access to Rudee Inlet.

The Eastern Shore. No single area in the United States and possibly the world offers as many fishing possibilities as the Eastern Shore of Virginia. The season runs all year, and the variety of species available is overwhelming.

The Eastern Shore of Virginia is divided into the ocean side and the bay side. Fishermen can troll for tuna on the ocean side in the morning and cast for speckled trout on the bay side in the afternoon.

Accomac and Northampton Counties divide the narrow tip of the Delmarva Peninsula, which is Virginia's Eastern Shore. Both counties and the state have built numerous boat ramps on both the bay and ocean sides, so access to this good fishing is never a problem. Finding a way across the shallow waters on either side is a dilemma solved only by experience.

Beginning on the bay side, Saxis is the jumping-off point for fishing in Pocomoke Sound. Anglers find weakfish, flounder, croaker, spot, and striped bass over the numerous rocks in the sound. Bottom fishing with peeler crabs or squid is the most popular activity, but trolling bucktails, plugs, and spoons occurs in the spring and fall.

Onancock, at the head of Onancock Creek,

is close to the good fishing in the lower part of Pocomoke Sound and the open waters of the Chesapeake Bay. In the spring, anglers soak peeler crabs on night tides near Half Moon Island between Saxis and Onancock. At times, the mosquito bites are more frequent than the fish bites, but when a speck is caught it is usually a big one. Pungoteague and Nandua Creeks below Onancock also hold good numbers of speckled trout in the spring and fall.

Nassawadox Creek is also known for speckled trout, but the channel edge that lies just offshore between Buoys C20 and CB is a good location for channel bass in late summer and early fall. A good tactic is to anchor along the dropoff and soak chunks of spot, croaker, or menhaden about a hour or two before dark.

The junction of Hungars and Mahawoman Creeks forms a shallow grassbed surrounded by sandbars. Many speckled trout anglers feel this is the best area for their favorite quarry. Casting jigs and plugs begins in the spring and peaks in late fall. A light rain on an east wind is considered ideal weather for speckled trout.

Cape Charles is the last town on the bay side, and it is a center for fishing in the lower bay. Black drum draw the first anglers here each spring, and striped bass keep them coming into December. Old Plantation Light, the Cabbage Patch, the Concrete Ships, and Latimer Shoal are a few of the good fishing spots located just a short run from Cape Charles Harbor.

The cobia run on Latimer Shoal has been spectacular. Fish approaching 100 pounds are caught from June through September. Hundreds of boats anchor up and chum, creating a slick that goes on for miles. Cobia follow the slick and may or may not eat the baits waiting for them on the bottom.

Kiptopeke State Park on the bay side south of Cape Charles offers excellent camping facilities, a boat ramp, and a fishing pier. Cherrystone Campground just above Cape Charles has year-round camping, a fishing pier, a marina, and many family activities.

As one moves over to the ocean side, Oyster is the first town with access to the sea. As with all ocean-side access points, the run to the sea from here can be a challenge. Channels are marked, but they are narrow and subject to change without notice. Study the latest charts before departure, and do not stray from the channel until you know where you're headed.

The outlet from Oyster is Sand Shoal Inlet, where flounder, weakfish, and blues are caught throughout the spring, summer, and fall. The dropoff next to the 224 Day Marker is a great location to drift minnows, squid strips, or cut bait.

The marshes and channels between the mainland and the barrier islands produce several big tarpon each summer. All are taken on chunks of cut spot or menhaden, and the best action is during the hottest days of summer.

Quinby and Wachapreague are famous for spectacular flounder fishing, especially in the spring, when big doormats enter the channels between these two ports and the ocean. Drifting along the edge of the channels with live minnows is the best way to find a big flounder.

Wachapreague has a charter fleet that specializes in flounder fishing as well as working the offshore grounds for tuna, king mackerel, and big bluefish. Chunking with cut-up butterfish has become a popular technique for catching tuna. Most of the action occurs on the 26 Mile Hill or the Parking Lot.

Chincoteague lies just below the Maryland line and is the largest town along the sea side. It offers numerous motels and restaurants as well as several campgrounds. Rental boats, charter boats, marinas, and launch ramps provide access to every type of angler.

A lack of motorized transportation does not prevent folks from fishing the rest of Virginia's beautiful coastline. Most of the barrier islands from Assawoman down to Smith are owned by the Virginia Coast Preserve, a division of the Nature Conservancy. They are open to the public for surf fishing, but overnight camping is prohibited.

The best surf action takes place in the spring and fall, when big red drum move close to the beach. Peeler crabs are the top bait in the spring, and cut mullet or menhaden are preferred in the fall. Access is by small boat, and the islands are undeveloped.

VISE
A tool, also known as a fly tying vise, with adjustable clamping jaws to secure a hook for dressing with fly tying materials.
See: Fly.

VOMERINE TEETH
Teeth located on the vomer, a median bone in the front of the roof of the mouth of fish.
See: Anatomy.

WADE FISHING

Fishing by means of wading in the water.
See: Waders.

WADERS

Anglers who fish from the bank, who wade, or who get in and out of boats during the course of fishing (such as river drifters), often need to cover that portion of the body that will be in the water. Such a covering is generically called waders, which are chest- or hip-high products with connected or separate boots that keep anglers dry and sometimes warm, and which also help provide good footing. Waders also may serve a subordinate function as protection from such natural, and sometimes problematic, elements as leeches, bugs, snakes, prickly bushes, and poisonous plants along the waterway.

Some warmwater fishing situations permit anglers to "wade wet" by walking in the water in their clothes or bare-legged; however, this generally occurs when both the water and air temperatures are sufficiently warm, or when the angler will be wading for a relatively short period. In cool or cold water, when the air temperature is cool or cold, when a cool breeze is blowing, and when the angler must spend a long time in the water, it is usually appropriate, if not absolutely necessary, to wear some type of waders. In these circumstances, few pieces of equipment can be as valuable as a pair of warm, dry waders. For anglers who get into the water, waders are literally one of the most important pieces of fishing equipment that they own, and they will likely own many pairs during a lifetime of fishing, especially if they are guides, or have the enviable ability to fish on a very frequent basis.

The ideal wader has several obvious features: It should be totally waterproof, warm in cold water yet cool in hot weather, durable or long-lived, lightweight, supple and stretchable, tear- and puncture-proof, not bulky, not damp inside when worn, and low in cost. No wader achieves all of this, but in order to achieve these features, waders have been evolving since the late nineteenth century. Due to modern technology, they have taken quantum leaps since the late 1970s, and great strides have been made in most of these features. As a result, today's waders are extremely functional products, and there are waders now to suit nearly all angling situations; some anglers have two or three pairs of waders to use for different conditions.

History

In 1839, Charles Goodyear stumbled on a rubber treatment process he named vulcanization. Vulcanization is the combination of heat and pressure over time combined with ammonia, and in some cases sulfur, to create rubber products that are completely stable. Before vulcanization, rubber products would melt on a hot day and crack on a cold one.

Until the development of vulcanization, there was no reliably waterproof footwear. Thus, when the first vulcanized rubber boot was created, a revolutionary product was born. The success of waterproof rubber footwear eventually lead to the development of rubber waders, which were made by the Uniroyal Company in 1896. They were stiff and heavy, but waterproof. At the beginning of the twentieth century, a lighter, more comfortable wader was created by combining cotton canvas with rubber.

Few changes occurred in waders until manufacturing technology improved in the mid-1960s, and makers used extrusion laminates to produce far more supple and forgiving products that were much more comfortable to wear. In the extrusion process, materials are heated until their molecules change, and they are bonded completely together without depending on adhesives. Shortly after this improvement came the use of polyvinyl chloride (PVC) materials in boot bottoms, which made this component of waders lighter and less expensive.

A complete rethinking of wader materials and construction was reflected in the 1978 introduction of chest-high stocking foot waders made from nylon that weighed only 10 ounces. They had stocking-style feet and were meant to be worn with separate wading shoes or boots. These featherweight waders proved to be durable and far more comfortable to wear than pre-existing waders, and created a whole new category of wader, as well as opened the doors to achieving products that made wader-wearing anglers much less stiff-legged and encumbered.

The advent of neoprene, and its use in wetsuits, started a demand for neoprene waders, and the first national distribution of neoprene waders occurred in 1981. Neoprene wader manufacture—all of the stocking foot variety, which had to be worn with separate boots—rapidly advanced thereafter with lighter, less absorbent closed cell fabrics.

Early neoprene waders were tight fitting and had to be rolled down instead of pulled off. There was little room for wearing extra clothing underneath, but they were eagerly embraced by the coldest water waders. Neoprene waders are the warmest waders for severe cold because this material not only keeps water out but body heat in.

In just a few years, wader manufacturers quickly moved into neoprene production to meet growing demand. The greatest improvement for severe cold weather anglers was the development of boot foot neoprene waders, which featured a traditional insulated rubber boot bottom attached to upper full-cut neoprene.

Releasing body heat but still keeping dry and reasonably warm in appropriate conditions became the next goal of wader manufacturers, and in 1993 the first breathable wader, made of Gore-Tex, became available. This product allowed human body heat to be released through the material, even while standing in the water. Like most truly new designs, the first year of production saw many returns and field problems that were quickly resolved, and today this type of product is well accepted, without the flaws that marked the first items, and it is likely the wave of the future for wader manufacturing technology.

Waders are now made from even newer high-tech materials, and by using complex adhesives. Anglers today have a far greater choice in wader wear as a result of these developments, and can find a good product to meet virtually any use and season. Rubber hip waders for shallow stream wading, lightweight breathable chest waders for warm or cool water wading, rubber chest waders for general purpose wading, and neoprene chest waders for the coldest water fishing, are among the major possibilities.

Types

Chest and hip. Irrespective of the material they are made from, there are two general types of waders: chest and hip.

Chest waders are similar to pants in that the material extends from the legs up over the hips and waist to the upper part of the chest. Chest-high waders have straps or suspenders that loop over the user's shoulders, but they should also be worn with a waist-level outer belt to help keep water out and trap air inside in the event of a spill. Quite simply, chest waders are meant to be worn in water that is too deep for the use of hip waders—large rivers or ocean surf—and for extra water and weather protection in cold weather.

The biggest advantage of chest waders is that they get you to deeper fishing holes, either by allowing you to wade deeper to cast or to ford deep places to get to locales that can't be accessed otherwise. They are a bit heavy and bulky, however, which provides more warmth but makes for more difficult distance walking or climbing. A modified version, referred to as a waist-high wader because it extends only to the waist, is made for anglers who get in and out of boats frequently (especially guides), wading in cold water but otherwise being in warm air temperatures. Most chest waders actually do extend to the breast area of the chest, but some extend to the upper chest and armpits for the deepest possible wading.

Hip waders are all that are necessary for many fishing situations.

Hip waders are short and more like boots, and are also called hip boots, or hippers. They are fitted to each leg, with the material of each leg extending up to the hips and held up by a strap that loops onto the wearer's belt. Though they are often synonymously referred to as hip boots, they are technically slightly different; hip boots cover the same area, but technically they are made from heavier material from top to bottom.

Hip waders are meant for wading in relatively shallow water. It is easier to get in and out of a boat or car in them, and they are easiest to take off or put on. They are also cool to wear in warm weather, and, if fitted properly, good for long distance walking on land.

Boot and stocking foot. Both basic wader types can be further categorized by the nature of their bottom, or foot section. Those with integral boots are known as boot foot models. The boot section of the wader, usually a heavy-soled boot, is part of the legs and permanently attached to a chest- or hip-high upper section (called uppers), forming a single unit. Boot foot waders are generally popular with anglers who do a moderate amount of wading and are found on virtually all rubber chest and hip waders and on many neoprene chest waders. They are easier to take off or put on than stocking foot waders because of their one-piece construction, and are warmer in the coldest water. They generally are not as comfortable as, and are heavier than, stocking foot waders with wading shoes. The ankle portion of the boot provides support as good as that of a wading shoe. The ridge where the stiffer boot area joins the upper wader material can be a source of leaks, as well as of chafing to the angler who has to walk considerable distances.

Those waders that require separate boots are called stocking foot models, or sometimes pants.

The actual wader itself is a separate component from the boot, and features an integral stocking-style foot section that is worn inside a pair of wading boots or shoes; these may be chest- or hip-high products, mostly the former. Stocking foot waders fit the lower body closer, which can mean less drag in the water and easier climbing; the wading shoes worn with them often provide better ankle and foot support and traction; the soft ankle and calf section of the wader provides for more comfortable walking over distances. They take more time to get on or off, there is a greater chance of grit working into the boot, and they are not as warm in extreme cold water wading.

Materials and Styles

Rubber. With the exception of soles, rubber waders are much like they were a hundred years ago. They are generally stiff, bulky, and relatively heavy. Their greatest benefit is the sturdy construction of their integrated boot, and the capability of the boot to provide warmth in severe cold conditions. Lug-soled rubber boots are very durable, offering excellent support and protection from rocks. Rubber waders are also economical, which, coupled with durable boots, is why people who do construction and hard labor around docks and the like often use rubber waders, especially hip models.

In recent years, better quality rubber waders have added hi-tech tennis shoe–style air insole and air grip outsoles for better traction. These innovations have made the boots much more comfortable to walk and stand in. There is no getting around the fact that they are heavy, however, and it is also difficult to repair large tears in the rubber. Despite being low in cost, they do not tend to last long (especially the upper section), and they do not breathe, making them clammy inside.

Rubber hip waders and chest waders, as well as knee-high boots, are common in stores and economically priced. Each can be obtained in either full-cut boot bottoms for warmth or ankle-fit boot bottoms for walking support, both of which are available in insulated and non-insulated varieties. Some brands also have models that are factory-equipped with felt soles.

Canvas. The canvas wader is still readily available in the extrusion form that is lighter and more supple than rubber-canvas combination waders. However, some traditional rubber-canvas combination waders can still be purchased. Most extrusion canvas waders have PVC boot foot bottoms that make them lighter and less expensive than waders with rubber bottoms. Unfortunately, they do not offer the same support that traditional rubber boots offer. The modern canvas wader is very supple and light compared to full-rubber waders.

Canvas waders can be purchased in both insulated and non-insulated hip and chest models. Some brands offer felt-soled versions.

Nylon ultralights. Nylon stocking foot models make up the majority of ultralight waders. A few manufacturers make ultralight waders with PVC boot foot bottoms. Both configurations can be found in hip and chest waders with or without felt soles, but generally non-insulated.

Nylon waders are comfortable in warmer weather and are the lightest waders an angler can purchase, which is especially good for travel purposes. They are also comparatively low in cost, and durable enough to provide long life. They have no insulating properties, however, are not stretchable or breathable, and can be difficult to repair.

PVC. The PVC wader is usually less expensive than ultralight models and is sold primarily as a stocking foot wader. It is not very durable and is often used as a backup wader or for first-time anglers looking for an inexpensive solution to a day's wading.

Neoprene. Stocking foot and boot foot neoprene waders make up a significant portion of wader sales, despite the fact that they are more expensive than all other wader styles except breathables. They are commonly offered in 2 mil. (millimeter), 3.5 mil., and 5 mil. thicknesses. Many manufacturers offer models with felt soles. Most waders made from neoprene are chest-high models, and in stocking foot style.

Neoprene stretches in a 360-degree radius that substantially reduces fatigue and increases the angler's mobility. Bending, casting, and moving in general is essentially unimpeded in well-made products. Neoprene chest waders are generally form fitting, which is also comfortable and reduces drag in the water; more neoprene waders are currently available in wider cuts, the lack of which used to be a problem for larger-bodied anglers.

The greatest benefit of this material is its ability to keep an angler warm in cold conditions. Furthermore, neoprene is resistant to punctures, and repairs are easily accomplished even when

Neoprene waders, such as the chest-high model worn by this steelhead angler, are invaluable for cold-weather fishing.

the repair is over a large area. Neoprene itself, though bulky, has some flotation value. Existing mil thicknesses continue to become lighter and less absorbent.

The very attribute that makes neoprene warm also contributes to its greatest drawback. Because this material does not disperse heat outwardly, it produces interior wetness or dampness from perspiration; it is common for a neoprene chest wader wearer to be damp from waist to feet at the end of a day's use in anything but cold weather, and especially if exertion is required. Some brands have pile linings for displacing perspiration. Many brands also offer waist-high models that are ideal for anglers getting in and out of boats in cold water, but facing warmer air temperature when out of the water.

Neoprene waders can therefore be very uncomfortable in warm weather wading, or if significant walking is required. This is especially a problem when fishing where the air temperature is warm but the water cold. In heavy use, stocking foot neoprene can develop compression leaks in the bottoms of the foot portion of the wader.

Breathable. Breathable waders are heavier than ultralights, and a relatively new wader category that is likely to be the wave of the future as manufacturers perfect them and overcome some of the present disadvantages, which include being baggy, not stretchable, and easy to puncture.

The big advantage of breathable waders is that they disperse body heat, leaving the wearer much drier (no clamminess from condensation) than when wearing other types of waders. Most anglers can walk and fish all day with little condensation in their clothes.

This so-called "breathability" is derived from sophisticated breathable-membrane and breathable-coating products that allow water vapor (perspiration) to migrate outward from the interior of the garment but prevent water molecules (H_2O) from migrating inward from the exterior of the garment. The result, simply put, is that perspiration goes out and external water stays out.

For summer fishing, which is obviously when the majority of anglers are astream, these waders are very comfortable. They do not in themselves have any insulating property (more like nylon ultralights and less so than rubber). Because breathable waders are not form fitting, however, there is room for wearing warm clothes underneath, and it's possible to gain warmth for cool and cold water fishing, up to a point. For the coldest conditions, breathables do not compare in warmth to neoprene waders.

Breathable waders are expensive and can be difficult to repair (in fact, self-repair may void the warranty), which is a problem as these items have not proven to be very puncture-proof to date. The outer shell provides puncture resistance, and this material varies with different manufacturers.

A number of companies manufacture breathable waders in chest- and waist-high stocking foot models; there is little advantage to having these in hip waders. A few boot foot versions are available. Some stocking-foot models feature neoprene feet and are primarily found in fly fishing shops and specialty mail-order catalogs.

Other Gear

Soles. The purpose of the soles on a pair of waders or wading shoes is to provide stable nonslip footing. However, each sole type has limited application and will not function efficiently in every situation.

Traditional hard rubber-bottomed soles with lug-like gripping tread are best suited to traversing soft bottoms and gravel. Soft felt soles and similar woven polypropylene soles are a vast improvement for boulders and slick rocks, though not a help on wet shore grass or icy banks; felt wears out, however, and has to be replaced or at least reglued from time to time. Applying felt to rubber soles may require grinding down the rubber lugs and strapping or clamping replacement felt down until the cement cures, and the job is difficult on PVC soles because they don't mix well with many cements. Nevertheless, it's best to get boots with felt soles rather than to apply them yourself, even though you may need to replace the felt in time.

A recent option to smooth felt, though presently of limited availability, is a flat compressible soft rubber sole that is akin to rock-climbing shoe soles and grips as well or better than felt on slippery stream bottoms and better on other surfaces, and is far more durable. These are worth trying as resoling options, and are available on select wading shoes.

Metal gripping cleats, or creepers, which are either permanent attachments or strap-on metal studs of various shapes, provide the most stable walking on boulders and slick rocks, but are cumbersome to walk in and not welcomed in some situations (fiberglass boats, dune boardwalks, and so on). Metal cleats are absolutely essential for jetty fishing, where jetty rocks are moss covered and extremely slippery. They are also vital where wading anglers have to engage ice along rocky banks.

Some jetty anglers have a shoemaker cement golf shoe soles to the bottom of waders. Golf shoe spikes do not last long, but they can be replaced; always lubricate the threads of the cleats when inserting them; this prevents them from becoming corroded and makes replacement easier.

Wading boots/shoes. Wading boots (worn with stocking foot waders), which are often called wading shoes, should always be a consideration for fishing that requires wading in large, turbulent, or fast waters. They provide hiking boot–like support for walking on unstable ground, and superior protection from falls and below-ankle collisions. It is much easier to walk longer distances in wading boots (than in boot foot waders or booties), and they come in a varied selection of soles, making it possible to choose the best sole for the best application.

Using cormorants to fetch fish—a collar around the neck keeps the bird from swallowing its catch—is still done today and was practiced by Chinese fishermen back in 902 A.D.

Wading boots are fairly heavy and rugged products; most are of high quality and truly boot-like, made from leather or synthetic materials. Leather versions are becoming less popular because they absorb water and become heavier, are subject to rotting and cracking, shrink, and can be difficult to put on when dry.

There are various grades of wading boots, and you should choose one based upon the degree of wading difficulty that you will most likely encounter. An angler who has one pair of stocking foot waders and fishes easy wading streams most of the time can get a lightweight boot for everyday fishing, and also have a more solid and heavier boot for occasional fishing on swifter rivers and where there is more slippery and rugged bottom terrain. Obviously, outer sole considerations apply to wading boots, as previously discussed.

When wading wet in warm waters, including beaches, flats, and streams, special booty-style wading shoes are available that provide a tight ankle fit to keep gravel and sediment out, and offer overall foot protection. Many are made of neoprene, are calf-high in design, and have sturdy rubber composition bottoms. Wet-wading shoes with hard, ridged soles are good for varying applications, while those with felt bottoms are best for stream usage. Some have a zippered entry, which can be annoying when fine grit lodges in the zipper teeth. Most also have a heel bump that helps secure swim fins, which are used when fishing from float tubes *(see)*. Dark colored booties work fine for continuous wading, but not for saltwater flats fishing where you may spend a lot of time in a boat, subject to the sun heating the dark boots.

Accessories. Additional items that are useful if not necessary for waders include wading belts, staffs, PFDs, and gravel guards.

Wading belts keep chest waders from filling with water if you take a spill. Any belt that is large enough and which you don't mind getting wet can do, although easily adjustable synthetic belts with snap closures are excellent for this purpose. Some premium chest waders have lever or pinch latches in lieu of belts, and some have belt channels for handy enclosure of belts (auxiliary belts tend to get mislaid), but are also an added stress and point-prone to leaking.

Wading staffs, which allow an angler to be more sure-footed in fast water, are very helpful. A staff can be simply a sturdy green stick found at streamside, although finding a good stick isn't always possible. Multi-sectioned folding staffs are available, and many anglers make their own out of old ski poles (with the basket taken off).

Light inflatable personal flotation devices *(see)*, which do not hinder wading or casting, are good options for some people and in some circumstances. If worn (they are no good in the back of your vest), they can be instantly inflated in an emergency and will keep your head above water.

Gravel guards or cuffs (also called gaiters) are worn by some users of stocking foot waders or booties to help keep sand and gravel out of the boots, which can abrade the bottoms of the waders and cause water seepage. If long enough, the guards can also cover boot laces, which might catch loose fly line.

Selecting Waders
Just because you're a person of medium-average build who wears a size 9 shoe doesn't mean that a pair of medium waders will fit you. The best way to get proper fitting waders is to try them on to see how they fit. Mail-order catalogs offer extensive product lines, but even within the same brand, fit and last sizes (shoe sizes) will vary from product line to product line, so choosing by mail may be difficult.

Always try waders on with the clothing you will wade in. Make sure they are comfortable in all respects and you have enough room. Try bending over, squatting, sitting, and raising your leg as if you were climbing up a bank or out of a boat. Pay special attention to the boot and its fit; use the same sock(s) that you will wear when wading to determine proper fit. When you try on the waders make sure that your feet slip in the boots easily without a struggle, and that there's enough room to wiggle your toes. If not, you probably should go up to the next size. If you use stocking foot waders in extreme cold, consider a larger size wading shoe to accommodate the need for extra room.

If you order from a mail-order catalog, make sure you can return or exchange the wader if it doesn't fit you properly. If you absolutely cannot find a pair that fits properly (which especially happens to large individuals), check with manufacturers directly. A select few manufacturers offer custom waders at 40 to 60 percent above the retail price.

When buying waders, always keep your intended use in mind, and look for features that benefit your most common applications. If durability is an issue, for example, then you may want to consider models that are reinforced in the knees.

Ladies' waders. Women have been challenged to find waders that are made specifically for them, since the majority of anglers are male, and manufacturers have generally taken a one-size-fits-all design approach.

Some waders are cut for women, however. These are generally made in neoprene, ultralight, and breathable styles. The best place for women to be fitted is in a fly fishing shop; the selection and service is worth it.

Children's waders. Buying waders for children can be both challenging and expensive. The greatest frustration is that they will change sizes so quickly that they'll outgrow a good and otherwise usable pair of waders.

A few companies manufacture sizes as small as a children's size 1, but the most common sizes start at a children's size 3. One option is to purchase a size

small nylon stocking foot wader that a child could wear with old tennis shoes as an alternative to an expensive wading shoe; this would allow the wader to last through several size changes in the child.

Consider chest waders instead of hippers for children, since children are shorter to start out with and are prone to stumbling into the water with hippers on and likely to get wet enough to spoil the outing. If they're wearing chest waders, they stand a substantial chance of staying dry. Children should always wear a wader belt and a proper personal flotation device when wading, and they should avoid swift current.

Care and Repair

It's a good idea to clean and properly dry your waders after each use; many freshwater anglers do not need to clean their waders, but saltwater anglers should give them a freshwater rinse. Don't walk in stocking foot waders without boots on, as this is guaranteed to abrade them and diminish their life.

Storage. Taking good care of a pair of waders will pay you back in years of service. The first consideration in all wader care and storage is drying your waders by hanging them or otherwise storing them in an unfolded position. Always try to dry both the inside and the outside before storing for long periods of time. Except for short-term drying, keep waders out of direct sunlight. Do not store them where they will be under direct fluorescent lighting. Never fold waders for long-term storage. If you must fold them, try not to do so the same way each time. This will prevent permanent crease marks that can weaken the wader over many years.

Boot foot waders and wading boots should be dried as much as possible before long-term storage. If the boot has a removable insole, lift it up and set it sideways in the boot so air can circulate. Store boot foot waders hanging upside down with commercial boot hangers so the weight of the boot is supported by the hanger and not the wader. If hung by their suspenders, most boot foot waders will weaken at the suspender connections due to their heavy weight. Rinse wading boots to remove any grit or dirt inside, tie them together by their laces, and hang them where they can air dry. Short-term storage of wet boots, as when traveling, is best in a ventilated bag.

Stocking foot waders can be hung on a regular heavy duty plastic hanger by their suspenders. They are much lighter in weight and will not stress the suspender areas. Instead of folding stocking foots, roll them whenever possible to relieve stress cracks.

Finding leaks. With a little practice repairing waders can be efficient and easy. The key is finding the leak. Whether working with neoprene, nylon, or rubber, the leak can be found no matter how small. Holding the wader up to a light or using a flashlight will work for an easy leak, but seepage leaks demand more careful testing to ensure a quality permanent repair. When using the light methods, it is possible to miss the area entirely, and these may not show additional small leaks.

The trick to clearly identifying a leak is to fill the suspect section of the wader from the inside with water. This creates the same or greater pressure that is happening when they are being worn. One of the best places to do this is in a bath tub. Make sure that the bath tub is bone dry. Even the slightest moisture in the tub will leave a small damp mark on the outside of the wader creating the impression that the wet spot is a leak. Put the wader up to the spigot and begin to fill the inside of the wader with cold or barely warm water. Do not use hot water. Again, you must not spill any water while completing this procedure.

If the leak is in the right foot, direct all the water down the right leg filling the inside of the wader several inches above the estimated area that the leak is in. Stop the water flow and squeeze the area until water starts to seep outside. In most cases, the pressure created by the volume of water instantly shows the leak without any pressure being applied. Use a waterproof marker to draw a circle around the area so it will be easy to find during the repair process. This test often shows more than one culprit causing moisture to enter your waders.

Off-site repair. Make sure you save the kit that comes from the manufacturer and refer to it before repairing. In the case of breathable waders, making your own repair can invalidate the warranty and also create an area that will not breathe, but condensate. This may give the angler the impression that there is a small leak even after the repair is complete. Refer to the manufacturer for instructions.

For all other types of waders, an efficient repair can be easily made that will last the life of the wader. When making a repair it is important to determine whether or not the repair requires an added piece of material. Adhesives that work well and with all types of wader materials include GOOP, which can be purchased in a hardware or sporting goods store, and Aquaseal, which can be purchased in a sporting goods store. Both adhesives dry flexible and, if properly cured, will repair areas that might otherwise require a small piece of material.

When making the repair, make sure you mark the inside of the wader so the same repair can be made inside as well as outside. Be sure you're in a well-ventilated area and that the wader is completely dry and turned inside out. When the wader is ready, complete the inside repair first, using as little adhesive as necessary. If the wader has to be turned right-side out before the adhesive is dry, put a block of wood inside to keep the sides separate and apart. You don't want to glue the inside of the waders shut. Make sure you follow the curing instructions, which can be an hour to 24 hours depending on the formula. Follow the same procedure on the outside of the repair.

On-site repair. Depending on the adhesive for-

The blood of horseshoe crabs provides a vital test for the toxins that cause septic shock; coral has been used to replace bone grafts in humans.

mula, an emergency streamside repair can be made by drying the wader as much as possible and using a quick dry formula from GOOP. In most cases the repair will set immediately from the cold temperatures of the water. However, it is best to repair the site again for a long-term permanent solution.

Rubber sticks that can be lit by a match to melt over the needed area are another option. If done properly, this method can work efficiently if the area is small and has little stress from movement.

Tears. In the case of larger tears, repairs can be made with the same adhesives used for small repairs. Tears can be repaired effectively on neoprene, nylon, and some canvas waders. Rubber waders are most difficult and not always salvageable. The longer-curing formulas are recommended. The other challenge is to find the same material that the wader is manufactured from. If you can't find the extra piece the manufacturer gave you, most waders have an internal pocket that could be cut for the material required to make the repair.

For larger tears (1 to 3 inches), find a well-ventilated area with a clean, flat working surface. Turn the wader inside out, completing the inside repair first. Carefully rough up the area with 100 grit or finer sandpaper, just enough to raise the grain of the material. Precut the selected repair patch, making sure to generously cover the tear, and round the edges.

Clean the surface and apply a light coating of adhesive using a Popsicle stick or similar tool. Make sure not to get any of the glue inside the wader, risking gluing it together. Allow it to dry until tacky (see adhesive instructions), then firmly apply the patch material to the repair area, working the excess adhesive away. Wait 10 minutes and apply the outside final layer of adhesive. Let dry for 24 hours.

Wading Issues

Most anglers give little thought to safety while wading, until they fall when they least expect to or when they're washed down a turbulent stream with their waders perilously filling up with frigid water. The latter can be a frightening and possibly fatal experience, which most anglers can avoid through common sense and the correct equipment. By learning to read and judge waters, you'll become adept at sensing when to move forward and when to step back.

Swift flowage poses the most obvious difficulty, of course, and rivers that have steep drops and whitewater are most dangerous and allow only edge wading (and maybe not even that). Likewise, some flows may have objects floating down them, such as ice chunks or logs, that you need to look out for, especially if you are not facing upstream (keep looking behind you). Many rivers have sections that are easy to wade, and sections that are difficult, and some that look easy are actually not because their bottoms are slippery and put a lot of pressure on your feet. Surf anglers generally need waders so they can stand on the surf edge and gain extra casting distance without getting wet, but sometimes they need to wade out in the surf and have to beware of underwater tow. So, wading is different depending on the circumstances. Nevertheless, there are some general guidelines to follow.

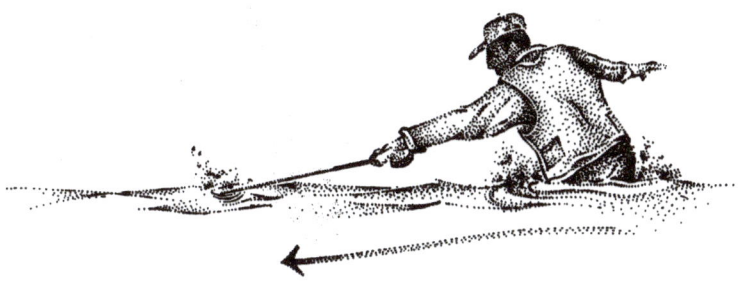

When wading across a river, to help maintain balance when footing is uncertain or the current is swift, lay the tip of your fishing rod into the water directly downstream of your position, and keep the rod in the water while wading across the flow.

Techniques. Wading is a skill. The more you do it, the better you become. Consideration should always be given to depth, water speed, bottom configuration, and whether it is prudent to wade through the fast or deep areas at all. Many anglers have taken one step too many and found themselves slipping into deeper water over the top of their waders; in rivers, this may result in a floating trip though the rapids or pool, which is not worth the fish you might have caught.

Always respect water. Go slowly. Make sure that your foot is firmly planted and stable before taking the next step. Crablike steps are much better than reaching strides. Concentrate on the task at hand. Wearing polarized sunglasses helps make the trail under the water more visible, although the deeper you wade and the murkier the water, the less this helps. In clear water, polarized sunglasses are a great aid.

Scout an area that you intend to wade across before starting to do so. Often, you will find a better route, usually shallower, a little distance upstream or downstream; often, the tail of a pool is best to cross because the water is shallower at the bottom lip and the velocity is less. Do not cast and wade at the same time; better to get into position and then cast. Don't walk or leap from one large rock to another, which is asking for trouble; don't wade in the turbulent water upstream of a large rock; and beware of deep holes below large rocks. In tailwater rivers, beware of rising water; dam releases can suddenly raise the water level, and if you notice the water coming up, waste no time in getting to shore.

In swift, deep, or unfamiliar water, you should plan every step, and take slow steps by sliding your foot along, rather than lifting it. If you lift your feet in swift water, the current can push your leg away and throw you off balance. Also, place your feet between rocks instead of on top of them, which is an invitation to slipping or moving too deep with the next step.

In rivers, you should wade with your body and

feet sideways to the flow. Even a slight turn in fast water can spin you or knock you over. Wade across at an angle, preferably slightly quartered upstream. Remember that the more you weigh, the easier it is to wade fast water; the lighter you are, the harder. A light person should draft below a heavier one if the two can cross swift water together; a better idea for two people in swift water may be to link elbows and cross

Using a staff is a good way to maintain balance when wading in swift flows; place the staff on your upstream side and don't extend it too far from your body.

slowly, having the stability of four feet on the bottom.

Using a wading staff or stick can be very helpful. It acts as a stabilizing third leg, and is also valuable for probing depth and poking for rocks. Most people find that it's best to place the staff upstream.

Without a stick, you can use your fishing rod to help stabilize you in deep swift current, especially when you start to feel unbalanced or are about to stumble or fall. Hold the rod in your downstream hand and keep it pointed directly downstream. Place the tip section in the current to act as a stabilizer. Obviously, you need to have the rod in the proper hand to start with, so when you don't have a staff, start wading with the rod in your downstream hand. In the worst cases, use both a staff in your upstream hand and the rod in your downstream hand.

Once you get across a rough spot, or are about to leave the water, don't let up your concentration.

If you fall into a swift flow, get your feet headed downstream and float with the current so you can fend off objects and see where you're headed; work toward the shallows or light-current areas where you can get your footing and leave the water.

Many people fall on their way out of the water by taking their last steps for granted. High and slippery stream banks are also a problem.

When you're getting out of a boat to wade, especially if you're not right on shore in shallow water, don't be fooled by the illusion of depth that comes with clear water. The water is often deeper than it looks, and many people have gotten out of boats to find that they are over the top of their waders, or sometimes their heads.

If you start heading into soft-bottomed areas, which may happen in stillwater, do not keep going forward, as you may find your feet so deeply buried in muck that suction keeps your feet mired. If you start sinking into soft bottoms, retreat to firmer ground and find a better route.

When you hook a strong fish, gradually retreat from deep water and get to shore. You can follow a fish easier, if necessary, from the shallows, where you have more maneuverability, and also can effect a higher rod angle.

If you do find yourself floating downriver in current while wearing chest waders, don't panic. Get your feet pointed downstream so they can be used to deflect your body, and especially head, from objects, and go with the flow on your back with your head up. Use your arms to try to maneuver toward the bank and water that is calm and shallow enough for you stand up in. Do not float head first or try to fight the current.

It is a good idea to test your waders sometime in a swimming pool or warm safe stream or lake to see what happens to them when they fill with water, and how you are able (or not able) to maneuver. A wet, fully clothed person in waders full of water is very heavy, barely able to move, and a candidate for drowning, so this is a matter to be taken very seriously.

Staying warm. Staying warm has never been easier. Tremendous strides in wader manufacturing and clothing have made it possible to stay out in weather that your fishing gear won't even work in.

Anglers who venture out when the air temperature is subfreezing and water temperature is at the freezing mark must take special precautions and wear specialized equipment. Waders must be open cut, allowing the angler to comfortably wear clothing made of noncotton-based polypropylenes, piles, or their equivalents.

The foot is the most important design feature of a wader. A full-cut rubber boot foot bottom on any wader is superior to even heavy stocking foot neoprene waders for warmth and comfort in severe cold. Boot foot bottoms offer superior insulation and, most importantly, open space for your toes and feet to move. Stocking foots tend to constrict blood flow from the tight "walking fit" that happens when you lace your wading shoes. Even full-cut rubber and canvas waders can provide adequate warmth if the angler has enough room to wear the proper clothing.

Most people can stay warm all day if they can keep their feet warm. To make sure that your feet stay warm, wear a light polypropylene liner sock with a heavy poly or wool sock over it. This combination will keep you much warmer than two heavy wool socks, which will most likely fit your feet too tightly, constricting blood flow. Do not wear cotton socks, which absorb perspiration and make feet damp and cold. When you put the waders on, your feet should slip into the boots easily without a struggle, and there should be enough room to wiggle your toes. If you use stocking foot waders in extreme cold, consider a larger size wading shoe to accommodate the need for extra room.

Even the warmest waders will not keep you dry if you sweat and soak your cotton-based underclothes. This is a common mistake that can ruin a day of fishing quickly. Always wear an undergarment made from polypropylene or other micro fibers. Expedition-weight underwear can even substitute for pants if worn with thin poly liner underwear. The same is true for the upper half of your body. Wear layered poly or other micro fibers, and never wear cotton. When taking long walks, remove as much upper clothing as possible to let hot air escape to keep you from perspiring.

It is true that most of your body heat can be lost through your head. Always wear warm hats in the winter. If it's a long walk to your destination, take the hat off while walking to release more heat and to keep you from perspiring.

WADING BOOTS
See: Waders.

WADING STAFF
See: Waders.

WAGGLER
A float attached to fishing line by its bottom only, used with a rod and reel for stillwater angling.
See: Float.

WAHOO *Acanthocybium solandri*.
Other names—barracuda, oahu fish, ocean barracuda, Pacific kingfish, pride of Bermuda, queenfish, tigerfish; Arabic: *kanaad znjebari*; Creole: *bécune grosse race, kin fis, thazard raité*; French: *paere*; Hawaiian: *ono*; Japanese: *kamasu-sawara*; Portuguese: *cavala gigante, cavala-da-India, cavala empinge*; Spanish: *guacho, peto, sierra*; Tuvaluan: *tepala*.

The wahoo is a popular gamefish and a close relative of the king mackerel. It is reputedly one of the fastest fish in the sea, attaining speeds of 50 miles per hour and more, and no angler who has hooked a large wahoo and watched it sizzle a hundred yards of line off the reel in a few seconds will dispute this.

The wahoo was originally plentiful off the Hawaiian island of Oahu, once commonly spelled "Wahoo," and this accounts for the fish's name. The Hawaiian word for this fish, *ono*, meaning "good to eat," is an appropriate description of the wahoo's sweet, white, flaky flesh. It has a more delicate texture than the meat of other fast-swimming pelagic species, as it contains less of the strong-tasting "blood meat" muscle—used for long-distance swimming—found in tuna and marlin. The wahoo has commercial importance in some countries and is marketed fresh, salted, spice-cured, or frozen.

Identification. A long, slender, cigar-shaped mackerel with a sharply pointed head and widely forked tail, the wahoo is a brilliant or dark blue color along its back. It has 25 to 30 bright or dusky blue vertical bands, or "tiger stripes" that extend down the bright silver to silvery gray sides and sometimes join into pairs below. The stripes are not always prominent or even apparent in large specimens, although they may become more noticeable when the fish is excited. A distinguishing feature is the movable upper jaw, which has 45 to 64 teeth, of which 32 to 50 are on the lower jaw; these teeth are large, strong, and laterally compressed. The gill structure resembles that of the marlin more than it does those of the tuna or mackerel, and it lacks the characteristic gill rakers of the latter fish. The lateral line is well defined and drops significantly at the middle of the first dorsal fin and extends in a wavy line back to the tail. The first dorsal fin is long and low and has 21 to 27 spines. It is separated from the second dorsal fin, which has 13 to 15 rays; the anal fin has 12 to 14 very small rays.

Wahoo

There are a series of 9 dorsal finlets both above and below the caudal peduncle.

Size. The wahoo grows rapidly, reaching on average 10 to 30 pounds, and 4- to 5-foot lengths are not uncommon. Its maximum size is 7 feet in length and more than 180 pounds in weight. The all-tackle world record is a 158-pound, 8-ounce fish taken off Baja California, Mexico, in 1996.

Distribution. Wahoo occur in the Atlantic, Pacific, and Indian Oceans in tropical and subtropical waters, including the Caribbean and Mediterranean Seas. Seasonal concentrations are thought to exist off the Pacific coasts of Panama, Costa Rica, and Baja California during the summer, off Grand Cayman in the Atlantic during the winter and spring, and off the western Bahamas and Bermuda during the spring and fall. Some of the best sportfishing and largest specimens occur off San Salvador in the Bahamas, and off Baja California, Mexico.

Habitat. An oceanic species, wahoo are pelagic and seasonally migratory. They are frequently solitary or form small, loose groupings of two to seven fish rather than large compact schools. They are known to associate around banks, pinnacles, and even flotsam. They are occasionally found around wrecks and deeper reefs where smaller fish are abundant.

Life history. Both sexes reach sexual maturity during the first year of life. Depending on their size, females may discharge from hundreds of thousands to tens of millions of eggs.

Food. Wahoo feed on such pelagic species as porcupinefish, flyingfish, herring, pilchards, scad, lanternfish, and small mackerel and tuna, as well as on squid.

Angling. This speedy member of the mackerel family is caught in a variety of ways, although trolling is by far the number one activity. A great many fish are caught incidental to other fishing activities, although they can be targeted specifically where they are abundant. As mentioned, wahoo are often solitary but may travel in small groups in some areas, especially in hard-fished waters where they can be less numerous and wary.

Wahoo are mostly caught in waters that range from 72° to 77°F. They are located over or along humps, ledges, seamounts, and other structure that causes current to well up and provide good feeding opportunities, as well as along current edges and around floating objects and sargassum. Near-surface trolling at high speeds is a standard ploy for wahoo-seeking anglers, as is deeper trolling via planers, downriggers, and wire line. Because wahoo are seldom found in the concentrations typical of other mackerel and tuna, trolling is a good way to cover a lot of territory. In addition, the fast swimming ability of this species allows for speedy boat travel; wahoo are typically caught at boat speeds of 6 to 10 knots, and a few anglers troll at up to 14 knots.

Trolled offerings include whole, rigged Spanish mackerel; mullet, ballyhoo, squid, or other small baits; strip baits and diving plugs; or heavy bullet-head trolling lures and other assorted offshore trolling lures. Live-bait fishing and kite fishing are less practiced but sometimes productive, and on occasion opportunities for casting with plugs, spoons, metal jigs, and flies exist. In the Pacific, long-range anglers use heavy plastic- or vinyl-skirted trolling or casting heads—called bombs—for trolling and for casting to secondary-strike fish; these usually feature a spinning willowleaf blade on the main hook, and sometimes a trailer hook, and weigh 3 to 8 ounces.

Wahoo are most likely to be active early in the day, so anglers who specialize in wahoo like to beat the competition to productive spots and commence fishing at dawn. Although wahoo are caught by trolling in the upper levels, trolling at deeper levels is the way to target larger fish. Appropriate depths range from just under the surface to 120 or more feet, and anglers use varied approaches to cover different depths. Weighted natural baits, deep-running plugs, and spoons are favored. Some anglers prefer wire line (60-pound) for this deep work, whereas others use planers that can take fast trolling as well as downriggers.

Other anglers use 50- to 60-pound nylon monofilament, although lighter line can be employed off downriggers. Reels must have an excellent drag and plenty of line capacity; 4/0 to 6/0 conventional reels and comparable lever drags are standard. Where the fish may not be really deep, spreading the lures horizontally in a trolling pattern is necessary; in a four-line setup, two center lines are fished at a shorter distance in the boat wake (which often attracts fish), and the two outside lines are fished twice that distance back in the wake.

Dark lure colors—especially green, mackerel patterns, purple and black bodies, and dark-combo bodies—are effective on these fish. Deep-running plugs must be capable of tracking straight at high speeds, which limits the possibilities. Heavy-duty wire leaders are a necessity owing to the toothy mouths of these fish.

Where there are groups of wahoo, continued trolling over likely structure is a good tactic, and when a fish is hooked, it may be possible to get a second hookup by casting out a metal jig after the other trolling lines have been cleared.

The first scorching run of a wahoo may peel off at least a hundred yards of line in seconds, and the heat generated by the friction has been known to burn out the drag on some reels. Keep your hands off the spool. Occasionally these fish jump on the strike and often shake their head violently when hooked in an effort to free themselves. Be careful when handling these fish, as you may otherwise put your fingers in jeopardy.

See: Mackerel; Offshore Fishing.

WAKE

The waves created by a passing boat; the visible track or trail behind a moving boat.

WALES
Gamefishing

Trout. The mountains of Wales give rise to dozens of rivers and streams holding brown trout, and many of these also have a sea trout and salmon run. Fishing for brown trout is relatively inexpensive, and permits are available locally. It is also possible to enjoy good salmon and sea trout (often called sewin) fishing at a reasonable cost, and assistance is available on some beats from a local gillie (guide) or fishing instructor.

In the 1980s, the trend to start up commercially stocked put-and-take stillwaters (in a broad sense, a stillwater is anything that is not a river, stream, or tributary) fisheries spread from England to Wales, and the south in particular now has a proliferation of these waters, some holding rainbows in excess of 20 pounds. Big brown trout are more expensive, because they take twice as long as rainbows to grow to any given weight and are therefore in shorter supply. It's difficult to land and return these big fish alive, so captured fish are seldom allowed to be released.

Of the biggest rivers, the Teifi holds wild brownies, and the Towy, Welsh Dee, Wye, and the upper reaches of the Severn are among the best-known rivers inhabited by wild browns and grayling. Day tickets are available on most at a very reasonable cost, usually from a local shop. Much of this fishery is fly angling only.

Salmon and sea trout. The best Welsh rivers for sea trout and salmon are the Towy, Conwy, Mawddach, Wnion (pronounced Oonion), Usk, Teifi, Welsh Dee, Wye, and Dovey. Three good smaller rivers are the Seiont, Gwyrfai, and Llyfni, near the Menai Straits, for which day tickets are easily available.

Welsh rivers tend to be shorter and faster than many English game rivers, and more of them have pools. It is easier to obtain fishing tickets here than on rivers in either England or Scotland. Some have private and expensive beats, however, including the Towy, which is reputed to be the best sea trout river in the UK; individual specimens run as big as the salmon and approach 20 pounds. Also worth trying is the Taf in South Wales. This venue was badly polluted, but a dedicated restocking policy has resulted in the return of salmon and the development of a good run.

Coarse Fishing

Coarse fishing in Wales plays second fiddle to gamefishing, but excellent venues do exist. The River Wye in particular can produce spectacular fishing for barbel, chub, and dace, and many experts have predicted that this river will produce a barbel weighing more than 17 pounds. The stretch below Symonds Yat has reportedly yielded such fish to salmon anglers, and there are loads of barbel from Hereford downward. The Wye is also famous for big catches of one of Britain's smallest fish, the bleak. It weighs only a couple of ounces on average but is present in such numbers that 50-pound catches have been taken in five-hour matches.

When the River Wye floods, tributaries such as the Rivers Lugg and Monnow become productive for dace, chub, and barbel. The nearby River Usk is dominated by gamefishing concerns, but where coarse fishing is allowed, the action is spectacular. Usk town center and Newbridge produce 100-plus-pound catches of dace and chub regularly, and roach exceeding 3 pounds are present. The river holds many specimen (large or trophy) dace, and the fish average nearly 1 pound in places.

The River Severn rises in Wales before making its way into England above Shrewsbury. The Welsh section is mainly fast and clear, but if you can find the slower, deeper stretches, you can enjoy great sport for medium-size barbel, chub, grayling, and roach. Welshpool and Newton are good spots. Farther north, the River Dee is full of chub, but this river has been hit hard by cormorant predation, and local knowledge is needed for success. These fish do tend to congregate near bridges.

Probably the most famous coarse fishing venue in Wales is not a coarse venue at all, but a trout reservoir. When a pike fishing trial was first held at Llandegfedd Reservoir in South Wales in the 1980s, it became known that these waters held big pike, but few people could have guessed what would follow. The venue yielded more 40-plus-pound pike than any other in UK history. The British record fell several times in quick succession and finally settled at a massive 46 pounds, 13 ounces. The pike at Llandegfedd Reservoir grow incredibly fast on a diet of stocked trout, and the big catches sparked the opening of a string of trout venues and changed the face of pike fishing for good.

Another worthwhile venue in South Wales is the Monmouthshire and Brecon Canal in Cwmbran, which is known to hold huge chub and carp. For big roach, pike, eels, and perch, giant Bala Lake near Oswestry is a hard stillwater to better. This ancient, deep glacial lake is also home to the rare gwyniad, a protected fish from the days when the country was dominated by glaciers and snowdrifts.

In Cardiff, the mile-long East Bute Dock is well worth a visit. This site holds an enormous number of small roach and bream (called skimmers), and 20-plus-pound catches are easily taken. It's also home to specimen eels weighing more than 5 pounds; these are taken at night. Other stillwaters worth mentioning are Ponsticill Reservoir in the Brecon Beacons, home to some enormous perch, including a rumored fish of 7 pounds; Llangorse Lake, where second-to-none bream and pike fishing can be enjoyed with stunning scenery as a back-

In Botswana, the climbing perch can breathe atmospheric air, crawl out of the water, and "walk" across muddy and moist land to find suitable spawning grounds; it has traveled as far as 9.4 kilometers.

drop; and Roath Park Lake in Cardiff, for summer roach fishing.

Coarse fishing in Wales is covered by the same national license as in England.

Sea Fishing

The south coast of Wales has a considerable number of charter ports, whose boats fish the Bristol Channel and regularly make the trip south to fish off the Devon coast. The ray fishing is exceptionally good from spring to midwinter, and anglers regularly land big cod as well. Other main species include conger, ling, and bass, which are usually taken inshore. The main ports are Penarth, Swansea, Tenby, and Pembroke.

Shore fishing from Penarth around the peninsula to Fishguard is especially productive, offering bass and flounder in summer and great numbers of codling (small cod) in winter. Mullet favor the waters around the many marinas. Anglers can avail themselves of a variety of sites, ranging from sandy beaches to rocky headlands, and many local clubs exist should the visitor need help.

Curiously, the west coast is little fished when compared with the rest of Wales, although some well-known storm beaches produce bass, as well as flounder in the estuaries. The long sweep of Cardigan Bay, however, is open to the prevailing westerly winds, at times rendering most of it almost unfishable. The main charter ports are Newquay, Aberystwyth, Barmouth, and Pwhelli; they get fantastic catches of rays, tope, cod, black bream, sharks, and other species from the Gulf Stream, rivaling most other areas of the UK on their best day.

To the north is the Lleyn Peninsula, known in particular for bull bass in spring, when pregnant females come close to shore and near-record fish are taken every year. Some of the marks are especially dangerous, and anglers fishing here should always be accompanied by a companion who has local knowledge. On the north coast, flounder, codling, and bass are the main species, and the established charter ports are Bangor, Conway, Colwyn Bay, Rhyl, and Rhos.

The island of Anglesey, off the northwest tip of Wales, offers exceptional fishing from its rocky shoreline all around the island. Species include pollack, rays, codling, whiting, and conger. Conger and bass are plentiful from the narrow, fast-running Menai Straits. Local knowledge is essential here. The main ports are Amlwch and Holyhead. There's year-round fishing from Anglesey, which is easily reached by road across one of two bridges. No license is required for saltwater angling.

See: England; Scotland.

WALKING THE DOG

One of the few lure retrieval techniques that actually has a formal name, walking the dog is a slow and tantalizing method of manipulating so-called walking surface plugs or stickbaits *(see: surface lure)*, which are designed to swim from side to side. The term and the method derive from the infamous Heddon Zara Spook plug, and this method is particularly effective at tempting larger-than-average-size bass out of woody cover and thick vegetation, and up from deep clear-water hideouts. However, it is also effective for other freshwater and saltwater fish that may strike a surface lure.

Because of their tail-weighted design, these types of lures are distinctly unimpressive and ineffective if not worked right, and practice is needed to develop the most effective action.

To effect the right retrieval, begin with the rod tip pointed down. It's helpful to stand or be seated high, to have most of your line on the water to help create drag, and to tie the fishing line to the lure with a rounded snap or a loop knot.

To walk the dog, you need to make rhythmic short jerks with the rod tip while simultaneously advancing the reel handle a quarter turn or so with each jerk to take up line. Done slowly, the lure's travel path widens; done quickly, it narrows. The line should lie slightly slack in the water to avoid pulling the lure ahead. The right cadence allows the lure to swim from side to side, but a taut line jerks it ahead. A skilled retriever can slow-fish a walking plug so that it almost stays in place, nodding from left to right, an action that can be highly seductive to otherwise disinterested fish.

"Half-stepping" is an advanced technique for working a walking plug very close to logs, bushes, docks, and so on. Here the plug swims repeatedly

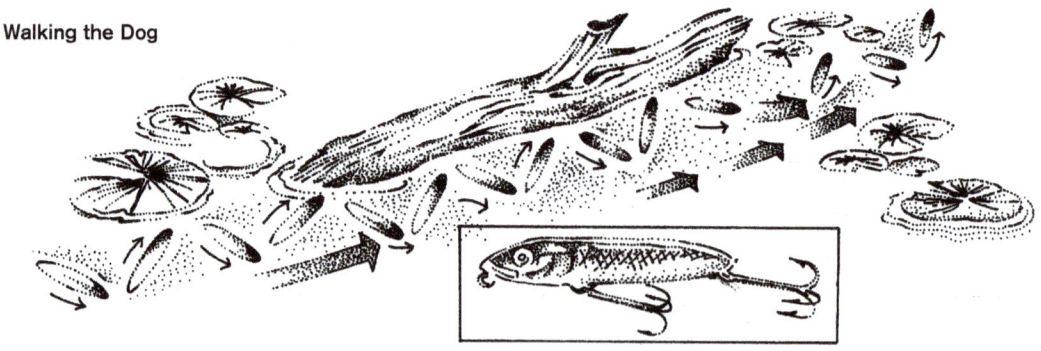

Walking the Dog

Walleye

to one side instead of from left to right. To do this, you must first get into proper casting position by aligning your line with the object being fished. Walk the lure up to the object so that the plug faces it. Barely nudge the rod tip so that the head of the plug turns away. Now jerk the rod tip; the plug heads inward toward the bush. Nudge again; jerk again. The lure continues to swim toward the bush and actually works around it as if using it for protection. Done right, this tactic is almost irresistible to a bass that is in or under that object.
See: Plug.

WALLEYE *Stizostedion vitreum.*
Other names—pickerel, yellow pickerel, walleyed pike, yellow walleye, jack salmon, jack, pike-perch, walleyed pike-perch, pike, gray pike, green pike, 'eye, marbleye, glass-eye; French: *doré*.

The walleye is the largest member of the Percidae family of perch *(see)* in North America and a close relative of the sauger *(see)*. It is also closely related to the larger-growing zander *(see)* of Europe. A popular freshwater sportfish, the walleye is relatively abundant in many waters, grows to large sizes, and is renowned for its delicious, sweet, and fine-textured meat. As a food fish, the walleye has few peers in freshwater, which helps counterbalance its reputation as a sluggish battler when hooked. It struggles on or near the bottom rather than making long or sustained runs or leaping out of the water.

The walleye has received considerable commercial interest in the past and is still sought commercially in Canada, where Manitoba and Ontario provide the bulk of the commercial harvest. It is also that country's leading inland sportfish, vying with coastal salmon species for overall honors. It is likewise hallowed in upper Midwestern U.S. states. In many parts of Canada, walleye are primarily referred to as "pickerel," which is a misnomer and a source of some confusion. The walleye is sometimes incorrectly associated with the true pickerel *(see: pickerel, chain)*, which, unlike the walleye, is a member of the Esox, or pike, family of fish.

Identification. The walleye has a slender and cylindrical body with a tapered head. Its first dorsal fin has needle-sharp spiny rays and is separated from the soft-rayed second dorsal fin. The cheeks are sparsely scaled, the gill covers are sharp, and the teeth are sharp. When handling the fish, anglers must take care around the teeth, gill covers, and spiny dorsal fin to avoid cuts and stab wounds.

The walleye has a dark green back, golden yellow sides, and a white belly. The lower lobe of the caudal fin is white, and there is a large black blotch at the rear base of the spinous first dorsal fin. Young walleye usually have dark blotches across their backs and down their sides, but these patterns are absent in adults. As with many fish, the color of the walleye is highly variable depending on habitat, with golden color characteristics in many populations. Typically, fish in turbid or off-color waters are paler with less obvious black markings; clear waters produce more definitively marked specimens.

Perhaps the most prominent feature of a walleye is its large, white, glossy eyes. The special reflective layer in the retina of the eye is a characteristic known as tapetum lucidum; it gathers light that enters the eye, making it extremely sensitive to bright daylight intensities but is conducive to nocturnal vision. This attribute is also present in the sauger. These two species thus have the best night vision among freshwater gamefish, with a light-gathering eyesight similar to that of cats, raccoons, and deer.

Size. The size of walleye varies with their environment, but anglers commonly encounter fish in the 10- to 18-inch range and weighing about 1 to 3 pounds. Some waters support fish that are larger on average, and it is not uncommon to catch walleye exceeding 5 pounds in many places. Fish exceeding the arbitrary trophy size of 10 pounds are hard to come by in many places, although some waters have an abundance of such fish. Walleye are capable of achieving a maximum size of at least 23 pounds and possibly 25 pounds. The only one known to have exceeded 23 pounds is the Tennessee state record and International Game Fish Association (IGFA) all-tackle world record—a 25-pound fish caught in Old Hickory Lake, Tennessee, in 1960. It has been the subject of revisionist dispute in recent years and is followed in the record annals by a 22-pound, 11-ounce walleye from Greers Ferry Lake, Arkansas, in 1982, and a 22-pound, 4-ounce specimen caught at Fort Erie, Ontario, in 1943.

Distribution. The walleye is widely distributed in North America. Its native range in the north extended from Great Bear Lake in the Northwest Territories easterly to James Bay and the Gulf of St. Lawrence. In the east it extended southward along the Allegheny Mountains to Georgia and Gulf Coast drainages in Mississippi and Alabama. In the west it extended from Saskatchewan throughout the Dakotas to Arkansas. Through some natural expansion and extensive introduction, the range has been extended eastward to Atlantic coast drainages from Vermont to South Carolina and westward to all western states except California, as well as southern Alberta and British Columbia. With few exceptions, the significant walleye fisheries exist in waters within its native range; the walleye forms a dominant part of the fish fauna of central Canada, particularly in the boreal forest zone. In that region, it is clearly the dominant and most popular game species.

Habitat. Walleye are tolerant of a great range of environmental situations but seem to do best in the open water of large lakes and reservoirs, as well as the pools of large rivers. They inhabit many smaller bodies of water but are not typically prolific in the most turbid environs, preferring somewhat clearer water than their sauger cousins. Gravel, rock, and firm sand bottoms are preferred, and they may associate with various weed cover; they will also use sunken trees, standing timber, boulder shoals, and reefs as cover and foraging sites. Although they can survive temperature extremes from 32° to 90°F, they prefer waters with a maximum temperature of roughly 77° and are commonly associated with 65° to 75° water in summer.

In clear lakes, walleye often lie in contact with the bottom during daytime, seemingly resting. In these lakes, they usually feed from top to bottom at night. In turbid water, they are more active during the day, swimming slowly in schools close to the bottom. Walleye frequently are associated with other species such as yellow perch, northern pike, white suckers, and smallmouth bass. During the winter, walleye do not change their habitat except to avoid strong currents. In large water bodies, they will orient to open water in schools that coincide with the presence of baitfish, especially alewives but also shad and perch.

In the spring, the fish have a spawning run to shallow shoals, inshore areas, or tributary rivers; at other times they move up and down in response to light intensity. They also move daily or seasonally in response to water temperature or food availability. For the most part, walleye seem to remain in loose but discrete schools with separate spawning grounds and summer territories.

Life history/Behavior. Spawning occurs in the spring or early summer, depending on latitude and water temperature. Normally, spawning begins shortly after the ice breaks up in lakes that freeze; water temperature is usually in the mid-40s, but spawning may occur at a range between 38° and 50°F.

The males move to the spawning grounds first. These are usually rocky areas in flowing water below impassable falls and dams in rivers and streams, coarse-gravel shoals, or (least common) along rubble shores of lakes at depths of less than 6 feet. Spawning takes place at night, in groups of one large female and one or two smaller males or two females and numerous males.

The male walleye is not territorial and does not build a nest. Prior to spawning, there is a lot of pursuit, pushing, circular swimming, and fin erection. Finally, the spawning group rushes upward into shallow water and stops, the females roll on their sides and release their eggs, and simultaneously, milt is released by the males. Apparently, females deposit most of their eggs in one night of spawning. The fertilized eggs are dispersed at random over rocks and gravel and fall into crevices in the stream or lake bottom where they adhere. Hundreds of thousands of eggs (as many as 600,000) may be dispersed.

The eggs hatch in 12 to 18 days on the spawning grounds, and by 10 to 15 days after hatching the young have dispersed into the upper levels of open water. By the latter part of the summer, young-of-the-year move toward the bottom. Growth is fairly rapid in the south but slower in more northerly latitudes. Females grow more quickly than males.

Juvenile and adult walleye are themselves important food sources for various predatory fish at various stages of their life. The northern pike is probably the dominant predator of the walleye over much of its range, and muskellunge will also consume adults to some degree. Adult perch, other walleye, and sauger prey on young walleye, and yellow perch, sauger, and smallmouth bass are the walleye's main competitors for food.

Food and feeding habits. The walleye can be a voracious feeder and primarily consumes other fish. The wide diet includes alewives, smelt, shad, cisco, shiners, sculpin, suckers, minnows, darters, perch, and crayfish, as well as many other items. Their diet shifts rapidly from invertebrates to fish as walleye increase in size. Some populations, even as adults, feed almost exclusively on emerging larval or adult mayflies for part of the year. The relative amounts of the various species of fish that walleye feed on apparently is determined by their availability. Yellow perch and cyprinids are particularly favored when these species are present.

Angling. In addition to being good food and fairly abundant, the walleye is popular because it is a schooling species often found in concentrations, it does not tend to be an aggressive feeder so it can be challenging to catch, and it is susceptible to a wide range of angling techniques. Although they have light-sensitive eyes that theoretically make them most active in low-light and dark conditions in many environments, they do feed during daylight hours and can be caught during the day.

Walleye abundance relates to baitfish presence and to structure. Their prey varies with the body of water, often being whatever small fish are most prevalent. The activities of the predominant food have a bearing on where walleye are located—suspended in open water, hugging the bottom along sandbars or reefs or points, waiting along weedlines, and so forth. The structure they favor includes rock reefs, sandbars, gravel bars, points, weeds, rocky or riprap causeways or shorelines, and creek channels. Walleye are particularly known for congregating in or along the edges of vegetation. Walleye weeds, for the most part, are submerged, sometimes slightly visible on or near the surface, especially in shallow water, and often deeper and out of sight. Thick clumps of weeds are preferable to scattered weeds because the former offer more cover. Fishing clumped weeds is easiest. When these are not available, scattered weeds are the second choice. Walleye often prefer shorter weeds in moderately deep water than taller weeds in the same depth. Knowledgeable walleye anglers always look for the weedline and its depth. An excellent situation, although not as readily fished, is where the weeds are thick and the edge is close to a sharp bottom dropoff. Working the edges of the weeds is particularly effective.

In some waters, particularly large lakes, walleye are also found in deep water, suspended or on the bottom where there are open, basinlike flats. Some walleye, especially big specimens and those that are likely to be feeding, do not hold to the traditional bottom and cover-providing structure; instead, they roam open water to take advantage of migratory schools of baitfish—mainly smelt and alewives—prevalent in those waters. Depending on the location of the baitfish, walleye may be in a few feet of water or in 20 to 30 feet, over a bottom that is much deeper.

Fishing presentations for walleye run the gamut, but they largely center on jigging, stillfishing or drifting with live baits, trolling with bait rigs, casting crankbaits, and trolling with plugs. Jigs are typically used with baits (leeches, minnows, and worms), although hair- and grub-bodied jigs are popular as well. Fixed and slip bobbers are used for live-bait fishing, although sometimes a jig and worm is fished below a bobber. Trolling rigs include weight-forward or June-bug–style spinners, as well as spinner-and-worm/leech harnesses, and walking or bottom-bouncing sinkers. Many walleye anglers have employed a controlled wind-drifting and boat-movement technique called backtrolling *(see)*—using a tiller-steered outboard motor or an electric motor—to keep the boat in proper position. Jigs and rigs are used and almost always fished very slowly.

Walleye anglers on big waters predominantly

A slow-trolled diving minnow plug fooled this walleye.

employ forward trolling, primarily using shallow to deep-diving plugs (and sometimes spoons). They troll them on flatlines, in-line planers, large side-planer boards, and even downriggers. The offerings are presented at precise depths for suspended and mobile walleye; locating the fish, getting to the precise depth, and having good lure action are paramount.

When walleye are spawning in rivers, other tributaries, and in shallow bays, fishing, where legal, is relatively easy. It becomes more difficult after spawning, however, when the fish migrate out of rivers and bays into main-lake structure and disperse. Throughout the summer, anglers work various forms of structure, as well as deep water. In the fall, walleye become more concentrated again and are especially found on main-lake points that are close to deep water. In large lakes, they will migrate toward the upper end where a river comes in, or to a dam end. This is a good time to prospect for bigger fish.

Walleye fishing is different in rivers than in lakes. The fish spawn throughout the same temperature range, and they migrate after spawning, although they may not go particularly far in smaller systems. In both spring and fall they may be located off the mouths of tributaries; in spring, they are drawn by spawning needs; in fall, by baitfish. They do not suspend, however, and almost always respond to bottom-oriented presentations.

In large river systems, anglers land walleye close to dams in winter and spring. At other times, they work the deep water off wing dams, island channel cuts, deep-water bridge abutments, and center-channel edges. Look for walleye along a river channel that has considerable depth as well, especially in midsummer.

Riprap is an especially favored walleye haunt in rivers, particularly in the evening and if there is deep water nearby. Other prominent locales include cuts, where currents meet each other; eddies and slicks; along and behind islands; large rocks; and the head and tail of pools. River walleye feed on assorted forage, including crayfish, hellgrammites, and minnows. They are caught by jigging, casting, and trolling with spoons, spinners, and plugs; and fishing with live baits.

Jigs are the most effective river lure, probably because they are worked close to the bottom and represent minnows or crayfish. Small and shallow rivers generally require $1/8$- to $5/8$-ounce jigs; in fast water, you should increase the weight. Fish jigs with the current; there is no need to actually jig them, and a slow rolling action is best. In spring and fall, use white, yellow, chartreuse, and silver colors; in summer, use brown, black, green, or orange-and-brown.

Live baits are also effective. A live-bait rig, weighing $1/4$ to 1 ounce and rigged with 20 inches of dropback leader and a No. 2 short-shanked hook, is a popular offering. Minnows, nightcrawlers, leeches, salamanders, waterdogs, and crayfish are used for bait, as are assorted minnows. Sinker style can be split shot, egg, or a different bottom-bouncing type.

Tackle needs for walleye in lakes and rivers are not especially complicated. Medium-action spinning rods from $5\frac{1}{2}$ to 7 feet long, and reels filled with 8- to 12-pound line, are standard. For trolling, especially when planer boards are used, longer rods and stouter gear may be necessary. Baitcasting tackle can be employed but is usually not necessary, except when using long lines off planers in rough water. Fly tackle is seldom appropriate, although fly fishing is possible when the fish are shallow and concentrated.

WALLEYE BOAT

The term "walleye boat" refers to a boat that is similar in many respects to a bass boat *(see)*. Walleyes

These anglers, on Lake Erie in Ohio, have a walleye boat that is "dressed to the nines" for big-water fishing.

can be caught from any type of craft that suits the necessary angling method and the water conditions, but so-called walleye boats are a type of craft that is popular for walleye angling in big lakes and rivers, and has evolved in part due to the wide-ranging demands of fishing tournaments. Walleye boats are not as widespread as bass boats, but are a fishing machine that is particularly functional where a lot of freshwater trolling, stillfishing, jigging, and bottom fishing is required; where presentation and boat positioning are especially important; and where fishing is done on large bodies of open water that can get rough. In truth, a so-called walleye boat is really a multi-species freshwater fishing boat that can be useful almost anywhere and used with a variety of techniques, although it is not as functional in shallow rivers.

Walleye or multi-species boats look a bit like

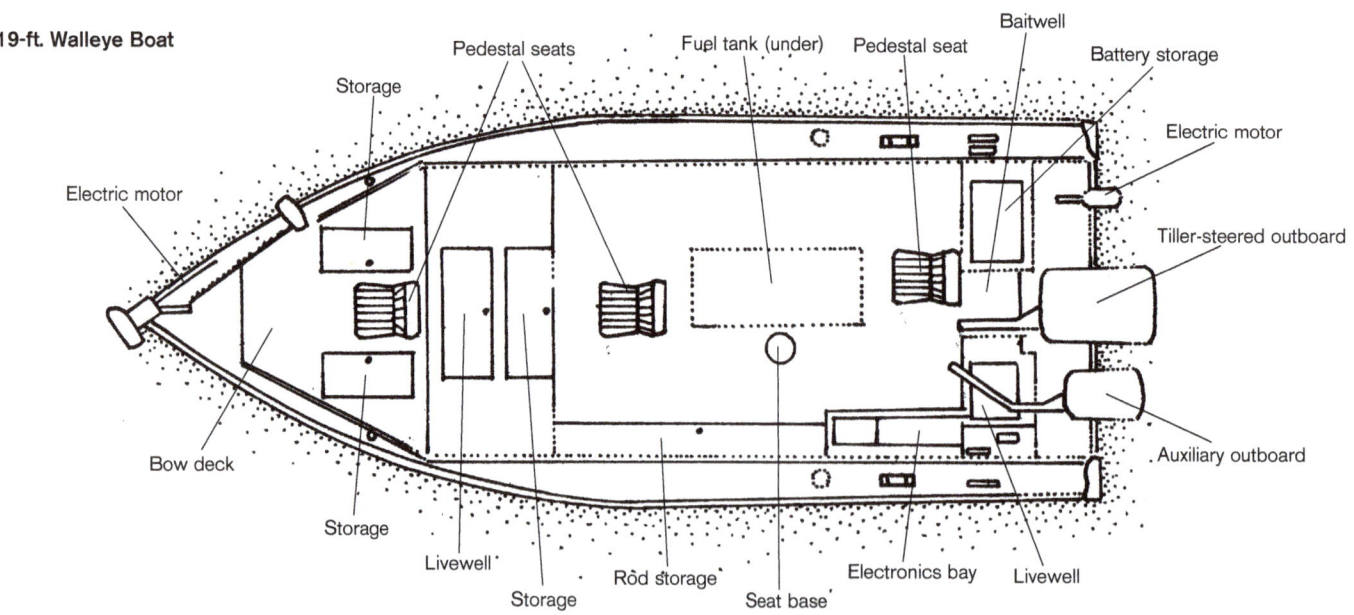

Warmouth

bass boats, but they have a deeper design and are better appointed for sustained fishing in wave-whipped water. Generally, they range from 15 to 18 feet in length, with a hull style from semi-V to deep-V, with a deeper interior design and greater freeboard than a bass boat.

Walleye boats are made of both aluminum and fiberglass, and may have tiller or console steering, although bigger versions, suited for large-horsepower motors, employ console steering. With tiller-steered models, 50- to 60-horsepower motors are standard, in part because they gear down and perform well at slow speeds for long periods of time.

Walleye boats sport many of the same features as bass boats, including high-speed bow-mounted electric motor, console and bow sonar devices, livewells, and rod and tackle storage. Some models have a baitwell in addition to a livewell, an auxiliary outboard motor on a kick-up transom bracket, a transom-mount electric motor, GPS navigational device, and possibly a platform foredeck with pedestal seating, although this is well below gunwale height. They are usually stored on a trailer for transport to and from the water.
See: Boat; Sonar; Trailer, Boat.

WALLOP-BREAUX AMENDMENT
See: Federal Aid in Sport Fish Restoration Act.

WARMOUTH *Lepomis gulosus.*
Other names—goggle-eye, openmouth, perch.

The warmouth is a member of the Centrarchidae family of sunfish *(see)* and is typically encountered by anglers fishing for other panfish *(see)* species. It has white, flaky flesh and is good table fare.

Identification. The warmouth has a deep, stout body and is olive brown above and cream to bright yellow below, often with an overall purple luster and a dark brown chainlike mottling on the back and upper sides. Dark, red brown lines extend from the back of the eye. On breeding males, there is a red orange spot on the yellow edge of the short ear flap, and there are dark brown spots and wavy bands on the fins. The warmouth has a large mouth and a patch of teeth on the tongue, and the upper jaw extends under or past the pupil of the eye. It also has a short, rounded pectoral fin and a stiff rear edge on its gill cover.

Size/Age. The warmouth can reach a weight of 1 pound and a length of 12 inches. It is capable of living for six to eight years. The all-tackle world record is a 2-pound, 7-ounce fish taken in Florida in 1985.

Distribution. Originally found in the Great Lakes and Mississippi River basins from western Pennsylvania to Minnesota and south to the Gulf of Mexico, warmouth occur in Atlantic and gulf drainages from the Rappahannock River, Virginia, to the Rio Grande in Texas and New Mexico. They are abundant in lowland areas and less common in the uplands, and they have been introduced in many places, including the lower Colorado River drainage, where they are common.

Habitat. Warmouth inhabit relatively shallow, vegetated, slow-flowing, mud-bottom creeks, ponds, lakes, swamps, and reservoirs. They are often found around weedbeds, snags, hollow trees, or stumps, and under the banks of streams and ponds.

Spawning behavior. Warmouth begin spawning from April through August when they are 3 to 4 inches long and from one to three years old.

Spawning peaks in early June, when waters warm to about 70°F. The male builds a shallow, bowl-shaped nest in water less than 5 feet deep, often in the company of others so that a small colony of nests is formed. Preferred nesting sites are in sand or rubble bottom with a thin covering of silt near patches of lily pads, cattails, and grasses, or at the base of trees standing in shallow water.

Food. Because of their large mouths, warmouth have more variety in their diet than do some of their sunfish relatives. They feed on invertebrates, small sunfish, darters, mosquitofish, crayfish, snails, freshwater shrimp, dragonflies, and other insects.

Angling. These fish are caught with standard panfishing methods.

WARMWATER FISH

A term for freshwater species whose optimum environment contains warm water, usually over 70°F, and that can tolerate warm and even turbid or poorly oxygenated water during summer; largemouth bass, various sunfish, crappie, bullhead, and catfish are among this group. They primarily inhabit warm rivers and streams and very fertile lakes and ponds, many of which are shallow.

See: Coldwater Fish; Coolwater Fish.

WASH

The disturbed water close to and immediately behind a moving boat, created by the action of the propeller; often referred to as prop wash.

WASHDOWN

The practice of cleaning fishing equipment, boats, and boat trailers with freshwater after use; this is especially important when this equipment is used in marine environments.

See: Tackle Care/Maintenance/Repair.

WASHINGTON

If angling variety is the deciding factor, then Washington ranks very highly with other states in the U.S. The Evergreen State's list of significant sportfish includes 23 freshwater, 20 saltwater, and 8 anadromous species. Some of these, in fact, have been successfully transplanted to form important fisheries elsewhere. Rainbow trout, for example, flourished in Washington lakes and streams for thousands of years before people transported them to the far corners of the earth. The Skamania steelhead that delights Great Lakes anglers is a Washington native. Chinook and coho salmon from Washington waters have been used to help establish thriving sportfisheries elsewhere as well.

Washington's angling opportunities, on the other hand, have been greatly enhanced by the introduction of several fish species from other parts of the country and the world. Shad were brought from New England in the 1870s and 1880s, largemouth bass came from Ohio and elsewhere a few years later, and smallmouth bass were imported to Washington from various places around the turn of the twentieth century. No one seems to know exactly where Washington's walleye population came from, or when, but anglers have been catching them from the Columbia River since the early 1970s.

As for places to fish, the possibilities are many and varied. As if more than 150 miles of Pacific Ocean coastline weren't enough for saltwater anglers, the 80-mile-long Strait of Juan de Fuca and the inland waterways of Puget Sound offer both marine fishing variety and protection from all but the worst of Northwest storms. Chinook, coho, and pink salmon are among the primary targets of Washington's saltwater fishing fleet, but the possibilities also include Pacific halibut to 100 pounds, ill-tempered lingcod, and many species of rockfish, flounder, sole, and saltwater perch.

Freshwater fishing is virtually unlimited in this state, which has roughly 5,100 lowland lakes and reservoirs, 2,800 high-country lakes, 140 rivers, and more than 1,600 creeks. Rainbow and cutthroat trout inhabit most of these lakes and streams, and a majority of the rivers are home to the big sea-run rainbow trout called steelhead. Anglers searching for warmwater fish don't have to look far, as largemouth and smallmouth bass, walleye, black crappie, yellow perch, brown bullhead, and other species inhabit hundreds of Washington lakes and reservoirs.

Saltwater

Pacific coast. Nothing better personifies the wild and woolly nature of the rugged northwestern United States than its sometimes stormy, always beautiful, Pacific Ocean coast. From the mouth of the Columbia River at Ilwaco to the Strait of Juan de Fuca entrance near the village of Neah Bay, Washington's 157-mile-long coastline is largely undeveloped and uninhabited, but the angling opportunities are many.

Most of the world knows this area for its salmon fishing, but salmon seasons are shorter, bag limits more conservative, and salmon fishing regulations more restrictive than they were just a few decades ago. Changes in salmon fishing, though, have led to diversification along Washington's coast, and anglers now visit the state's fishing ports in search of many important species. The chinook and coho salmon are still there, along with occasional chum and pink salmon, and anglers also catch good numbers of albacore, Pacific halibut, lingcod, sablefish, and several species of rockfish. Of the rockfish species, the black rockfish is the most abundant and is a mainstay of the coastal charter fishery, but blue, yellowtail, canary, yelloweye, and Boccaccio rockfish also are popular.

Ilwaco, near the mouth of the Columbia River in the extreme southwest corner of the state, is a point of departure for anglers headed for the open Pacific, as well as for those who stay in the Columbia River estuary to try their luck. Both charter and private-boat anglers fish here, but boaters must be alert to the strong currents and tricky bottom contours. Depending on weather and seasons, which vary from year to year, Ilwaco salmon anglers might concentrate their efforts on the open ocean, the Columbia River, or both. Chinook and coho salmon are available, and both are most commonly caught on fresh or frozen herring. August is the prime salmon fishing month in the Ilwaco area.

Interest in bottom fish begins in the spring and runs into early fall, and lingcod and various rockfish species are the most popular targets. Submerged rockpiles and ledges to the south and west of the river mouth are the most productive for bottom fishing. Ilwaco anglers also catch Pacific halibut around offshore breaklines and underwater plateaus.

The lower Columbia River is the source of spectacular sturgeon fishing, and Ilwaco provides easy access to many good sturgeon holes. White sturgeon can grow to 12 feet or longer, weigh over 500 pounds, and account for a bulk of the catch, but the smaller green sturgeon are also caught from the Columbia estuary. A slot limit protects smaller, immature sturgeon and large females.

Willapa Bay, the large estuary between the Columbia River and Grays Harbor, was long overlooked by Northwest salmon anglers. It has come into its own since the early 1990s, however, thanks to impressive returns of hatchery chinook and coho bound for the Willapa, Nemah, and Naselle Rivers, all of which empty into Willapa Bay. Anglers troll herring or flasher-and-fly combinations throughout the western end of the bay for coho, whereas many of the bigger chinook are taken on herring bounced along the bottom, right up against the beach near the bay's north entrance.

Grays Harbor is home to Westport, Washington's most well-known fishing port. Westport's famous party boat fishery had its start in the 1950s and grew to as many as 400 boats by the mid-1970s. The charter fleet is smaller now, but charter skippers who remain are among the best at what they do. For those who prefer to fish from their own boats, Westport has launch ramps, fuel docks, moorage, and other facilities, but the treacherous Grays Harbor Bar is no place for incompetent or inattentive navigators.

Salmon fishing still is a main attraction here, even though the seasons are now measured in weeks rather than months. July and August are the best months for salmon. The season for bottom fish is open year-round, but winter storms make fishing a tough proposition from October through March. Spring fishing for lingcod of 5 to 30 pounds can be very good around the many rock pinnacles and ledges to the north of Grays Harbor. Deeper waters around those same rockpiles produce yelloweye and canary rockfish, sablefish, and other bottom fish. Large schools of 1- to 3-pound black rockfish provide fast action for Westport anglers from spring through fall.

Albacore tuna cause excitement for Westport anglers nearly every summer, especially when the tuna's northward migration brings them to within 60 or 70 miles of the coast, where party boats and larger private craft can reach them. A typical August or September tuna trip is an overnight affair, and two-day trips are common. Trolling hex-head jigs on heavy tackle helps anglers locate the fish. When a school is found, the anglers swing into action with lighter outfits and single hooks baited with live anchovies. A Westport albacore trip can produce 10 fish or more per rod.

Most people fish Westport-area waters from a boat, but the area also holds a lot of promise for bank anglers. The Grays Harbor South Jetty and the six finger jetties at Westport offer year-round fishing for lingcod, black rockfish, kelp greenling, starry flounder, pike-perch, striped seaperch, and Dungeness crab. The sandy ocean beaches to the south have good numbers of redtail surfperch. The perch, flounder, and crabs will take almost any small bait fished on a No. 4 or 6 hook, but leadhead jigs with plastic grubs work better for rockfish. Larger grub bodies on a leadhead will work for the ling, or try whole herring or a live greenling fished beneath a large foam float.

Once home to several fishing resorts, LaPush is a small Indian village at the mouth of the Quillayute River. It now has only one thing to offer anglers: access to some of the most rugged coastline and most intriguing fishing spots in Washington. Salmon fishing used to be the big draw here, and it still can be very good in August. Rocky ledges and submerged pinnacles are common throughout the area, and they host to some of the largest lingcod remaining in Washington. The area also has several less-severe offshore rockpiles and underwater plateaus that hold good numbers of Pacific halibut. Nearshore coves, boulder piles, and small islands teem with schools of black, blue, and copper rockfish, kelp greenling, small lingcod, and other bottom fish well suited to light-tackle jigging or even fly fishing.

Strait of Juan de Fuca. Connecting Puget Sound to the Pacific Ocean, this 80-mile-long waterway separating the north end of Washington's Olympic Peninsula from British Columbia's Vancouver Island offers great angling variety. At the extreme northwestern tip of the Olympic Peninsula, Neah Bay provides access to excellent fishing both in the Strait of Juan de Fuca and the Pacific Ocean. The summertime fishing for chinook salmon "around the corner" on the Pacific Ocean side is legendary, and such spots as Skagway, Father and Son Rocks, and Spike Rock offer anglers a chance to fish for 40-pound salmon. A little later, usually around Labor Day, large, adult coho become the

American fisheries research first began in 1871 at Woods Hole, Massachusetts, with the creation of the U.S. Commission on Fish and Fisheries.

prime attraction, and they are often caught right on the surface with a fast-trolled streamer fly.

Halibut fishing draws thousands of anglers to Neah Bay every spring and summer. Some fish Swiftsure Bank and Blue Dot, both offshore banks 20 to 30 miles out; some try Garbage Dump and other spots closer to port where halibut are less abundant but where a better chance of hooking a barn-door fish of 100 pounds or larger may exist. Standard baits and lures in both locations include whole herring or squid fished on wire spreaders, homemade pipe jigs or metal slab-type jigs of 12 to 32 ounces, and huge leadhead jigs adorned with 8- or 10-inch plastic grub bodies.

Lingcod are another big Neah Bay attraction, especially during the spring and early summer, when adult ling are still found around the shallow-water rockpiles where they spawned earlier in the year. Huge ling of 40 pounds and larger are fairly common, but more and more anglers are releasing the big ones (which are females) to target the 10- to 15-pound males, which are better table fare. A small greenling, worked just off the bottom with a hook through the lips and another near the tail, will coax ling to hit when all else fails.

The waters around the entrance to the Strait of Juan de Fuca are famous for huge populations of black rockfish, which are found at almost any depth, depending on the food supply. When near the surface, they can be caught on light spinning tackle and 4- or 6-pound line, and will take virtually any bait, lure, or fly thrown in their direction.

About 12 miles east of Neah Bay lies Sekiu, pronounced "CQ," which offers a slightly toned-down version of the angling potpourri found farther west. Salmon, halibut, and lingcod are the primary draws, but shoreline kelp beds also hold fair numbers of rockfish, greenling, and various smaller game. In the summer of each odd-numbered year, Sekiu is also a staging area for anglers in search of pink salmon, the smallest of the five Pacific salmon species but the most abundant when it makes its biennial appearance. Trolling near the surface with small wobbling plugs or spoons in pink, orange, or red accounts for the best catches of pink salmon, or humpies, as they're often known.

The odd-year pink salmon runs are also big news farther east, where anglers depart from boat ramps in Freshwater Bay, Port Angeles, and Sequim (pronounced "Skwim"). These areas provide fair fishing for chinook and coho salmon, as well as for halibut. There is good spring fishing for lingcod here. Sequim is also a point of departure for anglers fishing several productive banks near the east end of the Strait of Juan de Fuca. Hein, Middle, and Eastern Banks are the best known, especially for late-winter chinook salmon, and spring lingcod and halibut fishing.

San Juan Islands. One of the Northwest's most beautiful fishing destinations, the San Juans have been loved to death by anglers in search of bottom fish. Trophy lingcod and yelloweye rockfish, and huge schools of quillback rockfish, once made these islands near the U.S./Canada border a can't-miss destination, but too many people got too good at the game, and fish managers were slow to respond. Now, lingcod regulations are extremely restrictive, and it's a little tough to find an underwater rockpile with a good population of rockfish.

On the bright side, salmon fishing in the San Juans remains good, and the variety is some of the best in Washington. Chinook are available here year-round, and the west side of San Juan Island is one of the state's better summertime spots for kings in the 15- to 30-pound class. Fishing is good for blackmouth (immature, resident chinook) all winter throughout the islands, but the east and west sides of Orcas Island and the east side of Blakely Island are among the favorite spots for blackmouth. Fishing for coho and odd-year pink salmon is excellent during the summer. Even sockeye salmon pass through the islands on their way to British Columbia's Fraser River, and lucky anglers pick off some of these delicious fish.

Puget Sound. Salmon fishing is a year-round activity throughout much of this inland waterway, along whose shores more than 60 percent of the state's population lives. From Admiralty Inlet on the north to Hood Canal on the west and down to Anderson Island at the south end, Puget Sound has dozens of productive salmon fishing spots.

Resident chinook salmon—known locally as blackmouth because of the black gumline that helps distinguish them from other salmon species—are especially popular. Among the top blackmouth fishing area in the sound, from north to south, are Port Townsend's Mid-Channel Bank, Possession Point (south end of Whidbey Island), Point No Point (northeast corner of the Kitsap Peninsula), Point Jefferson (east side of the Kitsap Peninsula), Manchester (northeast of Bremerton), Point Defiance/Point Dalco (just north of Tacoma), and Anderson Island and Johnson Point (both near Olympia). Trolling with flasher-and-fly or flasher-and-squid rigs, mooching with whole or plug-cut herring, and jigging with any of several baitfish-imitating metal jigs are productive blackmouth fishing techniques, and the key usually is to fish within a few feet of bottom in 80 to 200 feet of water.

Puget Sound's salmon fishing variety improves in late summer, when adult chinook and coho begin returning from the Pacific. Pink salmon add to the possibilities during odd-numbered years, especially in the northern third of the sound. By mid-October, the chinook and pinks have entered the rivers where they started their lives, but there are still coho to be caught in saltwater. That's when chum salmon, the second largest and hardest-fighting of the five Pacific salmon, make their appearance. Although somewhat difficult to catch in saltwater, chums provide good fishing when they congregate in the estuaries and lower portions of

Smallmouth bass fishing on the Columbia River.

most Puget Sound rivers, where they favor small, sparsely tied green flies or little tufts of green nylon yarn on a No. 2 or 4 hook. The most popular chum fishery of all is near the Hood Canal Salmon Hatchery, at the town of Hoodsport.

Freshwater

Columbia River system. Draining nearly three-quarters of the state, the Columbia River and its many tributaries constitute not only Washington's largest river system, but the second largest river system in the country. The Columbia flows north to south, to bisect eastern Washington all the way from the British Columbia border to Oregon, then turns west to comprise most of the Washington-Oregon border. All that water provides plenty of angling opportunity for a wide range of freshwater and anadromous species.

The Columbia River system was once the world's top salmon producer, and even though hydroelectric dams, careless agricultural practices, overfishing, and other abuses have taken their toll, at certain times and in certain places salmon fishing can range from good to excellent.

Spring-run chinook salmon return to hatcheries on several lower Columbia tributaries from April through June, and these "springers" are a favorite of Washington anglers. The Cowlitz River from Longview upstream to the salmon hatchery near Salkum has long been a top spring chinook spot, and the North Fork Lewis River is another good bet. Farther up the Columbia, good springer fishing exists around the mouths of the Wind, Little White Salmon, Big White Salmon, and Klickitat Rivers. Trolling various diving plugs and spinners or bouncing large roe clusters along the bottom are the preferred fishing techniques.

Fall-run chinook also inhabit the Columbia, and the techniques that work for springers also are effective for fall fish. Fall chinook anglers congregate in dozens of places along the lower 250 miles of the Columbia, from its mouth to Kennewick. They especially gather around the mouths of major tributary streams, but one of the best fisheries occurs some 300 miles from the ocean, along the last free-flowing section of the river, known as the Hanford Reach. Anglers here commonly catch fall kings of 30 to 50 pounds, and even bigger fish are possible.

The steelhead trout is another sea-run favorite of Columbia River anglers, and there's a steelhead fishery happening somewhere on the main river or several of its tributaries throughout the year. Boaters find good summer and early fall steelheading on the lower Columbia around Camas and Washougal and also in McNary Pool and some of the other reservoirs behind main-stem dams. Bank anglers do well casting from the east side of the Columbia in the Ringold area upstream from Richland. As for the tributaries, the Elochoman, Cowlitz, Lewis, Washougal, Klickitat, Wenatchee, and Methow all are well-known steelhead producers.

White sturgeon thrive throughout the Columbia-Snake River system and have enjoyed increasing popularity over the past decade or two. The lower 200 miles of the Columbia is especially popular with sturgeon anglers. They anchor smelt, shad, shrimp, and other baits to the bottom in areas of moderate current and wait for one of the big bottom feeders to come along. A slot limit protects small and large fish, but many anglers enjoy catching and releasing the bigger females, some of which measure 8 to 12 feet and larger. These large fish often jump when hooked.

American shad were released on the West Coast a century ago, and a shad run of several million fish now occurs in the Columbia every summer. Some of the best shad angling occurs immediately downstream from Bonneville Dam in June.

Walleye began to appear in the Columbia River system around 1970, and now the river and some of its impoundments support good walleye fisheries. Lake Roosevelt (the pool behind Grand Coulee Dam), nearby Banks Lake, Rufus Woods Lake (behind Chief Joseph Dam), all three lower river reservoirs, and the free-flowing portion of the Columbia below Bonneville Dam are all good walleye fisheries.

The Columbia also offers smallmouth bass, especially in the Hanford Reach, in Lake Celilo (Dalles Dam), and in Lake Wallula (McNary Dam). The Columbia, in fact, produces trophy smallmouths; a state-record 8-pound, 12-ounce bronzeback was caught from the Hanford Reach.

The Snake River, the largest tributary to the Columbia, provides even better smallmouth fishing and is also home to a thriving fall and winter steelhead fishery. Channel catfish also are abundant in the Snake, and the catch-and-release fishery for white sturgeon has been a big draw here for decades.

Another important Columbia tributary, the Yakima River, has a little of everything to offer anglers, from its blue-ribbon trout fishing between the towns of Ellensburg and Yakima to the channel catfish and crappie in the lower reaches. Between the two exists an excellent winter fishery for mountain whitefish, and good smallmouth bass angling.

West-side steelhead streams. Big rainbow trout start their lives in freshwater; migrate to the Pacific to feed, grow, and become belligerent; then return to their natal river as 5- to 25-pound trophies. Such fish are the favorites of about 100,000 Washingtonians as well as visiting anglers from all over the world. Luckily for all those anglers, dozens of rivers here offer opportunities to try their luck whenever the steelhead bug bites them. The best of those steelhead streams are in western Washington, where there is always plenty of rain to keep the rivers flowing and the steelhead runs moving.

The Steelhead rivers flowing into the Pacific from the west side of the Olympic Peninsula are among the most famous in the world. Near the north end of the Peninsula is the Quillayute system, which includes the Bogachiel, Sol Duc, and Calawah Rivers. All three are favorites of river guides, private-boat anglers, and bank anglers alike; and all do well, thanks to generous plants from the system's hatchery facilities. Winter-run steelhead are the big draw, but summer steelies also are available.

It's the same scenario on the Hoh and Queets Rivers to the south, except that the fishing pressure may be a little lighter on these rivers. Even farther down the coast, the Quinault River is perhaps the best of the bunch. Anglers can fish the lower Quinault only with a tribal fishing guide. The Humptulips, Satsop, and Wynoochee Rivers, all of which eventually flow into Grays Harbor, are good possibilities for winter steelhead, and the Wynoochee also offers fair to good summer steelheading.

The crowds are bigger on steelhead streams flowing into Puget Sound, but the fishing, especially for winter-run steelies, can be quite good for hatchery steelhead, especially from December through early February. The Skagit River is the biggest and one of the best known, but good fishing is also available on the (from north to south) Stillaguamish, Skykomish, Snoqualmie, Green, and Puyallup Rivers.

Drift fishing is the most widely practiced steelhead-fishing technique. This entails casting slightly upstream and using just enough weight on the line to bounce a bait or lure along the bottom, moving with the current. Other possibilities include casting weighted spinners and wobbling spoons, working diving plugs along the bottom, and drifting leadhead jigs beneath floats.

Western Washington lakes. A large percentage of the more than 2,000 lakes on the west side of Washington's Cascade Mountains are open to year-round fishing, but that doesn't stop some 300,000 anglers from turning out for the traditional "opening day" on the fourth Saturday of April every year. If you like crowds, that's the day to fish. Otherwise, it's a good idea to check the annual regulations pamphlet and hit the water some other day, either earlier or later in the year, depending on the season details for the particular lake.

Rainbow trout are the biggest draw for western Washington anglers, and the State Department of Fish and Wildlife stocks well over a million hatchery rainbows every year in west-side lakes alone to help meet the demand. Most are pan-size trout, planted in the spring, but a few lakes receive fall plants of fingerlings that tend to provide bigger trout for anglers over the long term.

Some of the top rainbow lakes, in terms of both popularity and catch, are Whatcom County's Padden and Silver Lakes; San Juan County's Cascade and Mountain Lakes; Skagit County's Erie, Pass, and McMurray Lakes; Clallam County's Lake Sutherland; Jefferson County's Anderson Lake; Grays Harbor County's Duck and Failor Lakes; King County's North Lake and Lake Wilderness; Pierce County's Silver and Tanwax Lakes; Thurston County's Clear

The St. Johns River in Florida, long renowned for its largemouth bass, is also one of the few rivers in the United States that flows north.

Lake; Lewis County's Mineral Lake; and Mason County's Phillips, Spencer, and Price's Lakes. More and more west-side lakes also are stocked with hatchery brown trout, and many contain small populations of native cutthroat trout as well.

Although not recognized as a world hotbed of bass fishing action, western Washington does have some good bass lakes, and both largemouth and smallmouth bass are available. Some of the best largemouth waters are Big Lake in Skagit County; Lake Stevens in Snohomish County; King County's Lake Sawyer; Mason Lake in Mason County; Pierce County's Lake Kapowsin; Thurston County's Black Lake; Silver Lake in Cowlitz County; and Lacamas Lake in Clark County. Western Washington's best smallmouth lake is King County's Lake Sammamish.

Anglers willing to hike into the high country of the Cascade Range and the Olympic Mountains may choose from among some 1,500 fishable lakes that most anglers never see. The bulk of these high lakes (located at 2,500 feet of elevation or higher) hold trout, thanks to the efforts of State Department of Fish and Wildlife personnel and volunteers who pack trout fry and fingerlings on their backs to stock these waters. Some high lakes contain rainbows, some cutthroats, some brookies, and still others golden trout.

Eastern Washington lakes. Although western Washington hosts lots of trout, the drier two-thirds of the state east of the Cascade Range has some of Washington's best trout waters. Okanogan County's Wannacut, Spectacle, Conconully, and Chopaka Lakes draw rainbow trout anglers from throughout the Pacific Northwest. Douglas County, a little farther south, has only two significant lakes, but both are famous for their trout fishing; Jameson Lake is a top rainbow producer, and Grimes Lake offers excellent fly fishing for Lahontan cutthroats to 8 pounds. Yakima County's Wenas Lake has both husky rainbows and trophy-class browns. Farther east, Waitts Lake in Stevens County, Lincoln County's Fishtrap Lake, and Spokane County's Medical and West Medical Lakes all provide excellent fishing for big rainbows.

The best place to fish for trout in all of Washington, though, might be Grant County, right in the center of the state. Some of that county's prime trout waters include Dry Falls, Blue, Park, Perch, Lenice, Nunnally, and Merry Lakes, all of which have big rainbows, or Lake Lenore, where Lahontan cutthroats grow to 7 or 8 pounds.

Some lakes offer even larger game. Lake trout, known as mackinaws by most Washington anglers, grow to 30 pounds here and are available in several eastern Washington lakes. The best mackinaw lakes include Chelan in Chelan County, Loon and Deer Lakes in Stevens County, and Bead Lake in Pend Oreille County.

Largemouth and smallmouth bass, walleye, crappie, bluegills, and other warmwater fish also inhabit many east-side lakes. Again, Grant County is a leader, offering such possibilities as Banks Lake (largemouth and smallmouth bass and walleye), Potholes Reservoir (largemouths, smallmouths, walleye, black crappie, yellow perch, and bluegills), Moses Lake (largemouths, walleye, and bluegills), and Soda Lake (crappie and perch).

Spokane County's Eloika Lake also offers a mixed bag of warmwater angling ranging from bluegills to largemouths. But for shear variety it's hard to beat Sprague Lake, located near the town of Sprague. Here you'll find largemouth and smallmouth bass, walleye, bluegills, crappie, and channel catfish; their presence is the result of an extensive rehabilitation project that reclaimed the lake from hordes of carp in the mid-1980s.

WATER CLARITY

Water clarity, or transparency, in both freshwater and saltwater ranges from crystal clear to muddy; it is most likely to be turbid in large rivers and in lakes and ponds, where runoff, tributaries, erosion, plankton blooms, and various factors influence the transparency of water.

Biologists measure clarity or transparency by lowering a circular black-and-white plate called a secchi disk into the water to the depth at which the disk just disappears. At this depth, approximately 95 percent of sunlight has been eliminated because of shading from particles in the water; a small amount of light can penetrate two to three times this depth.

Clear water is generally more productive than muddy water for sight-feeding fish and for most aquatic life; muddy water is best suited to species that feed primarily through sense of feel or smell. If clear water is classified (as it is by some biologists) as having visibility over 30 inches, this water may be many times more productive for certain species, such as bass and bluegills, for example, than water with only 5 to 6 inches of visibility.

Water clarity is a factor in angling, both in the sense of where to locate some species as well as how to fish for them. However, the clarity of freshwater varies markedly from one lake to another and even varies in a particular lake through the course of the fishing season. Using largemouth bass in freshwater lakes as an example will illustrate this.

In North America, many of the larger lakes and reservoirs in northern areas are reasonably clear. Light penetrates deep there, and bass either are well secured in what thick cover might exist or are more likely deep enough to avoid the discomfort of light. In such waters, you can see a brightly colored lure 6 or more feet below the surface. Here, bass tend to be spooky, and a refined fishing presentation, using small- to moderate-size lures and light line, is very beneficial. Other waters may be blue-green colored and allow visibility for 3 to 6 feet below the water's surface. Such a condition is considered very clear by many Southern anglers, who never see the ultraclear waters of mountain-region lakes.

Many bass waters are more off-colored, however, allowing limited visibility. This is the only type of condition some anglers see, and it does not require such a stealthy approach or use of light line as clearer waters do. Muddy, milky, slate gray, and tea-colored water is common in many reservoirs after heavy rains; farmland runoff, sediment from tributaries, and bank erosion cause this condition. You may be able to see a light-colored lure if it is only a few inches below the surface. In some large lakes, only the upper ends are affected like this, and the lower ends remain relatively unchanged, or at least unaffected for several days. In still other bass waters, particularly in Florida, the high tannic acid content gives the lake a blackish brown tint.

In highly turbid waters, where visibility is limited, bass are likely to be relatively shallow and holding tight to cover, especially in the early part of the season and when water temperatures are not excessively high. Turbid water can be good for bass fishing success because of the nature of this fish; certain types of lures, such as big spinnerbaits, crankbaits with good vibration qualities, and noisy surface baits, are well suited to angling under these conditions because they appeal more to the bass's sense of sound than to its vision.

Naturally the clarity of any given water is important to the color of lures that are fished, and this is also intertwined with issues pertaining to depth and the intensity of the light.
See: Finding Fish; Lure.

Major fluctuations in sea level and climate eons ago are believed to have been responsible for the extinction of many ancient fish species, as well as the evolution of present fishes

WATER FLEA
See: Daphnia; Spiny Water Flea.

WATERLINE
(1) That section of the boat's hull that intersects the water's surface; also a painted line separating the hull and topsides of a boat, or a painted line that depicts the point to which a properly loaded boat sinks in the water.

(2) The horizontal line on a shore or bank that reflects maximum high-water level. In areas that are regularly flooded, because of high water or tides, there is an identifiable band on tree trunks, bushes, vegetation, and rocks that serves as a high-water mark. In some places, especially rivers, this line is accompanied by brush and debris in the trees at the waterline. In rivers, periodic water releases from dams may cause sudden fluctuations in water level; anglers wading downstream in such places need to observe this waterline in order to retreat to safety if there is a sudden surge of rising water.

WATERSHED
An area of land from which water drains to a given point, usually a larger body of water. Smaller watersheds make up larger watersheds, creating a series of watersheds, which is known as a drainage basin *(see: drainage).*

WATERSPOUT
A waterspout is a spinning, funnel-shaped column of water pulled up by a whirling wind from the surface of the ocean, resembling a tornado. Waterspouts are formed in humid, hot, tropical air, though they are sometimes found in more middle latitudes. They do not last long if they move over land.
See: Safety.

WAVES
For the most part, waves are generated by friction created by wind blowing over the water surface. This includes the ripples on a creek or pond, the crests and troughs that run across a lake, the rhythmic pounding of surf against the beach, and the rolling of swells in the open ocean. Generically these are called wind waves. There are other types of waves, such as tsunamis, which are very long waves produced by seismic disturbance, and internal waves, which are waves that occur within the sea rather than at the surface, but these types of waves are seldom encountered by anglers.

Waves are a common fact of life for all open-water anglers. They have a great bearing on boating and boat manipulation in saltwater and freshwater, and they interact with currents and with tidal movement. They can have significance for angling, especially when trolling and drifting activities are influenced by the height or frequency of waves, and especially for those fishing from beach, shore, jetty, or pier. It is therefore useful to understand how waves work, whether for safety, general boating, or varied angling reasons.

Height and length. Wind waves, tsunamis, and internal waves are all considered progressive waves; they appear to progress in a definite direction. The other major wave type is called a standing wave because it appears to oscillate without forward movement. All progressive waves have similar characteristics in form and motion. They have crests and troughs, with the vertical distance between the two called the wave height, and the horizontal distance between crests called the wave length. The wave period is the time it takes for two consecutive wave crests to pass a given point. The speed of a wave's travel can be calculated by dividing the wave length by the wave period.

Wind waves begin as ripples or capillary waves formed as the water surface is deformed by variation in wind pressure. Thus, ripples provide surface roughness necessary for the wind to push the water into larger waves. Ripples disappear almost immediately if the wind dies. However, with continued wind, ripples grow into larger, steeper crested waves. As long as energy is supplied, waves will continue to develop. Once formed, waves persist for a while even after the wind ceases, but the steepness decreases and, in the ocean or large inland lakes, the waves become "swells." Swells can travel thousands of miles without losing much energy.

Speed. The size of waves is dependent on the speed of the wind that formed them, the duration that the wind blew, and the fetch (the length of water surface over which the wind blows in a constant direction). For example, if the wind is blowing across a barrier island toward the mainland at a constant speed, the water in the lee of the island will be relatively free of waves, while that on the opposite side of the sound will have large waves because the winds will have acted across a greater distance of water surface. Given the wind speed, duration, and fetch, it is possible to predict the size of the waves generated by a given storm. Conversely, wind speed at sea can be estimated by the wave conditions produced. This relationship is presented in the Beaufort scale, which assigns numbers that correlate to specific wind speeds and sea conditions from calm to hurricane.

A summary of lesser conditions of wind speed in miles per hour and sea conditions is as follows:

Under 1	Calm; mirrorlike sea
1–3	Light air; ripples with scalelike appearance, no foam crests
4–7	Light breeze; small wavelets, crests glassy and not breaking
8–12	Gentle breeze; large wavelets, crests begin to break with scattered whitecaps
13–18	Moderate breeze; small waves (to 4 feet high) becoming longer, more whitecaps
19–24	Fresh breeze; moderate waves (to 8 feet high) taking longer form, many whitecaps and some spray
25–31	Strong breeze; larger waves (to 13 feet high), whitecaps everywhere and more spray.
32–38	Near gale; sea heaps up (to 20 feet), white foam from breaking waves blows in streaks

Most anglers, especially in freshwater, overestimate the height of winds and thus the size of waves that they see or encounter. Nevertheless, most small boaters are off the water when waves are at the 4-foot stage, especially in freshwater, either for personal comfort or for safety, and should not be on the water under fresh breeze conditions. Many large boats do not stay out under the latter conditions. Strong winds have the ability to quickly move sea conditions right up this scale, so anglers in boats should be watching wave and sea conditions for changes, in order to make appropriate moves to shelter in a timely manner. Regardless of wave height, when whitecaps become increasingly prominent, it's time to evaluate the situation. When there's spray on the tops of waves, you probably should be heading for port or not far from it, because the sea will likely keep building. Using a VHF radio *(see)* or weather radio to be forewarned of advancing conditions is a good idea.

Motion. Two types of motion are associated with waves: that of the wave form and that of the water particles. It is important to realize that waves transport only energy, not water. Thus, the wave form moves across miles of sea, but the water does not. Storms make waves of different wave lengths. Since waves travel at different speeds, the longer waves move out ahead of the shorter waves. Long waves may even run ahead of the storm itself. Long, low waves crashing on a beach often warn of approaching storms.

Individual water particles in a wave travel in circular orbits with diameters (at the surface) equal to the wave height. These water particle orbits get smaller with depth but are still measurable at depths of about one-half the wave length.

In deep water, surface waves with long wave lengths travel faster than those with shorter wave lengths. Shorter wave lengths may be encountered in shallow bodies of water and may cause bumpy riding, as boats bounce and plow through them. If large waves with steep troughs are generated in shallow areas, they can be very dangerous for boaters, especially in places with reefs or bars; being in a trough might cause the boat to bottom out.

In water shallower than half the wave length, waves begin to drag along the bottom. The circular motion of the water particles becomes flattened. The bottom of the wave moves more slowly than the top, causing the wave to steepen, become unstable, and eventually "break" on the beach. Water from a breaking wave running up a beach is known as "swash." After dissipating its energy

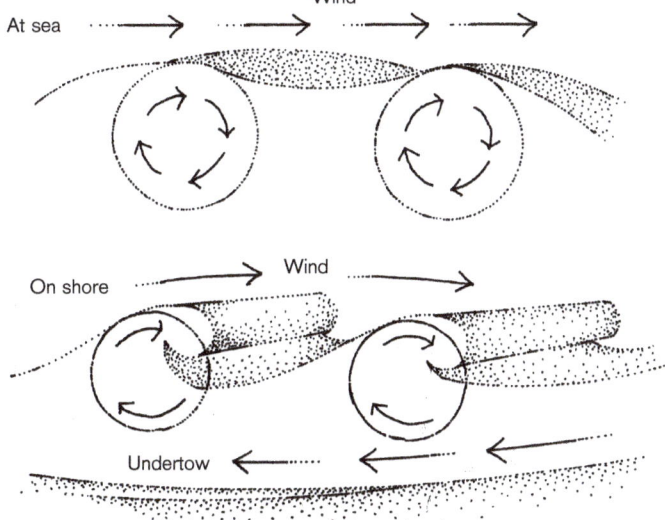

The effect of wind in creating waves is different at sea than on shore.

on the beach, the swash runs back down the beach and under the next breaker producing a flow often called "undertow." This back and forth motion of the swash stirs up sand and sediment.

Breakers occur as several types. Spilling breakers are over-steepened waves in which the unstable top spills down the front of the wave as it travels toward the beach. Spilling breakers occur on relatively flat beaches and are good for surfing. Plunging breakers are more spectacular. The wave crest curls over,

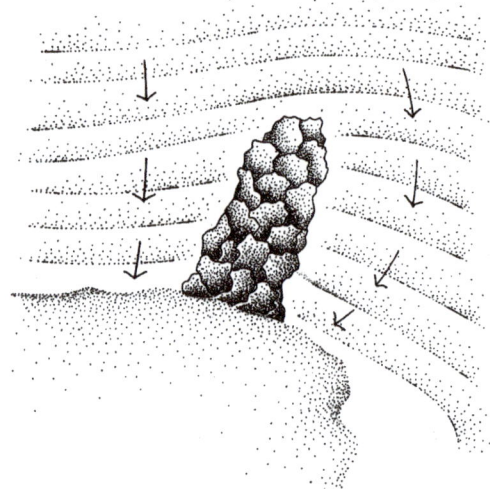

The bending of waves, called diffraction, is evident in this depiction of how waves approach a shoreline at either side of an angled jetty.

forming a large air pocket. When the wave breaks, there is usually a large splash of water and foam. These waves are even better for surfing, and they occur on steeper beaches.

In shallow water, long waves travel at the same speed as short waves, but the speed of all waves slows as water depth decreases. If one part of a wave is in deeper water than another part, the shallow water section will slow down and the wave crest will bend. Although most waves approach the beach at an angle, the influence of the bottom causes waves to refract toward the beach. Refraction results in waves with crests almost parallel to the shoreline. Wave refraction causes wave energy to be concentrated on a headland because the crests on either side bend so that the energy of the wave is dissipated along a greater distance of the coast. Wave diffraction occurs when waves bend around objects, such as when they move past a barrier into a harbor; wave reflection occurs when waves strike objects, like a seawall, with the most reflection happening when the wave is at a right angle to the object.

Waves are also the originators of two types of currents: the longshore current and the rip current. The longshore current is caused by waves that approach the shore at an angle. As these waves break, they move water and sand grains along the beach in the direction of their travel. This longshore transport exists in the surf zone where waves are breaking. Longshore current is responsible for much of the erosion on barrier islands. Attempts to stop longshore sand transport, such as with jetties and groins, usually result in deposition in one area coupled with increased erosion in another.

Rip currents are localized seaward flows of water from the surf zone. They occur when wave action forces more water into the surf zone than can escape by normal swash run back. As a result, the excess water accumulates and eventually flows seaward in a strong localized current, which can be dangerous to swimmers, who are carried seaward. Such rip currents occur when longshore currents converge in a bay, where water builds up as breakers coming across an underwater sandbar, or where some barrier obstructs longshore currents. Discolored water due to suspended sand, premature steepening of the waves, and accumulation of foam at the head of the rip are signs to watch for.
See: Boat; Jetty Fishing; Surf Fishing.

WAXWORM
See: Maggot.

WAYPOINT
A specific location, as represented by latitude and longitude coordinates, stored in the memory of an electronic navigational device such as GPS or Loran.
See: GPS; Loran.

WEAKFISH *Cynoscion regalis.*
Other names—squeteague, common weakfish, northern weakfish, common seatrout, northern seatrout, gray trout, summer trout, tiderunner, yellowfin, weakie; French: *acoupa royal;* Portuguese: *pescada-amarela;* Spanish: *corvinata real.*

The weakfish is a member of the Sciaenidae family (drum and croaker), named for drumming noises made by their swim bladder. The name "weakfish" refers to the tender, easily torn membrane in the fish's mouth, not its fighting ability. It is the gamest of the *Cynoscion* species in North America, striking hard and making one or two strong runs after being hooked.

The weakfish is highly sought, although it experiences dramatic fluctuation in stocks. When abundant, it is a popular gamefish. Commercial overfishing, especially in the Carolinas, however, has had drastic impacts on the overall biomass of this species, and recreational fishing for this species throughout much of the 1990s was extremely poor. Larger fish have been particularly scarce.

The meat of weakfish is white, tender, and moist and has an excellent flavor. The skin is usually left on during cooking to hold the meat together, and the bones are easily removed once the meat is cooked. It does not keep well, so it must be stored properly upon capture and prepared for consumption soon afterward.

Identification. Weakfish are considered a beautiful fish by many anglers. Their body is slim and shaped somewhat like a trout's. The lower jaw projects beyond the upper jaw. There are two large, protruding canine teeth in the upper jaw, and no chin barbels. The first dorsal fin has 10 spines, and the second has 1 spine and 26 to 29 soft rays. The anal fin has 2 spines and 11 to 12 rays. Its coloring is dark olive or greenish to greenish blue on the dorsal surface, and blue, green, purple, and lavender with a golden tinge on the sides. Numerous small black spots speckle the top, sometimes forming wavy diagonal lines. There is sometimes a black margin on the tip of the tongue.

The weakfish is distinguished from the closely related spotted seatrout *(see: seatrout, spotted)* because its spots do not extend onto the tail or the second dorsal fin, and are not as widely spaced. The scales also do not extend onto the fins on the weakfish.

Size/Age. This species' average size varies with locale. In southerly U.S. waters, weakfish tend to be smaller on average, generally 1 to 4 pounds. In the upper mid-Atlantic, they typically weigh 4 to 7 pounds on average. Their weight will also vary according to relative abundance. The all-tackle record is 19 pounds, 2 ounces (shared by fish from New York and Delaware), and the maximum possible growth is believed to be higher, as larger fish from commercial catches have been reported. Weakfish of 15 inches in length are between 3 and 5 years old, and those of 24-inch length are 9 to 12 years old. The average life span is roughly 10 years, but some weakfish reportedly live twice that long.

Distribution. Weakfish inhabit the western Atlantic Ocean from Florida to Massachusetts, and records show isolated populations occurring as far north as Nova Scotia. They are most abundant from North Carolina to Florida in the winter, and from Delaware to New York in the summer.

A weakfish from the northern New Jersey shore.

Habitat. Preferring sandy and sometimes grassy bottoms, weakfish are usually found in shallow waters along shores and in large bays and estuaries, including salt marsh creeks and sometimes into river mouths, although they do not enter freshwater. They can be found in depths of up to 55 fathoms in the winter.

Life history/Behavior. Mature weakfish are three to four years old. Spawning occurs in the nearshore and estuarine zones along the coast from May through October. The eggs drift on the surface and hatch within two days. A schooling species, weakfish migrate northward in the spring, spending the summer inshore, then moving southward again in late autumn.

Food and feeding habits. Weakfish are omnivorous and feed on crabs, shrimp, other crustaceans, and mollusks. They also consume small fish like herring, menhaden, silversides, killifish, and butterfish, which are caught in midwater levels or near the surface. Because of their varied diet, weakfish forage at different levels and adapt to local food conditions, feeding at the surface or deeper as necessary. Many anglers believe that weakfish and bluefish

Weakfish

cannot share the same habitat, the voracious blues eating the fry and food of the less-aggressive weakfish and driving them out of the area. Indeed, in past periods of abundance of both these species, the mid- to late-summer arrival of large numbers of bluefish seemed to coincide with a disappearance of weakfish.

Angling. With such a broad diet and feeding range, weakfish are susceptible to an equally wide variety of angling methods, lures, and baits. Drifting or stillfishing with an assortment of live or dead baits is extremely popular. The most common natural baits for weakfish are shrimp, squid, shedder or peeler crabs, worms, eels, mullet, and other small fish, or pieces of such fish as mackerel or bunker. Chumming is also effective, especially with a grass shrimp mix, ground up fish, or conglomerations of fish, shrimp, clams, and the like.

Jigging with metal jigs, grubs, or bucktail jigs garnished with a plastic worm body is also a favorite method, again either drifting in a boat or anchored. Bucktail jigs, usually garnished with a soft-action tail or with a strip of squid or other bait, are highly favored lures, as are leadhead jigs with soft bodies. The latter come in many effective varieties and are also often tipped with a piece of squid or shrimp. Other lures include spoons, tube lures, diamond jigs, and surface and shallow-running plugs. Trolling with plugs and spoons is another technique, although shore fishing, from the surf and by wading, or by casting from piers and jetties, is just as effective. Casting with plugs or streamer flies is usually done when the fish are fairly shallow, and in bays and estuary environs.

Weakfish will move into brackish water, and the shallow bay areas of estuaries is a common hangout, particularly in brackish rivers or creeks. In the northerly parts of their range, weakfish are seldom taken deeper than 20 feet in bays or open-water areas.

They will move onto shoals in schools to feed, and concentrate around oyster bars, bridges, and inlet jetties. Anglers should especially focus on structure and edges to locate weakfish, including such places as a channel in a shallow bay; a slough, cut, or trough in the surf; the edge of a tide rip, flat, and dropoff; deep holes in a bay; and along a sandbar. In daytime, these fish will usually hold deeper than at night or in low light.

Once weakfish are located in a given spot, it is a good bet that they will be there the following day as well but an hour later, taking into consideration the change in the timing of the tides. Areas that attract weakfish usually continue to do so until a weather change moves the fish, or until something else occurs to affect the site. When the fish are abundant, the same places will produce year after year unless the structures themselves are changed due to some phenomenon.

Light to medium spinning or baitcasting tackle is usually just right; weakfish are able fighters, but a lot of line capacity isn't necessary, and there's fun to be had by using ultralight gear and fine line. Small-boat anglers commonly use 6- to 12-pound line, often on standard freshwater tackle. Slightly heavier gear (15- to 20-pound line and comparable outfits) can be employed for trolling and also for surf fishing. Boat anglers don't need as long a rod as those fishing from shore. Tackle for party boat weakfishing runs to the heavier side, as other species may be encountered, lots of people are on board, and light tackle becomes more problematic in this situation.

WEAKFISH, ACOUPA *Cynoscion acoupa.*
Other names—French: *acoupa toeroe;* Portuguese: *pescada-amarela, pescada-ticupá;* Spanish: *corvinata amarilla.*

The acoupa weakfish is a member of the Sciaenidae family (drum and croaker), named for drumming noises made by their swim bladder. The name "weakfish" refers to the tender, easily torn membrane in the fish's mouth, not its fighting ability.

It occurs in the western Atlantic from Panama to Argentina and is abundant along the Brazilian coast. It generally inhabits muddy or sand bottoms near river mouths and feeds on shrimp and fish. Juveniles are restricted to brackish- or freshwater environs.

The acoupa weakfish is similar in appearance to the weakfish *(see)* of North America, although found in considerably larger sizes. It is a popular food fish and sportfish, and is highly respected by anglers.

The maximum size of acoupa weakfish has been reported at 43 inches and 29 pounds; the common length is 18 inches. The all-tackle record is a Brazilian fish of 29 pounds, 5 ounces, caught in Guanabara Bay near Río de Janeiro in 1997; in the late 1990s, various specimens exceeding 25 pounds were caught in Brazil.

WEATHER
Obviously anglers are affected by weather every time they go fishing. The extent to which fish are affected by the weather has been a source of uncertainty and speculation for ages. Some elements of weather are known to have certain general effects on fish, but there is no clear scientific proof, nor is there solid evidence that all fish are affected in the same way; if anything, it may be just the opposite. Freshwater species, for example, are more adversely impacted by exceptional weather events than saltwater fish, and deep dwellers seem less affected by most weather than residents of shallow environs.

Certainly some elements of weather are most significant because they impair fishing techniques or angler effectiveness. And some types of weather evidently affect the personal comfort of anglers more than they do the fish, since the majority of fishing is done when conditions are most suitable to humans. Yet, fishing is a four-season sport, and the entire gamut of weather possibilities can come into play for different anglers in different geographical areas.

Weather plays a major role not only in actual fishing activities, but also in boating. This is especially true on large bodies of water, when great distances are traveled by boats, and in places where storms are likely to occur. Weather events can imply safety concerns, which is a far greater issue than how the weather affects fish or fishing conditions.

Most anglers don't know as much as they should about the weather, and even though you can do nothing to change the weather, you can gain basic weather knowledge to understand the significance of cloud patterns, wind direction, barometric pressure, and the like, as well as abnormal events like storms.

There are numerous sources of information about atmospheric conditions and weather events, as well as basic meteorology, not the least of which are various materials provided in the United States by the National Weather Service, which is part of the federal government in the National Oceanic and Atmospheric Administration (NOAA). In addition, much can be learned from professional meteorologists and the weather maps and satellite imagery that are widely televised. Weather forecasting today has greatly improved, and technological advances are taking it to new heights annually.

Watching or listening to standard media weather forecasts, however, is largely of general significance and is often not adequate for boating and fishing activities. For these activities, the best reports are issued by National Weather Radio (NWR), a mariner's service of NOAA on weather band frequencies that is broadcast on VHF radios *(see)*. In the United States, NWR has more than 425 stations; reports are given every four to six minutes and updated every one to six hours, with an excellent warning system for local events; broadcasts are continuous all day all year. In addition to reports about general conditions, NWR gives a synopsis of prevailing regional weather patterns, which can be a clue for the astute listener as to conditions that may affect fishing plans not just for the present time but for a while to come. No big-water boater should be without a means of getting reports from this source.

Reports from any source are just one piece of information, and the wise person is observant of the weather all the time; such observance increases understanding of basic weather patterns and cycles that happen continuously. If you keep in tune with local weather patterns, you'll probably lose less fishing time than the person who doesn't, since you'll understand what the real effect of changing weather means. The important point is to develop your own ability to understand what the best weather forecast information means so that you can assess factors before you go on the water, and also so that you can assess them while you are on the water.

It is beyond the scope of this entry to provide a review of weather development as it pertains to cloud identification, wind *(see)*, barometric pressure changes, and fronts, or to events like thunderstorms, tornadoes, waterspouts, and hurricanes. However, all of these components of weather can have impacts on fishing, boating, and safety. The safety implications of storm events are addressed elsewhere *(see: safety)*, but some general comments can be made about the fishing significance of these factors.

The presence or absence of sunlight is a basic element of weather. Clear skies and bright sun is indicative of a high pressure system, and it often brings with it a strong wind. Cloudy conditions can cause light-sensitive fish to be more active, especially in shallow freshwater; in freshwater fishing this is generally viewed favorably; in most saltwater fishing it is not as significant. Cloudy cover makes it harder to see shallow saltwater fish that are caught by sight fishing methods, so good light with low wind is preferred. In freshwater, strong overhead light from the sun is often poor for shallow water fishing activities.

Rain or fog is similar in effect to clouds. Light and warm rains are often more conducive to fish activity than heavy or cold rains, although warm heavy rains in the spring in freshwater do a lot to move feeding and spawning activities along.

Wind, or the absence of it, is often the most influential factor in fishing activities. A strong wind makes many presentation methods, particularly casting and drifting, very difficult. If the waves are high enough, wind can make trolling very unpleasant, and proper boat control difficult. The total absence of wind, however, allows light penetration and causes shallow, light-sensitive fish to go deeper or seek shade, and makes many fish more wary. A light breeze, just enough to ripple the surface, can make a positive difference in fishing; moderate winds that chop up the surface are rarely unfavorable.

Some marinas provide computerized weather information; this angler is checking a Doppler system at a marina in the Florida Keys.

A cold front is less favorable than a warm front and may be very unfavorable for some fish (shallow water residents in particular). In North America, most cold fronts arrive from the northwest, and most warm fronts arrive from the south and southwest. Severe storms are usually poor for most fishing, because they cause great changes in the environment. It often takes a few days to a week or more to improve fishing after some severe storms. Periods of stable weather tend to produce good fishing, and a continual series of unstable weather and cold fronts, accompanied by high winds, tends to sustain poor or at least sub-par fishing.

WEATHER RADIO
A radio equipped to broadcast weather information issued on three specially designated frequencies by the National Weather Service; also, the system created by the National Weather Service which broadcasts weather information on an all-day, everyday basis.
See: Communications; Weather.

WEEDGUARD
A piece of plastic, metal, or rubber that covers a fish hook to help prevent snagging in cover.

WEEDLESS HOOK
A hook with a wire, plastic, or rubber cover over the hook point to keep it from hanging on objects.

WEEDLESS LURE
A lure with some type of a guard covering the hook to help prevent it from getting caught on objects, especially weeds, but other items as well; also, a lure that by its own design and nature is generally free from inadvertent hanging on objects.

WEEDLINE
The edge of aquatic vegetation.
See: Aquatic Plants.

WEEDS
The terms "weeds" is often used to refer to all types of aquatic plants, although technically a weed is a plant that grows where it is not wanted. A native aquatic plant that has spread to an area where it affects navigation or has become so abundant that it hinders fish populations is considered a weed. Any aquatic plant that is not native to a water body is a weed. In North America, such exotic aquatic plants as water hyacinth and hydrilla, which came from other countries, are considered weeds and have become problems because of uncontrolled growth.
See: Aquatic Plants.

WEIGHING FISH
See: Measuring Fish.

WEIGHT
(1) An object used to sink a lure or bait, often referred to as a sinker *(see)*.

(2) A heavy lead object essential to downrigger *(see)* usage and commonly referred to as a weight or cannonball.

WEIGHTED LINE
Weighted lines are core-heavy products that sink and are used for deep trolling, the objective being to bring a lure or bait (mostly the former) to depths that cannot be reached by flatlining *(see)*, and where other devices are unavailable. Lead core is the foremost type of weighted line, but similar products have a flexible non-toxic lead substitute.

These are not lines to which some external weight has been added. They feature a pliable, dense core that is covered by braided nylon or Dacron. They are available in a somewhat limited range of strengths, from 15- to 60-pound-test, mostly from the upper 20s on up. Weighted lines have the density to sink on their own without the addition of external objects, although the bulky diameter of the line offsets some of the sinking ability at trolling speed, usually meaning that to get very deep, great lengths of line have to be trolled or the boat moved very slowly. In saltwater, and in some freshwater applications, trollers who desire to get lures deep prefer wire line *(see)*.

Weighted lines are not as useful at high speeds and where there is current, but they are much easier to use than wire. They rarely create kinking or jamming problems, and can easily be wound on a reel and set out (they cannot be cast). They are color-coded every 10 yards so you can easily determine how much is out, although this won't necessarily tell you how deep the lure is.

Weighted lines are available in coated and uncoated versions, the former using some type of plastic. Coating may help abrasion, but generally these lines are not very abrasion resistant. They have less stretch than some similar strength nylon monofilaments, but they do stretch. They will corrode in saltwater, and have to be taken off the reel spool and rinsed, in part explaining why wire line is universally preferred in saltwater.

No special tackle is required for weighted lines, although the rod should be relatively stout and the reel large enough to hold this bulky product and some backing. Levelwind reels can be used. A leader of monofilament line is tied to the business end of the weighted line, and then a lure is attached to that.

Weighted-line trolling was a principal means of fishing deep in freshwater but has decreased greatly in popularity with the increased use of downriggers

and diving planers, and is primarily employed for lake trout and salmon angling. To many anglers, weighted-line trolling is not as satisfying as other trolling techniques using lighter and more challenging tackle. The problem is that weighted lines make fish landing mostly a reel-cranking, winch-the-fish-up affair. If you catch a really large fish, it will surely fight well enough for you to know it's there. But for every large fish you hook, you'll catch a lot of small- to medium-size fish, which just don't give as good an account of themselves on weighted line as they do on finer line because they must resist the bulky drag of the line in the water.
See: Line; Trolling.

WEIGHT-FORWARD LINE
A fly line that is tapered only at the fishing end.
See: Flycasting Tackle.

WEIGHT-FORWARD SPINNER
See: Spinner.

WELS
A Eurasian catfish and one of the largest of all freshwater fish.
See: Catfish.

WEST INDIES
See: Bahamas; Cayman Islands; Cuba; Jamaica; Lesser Antilles; Puerto Rico; Virgin Islands.

WEST VIRGINIA
Since the early 1970s, West Virginians have proclaimed far and wide the "wild, wonderful" nature of their state. Visitors quickly discover that it's not just a tourism marketing slogan. Pristine trout streams tumble from tall, forested slopes; scenic whitewater rivers cut deep gorges through the mountainous landscape; broad-shouldered waterways meander placidly through farm-dotted valleys.

The rivers' scenic value attracts tens of thousands of tourists each year. Their angling value draws tens of thousands more. Although not widely considered a destination for traveling anglers, the Mountain State nonetheless boasts several national-class, and at least a handful of world-class, fisheries.

Born of the great tectonic collision that formed the Appalachian Mountain chain, West Virginia exhibits all the characteristics of a land squeezed between two continental plates. The rock strata under its highest peaks have been shoved to, and sometimes even past, the vertical. Eons of erosion have carved deep, steep-sided valleys into the sandstone, limestone, and shale. As a whole, the landscape resembles a piece of emerald construction paper that someone wadded up and only haphazardly attempted to straighten.

Like the landscape, West Virginia's rivers and streams vary widely in water quality; quirks of geology render some vastly more fertile than others. The presence or absence of industry plays a significant role in the quality of the rest.

West Virginia has long been known for its natural resources, primarily coal, timber, and natural gas. Where those resources have been heavily exploited, water quality inevitably has suffered. Still, some waters have managed to maintain their fisheries despite decades of industrial degradation. In fact, some of the state's best angling exists in rivers that have been reclaimed through voluntary and government-mandated efforts.

Warmwater Rivers
One need look no farther than West Virginia's western boundary, the Ohio River, to find a sterling example of one of those restored fisheries. Once a troubled waterway that harbored little more than catfish and carp, the Ohio began its comeback after the Clean Water Act of 1970 forced the many heavy industries located along its banks to reduce their pollution levels.

The longest fly-distance double-handed cast in competition is 319 feet 1 inch, set in 1984.

Today, the Ohio ranks as the state's finest mixed-bag fishery. Anglers can fish for largemouth bass, smallmouth bass, spotted bass, white bass, and hybrid striped bass, as well as walleye, sauger, freshwater drum, channel catfish, flathead catfish, and carp.

Anglers familiar with the Ohio tend to concentrate most of their attention at the seven U.S. Army Corps of Engineers navigation locks scattered along the river. Outflows from low-head hydropower plants create ideal fishing conditions in the dams' tailwaters. In addition, most of the power companies have built special piers that bridge the outflows and give anglers access to particularly productive spots. Some angler-access locations even have special parking areas, lights, and fish-cleaning stations.

The Ohio's principal West Virginia tributary, the Kanawha River, boasts a remarkably similar fishery. Once so polluted that carp couldn't even survive in it, the Kanawha now rivals the Ohio in angling variety and productivity.

Fishing began to return to the Kanawha when the many chemical companies located near Charleston started reducing their pollution. Almost instantly, the river recovered. Bass clubs now routinely hold tournaments in areas once devoid of gamefish.

The Kanawha's fishery is even more varied than that of the Ohio. In addition to largemouth, smallmouth, spotted, white, and hybrid striped bass, the Kanawha tosses pure-strain stripers into the mix, plus walleye, sauger, and muskellunge. There aren't many muskies here, but there are enough to pique anglers' interests. Other species of note include freshwater drum, channel catfish, flathead catfish, carp, a rich variety of sunfish, and an occasional crappie.

Three navigation dams interrupt the Kanawha's journey northwest to its junction with the Ohio, and each is home to a first-class angler-access facility. When 3- to 9-pound hybrid stripers begin running in June, it is sometimes difficult to find casting space on the piers.

The Kanawha's main tributary, the New River, easily ranks as the state's most famous warmwater fishery. Although not as varied as either the Ohio or the Kanawha, the New River offers scenic beauty, difficult rapids, and world-class smallmouth bass fishing that make it West Virginia's premier tourist attraction.

Dubbed "River of Death" by Native Americans, the New is a broad, powerful river that roars through a steep-sided gorge for almost its entire journey through the state's southern mountains. From Hinton to Sandstone, its rapids are gentle enough to be navigated by experienced canoeists; from Sandstone to Thurmond, the rapids' size and violence require substantial whitewater skill. From Thurmond to Fayette Station, river navigation is strictly for experts.

Fortunately for anglers, many of the river's whitewater rafting outfitters also offer fishing guide services. With the help of an experienced guide, even novice anglers can experience the thrill of hauling a 3- to 5-pound bronzeback out of a Class IV set of rapids—a double adrenaline rush that shouldn't be missed.

The New River owes a great deal of its water quality to the limestone-rich waters of one of its principal tributaries, the Greenbrier River. As do its larger sister's, the Greenbrier's riches lie in the river's scenic beauty and an abundance of hard-fighting smallmouth bass.

From Bartow to Hinton, the Greenbrier flows through bucolic farmland bounded on each side by the lofty ridges of the Allegheny Range. For anglers who prefer to float-fish, it is paradise. With the exception of a few minor falls near Talcott on its extreme downstream end, most of the Greenbrier can easily be floated in canoes or jonboats.

The Greenbrier's smallmouth, although not as large as those found in the deep, swirling rapids of the New River, tend to make up in aggressiveness what they lack in size. Rock bass and channel catfish add spice to the fishery.

No description of float fishing in West Virginia would be complete without a mention of three phenomenal sections of the smallmouth-rich South Branch of the Potomac River in the state's Eastern Panhandle.

The first is an 8-mile stretch from the U.S. 220 bridge east of Petersburg to the County Route 13 bridge near Fisher. The second is the most famous: "The Trough." In the Trough, the South Branch tumbles almost straight as a string for 6.5 miles through a road-free, dwelling-free gap where deer, turkeys, and bald eagles appear more often than humans. The third section, nearly 9 miles long, extends from the U.S. 50 bridge west of Romney to the State Route 28 bridge at Blues Beach. All three sections boast some of the state's highest smallmouth catch rates, and all are scenic delights.

Although most productive mainly during early spring, the Elk River in central West Virginia shouldn't be overlooked. Few other rivers offer anglers the chance to catch a trophy smallmouth, a trophy walleye, and a trophy muskellunge from the same pool.

From Sutton Dam downstream to Clendenin, the Elk harbors fine populations of all three of these gamefish. Warmwater discharges from the dam have dramatically improved the river's bass fishing, and 2- to 3-pound bronzebacks have become fairly commonplace. Add to that the potential of catching walleye up to 10 pounds and muskies of 15 to 30 pounds, and one understands why the Elk's live-bait anglers load their minnow buckets with 6-inch chub and suckers during the months of March and April.

Large Impoundments

Since West Virginia's largest and only natural lake measures less than 2 acres in surface area, stillwater anglers must seek recreation at one of the state's many man-made lakes. The U.S. Army Corps of Engineers, through its flood-control system, manages many of the larger impoundments.

Perhaps the best of the lot is 2,500-acre Stonewall Jackson Lake near Weston. Widely acknowledged as West Virginia's finest largemouth bass fishery, Stonewall is a relatively shallow lake with an abundance of flooded timber. In addition to largemouths, the lake also harbors smallmouth bass, muskellunge, walleye, saugeye, and an abundance of crappie, plus channel catfish and other less-desired species.

Located just a few miles northeast of the state's geographic center, and just a stone's throw off Interstate 79, Stonewall is within a single day's drive of every West Virginian. Small wonder that, as its 1988 impoundment, it has become the darling of bass clubs throughout the state.

For sheer scenic splendor, Summersville Lake has no equal within the state. Formed in 1963 when the Corps of Engineers dammed the wild Gauley River near its namesake town, Summersville today is a sprawling complex of quiet coves set in a landscape of sandstone cliffs and thickly forested hillsides.

It is the state's largest, deepest, and clearest lake, and its smallmouth bass and walleye are difficult to locate and to catch. Most of the really productive walleye fishing occurs during the winter, when officials shrink the lake from 2,700 to just 920 acres to catch spring snowmelt from nearby mountains. Smallmouth anglers tend to do better in early fall, when bronzebacks are known to hurtle up through 20 feet of hydrogen-clear water to smash well-presented surface lures.

The first published description of the use of lures to catch fish appeared in 1496 in Dame Juliana Berners' The Boke of Saint Albans; a dozen artificial flies were mentioned.

Most of Summersville's walleye average 18 to 24 inches in length, although larger specimens have been caught. Smallmouths and largemouths of up to 5 pounds are not uncommon. Occasionally, lake anglers catch large brown or rainbow trout; these fish have migrated into the lake from tributary streams and grown large on the impoundment's abundance of forage.

Summertime fishing is difficult at Summersville, mainly because the lake's scenic charms attract so many pleasure boaters and water-skiers. Quiet coves, although abundant, aren't likely to remain secluded for long amid the crowds that flock to Summersville between Memorial Day and Labor Day.

A similar situation, although not quite as severe, exists at Bluestone Lake near Hinton. The 2,040-acre impoundment harbors fine populations of smallmouth, largemouth, and striped bass, but anglers must work hard to find peace amid all the recreational boaters.

Perhaps the best bet for fishing success at Bluestone is to wade into the dam's tailwaters and cast for smallmouth bass. Bronzebacks of up to 4 pounds abound in the rich, highly oxygenated tailrace, and the fishery never seems to become depleted despite heavy pressure. The lake's Bluestone River arm also produces some fine smallmouth fishing, as well as a scenic treat.

One of the state's few major lakes not managed by the Corps of Engineers, 550-acre Stonecoal Lake offers visitors to the Weston area one of the state's most unique fisheries. Deep and unusually cold, Stonecoal is known less for its bass than for its trout and muskellunge. Muskie aficionados consider it West Virginia's finest lake-based fishery, bar none. Every year, anglers haul muskies in the 45- to 50-inch class from its waters.

Cynics believe the lake's muskies grow so large because fishing clubs continue to stock the lake with trout. But enough 4- to 6-pound trout show up in anglers' creels to make it abundantly clear that not all the stocked rainbows and browns end up in the stomachs of toothy predators.

Despite water quality problems caused by the infertile hills that surround it, Beech Fork Lake near Huntington produces remarkably good catches of hybrid striped bass. This 720-acre impoundment averages less that 20 feet in depth, so its hybrid schools remain within easy reach of anglers regardless of season. Trolled live minnows work remarkably well on schooling fish.

Beech Fork's headwater tributaries harbor most of the lake's largemouth bass. Early evening forays up those thin water tributaries with fly tackle and poppers have been known to bring unforgettable surface action.

Small Impoundments

Lake-based fishing took a sharp turn for the better in West Virginia during the 1980s when local soil-conservation authorities began building small-scale flood-control lakes in the headwaters of flood-prone creeks.

None has captured the public's fancy more than Woodrum Lake, a 240-acre impoundment near Kenna. Only the state's 10-horsepower outboard motor limit for small impoundments keeps Woodrum from being "the" destination for West Virginia's bass clubs.

Built specifically with anglers in mind, Woodrum features dozens of acres of flooded timber. Its deep creek channels, rocky cliffs, and steep hillsides comprise some of the state's most productive bass habitat. Catch rates at Woodrum are among the state's highest, and nowhere in West Virginia do largemouths grow any larger. Fish of 3 to 4 pounds are common, and 6- to 8-pounders show up often enough to keep things interesting.

Just a few miles to the northeast, 217-acre O'Brien Lake boasts a remarkably similar fishery. Although shallower and less clear than Woodrum, it nonetheless harbors a fine largemouth population. O'Brien's fish are a little smaller, on average, and they aren't quite as easy to catch. But they do come often enough to make anglers speak of the two lakes almost as if they were identical twins instead of merely sisters.

The largest of the Mountain State's small impoundments, 300-acre Stephens Lake west of Beckley is home to some of the area's finest fishing for trophy-class tiger muskellunge. For a while in the mid-1980s, Stephens Lake "regulars" swapped the state tiger muskie record back and forth among themselves. The hot streak eventually cooled off, but the lake remains one of the state's three best fisheries for these northern pike/muskie hybrids. Stephens also produces trophy-class largemouth bass and channel catfish on occasion.

A few miles to the northeast, Plum Orchard Lake offers anglers something they rarely get to experience in West Virginia: the pleasure of casting to lily pad cover. Most Mountain State impoundments simply don't possess the proper habitat for lily pads to grow. Plum Orchard, with its stable lake level and shallow coves, does. The pad-covered coves consistently produce trophy largemouth bass and slab-sided bluegills. Big channel cats lurk in the lake's deeper areas. Unlike most small impoundments, Plum Orchard has no horsepower restrictions for boats.

Trout Streams

West Virginia's higher elevations are home to more than 1,200 miles of trout streams. Nearly half that mileage is composed of tiny native brook trout waters small enough to be jumped across. Mountain State anglers are far more familiar with the other 600 miles, which include many of the state's most storied trout streams and rivers. Of those, none has a more gloried or checkered past than the Cranberry River.

Born amid the soaring 4,000-foot ridges of western Pocahontas County, the Cranberry flows more than 26 miles through some of the state's most remote backcountry. From 1930 to the late 1960s, it harbored self-sustaining populations of brook, rainbow, and brown trout. In the early 1970s, though, the fishery began to decline. Acid rain had soured the waters so badly that trout could no longer survive. The state Division of Natural Resources (DNR) continued to stock trout in the river, even though surveys showed that none of the fish would live through the spring snowmelt.

All that changed in 1988, when the DNR placed an acid-treatment station on Dogway Fork, one of the Cranberry's principal tributaries. A second station, added in 1992 to the river's North Fork, completed the transformation.

Brook and brown trout already have begun to reproduce in the Cranberry, and catches of trophy fish continue to increase. Once insect and baitfish populations expand to their respective carrying capacities, researchers expect the river to match or exceed its former status as the state's finest trout stream.

The current holder of that title, the upper Elk River, won't yield it easily. Nowhere else in the state can an angler legitimately expect to catch an 11-inch native brook trout, a 15-inch stream-spawned rainbow trout, and an 18-inch wild brown trout all in the same day.

Such catches don't often occur, but they could. All three species exist in the Elk watershed, and all three have been known to grow to even larger sizes. From the Elk's birthplace near the little town of Slatyfork, it races 4 miles through a remote canyon, sinks into an underground cavern, runs underground for nearly 2 miles, then rises as a full-blown river at Elk Springs.

From Elk Springs 20 miles downstream to Webster Springs, the Elk is trophy brown trout water, home to fish that occasionally top 6 pounds. Most of the fish caught, however, are hatchery fish planted during weekly stockings by the DNR.

Shavers Fork of the Cheat River has been described as "the poor man's Madison" because of its strong currents and its boulder-littered bottom. It's an apt description. Like its Montana counterpart, Shavers seldom pauses to rest during its descent from the slopes of Bald Knob to its confluence with the Black Fork at Parsons. For more than 40 miles, it slips straight along the ridge of Cheat Mountain like a needle through the teeth of a saw before it at last tumbles out and assumes a more meandering route.

Recent acid-treatment efforts on its tributaries promise to return Shavers to its once-held status as a top trophy trout producer. For the time being, it will remain one of the state's most popular and productive stocked trout streams.

Anglers might similarly describe the Williams River. A sister to the Cranberry, the Elk, and Shavers Fork, the Williams originates in a portion of western Pocahontas County known locally as the "Birthplace of Rivers." Seven major rivers originate in less than 500 square miles of rugged mountains, and all of those rivers harbor trout.

The Williams might just be the most popular of all. Although it parallels the storied Cranberry for almost its full length, the Williams went unaffected by acid rain because fertile limestone soils underlie its headwaters.

From the Monongahela National Forest's Day Run Campground downstream to Dyer, the Williams harbors both stocked and wild trout. A Forest Service road parallels the stream for almost its entire length, providing easy angler access to every stretch. Anglers can camp at the Day Run or Tea Creek campgrounds, or at any of dozens of designated sites along the stream.

Gandy Creek and the Dry Fork of the Cheat are every bit as accessible as the Williams, and every bit as productive. Practically, the two streams should be considered as one. Gandy forms the drainage's headwaters, although the stream assumes the aptly named Dry Fork's name immediately after the two join together.

Gandy begins as a brook trout limestone stream that actually runs underground for a mile through the famous Sinks of Gandy. Below the Sinks, it assumes a freestone character and harbors native brookies and wild browns as well as stocked rainbows.

After the Gandy's confluence with Dry Fork, browns begin to dominate the species mix. The river's boulder-lined pools produce a few enormous browns each year. Three- to 5-pound fish show up fairly regularly, and 10-pounders have been caught. Roads parallel the two streams for nearly their entire length, providing easy access.

Just the opposite is true for the Blackwater River, a tannin-stained stream that drains the huge high-altitude wetlands complex known as Canaan Valley. A meandering, slow-paced brown trout stream in its headwaters, the Blackwater picks up speed and difficulty shortly after it vaults over 63-foot-high Blackwater Falls and plunges into the steep-walled Blackwater Canyon.

Anglers who venture into the roadless, nearly trail-less canyon often are rewarded with oversize browns and rainbows. The hike out, however, inevitably exacts a toll not many wish to pay. Perhaps more than any other fishery in the state, the Blackwater Canyon stands as the living embodiment of West Virginia's "wild, wonderful" character.

WET FLY

A sinking artificial fly that primarily represents subsurface forms of aquatic insects in freshwater. See: Fly.

An angler fishes near a freshwater marsh in Ontario's Kawartha Lakes.

WETLANDS

Although a wetland is generally thought of as a swamp, the technical definition of a wetland is a debatable one; it is generally viewed as an area between land and water where the water table is at or near the surface, or the land is covered by shallow water. Ponds and lakes less than 6 feet deep may be considered wetlands, as may bogs, swamps, or marshes *(see)*. In the broadest sense, wetlands must have soils that are saturated with water or periodically flooded and have an abundance of plants that can live in wet soils or water. This covers a lot of places along and around freshwater lakes and rivers, and in salt or brackish regions of tidal rivers and estuaries.

Tidal salt marshes are flooded regularly by the rise and fall of tides, but they are not flooded during low tide. They are highly productive ecosystems that support many marine organisms as places for breeding, feeding, and sheltering young. Mangrove *(see)* swamps or forests are also a form of salt marsh in tropical and subtropical areas.

Tidal freshwater marshes are coastal wetlands that maintain freshwater conditions through high amounts of rainwater or because of their location along a river. They also are affected by the tides but are never inundated by saltwater because of their elevation. Tidal freshwater marshes combine the features of salt marshes and inland freshwater marshes. Because they have a concentration of salt lower than tidal salt marshes, there is greater biodiversity. Many species of fish use freshwater tidal marshes to spawn and as a nursery for their young. Anadromous fish, which live their adult lives in the ocean, and fish that spend their adult lives in estuaries, travel through these marshes on their way to freshwater streams to breed.

Nontidal freshwater marshes are of various types. They may be emergent, such as marshes and meadows, and comprised of mostly grasses and sedges, or they may be scrub-shrub wetlands, such as bogs, pocosins, and shrub swamps. Some are small, like a prairie pothole, or large, like the Florida Everglades. Emergent wetlands are thought to be the most diverse of all wetland types. Many insects and animals inhabit these nontidal inland marshes. In general, more fish are found in marsh systems with deeper, open water.

Northern peatlands are wetlands called bogs and fens. Bogs have acidic peat deposits, a high water table, no inlets or outlets, and plants that thrive in acidic soils or water. Fens are fed by groundwater, are dominated by vascular plants, and have grasses, sedges, and reeds as opposed to sphagnum and true mosses. Plants and animals that inhabit bogs and fens have developed some unique characteristics and adaptations. They must deal with many stresses, such as acidic water, low nutrient levels, extreme temperatures, and being waterlogged. Because of low levels of productivity and the apparent unpleasant taste of bog plants, very few wildlife species inhabit the waters of bogs and fens.

Southern deep-water swamps, on the other hand, have a lot of aquatic species, including crayfish, snails, freshwater shrimp, midges, insect larvae, and clams, which use the large amount of detritus found in these swamps. Mayflies, caddisflies, and stoneflies can be found near in-flowing streams in these wetlands. Fish also use these swamps as temporary and permanent residences, where deep-water areas provide optimum habitat. In the southeastern United States, bald cypress, water tupelo, and black gum are the dominant trees in this type of wetland, and there is permanent or almost permanent standing water.

In the aggregate, wetlands are vital resources for a wide array of plant, fish, and animal life. Many prominent species of fish, including bass, trout, stripers, and salmon, need and use wetlands. Most wetlands provide shelter and food for fish species, and some harbor gamefish sought by anglers and thus provide recreation. However, wetlands are equally important as areas that absorb pollutants and filter human sediments and waster, thus maintaining and improving water quality. Some also reduce erosion and flood damage. Many endangered species directly or indirectly rely on wetlands for survival. Wetlands themselves have been threatened or lost because of myriad factors. It has been estimated that more than 100 million acres of wetlands have been destroyed in the United States over the past two centuries, and it is clear that continuing loss or degradation will adversely impact all natural resources, including fish species, as well as angling opportunities.

WET WADING

Fishing by means of wading in the water without the aid of waders *(see)*.

WHIP FINISH

A knot that is used to finish off thread winding and

that prevents the thread from unraveling; if done correctly, the whip finish is smooth without bulges or lumps. The whip finish is employed in tying flies, wrapping rod blanks, and tying skirts onto jigs or lure hooks.

See: Fly Tying; Lure Modifying/Repairing.

WHIRLING DISEASE

An infection of young salmonids caused by a microscopic, water-borne, protozoan parasite that attacks the cartilage and causes the fish to chase its own tail. Whirling disease spores *(Myxobolus cerebralis)* are released into the water when infected fish die and decompose, or when the spores are consumed and excreted by predators or scavengers. The parasite has a complex, two-host life cycle that involves a trout or salmon and the bottom-dwelling tubifex worm, which is found in streams, rivers, and lakes.

This parasite is not harmful to humans but has been disastrous on some trout populations, particularly rainbow, and has spread rapidly in northeastern and western North America in the 1990s, although it originated in Europe. It does not directly kill fish, but an infected fish's erratic tail chasing makes it extremely vulnerable to predation. The whirling activity of the fish also makes it unable to feed normally, which eventually results in starvation and death. This disease primarily infects fish smaller than 4 inches long.

See: Diseases and Parasites.

WHITEFISH, LAKE *Coregonus clupeaformis.*

Other names—high back, bow back, buffalo back, or humpback whitefish; common whitefish; eastern whitefish; Great Lakes whitefish; inland whitefish; Sault whitefish; gizzard fish; Cree: *atekamek;* French: *grand corégone.*

The lake whitefish is a larger and more widespread fish than are the mountain (see: *whitefish, mountain)* and the round whitefish (see: *whitefish, round),* and it is more highly regarded among anglers. A member of the Salmonidae family, the lake whitefish is a valuable commercial freshwater fish in Canada, although its numbers have declined due to environmental factors and overfishing, especially in the Great Lakes. The flesh—prepared fresh, smoked, and frozen—is considered superb in flavor, and its roe is made into an excellent caviar.

Identification. A slender, elongated species, the lake whitefish is silvery to white with an olive to pale greenish brown back that is dark brown to midnight blue or black in some inland lake specimens; it also has white fins and a dark-edged tail. The mouth is subterminal and the snout protrudes beyond it, with a double flap of skin between the nostrils. The tail is deeply forked, and an adipose fin is present. The lake whitefish is occasionally referred to as "humpback" because the head is small in relation to the length of the body, and older specimens may develop a hump behind the head. It has 10 to 14 anal rays, 70 to 97 scales down the lateral line, and 19 to 33 gill rakers. The body is more laterally compressed than that of the round or mountain whitefish, which belong to a separate genus of "round whitefish."

Size/Age. The lake whitefish is commonly 18 inches long and weigh 2 to 4 pounds. Some are said to reach as much as 31 inches, and the all-tackle world record is a 14-pound, 6-ounce fish caught in Ontario, Canada, in 1984. The average whitefish caught by anglers is in the 1- to 2-pound range. Fish of 4 or 5 pounds, and even larger, are sometimes caught. This species can live for 18 years.

Distribution. Lake whitefish occur throughout Alaska and Canada; in the mainland United States, they occur throughout central Minnesota and the Great Lakes and from New York to Maine. Transplanted populations exist in Washington, Idaho, and Montana. They have been stocked into high Andean lakes in a few countries in South America.

Habitat. Lake whitefish are named for their primary habitat of large, deep lakes, but they are also residents of large rivers. They prefer water temperatures of 50° to 55°F and will enter brackish water.

Life history/Behavior. Spawning occurs in late fall, when fish migrate into shallow areas over sandy bottoms or shoals in large lakes or tributary streams. Eggs are randomly deposited over the bottom by females laying up to 12,000 eggs per pound of body weight. These fish do not build nests, and parents return to deep water after spawning, leaving eggs unprotected on spawning grounds until they hatch the following spring. By early summer, the young move from shallow inshore areas to deeper water.

Food and feeding habits. Mainly bottom feeders, adult lake whitefish feed primarily on aquatic insect larvae, mollusks, and amphipods, but also on other small fish and fish eggs, including their own. Young fish feed on plankton.

Angling. In lakes, whitefish are readily taken when schooled and when rising to flies, but they are often hard to catch otherwise. Although many open-lake anglers catch them accidentally while seeking other game, these fish are successfully pursued through the ice. In rivers where whitefish are abundant, flycasters are routinely successful in landing them; sometimes they are a nuisance rather

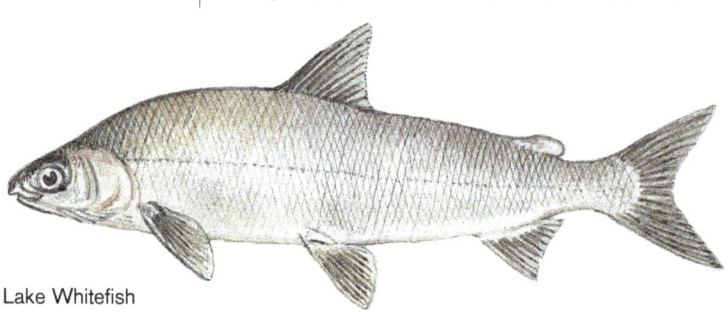

Lake Whitefish

than a pleasure. They linger in slow pools, beneath waterfalls, and along back-switching bank eddies.

Whitefish are principally an insect feeder, and this is reflected in fishing tactics. They are most likely to be caught on nymphs or dry flies, the latter especially in lakes when these fish rise to the surface in large schools that travel along the shores of a deep-water bay.

Whitefish rise gently when feeding on floating insects, and often one sees the dorsal fin cutting through the surface momentarily. A dry fly presented slightly ahead of the cruising fish will usually be taken, but the hooksetting motion need not be vigorous. The whitefish has a soft mouth, so a smooth rod-lifting action will set the hook without tearing it away from the fish.

Methods other than fly fishing can be productive, but not reliably so. A whitefish will occasionally strike a spoon or small plug, although a jig is far more likely to be effective. A small dark jig is best; it can be fished plain or it can be tipped with a small insect or grub. Grubs are popular for ice fishing, as are small live or salted minnows, and small jigging lures. Chumming is also effective.

Whitefish fight well, occasionally jumping and characteristically making a diving run and shaking near the surface. They are a fine light-tackle fish; light or ultralight spinning rods equipped with 2- to 6-pound line are suitable, as are light, medium-length fly rods for 5- to 7-weight fly lines.

WHITEFISH, MOUNTAIN *Prosopium williamsoni.*

Other names—Rocky mountain whitefish, Williamson's whitefish, grayling; French: *ménomini des montagnes.*

Although not as significant a gamefish as the lake whitefish *(see: whitefish, lake),* the mountain whitefish has gained popularity and provides an important winter fishery in certain areas, especially where steelhead are absent. A member of the Salmonidae family, it is a very good table fish, particularly when smoked.

Identification. Possessing an adipose fin and an axillary process, the mountain whitefish is long, slender, and nearly cylindrical, although not quite as cylindrical as the round whitefish *(see: whitefish, round).* It is nevertheless among the species referred to as "round whitefish" and can be distinguished from the lake whitefish, which is more laterally compressed than the mountain whitefish. Silvery overall, it is dark brownish to olive or greenish to blue gray above, with scales that often have dark borders and ventral and pectoral fins that may have an amber shade in adults. The small mouth is slightly subterminal, and the snout extends clearly beyond it. The caudal fin is forked, and there are 74 to 90 scales down the lateral line and 19 to 26 gill rakers. Young fish have 7 to 11 large, oval, dark parr marks.

Size/Age. The mountain whitefish can grow to

Mountain Whitefish

$22\frac{1}{2}$ inches and 5 pounds. The all-tackle world record is a 1988 5-pound, 6-ounce fish from Saskatchewan. It can live for 18 years.

Distribution. The mountain whitefish is endemic to the lakes and streams of the northwestern United States and southwestern Canada, from the Lahontan basin in Nevada north to the southern border of the Yukon Territory. It occurs inland into Alberta in Canada and Wyoming in the U.S., overlapping the range of the lake whitefish in British Columbia and Alberta, and slightly overlapping that of the round whitefish in extreme northern British Columbia near the Yukon border.

Habitat. Generally inhabiting rivers and fast, clear, or silty areas of larger streams as well as lakes, mountain whitefish usually occur in stream riffles during the summer and in large pools in the winter. They prefer temperatures of 46° to 52°F and are found in the deep water of some lakes, although in northern lakes they usually hold no deeper than 30 feet.

Spawning behavior. Spawning takes place from October through December in shallow, gravelly streams or occasionally in lakes at water temperatures of 42°F or less. Parents do not guard the eggs, which number about 5,000 on average and incubate over winter to hatch in spring.

Food and feeding habits. Mountain whitefish feed primarily on benthic organisms like aquatic insect larvae, mollusks, fish, and fish eggs (including their own), as well as on plankton and surface insects when primary food sources are unavailable.

Angling. Mountain whitefish are underutilized by anglers. Similar to the lake whitefish, they are good fighters and are caught on flies, natural baits, and some artificial lures that they can fit in their small mouths. They bite especially well during the winter months.

WHITEFISH, ROUND *Prosopium cylindraceum.*
Other names—menominee, round fish, frost fish, pilot fish, grayback; French: *ménomini rond.*

Round Whitefish

A member of the Salmonidae family, the round whitefish seldom exceeds 2 pounds and has considerably less commercial value in Canada than the lake whitefish *(see: whitefish, lake)*, although it is sought to a limited degree by anglers. Its flesh is of good quality.

Identification. The round whitefish is mostly silvery and has a dark brown to almost bronze coloring with a greenish tint on the back. It has black-edged scales, particularly on the back. The lower fins are an amber color, becoming slightly more orange during spawning, and the adipose fin is usually brown spotted. Young fish have two or more rows of black spots on the sides that may merge with a row of black spots on the back. The round whitefish has a small head and a fairly pointed snout, and a single flap of skin between its nostrils. It also has a forked caudal fin, 74 to 108 scales down the lateral line, and 14 to 21 gill rakers. The round and lake whitefish can be easily distinguished because the round whitefish has a very cylindrical body, whereas the body of the lake whitefish is laterally compressed; the mountain whitefish *(see: whitefish, mountain)* is almost cylindrical, although slightly more compressed than the round whitefish.

Size. Usually about 8 to 12 inches long and weighing $1/2$ pound or less, the round whitefish can grow to more than 20 inches long and weigh several pounds. The all-tackle world record is a 6-pounder taken in Manitoba in 1984.

Distribution. The round whitefish occurs in arctic drainages in northeastern Asia from the Yanisea River to Kamchatka and the Bering Sea. A wide-ranging species in the northern portions of North America, it has disjunct populations, one of which is found through the St. Lawrence–Great Lakes basin (with the exception of Lake Erie) north to the Arctic Ocean east of Hudson Bay; the other is found throughout the northern Canadian provinces and Alaska west of Hudson Bay. It also occurs in limited areas directly south of Hudson Bay and in East Twin Lake in Connecticut.

Habitat. Occurring in the shallow areas of lakes and streams, round whitefish may also inhabit rivers with swift current and a stony bottom. They rarely enter brackish water or water more than 150 feet deep.

Spawning behavior. Spawning takes place during the fall in lakes, tributary mouths, and occasionally in rivers over gravelly shallow areas. Fish spawn in pairs, with females releasing from 2,000 to 12,000 eggs, which are abandoned after spawning and hatch in early spring.

Food. Round whitefish feed on benthic invertebrates and occasionally on fish and fish eggs.

Angling. *See: Whitefish, Lake.*

WHITING

(1) A term commonly and primarily used for silver hake *(see: hake, silver)*.

(2) A term for members of the *Menticirrhus* genus of the Sciaenidae family of drum *(see)* and croaker *(see)*. These include the gulf kingfish *(M. littoralis)*, southern kingfish *(M. americanus)*, northern kingfish *(M. saxatilis)*, and minkfish *(M. focaliger)*. These bottom-feeding fish seldom exceed a half pound in weight or more than 10 inches in length and are generally ignored by anglers. They are found close to shore, lack air bladders, and are unable to make the croaking sounds produced by other Sciaenids.

WHITING, KING GEORGE *Sillaginodes punctata*

Other names—spotted whiting, South Australian whiting, spotted sillago.

One of a number of species of whiting found in Australian waters, and one of the best-known fish along the southern coastline of Australia, the King George whiting is a favorite with anglers. A superb table fish, it is also the target of commercial fisheries in Victoria, South Australia, and Western Australia.

Identification. This species is readily identified by scattered bronze or brown spots on the back and upper sides that extend to the long dorsal fins. Its body coloring shades from light to dark brown on the back to silvery white on the belly. The body shape is rounded and elongate. The forked caudal fin is yellow, and the pectoral and anal fins are white. This species has a small mouth and extremely small scales.

Size. King George whiting can exceed 4 kilograms in length and 70 centimeters in length, but the average fish taken by anglers weighs roughly 500 grams.

Distribution. These fish are an indigenous species confined to temperate waters from Jurien Bay in Western Australia, across the bottom of Australia, including the northern coastline of Tasmania, and along the East Coast to as far north as Sydney, New South Wales.

Habitat. King George whiting dwell along ocean beaches and in shallow offshore waters, but anglers land greater numbers of them from bays and tidal estuaries, where they live in fairly shallow water (down to 1 or 2 meters) in areas of seagrass beds and sandy bottoms.

Life history/Behavior. King George whiting are serial spawners. Spawning takes place in offshore waters from May through July, and fecundity can be as high as 800,000 eggs. The eggs float, and the larvae are planktonic until they're about 15 millimeters long; then, they move into sheltered areas where they remain for two to three years. After that, they move to deeper waters where they are targeted by both recreational anglers and commercial fishermen. They reach maturity after three to four years, and are reported to live for 15 years.

Food and feeding habits. The shape of the King George whiting's mouth identifies it as a bottom feeder. It has a varied diet that includes bivalves, crustaceans, and worms.

Angling. Recreational anglers of all ages seek the King George whiting because it is relatively easy to hook, provides exciting fishing due to its vigorous attempts to escape, requires the simplest of tackle, and is tasty. Anglers do well with light to medium tackle, light lines to 4 kilograms, and hooks from No. 4 to 1/0, depending on the size of the fish pursued. Handlines are frequently used, especially by boat anglers.

Favorite baits are cockle or mussel flesh, sandworms, and strips of squid. Rigs are either fixed or running; attaching two hooks to leaders is common, and sinker weight varies with conditions but must be enough to take the bait to the bottom, where these fish feed. Boat anglers find that judicious use of chum will attract the fish and hold them in the vicinity of the boat.

Although the shore-based angler is usually limited to a certain area due to the terrain, the boat angler can cover much more of the whiting's territory by drifting over sandy bottom covered in patches of seagrass.

WINCH

A device for helping to load a boat on a trailer and secure it to the trailer for transport. There are single and dual speed manual winches as well as electric winches.

See: Trailer, Boat.

WIND

Without doubt, wind is one of the most significant natural elements that affects sportfishing. No matter which direction it comes from, wind is one of nature's phenomena that can be a blessing or a curse to anglers, although usually more of the latter. When there is no wind, anglers usually wish for a light chop on the surface to make it easier to dupe fish. Yet when there is too much wind, boat handling and lure presentation can be so difficult that fishing may be impaired. Wind can direct a cast fly into your hat or your ear. It makes you throw more forcefully with a baitcasting reel, increasing the chance of backlash. It may cause you to troll too fast or too slow, depending on whether you're headed with it or against it. When the temperature is low, wind makes an angler cold and often uncomfortable and less able to fish properly.

Anglers often face the dilemma of whether to get out of the wind or fight it. If the wind is a precursor to a front, changing several days worth of stable weather, it may signal the beginning of fish activity that you don't want to miss because that period before a new frontal system is often a good angling time.

In some places, you have no such choice. In winding or island-studded bodies of water, you often do. However, even though getting in the lee may allow you to fish comfortably, you may not

Wind is more of a problem for anglers than for fish, and it can stimulate fish activity.

be very successful there or you may have to pursue a species of fish that you were not already after. However, the wind-whipped shore may be, and often is, a good place to be fishing. Small fish and baitfish can be greatly disturbed by hard-driving winds, becoming disoriented or finding it very difficult to move, sometimes even being pinned against wind-driven shores. Wind pushes minute organisms into the windward shore; the organisms attract small fish and in turn larger fish. Oxygen is enhanced on windward shores because of the continued wave-beating. Fish may be facing out toward deep water here, and a controlled drift or troll is a good idea.

Fishing along those shores, or around the sides of wind-driven islands or shoals, may also be a good move. Baitfish may try to move out to deeper water to escape the turbulence, and predators sense this and move from deeper water to shallows to capture their prey. Casting crankbaits and jigs into the shallows and retrieving them outward may be the ticket, provided you can hold boat position. Keeping position is often hard, however, and sometimes impossible.

There will be times when you can't make any headway into the wind or are constantly being blown about, and fishing becomes a hardship. You can't make the right presentation or retrieval, and you can't detect strikes properly. You feel like your efforts are wasted. Dedicated anglers learn to deal with it.

Trolling *(see)* is one activity that can be done quite well in the wind if your boat is suitable, but you have to be mindful of several factors in order to make an effective trolling presentation. Probably the most important of these is the effect of the wind on speed.

A boat moving with a motor at a constant engine speed of 500 rpms, for example, will go much faster with the wind than when headed into the wind. Often, fish are caught only when the boat is headed in one direction; this is because the lures

being used aren't traveling at a suitable speed in the opposite direction (and don't have the proper action). Traveling into the wind at a moderate speed may bring lures deeper or shallower, depending on the lure, so depth attainment, rather than speed, can be the main factor. The worst thing you can do is troll blindly in one direction, then turn around and head blindly in the other direction, not knowing much about either the real speed or the depth at which your lures are working.

Maintaining a course is another matter that trolling anglers don't anticipate as a problem, but which is affected by wind speed and direction. To counter the tendency of a quartering wind to push a boat forward and away, for example, you must get the boat slightly sideways to the wind. This can be a difficult position to steadily maintain.

Because it helps maintain boat position even in wind, backtrolling is popular with walleye anglers. By using some type of sonar unit, a backtroller can maintain position along specific depths, nearly hover over selected spots, and maneuver the boat to use whatever wind direction is present to position the boat in such a way that a following bait is kept in the proper place and worked very slowly.

Casting is an altogether different story than trolling. Depending on what you are tossing to the fish, the act of casting is itself difficult in a brisk wind; accuracy and distance are often sacrificed. With lures you may have to cast farther upwind, or cast low and sidearm, to be more accurate, or use a heavier lure. You may have to cast only with, or quartering into, the wind instead of directly into it. With flies, you may have to position yourself much closer to your target than you would otherwise, since you may be unable to get the necessary distance.

High winds impact on just about every form of cast-and-retrieve angling, primarily because boat control and lure presentation are made much more difficult the greater the velocity of the wind is. Wind particularly affects jig and plastic worm fishing, which are games of feel and depth attainment. With a bow in your line, you don't have the sensitivity you need, and often your lure spends far too little time in the places it should be.

Anchoring is one way to deal with the wind for casting, but few anglers who are accustomed to positioning with an electric motor and casting to cover a good deal of water are satisfied with repeated anchoring and re-anchoring. Electric motors are certainly very helpful for fishing in the wind and maintaining position, provided the motor is powerful enough to move your particular boat (the more weight the harder) and the battery has enough juice. An electric motor's energy reserves are depleted more quickly in brisk wind because you run the motor more often and at higher speeds. With a bow-mounted electric motor, it may be necessary to have a long shaft to keep the motor in the water as the bow lurches up and down.

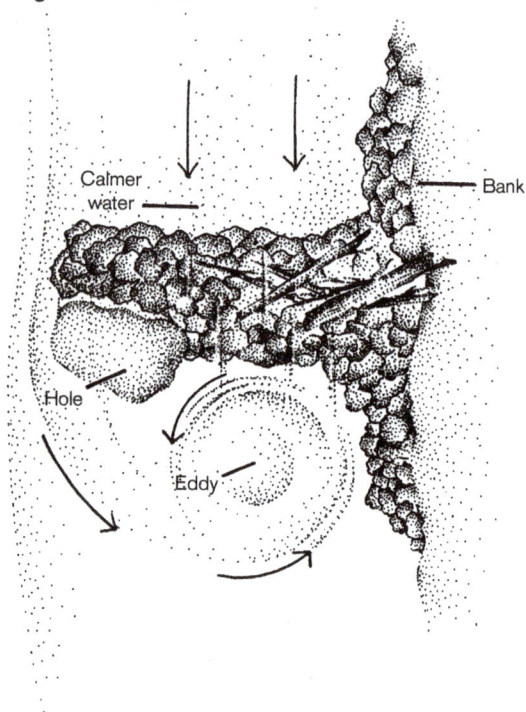

Wingdam and Current

These are some of the typical problems to be overcome when the wind is rough. Fishing in heavy winds also raises concerns about safety issues, which are addressed elsewhere.
See: Safety; Weather.

WIND KNOT
A simple overhand knot that is inadvertently formed on fly line or (usually) leader while casting. It is attributed to the wind, hence the name, but is likely due to the formation of a loop that causes fly line and leader to cross. Such a knot greatly weakens the breaking strength of the line and should be removed, especially if it occurs in a light tippet.

WINGDAM
In a river, a man-made arrangement of rocks that extends from shore a variable distance perpendicular to the river and is intended to deflect current and prevent bank erosion. A wingdam is often submerged, especially in spring and in periods of high water, and thus a navigation hazard; but in normal to low water levels, it may protrude enough to be visible. It is not actually a dam, since it does not cross a river entirely (although a form of wingdam is an eel weir, which may extend across most of the shallow section of a river), and it may gather tree branches, logs, or other debris for a period of time until swept away.

Where the water is deep enough and current flow great enough, there is likely to be an eddy (see) behind the wingdam, and a deep hole alongside or just behind the leading edge that has been scoured out of the bottom. There is also a patch of calmer water on the upstream side of the wingdam. Such species as smallmouth bass, walleye, and catfish will use these key parts of a wingdam for feeding or resting.

WINTERKILL
See: Fishkill.

WIPER
See: Bass, Whiterock.

WIRE LEADER
See: Leader.

WIRE LINE

Wire line is used by a relatively small but ardent number of both freshwater and saltwater anglers. There is some minor use of it in saltwater for jigging, but it is almost exclusively used for trolling. Wire line trolling is essentially a form of flatlining (see), except that the density of wire causes it to sink, bringing a trolled lure or bait down to specific depths. It is used for deep-water probing in freshwater, primarily for lake trout, and for mid- to deep-water bottom probing by inshore saltwater anglers, primarily for striped bass but also for bluefish, wahoo, and king mackerel. Some people do not think there is much sporting virtue in using wire line, and fish caught on wire line are not recognized by the IGFA for world records.

Wire lines are primarily made of single or multiple strands of Monel or stainless steel. Monel is a corrosion-resistant alloy that is more expensive than stainless steel, more pliant, and less prone to kinking. Multiple strand wire is easier to handle but poses difficulties when burrs develop; because it sinks less readily than single-strand wire, it is used less. It's necessary to use gloves when working with it, because of the possibility of burrs that could slice your flesh.

Wire line doesn't stretch very much and it is very resistant to abrasion; therefore, it makes hookups a little surer and there is less chance of breaking it during a fight with a fish than if you were using other types of line, provided that it doesn't have a kink. Because of low stretch, however, it can contribute to pulling the hooks out of big fish.

Found in various strengths, but primarily used in 30- and 40-pound test, wire line is not as difficult to work with as believed, but it is certainly not as easy as nylon monofilament or weighted line (see) like lead core, and does require some precautions. Wire must be wound on a reel spool under tension, or it will spring off and create a terrible tangle. Tangling, in fact, is possible whenever tension is removed, so when trolling, it's imperative that wire be let out carefully and under controlled tension, usually keeping a thumb on the spool as the line is paid out. You have to get some tension on the lure to be trolled before slowly letting line out. Make sure that the leader, swivel, and any terminal tackle has cleared the rod guides before doing this, or an abrupt stop in the spool will cause an overrun that could be a problem. It helps to hold the rod in your hand and put the tip in the water to get the lure and terminal gear out.

Wire sinks quickly, and if the boat is traveling slowly, it's possible that the wire will sink so fast it gets the lure to the bottom and hangs up. With the boat in forward gear, while letting line out, put your thumb tightly on the spool several times to stop it and to keep the lure from getting hung up. Once underway, on a standard troll, wire will take a lure down 10 feet for every 100 feet let out. To get down 30 feet, therefore, you'd have to let out 300 feet of wire, although you can obtain more depth by using some extra weight and fishing slowly or making turns. Weights up to a pound are used; when using a weight, the length of line out needn't be as great. The tactic here is to troll very slowly and let line out until you feel the sinker hit the bottom. Reel up a turn or two and set the rod in a holder.

One of the benefits of trolling wire is the ability to let out and bring in more as necessary when the bottom depth changes. To know where the lure is you have to know how much line is out. Wire line doesn't hold paint and isn't marked by the manufacturer in lengths, so you have to do this

Wire line lays evenly on a conventional reel; it is attached to a nylon leader and a feathered trolling jig.

yourself. Because there is no levelwind, you can't count passes to estimate the length of line out, and the pull system isn't practical with such heavy gear, so you'll have to mark wire in specific intervals, usually every 50 feet, to know how much you've set out. One way to do this is to put a short piece of colored adhesive wrap around it.

Some anglers will put a small metal clip on this first wrap to keep leaves, grass, and debris from sliding down the line and fouling the lure. A good thing about wire line fishing is that, if you have the right kind of rod, you can readily tell if a lure is working properly and when it has gotten some debris on it. It is often not necessary to reel all the line in to remove the debris; jerking the rod back several times may free it. This is one of the big reasons why anglers, especially saltwater anglers, opt for wire over a downrigger. They can tell by watching the rod if a lure is working right, and they can readily adjust for depth and bottom contour changes.

This is heavy-tackle fishing, and big, star-drag reels and stout rods with carbide guides are mandatory. In saltwater, anglers use up to 4/0 to 6/0 reels, in part because they need a lot of winching power to work a fish when a boat keeps moving (if you have a couple of rods out and stop, the wire will take the other lures to the bottom and hang up, or they have to be reeled in). Smaller reels will do the job, however. They needn't be filled entirely with wire line, and usually are filled with 100 yards of wire followed by backing of braided or nylon monofilament. The reel should be nearly full, primarily to let you wind as much as possible on with every turn of the handle. This has to be done under tension. Some tackle shops can wind the line on for you.

Rods need to be equipped with guides that can withstand harsh use. Steel or stainless steel guides will be grooved by wire and can't be used. Silicon and tungsten carbide guides are necessary. Rods must have a lot of power, and actions can charitably be described as stiff, although the tips must be limber enough to reflect lure action. Rods specifically meant for wire line trolling are sold by several manufacturers.

Although wire line is very durable, it is subject to kinking and to fatigue. Wire seldom breaks under direct tension but can suddenly break when it is being set out. Kinks are a big problem. If they are severe, the line has to be cut; if they are not too serious, they can be straightened out. If the line is cut, you'll need to use a Haywire Twist (see) to rejoin the sections. Avoid setting the line out in the same spot all the time. Repeated stress (like at the tip guide) in one spot can cause fatigue.

To many anglers, wire line trolling, like trolling with other weighted lines, is not as satisfying as other trolling techniques using lighter and more challenging tackle because fish landing is mostly a reel-cranking, winch-the-fish-up affair. If you catch a giant, it will surely fight well enough for you to know it's there, and you will definitely have a good feel for strikes (although few wire users actually hold the rod when trolling) and for head shakes when a fish is on. But for every giant you hook, you'll catch a lot of smaller fish. On some charter boats, anglers tire quickly of cranking wire lines in.
See: Line; Trolling.

WISCONSIN

Few states have the diversity of freshwater habitat that exists in Wisconsin. From the cold depths of Lakes Superior and Michigan to the 231 miles of the Mississippi River to the 15,057 lakes and ponds and 9,560 miles of trout streams, almost every popular species of North American freshwater fish can find a suitable place to thrive. Anglers migrate to Wisconsin like salmon up a river to pursue their sport, and for many years the Badger State has led all other states in the sale of nonresident freshwater fishing licenses and stamps.

Wisconsin straddles the subcontinental divide between the Great Lakes and the Mississippi River drainage basins. Water from the northward-flowing trout streams that enter Lake Superior eventually joins the flow from eastern Wisconsin rivers that drain into Lake Michigan, and exits the Great Lakes via the St. Lawrence River to the Atlantic Ocean. The remaining two-thirds of Wisconsin drains south and west into the Mississippi River and into the Gulf of Mexico. These two great systems each have their own complement of fish species, which contribute to the great variety on the Wisconsin sportfishing menu.

Panfish, which include bluegills, crappie, yellow perch, and white bass, are the most widespread of the angler's quarry, and their tasty fillets make them a perennial favorite. They are found in thousands of lakes and streams and provide both open-water and winter sport.

But it is the large predator fish who live at the top of the aquatic food chain that provide the real excitement. The "big five" in Wisconsin—walleye, muskellunge, northern pike, largemouth bass, and smallmouth bass—steal the spotlight in the cool inland waters.

Walleye have always been extremely popular and inhabit almost all of Wisconsin's 1,107 larger lakes and rivers. Good walleye fishing is available all across the state, led by huge Lake Winnebago, the premier water for this species and home to more than a million adult walleye.

Largemouth bass, smallmouth bass, and northern pike also enjoy a statewide distribution. They thrive in marshy Mississippi River backwaters that are reminiscent of Southern bayous, as well as in crystal-clear lakes of the northern forests that look like the Canadian wilderness.

The muskellunge, however, is the official state fish of Wisconsin. This species is unique to North America, and northern Wisconsin lies in the heart of its original range. For well over 100 years, anglers have pursued these fish, and they have always been viewed as trophies. Wisconsin began propagating and stocking muskellunge fry in 1900, and through stocking has expanded this species' range to more than 700 waters. Nowhere do anglers catch more muskellunge than in Wisconsin.

The inland trout enthusiast has the choice of fishing in 2,674 streams. Brook trout and brown trout are the most common species, and a handful of streams contain rainbow trout. The bulk of these fish are naturally reproducing, and most of the better rivers require no stocking to maintain excellent populations. A few small lakes that are tucked away in the Chequamegon and Nicolet National Forests are stocked annually with trout and offer good fishing.

Wisconsin was one of the first states to protect its most pristine trout streams through the creation of a state wild rivers acquisition program that began in 1965. Almost 50 miles on the Pine, Popple, and Pike Rivers in northeastern Wisconsin have been protected from development and will remain free flowing forever. More than 12,000 acres of adjoining lands are open to the public for fishing and other outdoor recreation.

Across the state, at the western boundary, lies the St. Croix National Scenic Waterway. This wilderness gem was one of the original eight rivers established under the 1968 National Wild and Scenic Rivers Act. The St. Croix flows 25 miles through Wisconsin before it becomes the border river between Minnesota and Wisconsin. The beautiful Namekagon River, which lies completely within Wisconsin, is a part of this system and provides excellent trout fishing. Both rivers have good canoe access sites and offer primitive camping opportunities.

For really large trout and salmon, anglers head to Lakes Superior and Michigan. Lake Superior's waters are best suited for native lake trout, which have rebounded from sea lamprey depredation and overfishing. On Lake Michigan, introduced chinook salmon steal the show, but all the trout species grow to mind-boggling sizes in this forage-rich environment. Summer fishing derbies at Lake Michigan ports like Racine, Sheboygan, Manitowoc, Sturgeon Bay, and Marinette attract crowds of onlookers who come to view the trophies as they are registered. It is not uncommon for the winning fish of each species of brown trout, steelhead, and lake trout to all exceed 15 or 20 pounds in a weekend contest. The chinook salmon winners almost always exceed 25 pounds each. Numerous charter boats operate out of these ports, offering a safe and effective way for visiting anglers to sample the fishing on this inland sea.

Although Wisconsin is a relatively small state of 54,000 square miles, it offers great fishing opportunities, and fishing is an important part of its culture. Twenty-five percent of Wisconsin's adult citizens go fishing. They are joined each year by half a million nonresident anglers. The variety of fish available and the excellent access to its lakes and streams fuel Wisconsin's popularity as a fishing destination.

Northern Lakes
State Highway 64 slices across Wisconsin east to west from Marinette to New Richmond. The third of the state that lies north of this road is largely forested and dotted with thousands of inland lakes. Vilas County alone has 1,327 lakes. These lakes are part of the legacy left by the last glacier to cover northern Wisconsin.

Many of the northern lakes appear to be quite similar, but that is not the case. Each has unique qualities, and lakes vary based on physical characteristics like size, depth, and shape. But more important, it's the chemical characteristics of the lake that determine the clarity, productivity, and fishery. Lakes near acidic bogs are stained with natural tannic acid that leaches from surrounding vegetation. The water in these lakes may be as dark as coffee but still harbor a good population of northern pike, yellow perch, crappie, and smallmouth bass.

Just across the ridge from a brown-water lake may be a gin-clear spring lake that gets its water from an underground aquifer. It won't warm up as quickly in the sun as a brown-water lake, and it will probably have a different complement of fish, yet it's just a stone's throw from its neighbor.

When anglers get a hot tip to fish a particular lake in Wisconsin, they had better get an exact location, too, because many bear the same name. There are 116 Mud Lakes, 82 Bass Lakes, 59 Long Lakes, 45 Spring Lakes, and 42 Lost Lakes, plus many that are unnamed.

When the general inland fishing season opens in early May, both northern pike and walleye have usually completed spawning. Water temperatures are still cold, usually near 50°F. Northern pike may remain in shallow waters. When the first warm weather makes its appearance and the water warms up just a bit, these fish feed heavily. Male walleye may still congregate alongshore near spawning grounds. The spent females may be nearby but in deeper water.

By June, muskellunge start to feed aggressively. Panfish move into shallow water in June, and anglers search for their spawning beds in gravel-bottomed areas. Walleye begin to move offshore to deeper rock bars at this time and are predominantly caught on slowly fished nightcrawlers, minnows, and leeches.

Midsummer fishing is never a sure bet anywhere, as northern pike and panfish are tougher to find when they move to deeper water. Two exceptions are muskellunge and smallmouth bass; both species feed heavily during the warmest months. Early morning or late evening is best on lakes with busy boat traffic and water-skiers. In some lakes, walleye move right into the submergent vegetation in 2 to 3 feet of water during the hottest weather, providing fast action on leeches.

Why do prey fish school? Individuals are more vulnerable; flashlike escape maneuvers can confuse predators; and usually the slow, sick, or disabled fish become victims.

Autumn in Wisconsin is not only a beautiful time, but this is also when many of the largest fish of the year are boated. Muskie hunters soak 2-pound suckers trussed up in quick-strike rigs, waiting for that 40-pound fish of a lifetime. Most of the fish species seem to feed heavily in preparation for winter as the days shorten.

Winter fishing can be the most productive of the year for anglers hardy enough to drill through 30 inches of ice and brave the elements. Both walleye and northern pike feed all winter. Live minnows are the most successful bait, but vertically jigging an ice-jig takes plenty of fish. Muskellunge are not legal fare in winter. They are rarely taken through the ice by accident and don't seem to feed in the winter, as do their northern pike cousins. Meanwhile, panfish anglers do well on bluegills, crappie, and perch using light line and tiny, colorful jigs tipped with a tiny grub.

A brief review of the northern counties and opportunities follows.

Oconto County (200 named lakes). The area around Lakewood is famous for clusters of smaller lakes. Many offer excellent northern pike, bass, and panfish angling and are located in the beautiful Nicolet National Forest.

Marinette County (242 named lakes). Big and wild Caldron Falls Reservoir and High Falls Reservoir are angler favorites for walleye and muskies. Lake Noquebay is a well-known panfish lake.

Forest County (194 named lakes). Lake Metonga at Crandon is good for perch and walleye. Beautiful Lake Lucerne and Pine Lake are favorites.

Florence County (101 named lakes). Many of the smaller wildernesslike lakes offer opportunities for northern pike, muskellunge, walleye, bass, and panfish.

Oneida County (428 named lakes). There are many great muskellunge spots among Oneida County's 66,000 acres of water. Excellent fishing abounds for walleye, northern pike, largemouth and smallmouth bass, and panfish.

Vilas County (561 named lakes). In places, there seems to be more water than land in Vilas County. Many of its lakes are located in the beautiful Northern Highland–American Legion State Forest. All of the popular species are common, including walleye, muskie, northern pike, large- and smallmouth bass, crappie, bluegills, perch, and whitefish.

Iron County (217 named lakes). In Iron County, the sprawling and wild Turtle-Flambeau Flowage covers 14,000 acres. Sixteen natural lakes were flooded when it was created in 1926. It has a super walleye population, but smallmouth bass and muskies are also good. Another wild beauty is the Gile Flowage near Hurley.

Price County (161 named lakes) and **Taylor County** (98 named lakes). Many of the lakes in Price and Taylor Counties are located within the unspoiled Chequamegon National Forest. Anglers willing to carry a canoe can find solitude and great bass fishing on numerous smaller lakes.

Bayfield County (339 named lakes). Best known are Lake Namekagon, Lake Owen, and the Eau Claire Chain, but the whole area is known for walleye fishing.

Ashland County (84 named lakes). Much of this county is wilderness quality with pristine lakes and great trout streams. Day Lake is known to be a good muskellunge water.

Sawyer County (244 named lakes). Most famous is the 15,000-acre Chippewa Flowage, site of the 69-pound, 11-ounce world-record muskellunge. Several other great muskie lakes are Round, Grindstone, Lac Court Oreilles, Chetac, Lost Land, and Teal. Northern pike and walleye are also abundant in these and other waters.

Washburn County (267 named lakes). Excellent fishing for walleye, muskellunge, and northern pike are found here. The bigger lakes like Shell, Long, Spooner, and the Minong Flowage get the most publicity, but knowledgeable anglers explore the lesser-known lakes and do very well.

Burnett County (228 named lakes). Top-notch muskie lakes abound here, but there are good populations of large- and smallmouth bass, and the area is favored by bass anglers.

Polk County (222 named lakes). Many large lakes here provide good action for bass, walleye, and muskies. Best known are Balsam, Deer, Cedar, Wapogasset, and Bone Lakes.

Barron County (124 named lakes). Red Cedar, Bear, Rice, Chetec, and Prairie Lakes offer a wide variety of fish species.

Lake Winnebago

Lake Winnebago is Wisconsin's premier walleye lake and is home to a wide variety of other gamefish, including white bass, sauger, northern pike, smallmouth bass, channel catfish, crappie, and yellow perch. Perhaps its most unusual resident is the lake sturgeon, a freshwater behemoth that can exceed 100 pounds. Although several species of sturgeon are endangered across the United States, Winnebago's lake sturgeon are thriving, and each winter the lake draws thousands of trophy seekers out on the ice for a unique spearing season.

Wisconsin's largest inland lake, at 137,708 acres, measures 28 miles long and 11 miles wide. The average depth is 15 feet, and it doesn't stratify, which makes it good walleye habitat from the surface to the bottom. Being shallow and windswept, Winnebago kicks up rapidly in a wind, so sturdy deep-vee boats are recommended.

Winnebago is not known for producing many huge walleye. Most angler-caught fish are less than 18 inches in length, which is perfect for eating. But 3- to 5-pound fish are common, especially during the spring, when the larger females run the Fox and Wolf Rivers to their spawning grounds.

An occasional 10-pound fish is creeled. Although most North American walleye spawn on rocky or gravel shoals and shorelines, Winnebago fish seek out flooded marshes in which to drop their adhesive eggs, sometimes venturing as far as 75 miles upriver from the main lake.

In the spring, some walleye stay in the lake along with the immature fish, but anglers do best when they follow the fish upriver. In April and early May, this means that the best fishing occurs near Oshkosh in and around where the Fox River enters Lake Winnebago. Tens of thousands of spawning-minded walleye and white bass begin to concentrate here in late winter.

A favored fishing technique in the heavy, cold current of April include a three-way swivel rig with live minnows, known locally as a Wolf River rig. A slowly fished jig and a minnow are also popular. As the fish work upstream (the walleye go first and the white bass later in May) to spawn, anglers follow them up the Fox and Wolf Rivers past Winneconne, Fremont, New London, and Shiocton. White bass provide fast and furious action, and crowds of boats get in on the action.

By late May and early June, the walleye are back in Winnebago and feeding actively. Excellent fishing occurs from the many rocky reefs that line the western lakeshore. Trolling works well; wind and rough water will spur a bite. Casting the shallow-water weedbeds is also productive, and a strike could come from not only a walleye but also a smallmouth bass, northern pike, channel catfish, or freshwater drum.

Later in summer, many fish take up a pelagic lifestyle all across the lake. Trolling with bait-imitating plugs and planer boards puts white bass and walleye in the boat. Many freshwater drum are taken this way. Called sheepshead by the locals, most are released, but the skinned fillets are quite good when battered and deep-fried.

Yellow perch are located on the reefs in mid-summer. Natural bait work best, followed by nightcrawlers, but local experts use hellgrammites (dragonfly nymphs) when the going gets tough. Slip floats work well for perch, as the bait can be suspended near the bottom without its getting hung up on the rocks.

In winter, the lake's frozen surface becomes a playground for anglers and snowmobilers. Thousands of fishing shacks dot the surface, now covered with 2 feet or more of ice. Clubs plow roads so anglers can drive out with their vehicles to fish. Popular spots include Oshkosh, Stockbridge, Brothertown, and Fond du Lac. Tip-ups with minnows fished tight to a silt or clay bottom work well in winter. Jigging also takes many walleye.

Southeastern Lakes

One of the most scenic areas in Wisconsin is the hilly and forested Kettle Moraine region, which was created when the two huge lobes of the last glacier

Salmon, trout, and walleye draw many boaters to Lake Michigan.

pushed south. Numerous lakes were formed in what is now Manitowoc, Sheboygan, Washington, Waukesha, and Walworth Counties.

Waukesha County has several large and productive lakes with excellent fishing for largemouth bass and panfish. Northern pike are common, walleye are present in some waters, and a few hold muskies. The most popular lakes include Pewaukee, Okauchee, Lac LaBelle, Nagawicka, and Nemahbin. Pewaukee lies just 20 miles due west of downtown Milwaukee. It produces a 40-pound muskie every year or so despite intense fishing pressure.

Farther south in Racine County are Wind, Eagle, and Browns Lakes, all of which have good fishing. Walworth County has two excellent large lakes. One, Delavan Lake, has a thriving walleye population and good numbers of northern pike, largemouth bass, and large bluegills. The other, Lake Geneva, covers 5,262 acres of clear water and is known for smallmouth bass.

To the west, the Yahara Chain of Lakes offers 18,000 acres of highly productive water. Lakes Mendota, Monona, Waubesa, and Kegonsa are most famous for excellent fishing for bluegills, crappie, yellow perch, and white bass. Other species are plentiful, too, and it is not uncommon to hook a 40-inch muskie or a 4-pound largemouth bass with the dome of the state capitol of Wisconsin in downtown Madison in the background.

Big Green Lake near Ripon is Wisconsin's deepest natural lake at 236 feet. Its 7,346 acres of clear, cold water contain an amazing variety of fish. Lake trout provide an excellent trolling fishery in mid-summer, plus good ice fishing. A huge population of cisco also provide some unusual action through the ice. These silvery members of the whitefish clan go berserk when hooked, and the fish run from 12 to 18 inches in length. Big Green also contains good numbers of smallmouth bass, northern pike, walleye, yellow perch, white bass, bluegills, and channel catfish. Nearby Lake Puckaway is much shallower and offers largemouth bass along its marshy shores; it is a completely different fishery, just 2 miles west of Big Green Lake.

The Wisconsin River and Reservoirs

The Wisconsin River arises in Lac Vieux Desert, a lake straddling the state border with Michigan's Upper Peninsula, and begins its 430-mile journey to the Mississippi River. Smallmouth bass, muskellunge, and walleye are common residents. Huge pines line its banks, and bald eagles nest high in their branches.

The 2,035-acre Rainbow Flowage in Oneida County is the first impoundment of the Wisconsin. This wilderness-type flowage is known for walleye and perch fishing and has excellent boat landings.

Below the dam, the Wisconsin glides around granite boulders on its way south; here it is home to muskellunge, walleye, and smallmouth bass. It passes through the Rhinelander Flowage and bends southwest for about 15 miles over several rapids before it flows through Lake Alice and then Lake Mohawksin in Tomahawk. Both of these flowages have walleye, northern pike, smallmouth bass, muskellunge, and crappie.

From Tomahawk to Wausau are several great areas to float a canoe and fish the river, casting for smallmouth bass that run 12 to 18 inches. The occasional muskie is here, too. Downstream of Wausau lies the Mosinee Flowage, Lake DuBay, and the Wisconsin River Flowage at Stevens Point. Smallmouth bass and walleye are abundant in these reaches.

Below the City of Wisconsin Rapids, the river flows into two of the largest man-made lakes in Wisconsin: 23,000-acre Petenwell Flowage and 14,000-acre Castle Rock Flowage. Both are home to walleye, northern pike, crappie, and muskellunge.

Continuing south, the river is dammed at scenic Wisconsin Dells and again at Prairie du Sac; the latter forms Lake Wisconsin, a popular fishing area for walleye, large- and smallmouth bass, and lake sturgeon. To reach this point, the river has flowed through 21 storage reservoirs.

Downstream of Lake Wisconsin, the river runs free south and west 92 miles to the Mississippi River. The valley along this reach is a scenic marvel of stately bluffs, damp-wooded bottom land, and hundreds of miles of sandy beaches, islands, and sandbars. It will always be permanently preserved in a wild state, because it was established by the state in 1989 as the Lower Wisconsin State Riverway. Plans include the acquisition of 79,000 acres of land to protect the river's environmental corridor.

Fish can and do move all the way from the Mississippi River up to the dam at Prairie du Sac. An amazing 84 species of fish have been recorded in this portion of the river. The angler never knows what may strike here—northern pike, walleye, smallmouth bass, muskellunge, dogfish, drum, longnose gar, carpsuckers, or mooneye. The current can flow upward of 5 miles per hour at times, so the fish usually hide behind the numerous downed trees and in the lee of sandbars. Smallmouth bass will hit within inches of the shore, but for walleye you must fish the bottom. Northern pike like the still backwaters.

Mississippi River

This incredible natural resource defines the boundary between Wisconsin and Minnesota for a distance of 231 miles. The upper Mississippi River is huge, and in most places measures 2 to 3 miles wide.

The Mississippi is much more than a river in this region. It is many rivers, huge riverine lakes, and thousands of potholes, sloughs, and ditches. There are fish everywhere, and more places to fish than an angler could visit in a lifetime. Many of these spots are accessible to the shore angler.

Anglers should become familiar with special features of the river environment that influence the distribution of fish, particularly wing dams and locks. Hundreds of wing dams were constructed during the 1800s to force water to the center of the river to aid navigation. These "piers" of rock rubble were placed perpendicular to the shore and extended out as much as 100 yards.

During the 1930s, the U.S. Army Corps of Engineers constructed a series of locks and dams to create even deeper water for commercial navigation. These dams reconfigured the river into a series of "pools" that lead into one another. The higher water levels now flood over the wing dams, hiding them.

There are 10 locks and dams along the Wisconsin portion of the river; some are only 9 miles apart, whereas the longest span is 44 miles. These are located at or near Red Wing, Minnesota (No. 3); Alma, Wisconsin (No. 4); Buffalo, Wisconsin (No. 5); Winona, Minnesota (No. 5A); Trempealeau, Wisconsin (No. 6); La Crosse, Wisconsin (No. 7); Genoa, Wisconsin (No. 8); Lynxville, Wisconsin (No. 9); Guttenburg, Iowa (No. 10); and Dubuque, Iowa (No. 11).

In essence, the locks and dams modified much of the "wild" or natural appearance of the Mississippi and transformed "Old Man River" into four main types of habitat. Species like largemouth bass and bluegills responded favorably to stillwater, whereas truly riverine fish like paddlefish and sturgeon have suffered.

Tailwaters. Turbulent tailwaters extend about a half mile below each structure. Although fish can migrate upstream through most of the dams during high water, they still temporarily block fish movement, and large numbers of fish build up below all of the structures. This makes for excellent walleye and sauger fishing in late winter. Anglers look for eddies or current breaks where fish are resting in the cold water. These areas, depending on river levels, are good all summer for a host of other species, including channel and flathead catfish, white bass, and freshwater drum.

Backwaters. The upstream sections of each pool look somewhat the same today as they did before the dams. In some instances, there is a maze of sloughs, side channels, flooded forests, and muck-bottomed wetlands. Largemouth bass, bluegills, and northern pike thrive in these still-waters. Some of the side channels with water flow harbor huge flathead catfish of 25 to 40 pounds. In winter, these backwaters concentrate bluegills, crappie, and yellow perch.

Main channel. Heavy current and copious commercial and recreational boat traffic present challenges to anglers. The navigational channel itself is extremely narrow, and by staying outside the navigational buoys the angler can fish riprap banks for smallmouth bass. The submerged wing dams are the scourge of the boater and ruin hundreds of outboard motor lower units each year because they are unmarked. But walleye and bass anglers love them. As the current slides over the wing dam, some of which are only a foot below the surface, walleye like to lie upstream and bushwhack forage. Crankbaits of all kinds work great along wing dams, and a solid strike could turn out to be any one of a dozen species.

Riverine lakes. Generally, the waters become more open and lakelike as you move downstream toward the dams. There are submerged stump fields out of the channel, which can be great fish habitat for largemouth bass and crappie.

Several of these riverine lakes are so huge they have been given names. Lake Onalaska near La Crosse is a 7,688-acre site and has excellent fishing for largemouth bass and bluegills. Much larger at 25,060 acres, Lake Pepin is of natural origin but is considered part of Pool 4. The Lake Pepin fish community comprises 85 species of fish, including many lesser-known members of the sucker family, such as redhorse and buffalo fish. Dominant gamefish species are sauger, white bass, walleye, northern pike, channel catfish, largemouth bass, and smallmouth bass.

Stream Trout Fishing

Wisconsin's 2,674 trout streams provide nearly 10,000 miles of trout habitat, and hundreds of miles of top-quality trout fishing water is publicly accessible. These trout streams are found in six general areas.

Northwest forested area. The northwest forest area is wild country for the Midwest. It is home to resident timber wolf packs, deer, elk, and even the occasional moose. Streams in this region drain into the St. Croix and the Chippewa Rivers, and the best-known trout stream is the Namekagon River, a St. Croix National Scenic Riverway. It contains brook, brown, and rainbow trout and has hatches similar to other freestone rivers in Wisconsin. Dozens of tiny native brook trout streams flow through this area and ultimately into the St. Croix and Chippewa Rivers. Many of these sparkling little gems are less than 5 miles in length but contain good numbers of small brook trout. Farther south, other notable streams include the Willow River and the Kinnickinnic near the City of River Falls, and Duncan Creek near the City of Chippewa Falls.

Northeast forested area. The northeast forest area contains big and brawny freestone trout streams that tumble rapidly over large boulders. The streams flow easterly into the Menominee River or into Green Bay of Lake Michigan. The Peshtigo River in Forest and Marinette Counties is big and fast. Its upper watershed is a maze of feeder streams in the nearly wilderness setting of the Nicolet National Forest. Just north lie the drainages of the Pine/Popple and Pike wild rivers, which are fast waters with numerous rapids and waterfalls. Brook trout occupy the headwaters of these rivers, and brown trout predominate in the lower reaches. Anglers who can deal with some brush have no problems finding a place to fish in solitude.

The famous Wolf River is to the west toward Antigo. This is a big, fast, and picturesque freestone river. At 50 yards wide, it rambles through hilly pine forests. The Wolf starts out as a warmwater stream and has numerous whitewater sections in northern Wisconsin. It becomes trout water near Pearson, where the Hunting River joins it. The Wolf offers 34 miles of public trout water. Once it flows into the Menominee Indian Reservation, access is denied. Special regulations protect the river's trout fishery.

Southwestern coulee country. Southwestern Wisconsin is hill country, with steep terrain and almost no lakes. But each valley has a stream, and from Buffalo County all the way south to the Illinois border, there are hundreds of trout streams hidden away in the deep creases of the landscape, all of which drain into the Mississippi River. Brown trout are the most abundant fish in these spring creeks, but both brook and rainbow trout are also present. In the better creeks, the clear but fertile waters support up to 5,000 trout per mile.

In Buffalo and Jackson Counties, the Buffalo River, Elk Creek, the Trempealeau River, and their numerous tributaries are all trout waters. Farther south in Trempealeau and La Crosse Counties, Beaver Creek, the La Crosse River, and Robinson Creek are good streams. Still farther south are the fine waters of the Coon Creek Drainage, Kickapoo, and Bad Axe. Flowing north into the lower Wisconsin River in Grant and Iowa Counties are several popular fly fishing streams: the Big Green River, Crooked Creek, Castle Rock, the Blue River, and Otter Creek.

Central sand country. Glaciers left an indelible imprint in the central sand country. Springs in Portage, Waupaca, Waushara and Marquette Counties are born out of a glacial moraine and flow east into the Fox River or Wolf River drainage basins. Well-known streams like the Tomorrow River, Emmons Creek, the Waupaca, Pine, White,

 Fossils indicate that over five million years ago the Pacific Ocean contained a giant salmon that was 6 feet long and weighed over 250 pounds.

Waters throughout Wisconsin are home to muskellunge.

and Mecan Rivers, and Lawrence Creek are like mecca to the trout angler.

Brook, brown, and rainbow trout exist here, and few of these streams require stocking. Much of their required habitat has been permanently preserved through state acquisition, and the trout populations are viable and self-sustaining. Brown trout exceeding 20 inches are caught each year, but the bulk of the fish run from 9 to 15 inches in length. A few sand country streams, like the Mecan and the White River, are famous for large hexagenia hatches in June. Public fishing areas along them provide easy access in many reaches. Warm June evenings find the best spots lined with fly fishers in the twilight, waiting for the hatch.

Lake Superior tributaries. Lake Superior's tributaries are northward-flowing streams with dual personalities. Their upper reaches contain native brook trout and wild brown trout populations, but their lower portions receive migratory runs of steelhead and brown trout, and chinook, coho, and pink salmon.

The most famous is the Bois Brule, a beautiful river almost entirely preserved within the Brule River State Forest. Special early seasons allow the angler to fish the spring run of steelhead, which begins in early April. Steelhead, or migratory rainbow trout, spend the first year or two in the stream and then move to Lake Superior to feed. The males return at 17 inches and larger, but it is common to encounter specimens up to 23 inches in length and an occasional fish to 30 inches and 10 pounds. Large (21 inches) brown trout enter the Brule in August and are soon joined by a fall run of steelhead and the three species of salmon. Hooking a big salmonid in a fast-flowing and often very clear river is hard enough, but landing one among the boulders and fallen logs is a real challenge.

Other streams with Lake Superior runs include the Nemadji, the Flag River, the Cranberry River, Pike's Creek, and the Sioux River. Two systems that are not known for lake-run salmonids are the White and Marengo Rivers, but their headwaters and upper tributaries are superb water for resident brown and brook trout.

Lake Michigan tributaries. The rivers that drain eastern Wisconsin's heavily populated regions are too warm to harbor trout populations year-round. Migratory trout and salmon from Lake Michigan, however, are drawn to their temporarily cold waters by the thousands from March through May and again from September through December. Some fish even spend the whole winter in the rivers under the ice.

Three strains of steelhead and both chinook and coho salmon are stocked in Lake Michigan by the Wisconsin Department of Natural Resources (DNR) and by the other states that border Lake Michigan. Most popular of the streams are the Kewaunee, Manitowoc, Sheboygan, Milwaukee, and Root Rivers. Several small tributaries also receive nice runs of fish. The Oconto River, which flows into Green Bay, has a fine run of trout and salmon.

Anglers are surprised to learn that a 10-pound steelhead can be taken on a fly in downtown Milwaukee, literally in the shadow of a freeway overspan or a baseball stadium. These streams have a continuous open season, and a few thousand trophy steelhead and salmon are taken annually. Most of the steelhead run 3 to 7 pounds, but each year several 15-pounders are landed. Spinning gear is popular, and 10- to 15-pound line is a must. Fly anglers use 7- to 9-weight rods with a lot of backing beneath their fly line. Tippets can be 8 or 10 pounds, as these brawny fish are not leader shy in the often murky waters of April. In autumn, the rivers are low and clear and the fish more skittish.

Lake Michigan

Lake Michigan is the sixth largest lake in the world. Wisconsin occupies 495 miles along its western shore, where 25 permanent streams flow into the lake. The main lake almost never freezes over but can become partially covered with floating pancake ice. Most of Green Bay freezes solidly, depending on the year.

Historically, lake trout and burbot were the top predators of western Lake Michigan. These fish feed mainly on seven species of deep-water cisco and sculpin. The invasion of numerous exotic species changed the mix, and by 1950 the sea lamprey had decimated a lake trout population that was already on the ropes from commercial overharvesting.

The U.S. Fish and Wildlife Service used a selective toxicant to treat the lamprey spawning streams, and federal hatcheries began to restock lake trout in Lake Michigan in 1965.

Wisconsin began its own fisheries rehabilitation program in 1963 by stocking rainbow trout, and then brown trout in 1966, in some of its tributary streams and harbors. Following the State of Michigan's lead, Wisconsin introduced stocks of coho salmon in 1968 and chinook salmon in 1969. With the exotic alewife as forage, the stocked salmon grew rapidly, and a large new sport fishery developed during the 1970s.

Today almost every port has renovated its harbor and launching area. Most provide fish-cleaning facilities and other support services. Hundreds of charter boats are available for those anglers without a boat of their own sturdy enough to tackle a Great Lake.

The fishing season on Lake Michigan is continuous. Even in midwinter, anglers catch brown trout off warmwater discharges such as those at Oak Creek, Port Washington, and the nuclear power plants near Point Beach.

Open-water fishing begins in late March or early April, as trollers dodge icebergs off Door County ports like Baileys Harbor and Sturgeon Bay. Trolling with plugs on light line takes the most browns. The fish average 2 to 3 pounds with an occasional 15- to 20-pound heart stopper. The same technique works well in Green Bay as soon as the ice leaves at Marinette and south.

Coho salmon migrate north from Illinois water in late April or early May. Trolling in the top 30 feet of water with bright-colored flashers and flies produces fast action. The coho average 1 to 3 pounds at this time, and their red orange fillets are excellent table fare.

Anglers land chinook salmon from May through October, but the fastest fishing usually occurs in July. Ports like Kenosha, Racine, Milwaukee, Sheboygan, Manitowoc, Kewaunee, Algoma, Sturgeon Bay, and Marinette all produce chinook over 20 pounds. Trollers often fish 60 to 100 feet below the surface.

Steelhead are taken all summer almost anywhere out in the open water near the surface. Trolling takes these silvery acrobats, which average 3 to 7 pounds but may approach 20 pounds.

Lake trout remain near bottom in 75 to 150 feet of water for most of the summer and are caught by anglers slow-trolling tight to the bottom. These long-lived fish are getting larger, and each year 30-pounders are landed.

Yellow perch frequent the shallow water of Lake Michigan and are a favorite of the shore angler. Perch have been cyclic in Lake Michigan, and alternate between being extremely abundant to almost rare, depending on their degree of spawning success each June.

Fishing for both yellow perch and salmon is influenced by water temperatures. A strong west wind blows the warm surface water out over the lake, and the cold water upwells along shore; sometimes it is as cold as 46°F in July. This enables salmon to come right into the beach in search of food, so even shore anglers can cast to them. Perch become inactive in this cold water, but a prolonged east wind pushes the warmer water back to shore. This will cause the perch to bite, but it drives the trout and salmon sometimes 8 to 10 miles offshore in search of cooler temperatures.

Door County is the most easterly part of Wisconsin and the peninsula that juts northeast into Lake Michigan. This county alone has 250 miles of shoreline, offering a wide variety of fishing opportunities. Salmon and trout are available, and the shallow, warmer bays of this vacationer's paradise offer superb smallmouth bass fishing. Catches of 30 to 40 bass per day are not uncommon for the experienced angler working out of Sturgeon Bay, Fish Creek, Sister Bay, or Detroit Harbor on Washington Island.

Nearly 100 miles long, Green Bay is the largest bay on Lake Michigan. It behaves differently than the main lake because it is more fertile and shallower. The fish population in southern Green Bay is more typical of the western basin of Lake Erie and contains walleye, yellow perch, white perch, drum, northern pike, carp, white suckers, and channel catfish. In summer, fleets of boats anchor over limestone reefs in search of perch. Farther north at Peshtigo and Marinette, anglers will find excellent fishing for trout, salmon, and smallmouth bass. Brown trout derbies at Marinette in July consistently produce hundreds of huge browns, and it's usually a fish weighing more than 20 pounds that wins.

Lake Superior

Lake Superior is the largest lake on Earth in terms of surface acres (31,800 square miles). It is the deepest, coldest, and most pure of all five of the Great Lakes. Although the 156 miles of its shoreline that lie in Wisconsin are a relatively small part of the lake, it is a very diverse part.

The St. Louis River enters the lake at the extreme western end and forms the border between Minnesota and Wisconsin. A sizable population of the Great Lakes' walleye, nearly 100,000 adults, leave the Wisconsin waters of Lake Superior each April to spawn in the river. The huge St. Louis "estuary" also provides sport for northern pike and yellow perch. It was here that a Wisconsin fisheries biologist discovered the first European ruffe, a small member of the perch family, in 1987. This potential pest continues to expand its range in the Great Lakes.

Fifty miles to the east, the beautiful Bayfield Peninsula juts into the lake, and off its tip lie the spectacular Apostle Islands. This scenic archipelago consists of 22 islands, 20 of which form a national lakeshore managed by the National Park Service. The waters around these islands contain lake trout, brown trout, and steelhead.

The city of Ashland lies at the head of

The Pere Marquette River in Michigan was the first stream to be stocked with brown trout in America; the fish were instantly seen as more difficult to catch than native brook trout.

Chequamegon Bay, a large but protected bay that warms up much more than the open lake and is home to a diverse fishery including smallmouth bass, walleye, and perch. Just to the east is the famous Kakagon Slough, a huge maze of wild rice beds and side channels that arise near the entrance of the Bad River. This is part of the Bad River Indian Reservation and is not open to the public without tribal approval.

Much of the Wisconsin portion of Lake Superior freezes over during winter. At ice out in late April, the open-water fishing season begins in Chequamegon Bay, where small coho salmon are caught by trollers. The best fishing is from Washburn to Bayfield, but anglers find coho in many other spots along the shoreline, including the Saxon area and off the city of Superior.

At about the same time, walleye run up the St. Louis River to spawn. These are slow-growing fish, but they can be large and beautiful. The best fishing is in mid-May.

As the water warms up a bit, lake trout move to the surface to feed and are taken high in the water column until mid-July. Trollers must spread out their lines to avoid spooking fish in the crystal clear water. Chinook salmon are taken on spoons in June in many areas, but not in great numbers.

Increasing numbers of siscowet are also taken this way. Siscowet are a subspecies of lake trout found only in Lake Superior that have evolved to survive in its deepest waters, below 55 fathoms. Their extremely high fat content makes them inedible once they exceed about 17 inches in length. It takes experience to identify their slightly rounded snout from that of their close cousin, the lean lake trout, which has excellent flesh.

With the warm weather, a thriving population of smallmouth bass moves into Chequamegon Bay to spawn and spend the summer. This is a trophy fishery with some bass over 20 inches in length. Thirty-fish days are common, and many of the smallmouth run 14 to 18 inches.

In September, chinook and coho salmon concentrate off the mouths of rivers like the Brule, Sioux, and Onion.

Water temperatures always greatly influence fishing success in Lake Superior. The open lake rarely warms above 50°F, and when it does, the warm water is just a thin layer on the surface. Strong winds push the water around, so that a fluctuation of 20°F in a day is not unusual. These fluctuations induce the fish to move around. It pays to have a thermometer in the boat.

Ice fishing on Lake Superior is very productive and begins in December, when splake are taken from Washburn to Bayfield in 20 to 50 feet of water. Walleye, northern pike, and perch provide action farther south in Chequamegon Bay. Ice fishing for lake trout, or "bobbing" as the locals call it, starts in late January in water from 70 to 170 feet deep. Ice conditions are often dangerous, and only the experienced or those with a fishing guide should venture out across the numerous cracks and pressure ridges to the bobbing grounds.

Wisconsin Muskellunge

The muskellunge is special in Wisconsin; it has its own following and is the official state fish. Muskie addicts wear T-shirts that proclaim, "To a muskie fisherman, everything else is just bait." Perhaps nowhere else is this species pursued with such fervor.

Although it is closely related to the northern pike in appearance, a muskellunge behaves quite differently. Muskies were never as abundant as pike, and even a good muskie lake today may have only one adult fish for every 2 acres of water. Muskellunge will follow a lure to the boat, often more than once, and sometimes lie on the surface in an unconcerned manner. They are much more inclined to jump than a pike, and grow much larger. Yet, there are plenty of tiger muskies, which are northern pike–muskellunge hybrids. "Natural" tigers are common in Lac Vieux Desert and Big St. Germain in Vilas County, and in several other waters in the upper Wisconsin River drainage.

Wisconsin is the home of the often disputed world-record muskellunge of 69 pounds, 11 ounces, taken in the Chippewa Flowage in 1949. The undisputed world-record tiger muskie was also caught in Wisconsin, a 51-pound, 3-ounce fish that was caught in Lac Vieux Desert in 1919.

Wisconsin lies in the heart of the original range of the muskellunge, and in many lakes here these fish still reproduce naturally. The DNR supplements their populations through stocking. It raises large muskie fingerlings at its two huge fish hatcheries at Spooner and Woodruff. Annual production approaches 100,000 10- to 14-inch fish. These hatcheries also rear the Great Lakes strain of muskellunge, commonly called the spotted muskie. They have been reintroduced into Green Bay waters, where they are becoming a more common catch among anglers.

As a result, Wisconsin leads the world in muskie fishing. These fish are present in 711 lakes and numerous rivers. Anglers land an estimated 100,000 muskellunge a year, 90 percent of which are released. Most fish run between 30 and 40 inches in length, or from 7 to 20 pounds each. A few fish weighing more than 40 pounds are caught each year.

Wisconsin waters receive heavy angling pressure for these fish, and varying length limits have been instituted in an effort to grow more trophy muskies. Some lakes have 45-inch and 50-inch minimum length limits. With these measures, coupled with a growing catch-and-release ethic, the numbers of larger muskies should increase steadily in Wisconsin.

Fishing for muskellunge in Wisconsin begins in late May and runs through November. Smaller baits are preferred in the cold waters of early June, but later, most anglers turn to full-size bucktails and large plugs. Muskie action always picks up in

July and August, when anglers use surface lures as well as huge stickbaits or jerkbaits. They take some of the biggest fish in autumn, right until ice-up. Live bait in the form of suckers are preferred, and trophy hunters will use a 17-inch-long sucker in a quick-strike rig.

Although muskies have been known to eat mice, frogs, and even ducks, anglers will do well to remember their preferred foods in Wisconsin are yellow perch, white suckers, and large minnows.

Most anglers use baitcasting reels and stiff rods to handle the heavy baits. Many prefer a nonstretch line to get a better hookset. It is common to see two anglers, each standing in opposite ends of their boat, flinging their lures in an arc over a submerged weedbed. They vigorously work the lure in a figure-eight pattern at the end of each retrieve, hoping to get a strike from this elusive fish.

See: Spoon.

WOBBLER
(1) A generic word for any thin metal spoon, often used for trolling, sometimes for casting; small- and medium-size spoons, especially those used in fishing for lake trout and landlocked salmon, are sometimes referred to as wobblers, especially by anglers in the northeastern U.S., eastern Canada, and in Great Britain.

(2) A generic word for crankbaits or diving plugs, primarily used in Scandinavian countries; plugs that exhibit a strong side-to-side action while diving and swimming may be called wobblers but are distinguished in shape from those with minnow-like bodies.

WOLFFISH
Eel-like in body shape, wolffish are blenny relatives that live in the cold to arctic waters of the Atlantic and Pacific. They are members of the Anarhichadidae family, which encompasses seven species. Wolffish lack pelvic fins, and the dorsal fin, which begins just behind the head, extends to the caudal fin but is not joined to it. The anal fin extends about half the length of the ventral surface. Wolffish have powerful jaws and numerous broad teeth that are used to crush the shells of mollusks and crustaceans. They also have sharp canine teeth, which makes them dangerous to handle.

The Atlantic wolffish (*Anarhichas lupus*), inhabits the western Atlantic from southern Labrador and western Greenland to Cape Cod, rarely occurring as far south as New Jersey. In the eastern Atlantic, it ranges from Spitsbergen south to the White Sea, along the Scandinavian coasts, into the North Sea, the British Isles, Iceland, and southeastern Greenland. It is also known as, in Danish: *havkat;* Dutch: *zeewolf;* Norwegian: *gråsteinbit;* and Swedish: *havskatt.*

The sides of its brownish gray to purplish body are crossed by as many as a dozen vertical black bars. It is sedentary and rather solitary in habit, and is commonly found at depths of 45 to 65 fathoms. Populations tend to be localized. Although it appears sluggish, it is easily provoked, can move rapidly for short distances, and gives severe bites. Little is known about the biology of this species. Individuals can attain a length of 5 feet and a weight of 40 pounds. They prey on mollusks, crabs, lobster, and sea urchins. The Atlantic wolffish is seldom caught by anglers and is usually taken commercially by otter trawls. It is overexploited and depleted in the western Atlantic.

Also in the North Atlantic and with similar ranges are the spotted wolffish (*A. minor*) and the northern wolffish (*A. denticulatis*). In the North Pacific, the very similar Bering wolffish (*A. orientalis*) occurs in the Sea of Japan and from the Aleutian Islands in Alaska southward to central California. The wolf-eel (*Anarrichthys ocellatus*) has a similar range; it reaches a length of 6 feet, 8 inches. These species are also caught by commercial trawlers, as they all make excellent eating despite their ugly appearance.

WOLF RIVER RIG
A bottom fishing bait rig featuring a three-way swivel, weight, and live minnow, derived from anglers fishing for walleyes on the Wolf River in Wisconsin.

WORLD-RECORD FISH
See: Records.

Atlantic Wolffish

WORM

Any natural earthworm or marine worm; also a soft imitation of the natural object, usually made of plastic. Many types of natural worms exist and are suitable for use as bait, whether whole or in pieces. Imitation worms are primarily used in fishing for largemouth bass, where they are extremely popular and effective, and other soft wormlike lures are used for a variety of fish in freshwater and saltwater.
See: Lure; Natural Bait.

WORM HOOK

A hook for use with various soft lures, especially artificial worms.
See: Hook; Soft Worm.

WRASSES

Wrasses are members of the Labridae family, an extremely varied group of some 500 species that are most abundant in warm seas around the world, although some occur in temperate to cool waters. Projecting canine teeth and thick, protrusible lips give the face a distinctive profile. Many species are brightly colored, and the body is elongated. The spiny and soft dorsal fins are united as one, and the anal fin is the same size and shape as the soft-rayed portion of the dorsal fin. Typically, the pectoral and caudal fins are rounded, and the caudal peduncle is clearly set off from the body.

The color of wrasses varies greatly, often differing from young to mature fish and becoming different during the breeding season, as well as changing with the background over which the fish swim. Most species are greenish, but they may be marked with red, yellow, or blue. Smaller species are collected for aquariums. Many smaller wrasses of tropical reefs practice the unusual habit of cleaning parasites from the bodies of larger fish.

Prominent angling wrasses along North American coasts are the California sheephead *(see: sheephead, California)* and the tautog *(see)*. Some species are prominent in the warm waters of Florida, the Bahamas, and Bermuda, including the hogfish *(Lachnolaimus maximus)*, which is one of the larger-growing members of the clan and has been caught to nearly 20 pounds. The largest of the family is the humphead wrasse *(Cheilinus undualtus)*, which is also known as the giant wrasse or giant Maori wrasse; the all-tackle world-record fish weighed 43 pounds, 10 ounces, but these fish can attain much greater weights and have been reported to exceed 6 feet in length. They inhabit Indo-Pacific waters. The ballan wrasse *(Labrus bergylta)* is a common eastern Atlantic species that occurs from Norway and Scotland to northwestern Africa, and grows to roughly 10 pounds.

Wrasses are predominantly reef, rock, and wreck dwellers. Anglers catch them principally by bottom-fishing with baits. They are caught from small boats inshore, from party boats, and from some piers or jetties.
See: Inshore Fishing.

WRECK

Shipwrecks are a type of man-made structure common to the coastal continental shelf waters of many oceans. Resting on the ocean floor, often near bare stretches of mud bottom, they are conspicuous fish attractants and may hold a variety of pelagic as well as bottom species during the season, some offering year-round fishing.

The general location of some wrecks is well known and published on charts and in various publicly available literature. Many are unpublicized, found by luck or by plenty of searching, and their locations are shared with relatively few others. The locations of some are zealously guarded, especially by party boat and charter boat captains.

When the Loran or GPS coordinates of wrecks are known, they are located by using these navigational devices; this is not an automatic thing, because a grid search pattern is usually necessary to pinpoint the exact location of the wreck. Pinpointing these locations is done in combination with using narrow-cone-angle sonar both to find the main or high point of the wreck as well as to find nearby rubble and baitfish.

Wrecks may be fished via trolling and drifting, but the primary tactic is to anchor and chum. Precise anchoring over the high point of the wreck is essential to properly fishing it. When anchored, some fishing occurs near the surface when fish are attracted to the chum, but most fishing is deep—on or close to the bottom—with bait, baited jigs, or heavy metal jigs, although many of the latter are lost owing to hangups.

Depending on current, fish may be on one side or the other of the wreck, although some species cluster in the wreck and others are found nearby. Some of the best wrecks have large fields of debris within a few hundred feet of the main wreck location.
See: Anchor; Chumming; Drift Fishing; Inshore Fishing; Jigging.

WRECKFISH *Polyprion americanus.*

Other names—bass, stone bass, wreck bass, hapu-

Ballan Wrasse

ku; Afrikaans: *wrakvis;* Danish: *vragfisk;* Dutch: *wrakbaars;* Finnish: *hylkyahven;* French: *chernier commun, mérot gris;* Greek: *vláchos;* Icelandic: *rekaldsfiskur;* Italian: *cherna di fondale;* Norwegian and Swedish: *vrakfisk;* Portuguese: *cherne;* Spanish: *cherna;* Turkish: *iskorpit hanisi.*

A member of the Polyprionidae family and relat-

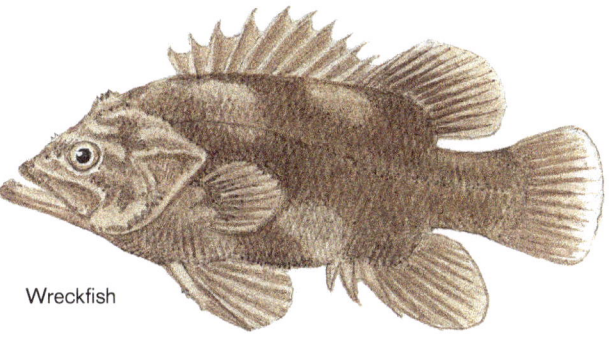
Wreckfish

ed to the giant sea bass, the wreckfish is a very deep-dwelling and large-growing species occasionally caught by heavy-tackle anglers probing extreme depths. It is marketed fresh or frozen, sometimes as sea bass or stone bass, although it is susceptible to overfishing and is regulated in U.S. federal waters.

Identification. The wreckfish has a deep, strongly compressed body and a very bumpy head with a ridge and bony protuberances above the eye. Adult fish are uniformly dark brown or bluish gray, and the young are mottled. The second dorsal, as well as the caudal and anal fins, are often edged in black, although the rounded caudal fin is otherwise edged in white, as are the pectoral fins. The spinous and soft parts of the dorsal fins are notched, and the lower jaw projects past the upper jaw.

Size. The wreckfish grows slowly but can eventually reach 7 feet or more in length and weigh 100 or more pounds. The all-tackle world record is a 106-pound, 14-ounce fish taken off Portugal.

Distribution. In the eastern Atlantic, the wreckfish is found from Norway to South Africa, including the Madeira, Canary, and Cape Verde Islands, and the Mediterranean. In the western Atlantic, it ranges from Newfoundland to North Carolina. In the western Indian Ocean, it inhabits the St. Paul and Amsterdam Islands and has been reported from New Zealand.

Habitat. Found in the deep part of the continental shelf, at up to 2,000-foot depths, wreckfish prefer rocky ledges, pinnacles, and outcroppings around shipwrecks. They are solitary fish and are sometimes found drifting with floating timber or other objects.

Food. Wreckfish feed on crustaceans, mollusks, and deep-dwelling fish found around wrecks or underwater objects.

Angling. Wreckfish are typically caught by anglers using very heavy gear, strong lines, heavy weights, and large hooks baited with fish strips or chunks. They land wreckfish primarily by fishing at the right depth over an irregular bottom. The appropriate depth can vary from 200 feet to 1,000 or more feet; keeping large specimens from cutting the line on bottom obstacles and then winching them to the surface are tough requirements. The amount of weight to use varies with depth, current, and site, but it's important to present the offering right on the bottom.

See: Inshore Fishing.

WYOMING

Wyoming is a big place with no large cities, few people, and little industry. This western state has more pronghorn antelope than people and ranks 50th among the states in population. Yet its open spaces and fish and wildlife draw tourists, who flock to such national forests as Shoshone, the first national forest preserve, and Yellowstone National Park, the first national park. People also come to view the unique and spectacular scenery and to participate in the state's phenomenal hunting and fishing opportunities.

Within its 97,809 square miles, Wyoming boasts high plains, mountains, deserts, and badlands. There are many plateaus with elevations between 4,500 and 7,500 feet. In the southeast corner, the Laramie Mountains rise to more than 10,000 feet, and the Medicine Bow Mountains reach 12,005 feet at Medicine Bow Peak. In the north-central area, the Bighorn Mountains jump to 13,165 feet on Cloud Peak. In the northwest corner, Francs Peak in the Absaroka Range rises to 13,140 feet. The Grand Teton in the Teton Range points to 13,766 feet, and Wyoming's highest mountain, Gannett Peak, is in the Wind River Range and rises to 13,785 feet. Many other peaks in the Wind River Range eclipse 13,000 feet.

Just about everything runs downhill out of Wyoming. The state's headwater status provides water for four important drainage systems—the Missouri-Mississippi, the Great Basin, the Columbia, and the Colorado.

Most of Wyoming drains to the north and east into the Missouri-Mississippi system. Tributaries of the Missouri River include the Yellowstone, Clark's Fork, Bighorn, Tongue, and Powder Rivers flowing north, and the Cheyenne, Niobrara, and North Platte Rivers flowing east. The major source of the Colorado River is the Green River. The Snake River and Salt River join and flow into the Columbia system. And the Bear River, part of the Great Basin system, flows along Wyoming's western edge and dumps into the Great Salt Lake in Utah.

Wyoming's fishing bounty derives from hundreds of small, clear mountain streams and lakes. The state's largest freshwater mountain lakes are the Yellowstone, Shoshone, Fremont, and Jackson. Other small bodies of water are man-made due to reclamation projects. The major reservoirs include

Seminoe, Pathfinder, Alcova, Glendo, and Guernsey Reservoirs in the North Platte River system, and Boysen Reservoir and Bighorn Lake (Wind River/Big Horn River), Buffalo Bill (Shoshone River), and Flaming Gorge Reservoir (Green River).

Southeast

North Platte River (Colorado line to Seminoe Reservoir). The North Platte River cuts a 300-mile swath through the mountains to the plains and defines fishing in Wyoming's southeast corner. Almost 90 miles of the North Platte are classified by the Wyoming Game and Fish Department as Class I, or blue-ribbon, waters. This classification means that these 90 miles are premium trout waters and fisheries of national importance. Float-fishing for rainbow and brown trout down the undisturbed upper river is one of the most beautiful adventures in the West. The best time for float fishing is from mid-June through July.

Seminoe Reservoir. The first impoundment on the North Platte River system, Seminoe Reservoir spans 21,000 acres and is one of the best fisheries in Wyoming. It produces big rainbow and brown trout, as well as walleye. Spring is a good time for big trout, and walleye fishing improves as the water warms.

Miracle Mile. Two trophy-trout tailwater fisheries draw the most attention from anglers pursuing big rainbow and brown trout: the famous so-called Miracle Mile between Seminoe and Pathfinder Reservoirs, and the Gray Reef area below Alcova Reservoir.

Today, the Mile rarely offers a solitary experience. No matter what Wyoming's weather, a few anglers always seem to be on the Mile, although the fishing can still be very good. The Mile actually averages 5 to 8 miles in length, from Kortes Dam below Seminoe Reservoir to the backwaters of Pathfinder Reservoir; in drought years, it can be up to 15 miles long.

Pathfinder Reservoir. You can't see the North Platte River make its big turn to the east anymore, because all 22,000 acres of Pathfinder Reservoir conceal the evidence. That's good news for anglers in search of trophy rainbow trout and big walleye.

Alcova Reservoir. Good fishing for trout and walleye can be found at 2,260-acre Alcova Reservoir, which produces among the biggest walleyes in the North Platte system. Fishing for brown trout can yield impressive results, especially in the fall. Don't expect a quiet trip to Alcova during the summer; weekends draw Casper-area people who own personal watercraft and speedboats.

Gray Reef. Some of the state's best year-round trout fishing occurs on the tailwaters of Gray Reef Dam. Large trout are often caught between November and March in the river's warmer waters that don't freeze. Even during high periods, the water below Gray Reef Dam stays clearer and more fishable than in other places on the Platte.

North Platte. (Alcova to Glendo Reservoir). From Alcova Reservoir to Edness Kimball Wilkins State Park at Casper, the North Platte is one of Wyoming's best stretches of big river. Fishing here is good for rainbow trout, and big browns are sometimes taken. The highest trout densities are in the stretch of river from Lusby public fishing area to Gray Reef, and at The Narrows. Below Casper, the North Platte is a marginal trout fishery because its flow slows and the water warms. Persistent anglers can catch catfish and walleye throughout this stretch.

Glendo Reservoir. There's good fishing for walleye, catfish, and yellow perch on Glendo Reservoir's 15,000 acres. Most Glendo walleye are taken around islands and rocky points in the upper part of the reservoir, and downstream they're taken near the dam. Catfishing is best near where the North Platte River flows into the reservoir. Yellow perch fishing on Glendo can be good almost anytime or anywhere. Like other Platte reservoirs, Glendo is a busy place on the weekends, so weekdays offer the best fishing.

North Platte below Glendo Reservoir. Between Glendo Dam and Wendover Siding, almost the only fishing pressure is applied by floating anglers. The fishing can be good for rainbow, brown, and cutthroat trout from April through early May, and in September and October. Several miles of publicly accessible water below Glendo Dam can produce good fishing for bank anglers, too.

Encampment River. For those who are prepared to walk, the Encampment River is a good bet for brown, rainbow, cutthroat, and brook trout. The Encampment begins on the Continental Divide in Colorado and flows north into Wyoming along the eastern flank of the Sierra Madre. It flows gently through Commissary Park to Entrance Falls, where, for the next 18 miles, it drops through a steep, forested canyon known as the Encampment River Wilderness Area. Here, fishing for brown and rainbow trout is best usually in late summer or fall, after the runoff peaks.

The lower part of the Encampment River flows through a series of ranches as it nears its confluence with the North Platte River, and public access is limited.

Hog Park Reservoir. Above the Encampment River is 695-acre Hog Park Reservoir and the creek bearing its name, Hog Park Creek. The creek merges with the Encampment River near Entrance Falls. Brown, rainbow, and brook trout inhabit the creek and are a challenge to catch. The creek's undercut banks and pools provide refuge for some of its bigger trout. Nearby beaver ponds and other small creeks offer good fishing for brook trout.

Hog Park Reservoir is a popular place for families to fish. Productive angling for cutthroat, rainbow, and brook trout keeps these families coming back year after year.

Little Snake River. Several branches of the Little Snake River flow off the west slopes of the

Sierra Madre. The rare Colorado River cutthroat calls them home, and these colorful trout are protected by catch-and-release regulations. The best fishing is in the higher elevations for cutthroat and brook trout. Rainbow trout are common on the river near the Colorado border. Public access is very limited on the lower stretches of river.

Sweetwater River. The North Platte's largest tributary, the Sweetwater River, flows into Pathfinder Reservoir. Fishing for rainbow and brown trout is fair to good on the Sweetwater in the late summer and fall, after the runoff ends and the water clears. Be prepared when planning a fishing excursion on the Sweetwater—it's a long way from the Sweetwater to any town. More than 75 miles of public-access fishing is available on the Sweetwater, but these public areas are in some of Wyoming's most remote places. The lower parts of the river, below Sweetwater Station, meander through ranching country. Permission to fish is required in the lower parts of the river.

Laramie Plains lakes. The Laramie Plains lakes are north, south, and west of Laramie, and they are known for producing fat, fast-growing trout. They are also famous for their winds, and are fished fairly hard all year. They produce nice fish for people with patience, who show up early and stay late in the day.

Lake Alsop is west of Laramie on Herrick Lane. The action is usually slow for rainbow and cutthroat trout, splake, and grayling. Early mornings and late evenings are the best times to fish on points bordered by deep water.

Fishing at Lake Hattie west of Laramie offers particularly diverse fishing. Anglers can catch yellow perch, rainbow, cutthroat, and brown trout, kokanee salmon, and lake trout. The action isn't as good at 1,500-acre Hattie as at other Plains lakes, but the chance of catching a big fish is better. Action is usually best when the wind isn't blowing, making early morning and later afternoon best bets.

Lake Gelatt, west of Laramie, offers fair fishing for rainbow trout and grayling. The lake's bigger fish are generally caught just after the ice melts. Action during the fall is usually fair.

Twin Buttes Reservoir can provide fast action for yellow perch early and late in the day. Fishing for trout is only fair, because the yellow perch are doing so well in the lake.

Spring is usually the best time to fish Sodergreen Lake, west of Laramie. The lake is stocked early each year with rainbow trout. Fishing is best early in the day when the winds are calm.

Pole Mountain beaver ponds. More than 100 beaver ponds dot the Sherman Mountains between Cheyenne and Laramie. Fishing varies depending on water conditions and beaver activity, but where there's a pond, the fishing is usually good for brook trout. Big fish are unusual, but catching lots of little ones is the norm. Fishing is good throughout the season and is best at sunrise, sunset, and after dark.

Snowy Range waters. The Snowy Range is roughly 50 miles west of Laramie. Nearly 100 lakes and several hundred streams are there. Fishing is good for small trout, especially in areas accessed by a considerable hike. Lake Owen and Rob Roy are the largest reservoirs in the Snowy Mountains and provide good seasonal trout fishing.

Laramie Peak country. Wheatland Reservoir No. 3, at 7,600 acres, is one of Wyoming's best reservoirs for big rainbow, brown, and cutthroat trout. The fishing is best in April and early May, and from late September until the lake freezes. Angling pressure is high in the spring.

Toltec Reservoir is north of Wheatland No. 3 in one of Wyoming's most remote areas. Fishing can be good for medium-size rainbow and brook trout. Angling is usually best early and late in the day in spring and fall. Roughly 6 miles of public land allow access to Duck Creek, where there's fair fishing for small rainbow, brown, and brook trout.

Other sites. Hawk Springs Reservoir is southeast of Hawk Springs and the best fishery in the area, boasting good-size walleye, largemouth bass, catfish, yellow perch, and crappie. Anglers sometimes catch nice brown trout as well. Most people fish 1,100-acre Hawk Springs for its walleye, though, either early in the morning or in the evening.

Packers Lake east of Yoder offers fair fishing for walleye, catfish, and rainbow trout. Some bass are also caught. Grayrocks Reservoir east of Wheatland is the best walleye lake in Wyoming. Action for walleye is excellent all over this 3,500-acre lake, which also contains yellow perch, crappie, smallmouth bass, and tiger muskies.

Northeast

Tongue River. The rewards in fishing the Tongue River while viewing the scenery along the way are worth the extra effort required to reach this water. Anglers making the trip can expect to sample classic pocket water for cutthroat, rainbow, and brown trout.

Clear mountain streams, like the Little Laramie River here, provide good trout fishing throughout Wyoming.

The upper river holds good-size trout, and fall spawning runs bring larger brown trout upriver. Downstream, the river flows through private lands, and permission is required to access this area of good brown trout fishing.

The North Tongue is a gentle stream with a healthy population of Yellowstone cutthroat and smaller numbers of rainbow and brook trout. It receives a lot of pressure, as the size of its fish are steadily increasing due to catch-and-release efforts.

The South Tongue is a small, cascading stream. The best fishing is along the stream's 7-mile descent between Tie Plume and Prune Creeks for rainbow and brook trout.

Northern Bighorns lakes. Sibley Lake is between Dayton and Burgess Junction. It's a popular alpine fishery for cutthroat and brook trout, and requires a short hike to get there. Sawmill and Twin Lakes offer good to fair fishing for cutthroat, rainbow, and brook trout. Cutthroat and rainbow trout are usually part of the creel at Park Reservoir.

Cloud Peak Wilderness. The Cloud Peak Wilderness offers more than 189,000 acres of wilderness land in the Bighorn Mountains, and more than 200 trout-filled lakes are scattered like dots across the range. Hundreds of streams run through the drainages and fill the lakes. Although trout in the lakes are bigger than fish in the streams, the stream fishery is better. Anglers can catch rainbow, brook, and cutthroat trout, as well as grayling and lake trout in the Bighorns.

Among the popular destinations are Seven Brothers Lakes, Lake Angeline, and Willow Park Reservoir. Lake Solitude and West Tensleep Lake are especially scenic. Tensleep Creek and Meadowlark Lake on the west side of the Bighorns are popular, too.

Middle Fork Powder River. Public access to Middle Fork Canyon is southwest of Kaycee. It takes a little extra effort to get there, but it's worth it. Good-size rainbow and brown trout live in the deep canyon pools. Roughly 10 miles of public access water is available to anglers in the canyon.

Sand Creek. Sand Creek is a spring creek that flows through the eastern foothills of Wyoming's Black Hills and is home to a large population of brown trout. These fish, and their creek, pose a challenge. Undercut banks and a summer growth of weedbeds make the fishing tough.

Keyhole Reservoir. Between Sundance and Moorcroft lies Wyoming's premier northern pike fishery, 9,000-acre Keyhole Reservoir. It holds a variety of other warmwater species, including walleye, catfish, crappie, and smallmouth bass.

Fishing for walleye is best in May and June. Northern pike fishing is best early in the spring at Mule Creek Bay on the southeast side of the reservoir, at Eggie Creek Bay on the northern end, or at Cottonwood Bay between the dam and marina.

The reservoir's smallmouth bass are small but fun to catch and are best caught from June through August early and late in the day. The catfishing is good from spring through fall, mainly at night. Keyhole is crowded on summer weekends. Only a few diehard anglers fish the lake during the week.

Prairie reservoirs. Lake DeSmet, north of Buffalo, has a healthy population of Eagle Lake rainbow trout. Yellowstone cutthroat trout and large brown trout are also caught here. The 3,220-acre DeSmet is the most popular lake in the region, and fishes well until the water warms and forces trout deeper. DeSmet fishing is especially good in the fall.

Muddy Guard Reservoir No. 1, southeast of Buffalo, has rainbow and brown trout, as does its twice-larger sibling, Muddy Guard Reservoir No. 2; both fish easier in the spring. Healy Reservoir, east of Buffalo, is a small but popular site and receives significant pressure. Fishing for Healy's rainbow and cutthroat trout is best in the spring.

Northwest

Wind River. The Wind River originates at Wind River Lake at the base of Togwotee Pass northwest of Dubois. By the time it reaches Dubois, it's a good-size stream and the fishing, although challenging, can be good. This is the best stream in central Wyoming.

From Stoney Point northeast of Dubois, the Wind River offers excellent fishing for about 8 miles. Anglers can catch rainbow, brown, and cutthroat trout, plus whitefish. Fishing is best from mid-August through fall, when the water is low and clear.

Below Dubois, the Wind River enters the Wind River Indian Reservation. A special license is required to fish that section. Two miles of the Wind below Boysen is a popular but profitable tailwater fishery. It yields good-size rainbow and brown trout, walleye, and ling. The best time to fish this stretch is from March through early May.

At the end of this 2-mile segment, the Wind River again enters the Wind River Indian Reservation. This 15-mile section is a pocket-water secret, even though a main highway runs beside it through Wind River Canyon. A special permit is required throughout the canyon up to where the river flows under the highway bridge. There, at the Wedding of the Waters, the Wind River's name changes to the Big Horn River.

Big Horn River. The best fishing on the Big Horn River begins south of the town of Thermopolis and extends nearly 20 miles past Wind River Canyon. Fertile waters here produce trophy rainbow, brown, and cutthroat trout. The rest of its 130-mile trek travels north through sagebrush country to Bighorn Lake near the Montana border. The warmer water supports catfish, sauger, and a few brown trout as it nears Bighorn Lake and the Yellowtail Dam in Montana.

The best place to fish for walleye and catfish on Bighorn Lake is generally around Horseshoe Bend. Action is best in May and June.

Wind River Indian Reservation. The 2.3-mil-

lion-acre Wind River Indian Reservation receives very little angling pressure, but the fishing opportunities are some of the best in the West. The fishery is open during the spring and summer, and special permits are required. Many lowland and alpine venues exist on the reservation, and anglers catch big trout, grayling, and walleye.

Boysen Reservoir. Boysen Reservoir, north of Shoshone, features good rainbow and cutthroat trout fishing in spring. The face of the dam, the bay at the boat ramp, and rocky points along the northeastern shore are productive areas. Fishing for walleye heats up in June. It remains fair or good throughout the summer. The 15,000-acre lake also has ling, crappie, and its perch are particularly sought after. Pressure at Boysen can be heavy on holidays but is moderate the rest of the year.

Foothills fishing. Northwest of Dubois is Brooks Lake, situated in a breathtakingly scenic area. It offers good fishing for rainbow trout, lake trout, and splake. The fishing is best shortly after the ice melts, and in the fall. Upper and Lower Jade Lakes, Upper Brooks Lake, and Rainbow Lake are short hikes from Brooks Lake.

Three popular lakes are east of Dubois: Torrey, Ring, and Trail Lakes. All are home to rainbow, brown, and lake trout, and splake. These lakes fish best in the spring and fall. Near these is Jakey's Fork, a nice trout stream with good summer fishing for browns.

Northwest of Dubois is Horse Creek, which has fair to good fishing for brook, rainbow, and brown trout. The Wiggins Fork River, the East Fork River, and Bear Creek near Dubois have cutthroat trout, which are caught where there's decent cover.

Ocean Lake, 15 miles northwest of Riverton, is a 6,100-acre reservoir that offers fair walleye fishing from mid-May through June. A few perch, crappie, largemouth bass, and ling are also taken. Pilot Butte Reservoir, west of Kinnear, produces some rainbows as well as big ling.

Local anglers refer to Lake Cameahwait as Bass Lake for its good numbers of largemouth bass. Located near the west shore of Boysen Reservoir, Cameahwait also harbors rainbow trout and perch. The bass fishing is best in June. Middle Depression Reservoir is a rainbow trout fishery west of Lake Cameahwait.

Louis Lake, northeast of Atlantic City, offers fair to good fishing for brook and rainbow trout. Occasionally anglers catch nice-size lake trout. The action is best right after ice out. Northwest of Atlantic City, Rock Creek Reservoir offers good angling for small and medium-size brook and rainbow trout.

Frye and Fiddlers Lakes and Worthen Meadows Reservoir offer fair to good fishing for small and medium trout. The action is best in spring and fall, early and late in the day.

Carmody Lake, Antelope Springs Reservoir, and Silver Creek Reservoir are between Lander and Jeffrey City. All three fisheries produce nice rainbow trout in the spring and fall.

Popo Agie River. The Popo Agie forms at Lander after collecting the flows of its mountain tributaries. The Popo Agie and its tributaries provide good fishing for rainbow and brown trout. Larger brown trout run upstream from Boysen Reservoir to spawn in the fall, and walleye are also present in the river.

The Little Popo Agie—10 miles south of Lander—the North Fork of the Popo Agie, and the Middle Fork of the Popo Agie have good summer and fall fishing for rainbow and brown trout. The Middle Fork also has brook trout.

The high lakes. The waters on the east side of the Wind River Range are known for golden trout and long hikes. This country probably holds the world's best golden trout fishery. Unfortunately, perhaps, a hike of up to 20 miles is required to reach it.

Trips into the wilderness areas above Lander and Dubois probably shouldn't be attempted until after mid-July. Until then, hikers will likely encounter snowdrifts and frozen water. Anglers who make the trip find good fishing for rainbow, brook, lake, and brown trout as well. Fishing is best in August and September.

Clark's Fork River. The Clark's Fork, northwest of Cody, is Wyoming's only Wild and Scenic River. It runs south from Montana into Wyoming from the Absaroka Mountains. Its 66-mile run through Wyoming offers good fishing for Yellowstone cutthroat, rainbow, and brook trout. Grayling, whitefish, and brown trout add to the selection below Clark's Fork Canyon on the river's desert path back into Montana. The whitefish action is excellent.

Tributaries of the Clark's Fork, such as Sunlight, Crandall, and Dead Indian Creeks, offer good fishing for Yellowstone cutthroat, rainbow, and brook trout. Above Sunlight Creek's headwaters are the three Copper lakes, which harbor golden trout. Swamp Lake is home to some trophy brook trout.

Beartooth Wilderness lakes. More than 100 lakes are fishable in the Beartooths. The fishing is good after the snow and ice melts from the region. Anglers catch Yellowstone cutthroat, brook, rainbow, golden and lake trout, grayling, and splake.

Shoshone River. The North Fork of the Shoshone River and its tributaries offer excellent fishing for Yellowstone cutthroat throughout the year, and the fishing is best from spring through fall. The South Fork of the Shoshone River has good-size brown trout in the summer and fall, when anglers can catch them. Farther upstream, the South Fork has above-average brook and cutthroat trout.

The Shoshone River offers excellent fishing between Buffalo Bill Dam and Willwood Dam between Cody and Powell. This big tailwater river often gives up big brown, cutthroat, and rainbow trout, and the fishing is good throughout the year.

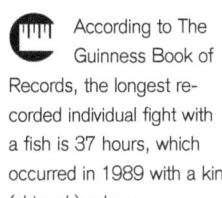 According to The Guinness Book of Records, the longest recorded individual fight with a fish is 37 hours, which occurred in 1989 with a king (chinook) salmon.

Buffalo Bill Reservoir. Buffalo Bill Reservoir west of Cody is the most popular fishery in the area. Excellent fishing for rainbow and cutthroat is the norm. The 4,900-acre lake also gives up arm-length lake trout. The best fishing times are spring and early summer, and during midweek. The reservoir receives a lot of angling pressure throughout the year.

Other sites. East Newton Lake, north of Cody, is famous for trophy rainbow and golden trout. West Newton Lake offers good fishing for cutthroat and brook trout.

Beck Lake, southeast of Cody, is known for rainbow trout, largemouth bass, yellow perch, and catfish. Fishing pressure is heavy on the weekends, and moderate during the week.

Deaver Reservoir, south of Frannie, has good fishing for small and medium rainbow trout. The reservoir also contains largemouth bass, sunfish, and bluegills.

Upper Sunshine and Lower Sunshine reservoirs are southwest of Meeteetse. Both have fair to good fishing for cutthroat trout and splake.

Luce and Hogan Reservoirs, both north of Cody, are home to good numbers of rainbow, cutthroat, and brook trout. The fishing is fair in spring and fall, and slow in summer.

Renner Reservoir, northeast of Ten Sleep, boasts a good population of largemouth bass. Fishing pressure is heavy on weekends, and angling is best in the mornings and evenings from spring to early summer. Wardell Reservoir, south of Otto, provides good fishing for walleye and crappie.

Yellowstone National Park

America's oldest national park offers better fishing than most states. That's because fish harvest is tightly regulated, the park has plenty of water, and it contains arguably the best trout habitat in the lower 48 states.

Yellowstone Lake is the most famous and most fished water in the park. This 87,000-acre lake provides a world-renowned Yellowstone cutthroat trout fishery. It also contains lake trout, and park officials encourage harvesting of this introduced species to minimize predation on cutthroat. Fishing success usually drops off on Yellowstone Lake several days before and after a full moon.

The Yellowstone River flows south to north from its headwaters above Yellowstone Lake until it leaves the park near Gardiner, Montana. This is a big, fast-moving river, so weight is handy in trying to reach the fish. Action is hot for cutthroat trout, usually around mid-July.

The Firehole River flows southwest of Old Faithful geyser until it joins the Gibbon River to form the Madison River at Madison Junction. The Firehole is full of rainbow, brown, and brook trout. Despite this, fishing can be slow. The action is usually best early and late in the season, the best locations are near the mouths of its tributaries, where the water is cooler.

The Madison follows the highway from Madison Junction to the park's boundary north of West Yellowstone, Montana. It's loaded with big trout, but they can be tough to catch. Anglers who avoid midday and midsummer fishing usually have the best success.

Slough Creek is accessible east of Tower Junction. Anglers can find good fishing all along the foot trail. It's easy to see and stalk Slough Creek's big cutthroat trout.

The highway follows Gibbon River east of Norris Junction until it joins the Firehole at Madison Junction. Anglers experience steady fishing along Gibbon for small rainbow and brook trout. Angling for whitefish and brown trout is better near the Firehole confluence.

Lewis Lake is north of the park's south entrance along the main highway. This fishery is good for lake and brown trout. Angling is best early and late in the season.

Gardiner River flows north to south through the park wilderness before joining Obsidian Creek south of Mammoth. The Gardiner is perhaps the park's best brook trout fishery, and some nice browns are caught in its lower section.

The Lamar River flows northwesterly across the northeast corner of the park. It offers almost 50 miles of good fishing for cutthroat and rainbow trout. Much of the good fishing requires a walk-in.

Shoshone Lake is an 8,050-acre backcountry lake that produces big lake and brown trout, plus a few brookies. In July and August, anglers catch more and bigger fish by fishing deep. This can be done from shore by working dropoffs and the mouths of inlets.

Soda Butte Creek, in the northeast corner of the park, offers particularly fast fishing for cutthroat and rainbow trout. The Gallatin River, in the extreme northeast corner of the park, offers good to excellent fishing for rainbow, brown, and cutthroat trout, as well as whitefish. Fishing is best during July and August.

Southwest and West

Jackson Lake. Jackson Lake is 30 miles north of Jackson. This 25,370-acre reservoir produces nice lake and cutthroat trout. Action is best right after the ice melts in late May, and in late September.

Snake River. The Snake River is the common link between Grand Teton National Park and Jackson Hole. It is fished heavily during its 52-mile trek from Jackson Lake Dam through Jackson Hole. It's still one of the top fishing streams in the West.

The Snake River is home to the Snake River finespotted cutthroat trout, and anglers enjoy catching a few of these during their trips to the Snake. Besides cutthroat trout, the river's upper section also produces numerous brown trout and whitefish. The middle section, which ends near Jackson, is good for cutthroat trout and whitefish. The lower section has good fishing for bigger cutthroats.

Other waters near Jackson. Pacific Creek

crosses the highway between Moran Junction and Jackson Lake. In the Teton National Forest, cutthroat trout fishing is excellent. The Gros Ventre River crosses the highway 6 miles north of Jackson. Its upper stretch, above Kelly in the Teton National Forest, provides good fishing for cutthroat, brook, and rainbow trout. The Hoback River enters the Snake 17 miles south of Jackson. Most of the time, anglers can experience fair fishing here for cutthroat trout and whitefish, and late summer is the best time to pursue these fish. Granite Creek offers fair fishing for small cutthroat trout and whitefish. Flat Creek runs through the National Elk Refuge, and this fishery is good from August through October. The Buffalo Fork River enters the Snake River at Moran Junction. Many sections of the Buffalo Fork offer good fishing for cutthroat, brook, and rainbow trout in late summer and early fall.

Grassy, Leigh, Jenny, Phelps, Lower Slide, and Two Ocean Lakes offer fair to good fishing for brook, cutthroat, and lake trout. At Two Ocean Lake, action is best in spring and late fall. The lake sometimes gives up trophy trout.

Teton high-country waters. The high-country fishing here is good for small brook trout. But even some of the heavily fished waters yield up nice-size trout. It is generally late June before most of the high-country trails open. The best fishing is usually in September.

Green River. Most anglers on the Upper Green River catch good quantities of rainbows, but some catch brook, brown, and cutthroat trout. Action on the Green River is usually good from spring through fall, and it can be excellent at times. From Fontenelle Reservoir to Flaming Gorge Reservoir, the Green offers fair to good trout fishing; the key is finding good fish habitat. In areas with good habitat, anglers can catch many big rainbow, brown, and cutthroat trout. Float fishing is popular on the Green.

Fontenelle Reservoir. Ten miles south of LaBarge, 7,000-acre Fontenelle Reservoir is one of Wyoming's top lakes for big brown and rainbow trout. On the weekends during the summer, it's a busy place although not usually crowded.

Flaming Gorge Reservoir. Half of Flaming Gorge Reservoir's 42,000 acres is in Wyoming, the other half in Utah. It is famous for its lake trout fishing and produces a tremendous number of 20-plus-pound lake trout. The reservoir also has trophy brown trout, nice-size rainbow trout, kokanee salmon, smallmouth bass, and catfish.

New Fork River. One of the state's best trout streams, the New Fork River yields good numbers of nice-size brown and rainbow trout. The fishing is usually good to excellent following spring runoff. The action is best in the evening.

Lakes near Pinedale. The Finger Lakes near Pinedale all offer good fishing for lake trout. These include the New Fork Lakes 20 miles north of Pinedale, Willow Lake 12 miles north of Pinedale, Fremont Lake 5 miles and Halfmoon Lake 8 miles northeast of Pinedale, Boulder Lake 10 miles east of Pinedale, and Burnt Lake 10 miles east of Pinedale. The action is fastest at Burnt and Willow Lakes, but Fremont and New Fork Lakes have the larger fish. Anglers also catch rainbow and brown trout in the Finger Lakes.

The Green River lakes are roughly 40 miles north of Pinedale. They provide good fishing for big lake trout and rainbow trout. Action is best early and late in the day. Soda Lake, 7 miles north of Pinedale, has brook and brown trout. Mid-May and late September are the best times to fish Soda Lake.

Meadow Lake is the best source of grayling eggs in Wyoming, and it is probably the best grayling fishery in the West. It lies halfway between Halfmoon and Burnt Lakes. Meadow Lake usually loses its ice in mid- or late May, when the fishing is best. Middle Piney Lake, 25 miles west of Big Piney, offers good fishing for rainbow and cutthroat trout and can have good fishing for lake trout. Optimal times to pursue these fish are early and late in the day. Dollar Lake is 10 miles below the Green River lakes and is easy to fish for rainbow trout. The angling is best right before dark.

Bridger Wilderness. There are hundreds of alpine lakes and streams to fish in the Bridger Wilderness and Wind River Range. Anglers can catch plenty of small brook and cutthroat trout, but they have to walk to get there.

Other waters. Lake Viva Naughton, 17 miles northwest of Kemmerer, is usually busy but not too crowded on spring and summer weekends. This 1,375-acre lake holds nice-size rainbow trout. Kemmerer City Reservoir northwest of Kemmerer produces good rainbow trout. About 700 acres of big Palisades Reservoir, 40 miles south of Jackson, spills from Idaho into Wyoming; fishing is best in spring and fall for cutthroat, lake, and brown trout.

The Greys River is one of Wyoming's best-kept secrets, providing good fishing for cutthroat trout below Palisades Reservoir. The Hamms Fork River below Kemmerer City Reservoir has fair to good fishing for rainbow and brown trout. The Salt River produces good-size cutthroat and brown trout near Afton. The Smith's Fork River has fair fishing for brown and cutthroat trout. LaBarge Creek, west of LaBarge, has fair to good fishing for rainbow, brown, cutthroat, and brook trout.

Sulphur Creek Reservoir, 10 miles south of Evanston, spans 699 acres and is known for rainbow, brown, and cutthroat trout. The action is best in May and September. Woodruff Reservoir, north of Evanston, is 1 acre larger and has fair action for rainbow, cutthroat, and brown trout. Anglers also catch a few channel catfish and tiger muskies here. The Bear River is mostly on private land, but it offers fair to good fishing for cutthroat, brown, and rainbow trout.

YARN FLY

An artificial fly tied with yarn, some of which are also called egg flies. See: Fly.

YEAR-CLASS

The fish spawned and hatched in a given year, also referred to as a "generation" of fish.
See: Fisheries Management.

YELLOWTAIL

Other names—kingfish, yellowtail kingfish, king yellowtail, kingie, amberjack.

Yellowtail are members of the Carangidae family and are closely related to amberjack. Although they are commonly referenced by anglers and scientists as three separate species—California yellowtail *(Seriola lalandi dorsalis)*, southern yellowtail *(S. lalandi lalandi)*, and Asian yellowtail *(S. lalandi aureovittata)*—it is currently believed that the worldwide yellowtail pool consists of one species, *S. lalandi*. The three varieties are recognized distinctly, however, because they are isolated from each other and do not appear to interact; there are also size differences with some populations, the southern variety growing larger (especially in New Zealand waters) than the others.

These are fast-swimming, hard-striking, strong-pulling fish that give anglers a great struggle, especially in large sizes, and are a great favorite with shore, boat, and light-tackle big-game anglers. They are a commercially important species and are highly regarded as table fare. The smaller specimens, especially the California population, are preferred, although the flesh of some southern yellowtail has been found to turn milky when cooked.

Identification. Yellowtail are readily identifiable by their deeply forked, bright yellow caudal fins. Their body coloring graduates from a purple blue on the back to a silvery white on the belly. The body is elongate and moderately compressed, and a brass-colored stripe runs the length of the body from mouth to tail. There is a small keel on either side of the caudal peduncle.

Size. The southern yellowtail is believed to grow to a maximum weight of 70 kilograms and a length in excess of 2 meters, although fish of this size are rare. An Australian record, taken off Sydney, New South Wales, stands at 51 kilograms, and a 52-kilogram New Zealand fish holds the all-tackle world record. The world record for the California yellowtail is nearly 36 kilograms, but the average fish is much smaller.

Distribution. The California yellowtail ranges throughout the Gulf of California and along the Pacific coast of North America from Baja California, Mexico, to Los Angeles, California. On occasion, it is found as far north as Washington. The southern yellowtail occurs off southern Brazil and Argentina, South Africa, Australia, and North Island, New Zealand. In Australian waters, it ranges from Perth in Western Australia, around the bottom of Australia, and up the East Coast to North Reef, just North of Brisbane. Lord Howe Island, off the East Coast, and nearby Elizabeth Reef, hold among the world's largest southern yellowtail.

Habitat. Yellowtail are primarily coastal schooling fish found in inshore waters and out to the continental shelf. In addition to schooling in and around offshore reefs and rocky shores, they frequent deep water around wharves and jetties and man-made structures such as sunken vessels or artificial reefs where baitfish are common. Occasionally they will venture along ocean beaches and into larger estuaries. Large specimens, especially of the southern variety, are encountered in deep water around rocky pinnacles.

Life history/Behavior. Few details of the yellowtail's life history are available. Southern yellowtail are of spawning age at about two to three years. It is known that spawning occurs off eastern Australia from July through February, the occurrence varying with the location. Eggs are pelagic and hatch within two or three days. Juveniles are frequently found around floating objects such as

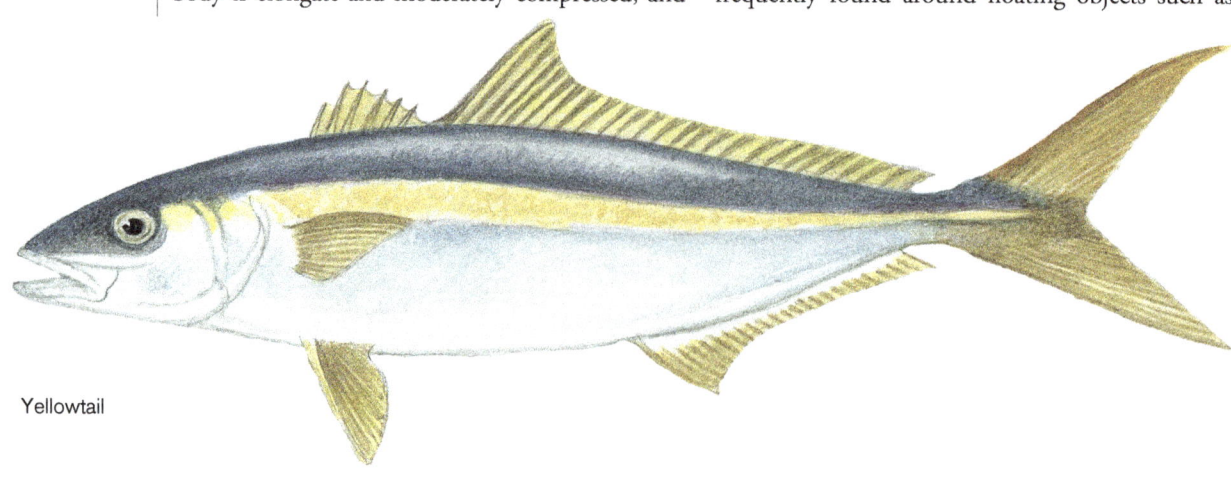

Yellowtail

A southern yellowtail from deep water off North Island, New Zealand.

buoys, traps, and channel markers.

Yellowtail can form large schools around reefs and will rise to the surface en masse to feed on schools of baitfish, as well as drive baitfish up against shore. Their migratory habits are not well known, although records tell of southerly moving spawning schools of southern yellowtail covering several square miles. Large individuals are believed to be less migratory.

Food and feeding habits. Yellowtail will eat whatever is available, but they feed predominantly on small fish, squid, and pelagic crustaceans. They are known to herd baitfish into shallow water off beaches, where they are vulnerable to the surf angler. Large specimens will tackle bluefish, salmon, and small tuna.

Angling. Various methods are used to catch yellowtail, including trolling, jigging, casting with lures, rock- and surf fishing, and fishing with baits. Tackle ranges from conventional gamefishing outfits in various classes to roller-tipped boat rods of various configurations to light and medium gear.

Lures can be large surface poppers, offshore trolling lures, plastic squid, metal spoons, metal jigs, skirted lures, feathered lures, artificial flies, dead fish, casting plugs, among others. Baits can consist of garfish; pilchards; squid; sauries; strips of mullet, tuna, and bonito; and live fish.

Slow to medium-fast trolling is most effective when close to deep-water rocky shores, around bomboras, along the dropoff from reefs, and over and around underwater pinnacles and wrecks. A well-known technique for southern yellowtail is using a flashing device rigged 1 to 2 meters ahead of a trolled bait.

Jigging requires repetitive lifting and dropping of a heavy metal jig and is very effective when used over offshore reefs. Once the school or reef is located by sonar, the jig is dropped over the side of the boat and allowed to sink to the bottom, then raised to the surface in a series of lifts. The procedure is repeated until a fish is hooked. Another strategy is to drop the jig to the bottom, then lift it up and down in one place. Both methods work well, although the former is preferred. Jigging can also be effective when using a strip bait hooked to the jig, or with a whole squid only.

Shore fishing from rocky platforms adjacent to deep water presents a real challenge to the shore-based southern yellowtail angler, as does fishing from man-made structures such as jetties and wharves. In these situations, lure casting with metal spoons or jigs demands physical stamina and finely honed casting skills. Fishing with live baits, using balloons to float the baits out from these areas, is also practiced.

Fly anglers are best served when schools of yellowtail swim close to the surface chasing baitfish. This is also when light-tackle anglers score well by tossing surface poppers. The excitement can be heightened by chumming to keep the fish at the surface, or by tethering a caught yellowtail behind the boat so that its efforts to escape attract the other members of the school and hold them in the vicinity. It's not unusual to see 50 to 100 trophy southern yellowtail swimming within meters of the boat; jigging a feathered lure or strip bait works especially well then.

Yellowtail don't concede easily when hooked. The first lengthy run is followed by several shorter ones, each impressing the angler with the power that this species possesses. In open water, they can usually be played out in a straightforward manner; however, if hooked from a boat over a reef, or from a shore-based location, the southern yellowtail will likely try to head to the nearest obstruction to break the line, often succeeding.

YUGOSLAVIA

The Federal Republic of Yugoslavia covers 102,173 square kilometers of territory and has more than 10 million inhabitants. It is situated in southeastern Europe, and nearly four-fifths of its landmass lies in the central area of the Balkan Peninsula, where the Rodope, Carpathian-Balkan, and Dinaric Mountains meet.

Yugoslavia is bordered on the north by Hungary, on the north and east by Romania, on the east by Bulgaria, on the south by Albania and the former Yugoslav Republic of Macedonia, and on the west by Croatia and Bosnia/Herzegovina. A southwestern strip of 153 kilometers borders the Adriatic Sea. Twenty-one percent of the country is in Middle Europe, that is, north of the Sava and Danube Rivers.

Yugoslavia consists of two republics: Serbia, which accounts for 86 percent of the land, and Montenegro, which is in the southwest facing the Adriatic. There are some 80,000 licensed anglers in the country, but at least twice that number fish without buying a license. There is almost no angling tourism due to water pollution, intensive localized sportfishing, legal and illegal commercial exploitation (on seas, rivers, and lakes), and a lack of angling guides, boat rentals, and other services; recent ethnic conflicts, as well as NATO military activities have obviously precluded visitation in any event. In better times, however, a tourist can still find some interesting fishing in Yugoslavia mainly for grayling, huchen, brown trout, and carp. The key is finding a local angler who is willing to help and with whom you can communicate. The chance of getting information from local tourist boards or angling clubs is slim.

James Heddon is credited with making the first artificial plug in the early 1900s, yet the first patent for a wooden lure was granted to David Huard and Charles Dunbar in 1874.

Land, Climate, and Resources

The northern part of Yugoslavia, from its border with Hungary and including the narrow zone to the south of the Sava and Danube Rivers, is part of the Panonian Flat. This area has a height of less then 200 meters and only two small mountains (Fruska Gora and Vrsacke Planine). The Danube, one of Europe's biggest rivers, enters Yugoslavia on the northwest and flows through the country for 588.5 kilometers, collecting 72.3 percent of its water and taking it to the Black Sea. Most of the Danube's big tributaries—the Sava, Tisa, and Tamis—are all slow flowing, with brown and muddy waters that are high in spring and low during summer.

A large network (hundreds of kilometers) of artificial canals connects the Danube and Tisa Rivers in the province of Vojvodina, north of the Sava and Danube. It is used for drainage, agricultural purposes, and water transport.

The climate in this region is continental; the summers are very hot and almost without rain (the daily temperature in July and August can reach 40°C, but is usually 30° to 35°C). Winters are sharp and long, with the lowest temperatures dipping to roughly –20°C. Vojvodina receives 500 to 600 millimeters of rain per year; the southern part of this flat region gets 700 to 900 millimeters of rain, mainly at the end of spring (May through June) and in autumn.

Mountains mainly in the range of 600 to 1,400 meters dominate the rest of Yugoslavia all the way south to the Adriatic coast. The highest mountain peak is Djeravica (2,656 meters) in the Prokletije Mountains in southern Yugoslavia.

Numerous streams, creeks, and medium-size rivers run down the mountains and through the valleys. Waters from this area primarily flow to the Black Sea, connecting to the Velika Morava River and then the Danube, and also via the Drina River to the Sava and the Danube. A few waters (26.6 percent) from this region flow to the Adriatic Sea, and very little (1.1 percent) to the Aegean Sea. All of the rivers get their water from rain and snow; levels are therefore extremely high in spring and extremely low in summer.

The climate of this region is continental; on higher mountains it is sharp, with long and cold winters (temperatures drop to –38°C). Snow is a possibility from 70 to 210 days a year in higher regions, where it can remain for four to five months. Summers are short and fresh. Rainy periods occur in autumn (October and November) and spring (March and April). The mountain area receives 1,000 to 1,500 millimeters of annual rainfall; the Krivosije area north of Boka Kotorska Bay on the Adriatic gets 5,317 millimeters annually.

The biggest Yugoslavian lake, Skadarsko, is located in the far southeast in the Republic of Montenegro. Its surface is 6 meters above sea level, and its bottom is 28 meters below sea level. The lake covers an area of 379 kilometers, 222 of which belong to Yugoslavia and the rest to Albania. It is 55 kilometers long and up to 14 kilometers wide, and has a maximum depth of 44 meters.

Skadarsko (known as Scutari to Italians) is part of a national park and contains many fish. Angling there can be satisfactory to good, especially for wild carp (up to 25 kilograms), eels, and mullet (in the Bojana River, which runs from the lake to the sea). There is a small hotel in the little town of Virpazar, and also private rooms to rent. There is no commercial boat livery, but wherever there are boats it is possible to rent them from the owners along the sea coast (this is true elsewhere in Yugoslavia as well).

The Adriatic coast has a mild Mediterranean climate. Winters are short and mild, and summers are long and hot; temperatures in autumn are 2° to 5°C hotter than in spring. The midsummer temperatures are between 20° and 26°C (July is the hottest month), and in winter the temperature never falls under 7°C.

Yugoslavia has a wide variety of fishing waters: deep, slow-running rivers; fast-running, well-oxygenated brooks and rivers; canals; reservoirs (water dams); small deep lakes; and small, shallow, brown ponds. Nearly all species of native European freshwater fish (some 70 in all) inhabit these waters, as do such introduced species as rainbow trout (generally small and not numerous), Prussian carp (which weigh up to 8 pounds but average well under 1 pound and have suppressed native cyprinids), grass carp, silver carp, bighead carp, largemouth bass, pumpkinseed, and small catfish (brown bullhead).

Largemouth bass probably came from fisheries in Hungary. This species has spread throughout a network of canals in northwestern Vojvodina around the cities of Sombor, Kula, Crvenka, and Vrbas, and is favored by spinning tackle enthusiasts. It is numerous in this area and spawns naturally. The average catch is under 1 pound, and a 4-pounder is rare;

the maximum weight of the species in Yugoslavia is thought to be between 6 and 8 pounds.

The brown bullhead, known here as an American catfish, was planted in some waters a few decades ago to make it a sport and food fish. It stays small, however, rarely exceeding 2 pounds. In nearly all the lakes in which it was stocked, it has caused an ecological catastrophe. It commonly grows to 10 centimeters and is so numerous that populations of all other fish in the same waters have sharply decreased, and some domestic species are disappearing.

The most popular species for coarse angling are: carp *(saran)*, Prussian carp *(babuska)*, pike *(stuka)*, pike-perch or zander *(smudj)*, barbel *(mrena)*, nose-carp *(skobalj)*, chub *(klen)*, and catfish *(som)*. Anglers using spinning tackle pursue pike, pike-perch, huchen *(mladica)*, and brown trout *(potocna pastrmka)*. The brown trout is favored by fly anglers, who also pursue grayling *(lipljen)*.

Generally, coarse fishing is more or less satisfactory throughout the country, grayling fishing is good in some areas, and huchen fishing is satisfactory in some areas. Saltwater trolling offers some good sport, especially in the hotter part of the year, around the mouth of the Bojana River (on the Yugoslavia-Albania border), where leerfish (garrick) weighing between 20 and 60 pounds can be numerous.

Except for huchen and grayling in some rivers, the concentration of fish throughout Yugoslavia is lower than it is in many other European countries. Traveling anglers looking for intensive fishing and a lot of trophy catches would be better served elsewhere.

Gamefishing

Yugoslavia offers good grayling fly fishing on the Drina River, especially around the city of Bajina Basta. This is a fast-running river with clear water. A tributary of the Sava, it courses through the mountains between Yugoslavia and the state of Bosnia/Herzegovina. There is a good grayling population here, and the fish average 35 centimeters in length, although some measuring 50 to 53 centimeters (approximately 4 pounds) were caught in the mid- to late 1990s.

The huchen is very popular in this region, too. Anglers who favor spinning tackle pursue it on the Drina and Lim Rivers (the latter being the same type of water as the Drina, shared by Serbia and Montenegro, in the mountainous area), and occasionally produce memorable catches. The visiting angler who hires an experienced local angler to share his spots, lures, and techniques stands a chance of catching a trophy huchen weighing between 10 and 20 kilograms. The largest huchen caught on sportfishing tackle since 1980 have weighed up to 25 kilograms.

The best period for this species is December and January, but autumn can bring good catches, too. The closed season for huchen is from February 1 through June 5 to 15 (depending on local regulations). Fishing with natural baits is prohibited for huchen, brown trout, and grayling on Yugoslavian waters; only lures and flies are allowed.

The Montenegrin mountains contain regions of exceptional scenic beauty that have been proclaimed national parks; these include Durmitor, with 16 lakes, 5 rivers, and 6 canyons, and Biogradska Gora. Some river canyons in Montenegro, namely Tara, Moraca, and Piva, are among the deepest in the world (up to 1,200 meters). These 3 rivers offer brown trout and grayling fishing, and brown trout also inhabit the Mlava, Rzav, Djetinja, Vapa, and Uvac Rivers, as well as numerous small rivers and streams in the mountainous part of Yugoslavia. The average size is well under 2 pounds. In some lakes, however—namely Lake Zavoj near the city of Pirot in southeastern Serbia—there are brown trout weighing 18 kilograms-plus, but such big fish are very rarely caught.

Pike, pike-perch, and wels catfish are caught on lures in slow-flowing rivers (Dunav, Sava, Tisa, and Tamis), but the average pike and pike-perch are small (under 2 pounds). Wels are respectably bigger (from about 4 pounds up to 200 pounds), but fish over 20 pounds are rarely caught.

Coarse Angling

Pike, pike-perch, and wels catfish are all predators favored by Yugoslav coarse anglers on slow-flowing rivers and brown-water lakes and are caught on natural baits as well as artificials. But the number one challenge for most resident anglers in the northern and central parts of the country is hard-fighting wild carp (common carp), which can grow to around 60 pounds, and mirror carp, which can grow to 75 pounds.

With constant feeding of a chosen spot on the river, canal, or natural or artificial lake, and lots of fishing hours, catches of around 10 pounds are possible on nearly all waters. The season for carp lasts from June 1 until winter, and they are caught on natural and processed baits. Generally, catching a trophy carp on Yugoslav waters today requires a lot of luck, as much skill, and weeks or sometimes even months of hard work. A visiting angler ultimately needs the assistance of a good local angler as a guide, just to locate a spot that has any chance of yielding a respectable catch.

Coastal Fishing

Sportfishing in saltwater is not popular with Yugoslavs, but commercial fishing, mainly with nets, is common. It is known, however, that trolling with lures can produce good catches of amberjack, leerfish, mackerel, and bonito. Big-game fishing is popular in the south on the Italian side of the Adriatic, which should mean that the Montenegrin region is worth trying, too. Some catches by Yugoslavian commercial fishermen confirm the presence of swordfish, tuna, and little tunny in local

waters. It is also possible to catch seabass while casting (even from the shore), and night anglers have experienced nice catches of hard-fighting conger eels, which favor dead baits. A boat is a must for almost all sea fishing on the Adriatic, and although no charter boats for angling are available, boats can be rented from individuals.

Regulations and Tourist Information
Both Serbia and Montenegro have their own fishing laws and regulations. One license covers fishing in all of Montenegro, with the exception of three national parks, but more than a dozen regional and local licenses are required for fishing on all Serbian waters.

Yearly and daily licenses are sold in fishing clubs and tourist centers, and sometimes in hotels. Prices vary considerably, but generally it is much cheaper to buy a yearlong license for a region than a series of one-day licenses, which are usually site-specific. Prices for residents and nonresidents are the same. The license for fishing on Montenegrin rivers and lakes is valid for boat angling on the sea as well. No license is required for saltwater angling from the shore.

Night fishing is illegal on almost all rivers and lakes, and regulations exist that govern size limits, catch limits, seasons, and equipment (mainly regarding the number of hooks). Ask about all of them when buying a license; it's a good idea to check on all regulations before going fishing to avoid difficulties with local authorities. It is not legal to use sonar anywhere in Yugoslavia, but this regulation does not seem to be enforced for those using sonar for sportfishing purposes, as local anglers use it.

All-inclusive angling tours are unavailable in Yugoslavia. Visiting anglers must rely on private contacts with local anglers. Contacting the local, regional, or state tourist boards can only help in making travel plans and reserving accommodations.

Many of the Yukon's top fishing grounds are only accessible by floatplane.

YUKON TERRITORY
Located in the northwest corner of Canada and bordering eastern Alaska, the rugged and mountainous Yukon Territory offers good fishing opportunities in a beautiful and pristine wilderness setting. Covering 479,000 square kilometers, the Yukon has a larger landmass than California. Yet it has just 33,000 inhabitants, two-thirds of whom live in the capital city of Whitehorse. It issues only 17,000 fishing licenses annually, to anglers who have approximately 4,500 square kilometers of freshwater to choose from.

Some of that bounty is easily accessed via 4,700 kilometers of roads, but the most notable and exciting opportunities to catch trophy fish are tucked away in remote areas accessible only by boat or plane.

Gamefish primarily inhabit the region's 12 principal lakes and 14 major river systems. These fish include four species of Pacific salmon, lake trout, arctic grayling, northern pike, inconnu, lake whitefish, kokanee salmon, arctic charr, bull trout, Dolly Varden, steelhead, and rainbow trout. Grayling, pike, lake trout, rainbow trout, and salmon are the most pursued species, and trophy specimens exist in numerous waters. An active rainbow trout and arctic charr stocking program exists in pothole lakes, most of which are easily accessible by road. A salmon stocking program has enhanced chinook salmon stocks in some tributaries of the Yukon River system.

Waters in the Yukon are generally cool due to the short summers and long ice-covered winters, which last late October into May. These cold waters keep the growth of fish slow and the flesh firm, making them excellent table fare and very active on the end of a fishing line. Due to rapidly changing weather and extremely cold water temperatures, fishing by boat in all Yukon lakes, especially the larger ones, should be approached with caution. It is wise to inquire with government representatives or local inhabitants about water and weather conditions before heading out onto an unfamiliar lake. All waterways are public and are also open to fishing by Yukon-licensed nonresidents.

Commercial airline service is available to Whitehorse from Vancouver, British Columbia, as well as from Anchorage and Fairbanks, Alaska. Primary road access is via the Alaska Highway from northern British Columbia. Many good fishing opportunities exist along this highway, as well as on other road systems within the territory. Guided and fly-in fishing services are also available, and some visitors take advantage of lodge and outfitter opportunities to reach distant waters.

Because much Yukon angling occurs in unspoiled wilderness, the most competition may come from local wildlife, including grizzly bears. During the salmon runs these creatures can add some exciting moments to an angling adventure, so it's important to be alert for bears and give them the right of way.

Catch-and-release fishing is encouraged for conservation throughout the Yukon Territory and is mandated in a few locations for certain species. Barbless single hooks are mandated on some waters as well, and encouraged elsewhere.

Major Species

Arctic grayling. Grayling inhabit most lakes, rivers, and streams of the Yukon. Their abundance, beauty, and fighting qualities on light tackle make them a popular quarry. They may grow as large as 60 centimeters in length and attain a weight of more than 2 kilograms, but the average grayling in the Yukon will be less than 50 centimeters long, with a weight of under 1 kilogram. Grayling are excellent table fare when fresh; these white-fleshed fish lose their taste when frozen for any length of time.

Terrestrial insects form the larger part of their diet, but they also feed on bottom nymphs, snails, and eggs. One of the more popular times to catch grayling in the Yukon is early spring, when they gather in numbers to spawn in shallow rivers and streams. Flies, spinners, and small spoons are all successfully used by anglers.

Fishing opportunities for arctic grayling exist along the Alaska Highway at the Rancheria, Swift, and Teslin Rivers. The Teslin offers excellent fishing at Johnson's Crossing in early spring. Grayling are caught at Kusawa and Kluane Lakes, as well as at Mendenhall Creek. Notable sites along the Campbell Highway are the Francis and Finlayson Rivers, as well as Frenchman and Francis Lakes. Other good sites are along the Klondike Highway at Fox Creek, the McQuesten River, and the Klondike River.

Lake trout. Lakers are also avidly pursued in the Yukon Territory for their trophy size, bulldog-like fighting abilities, and fine eating qualities. They are found in virtually all Yukon lakes. Ten- to 14-kilogram fish are not uncommon in the larger lakes.

The best time to catch Yukon lake trout is in early spring before the water temperature reaches 9°C. Throughout the month of June, lake trout feed in the shallows before heading to deeper, cooler water in summer. Fishing improves again in the fall, when lake trout move into the shallows to spawn. Methods to catch these fish include trolling and casting lures and flies, and Yukoners also take them through the ice in winter.

Notable lake trout sites along the Alaska Highway are Teslin, Kusawa, Aishihik, and Sekulmun Lakes; along the Campbell Highway are Frances, Little Salmon, and Frenchman Lakes; and along the Klondike Highway are Laberge, Braeburn, and Ethel Lakes.

Northern pike. Pike generally inhabit the shallow waters of lakes and streams in the Yukon, as they tolerate higher water temperatures, lower concentrations of oxygen, and higher concentrations of carbon dioxide than many species of freshwater fish here. Some reach the 12-plus-kilogram category.

Adults spawn in shallow marshy areas of lakes as soon as the ice goes out in the spring. When taken from cold water north of the 60th parallel, the northern pike is an aggressive gamefish and superb table fare. The most popular times to catch northern pike are in the spring and early summer, and a variety of methods are effective.

Good pike lakes along the Alaska Highway include Squanga, Marsh, Kusawa, and Kluane; along the Campbell Highway they include Frances, Finlayson, and Frenchman Lakes; along the Klondike Highway they include Laberge, Fox, Tatchun, and Ethel Lakes.

Probably the most exciting opportunities for Yukon pike exist in lakes and streams away from the beaten track, and these are also likely to yield the bigger fish. Most of those places are accessible only by air via floatplane service available throughout the Yukon. Great fly-in pike fishing exists in Toobally, Alligator, Tatlmain, Tshawsahmon, Tincup, Wellesley, Wolf, and Big Kalzas Lakes. There is good fishing in the Yukon River for relatively big pike, but except for a few spots it is hard to access, is mainly fished from a boat, and usually requires planning for an extensive trip into the wilderness. More people visit this big river for the unspoiled wilderness travel experience than for the fishing.

Rainbow trout. The Yukon offers opportunities for stocked and native rainbows. A small reproducing population of native rainbow trout inhabits the Kathleen River and McLean Lakes systems. These rainbows generally reach a size of 1.4 kilograms and are all subject to live-release regulations. The Kathleen River is a special site, originating from a deep mountain lake and heading to a chain of shallow nutrient-rich lakes downstream.

Because of an extensive stocking program in pothole lakes, stocked rainbows have reached more than 6 kilograms. These stocked fish can live up to 11 years, although their normal life span is 4 to 6 years. Adults feed mainly on freshwater shrimp, caddisflies, blackflies, mollusks, and occasional small fish. Their flesh ranges from bright salmon orange to pale pink and is very delicious.

Rainbow trout are caught year-round, but spring and summer are most popular. Spinners and dry flies are productive, and some stocked rainbows are taken through the ice during the winter.

Arctic charr. These fish share many of the characteristics that make rainbow trout so popular. Until the arctic charr was included in government stocking programs in the Whitehorse area, however, few Yukoners had had an opportunity to catch this powerful and good-eating fish, as native charr were so remote. Native charr populations are found in the northern part of the territory in the Firth and Blackstone River systems, and there they sometimes weigh up to 9 kilograms. They are caught on streamers and occasionally on dry flies, but a flashy spoon is generally most effective. Ice fishing anglers catch charr on spoons with a small roe bag attached.

There are no outfitters here, however, so this is do-it-yourself fishing. The Firth is very difficult to reach, although the Blackstone can be accessed via the Dempster Highway. You'll need your own river transportation.

Dolly Varden/bull trout. Dolly Varden in the Yukon are recognizable by their dark blue to olive green backs with white or dusky underparts. They have yellow spots on the dorsal surface and orange or red spots on the sides. Stella Lake on the Haines Road contains landlocked Dollies. They're in the Blackstone River along the Dempster Highway in the north, as well as in the southwestern part of the territory.

Bull trout, often confused with Dolly Varden, are aggressive feeders and are easily caught. They inhabit the Liard River basin and tributary lakes and rivers.

Salmon/steelhead. Salmon migrate into two main water systems in the territory, neither of which provides much access. The mighty Yukon River has chinook, coho, and chum salmon. The migration of chinook salmon in the Yukon River system is the longest in the world, extending more than 2,000 kilometers from their home in the Beaufort Sea to their spawning grounds in tributary streams of the Yukon River. The chinook salmon run usually reaches Dawson by mid-July, and Whitehorse by early August. One of the longest fish ladders in North America (1,200 feet) is located at the dam at Whitehorse Rapids, allowing fish to migrate to the headwaters.

Chum salmon are in many Yukon tributaries from August through October. A small number of coho salmon migrate into the Porcupine River tributary system in the northern part of the territory in September and October.

The Alsek-Tatshenshini River system in the southeast corner of the territory holds runs of chinook, coho, and sockeye. The best angling occurs throughout July for chinook, in late September and October for coho, and from late August until October for sockeye.

Adult chinook salmon average 7 to 10 kilograms, but fish up to 30 kilograms have been taken from both river systems. Coho returning from the ocean are in the 5-kilogram category, and sockeye seldom exceed 2 kilograms but are most prized as table fare.

Chum salmon spawn in the major tributaries of the Yukon, White, Stewart, Pelly, and Teslin Rivers. The Porcupine River and its tributary, the Fishing Branch River, contain a sizable spawning population (and also one of the densest grizzly bear populations). This is the least popular salmon species for anglers, and they are generally caught in nets for subsistence purposes. Chum salmon first appear in Dawson City around the middle of August and are still running after freeze-up. Adults average under 2 kilograms in weight.

Kokanee salmon (which are landlocked sockeye) are identical to anadromous sockeye except for their size. They're found only in Kathleen, Frederick, Stella, and Louise Lakes. They seldom exceed .5 kilogram in weight or 42 centimeters in length. During most of the year, kokanee are in deep water; they hold shallow in early June and again in August when they spawn. Flies and small spinners are usually the most successful lures in catching these fighters.

Steelhead are found only in the Alsek-Tatshenshini River system. These are anadromous fish and average better than 2 kilograms.

Other species. Whitefish are abundant in Yukon waters. There are six species here, and lake whitefish are of most interest to anglers (and also commercially). Mature adults average 45 to 50 centimeters long, reach a maximum weight here of 3 to 4 kilograms, and are found in all parts of lakes. From late September to November they move into shallow lake outlets to spawn.

Inconnu, which are also known as coney or sheefish, will take a lure, but they are not often caught by anglers and mostly appear in the gillnets of commercial fishermen. They generally range from 4 to 9 kilograms and are excellent fighters on rod and reel. Inconnu inhabit the Yukon, Pelly, Stewart, and Porcupine Rivers.

Burbot are popular fish with Yukoners for fish and chips, although they're not considered a gamefish. They are voracious, however, feeding mainly at night and primarily on aquatic insects, crustaceans, and fish eggs, and are easily caught on baited lines fished on the bottom. They are popular with ice anglers in early spring, when these fish come into the shallows.

ZAMBIA

Situated in the interior of south-central Africa, Zambia is bounded by several countries with varied angling opportunities (Zimbabwe and Mozambique in particular), and itself has or shares some prominent rivers and lakes. From a sportfishing standpoint, its most significant river is the Zambezi, which flows from Angola in western Zambia and then courses along a shared border with Zimbabwe, forming Lake Kariba in the process. The fisheries of this portion of the Zambezi are detailed elsewhere (see: *Namibia; Zimbabwe*).

Other important waterways include the Kafue and Luangwa Rivers, which are respectively eastern and western tributaries to the Zambezi; and the Lualaba and Chambeshi Rivers in the north. Other lakes include Mweru, shared with the Democratic Republic of the Congo (Zaire); the southernmost portion of Lake Tanganyika; and Bangweulu, which is surrounded by a vast swampy region. Lake Bangweulu covers more than 1,150 square miles during the dry season, and several times that in full flood, and is one of the headwaters of the Congo River.

Huge Lake Tanganyika is reputedly of great angling interest, but extremely limited information exists on locations, seasons, and, most importantly, availability of true sportfishing services throughout the lake. Several lodges are said to exist at Kasaba Bay in Zambia, and some boats are allegedly available for angling. Nile perch, tigerfish, and vundu (giant catfish) are reportedly the main angling species, but the lake has some 200 species of fish in all. Only a small portion of the southern lake is in Zambia. Tanganyika extends for 420 miles, making it the longest freshwater lake in the world. It has a maximum depth of 4,710 feet, which is second in the world only to Lake Baikal in Siberia. Game viewing is the main attraction for visitors to the area, mostly from Tanzania *(see)*, and the overall lack of knowledge about sportfishing possibilities here (as opposed to Lake Kariba in Zimbabwe, for example) is a cause for wonder.

Sportfishing opportunities throughout Zambia are at best limited and primitive, and primarily relegated to the Zambezi watershed. In addition to the common species of tigerfish, other waters in Zambia are said to contain the giant tigerfish *(Hydrocynus goliath)*, as well as vundu.

ZANDER *Tizostedion lucioperca*.

Other names—pike-perch, pikeperch, pike perch, perch-pike; Danish: *sandart;* Dutch: *snoekbaars;* Finnish: *kuha;* French: *sandre;* German: *schill;* Hungarian: *fogas süllö;* Italian: *sandra;* Norwegian: *gjörs;* Portuguese: *lúcio perca;* Russian: *sudak;* Spanish: *lucioperca;* Swedish: *abborrfisk, gös;* Turkish: *sudak baligi, levrek.*

This is a prominent member of the Percidae family of perch in Europe and an important sportfish. It is commonly known as pike-perch; this is a misnomer, as it is not related to pike nor is it a cross between a pike and a perch. It is very similar and related to the walleye *(see)* of North America, and to a lesser European and western Asian species, the Volga zander *(S. volgense),* which is also known as Volga perch, Volga pike-perch, and *bersh* in Russian.

Identification. The zander's body form and coloration is similar to that of the walleye, although coloration and patterns vary significantly with environment. It has a generally dark greenish back, yellow green sides, and a light belly; the caudal fin is moderately forked; and the spiked first and soft second dorsal fins are separated. There are muted blotches on the back extending down the sides, and the jaws

Zander

possess large and sharp pikelike canine teeth. The Volga zander is similar but with more distinctive dark markings on its back (somewhat like yellow or European perch) and with smaller teeth.

Size/Age. The zander is commonly found to 20 inches in length but may grow to a maximum of 51 inches and 33 pounds; it can live for 16 years. The Volga zander is much smaller, growing to only 16 inches and $4^1/_2$ pounds.

Distribution. The zander is native to eastern, northern, and central Europe, including Finland, Sweden, and westernmost Asia; it has been introduced into several western European countries, including England (where it was first introduced in 1878), and has been spreading. The Volga zander occurs in eastern Europe from the Danube River to the Volga and Ural Rivers.

Habitat/History. Zander are found in rivers, lakes, ponds, and canals, especially in vegetated areas, and they favor larger systems. They spawn between February and July, earliest in southerly areas, and are especially prolific. Their introduction to some nonnative environments has led to a depletion of native fish stocks. Volga zander primarily inhabit deeper nonvegetated areas of rivers but also occur in brackish water near river estuaries.

Food. These carnivorous species consume assorted small fish.

Angling. Although zander have excellent flesh, they are not as widely consumed in Europe as walleye are in North America. As a game species, zander are generally downgraded, falling below the more favored northern pike and above many coarse species, as they are sluggish fighters like walleye.

Sportfishing for zander throughout Europe is largely carried out from shore, although boats may be employed in large waters. Methods are similar to those used for northern pike, the exception being lighter lines and smaller baits and lures; however, zander are susceptible to many of the same tactics used for walleye.
See: Perch.

ZEBRA MUSSEL

The zebra mussel is a small, fingernail-sized mussel native to the Caspian Sea region of Asia. It was discovered in Lake St. Clair near Detroit in 1988. Tolerant of a wide range of environmental conditions, the zebra mussels have spread to parts of all the Great Lakes and the Mississippi River, as well as many other water systems in North America.

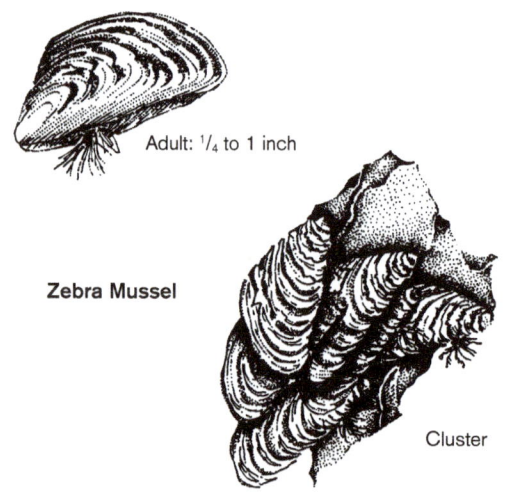

Zebra mussels clog water-intake systems of power plants and water treatment facilities, and the cooling systems of boat engines. They have severely reduced, and may eliminate, native mussel species.

Female zebra mussels can produce as many as 1 million eggs per year. These develop into microscopic, free-swimming larvae called veligers, which quickly begin to form shells. At about three weeks, the sand grain–sized larvae start to settle and attach to any firm surface using "byssal threads." They will cover rock, gravel, metal, rubber, wood, crayfish, native mussels, and each other.

Zebra mussels filter plankton from the surrounding water. Each mussel can filter about 1 quart of lake water per day. However, not all of what they remove is eaten. What they don't eat is combined with mucus as "pseudofeces" and discharged onto the lake bottom where it accumulates. This material may benefit bottom feeders while reducing the plankton food chain for upper water species.

Diving ducks and freshwater drum eat zebra mussels but do not significantly control them. Many methods of control have been tried, and continue to be tried. Minimizing the spread of zebra mussels is important, and anglers and boaters need to make sure they are not part of the problem.
See: Exotic Species.

ZIMBABWE

Described by some Africans as a small country, Zimbabwe is almost the same size as California. Situated in southern Africa and formerly known as Rhodesia, it is one of the most popular tourist destinations in all of Africa. This is not surprising, as Zimbabwe offers tremendous wildlife viewing opportunities, one of the largest waterfalls in the world, and some of the finest freshwater angling available on the continent. Several locations in Zimbabwe have excellent angling for the mighty native tigerfish, dozens of lakes with good populations of introduced largemouth bass, and highland waters with introduced rainbow and brown trout. The country's superb angling is often accompanied by close-up viewing of elephants, buffalo, crocodiles, and other wildlife, which does much to enhance the experience.

Zimbabwe is bordered by Zambia on the north, Botswana on the west, South Africa on the south, and Mozambique on the east. Various rivers span the country, and many of these are dammed to form reservoirs of various sizes.

The most prominent river in the country, which forms the northern boundary with Zambia, is the Zambezi River. The Zambezi winds through the valleys of southern Africa, originating in Angola and coursing through Zambia and the Caprivi Strip of Namibia (see) before entering easternmost Zimbabwe and falling through gorges and chasms to create one of the natural wonders of the world in Victoria Falls. At these dramatic falls, heavily visited but not as developed as Niagara, the Zambezi plunges more than 30 stories beforecontinuing to Lake Kariba, the third largest lake on the continent.

More than 120 indigenous fish species, and nearly a dozen introduced ones, thrive in Zimbabwe. Angling for sport has become more common only in the last few decades of the twentieth century, primarily because equipment was previously difficult and extremely costly to obtain. Sportfishing is gaining significantly here, however, among Zimbabweans as well as among visitors from other African countries, and to some extent among overseas visitors. Visiting anglers have more tourist operators, guides, and—in some places—boats and equipment providers ready to service them in Zimbabwe than in many other countries in southern Africa, although Zimbabwe is still regarded as an emerging market.

Tigerfish are undoubtedly the main attraction for anglers visiting from abroad and from other African countries. Although abundant, these fish have been heavily pressured by angling and poaching (via netting). Zimbabweans have placed greater emphasis on conservation and catch-and-release of this species, following the example set by bass anglers in the country. Largemouth bass have gained a great following with resident anglers since the mid-1980s, whereas trout, which are more limited in distribution, have inspired interest among local and visiting anglers. Popular fish for local and regional anglers also include various coarse species, including bream, barbel, tilapia, and large catfish.

Tigerfish

A number of species of tigerfish inhabit the African continent. The one found in Zimbabwe is *Hydrocynus vittatus,* which is not unique to Zimbabwe but is certainly more prolific here than elsewhere in Africa. The national all-tackle record stands at 34 pounds, 4 ounces. This specimen was taken from Lake Kariba in 1962. Many of these razor-toothed, hard-battling fish are caught in the 5- to 12-pound range; some weigh between 16 and 20 pounds.

The tigerfish is extremely streamlined, predominantly silver in color, with black lateral lines on the body. The fins are a mixture of blending reds and oranges, and these fish have a fine set of razor-sharp, pointed, interlocking teeth similar to the South American piranha. Although a vicious predator, it does not attack humans. It will readily strike at a variety of spoons, spinners, flies, and plugs, as well as at live or cut baitfish.

Tigerfish are found in various lakes and rivers in Zimbabwe. From a sporting perspective, they are most associated with the Zambezi River and its tributaries, and especially with Lake Kariba. Kariba is a man-made lake some 180 miles long and up to 20 miles wide in parts.

Filled in from 1960 to 1961, Lake Kariba covers 3,750 square miles of water and has an untold amount of shoreline. It is studded with islands and submerged timber. Anyone visiting Zimbabwe for the first time must include a visit to Kariba in their itinerary.

The shores of Kariba, especially along the southern portion in Zimbabwe, have numerous high-quality lodges and hotels. Game viewing is the chief activity. Elephants are commonplace, and there are abundant populations of many game and bird species, including buffaloes and eagles, and some lions. Boats are available for hire here, and numerous angling-oriented safari operators provide extremely worthwhile opportunities in this wild and beautiful country.

In recent years, Kariba has seen a burgeoning houseboat charter industry. Large (60 to 100 feet long) pontoon houseboats, fully equipped with cabins and staff and capable of trips lasting over a week, take out parties for game viewing and/or fishing. At least 100 such boats exist at Kariba. When towing a small fishing boat, the houseboat serves as a mother ship. This setup enables anglers to fish along vast and distant areas of shoreline.

The Kariba International Tigerfishing Tournament is held every October, and in recent years the three-day event has grown to include more than 600 anglers in 4-person teams. Numerous specimens to 13 pounds are landed, and sometimes the largest weighs around 20 pounds.

Nearly all conventional angling methods are successful in landing tigerfish. Medium-action rods of $6^1/_2$ to 7 feet are generally preferred, as is line of about 12-pound test. Terminal tackle must be protected by a wire leader to prevent the fish from severing the line with its sharp teeth. Trolling, casting, and baitfishing are all practiced, and fly fishing is enjoyed as well. Kariba anglers are especially fond of using dead baits, the best of which is the kapenta. This small sardine was introduced into Lake Kariba from Tanzania in the early 1980s for commercial harvesting. Tigerfish like this forage a great deal, and kapenta account for more than half their diet at Kariba.

Tigerfish travel in shoals of varying sizes, from a pair to 20 or more. They start biting suddenly and stay engaged for up to 30 minutes, then cease activity just as suddenly. The strike is strong and vicious and followed by a series of spectacular leaps. Tigerfish are extremely strong fighters, and they battle right up until boated. Many are lost when the line is accidentally cut or the hook simply doesn't get properly imbedded—both because of this species' sharp teeth.

Lake Kariba is a premier attraction for angling and wildlife viewing.

Tigerfish caught in fast water—whether on flies, lures, or baits—are even more tenacious than those taken from lakes, as this species is more vigorous in fast water. The Zambezi River above and below Lake Kariba has excellent opportunities for these fish, and a number of fishing camps line its banks. Some opportunities for self-guided safaris with 4×4 vehicles exist on the Zambian side. More angling is available along the lower river, below 400-foot tall Kariba Dam, and most notably at Mana Pools (and National Park), which is also a noted ornithological area. The middle river, from Victoria Falls to Lake Kariba, is a productive section that also offers whitewater rafting. The upper Zambezi River in Zimbabwe is lush and heavily vegetated; its width varies from 200 yards to a mile or more, and this stretch of river is especially commendable for both beauty and fishing.

Other Species

Both northern-strain and Florida-strain largemouth bass have been introduced into many, if not most, public reservoirs and rivers in Zimbabwe, and they have established self-sustaining populations. They are also present in privately owned ponds. Largemouth bass are believed to have been present here since 1932; Florida-strain bass were introduced in May of 1981. The Zimbabwe record stands at 13 pounds, 13 ounces. A big following for this species exists among organized fishing clubs, and catch-and-release is ardently practiced.

Reservoirs and rivers within 40 to 50 miles of

the cities of Bulawayo, Harare, and Masvingo, as well as others at Chinnoyi, Chegutu, the eastern mountains, and elsewhere, provide bass fishing. There may be as many as 60 good bass waters in the country. Near Masvingo, Lake Kyle is one of Zimbabwe's largest reservoirs and most prominent bass waters. Access sites at the lakes are generally poor, and most Zimbabweans must launch their boats along a muddy shoreline. Angling methods are similar to those in North America.

A flourishing bass angling industry since the early 1990s has resulted in a boom in fishing boat manufacture in Zimbabwe, and the country now has suppliers of boats with livewells, electronics, and assorted angling-related features. These are exported regionally in the continent as well.

Both brown and rainbow trout exist in the mountainous Eastern Highlands region along the Mozambique border. Described as the "Scotland of Africa," this region is a 180-mile-long series of mountain ranges that are representative Zimbabwe's greatest beauty.

Trout were introduced here in 1921 and inhabit various rivers and lakes. Accessibility is best in Nyanga National Park at Nyanga, near 8,500-foot-tall Mt. Inyagani, and at Chimanimani National Park south of Mutare. Clear waters here contrast with the lakes and rivers elsewhere in Zimbabwe. Fly fishing is the rule in the parks, and some hotels may offer private fishing to guests.

Zimbabwe hosts other species, many of which inhabit the same waters as tigerfish and/or largemouth bass. These include the tackle-busting vundu (giant catfish), which can grow up to 100 pounds but is now rare in the middle Zambezi yet prolific elsewhere, as well as tilapia, bream, barbel, and other coarse species.

ZOOPLANKTON

Minute suspended animals in the water column of seas and lakes.

Conversion Charts

THE SYSTEM OF WEIGHTS AND MEASURES USED IN MOST COUNTRIES AND IN ALL SCIENTIFIC work is the International System of Units (SI), which is commonly referred to as the metric system. A notable and influential exception to this is the United States, where the general public, and non-scientific publications, use the U.S., or U.S. customary, system of weights and measures. Throughout the *Ken Schultz's Fishing Encyclopedia & Worldwide Angling Guide*, there is a liberal use of both metric and U.S. customary weights and measures without parenthetical conversions to equivalent weights or measures. Some anglers, especially those who travel widely and those who pay close attention to world-record fish weights and fishing line classifications, are accustomed to both systems, which are often found mixed at boat docks, fish camps, and tackle shops throughout the world. The following information is provided to help the reader make the conversion from one system to another.

U.S. To Metric Conversion Formulas

When You Know...	Multiply By...	To Determine...
Inches (in)	25.4	Millimeters (mm)
Inches (in)	2.54	Centimeters (cm)
Inches (in)	0.0254	Meters (m)
Square Inches (sq in)	645.0	Square Millimeters (sq mm)
Square Inches (sq in)	6.45	Square Centimeters (sq cm)
Square Inches (sq in)	0.00064	Square Meters (sq m)
Feet (ft)	30.5	Centimeters (cm)
Feet (ft)	0.305	Meters (m)
Feet (ft)	0.0003	Kilometers (km)
Square Feet (sq ft)	0.093	Square Meters (sq m)
Fathoms (fath)	1.827	Meters (m)
Fathoms (fath)	0.0018	Kilometers (km)
Yards (yd)	0.914	Meters (m)
Square Yards (sq yd)	0.836	Square Meters (sq m)
Statute Miles (mi) (5,280 ft)	1.61	Kilometers (km)
Nautical Miles (n mi) (6,020 ft)	1.852	Kilometers (km)
Square Miles (sq mi)	2.56	Square Kilometers (sq km)
Miles per hour (mph)	1.61	Kilometers per hour (kph)
Knots per hour	1.84	Kilometers per hour (kph)
Acres	0.405	Hectares
Ounces of Weight (oz)	28.3	Grams (g)
Ounces of Weight (oz)	0.0283	Kilograms (kg)
Ounces of Fluid (fl oz)	29.6	Milliliters (mL)
Pounds (lb)	454.0	Grams (g)
Pounds (lb)	0.454	Kilograms (kg)
Pints (pt)—U.S.	0.473	Liters (L)
Pints (pt)—Imperial	0.568	Liters (L)
Quarts (qt)—U.S.	0.946	Liters (L)
Quarts (qt)—Imperial	1.14	Liters (L)
Gallons (gal)—U.S.	3.79	Liters (L)
Gallons (gal)—Imperial	4.55	Liters (L)
degrees Fahrenheit (°F)	0.555 (after subtracting 32)	degrees Celsius (°C)

Metric To U.S. Conversion Formulas

When You Know...	Multiply By...	To Determine...
Millimeters (mm)	0.039	Inches (in)
Centimeters (cm)	0.394	Inches (in)
Centimeters (cm)	0.0328	Feet (ft)
Square Centimeters (sq cm)	0.155	Square Inches (sq in)
Meters (m)	39.37	Inches (in)
Meters (m)	3.281	Feet (ft)
Meters (m)	1.09	Yards (yd)
Meters (m)	0.547	Fathoms (fath)
Square Meters (sq m)	1.2	Square Yards (sq yd)
Kilometers (km)	3,279.0	Feet (ft)
Kilometers (km)	1,093.0	Yards (yd)
Kilometers (km)	546.0	Fathoms (fath)
Kilometers (km)	0.621	Statute Miles (mi)
Kilometers (km)	0.545	Nautical Miles (n mi)
Square Kilometers (sq km)	0.386	Square Miles (sq mi)
Kilometers per hour (kph)	0.621	Miles per hour (mph)
Kilometers per hour (kph)	0.545	Knots per hour
Hectares	2.47	Acres
Grams (g)	0.035	Ounces of Weight (oz)
Grams (g)	0.002	Pounds (lb)
Kilograms (kg)	35.2736	Ounces (oz)
Kilograms (kg)	2.2	Pounds (lb)
Milliliter (mL)	0.034	Fluid Ounces (oz)
Liters (L)	2.11	Pints (pt)—U.S.
Liters (L)	1.76	Pints (pt)—Imperial
Liters (L)	1.06	Quarts (qt)—U.S.
Liters (L)	0.880	Quarts (qt)—Imperial
Liters (L)	0.264	Gallons (gal)—U.S.
Liters (L)	0.22	Gallons (gal)—Imperial
degrees Celsius (°C)	1.8 (and add 32)	degrees Fahrenheit (°F)

Table Of Metric and U.S. Equivalent Line Strengths

Metric	U.S. Customary	Metric	U.S. Customary
1 kg	2.2 lb	10 kg	22.0 lb
2 kg	4.4 lb	15 kg	33.0 lb
3 kg	6.6 lb	24 kg	52.8 lb
4 kg	8.8 lb	37 kg	81.4 lb
6 kg	13.2 lb	60 kg	132.0 lb
8 kg	17.6 lb		

Table of Fish Weights

Metric	U.S. Customary	Metric	U.S. Customary
1 kg	2.2 lb	60 kg	132.0 lb
2 kg	4.4 lb	70 kg	154.0 lb
3 kg	6.6 lb	80 kg	176.0 lb
4 kg	8.8 lb	90 kg	198.0 lb
5 kg	11.0 lb	100 kg	220.0 lb
6 kg	13.2 lb	200 kg	440.0 lb
7 kg	15.4 lb	300 kg	660.0 lb
8 kg	17.6 lb	400 kg	880.0 lb
9 kg	19.8 lb	500 kg	1,100.0 lb
10 kg	22.0 lb	600 kg	1,320.0 lb
20 kg	44.0 lb	700 kg	1,540.0 lb
30 kg	66.0 lb	800 kg	1,760.0 lb
40 kg	88.0 lb	900 kg	1,980.0 lb
50 kg	110.0 lb	1,000 kg	2,200.0 lb